quaderni di matematica

volume 1

edited by
Dipartimento di Matematica
Seconda Università di Napoli

Published with the support of
Seconda Università di Napoli

quaderni di matematica

Published volumes

1 - Classical Problems in Mechanics (R. Russo ed.)

Next issues

Recent Developments in Partial Differential Equations (V. A. Solonnikov ed.)
Recent Progress in Function Spaces (G. Di Maio and Ľ. Holá eds.)
Methods in Combinatorics (F. Mazzocca, N. Melone and U. Ott eds.)
Connections between Model Theory and Algebraic and Analytic Geometry (A. Macintyre ed.)
Advances in Fluidodynamics (P. Maremonti ed.)

Classical Problems in Mechanics

edited by
Remigio Russo

ARACNE

Authors' addresses:

Bruno Carbonaro
Dipartimento di Matematica
Seconda Università di Napoli
Piazza Duomo
81100 - Caserta (Italy)

Giovanni Paolo Galdi
Istituto di Ingegneria
Università di Ferrara
Via Scandiana, 21
44100 - Ferrara (Italy)

Paolo Maremonti
Dipartimento di Matematica
Università della Basilicata
Via N. Sauro, 85
85100 - Potenza (Italy)

Mariarosaria Padula
Istituto di Ingegneria
Università di Ferrara
Via Scandiana, 21
44100 - Ferrara (Italy)

Salvatore Rionero
Dipartimento di Matematica e
Applicazioni *R. Caccioppoli*
Università di Napoli *Federico II*
Complesso Universitario Monte S. Angelo
80126 - Napoli (Italy)

Remigio Russo
Dipartimento di Matematica
Seconda Università di Napoli
Piazza Duomo
81100 - Caserta (Italy)

Giulio Starita
Dipartimento di Matematica
Seconda Università di Napoli
Piazza Duomo
81100 - Caserta (Italy)

Photocomposed copy prepared from a TEX file.

ISBN 88-7999-187-6

To Raffaele Nogaro
Bishop of Caserta
who never spared himself
in fighting in favour of justice and culture
this volume is gratefully dedicated

Contents

AMS subject classification

The Principle of Virtual Velocities: 01-02, 34A40, 70-03, **70C20**, 70D05, 70D10.

On the Steady, Translational Self-Propelled...: 35D05, 35D10, 35Q30, 35R30, **76D05**.

On Existence and Uniqueness...: 35B50, 35D05, 35D10, 73C02, 73C15, **76D05**.

Steady Flows of Barotropic Viscous Fluids: 35D05, 35D10, **76N10**, 80A10.

On Magnetohydrodinamic Stability: 35Q35, 76E05, 76E30, **76W05**.

Preface

The first and most important objection to which may feel exposed whoever decides to start the publication of a new scientific — in particular, mathematical — magazine, is that it was not needed at all, and that there already exist even too many *showrooms* for the new, more ore less deep, meaningful and hidden, results with which the work of researchers almost daily enriches our heritage of knowledge.

Despite this objection, or rather actually guided by it, we are pleased and feel honoured to present to the mathematical community these *Quaderni di Matematica* of the Department of Mathematics of the Second University of Naples, published thanks to the financial support of the Second University of Naples and to the zeal of all the teachers of the Department. That is not, indeed, a magazine in the sense this word is usually given, and is not simply originated by the will to give the scholars a further tool to diffuse among their colleagues the product of their researches. It is a Series of volumes, each taking its inspiration and its form from an underlying thematic unity, with the explicit aim of inserting possible new results in a logical picture that could cleverly describe the origin of the problems, their relevance in the framework of present research, and the cultural value of their (either partial or total) solution. That's indeed the service this new Series intends to give to mathematical community: not only new theorems, but also new interpretations, new motivations and, as far as possible, connections.

In this way, it is also our hope to fuse the more specifically scientific objective of making professional mathematicians know some more novelty in their own research fields, with the objective, that could be defined as a didactic one, of delivering accounts which, when read by young graduate people wishing to discern the current problems of mathematical research, may give them not only an uptodated description of the present state of a number of these problems, but also a way to situate them in a thematic and historical view. This is what we feel to owe to all the students, with perhaps a bit of special regard to those coming from Caserta and its territory, which gives hospitality to the Second

University of Naples, as well as not only a reason of existence, but also — with its young people — a promise for the future.

In the above outlined perspective, and in conformity with the aims just briefly described, the present volume, which opens the Series of *Quaderni di Matematica*, is devoted to the study of some classical problems of Mechanics, concerning both systems with a finite number of degrees of freedom and continuous systems.

The first article treats the Principle of Virtual Velocities, better known nowadays in the didactic literature as the Principle of Virtual Works. It is one of the basic principles of Statics of constrained systems, widely used in the framework of engineering to determine the equilibrium configurations of structures. The article owes its birth to the fact that, in spite of the acknowledged intuitive character of the Principle, and of its great power in applications, that make of it a didactic subject of primary importance in almost all the modern courses of Rational Mechanics, it still offers some relevant ambiguities of interpretation, not only as regards its rôle in the establishment of lagrangean mechanics, but above all in connection with its *status* as a theorem in an essentially newtonian and eulerian axiomatic-deductive framework: such a *status* seems to be questioned by the lack of a complete and rigorous proof of the Principle for systems subjected to unilateral constraints, though in almost all the university treatises about Rational Mechanics its validity is taken for granted also in this case. Attempting to dissipate doubts and ambiguities, the article offers an historical *excursus* of the evolution of the Principle from the origin of Statics to the present day, and proposes for it a proof in the framework of uniqueness theorems for differential systems.

The second article tackles the problem, of great interest from both the mathematical and the applicative viewpoint, of the steady motion of self–propelled bodies in a viscous incompressible fluid. To be precise, a body moving in an infinite viscous fluid, undergoes a *self–propelled motion* if the net external force and torque exerted on it are identically zero. Typical examples of self–propelled bodies can be those performed by rockets, submarines, fishes, and by microrganisms, etc. This kind of movement is contrasted to a *towed motion*, where the body moves just because of a nonzero net external action. A characteristic example of towed motion is the fall of a body in the air, under the action of gravity. In spite of its importance, it is a problem not yet studied as deeply as it deserves: though it is a natural development of the fluid-dynamic studies started in the first half of this century, nevertheless the first researches explicitly devoted to give it a mathematical formulation and a first solution for two–dimensional flows seem to have been given only in 1957 by Garrett Birkhoff and Eduardo Zarantonello. More recent contributions have been obtained either for bodies of particular shape, as cylinders and spheres, or, for arbitrary bodies, within the Stokes approximation. In any case, no general and rigorous well–posedness theory is known for the full nonlinear Navier–Stokes problem. This problem is tackled here for the first time for bodies that are symmetric around a direction; this article can also be considered as a first step toward the solution of other problems of physical interest like, for example, whether any of the steady self–propelled solutions found by the author is stable or whether it can be obtained as a limit of unsteady solutions.

The third article tackles the problem of existence and uniqueness of classical solutions to the steady–state Navier–Stokes system and to the traction problem of linear elastostatics under the assumption that the boundary data be only continuous. Such questions date back to the original formulations of the mathematical problems to which they are related: precisely, to a fundamental research of 1933 by Jean Leray, the former, and to an equally celebrated paper of 1908 by Arthur Korn, the latter. After a review of the most meaningful contributions to the solution of such problems, the authors, thanks to the theorem of maximum modulus for the Stokes problem, previously proved by one of them in the case of bounded domains, and extended here to the case of exterior domains, are able to show that the boundary value problem associated with the stationary Navier–Stokes system has a unique classical solution if the velocity at the boundary is continuous, the viscosities are large and the usual *smallness* requirements of data and fluxes are met. Moreover, dealing with a homogeneous and isotropic elastic body, they first observe that in a neighborhood of the boundary the traction obeys a system of Stokes' type, then they prove that in this neighborhood the traction obeys a maximum modulus theorem. Finally, by using this result, they obtain existence and uniqueness of classical solutions to the traction problem for linearly elastic bodies, identified either with bounded or exterior domains or with the half–space, that turn out to be isotropic *near to the boundary*, under the single hypothesis of continuity of the boundary traction.

The objective of the fourth article is an investigation of some important properties of viscous barotropic gases: the validity of the mathematical model of barotropic fluids as well as existence, uniqueness, regularity and asymptotic behaviour in space of steady solutions. Though the mathematical theory of viscous compressible fluids goes back to the basic works by SIMÉON DENIS POISSON (1831) and GEORGE GABRIEL STOKES (1845), the mathematical study of their steady flows has started only recently, so that a number of crucial questions still remain unsolved. Accordingly, the article furnishes a so complete as possible landscape of the subject, aiming at finding the mathematical limits of validity of the barotropic model for several kinds of domains. It is shown here how the physical interpretation of ill-posed problems leads to paradoxical situations, and a new formulation of the classical well-posedness problem is proposed to avoid paradoxes. In this connection, a new iterative procedure is proposed, being a natural extension of the classical iterative procedures used for incompressible fluids, and mainly presenting the applicative advantage of being very efficient for numerical computations.

The aim of the last article is to give an account of the stability questions concerning some fundamental magneto-hydro-dynamical motions, whose relevance is easily acknowledged bearing in mind their applications in problems concerning the dynamics of plasma and the realization of machines to accelerate beams of charged particles. As is well known, the main difficulty of the problems lies in the continuous interaction between the motion of the fluid and the magnetic field in which it is plunged: the magnetic field influences the motion of each charged particle of the fluid and, simultaneously, this last influences the magnetic field, so that the hydro-dynamic motion may completely change its aspects, and even completely new motions can arise. Accordingly, the paper is mainly devoted to point out some ways to solve this difficulty. To give an as complete as possible view of the problem, Hall and ion-slip currents are taken into account, and the guide-lines of the linear stability of the classical magnetic Bénard problem are presented, that enable to recover — via the Lyapounov direct method — the same results obtained by means of the analysis in terms of normal modes.

Remigio Russo

The Principle of Virtual Velocities

Bruno Carbonaro and Giulio Starita

Contents

1. Introduction

The *Principle of Virtual Velocities* (also identified in the literature about Statics as the *Principle of Virtual Works* or *Principle of Virtual Displacements*) is one of the richest-in-contents statements of the mathematical theory of mechanical equilibrium. As a consequence, it is considered as one of the most powerful tools in the applications of Statics, used in the framework of engineering to obtain, with straightforward geometrical considerations, and by the aid of simplified calculations, the equilibrium configurations of structures, or to solve the problem of determining the loads they can withstand.

But its power in applications, ceals at least two more reasons of its great relevance in Mechanics from a cultural and logical viewpoint: first, since its explicit formulation in XVIIth Century, this Principle has always been, and is nowadays, conceived as the very basis of the whole Statics, at least as long as this science is considered — according to its historical development — as a theory quite independent of Dynamics; next, a clearly recognizable line of thought, which can be traced back to the work of d'Alembert, has made meaningful attempts to use it to found the whole theoretical construction of Dynamics on the concepts and the language of Statics.

In spite of this richness of both theoretical and technical contents, the rôle of the Principle of Virtual Velocities (PVV, from now on) in the structure of mechanical science, and in particular its relationship with newtonian-eulerian dynamics, still seem far from being really clear, so that they are matter of ever renewing discussions among researchers and teachers. As a matter of fact, it seems rather difficult to find, among the classical subjects of mechanics, a topic on which so many different, and often opposite, opinions find place in the literature.

To start with, as any statement proposed in the framework of a mathematical theory endowed with an empirical counterpart, it raises at least two basic questions: to what extent we can trust it? Is it to be taken as a primitive proposition, accepted without proof, or rather as a theorem? But it is readily seen that this latter is an ill-posed question, unless one specifies the theory within which the statement should be deduced: provided it is not self-contradictory, there will always be a system of axioms that imply it, so that all the question reduces to the choice of such axioms. If we think of axioms describing only some equilibrium conditions, as to embed PVV in pure Statics, we shall have a different answer from that we would have if we had chosen a system of axioms describing the laws of motion, as to consider PVV as a proposition of Dynamics.

Now, these questions cannot be discussed in a merely logical or mathematical fashion, without taking into account interpretation and teaching of both Statics and Dynamics and of their mutual relations in the present academic culture: actually, handbooks and University textbooks about Rational Mechanics tell the reader, more or less explicitly, that PVV is in fact a theorem of the lagrangean formulation of newtonian-eulerian dynamics; but such a statement is not supported by a complete and satisfactory proof of the Principle, except in the case of bilateral constraints. The lack of such a proof, on the other hand, has led some researchers to the conviction that PVV should instead be viewed as a true independent axiom of dynamics.

To shuffle further the cards, there is someone who denies the validity of PVV and exhibits, in this connection, a counterexample which could seem to show that there could be not equilibrium even when the assumption of PVV is satisfied. In this sense, PVV would be neither a Principle nor a theorem, neither in the framework of Statics nor in that of Dynamics. But these authors go actually farther: more or less consciously, they claim that Statics is not, as we all would expect, a special chapter of Dynamics (neither in its lagrangean nor, of course, in its newtonian-eulerian version).

The present paper has its cue in the authors' opinion that the above sketched debate is at least partly referred, further than to the attempt to answer the above outlined questions without distinguishing Statics from Dynamics, to an unhomogeneity in understanding terms as *principle*, *rest*, *equilibrium*, *ideal constraints*, *frictionless constraints* and, last but not least, the attribute *virtual*: once any ambiguity is dropped out from the language, it should be possible to formulate PVV as a theorem and to prove it rigorously, apart from the technical difficulties.

Dropping the ambiguities, and trying to establish whether PVV should be now proved or criticized as pertaining to Statics or to Dynamics, seems to be impossible without an accurate analysis of the long history which first led to the final version of the Principle, due to Bernoulli, then to the use made of it by Lagrange to support a dynamical theory of constrained systems of bodies, and finally to the present attempts to prove it as a theorem of Dynamics (either described by the Lagrange equations, or by the Newton and Euler ones).

Moreover, one cannot help asking why, though the history of PVV goes back for two thousand years and the attempts to prove it started at least two centuries ago, a complete proof does not yet exist. Getting a plausible answer to this question requires again an historical analysis, with special concern to the last period, from Lagrange to the present attempts to prove PVV.

Thus, it is only history what can give us a sufficient understanding of both the meaning and the logical *status* of PVV in modern Mechanics. It will show that this Principle is so ancient as Static itself, and that its first smell dates back to Aristotle.

As a matter of fact, the earliest documents about Statics that have arrived to us, can be found in the writings by Aristotle and Archimedes. These, dealing mainly with the way of working of lever, seem to suggest that Statics derives its birth to mercantile activity, and in particular to weighing problems. In fact, a lever works like a balance or a steelyard, and it is from these tools that the entire terminology of Statics owes its origin. *Libra* is the latin name of the equal-armed balance, but it also stands for the *horizontal position of a plane*, as well as the word *aequilibrium*. Two bodies on the plates of a balance are in *aequilibrium* if and only if they are at the same horizontal level: they are *pondera aequē librata*.

Beyond their intrinsic interest, the works of Aristotle and Archimedes are also of basic relevance since they clearly present themselves as the poles of a dualism, which characterizes the whole history of Statics, between two different approaches to equilibrium problems, that may be referred to as *synthetic* and *analytical*, respectively, whose development lines, though easily acknowledgeable through the centuries as distinct from each other, are nevertheless complementary and have strongly influenced one another.

As we shall see in more detail in the sequel, the evolution of PVV coincides with that of synthetic viewpoint, which arises with Aristotle, and, through the contributions of medieval mechanicians, takes its accomplishment with Descartes and Bernoulli.

Though the explicit statement of PVV is due to Bernoulli, this Principle is nevertheless universally linked to the name of Lagrange, to whom is due the introduction of an analytical method which really enables to derive from PVV all of its potential consequences.

At the same time, Lagrange first felt the need to prove the Principle, and gave it a proof his own way. Subsequently, several other scientists, as Carnot, Fourier, Ampère, tackled the same problem, and a careful reading of all their attempts of proof, clearly shows that their real common goal was to reduce PVV to simpler and more intuitive, though less general, principles of Statics.

But in the meantime, starting from the end of sixteenth century, the students of mechanics, besides their traditional studies in Statics, had turned their interest towards the dynamical phenomena. After Newton had established his dynamical theory for single mass-points on a principle of proportionality between acceleration and force, this interest essentially originated two currents of thought: from one side, Euler extended Newton's Dynamics to systems of points reliyng it on a postulate of proportionality between causes and effects; on the other hand, d'Alembert and, on his footsteps, Lagrange, tried to ground the whole body of problems and knowledges about the Dynamics of such systems on the principles of Statics.

This gave rise to a tortuous and troubled process, which only at the end of nineteenth century has led at least the most part of mechanicians to consider Statics as a particular case of Dynamics, and so the newtonian-eulerian viewpoint to prevail. In spite of this, most of the modern treatments of mechanics couple an apparently complete adhesion to the dynamical viewpoint with a traditional exposition of Statics as an independent theoretical system.

It is then not surprising that only in the last century the mechanicians have begun to look for a proof of PVV as a deduction of its statement from the principles of Dynamics rather then from some simpler principles of Statics, and — on the other hand — that most of these attempts be initially affected by such duplicity of viewpoint.

Finally, the complete embedding of lagrangean formalism in the framework of newtonian-eulerian dynamics, has made the proof of PVV, in the case of bilateral constraints, almost trivial, as an application of the classical uniqueness theorem for differential systems; on the contrary, the question becomes far more complicated in the case of unilateral constraints, in which one has to deal with a mixed system of differential equations and inequalities. Few authors have tackled the problem, still without covering the most general case.

The above considerations have induced the authors to plan a work where, after a detailed picture of the evolution of the concepts that underlie the formulation of the Principle, a precise statementof PVV be proposed as a necessary and sufficient condition for the equilibrium of systems of constrained mass-points and rigid bodies. In such a context, in order to prove PVV, it is necessary to show the uniqueness of the rest solution for a system of coupled differential equations and inequalities. The necessity of the principle is almost evident; on the contrary, its sufficiency is a very involved mathematical problem, where the handling inequalities rather than equations hides some of information needed to grasp the properties of possible nonzero solutions.

A quite general proof is presented here in the case in which the active force is independent on time and satisfies the standard Lipschitz condition ensuring existence and uniqueness of solutions to systems of differential equations. For time-dependent forces it is finally shown that sufficiency still holds true, provided some further assumptions are made on forces or on the geometric structure of the constraints. The proofs here proposed have, in our opinion, the advantage of being so simple as to be presented in an university textbook of Rational Mechanics.

In our opinion, this is a complete solution of the problem from a conceptual viewpoint, in that it coversall physycal concrete situations for which PVV was originally stated, though it is to be acknowledged that, from a pure mathematical viewpoint, some open problems are still left.

2. The greek origins of Statics

2.1 - Aristotle of Stagyra.

The first writing about Statics which has arrived to us is the tract entitled *Problems of Mechanics*, that presents the study of about fourty problems, mainly concerning Statics, having a common character: they all treat cases in which a great resistance is overcome with a little effort by the aid of suitable tools (see Giovanni Vailati [23]). The paternity of this work is a matter of controversy: it is usually attributed to Aristotle of Stagyra (384–322 B. C.), and appears in an edition of his *Opera Omnia*; but some historicians deny this attribution, yet agreeing that this work should be however due to some of Aristotle's direct scholars — maybe THEOPHRASTUS (about 372–about 287 B. C.) or STRATO (?–271 B. C.) (see MARSHALL CLAGETT [59] for a detailed discussion of this point). We leave aside this question: as we shall see, the way in which the statical problems are tackled in that writing appears permeated by the physical thought of the philosopher of Stagyra, so that referring to it — even conventionally — as a work of Aristotle's, is certainly allowed.

The relevance of the *Problems of Mechanics* lies not only in the results presented there, but also, and mainly, in its methodological approach, insofar the questions about equilibrium are discussed without introducing any independent system of statical postulates, but rather on the ground of the rules to produce motion: when no motion is produced, a body stays in equilibrium. Accordingly, it can be stated that the equilibrium conditions are determined by dynamic motivations.

In this connection, it is convenient to recall that, according to Aristotle's general views about mechanics, motion is not a natural condition of bodies: it is, as we could say with the historycian of philosophy G. DE RUGGIERO, an *imperfect* act, as it cannot be conceived without a power, for it needs either a movable object, either a motive power: bodies offer to it a resistance that must be overcome not only to produce motion, but also to keep it. To this end, a force, or motive power, must be applied to the body, and such power must be as greater as heavier is the body to be set in motion, and as greater is the speed we want to impart to it:

Whatever the force may be producing the motion, that which is smaller and lighter receives more motion from the same force ... indeed, the velocity of the lighter body will be to the velocity of the heavier body as the heavier body is to the lighter body.

(ARISTOTLE, *On the Eavens*).

And, more precisely,

Let α be the motive force, β the moved body, γ the distance traversed and δ the time employed for the motion. Then, the same force α will displace half of β by a length twice γ in an equal time δ and at distance γ in a time half of δ: such will be, in fact, the proportion.

(ARISTOTLE, *Physics*).

According to these two statements, two powers are quite the same if, when setting in motion two different weights with different velocities, they produce equal values of the product of weight by velocity.

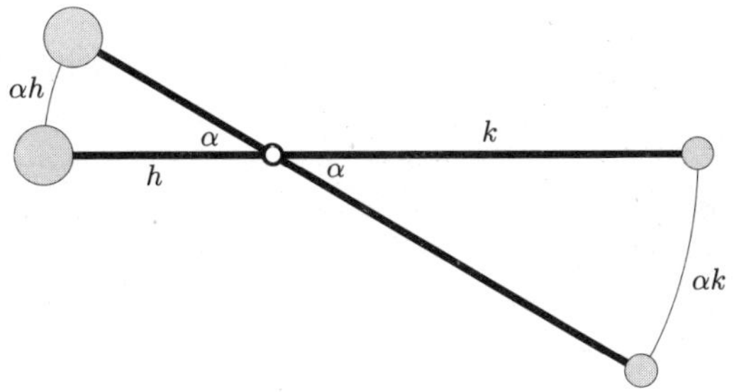

Figure 1.

These arguments contain the key to furnish an answer to the questions posed in the *Problems of Mechanics*, in particular to explain how is it possible, by the aid of a lever, to displace with a little effort weights that would be impossible to move without this tool, so perpetrating what Aristotle defines as "a fraud of man against nature". The author links this effect to the geometric properties of circle:

The original cause of all phenomena of this kind, is the circle ... The phenomena observed in a balance may be reduced to the circle, and those observed in the lever, to the balance, while in practice all other phenomena of mechanical motion are connected with lever.

(Aristotle, *Problems of Mechanics*).

Moreover,

Since there are not, on the same radius, two points that move with the same velocity, but of two points the one which is farther from the resting centre is faster, in the motions of circles many admirable phenomena are presented.

(Aristotle, *Problems of Mechanics*).

To be precise, Aristotle determines as follows the equilibrium condition for a lever: let us consider a stick divided by a fulcrum into two different arms, whose endpoints are charged with different weights. When the stick rotates around its fulcrum, the two weights move with different velocities, proportional to the lengths of arms (see Figure 1). As a consequence, in order to compare the motive powers, it will be necessary to multiply each weight by the length of the arm on which it is leaned. The motion will have the direction of descent of the weight corresponding to the greatest power. If the two products weight×radius turn out to be equal, then the stick will remain in equilibrium:

The weight which is moved is therefore to the weight which produces the motion in the inverse ratio to that of lenghts of lever arms: since each weight will produce the motion as more easily as farther it will be from the fulcrum. And the cause of this is always the same: that the trajectory at greater distance from centre involves a greater arc.

(ARISTOTLE, *Problems of Mechanics*).

We cannot but be affected by the originality of Aristotle, who — once he had understood that the fraud to the nature is only apparent, since the "marchandises" to be compared are not simply the motive powers, but what would be called nowadays *static moments* — devised to determine the equilibrium conditions by an *a priori* inspection of all potential motions of the system made of the lever and the weights, which should take place if the motive powers would put it into motion. It cannot escape that this inspection is exactly the method of virtual velocities, and it has not escaped indeed the attention of historicians:

Had Aristotle formulated only this single idea, he would deservedly have to be celebrated as the father of rational mechanics. This idea is, indeed, the seed from which the powerful ramifications of the Principle of Virtual Velocities will sprout over the next twenty centuries.

(P. DUHEM, *Les Origines de la Statique*).

It is difficult to read this passage of Aristotle without feeling that he has indicated, by his words, what once will become the main street of rational mechanics. Aristotle seems indeed to have realized the relation between the magnitude of the mutually equilibrating forces and the displacements that their points of application should undergo if equilibrium would be perturbed for any reason. In his thought is a first, rudimentary, maybe fuzzy, but precious germ of what we call nowadays the Principle of Virtual Work.

(G. COLONNETTI, *I Fondamenti della Statica*).

It is quite evident that, as pointed out by Clagett [59], some significant differences between the idea conceived by Aristotle and the modern version of PVV cannot be ignored: first, the virtual (or potential) displacement is not required to be infinitesimal; secondly, it is along an arc, not along a straight line. Nevertheless, the similarity seems to be far more important from the viewpoint of historical development of the Principle.

2.2 - Archimedes of Syracuse.

Besides the aristotelian dynamic approach, the purely static and geometric way of tackling the equilibrium problems develops independently a little later, in the so-called Alexandrine period: the earliest work in which a trace of such address may be found, could be perhaps *Euclid's book on the balance*, which however has reached us as an arabic manuscript of 970 A. D., so that the paternity of the proof of the Principle of Lever, which would be the first in the history at our knowledge, is not sure.

The most ancient work of certain attribution, on Statics as an independent theoretical system, is instead the treatise *On the Equilibrium of Planes*, due to ARCHIMEDES OF SYRACUSE (287–212 B. C.), who certainly presents himself as euclidean in methods and — if the book on the balance could be attributed without doubts to EUCLID OF ALEXANDRIA (about 365–about 300 B. C.) — also in the scope. In this writing, Archimedes develops Statics as an axiomatic-deductive theory based on its own postulates, of quite empirical origin. Four of them concern in particular the centres of gravity, and will not be reported here. We only point out, for the sake of completeness, that Archimedes does not even define, in the considered work, the notion of *centre of gravity*; this apparent lack is probably due to the fact that Archimedes, according an opinion widely diffused among the historicians, devoted to such definition and to the study of the main properties of centres of gravity a separated treatise. As a matter of fact, Archimedes' body of knowledge about this subject, may be reconstructed through the evidence left by Heron and Pappus in their works, where they quote several fragments of a lost work by Archimedes. PAPPUS OF ALEXANDRIA (about 290–about 350), in particular, reports the definition of the centre of gravity of a given body as

> ... a point such that, when the body is suspended from it [in such a way that the former cannot move but around the latter], the body remain at rest whatever its initial position may be.
>
> (PAPPUS, *Mathematical Collections*).

The remaining four axioms deal instead with the equilibrium of suspended weights, and — also in view of a comparison with aristotelian viewpoint — are of main interest to us:

1. Equal weights suspended at equal distances [from a fulcrum] are in equilibrium.

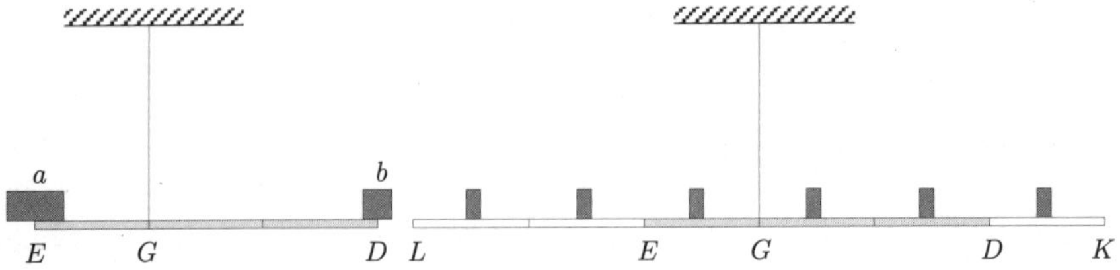

Figure 2.

2. Equal weights suspended at unequal distances are not in equilibrium; the one suspended at the greatest distance moves downward.
3. If weights suspended at given distances are in equilibrium ad if one adds something to one of the weights, they will no longer be in equilibrium, and the weight to which something has been added will move downward.
4. Similarly, if one removes something from one of these weights, they will no longer be in equilibrium, and the one from which nothing has been removed will move downward.

(ARCHIMEDES, *On the equilibrium of planes*).

Starting with these assumptions, Archimedes proves first that two commensurable weights suspended at extreme points of a lever are in equilibrium when their distances from the fulcrum are in inverse ratio with respect to the weights themselves. It is worth reconstructing Archimedes' reasoning in its essential lines, even confining ourselves, for the sake of simplicity, to the particular case of two weights a and b, the former being twice the latter. According to Archimedes, we want to prove that a and b are in equilibrium on a bar ED if — a and b being charged on E and on D respectively — ED is suspended by a point G such that $GD = 2EG$. Under this assumption, let us double the bar ED by adding to it a bar $LE = GD$ and a bar $DK = EG$. Marking the middle point of LE and GD, the bar turns out to be subdivided into six parts, all equal to EG. On the other hand, we may take — as unit measure for weights — one half of b. The bodies a and b may be therefore thought of as consisting on the whole of six parts of the same weight. If we load each segment of LK in its middle point with one of these parts, then the system will be in equilibrium, since its centre of gravity will correspond to the middle point of LK, which is just the fulcrum G. But now we can couple the weights: the first with the fourth, the second with the third and the fifth with the sixth; we then imagine each couple as suspended at its centre of gravity. And since the centre of gravity of the last couple is D, while the first two couples have the same centre of gravity at E, the proof is achieved.

By means of exhaustion method, Archimedes is able to extend his proof to the case of incommensurable weights, so showing the general statement that any two weights suspended at the endpoints of a lever are in equilibrium when their distances from the fulcrum are in inverse ratio with respect to the weights themselves. This statement is what is usually called *Archimedes' Principle of Lever*.

The above proof of the Principle of Lever was repeatedly examined, perfectioned and simplified in the centuries, until Galileo, seventeen centuries later, worked out an argument which allowed him to treat directly the most general case of two not necessarily commensurable weights.

It is worth remarking that the moravian scientist and philosopher ERNST MACH (1838–1916) strongly objected to Archimedes' proof in his treatise *Die Mechanik in ihrer historisch-kritisch dargestellt* ([17]), by remarking that it is based on an assumption not explicitly listed among his postulates (nor proved before); but, what is more important, this tacit hypothesis seems to Mach to be quite equivalent to the statement to show.

2.3 - Heron of Alexandria.

The latest greek work containing notions of Statics, which have reached us, is the *Elevator*, by HERON OF ALEXANDRIA (about 65–about 125), whose original greek version reached us in the form of some fragments, but of which we have an arabian version called *On the ascent of heavy things*.

It is a work of a less speculative character with respect to the *Problems of Mechanics* and to *On the equilibrium of planes*, and rather dealing with the equilibrium questions which the author cleems useful for applications.

The reasons why the *Elevator* is interesting from a scientific viewpoint, are several, but we want here to linger only over those which seem to be the most pertinent to the object of our study. It is in particular of great relevance to remark that, in this work, are very evident the references to Aristotle's as well as Archimedes' thought.

The influence of the latter on Heron is mainly of a methodological character, since the alexandrine scientist feels, as well as the Syracusan, the need to found his studies about Statics on a solid mathematical basis.

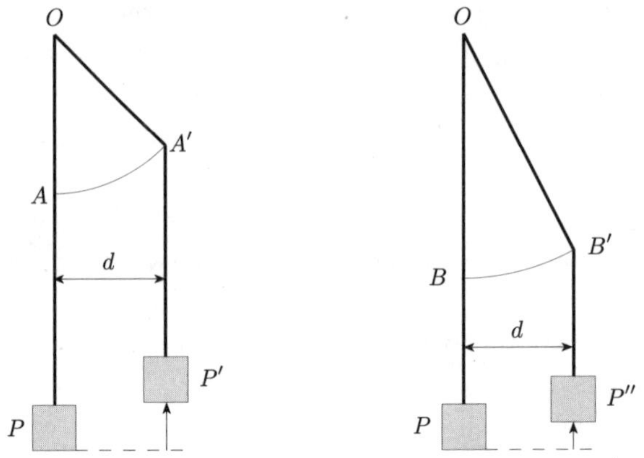

Figure 3.

As far as the most technical aspects are concerned, Heron seems to be indebted to Archimedes for the systematic use of the concept and of the properties of the centre of gravity; it is rather through his work that we may be able today to reconstruct many of Archimedes' reasonings about that concept (in this connection, see the article by G. Vailati [22]). Also the formulation of the principle of lever appears to be borrowed by Heron from Archimedes; but he applies this principle also to angular levers, showing to have clearly understood that the effect of a weight is related to his distance from the vertical line passing through the fulcrum of lever, *i. e.* to what we now call the moment of a force.

Equally evident is the connection of Heron with Aristotle, in particular when he brings the properties of the different mechanisms he analyzes — the winch, the lever, the hoists, the wedge, the screw — back to the properties of circle. But still more deserves attention what is defined as the *Principle of Slowing Down*, which Heron so states:

The ratio of force to force is [inversely] as the ratio of time to time.

(HERON, *Elevator*).

Though the meaning of this statement does not appear very clear, Clagett claims that an accurate study of how is it used by the author, shows that it may be rephrased in terms of space distances rather than time intervals. According to this remark, the Principle of Slowing Down turns out to be a restatement of PVV, or of the Principle of Work, as Clagett defines it: *When machines work, what is gained with respect to force, is lost with respect to time* (or, what is the same, with respect to distance). The following example clearly shows the use of this principle made by Heron: he wants to explain why the horizontal displacement of a weight suspended is as more difficult as nearer to the suspension point one picks the rope. The argument is as follows: if we want to displace the weight at a distance d (see Figure 3), and pull the rope by the point A, then the final configuration of the rope will be $OA'P'$, and the weight will have been raised by the length PP'; if instead we pull the rope by the point B, then the final position will be $OB'P''$, and the weight will turn out to be raised only by the length PP'', which is seen to be less than PP', so that also the work made in this latter case is less than that made in the former.

3. Statics from the Middle Age to Leonardo

3.1 - Jordanus de Nemore.

The Latin ancient times and the Middle Age have been considered for long time as a period in which the scientific activity was interrupted, so that, according to the views of historicians of science of XVIIIth and XIXth centuries, modern science starts with Galileo from the point where Greeks had leaved it.

It is PIERRE DUHEM [32] who brought at our knowledge the contributions of Middle Age students to the development of Statics: for this reason, he is considered by CLIFFORD TRUESDELL [65] as the first historician of science in the modern sense of the word. Thanks to him, we know that at least part of the scientific heritage of Greeks, preserved and transmitted by Arabian students, was worked out in the Middle Age by several authors, most of whom remain unfortunately unknown. They were able not only to organize the greek heritage, but also to transform it, with an ingenious and powerful work, which also led to the creation of new concepts whose fecundity, according to Duhem's words, is "unexhausted to this day", but will remain forever anonymous. Of the most important among them, JORDANUS DE NEMORE (around 1230), or Jordanus Nemorarius, considered by Duhem as "the master of them all", we know very little. He wrote important treatises about Arithmetics and Geometry, and a work, *De Ponderibus*, dealing with Statics. All historicians agree that this work

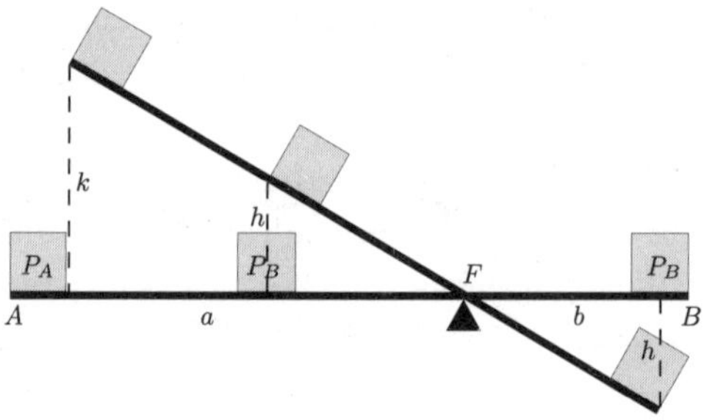

Figure 4.

derives from a previous greek treatise, but, with the only exception of Vailati [23], they also agree that it contains a good deal of original contributions. What is remarkable from our viewpoint is that its contents seem to be linked with those of the treatise *De ponderoso et levi* attributed to Euclid, and with certain passages of Aristotle's *Problems of Mechanics*. As a matter of fact, we learn from Duhem that Middle Age students seem to have been quite unaware of Archimedes' work. Thus, Jordanus de Nemore could not but develop an aristotelian viewpoint about equilibrium. And he did this in a very original way.

In particular, of great interest is the ingenious proof of the Principle of Lever given by Jordanus. Let us denote by A and B the endpoints of a lever, by F its fulcrum, by a and b the distances from F of A and B respectively, and by P_A and P_B the weights loading A and B, respectively (see Figure 4). Jordanus wishes to prove that, if the weights are in an inverse ratio with respect to their distances from the fulcrum, and the lever is horizontal, then it will stay at rest.

Assume as a postulate that all what can raise a weight p to a height h, will also raise a weight α times heavier than p to a height α times smaller than h. This stated, let us assume *per absurdum*, following Jordanus, that the lever is not in equilibrium. Then the whole system will rotate around F, in either direction. To fix ideas, assume that the weight P_B moves downward by a vertical distance h, thus raising the weight P_A by a vertical distance k. Then, according to the above postulate, it will be also able to raise by a vertical distance h a weight P_B set at the distance b from F on the side of P_A. But

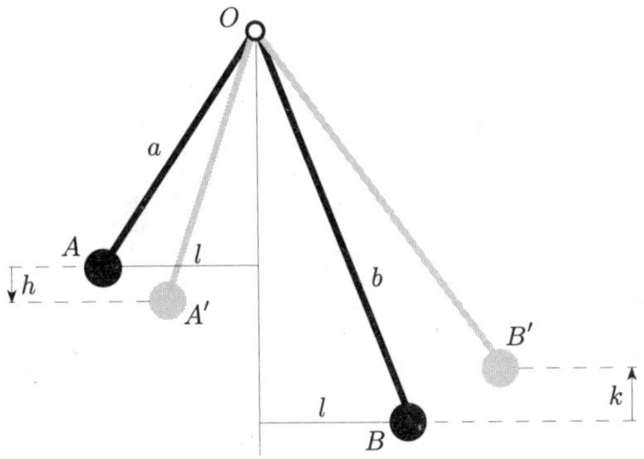

Figure 5.

this is impossible, since we know that equal weights at equal distances from the fulcrum are in equilibrium.

As a matter of fact, Jordanus does not state explicitly the postulate used in this proof, but his acceptance of it appears so clear that one of Jordanus' commentators in XIVth Century believes that this postulate is in fact legitimated by an obscure proposition in another work by Jordanus.

This is the first statement of a principle which prefigures PVV after Aristotle. It is as more important as it translates Aristotle's assertion in a rigorous and quantitative language.

3.2 - The school of Jordanus.

The graft of mathematical rigour into the aristotelian philosophical tradition, with the transformation of an essentially philosophical principle in a mathematical one, was to prove extremely fruitful in the solution of both theoretical and applicative problems. An excellent proof of this can be found in the work *De ratione ponderis*, written by an anonymous scholar of Jordanus (called by Duhem the precursor of Leonardo), in which the postulate reported in the previous subsection is used to solve a number of important and general problems related to the angular lever and the inclined plane.

Let us analyse in some details the arguments by which this author is able to establish the conditions of equilibrium for an angular lever whose endpoints be loaded with equal weights. He aims at proving that such a system stays at rest

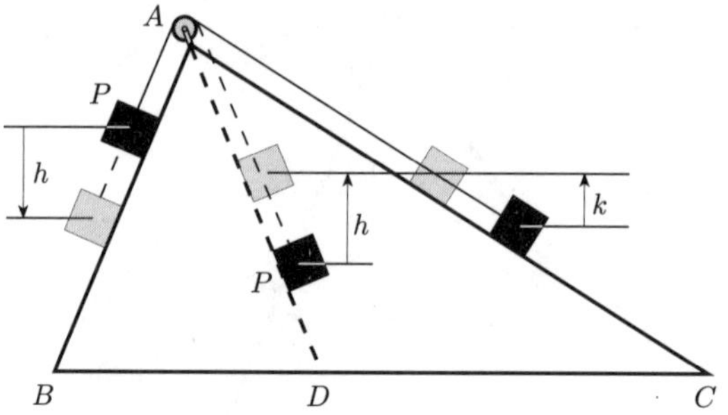

Figure 6.

when the two weight are at the same distance from the vertical line passing through the fulcrum. Indeed, let us consider an angular lever whose arms, having different lengths a and b respectively, form an angle φ, and denote by AOB the configuration of lever, in which its endpoints are at the same distance l from the vertical line through O (see Figure 5). Assuming *per absurdum* that this configuration be not of equilibrium, let for istance the weight at A prevail on that at B, so that the lever will assume the new configuration $A'OB'$. We would then obtain the result of raising a weight at an height k, by lowering an equal weight by a length h, evidently less than k. In a quite analogous way, one can prove that the weight at B cannot prevail on that at A.

Even more interesting is the way in which the scholar of Jordanus solves the problem of equilibrium of two linked weights on two inclined planes AB and AC with different slopes (see Figure 6). He wants to prove that they will be in equilibrium if they are in an inverse ratio with respect to that of the lengths of the planes. To this aim, he imagines once more that the weight at P go down by an height h; then the other weight will correspondingly go up by an height k. But this is equivalent to raise, along a plane AD symmetric to AB with respect to the vertical plane passing through A, a weight equal to the one at P by an height h. Since this effect is clearly impossible, because two equal weights on two equally inclined planes are certainly in equilibrium, the displacement of the initially considered system turns out to be all the same impossible.

Thanks to Jordanus and his school, the studies of Statics supported on the notion of work and on principles that, in our modern language, we could consider as precursors of PVV, reveal to have not a merely conceptual interest, but to be also fertile as well as the more analytical ones in the solution of problems of applicative nature.

3.3 - From Jordanus to XVIth Century.

In the period from XIIIth to the early XVIIth Century, Mechanics widened its horizont to include a new kind of problems: most of the students living and working from the late Middle Age to the rise of Modern Age turned indeed their attention toward very different problems, partly suggested by philosophical and theological questions (such as the shape and the motion of Earth, the motion of planets, the causes and the laws of fall of heavy bodies, and, as the most important among all these problems, the *inertia*, that is the property of thrown objects to keep themselves in motion for a longer or shorter interval of time). Still a number of names should be mentioned in connection with the statical problem we are dealing with.

Thus, after Jordanus, the first scholar quoted in [55] in connection with the study of Statics, as a critic of Jordanus himself, is BIAGIO PELACANI [BLASIUS OF PARMA] (about 1327–1416), whose contribution to Statics, given in a *Treatise on Weights*, known to us through a copy made by Arnold of Brussel and dated 1476, is reduced to relating Jordanus' idea of *gravitas secundum situm* with the tendency of bodies to follow the shortest path to reach their natural places, and to pointing out that the passive resistances should be taken explicitly into account, when dealing with equilibrium of a lever. As stated in [55], he deserves quotation only in that he "was one of the means by which the Statics of the XIIIth Century and the kinematics of the XIVth Century were handed on to the Italian School, which was destined to dominate mechanics" for more than one century since.

After Blasius, we directly arrive to LEONARDO DA VINCI (1452–1519) who is known as a genius who gave significant contributions to many branches of science and technics: he was interested in Statics, though in a not systematic way, but added nothing essentially new to what had been done by Jordanus and his anonymous pupil. He essentially considers and gives a solution to the problem of equilibrium of a lever and of the motion of an heavy body on an inclined plane, which he describes by making an essential use of the concept of "moment" (in the modern sense of the word) also, as it seems, to give a kind of explanation of what Jordanus had defined as *gravitas secundum situm*.

NICCOLÒ FONTANA (about 1500–1557), well-known with the surname of TARTAGLIA, also was interested in Statics, but his main merit in this field is to have published (and edited to some extent) in 1565 Jordanus' work, with the title *Jordani opusculum de ponderositate Nicolai Tartaleae studio correctum*. According to [55], "instead of giving his predecessors credit for their work, Tartaglia, who was not very scrupulous in matters of scientific propriety, claimed their demonstrations as his own".

GEROLAMO CARDANO (1501–1576) is usually considered as an interesting figure of this period, for he "was at once physician, astrologer, algebraist and a student of mechanics", but — as far as Statics is concerned — adds nothing to the work of Leonardo. As a matter of curiosity, it could be mentioned that he was probably the first to use the word *linkage* to describe the action of levers and inclined planes on the motion of an heavy body.

After Cardano comes GIOVANNI BATTISTA BENEDETTI (1530–1590), who belongs to the school of thought we have referred to Archimedes, as he rejected Aristotle's argument about the dependence of equilibrium on the (virtual) velocities of the bodies hanging at the ends of a lever, and simply uses the notion of moment.

We find next GUIDO UBALDO DAL MONTE (1545–1607), quoted also by Lagrange in the introduction to the statical part of his *Mécanique Analityque*, to whom is due the explicit consideration of the reaction of the support (as regards heavy bodies relying upon an inclined plane or upon an arm of a lever) to explain *gravitas secundum situm*. Thus he seems to be the first who introduced what are now called the forces of constraints.

A complementary contribution to the modern language of Statics is also due to JUAN BAPTISTA VILLALPAND (1552–1608), who introduced the concept of *polygon of sustentation*, and stated and proved a first form of the rule according to which an heavy body resting on an horizontal surface remains in equilibrium when the vertical projection of its centre of gravity on the surface belongs to the area covered by it (nowadays, we would say "is internal to the polygon of sustentation").

Finally, BERNARDINO BALDI (1553–1617) also rejected Aristotle's argument on virtual velocities, and gave a rule of the polygon of sustentation in connection with the problem of equilibrium of a tripod. But his main contribution was the discovery of the correct formula for the *stability* of the equilibrium of a lever.

4. The birth of modern Statics

4.1 - Simon Stevin.

The science of Statics, whose evolution we have outlined from the first greek contributions and, through Medieval students, until the results of the Renaissance scientists, makes a decisive progress thanks to the contribution given to it by two prominent figures: SIMON STEVIN (1548–1620) and the ingenious italian scientist GALILEO GALILEI (1564–1642).

The former was a geometer (in the sense Duhem gives this word) by inclination and culture, so that his work and his approach to Statics almost completely follows by method of study and exposition those by Archimedes. Accordingly, he conceives Statics as completely independent from any consideration concerning the possible motions of bodies whose equilibrium conditions are to be determined. His rejection of any contamination between Statics and Dynamics (or even kinematics, as for that) is very clearly summarized by the following syllogism:

> Something which does not move does not describe a circle. Two weights in equilibrium do not move. Therefore, two weights in equilibrium do not describe circles.
>
> (S. STEVIN, *Mathematicorum Hypomnematum de Statica*).

As a matter of fact, the attitude of the fleming scientist was opposite. In the same way as Archimedes, he wants to deduce, in a quite rigorous way, the main properties of equilibrium and the solution of problems of Statics from few principles whose truth could result as plainly evident. A very good sample of such attitude is furnished by his ingenious and original determination of the equilibrium condition for two heavy bodies linked by a string and posed on two differently inclined planes.

He imagines to surround two differently inclined planes by a chain of equal and equally spaced grains. This chain must certainly stay at rest, for if it started to move, then it could never stop: indeed, by the symmetry of the system, there

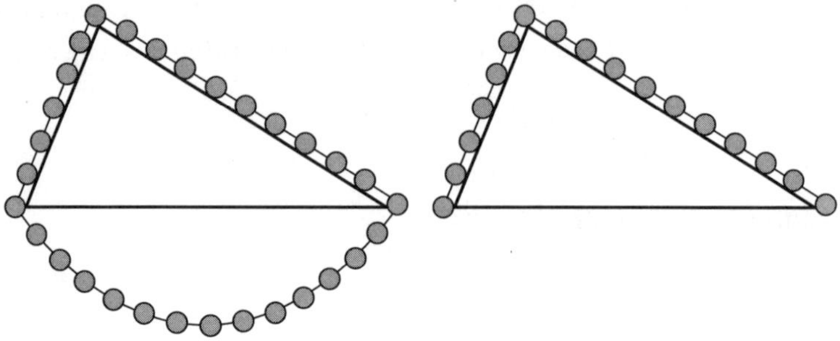

Figure 7.

would be no reason to stop, in contrast with the acknowledged impossibility of perpetual motion. Now, the piece of chain hanging under the planes may be cut off, since, again by obvious symmetry considerations, it does not affect any way the equilibrium of the whole system. The remaining piece of chain is now arranged in such a way that the weight lying on each plane is proportional to its length (the proportionality factor being the same for both planes, in virtue of the supposed homogeneity of chain): then the ratio between the weights is the same as that of the lengths of the planes. Accordingly, we may conclude, with Stevin, that two bodies, joined by a string and lying on two differently inclined planes, are in equilibrium when their weights are in the same ratio as the lengths of planes (see Figure 7).

In particular, when one of the two planes is vertical, then its length is the common height of them both; moreover, the action of the heavy body on the string pulling it, is measured by its own weight. As a consequence, for any inclination of the other plane, the action exerted on the same string by the body lying on it, must be measured by the product of its weight by the ratio of its height to its length, *i. e.* the product of the weight by what we call nowadays the sine of the angle of inclination. From a graphic viewpoint, this means that the magnitude of the vector expressing the counterpoise is the same as that of the projection of the weight on the plane itself.

Once stated this result, Stevin goes further. He observes that, in this last situation, the inclined plane may be replaced (Figure 8) by a string fixed at a point and perpendicular to the plane, since in this way the small displacement allowed to the heavy body remain the same. Thus, the weight is kept at rest

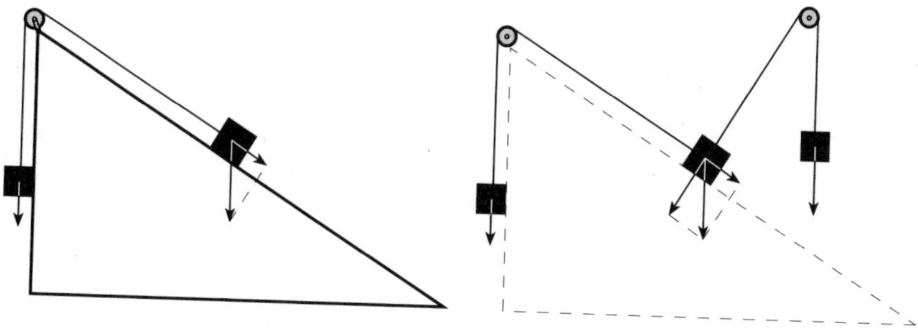

Figure 8.

by two strings; in order that the analogy between the two systems be complete, there is nothing more to do but replacing the fixed point by a pulley with a suitable counterbalance, which, by virtue of previous consideration, must have a magnitude equal to the projection of the weight along the direction of the string. Through this argument, Stevins arrives at drawing for the first time what will be called the *parallelogram of forces*, which will be later systematically used by DANIEL BERNOULLI (1700–1782) and PIERRE VARIGNON (1654–1722): this last, in particular, will assume it as a general principle of Statics.

4.2 - Galileo Galilei.

The fields covered by Galileo in his studies go far beyond statics; nevertheless, in view of the aims of the present paper, we confine ourselves to give a brief account of his important contribution to the statement of equilibrium conditions for weights on an inclined plane.

Galileo takes first on consideration an equal-armed angular lever, with an horizontal arm, being the other arbitrarily inclined. As this latter's inclination varies, so does the tendency of the weight charging it to go down, since its moment with respect to the fulcrum is also varied. The weights will be then in equilibrium when their moments will be the same. This stated, Galileo draws the straight line tangent to the circumference on which the weight could move (Figure 9) and claims that the tendency it would have to go down following this line is the same that characterizes its displacements on the circumference. Similarly, a weight running along a vertical plane has the same tendency to motion as the weight lying on the horizontal arm of the lever. It is then a

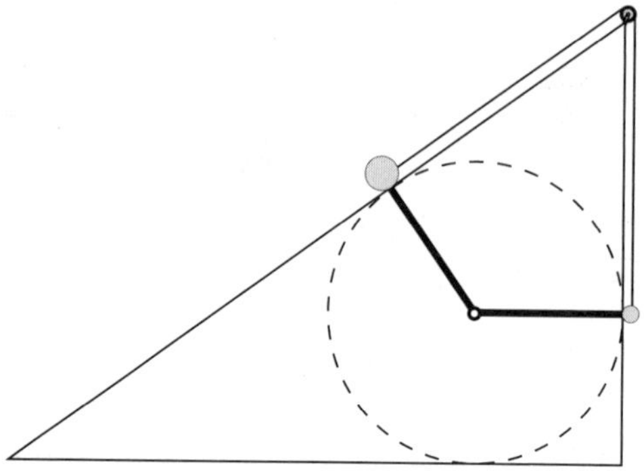

Figure 9.

simple matter of geometry to conclude that a weight lying on an inclined plane will be kept in equilibrium by another moving along a vertical plane, when the ratio of the weights will be equal to that of the length of the plane to its height.

The great interest of Galileo's reasoning lies in that he realizes that a constraint imposed to the mobility of any body, is not characterized by its explicit way of realization, but by the small movements it allows from any configuration of the body. This is the same idea used by Stevin in his construction of parallelogram of forces.

Thus, with the work of these scientists, the way of thought which we have conventionally identified as aristotelian seems to be overcome by the one originated with Archimedes. Nevertheless, rather paradoxically, it is just Stevin, the author of the above quoted critical syllogism to Aristotle, who recalled the equality of motive work and resistent work, from which Jordanus and his pupil had drawn inspiration. Indeed, in his study of systems consisting of several heavy bodies supported by a sole counterbalance, by means of a number of movable pulleys, he observes that it is possible to raise a weight P by an height h, by lowering a counterpoise equal to one α-th of P by an height being α times h. At a quite similar conclusion arrives Galileo, starting with the case of equilibrium on an inclined plane, then generalizing:

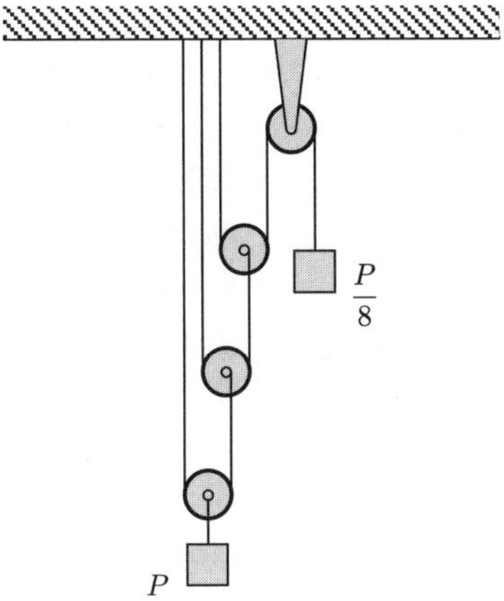

Figure 10.

We may assertively claim that, when equilibrium, that is rest, must take place between two movable things, their tendencies to motion must correspond to their gravities in a reciprocal way, according to what is proved in all cases of mechanical motions.

(G. GALILEI, *Addendum* to *Discourses and Mathematical Demonstrations about two New Sciences*).

Thus, we see that PVV is acknowleged by both Stevin and Galileo in its full generality, but seems to them as a property which manifest itself only when the equilibrium conditions have been already established, and almost as a corollary which adds nothing to the knowledge of phenomena.

4.3 - Evangelista Torricelli.

EVANGELISTA TORRICELLI (1608–1647) was a disciple and friend of Galileo, and succeeded him in the chair of Mathematics at the University of Pisa. He raised to the status of a principle a remark by Galileo, according to which a system of heavy bodies can start to move spontaneously only if its centre of gravity moves towards the common centre of all heavy things (*i. e.* that point towards which all heavy things are attracted by their weight). The statement of this principle, which is known today as the Principle of Torricelli, and is, as a matter of fact, a particular case of PVV, is contained in the treatise *De motu gravium naturaliter descendentium et projectorum*, published at Florence in 1644.

We may easily read this principle as a particular case of PVV as follows: provided the weight is vertical and directed downward, if the only allowed displacements (or velocities) for the centre of gravity of the system, starting at its position, are directed upward (or, what is the same, if the power of the weight corresponding to each of these *virtual* velocities is nonpositive), then the system cannot start to move and, consequently, remains in equilibrium.

Thus, the Principle of Torricelli, beyond its intrinsic interest, shows to us how and to what extent in the middle of XVIIth Century the intuition, or even the perception, of PVV, after an evolution of about two thousand years, had fully matured, and the world of mechanicians was ready to produce and to accept a general formulation of the Principle.

5. The formulation of the Principle of Virtual Velocities

5.1 - René Descartes.

As we have seen in Section 4, PVV was considered by Galileo and Stevin as a simple way to epitomize the knowledge about the equilibrium phenomena acquired by examining them case by case. It was René Descartes (1596–1650) who really reversed this viewpoint, and was able to understand the advantage of bringing all the cases of equilibrium back to a unique principle. He states this principle in the short treatise *Explication des engines par l'ayde desquels on peut, avec une petite force, lever un fardeau fort pesant*, published in the year 1637:

The work which is necessary to raise two different weights to different heights is the same if the same is the product of weight by height.

(R. Descartes, *Explication des engins par l'ayde desquels on peut, avec une petite force, lever un fardeau fort pesant*)

Also, in a letter dated October 5th, 1637, he writes:

The invention of all [simple machines] is only based on a single principle, which is that the same force that can lift a weight of, for example, a hundred pounds to a height of two feet, can also lift one of two hundred pounds to a height of one foot, or one of four hundred pounds to a height of half a foot, and so on, however this may be applied.

And this principle cannot fail to be accepted if it is considered that the effect should always be proportional to the action which is needed to produce it.

This principle is for Descartes the very startpoint of any study of problems concerning equilibrium, and as such he employs it in the above quoted treatise to discuss the equilibrium of a pulley, of a body on an inclined plane, and of a weight hung to an end of a lever.

One cannot help remarking explicitly that Descartes raises to the status of a principle that implicit postulate we have seen to have been so fruitfully used by Jordanus de Nemore and by his anonymous pupil (see Section 3). But his contribution to Statics cannot be thought of as reduced to this. There is more in his principle, that deserves to be carefully noted and at least briefly discussed. First of all, though Descartes uses almost always in his statements of the principle the word *force*, what he really means is the *work*, *i. e.* the expense in energy required to obtain the effect of raising a weight, as he explains himself in his letters to Father Mersenne:

The force of which I have spoken *always has two dimensions* and is not the force which might be applied at some point to mantain a weight, which always has only one dimension.
(R. DESCARTES, from a letter to Father Mersenne, September 12th, 1638).

At last you have understood the word force in the sense that I use it when I say that it takes as much force to lift a weight of 100 pounds to a height of one foot as to lift one of 50 pounds to a height of two feet. That is, that *as much action* or *as much effort* is needed.
(R. DESCARTES, from a letter to Father Mersenne, November 15th, 1638).

Accordingly, two different heavy bodies hunging from the ends of a lever with different arms are in equilibrium when and only when the same energy must be expended to raise any one of them. And it is such a conclusion what makes Descartes' principle a very formulation of PVV. But still, even explicitly stating an almost final form of PVV, which we have seen to be an evolution of Aristotle's description of the causes of equilibrium, Descartes was not aristotelian in his way of conceiving Statics. As we have seen (Section 2), Aristotle compared the velocities the weights on a lever would have acquired if it had left its equilibrium position. But Descartes claims that only displacements, not velocities, are to be considered. As observed by Colonnetti [47], since the (virtual) displacements to be considered in the study of equilibrium should be taken as being simultaneous, to speak about them or about the velocities should lead to the same result. But, according to Descartes, to speak in terms of velocities would imply a wrongful mixing Statics with Dynamics. And when Mersenne draws his attention to Galileo's results, perhaps attempting to point out some similarities between them and Descartes' ones, this latter sharply expresses his disagreement to the aristotelian (and galilean) viewpoint. He explicitly states that the consideration of velocities would necessarily lead to attribute three dimensions (instead of two) to the force, and adds:

As for those who say that I should consider the velocity as Galileo has done I believe, among ourselves, that they are people who only talk nonsense and that they understand nothing in this matter.

(R. Descartes, from a letter to Father Mersenne, October 11th, 1638).

Moreover,

I do not deny the material truth of what the students of mechanics are accustomed to say. Namely, that the greater the velocity at the end of the long arm of a lever is, in relation to the velocity at the other hand, the less force it requires to be moved. But I deny that the velocity or the slowness are the causes of this effect.

(R. Descartes, from a letter to Boswell, 1646).

Finally, that's how Descartes synthesizes the difference between his own principle and the methods of Galileo:

As for what Galileo has written on the balance and the lever, it explains the *quod ita fit* rather well, but not the *cur ita fit* as I have done with my Principle.

(R. Descartes, from a letter to Father Mersenne.

But, as we shall see, velocities would have worked very better than displacements, in a rigorous formulation of Descartes' principle. As we should say in our modern language, to project each force on the direction of the displacement of the point of the system on which it acts, means to project it on the straight line tangent to its trajectory at the equilibrium position, and this in turn means to take a vector parallel to velocity (not, in general, to any finite displacement of the point). This difficulty is solved by Descartes (though he would have probably not set it in these terms) by explicitly pointing out that his principle should be applied only to infinitesimal displacements, not to finite ones:

The relative weight of each body should be measured by the *start* of the movement which the power that mantains it can produce, either to raise or to lower it, rather than by the height to which it can rise after it has fallen down. Note that I say *start to fall* and not simply *fall*, because it is the start of the fall that must be taken care of.

It is this what enables him to describe a body moving along a curved surface rather than upon an inclined plane. And in connection to this problem, he explains that the tension a weight P would produce in a rope keeping it in equilibrium is the same either if the surface the weight relies upon is curved or if it is simply the tangent plane to the surface at the contact point M. According to Colonnetti [47],

> It is true that the motion of the body, should this go up or down by finite quantities, would be quite different from its motion along the tangent plane: nevertheless, the direction of the displacement at the initial instant would be the same in both cases.
>
> (G. COLONNETTI, *I fondamenti della Statica*)

Moreover, Descartes writes:

> And it is evident that the change occurring to this motion when [the body] has lost its contact with the point M cannot affect the weight it has when touching M.

Thus, in conclusion, Descartes stated and applied a Principle of Virtual Displacements (or of Virtual Work) rather than a Principle of Virtual Velocities. Nevertheless, his formulation, and above all his application and perception of the power and limits of the principle, are the first so near to our modern mathematical description as to deserve this name.

5.2 - Johann Bernoulli.

Descartes' Principle of Virtual Work was far from being plainly and diffusedly accepted in the mathematical and scientific world of XVIIth Century. It was supported by the english mathematician and mechanician JOHN WALLIS (1616–1703), who wrote a treatise *Mechanica, sive de Motu*, published 1669-1671, in which he not only accepted the principle, but also generalised it to forces other than the heaviness. Nonetheless, in the years immediately following the publication of Wallis' work, the method of virtual displacements was almost completely abandoned, so as the writers about Statics either ignored it at all or declared it to be not sufficiently assured to be taken as a foundation of Statics itself. In this last period of XVIIth Century, we find instead several attempts to reconstructs Statics as a deductive theory according to the model of euclidean geometry. In France, the mathematician PIERRE VARIGNON (1654–1722) wrote the treatise *Projet d'une Nouvelle Mécanique* (1687) and the treatise *Nouvelle Mécanique ou Statique*, only appeared posthumously in 1725. In the former, even acknowledging the influence of Descartes and Wallis, Varignon aims at showing that the whole Statics could be reconstructed upon the one principle of compositions of forces.

Thus, Varignon seems to disregard the Principle of Virtual Velocities. Nevertheless, it is him who gives this Principle the widest diffusion, by publishing the letter written to him by JOHANN BERNOULLI (1667–1748) (January 26th, 1717), in which this latter gives the first explicit statement of it. Bernoulli writes:

Imagine several different forces which act according to different tendencies or in different directions in order to hold a point, a line, a surface or a body in equilibrium. Also, imagine that a small motion is impressed on the whole system of these forces. Let this motion be parallel to itself in any direction, or let it be about any fixed point. It will be easy for you to understand that, by this motion, each of the forces will advance or recoil in its direction; at least if one or several of the forces do not have their tendency perpendicular to that of the small motion, in which case that force or those forces will neither advance nor recoil. For these advances or recoils, which are what I call *virtual velocities*, are nothing else than that by which each line of tendency increases or decreases because of the small motion. And these increases or decreases are found if a perpendicular is drawn to the extremity of the line of tendency of any force. This perpendicular will cut off a small part from the same line of tendency, in the neighbourhood of the small motion, which will be a measure of the virtual velocity of that force.

For example, let P be any point in a system which mantains itself in equilibrium. Let F be one of the forces, which would push or draw the point P in the direction FP or PF. Let Pp be a short straight line which the point P describes in a small motion, by which the tendency FP assumes the position fp. Either this will be parallel to FP, if the small motion is, at every point, parallel to a straight line whose position is given; or it will make an infinitely small angle with FP when this is produced, and if the small motion of the system is made around a fixed point. Therefore draw PC perpendicular to fp and you will have Cp for the *virtual velocity* of the force F, so that $F \times Cp$ is what I call the *energy*.

Observe that Cp is either *positive* or *negative*. The point P is pushed by the force F. It is *positive* if the angle FPp is obtuse and *negative* if the angle FPp is acute. But on the contrary, if the point P is pulled, then Cp will be *negative* when the angle FPp is obtuse and *positive* when it is acute. All this being understood, I form the following general proposition.

In all equilibrium of any forces, in whatever way they may be applied and in whatever direction they may act — through intermediaries or directly — the sum of the positive energies will be equal to the sum of the negative energies taken positively.

(J. BERNOULLI, from the letter to Varignon, January 26th, 1717)

The great philosopher and scientist Pierre Duhem who, among its merits, has also that of having been a great student of the history of Statics, claims that the above letter is the end of the *Origins* of this science and the start of its *Classical Period*. It is true that, as observed by Dugas [55], Bernoulli's statement is not quite general, nor quite precise, in that the virtual displacements he takes on consideration are simply translations or rotations, which may not be compatible with the constraints and, on the other hand, do not necessarily cover all allowed displacements. But nevertheless, it is the first true explicit statement of PVV (although in the form of a Principle of Virtual Displacements): after it, the two lines of thought which Duhem calls *analytic* and *synthetic* (roughly corresponding to the archimedean and aristotelian viewpoints, respectively) find a common perspective, which will be taken by Lagrange as a startpoint to develop not only the whole Statics, but also the whole Dynamics of (systems of) particles and rigid bodies. But to understand this issue, we must briefly turn our glance to the problems posed by Dynamics in XVIIIth Century, what will be done in the next Section.

6. The early rôle of the Principle in the rising modern mechanics

6.1 - Jean-Louis Le Rond d'Alembert.

At the end of XVIIth Century, and with the dawning of the XVIIIth, the history of PVV gets its own heart. From its earliest days and up to then, it developed in the pure framework of Statics, so that the subsequent refinements of the statement of PVV up to the one given, as we have seen in the previous subsection, by Bernoulli, simply mean achievements (even often through harsh polemics) of an ever better synthesis of the laws of Statics as a quite independent doctrine. But in the late years of XVIIth Century, the new theory of Dynamics, first outlined by Galileo, then brought to a mature axiomatic-deductive form by ISAAC NEWTON (1642–1727) and LEONHARD EULER (1707–1783), called the attention of scientist who looked for a mathematical description of physical phenomena. In particular, the french culture of XVIIIth Century, partly influenced by english empirism as it was introduce and diffused in France by Voltaire, partly still dominated by the authoritativeness of the german philosopher GOTTFRIED LEIBNIZ (1646–1716), or rather of the Academy of Science of Berlin, established by him in the year 1700, adopted the antimetaphysical perspective of the former, and the purely logical *a priori* method of the latter. This developed in it the trend to refuse the axiomatic foundation of newtonian (and, as far as systems of particles and rigid bodies are concerned, eulerian) dynamical theory. How this trend is linked with both the above described cultural influenced, is clearly expressed in the work of the philsopher and mechanician JEAN-LOUIS LE ROND D'ALEMBERT (1717–1783), especially in his *Traité de Dynamique*, published for the first time in the year 1743.

As a mechanician, d'Alembert did not give relevant contribution to the history of PVV, neither as concerns its statement, nor its proof. To be precise, as far as equilibrium is concerned, he goes back in his treatise to a refined form of the principle of the lever. Nevertheless, in view of our aims, his work is of the greatest relevance, insofar it furnishes a new perspective of use of the principles of Statics to solve a wide class of dynamical problems, in particular to write down the laws of motion of constrained bodies. And it is the use of PVV made in the dynamical context by Lagrange, which actually furnished the motivation for the not yet concluded debate about the rôle of PVV in Mechanics.

The work of d'Alembert takes place in the history of Mechanics between the researches of Newton (1688) and Euler (1736) about the dynamics of mass-points (bodies which may be considered as points, so that the motion of each of their parts with respect to the others may be disregarded), and Euler's work (1760) on the dynamics of rigid bodies. This is probably the first reason why his *Traité de Dynamique* shows a deep awareness of the open problem of describing the motion of bodies in a quite general fashion. According to his words,

> But how does it happen that the motion of a body follow this or that particular law? That is on which Geometry can teach us nothing, and is also what can be considered as the first Problem immediately pertaining to Mechanics.
>
> (J.-L. D'ALEMBERT, *Traité de Dynamique*).

These words, however, seem to go beyond the problems concerning only the bodies whose extension cannot be neglected, and to refer also to material points. This is likely to be due to the fact that d'Alembert rejects, as a *metaphysical* statement, the main principle of newtonian mechanics, that Second Principle which really enables to foresee the motion of a body by linking it to the forces exerted on the body itself by the external world:

> Why should we then appeal to that principle, which the whole world now uses, according to which the accelerating or retarding force is proportional to the elementary increment of velocity? A principle supported on that single vague and obscure axiom that the effect is proportional to its cause. We shall in no way examine whether this principle is a necessary truth or not, but we shall only acknowledge that the evidence till now produced to support such a hypothesis is not irrelevant; neither shall we accept it, as some geometers have done, as being of purely contingent truth, which would destroy the exactness of Mechanics and reduce it to being no more than an experimental science: we shall be content to remark that,

true or false, clear or obscure, it is useless to Mechanics and that, consequently, it should be banished.

(J.-L. D'ALEMBERT, *Traité de Dynamique*).

To get a correct understanding of these statements, one has to bear in mind the features of the french philosophical and scientific environment in which d'Alembert developed his way of thought. On one hand, the epistemologic views of english empirism induced most of french philosophers to try to abandon any metaphysical concept to found scientific knowledge, so that the concept of force itself was to d'Alembert still matter of reflection and critical re-examination, in that it needed to be purged of any nonempirical content. But, on the other hand, pure empirism could not fully satisfy d'Alembert, who otherwise could have accepted the idea that forces (or better, the laws of force) can be assigned by assumption, thus anticipating the interpretation of a dynamical theory which would have been asserted with Mach only hundred and fifty years later. He is also strongly influenced by the logical conception of a true description of the world proposed by Leibniz.

According to Leibniz, a rational and true description of the world must be of mathematical type, *i. e.* to be characterized by the same certitude of purely mathematical theories. On the other hand, the certitude of these latter lies in the *necessity* of their statements: these, of course, are of two kinds: the *premises* (axioms or principles, or hypotheses) and the *deduced statements*. The necessity of these latter is acknowledged to be guaranteed first by that of the rules of logic applied in their deduction, that are in turn considered as necessary by their very nature, then by that of the premises. Thus, in order to construct a truly mathematical theory, one has to be sure that its principles are *necessary truths*. A statement is a *necessary truth* when its truth can be acknowledged independently of experience, simply in virtue of its logical structure. Such a statement is said to be *self-evident*, and since its evidence does not lie on sensorial, but rather on intellectual experience (as, for example, the evidence of noncontradiction principle), it is also said to be true in all possible worlds. Roughly speaking, it corresponds to what is nowadays called — in the framework of Logic — a *tautology*: a proposition which is true independently of the value of truth of elementary (empirical) propositions composing it and whose negation is a contradiction. A statement which is not a necessary truth, is called a *contingent truth*, about which only experience may tell us whether it is true or not.

Thus, looking for a rational description of mechanical phenomena, d'Alembert assumes the task of relying it upon few principles that be so self-evident as those of Algebra were almost unanimously considered at his time. And Newton's equation

$$\text{force} = \text{mass} \times \text{acceleration},$$

conceived as an equation in which the forces were a datum, had not been proved to be a necessary truth, and could be neither stated nor used in a truly mathematical theory of mechanics. But d'Alembert discovered that the Principle of Inertia could. In fact, the first two principles of his *Traité de Dynamique* are:

> I. A body at rest will stay at rest, unless an external cause put it into motion.
> II. A body put in motion by any cause, must always continue its motion uniformly and on a straight line, until a new cause, different from the one which has moved it, will act on it; in other words, unless an external cause different from motive cause act on this body, it will perpetually move on a straight line, covering equal lenghts in equal times.
> (J.-L. D'ALEMBERT, *Traité de Dynamique*).

These statements obviously rephrase Galileo's Principle of Inertia by splitting it into two parts. And d'Alembert feels to be allowed to state them as principles, because he is able to prove them as consequences of a very old philosophical principle of logical nature, the so-called *Principle of Sufficient Reason*, thus proving — in agreement with the prescriptions of leibnizian rationalism — that they are necessary truths. Hereafter, he argues as follows: since only forces produce accelerations, then the acceleration of a body $\mathcal{B}$ is an evidence (even a measure) of the force acting on $\mathcal{B}$. As we would write in our modern symbolic language, the force F is a function of acceleration a:

$$F = f(a),$$

where the function f must satisfy the condition $f(0) = 0$. But there is no reason why it should be

$$f(a) = ma \tag{6.1}$$

(with some chosen $m > 0$, possibly equal to the mass of $\mathcal{B}$). This can be only an arbitrary choice of a measure of forces, a convention, a definition.

But, thus conceived, equation (6.1) gives no help to solve the Problems of Mechanics, unless we acknowledge that the force (or better acceleration itself) obeys a law of dependence on kinematic variables (position and velocity) and time. This dependence may be of course a merely contingent truth, and may be taken as an hypothesis of particular theorems of Mechanics aiming at the solution of particular problems. But, as it seems, there is only one case in which we are allowed by experience to formulate such a dependence: when the force acting on a body is reduced to its weight. On the other hand, according to d'Alembert, beyond this one, there is only one more type of force:

Now, which are the causes that may produce or modify the motion of bodies? Up to now, we don't know but two kinds: the former ones reveal themselves at the same time as the effects they produce, or rather of which they are an occasion; they have their source in the perceivable mutual action of bodies, which in turn results from their impenetrability: they reduce to the shock and to some more actions deriving from it; all of other causes are not known but through their effect, and we completely ignore their nature: such is the cause which leads the bodies to fall towards the centre of earth, keeps the planets on their orbits, etc.

(J.-L. D'ALEMBERT, *Traité de Dynamique*).

For this latter kind of forces, the law of gravitation may be directly assumed as a law of dependence of acceleration on position (possibly replaced, when dealing only with heavy bodies of daily experience, by the requirement that acceleration be constant and directed towards the centre of earth); but it is the solution of problems involving the former kind of forces, the *contact forces*, which draws d'Alembert's attention, as they are the only still open mechanical problems:

Bodies cannot act upon each other but in three different ways that are known to us: either by an immediate stroke, as in ordinary shock; or by means of some interposed body, to which they are attached; or finally by a reciprocal attraction, as the Sun and the Planets do in the newtonian system. Since the effects of this last kind of interaction have been sufficiently examined, I shall confine myself to treat the motion of bodies which shock in any way, or of those which pull each other by means of threads or inflexible sticks.

(J.-L. D'ALEMBERT, *Traité de Dynamique*).

And the solution of this kind of problems does not require, according to d'Alembert's opinion, the use of equation (6.1), which turns out to be quite useless in Mechanics, as it can be replaced by two more principles:

III. If any two powers move a body or a point A at the same time, the former from A to B uniformly during some time, the latter from A to C [not aligned with A and B]

uniformly during the same time, let us consider the parallelogram $ABCD$: I state that the body A will go along the diagonal AD uniformly in the same time it would have employed to cover the lines AB or AC.

IV. If two bodies, whose velocities are in the inverse ratio with respect to their masses, move in opposite directions, so that each of them could not move without displacing the other, they will be in equilibrium.

(J.-L. D'ALEMBERT, *Traité de Dynamique*).

These express the *Principle of Composition of Motions* and the *Principle of Equilibrium* respectively. As the above stated principles expressing the law of inertia, they also are, in a suitable sense of the word, theorems, *i. e.* propositions proved as consequences of purely philosophical principles, to be sure they are necessary statements.

The application of these principles is summarized in the solution given by d'Alembert to the general formulation of the kind of problems he aims at solving:

General problem: let there be given a system of bodies arragend in any way with respect to each other; and suppose that a particular motion is imparted to each of these bodies, which it cannot follow because of the action of the other bodies. Find the motion [the velocity, as d'Alembert has stated before] that each body must take.

Solution: let A, B, C, etc. be the bodies that constitute the system and suppose that the motions a, b, c etc. are impressed on them; let there be forces, arising from their mutual action, which change these into the motions a', b', c', etc.. It is clear that the motion a impressed on the body A can be compounded of the motion a' which it acquires and another motion α. In the same way the motions b, c, etc. can be regarded as compounded of the motions b' and β, c' and κ, etc.. From this it follows that the motions of the bodies A, B, C, etc. would be the same, among themselves, if instead of their having been given the impulses a, b, c, etc. , they had been simultaneously given the twin impulsion a' and α, b' and β, c' and κ, etc.. Now, by supposition, the bodies A, B, C, etc. have assumed, by their own action, the motions a', b', c', etc.. Therefore the motions α, β, κ, etc. must be such that they do not disturb the motions a', b', c', etc. in any way. That is to say, that if the bodies had only received the motions α, β, κ, etc. these motions would have been cancelled out among themselves, and the system would have remained at rest.

From this results the following principle for finding the motion of several bodies which act upon each other. *Decompose each of the motions a, b, c, etc. which are impressed on the bodies into two others, a' and α, b' and β, c' and κ, etc. , which are such that if the motions a', b', c', etc. had been impressed on the bodies, they would have been retained unchanged; and if the motions α, β, κ, etc. alone had been impressed on the bodies, the system would have remained at rest. It is clear that a', b', c', etc. will be the motions that the bodies will take because of their mutual action.* This is what it was necessary to find.

(J.-L. D'ALEMBERT, *Traité de Dynamique*).

This solution is known, and quoted in most subsequent treatises on Rational Mechanics, as the *d'Alembert's principle.*

The Mechanics of d'Alembert is then presented as a system quite alternative to Newton's and Euler's theory with respect either to the aims either to the methods. What d'Alembert — as he refuses in principle Newton's and Euler's method of axiomatisation — cannot realize, and that will be fully realized only hundred fifty years later, is that his principles, as leading to the same mathematical relations as Newton's and Euler's ones to describe the motion of any single point or rigid body, must be quite equivalent to the ones he rejects. And, in view of our attempt to achieve a complete understanding of the present logical *status* of PVV in Mechanics, it will be now important to acknowledge what hides to his eyes this equivalence.

The causes modifying the motion that are linked to the presence of material obstacles, are to d'Alembert — consistently with what has been stated in general about the causes of motion — to be considered as simply acting by means of geometric restrictions on the possible trajectories of the body. To treat them, no idea of force (at least, in the mathematical sense of the word) is needed at all. We may simply apply the Principle of Composition of Motion to split the supposedly unperturbed motion into the sum of the actual motion, unaffected by the obstacle, and another motion, which can be thought of as destroyed by the obstacle according to the Principle of Equilibrium.

We therefore see not only that it is d'Alembert who gives rise to the fully general theoretical study of constrained (systems of) bodies (and he confines himself only to such systems, too), but also the way in which he expunges the newtonian and eulerian notion of force from Mechanics. Even those contact forces that really motivate d'Alembert's work, and that we now call the forces of constraints, as mathematical expressions of the actions of obstacles on a body, are quite absent from his theory.

Thus, after the work of d'Alembert, two different and complementary theories of Mechanics are at disposal of the scientists: the former, developed by Newton and Euler, mainly dealing with free bodies and systems, and essentially relying upon a quite general notion of force; the latter, proposed by d'Alembert, almost solely devoted to treat constrained systems, and quite purged of this metaphysical concept (the phrase *force of inertia* could be interpreted as a linguistic bridge to translate in terms of motions a Principle of Equilibrium which, at least by tradition, should instead be expressed in terms of forces).

This is what completely ceals the equivalence between d'Alembert's mechanical theory and the newtonian-eulerian one. In the light of our present knowledge, and according to our modern language, we should state that such equivalence could result only, on one hand, by extending the dynamics of d'Alembert to consider actions at distance different from weight (and this will be one of the results of the work by Lagrange); on the other hand, by introducing in Euler's system of balance equations the forces of constraints among the external forces acting on a system of bodies, and setting them equal to zero for free bodies. That is why the mechanicians of XIXth Century, and of the early XXth Century, wishing to treat the dynamics of constrained systems in the framework of Euler's theory, shall feel obliged to write such a queer statement as *we may replace constraints by forces*, quite pleonastic in a theory in which any body (even if merely working as an obstacle) is assumed to exert a force upon any other. It is perhaps an acknowledgement to history, to remember the force free origin of the theory of constrained systems.

The forces of constraints will appear for the first time — without however being at first acknowledged as such — in Lagrange's *Mécanique Analytique*, as a side effect of the application of his method of multipliers: a sort of by-product.

6.2 - Joseph-Louis Lagrange.

It is almost impossible to overestimate the contribution given by Joseph-Louis Lagrange (1736–1813) to the birth of a truly mathematical theory of mechanics (or to the development of the whole body of mathematics, as for this). The figure he cuts in the history of mechanics must be discussed under at least three different aspects: first, as the scientist who was able to give PVV its final, comprehensive and precise form, which would have been not changed any more later, if not according to the evolution of mathematical language; second, as he established a mathematical theory of dynamics supported on a principle of equilibrium, choosing PVV to this aim; finally, as the mathematician who first perceived and tried to solve the problem of proving PVV or, at least, to give it a justification. These three aspects are of course strictly connected: nonetheless, they must be kept carefully separated, since mixing them is the shortest way to misunderstanding the rôle in Mechanics PVV would have been destined to have after Lagrange. Accordingly, we shall treat them separately, describing the first two aspects in this subsection, and the third one only in Subsection 7.1.

To start with, we report the lagrangean formulation of PVV, as it was presented in the treatise *Mécanique Analytique*, published for the first time in 1788, and again in a revised and enlarged edition (to which shall refer all of our quotations in the sequel) in 1811:

If any system of as many bodies and points as it can be desired, each pulled by whatever power, is in equilibrium, and is given any small displacement, by virtue of which each of its points travels an infinitely small distance which will express its virtual velocity, the sum of the powers, each multiplied by the space covered following its line by the point on which it acts, will be always equal to zero, if we take as positives the small lengths covered in the same directions of the powers, and as negatives the lengths covered in the opposite directions.

(J.-L. LAGRANGE, *Mécanique Analytique*).

Suitably generalized, this is the statement we have a confrontation with each time we discuss about PVV and try to prove or disprove it. Two remarks spontaneously arise about this form of the principle. First, it is clearly presented as only a necessary condition to equilibrium; next, it seems to be stated only for bilateral constraints. These features may be explained in connection with the kind of problems Lagrange had in mind as applications of the Principle, which seem to be the same suggested by d'Alembert as still left open after the creation of Newton's theory of gravitation and the related mathematical description of all phenomena solely involving freely falling bodies.

In particular, as far as the first feature is concerned, one could simply observe, at first sight, that Lagrange, though claiming PVV as only a necessary condition, still tries to give a proof also of its sufficiency, and, what is more, when using it in applications, he does not hesitate to treat PVV as both a necessary and sufficient condition.

One could now ask the reason why the necessity is pointed out in the statement while sufficiency is disregarded. In this connection, we may hazard an interpretation by noting that what Lagrange really aimed at doing, was to state a principle which, further than being sufficiently general, could be expressed by a single comprehensive formula easy to be specialized for particular problems. As he explicitly states the Foreword to his work,

I have intended to reduce the theory of this Science [Mechanics], and the art of solving the connected problems, to general formulas, of which the simple development could yield all the necessary equations to the solution of each problem.

(J.-L. LAGRANGE, *Mécanique Analytique*).

And in Section I of the statical part of his book, referring to his own formulation of PVV, Lagrange also states that

This principle is not only very simple and general in itself; it also offers a more precious advantage in that it can be expressed by a quite general formula which contains all the problems that could be posed about the equilibrium of bodies. We shall set this formula in all its extension, and shall try to present it in a still more general way than up to now, and to point out some new applications.

(J.-L. LAGRANGE, *Mécanique Analytique*).

Moreover, Lagrange does not — and cannot — argue as a modern mathematician would do, for he has not at his disposal, like this latter, two different mathematical conditions describing equilibrium, and whose equivalence is to be proved: he must start, rather than from a mathematical definition, from a mechanical, purely qualitative, description of equilibrium, namely,

Equilibrium results from the destruction of several forces that fight and mutually annihilate the action exerted by each on the others; and the aim of Statics is to give the laws according to which this destruction takes place.

(J.-L. LAGRANGE, *Mécanique Analytique*).

This description is quite non-mathematical as far as, at Lagrange's time, it cannot be expressed by making equal to zero a vector sum. Lagrange is then mainly interested in showing that, when this condition is met, then a general analytical formula may be applied.

Let us now turn our attention towards the complete absence from the above statement of any reference to unilateral constraints. This can also be explained by reminding that, according to the kind of problems concerning levers, pulleys and inclined planes, or even simply *large* free bodies, treated by the authors quoted by Lagrange in his introductory Section I, the constraints were to be solely viewed as devices diverting the force of gravity (or the force that a body could exert by virtue of its own momentum) from its direction. Starting from a rest position, which is to be checked whether it is of equilibrium or not, and referring to the sole gravity, the equilibrium problem lies in determining the residual, diverted force that could move the body along the constraint. This is equivalent to consider only bilateral constraints.

It will be only the mechanical science of XIXth Century which, with RUDOLF CLAUSIUS (1822–1888) will introduce the explicit consideration of unilateral constraints, thus taking into account the possibility of motions detaching from the constraints under the action of forces that can be different from the sole weight.

To conclude this discussion, it will be important to show how the above formulation of PVV may be expressed by a formula. To this end, consider some forces P, Q, R, etc. ..., having different directions, each acting on a point of a system. Then, denoting by dp, dq, dr, etc. ... the spaces that, if the system were not in equilibrium, could be covered by the points of the system in the directions of P, Q, R, etc. ..., respectively, the above formulation of PVV yields

$$P\mathrm{d}p + Q\mathrm{d}q + R\mathrm{d}r + \ldots = 0, \tag{6.2}$$

which Lagrange calls the *general formula of Statics*. This relation is used by Lagrange first of all to determine which kind of forces may assure the equilibrium; and, coversely, to derive a formula which could be used to check whether a given system of forces (the weights of the points of the system, say) keeps it in equilibrium at a given position. In the method used by Lagrange is fully revealed his mathematizing power. In fact, he gives an explicit analytical expression to d'Alembert's geometric considerations, by remarking that the constraints imposed to the points of the system (interposed bodies, sticks, pulling threads) may be expressed by a number (k, say) of *condition equations*

$$f_h(x_1, y_1, z_1, \ldots, x_i, y_i, z_i, \ldots) = 0, \tag{6.3}$$

where (x_i, y_i, z_i) are the coordinates of the i-th point of the system. Now, denoting by (X_i, Y_i, Z_i) the components

It should however be added that in the above statement there seems to be no reference at all to the concept of constraint, and, accordingly, no distinction between what we now call active forces and the forces of constraints, which seems to be completely absent even in what Lagrange considers as a proof of the principle. But the discussion of this point will be possible only once we have described why the Principle of Virtual Velocities came to Lagrange as a foundation for both Statics and Dynamics, and how was used by him to this aim.

This point is made clear, rather than in Lagrange's account of *The different principles of Statics*, where he confines himself to analyse the historical origins, the nature and the conceptual power of PVV, in the introductory Section to the dynamical part of *Mécanique Analytique*, *On the different principles of Dynamics*. Lagrange plots there a very accurate history of the principles that underlie the whole body of dynamics and, above all, of the evolution that led to them. It is of the main relevance his way of showing how and why and under which conditions the solution of dynamical problems needs the help of Statics:

> As regards the laws of acceleration of heavy bodies, they may be naturally deduced from considering the uniform and constant action of gravity, in virtue of which the bodies receive in equal instants equal degrees of speed along the same direction, so that the total speed acquired at the end of any time, must be proportional to this time; and it is clear that this constant ratio of speed to time must be itself proportional to the magnitude of the force exerted by gravity to move the body; so that, in the motion on inclined planes, this ratio cannot be proportional to the absolute force of gravity, as in the vertical motion, but to its relative force, which depends on the inclination of the plane, and must be determined according to the rules of Statics; this furnishes an easy mean to compare the motions of bodies descending along differently inclined planes.
>
> (J.-L. LAGRANGE, *Mécanique Analytique*).

This passage not only explains how Statics must be used in the description of dynamical problems, but also furnishes some matter of reflection on seventeenth century views about the forces and their link with the acceleration of bodies. We have seen that d'Alembert rejected as metaphysical the Second Law of Newton's Dynamics, according to which the acceleration of a body (at an instant, we would say nowadays) is proportional to the force acting on it. But Lagrange's words seem to set forth again Newton's view. On the other hand, he explicitly appeals to Statics as regards of the determination of the relative forces. In fact, he also states

> The Treatise on Dynamics by d'Alembert, which appeared in 1743, brought to an end this kind of challenges, as it offered a direct and general method to solve, or at least to put into equations, all the problems that could be imagined about Dynamics. This method reduces all the laws of motion of bodies to the ones of their equilibrium, and brings Dynamics back to Statics. [...] it was reserved to d'Alembert to represent this principle in a quite general fashion, and to give it all the simplicity and the fertility it could be given.
>
> (J.-L. LAGRANGE, *Mécanique Analytique*).

How can we understand this apparent contradiction? Does Lagrange share d'Alembert's rejection of Newton's Second Principle of Dynamics? Taking into account his scientific and philosophical environment, we could dare answer yes, and no as well. Of course, the wonderful agreement of this principle with the law of fall of heavy bodies discovered by Galileo, and with the three laws of revolution of planets formulated by Kepler, could not help raising in the scientifical world a widespread admiration towards it, or rather, towards the use made of it by Newton. On the other hand, and at the same time, one cannot forget the conception of forces inherited by modern scientists from the ancient people. According to it, by a force one tacitly meant a contact force, *i.e.* a traction or a pressure exerted on a body by another body touching it, or trasmitted by a number of intermediate contacts with interposed bodies. Bringing the law of fall of heavy bodies back to the action of a force, involved the conceptual jump to the existence of forces acting from a distance, without any contact: and this jump, in XVIIIth Century, was far from being accomplished (it would have been accomplished only one century later, with the full introduction of the notion of *field*). Newton could not but be admired in that he had been able to guess the existence of one force acting from a distance, and to determine its action depending on the distance itself. But this did not mean to accept his Second Principle in its full generality: in order to be used as an equation allowing to calculate, *i.e.* to foresee, the motion, it requires indeed the forces to be considered as a datum (at least as regards their dependence on the position and speed of the body undergoing them), so that, to write down it in a useful way to Dynamics, one needs to feel to be allowed to postulate a law of force; otherwise, d'Alembert is right, Newton's Second Principle is quite useless. And the contact forces, which probably seemed the most relevant part of the forces taking place in nature, were not, according to d'Alembert's and — as it seems — Lagrange's views, to be guessed, or arbitrarily assigned, but to be determined (at least in the absence of deformations of the body exerting the force: recall Hooke's law). As we shall see, this viewpoint, with suitable modifications of methodological nature, will be fully accepted in the framework of the Newton and Euler dynamical theory.

Thus, Lagrange concentrates himself on contact interactions between bodies (or parts of the same rigid body), and confines the use of the Newton equation of motion to the case of gravity and of possible other forces acting from a distance. When he states that force must be proportional to acceleration, he does not contradict d'Alembert's anti-metaphysical views (see Subsection 6.1):

he simply seems to express the purely mathematical fact that acceleration is one of infinitely many possible measures for the force (what is hard to suppose to have escaped d'Alembert). For the rest, he fully agrees to d'Alembert's Principle of Equilibrium that, joined with the Principle of Inertia and the Principle of Composition of Motions, should lead to determining both the motion of a body undergoing contact forces and, as a consequence, these forces themselves. But he also wants to give this principle a fully general mathematical form, through a formula allowing to achieve the desired results in any particular concrete case by means of pure calculations.

To Lagrange, the Principle of Equilibrium clearly appears as a very restricted, and difficult to handle, version of PVV. Once it is replaced by this latter, expressed as a mathematical equation, one can build the whole Dynamics in the same logical line as d'Alembert's, by simply calculating a suitable special form of the general relation, with a great economy of thought and for much more general and complicated systems of bodies. That's what Lagrange actually does: as a matter of fact, what is nowadays called the *d'Alembert-Lagrange equation* is nothing more and nothing less than PVV itself, where amongst the forces acting on the body under consideration, besides the contact forces (to be determined) and, as a datum, possible forces acting from a distance (typically, the weight), the forces of inertia (also to be determined) are taken into account.

Nevertheless, Lagrange was not a philosopher, but a mathematician, probably perceiving the philosophical instances of his time rather as a frame of thought than as a rigid system of methodological directives. Furthermore, he writes down the whole body of his theory for the first time forty-five years after d'Alembert. So, he does not hesitate to use the notion of a force as a mathematical concept (what d'Alembert had avoided as possible). As a mathematician, he shows to have clearly understood that, in the framework of Statics, forces can be measured, by simply taking any arbitrarily assigned of them as a measure unit: this makes them true mathematical objects, and that is one more reason to found the whole Mechanics on Statics. On the other hand, he is also fully aware that a standard measurement procedure for any force is based on the geometrical and kinematical description of the motion it would have produced if it had been not equilibrated by other forces. And this is the key step to the introduction of concepts like *virtual displacement* and *virtual velocity*, which did not mean to Lagrange what they mean to us nowadays. They were exactly any displacement and any velocity that would have been instantaneously imparted to a material point by a force acting on it, if this latter were not equilibrated by other forces. From this viewpoint, it does not matter at all whether such displacement or such velocity is allowed or not by supposed constraints. On the contrary, the explicit consideration of displacements, or velocities, forbidden by these latter, is in agreement with the basic idea that what we now call constraints, though described in a purely geometric language according to the above outlined methodological views, are simply bodies exerting contact forces on the material particles under consideration. As we shall see in more details in subsection 7.2, the geometrical description of constraints, which is nowadays presented in handbooks and textbooks purely as a mean to discriminate allowed velocities and displacements from the forbidden ones, was instead adopted by Lagrange to apply PVV to determining which forces are to be equilibrated by which ones.

As a matter of fact, in Lagrange's work there is no reference at all to constrained bodies in opposition to supposed free ones, for the very simple reason is that a free body is nothing more and nothing less than a freely falling body, about which, after Galileo, we know all what there was to know.

The distinction between free and constrained bodies will make sense only in the framework of Newton's and Euler's dynamical theory, when the idea of a law of force will dominate the whole world of mechanics, and it will be necessary to discriminate the case in which the law of all forces acting on a body may be assigned from the case in which some forces (just the forces of constraints) are to be left unknown.

7. Attempts to prove the Principle in the framework of Statics

7.1 - Lagrange and the reduction of PVV to the Principle of Pulleys.

In the first section of *Mécanique Analytique*, wholly devoted to the exposition of the principles of Statics, Lagrange states PVV and assumes it as the general principle of Statics, explicitly claiming that any other principle which might be taken as a foundation of this discipline, could not differ from PVV but in the expression:

> And in general I believe to be allowed to claim that all the general principles, which in the future could perhaps be discovered in the science of equilibrium, will be nothing but the same principle of the virtual velocities considered from a different viewpoint, and will not differ from it but in the expression.
>
> (J.-L. LAGRANGE, *Mécanique Analytique*).

And more, as we have seen in the foregoing Section, PVV was to him a foundation of Dynamics, when joined with the Principle of Inertia and the Principle of Composition of Motions. Once this is understood, one cannot expect that Lagrange would have tried to prove it in a quite formal way, especially relying upon some different law of Dynamics. A chain of propositions ending at the statement of PVV and starting with an unproved dynamical proposition is just the kind of thing we cannot expect, for it would lead to a vicious circle, in that any dynamical relation is to Lagrange a consequence of PVV, and cannot be taken as an unproved starting point for a proof of this latter without replacing it as a foundation for dynamics, so renouncing and nullifying all what Lagrange had in mind to do. But, as a proposition of Statics (a theory that, as we have seen in previous Sections, was conceived in XVIIIth Century as independent of Dynamics), was PVV again a foundation, that is, an axiom, or did it need a proof? To Lagrange's mind, it needed to be proved, and we shall now try to outline a motivation for this answer.

As a matter of fact, the need for a proof of PVV even in the pure framework of Statics, should be clear from our description (Subsection 6.1) of the contribution given by d'Alembert to the birth and development of modern Dynamics. We have seen, indeed (Subsection 6.2), that Lagrange shares at least the antimethaphysical views of d'Alembert: but he maybe follows even more faithfully d'Alembert's conception of what a principle of a mathematical theory should be. According to his words,

> One cannot but agree that it [PVV] is not so evident in itself as to be eriged to a primitive principle.
>
> (J.-L. LAGRANGE, *Mécanique Analytique*).

By these words, Lagrange seems to mean that PVV is not a necessary truth, so that it cannot be taken as a self-evident proposition, holding true in any possible world, and — accordingly — cannot work as a real principle,

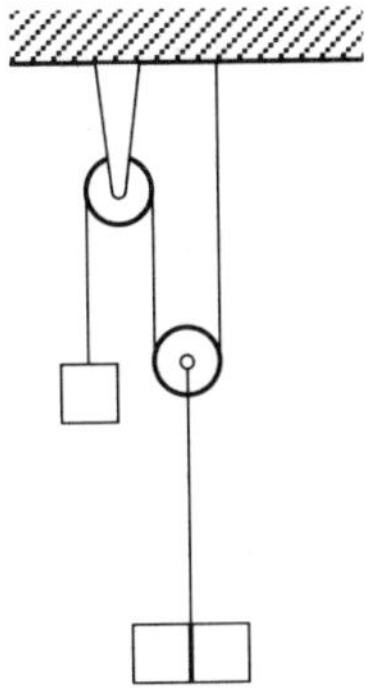

Figure 11.

to be accepted without proof. He therefore deems it necessary to point out the equivalence of this principle with some other, possibly more particular, but more intuitively evident and just for this reason more suitable to be adopted as a primitive principle. Such requirements, according to Lagrange, are fulfilled by what he calls the *Principle of Pulleys.* A pulley is a wheel which can turn around its own axis, and endowed with a groove in which a rope may slide; by combining a suitable number of pulleys, either fixed to a ceiling by a stirrup, or left free to go up and down, one can build machines allowing to raise great weights with small forces.

The way of working of these devices, widely studied, *e. g.*, by Guido Ubaldo dal Monte and Stevin, may be explained by starting with the assumption that an heavy body hanging from the end of a tightened rope produces in it a tension equal to the weight, which is transmitted without changing in the rope until its other end. In such a way, with the help of the machine illustrated in figure 11, a counterweight P may sustain a weight $2P$, since this last is suspended to two parallel ropes, each exerting on it a tension P. In the same way, if the rope is winded n times around the couple of pulleys supporting the weight, then the same counterweight P will be able to sustain a weight $2nP$.

This stated, Lagrange assumes that the points P_1, P_2, ..., of a mechanical system are acted upon by forces F_1, F_2, ..., which are supposed — as a first step — all commensurable, so that, denoting by $2f$ any of their common divisors, one can put $F_1 = 2n_1 f$, $F_2 = 2n_2 f$, etc., for some suitable natural numbers n_1, n_2, etc.

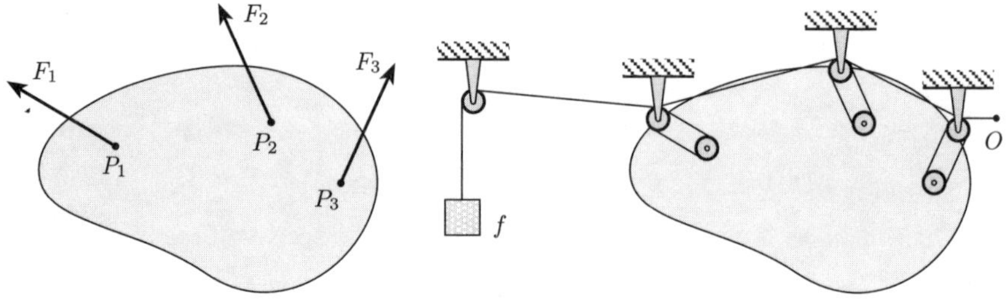

Figure 12.

Next, for any point P_h, he considers a pair of pulleys: the former occupies the position of P_h and is free to follow the small displacements allowed to P_h by the constraints; the latter is fixed at a point belonging to the action line of the force F_h (Figure 12). An unextensible rope, an end of which be fixed at a point O of the space, embraces n_1 times the couple of pulleys corresponding to the point P_1, n_2 times the one corresponding to the point P_2, and so on. To the free end of the rope is suspended a body of weight f, producing a tension of the same value at each point of the rope.

In such a way, each point P_h is pulled by a force equal to twice the product of tension f by the number of windings around the pulleys corresponding to it, and the device just described allows to replace by the sole weight f all the forces initially applied to the system.

If we now assume that the system be in equilibrium in a given configuration, then we conclude that there cannot exist any displacement of the points $P_1, P_2, \ldots$, allowed by our device, which makes the weight f go down; indeed, if such a displacement were allowed, the system would actually be displaced, and could not be in equiluibrium. On the other hand, also displacements raising f are not allowed: if any of them were allowed, since the constraints are bilateral, there would be also an allowed displacement lowering f. In conclusion, any allowed displacement of the points of the system must leave the height of f unchanged.

In order that this be possible, denoting by $s_1, s_2, \ldots$, the displacements of the points, as measured along the directions of the forces acting upon them, it must result

$$2nfs_1 + 2nfs_2 + \ldots = 0,$$

or, equivalently,

$$F_1 s_1 + F_2 s_2 + \ldots = 0. \tag{7.1}$$

This last identity coincides with the analytical formulation of PVV, which is therefore a necessary condition to the equilibrium of the system.

Conversely, if (7.1) is satisfied corresponding to any possible displacement of the points of the system, then this last stays in equilibrium: indeed, the weight f does not move for its height cannot change, and the remaining points also stay at rest because there is no reason why each of them should move according to one rather than to the other of the two displacements characterized by the numerical values $s_1, s_2, \ldots$ or by their opposites.

Lagrange concludes his proof by remarking that, once the principle is proved in the case of commensurable forces, the demonstration may be extended to the general case by means of a *reductio ad absurdum*.

The lagrangean proof of PVV lays itself open to some interesting remarks. It is based upon the replacement of the forces acting upon a system with the ones produced by a device consisting of a number of pulleys linked to a weight; in virtue of such a replacement, stating that PVV is verified for the real system, is fully equivalent to claiming that it is true for the machine which has taken its place. The necessity of PVV for this simpler system is guaranteed by the evident property according to which an heavy body which can go down will actually go; the sufficiency is proved instead by invoking the logical argument of the sufficient reason. These remarks induce first E. JOUGUET [36], then Colonnetti [47], to state that Lagrange's proof has a physical rather than a mathematical character.

This stated, we may however leave aside this aspect, to acknowledge that the conceptual meaning of Lagrange's proof consists in the statement that PVV holds true in general, provided it is verified in the particular case of the considered system of weight and pulleys.

Once he had achieved his comprehensive and general formulation of PVV, Lagrange also opened a new period, in which many attempts to reduce this principle to one or another of previous principles of Statics, were performed, after Lagrange himself, by several prominent Authors as, for instance, Ampère and Fourier. During that period, PVV met the strange destiny of being considered as a theorem in Statics and as a sort of axiom in Dynamics. It kept this ambiguous position during the whole XIXth Century until the first years of XXth Century. This, as we shall see in the sequel, will produce an as much ambiguous way of describing its real rôle in mechanics.

7.2 - Fourier and the reduction to the Principle of Lever.

It would be impossible to account for all the attempts to prove PVV by means of purely statical reasonings, that were performed after Lagrange at the beginning of XIXth Century. We simply confine ourselves to report two samples that seem of particular interest to understand which properties of forces were then accepted and used to deduce PVV.

To start with, we consider the proof presented by JOSEPH FOURIER (1768–1830) in his *Mémoire sur la Statique*, published in the *Journal de l'Ecole Polytechnique* in the year 1798. This work is divided into several parts, the first two of which are in particular devoted to the problem of proving PVV, and follow two different lines of reasoning. In the first part, that we confine ourselves to simply mention, Fourier gives rise to a line of thought which will be diffused in almost all the treatises about Rational Mechanics of XIXth Century, and according to which any system can be regarded as composed of points; it is permissible to apply to each of these the ordinary equilibrium condition holding for free points, provided the constraints are replaced by suitable forces, the forces of constraints, satifying the condition that, when the friction is disregarded, their total work corresponding to any infinitesimal displacement allowed by the constraints is less or equal to zero (it must be pointed out that Fourier uses a convention about signs which is opposite to the ours).

The second part of the paper turns out to be of particular interest in that it offers a very different way to tackle the same question, which appeals to the principle of lever. As already done by Lagrange, Fourier leaves the nature of the system under consideration undetermined, and confines himself to assume that the forces act upon the points P, Q, ... In order to show that PVV holds true, he must prove that, if the total work of the forces corresponding to an

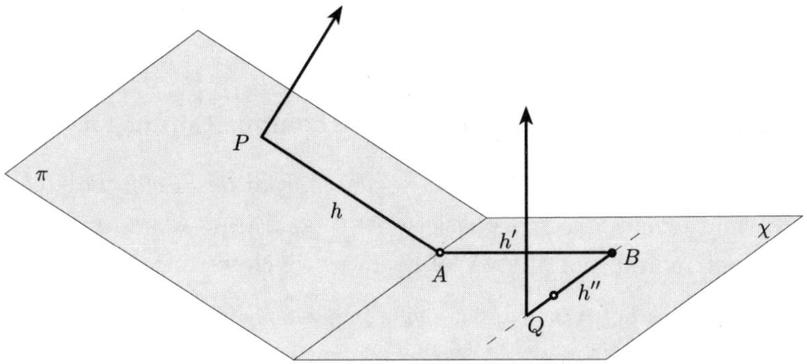

Figure 13.

assigned displacement of the system, allowed by the constraints, is zero, then such a displacement is impossible.

This goal is achieved by means of a reasoning which can be epitomized as follows: let us fix our attention on the points P and Q, and consider the planes π and χ passing through P and Q and orthogonal to the direction of their displacements, respectively; let us draw the perpendicular h from P to the intersection r of the planes, and denote by A the common point of h and r; next, starting from A, consider the perpendicular h' to r in χ; finally, draw the perpendicular h'' from Q to h', and denote by B the intersection between h' and h'' (see Figure 13). We may consider PAB as an angular lever with fulcrum at A and, similarly, QB as a rectilinear lever whose fulcrum is a point to be specified later. It is now clear that, if P undergoes the infinitesimal change of position pertaining to it in the assigned displacement of the system, then it communicates the motion, by means of lever PAB, to the point B, which in turn produces a motion of the point Q. Thus, provided the fulcrum of BQ is properly chosen, Q will in turn undergo the the infinitesimal change of position pertaining to it in the assigned displacement of the system. This construction may of course be extended in an obvious manner to all the points of the system.

The proof then follows from the equilibrium condition for the system of levers. Indeed, by a rather elaborate argument, whose details are not essential in this context, Fourier shows that if the original system were actually set in motion, then the same would happen for the system of levers, which is impossible, since this last cannot undergo any displacement for which the total work of the forces is zero.

7.3 - Ampère and the reduction to the composition of forces.

In a Memory published in 1806 in the *Journal de l'Ecole Polytechnique*, the great mathematician and physicist ANDRÉ-MARIE AMPÈRE (1775–1836) presented one more proof of PVV of his own, which were founded

> ... uniquely on the theory of composition and decomposition of the forces acting on the same point, and ... free from the consideration of infinitely small quantities ...
>
> (A.-M. AMPÈRE, *Démonstration générale du Principe des Vitesses Virtuelles dégagée de la considération des infiniment petits.*)

He achieves his goal by examining first the case of a system with only one degree of freedom, and subsequently bringing the general case back to this one, by means of a perspicacious analytical method.

Ampère starts with introducing the concept of the *moment* of a force acting on a point, which is what we now call its *power* corresponding to the unit virtual velocity. After this, he states PVV as follows:

> Let us take the sum of the moments of all the forces acting upon the system taking with opposite signs those for which the forces and their projections fall on the same part, and those for which the forces and their projections fall on opposite parts; let us add to this sum that of the equations deduced from all the given equations [the constraints], each multiplied by an arbitrary factor and reduced in such a way that they contain in all of their terms the derivatives x', y', z', at the first power; let us equate separately to zero the quantities multiplying each derivative and eliminate all of the arbitrary factors; the remaining equation or equations will express all the equilibrium conditions.
>
> (A.-M. AMPÈRE, *Démonstration générale du Principe des Vitesses Virtuelles dégagée de la considération des infiniment petits.*)

This rather involved statement simply expresses the procedure already described in Subsection 6.2 and consisting in writing equation (6.4), then deriving from it system (6.5) and finally calculating from it first the values of the arbitrary multipliers, then those of the coordinates of the equilibrium positions.

Since we consider a system with only one degree of freedom, we may claim that each of its points moves on an assigned trajectory, under the action of a given force. Now,

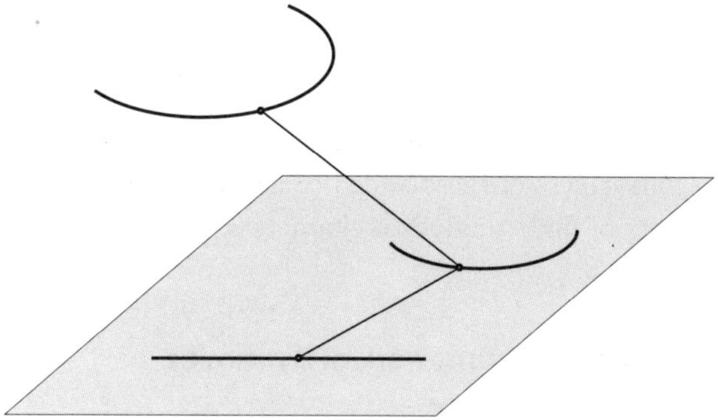

Figure 14.

There is a case in which the equilibrium law is evident for a system of forces applied to points that can move only simultaneously and in a prescribed fashion; this happens when the conditions are such as to allow the points only to slide, simultaneously and without changing their mutual distances, over the straight line along which are directed the forces acting upon them. The equilibrium then requires that the sum of these forces, when those acting in opposite directions are taken with contrary signs, be equal to zero; and if this condition is satisfied, equilibrium necessarily follows.

(A.-M. AMPÈRE, *Démonstration générale du Principe des Vitesses Virtuelles dégagée de la considération des infiniment petits.*)

This stated, the heart of Ampère's argument lies in the remark that, when a point is moving on a given trajectory under the action of an assigned force, the same effect of this force may be reproduced by linking the point, by a rigid stick, with another one moving on an arbitrarily chosen curve under the action of an arbitrarily directed force, provided this last has the same moment of the original one. Thus, by applying this construction to each of its points, any system may be in fact replaced by another one in such a way that

... the force are directed as it can be desired and the moving points slide on arbitrarily chosen curves; this in such a way that: 1) if there is equilibrium for the former system, then there still be for the latter, and conversely, since the forces may be replaced one by another with no change in the state of the system; 2) the sum of the moments be the same in both systems...

(A.-M. AMPÈRE, *Démonstration générale du Principe des Vitesses Virtuelles dégagée de la considération des infiniment petits.*)

In particular, any system may be replaced by a system of the kind for which the equilibrium condition, according to the above remark, is quite evident.

The extension of the result to systems with several degrees of freedom adds nothing, from a conceptual viewpoint, to the structure of the above reasoning. It is based indeed on the idea of adding, in a quite arbitrary way, as many constraints as it can be needed to reduce the system to one degree of freedom. By using the arbitrariness of these added constraints, Ampère is able to prove PVV by arguments of quite analytical character.

8. Towards a proof in the framework of Dynamics

8.1 - Statics as a particular case of Dynamics.

Thanks to the work of d'Alembert, Lagrange, Fourier, Ampère and others, the XIXth Century presents a picture of Mechanics in which not only Statics and Dynamics stay each beside the other on a ground of full parity and mutual independence, but also the latter uses as a basic principle, by a suitable change or reinterpretation of terms occurring in it, a theorem of the former. But at the beginning of XXth Century Statics lose its independence from Dynamics, to became a part of it. This drastic change of perspective is of the main relevance to understand which is the proper way to set today the problem about the provability of PVV and about its epistemological status in the framework of modern Dynamics.

In his paper *Über ein neues allgemeines Grundgesetz der Mechanik*, published in the year 1829 in the *Crelle's Journal für Mathematik*, KARL FRIEDRICH GAUSS (1777–1855) wrote that

> It is to be expected that, when the science will have reached an higher level, Statics will be presented as a particular case of Dynamics.
>
> (K. F. GAUSS, quoted by Mach in *Die Mechanik in ihrer Entwickelunghistorisch-kritisch dargestellt.*)

This forecast, due of course to the acumen of the great mathematician, seems today quite natural, in that we have at our disposal a dynamical theory which enables us to give an explicit mathematical form to the quite non-mathematical definition of equilibrium according to which any system of forces is in equilibrium if (and only if) their joint actions produce no effects, implicitly used — as we have already pointed out in previous Sections — by ancient students of Statics in their research of equilibrium criteria. In such a dynamical theory equilibrium is no more a property of systems of forces, but a property of positions: a position is said to be an equilibrium position if and only if a body occupying that position with zero speed at any instant, stays there at rest after that instant. Second, by using the dynamical equations of motions, one can show that if and only if a body is in equilibrium (at rest) in a position, then the system of forces acting on it in that position is equilibrated according to any one of the conditions of equilibrium determined in the framework of pure Statics.

As a matter of fact, we are today in a position to see that all the difference between the dynamical and the statical viewpoints lies in the direction of arguing. If one wants to give a logical and epistemological value to the preceding historical development of Statics with respect to that of Dynamics, then one cannot but take the principles of the former as very axioms of the latter, and deduce from them the equations governing the motion of any mechanical system under the action of whatever system of forces. If, instead, one is disposed to write the equations of motion without any justification other than some form of the Principle of Inertia, then one may deduce from these latter the principles of Statics, by simply determining under which conditions the equations of motion admit only the rest solution. In both cases, a basic problem is to be solved: the forces appearing in the equations of motion (be they deduced, as according to the former viewpoint, or assumed, as according to the latter) cannot be all unknown. At least some of them must be assumed to have been measured, at least as functions of the position and of the velocity. The full understanding of this problem led to the introduction of the concept of *law of force* as a prescribed dependence of external forces acting on a body, or on a system of material points, on its position and velocity. This, of course, solved the problem for both the procedures: but also, it deprived the choice of founding Dynamics on Statics of its main motivation, *i.e.* the rejection of any possibility of knowing forces without measuring accelerations. Thus, Dynamics was given the prominent and unifying rôle it has nowadays, and started the process leading Statics to be considered as a part of Dynamics.

Before this, for the whole XIXth Century, and until the first years of 1900, the most part of University textbooks and treatises about what is today called *Rational Mechanics*, developed the Dynamics founded by d'Alembert and Lagrange on the Principle of Virtual Velocities beside the one based by Newton and Euler on the Second Law, and independently of it: this latter was used indeed (together with a quite tacitly accepted idea of a law of force) only in the newtonian form dealing with single, freely floating or falling bodies, envisageable as material points, *i. e.* to solve problems involving uniquely gravity and other possible forces acting at a distance analogous to the weight; for rigid bodies and systems of material points subjected to mutual or external contact forces, the Principles of d'Alembert and Lagrange evidently seemed to be better founded. This was probably to be expected for the books written by scholars who developed their way of thinking in the cultural environment of continental Europe: but it also happened in some important treatises written by Authors of english culture, who should have supported instead the newtonian structure of mechanics, also in its eulerian generalization (see *e. g.* E. J. Routh, [37]).

But Gauss himself gave (together with Nicolaj Ivanovič Lobačevskij (1793–1856), János Bólyai (1802–1860) and G. F. Bernhard Riemann (1826–1866)) one of the deepest contributions to the evolution he had foreseen. The discovery of non-euclidean geometries, in fact, first put the mathematicians in front of the hard reality that no mathematical theory — not even euclidean geometry, which, together with what was then called *the science of numbers*, seemed the most certain among mathematical doctrines — develops from necessary truths or really self-evident propositions. In 1899, following this new epistemological address, David Hilbert (1862–1943) published his *Grundlagen der Geometrie*, where *points*, *straight lines* and *planes* were thought as arbitrary objects, having no intuitive nor experimental counterpart, and simply implicitly defined by the axioms they were supposed to satisfy. This was the official Death Act of necessary truth in Mathematics. Three years later, Henri Poincaré (1854–1912) wrote:

> The geometric axioms are neither a *priori* synthetic sentences, nor experimental facts. They are positions that rely upon an agreement.
>
> (H. Poincaré, *La science et l'hypothèse*).

And, only one more year after, the philosopher and mathematician Bertrand Russell (1872–1970), partly joking and partly seriously, echoed:

> Thus, mathematics may be defined as the matter in which we never know what we are talking about, nor whether what we say is true or not.
>
> (B. Russell, *Mathematics and metaphysicians*, quoted from memory).

While this ever more widely accepted epistemological position about mathematics destroyed the philosophical basis of any attempt to found Dynamics on Statics and of any consequent need to prove PVV in the framework of this latter, the *cardinal equations* proposed by Euler in 1760 for systems of material points and continuous (rigid) bodies, had proved — also thanks to the wonderful work made by LOUIS MARIE HENRI NAVIER (1785–1836), LOUIS AUGUSTIN CAUCHY (1789–1857), and many others — their great pragmatic value in the dynamical study of deformable continua. Thus, on one hand, Rational Mechanics turned out to be only conceivable as a deductive system based on mere hypotheses, that were to be checked only by the agreement of their consequences with experience; on the other hand, the theoretical scheme built on Newton's and Euler's axioms seemed to join an high degree of syntactic clarity and simplicity with a great richness and exactness of results. This prepared the way to the acknowledgement of the epistemological value of the law of force and to the dominance of Dynamics on Statics.

8.2 - The literature about Rational Mechanics in the second half of XIXth Century.

The treatises about Rational Mechanics published in the late XIXth Century and at the beginning of the present century, reflect rather faithfully not only the above outlined evolution, but also the consequent fight and overlap of principles for Dynamics: a number of them [5,7,9,10,13,31,44,46], evidently willing to apply as cleverly as possible the method of reduction to Statics for the Dynamics of systems of interacting material points, start from Newton's laws for a single free material point, but use them only as a mathematical tool to write in a formally manageable way the d'Alembert principle and PVV, that they invoke as such, without any attempt to give them a proof, to obtain the (Lagrange) equations governing the motion of an either constrained or free system; but most of them [11,12,14,18–21,25–28,37,38,41,45], also starting from the same Newton's laws, try in fact to give a methodological justification of Euler's method, by deriving from them at least the laws of equilibrium of both, free systems of material points and free rigid bodies. More precisely, still trying to establish Dynamics on Statics, they obtain from Newton's laws, further than the equilibrium conditions for a single free material point, also those for a point constrained to move on a surface or on a curve, and those for a free rigid body or system of points. Then, they take these conditions as a startpoint to give a proof of PVV, and use this latter, jointly with d'Alembert's principle of composition of motions, to get the equations governing the motion of a free rigid body or rigid system of points and — finally — of any system of constrained material points and rigid bodies (cf. mainly [18,20,37]).

It is to be noted that the application of such method forces these latter Authors to perform a statical proof of PVV, since they cannot appeal — in the general case of a constrained (or free but rigid) system of material points — to the laws of motion that they aim at determining. Nevertheless, or rather just as a consequence of their methodological approach, they need to take explicitly into account the so-called *forces of constraints*, *i. e.* the forces exerted on the system by the bodies that realize the constraints, and to make some assumptions on them or to prove for them, by appealing to a number of simple special cases, some characteristic properties. This, as we shall see in the next Section, seems to be an unavoidable price to pay in order to get at least a startpoint for a deduction of PVV from a different but formally expressed equilibrium condition. On the other hand, this also requires a careful distinction between free systems and those ones that are to be considered as constrained. The theoretical structure adopted by these Authors seems to betray the original method proposed by d'Alembert, who explicitly aimed at disregarding the forces of constraints. The statement of mathematical equilibrium conditions from which PVV could be deduced seems then one more step from d'Alembert's statical viewpoint towards Newton's and Euler's dynamical one.

9. A proof of the Principle of Virtual Velocities

9.1 - The statement of PVV for bilateral constraints.

In the second half of the present century, the evolution foreseen by Gauss is accomplished, and the first University textbooks appear presenting Analytical Dynamics as a consequence of a suitably formalized and generalized version of Euler's balance equations for systems of constrained material points and rigid bodies, and accordingly reversing the relationship assumed until then between Statics and Dynamics of systems subjected to constraints (see Walter Noll, [64], Clifford Truesdell, [67]).

The key step to this inversion is the remark that, when one is prepared to take explicitly into account, among the forces influencing the motion of a system, the contact interactions between the bodies of the system itself, and between them and the material devices realizing the constraints, and is not shocked by the need of making some assumptions about this kind of forces (though necessarily renouncing to the idea of giving for them a law of force), then the so-called *d'Alembert and Lagrange equation* does not need, to be deduced, any principle of equilibrium, but can be derived from the Euler system of equations. Once this step is made, the Lagrange equations become, as they were probably intended to be by Lagrange himself, the most general and complete formulation of d'Alembert's principle, PVV turns out to be quite useless as a principle of Dynamics and becomes a mere equilibrium criterion, whose provability in the framework of the dynamical theory is a new matter of study.

We shall now suitably rephrase in a quite formal and rigorous fashion the derivation of Lagrange's equations from Newton's and Euler's ones, as it is ever more diffused in the modern textbooks (we refer to [75] for a more detailed exposition of this subject). This seems convenient not only for the sake of completeness, in that this deduction is the final step of the above outlined evolution, but also because it will deliver all the technical tools for both the formulation and an attempt of solution of the problem of proving or disproving PVV, as it has nowadays taken shape.

To be more precise, let $\mathcal{X}$ be any material system consisting of K mass points $p_1, \ldots, p_K$ and H rigid bodies $\mathcal{B}_1$, $\mathcal{B}_2, \ldots$, $\mathcal{B}_H$. As we have seen in Section 6, even d'Alembert would have been disposed to write the newtonian equation of motion for each particle p_i,

$$m_i \ddot{\boldsymbol{x}}_i = \boldsymbol{f}(\{p_i\}, \{p_i\}^e; t) \tag{9.1}$$

($i \in \{1, 2, \ldots, K\}$) though taking it as a mere definition. On the other hand, according to Euler's description of the dynamics of rigid bodies, each $\mathcal{B}_j$ obeys a system of the form

$$\begin{aligned} M_j \ddot{\boldsymbol{x}}_{G_j} &= \boldsymbol{f}(\mathcal{B}_j, (\mathcal{B}_j)^e; t), \\ \dot{\boldsymbol{K}}_{G_j} &= \boldsymbol{M}_{G_j}(\mathcal{B}_j, (\mathcal{B}_j)^e; t), \end{aligned} \tag{9.2}$$

($j \in \{1, 2, \ldots, H\}$). In equations (9.1) and (9.2), $\{p_i\}^e$ and $(\mathcal{B}_j)^e$ respectively denote the complements of $\{p_i\}$ and $\mathcal{B}_j$, *i.e.* the remaining part of $\mathcal{X}$ and the external world $\mathcal{B}^e$ interacting with $\mathcal{X}$. Moreover, for any $i \in \{1, 2, \ldots, K\}$, m_i is the mass of $\{p_i\}$ and $\boldsymbol{f}(\{p_i\}, \{p_i\}^e; t)$ is the total force exerted on $\{p_i\}$ by $\{p_i\}^e$ at instant t; for any $j \in \{1, 2, \ldots, H\}$, M_j is the mass of $\mathcal{B}_j$ and $\boldsymbol{f}(\mathcal{B}_j, (\mathcal{B}_j)^e; t)$ and $\boldsymbol{M}_{G_j}(\mathcal{B}_j, (\mathcal{B}_j)^e; t)$ are the resultant and the total moment tensor, with respect to the center of masses G_j, of the system of forces exerted on $\mathcal{B}_j$ by $(\mathcal{B}_j)^e$ at instant t.

As we have seen in Section 6, d'Alembert would have never accepted equations (9.2), if not as derived from some necessary truths, namely, his own principle and a principle of equilibrium. But we, coming after the logical and epistemologic revolution shortly outlined in Subsection 8.1, neglect any preoccupation about necessary truths, and accept equations (9.2) as axioms. Doing so, we also keep in mind that, in order to construct a real dynamical theory, forces (and their moments, of course) must be always taken as data, at least as far as their dependence on the motion of $\{p_i\}$ and $\mathcal{B}_j$ is concerned.

This stated, our aim is now to show how we can derive from these premises the Dynamics of those constrained systems that HEINRICH HERTZ (1857-1894) calls *holonomic*. To this aim, we confine ourselves, mainly in view of our interest in criteria of equilibrium, to the case in which the constraints do not vary with time.

Let E be the vector space associated to the reference (inertial) space of positions and denote by $\boldsymbol{x}_i \in E$ the position vector of $\{p_i\}$, by $\boldsymbol{x}_{G_j} \in E$ the position vector of G_j and by $\boldsymbol{Q}_j \in \mathrm{Orth}^+(E)$ the positive orthogonal endomorphism of E expressing the orientation of $\mathcal{B}_j$; similarly, denote by $\boldsymbol{v}_i \in E$, $\boldsymbol{v}_{G_j} \in E$ and $\boldsymbol{A}_j \in \mathrm{Lin}(E)$ the velocity of $\{p_i\}$, the velocity of G_j and the endomorphism of E expressing the rate of change of $\boldsymbol{Q}_j$. Finally, let us put

$$\boldsymbol{X} = (\boldsymbol{x}_i, \boldsymbol{x}_{G_j}, \boldsymbol{Q}_j) \in E^K \times (E \times \mathrm{Orth}^+(E))^H$$

and

$$\boldsymbol{V} = (\boldsymbol{v}_i, \boldsymbol{v}_{G_j}, \boldsymbol{A}_j) \in E^K \times (E \times \mathrm{Lin}(E))^H.$$

We assume — according to the mathematical description proposed by Lagrange (see Section 6) — that any motion of the system $\mathcal{X}$ must obey a set of conditions

$$\begin{aligned} f_\alpha(\boldsymbol{X}) &= 0 \qquad (\alpha = 1, \ldots, r), \\ g_\beta(\boldsymbol{X}) &\geq 0 \qquad (\beta = 1, \ldots, s), \end{aligned} \tag{9.3}$$

where f_α and g_β are sufficiently smooth functions. Then, to be consistent not only with the spirit, but also with the logical structure of the theory we are building on the basis of equations (9.1)–(9.2), we cannot but acknowledge the presence of the contact forces exerted on $\mathcal{X}$ by any kind of material devices (obstacles) which be able to confine it in the region of space defined by conditions (9.3) and, accordingly, split the force terms at right hand sides of (9.1) and (9.2) as sums of these actions (that will be identified by the apex (c) and will be referred to as the *forces of constraints*) and some forces acting at a distance (that we shall mark with the apex (a) and identify as *active forces*):

$$
\begin{aligned}
m_i\ddot{\boldsymbol{x}}_i &= \boldsymbol{f}_i^{(a)} + \boldsymbol{f}_i^{(c)} \\
M_j\ddot{\boldsymbol{x}}_{G_j} &= \boldsymbol{F}_j^{(a)} + \boldsymbol{F}_j^{(c)} \\
\dot{\boldsymbol{K}}_{G_j} &= \boldsymbol{M}_{G_j}^{(a)} + \boldsymbol{M}_{G_j}^{(c)}
\end{aligned}
\tag{9.4}
$$

($i \in \{1,2,\ldots,K\}$, $j \in \{1,2,\ldots,H\}$). Here, the forces $\boldsymbol{f}_i^{(a)}$, $\boldsymbol{F}_j^{(a)}$, $\boldsymbol{M}_j^{(a)}$ are assumed to be calculated, according to a prescribed law of force, as functions of the position $\boldsymbol{X}$ and of the velocity $\boldsymbol{V}$ of $\mathcal{X}$, further than of time, so that

$$
\begin{aligned}
\boldsymbol{f}_i^{(a)} &= \boldsymbol{f}_i^{(a)}(\boldsymbol{X},\boldsymbol{V},t) \\
\boldsymbol{F}_j^{(a)} &= \boldsymbol{F}_j^{(a)}(\boldsymbol{X},\boldsymbol{V},t) \\
\boldsymbol{M}_{G_j}^{(a)} &= \boldsymbol{M}_{G_j}^{(a)}(\boldsymbol{X},\boldsymbol{V},t),
\end{aligned}
$$

while the forces $\boldsymbol{f}_i^{(c)}$, $\boldsymbol{F}_j^{(c)}$, $\boldsymbol{M}_{G_j}^{(c)}$ are, at each instant t, just the contact forces exerted on $\{p_i\}$, and the total forces and moments exerted on $\mathcal{B}_j$, respectively, by the whole complex of obstacles.

As far as these latter are concerned, we must now recall that — though the underlying methodology of the theory requires, in view of the kind of problems we aim at solving, the explicit assumption that any force acting on a material system whose motion we want to foresee, may be expressed as a function, further than of time, also of the parameters describing position and velocity of the system itself — experience, and above all our reflection on continuum mechanics, shows instead that the contact forces can be assigned as functions of position, velocity and time, only by means of an intermediate dependence on the deformation of contacting surfaces. Since conditions (9.3) exclude (or at least hide) any deformation of the material devices realizing constraints, we can in no way prescribe the forces of constraints. Still, the development of a self-contained and consistent dynamical theory, which could be also sufficiently powerful for applications, prevents us from giving up any kind of condition on these forces: we must at least bound the class of possible actions of constraints on the system. Now, in exactly the same way as for the forces acting at a distance, it is experience what suggests to us at least a number of plausible statements about the forces of constraints, which turn out to have only two kinds of effects on the system $\mathcal{X}$:

(i) preventing the points and the bodies of $\mathcal{X}$ from leaving the set $\mathcal{V}$ of allowed positions and configurations;

(ii) opposing the motion of $\mathcal{X}$ in $\mathcal{V}$.

The true difference between these properties and a law of force, is that they seem far too general to be mathematically expressed as a dependence of the forces of constraints on space, time and kinematical features of the motion. But, once they will have been put in some mathematical form, the obtained functional relations will result in a kind of generalized laws of force, less restrictive, and obviously lacking in information if compared with an explicit functional link between force and kinematical variables, but certainly consistent with our methodological directive of deriving information about the motion from that about forces.

At this stage, the modern language of Differential Geometry will be to us of the greatest help in achieving our goal. To start with, we first consider the case in which only constraints of the form $(9.3)_1$ are present (case of *bilateral constraints*). Next, we observe that the vectors $\boldsymbol{X}$ and $\boldsymbol{V}$, that label at each instant the configuration and the kinetic field of $\mathcal{X}$ clearly belong to the manifold $\mathcal{M} = E^K \times (E \times \mathrm{Orth}^+(E))^H$ of dimension $N = 3K + 6H$. This enables us to treat $\mathcal{X}$ as a point moving in $\mathcal{M}$, which is locally euclidean, with inner product

$$\boldsymbol{U} \cdot \boldsymbol{V} = \sum_{i=1}^{K} \boldsymbol{u}_i \cdot \boldsymbol{v}_i + \sum_{j=1}^{H} (\boldsymbol{u}'_i \cdot \boldsymbol{v}'_i + \boldsymbol{U}_j \cdot \boldsymbol{V}_j)\,,$$

for any pair of vectors $\boldsymbol{U} \equiv (\boldsymbol{u}_i, \boldsymbol{u}'_j, \boldsymbol{U}_j)$ and $\boldsymbol{V} \equiv (\boldsymbol{v}_i, \boldsymbol{v}'_j, \boldsymbol{V}_j)$ belonging to the same tangent vector space $T_{\boldsymbol{X}}\mathcal{M}$ to $\mathcal{M}$ at $\boldsymbol{X}$.

Let us now consider conditions $(9.3)_1$. It is well known that each of them defines a $(N-1)$-dimensional submanifold of $\mathcal{M}$. If they are all independent, and their intersection is nonempty and connected, then system $(9.3)_1$ defines a submanifold $\mathcal{V}$ of $\mathcal{M}$ whose dimension is $n = N - r$. Its tangent vector space $T_{\boldsymbol{X}}\mathcal{V}$ at a position $\boldsymbol{X}$ is of course a n-dimensional subspace of $T_{\boldsymbol{X}}\mathcal{M}$.

Let us set

$$\boldsymbol{F}^{(m)} \equiv (-m_i \ddot{\boldsymbol{x}}_i, M_j \ddot{\boldsymbol{x}}_{G_j}, -\frac{1}{2}\dot{\boldsymbol{K}}_{G_j}\boldsymbol{Q}_j),$$

$$\boldsymbol{F}^{(a)} \equiv (\boldsymbol{f}_i^{(a)}, \boldsymbol{F}_j^{(a)}, \frac{1}{2}\boldsymbol{M}_j^{(a)}\boldsymbol{Q}_j),$$

$$\boldsymbol{F}^{(c)} \equiv (\boldsymbol{f}_i^{(c)}, \boldsymbol{F}_j^{(c)}, \frac{1}{2}\boldsymbol{M}_{G_j}^{(c)}\boldsymbol{Q}_j);$$

the vectors $\boldsymbol{F}^{(m)}$, $\boldsymbol{F}^{(a)}$ and $\boldsymbol{F}^{(c)}$ belong, at each instant, to the (N-dimensional) vector space $T_{\boldsymbol{X}(t)}\mathcal{M}$ tangent to $\mathcal{M}$ at the configuration $\boldsymbol{X}(t)$ of system $\mathcal{X}$ at instant t, so that system (9.4) may be written in the form of the single equation

$$\boldsymbol{F}^{(m)} + \boldsymbol{F}^{(a)} + \boldsymbol{F}^{(c)} = \boldsymbol{0} \tag{9.5}$$

on $T_{\boldsymbol{X}(t)}\mathcal{M}$, where, of course, the terms $\boldsymbol{F}^{(m)}$ and $\boldsymbol{F}^{(a)}$ are completely determined by the motion of the system. On the contrary, the sole information at our disposal about $\boldsymbol{F}^{(c)}$ is the purely qualitative one expressed by the above described effects (i) and (ii).

It is now time to give a precise mathematical form to those assumptions. The former of them states that $\boldsymbol{F}^{(c)}$ must prevent the detachment from $\mathcal{V}$ of the point representing $\mathcal{X}$ in $\mathcal{M}$. If we imagine that any material device realizing the constraints is so resistent as to support any charge without being broken, this condition amounts to stating that the component of $\boldsymbol{F}^{(c)}$ normal to $\mathcal{V}$ be not subjected to any restriction, so that it can equilibrate the active and inertia forces, whatever their values may be.

Effect (ii), which expresses the physical mechanism of friction, from a macroscopical viewpoint must be expressed by a phenomenological condition. It is well known that the condition suggested by experience is a proportionality between the amplitudes of the tangential and normal components of $\boldsymbol{F}^{(c)}$ by a constant depending on the physical features of the contacting surfaces (Coulomb's law). In particular, this constant may be made so small as to render physically meaningful the study of the ideal limiting case which consists in assuming the tangential component of $\boldsymbol{F}^{(c)}$ to vanish: a system satisfying such a condition is said to be *ideal*.

Hence, all the information we assume to possess about the forces of constraints may be simply epitomized by the requirement

$$F^{(c)} \in N_{X}\mathcal{V}, \tag{9.6}$$

where $N_{X}\mathcal{V}$ is the r-dimensional normal vector space to $\mathcal{V}$ at $\boldsymbol{X}$.

At this stage, we are in a position to formulate the

Fundamental Problem of the Dynamics of Systems. *To find a couple* $(\boldsymbol{X}(t), \boldsymbol{F}^{(c)}(t))$ *such that, for all* t *in a suitable interval* $I \subseteq \mathbb{R}$, $\boldsymbol{X}(t) \in \mathcal{V}$, $\boldsymbol{F}^{(c)} \in N_{\boldsymbol{X}(t)}\mathcal{V}$ *and, finally, equation* (9.5) *is satisfied.*

Now, projecting equation (9.5) on $T_{\boldsymbol{X}}\mathcal{V}$, and taking into account (9.6), we obtain at once

$$\boldsymbol{F}_{\tau}^{(m)} + \boldsymbol{F}_{\tau}^{(a)} = \mathbf{0}, \tag{9.7}$$

where the index τ denotes the projection on $T_{\boldsymbol{X}}\mathcal{V}$. In virtue of equation (9.7), we may reformulate the Fundamental Problem of the Dynamics of Systems in a simpler form. In fact, we can easily acknowledge its equivalence with the following one: *to find a function* $\boldsymbol{X}(t)$ *such that, for all* $t \in I \subseteq \mathbb{R}$, $\boldsymbol{X}(t) \in \mathcal{V}$, *and equation* (9.7) *is satisfied.* Once this last problem has been solved, it will be indeed possible to determine, by means of equation (9.5), a function $\boldsymbol{F}^{(c)}$ which will certainly belong to $N_{\boldsymbol{X}(t)}\mathcal{V}$ for all $t \in I$.

If we now choose a coordinate system $\mathbf{q} \equiv (q^1, q^2, \dots, q^n)$ for $\mathcal{V}$ in a neighborhood of $\boldsymbol{X}(t)$, and consider the *holonomic* basis $(\boldsymbol{E}_h)$ of $T_{\boldsymbol{X}(t)}\mathcal{V}$ defined by

$$\boldsymbol{E}_h = \frac{\partial}{\partial q^h}, \qquad \forall\, h \in \{1, 2, \dots, n\},$$

then it is a matter of straightforward calculations to acknowledge that, for any $h \in \{1, \dots, n\}$,

$$\boldsymbol{F}^{(m)} \cdot \boldsymbol{E}_h = -\frac{\mathrm{d}}{\mathrm{d}t}\frac{\partial T}{\partial \dot{q}^h} + \frac{\partial T}{\partial q^h},$$

(where T is the total kinetic energy of system $\mathcal{X}$), so that, taking the inner product of equation (9.7) by each $\boldsymbol{E}_h$, we obtain the well-known Lagrange equations

$$\frac{\mathrm{d}}{\mathrm{d}t}\frac{\partial T}{\partial \dot{q}^h} - \frac{\partial T}{\partial q^h} = Q_h(\mathbf{q}, \dot{\mathbf{q}}, t), \tag{9.8}$$

($h \in \{1, 2, \ldots, n\}$) where

$$Q_h(\mathbf{q}, \dot{\mathbf{q}}, t) = \boldsymbol{F}^{(a)} \cdot \boldsymbol{E}_h.$$

Equations (9.8) are obviously quite equivalent to equation (9.7) in that they simply represent a coordinate version of it. Accordingly, we are allowed to further reformulate the above Fundamental Problem of the Dynamics of Systems as follows: *to find a function* $\mathbf{q}(t)$ *satisfying system* (9.8). In fact, the function $\boldsymbol{X}(\mathbf{q}(t))$ will certainly belong to $\mathcal{V}$ by its very definition, and will certainly satisfy equation (9.7).

The procedure we have just outlined shows that Lagrange's equations may be simply envisaged as a translation in an appropriate language of Newton's and Euler's equations, when these are joined with relation (9.6), whose rôle deserves to be carefully discussed.

First of all, one cannot help remarking that equation (9.6) is something less than a law of force, since it obviously does not enable us to calculate even the values of the forces of constraints corresponding to possible positions and velocities of $\mathcal{X}$. But this simply means that the logical development of an independent and self-consistent dynamical theory is much less conditioned by the possibility of prescribing laws of force than one could believe. It is actually needed a weaker support, namely, some relations that be capable to group the whole body of dynamical problems into classes, or kinds: these relations define, or constitute, the different classes of problems we plan to deal with in the framework of Dynamics. When one or more of such relations are assumed to be universally satisfied by all the objects of the theory, then they constitute the maximal class of the problems that can be tackled within it. For this reason, according to the language introduced by W. Noll, B. D. Coleman, C. Truesdell *et al.* (see, *e.g.*, [67]), they are called *constitutive relations*. The laws of force are of course a particular kind of constitutive relations, but — obviously as well — the converse needs not to be true.

It seems now clear how, in our opinion, condition (9.6) cannot be considered as an added axiom reflecting a crossing over the fronteers of the dynamical theory of Newton and Euler, as some authors have suggested (see *e. g.* [74]), but simply as a selection criterion of a class of problems manageable within the theory.

It could be hard to escape the guess that this selection criterion (and the general notion of constitutive relation to which it is related) is used in this case as an *ad hoc* tool to solve the problem of deriving a general description of the mechanical behaviour of any constrained system, *i.e.* the Lagrange equations: and this guess is of course at least partly true, but only in that it reflects that axiomatic spirit which gave rise to the whole modern mathematics, and was so clearly expressed by the statement ascribed to Hilbert: "With nothing, nothing can be done". But still, it is to be remarked that this tool is not more necessary to the dynamical foundation of the mechanics of constrained systems, than to its statical foundation. As a matter of fact, condition (9.6) is nothing but a reformulation of the fundamental part of d'Alembert principle of composition of motions (see Section 6), as it was interpreted in XIXth Century: the motion the system would have had if it had not been constrained, must be decomposed into the sum of its actual motion and another motion whose force of inertia is completely canceled by the action of the constraints. Thus, the true difference between the statical and dynamical viewpoint is simply that, while the former is built on d'Alembert's principle and on an equilibrium principle which, thanks to Lagrange, was chosen to be the Principle of Virtual Velocities, the latter develops again on the ground of d'Alembert's principle, but rephrasing it as an information about forces and joining it with Euler's equations. The former aims first at showing that any constrained material particle must undergo a force of constraint, then at determining both its motion and the forces of constraints; the latter starts with assuming that any material device realizing constraints actually exerts a force on the particle, and aims at a reaction-free description of the motion, *i.e.* a deterministic description obtained by disregarding the forces of constraint. A synthetic comparative view of the two logical procedures may be obtained from figures 15–16.

It is worthy to be stressed that our deduction of system (9.8) from system (9.4) and condition (9.6) has made no use of such notions as "virtual displacements" or "virtual velocities", as they are still present in most treatises on Rational Mechanics. It seems now important to reinterpret the deduction in terms of power corresponding to virtual velocities, not only for historical reasons, but mainly for otherwise we could have not the tools either to restate or to prove PVV.

The statical foundation of Dynamics of Systems subjected to time-independent holonomic constraints

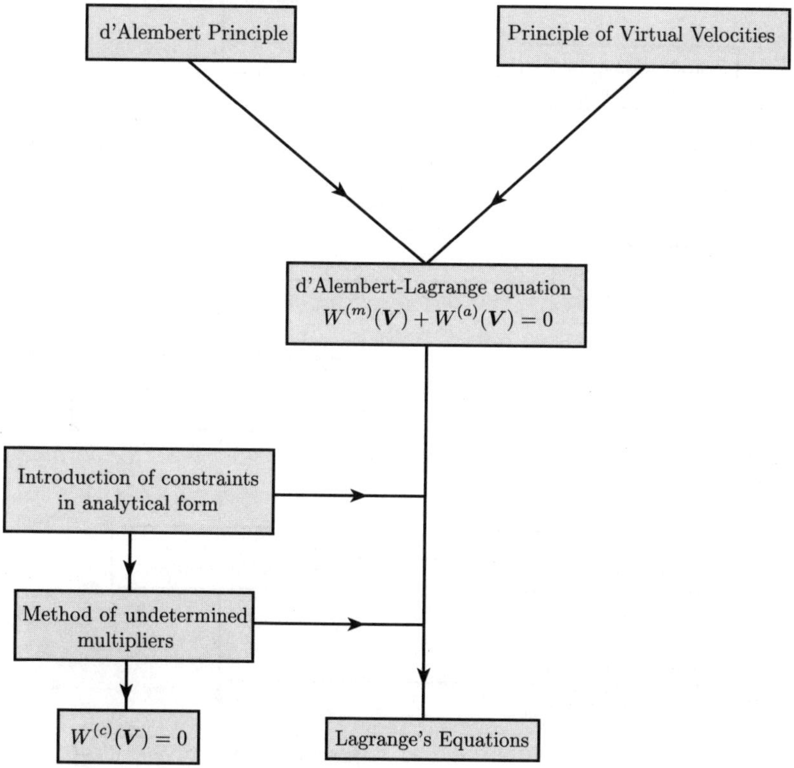

Figure 15.

The dynamic foundation of Dynamics of Systems subjected to time-independent holonomic constraints

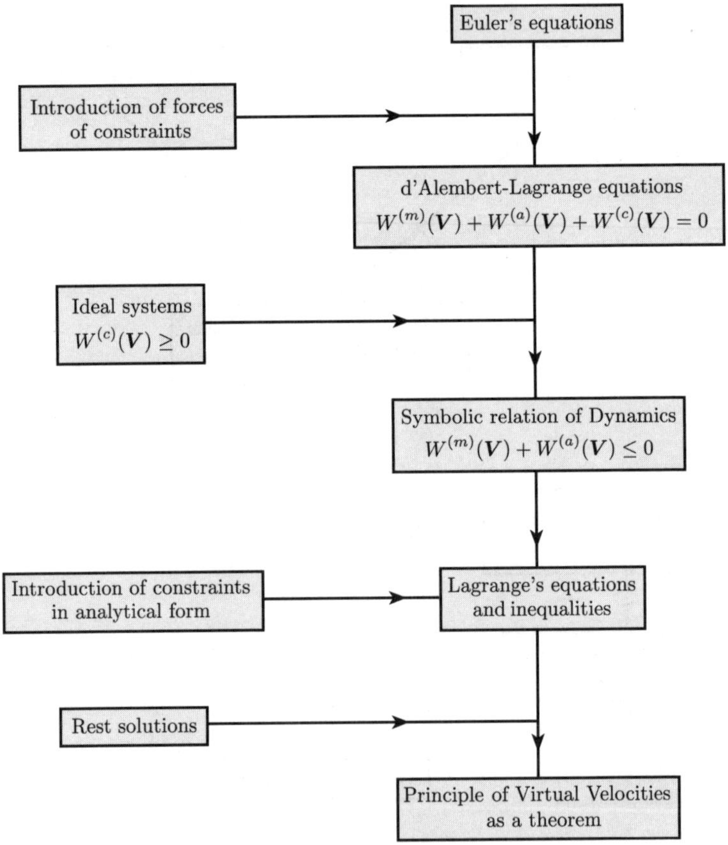

Figure 16.

To this aim, let us go back to (9.5). It is quite evident that, taking the inner product of both of its sides by any arbitrarily chosen $\boldsymbol{V} \in T_{\boldsymbol{X}(t)}\mathcal{M}$ and setting

$$(9.9)\quad W^{(m)}(\boldsymbol{V}) = \boldsymbol{F}^{(m)} \cdot \boldsymbol{V}, \quad W^{(a)}(\boldsymbol{V}) = \boldsymbol{F}^{(a)} \cdot \boldsymbol{V}, \quad W^{(c)}(\boldsymbol{V}) = \boldsymbol{F}^{(c)} \cdot \boldsymbol{V},$$

we find the equation

$$(9.10)\qquad W^{(m)}(\boldsymbol{V}) + W^{(a)}(\boldsymbol{V}) + W^{(c)}(\boldsymbol{V}) = 0,$$

and conversely, if this equation is assumed to hold for any $\boldsymbol{V} \in T_{\boldsymbol{X}(t)}\mathcal{M}$, then (9.5) follows at once. We have thus expressed the system governing the motion by a unique scalar relation: the one universally known as *d'Alembert-Lagrange equation.*

Quite analogously, condition (9.6) may be obviously written

$$(9.11)\qquad W^{(c)}(\boldsymbol{V}) = 0$$

for any $\boldsymbol{V}$ taken, this time, in $T_{\boldsymbol{X}(t)}\mathcal{V}$.

Now, a vector belonging to $T_{\boldsymbol{X}(t)}\mathcal{M}$ may be regarded as a displacement or a velocity of $\mathcal{X}$; correspondingly, the inner products (9.9) will respectively express the works or the powers of the inertia, active and reaction forces. Similarly, a vector belonging to $T_{\boldsymbol{X}(t)}\mathcal{V}$ may be always viewed as a displacement or a velocity among the ones allowed by the constraints: these are the *virtual displacements* and the *virtual velocities*. Correspondingly, the inner products (9.9), when evaluated for $\boldsymbol{V} \in T_{\boldsymbol{X}(t)}\mathcal{V}$, are the *virtual work* and the *virtual power*.

Now, for any $\boldsymbol{V} \in T_{\boldsymbol{X}(t)}\mathcal{V}$, the d'Alembert-Lagrange equation and condition (9.11) are both satisfied. This leads to the well-known symbolic equation of Dynamics

$$(9.12)\qquad W^{(m)}(\boldsymbol{V}) + W^{(a)}(\boldsymbol{V}) = 0, \qquad \forall \boldsymbol{V} \in T_{\boldsymbol{X}(t)}\mathcal{V}$$

and it is a matter of simple calculations to see that (9.12) is quite equivalent to system (9.8).

We must now turn back to the Fundamental Problem of the Dynamics of Systems, to tackle the question of its well-posedness: more precisely, it is usually expected that there is one and only one solution to such problem, once the values of $\boldsymbol{X}$ and $\dot{\boldsymbol{X}}$ have been assigned at a fixed instant t_0. This property may be actually proved to be true when we refer to the lagrangean formulation of the problem in terms of system (9.8), which — as is well-known — can be given a normal form in virtue of the fact that T is a positive definite quadratic form in the variables $\dot{q}^h$. As a consequence, the Cauchy problem for the Lagrange equations has a unique solution corresponding to any system of initial conditions, when the components Q_h of active forces satisfy the standard Lipschitz condition.

We may now try to understand the rôle of PVV in the dynamical context we have just constructed. First of all, as we have seen in Section 6, equation (9.10) itself was to be interpreted and used — in any attempt to found Dynamics upon Statics — as a formula expressing a special case of a very definition of equilibrium, according to which a system Σ of forces acting on a material system $\mathcal{X}$ is *equilibrated* or *in equilibrium* if and only if

$$W^{(\Sigma)}(\boldsymbol{V}) = 0,$$

for any choice of $\boldsymbol{V}$, where the meaning of the symbol $W^{(\Sigma)}(\boldsymbol{V})$ is the one introduced above. Definition, not condition, because there was no alternative formal definition of equilibrium to be compared with it: of course, such an alternative definition could have been suggested by the basic experimental fact that an equilibrated system of forces acting on a system $\mathcal{X}$ does not produce any motion of $\mathcal{X}$, if this last is initially at rest. This empirical observation was of course used more or less explicitly by all mechanicians, but it was never expressed by means of a mathematical formula, since they did not conceive rest as a particular motion with zero velocity, and had not at their disposal a general law of production of (variations of) motions by forces. As a consequence, how could they give a formal expression to the statement that an assigned system of forces acting on $\mathcal{X}$ does not produce a motion of $\mathcal{X}$? But our purely dynamical theory gives us the tools to express this statement in purely formal and mathematically unambiguous terms, according to the following

Definition (of an equilibrium position for a system subjected to bilateral constraints). *A position $\boldsymbol{X}^* \in \mathcal{V}$ is an equilibrium position starting from an instant t_0 for $\mathcal{X}$ if and only if equation* (9.7) *has only the rest solution*

$$\boldsymbol{X}(t) = \boldsymbol{X}^*, \qquad \forall t \in [t_0, +\infty) \tag{9.13}$$

corresponding to the initial conditions

$$\begin{aligned} \boldsymbol{X}(t_0) &= \boldsymbol{X}^*, \\ \dot{\boldsymbol{X}}(t_0) &= \boldsymbol{0}. \end{aligned} \tag{9.14}$$

Therefore, in view of recovering PVV as a proposition of the dynamic theory, its classical formulation must be translated by simply exploiting this meaning of the statement that a system is in equilibrium. As a consequence, in the modern language, the statement of PVV will be expressed as the following

Theorem of Virtual Velocities. *Let $\mathcal{X}$ be a material ideal system consisting of K mass points $p_1, \ldots, p_K$ and H rigid bodies $\mathcal{B}_1, \mathcal{B}_2, \ldots, \mathcal{B}_H$, subjected to holonomic and time-independent constraints* $(9.3)_1$. *A necessary and sufficient condition in order that equation* (9.7) *have only the rest solution* (9.13) *corresponding to the initial conditions* (9.14) *is that*

$$W^{(a)}(\boldsymbol{X}^*, \boldsymbol{0}, t; \boldsymbol{V}) = 0, \qquad \forall \boldsymbol{V} \in T_{\boldsymbol{X}^*}\mathcal{V}, \quad \forall t \geq t_0. \tag{9.15}$$

And at this stage we don't need to ask ourselves whether this statement is actually a theorem or not, since its proof is implicitly contained in the acknowledged well-posedness of the Fundamental Problem of the Dynamics of Systems, provided we remark that condition (9.15) assures that (9.13) solves equation (9.12). Nevertheless, an independent proof based on the method of energy was provided by FRANCESCO SBRANA [53] for the case of systems consisting only of material points.

Of course, to state that PVV is now a theorem of the Dynamics of Systems, means that a proposition (its thesis) is acknowledged to be true in virtue of the assumed truth of some premises (its hypotheses), so that it will hold only for systems belonging to a class defined by the assumptions. Now, the basic hypotheses underlying PVV are essentially two:

(i) all the constraints are time-independent;

(ii) the forces of constraints satisfy the ideality condition (9.6).

In connection with assumption (ii), we want to comment a supposed counter-example due to G. CHOBANOV & I. CHOBANOV [70], who consider an heavy hollow rigid ball σ constrained to rotate around its centre by a fixed ellipsoid whose greatest semi-axis is equal to the radius of the ball (see figure 17). The application of PVV shows in this case that every

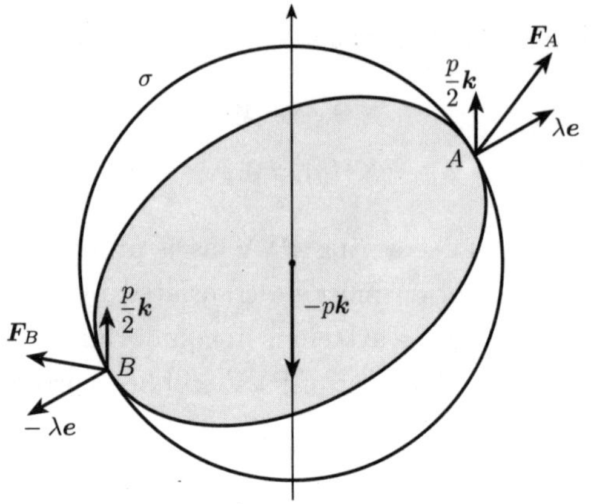

Figure 17.

position is of equilibrium for the ball. On the other hand, along a rest solution, the first Euler's cardinal equation becomes

$$-p\boldsymbol{k} + \boldsymbol{F}^{(c)} = \boldsymbol{0},$$

where p is the weight of the ball and $\boldsymbol{k}$ is the upward vertical unit vector. The force of constraint $\boldsymbol{F}^{(c)}$ is the sum of two contact forces exerted at the contact points A and B between the ball and the ellipsoid. Now, the Authors observe that, according to the absence of friction at A and B, both these forces should have the direction of the straight line containing A and B, so that, denoting by $\boldsymbol{e}$ a unit vector having this direction, they conclude that the following equation must hold

$$-p\boldsymbol{k} + (F_A - F_B)\boldsymbol{e} = \boldsymbol{0}.$$

But it is clear that this condition cannot be satisfied unless $\boldsymbol{e}$ is parallel to $\boldsymbol{k}$, so that, according to the Authors, "no position of σ is a position of equilibrium".

Obviously, this example does not contradicts, on a formal ground, the theorem of virtual velocities. It is based on the assumption that the unknown force of constraint has the form

$$\boldsymbol{F}^{(c)} = (F_A - F_B)\boldsymbol{e}. \tag{9.16}$$

While it is obviously true that a force of the form (9.16) satisfies (9.6), it is clear as well that (9.16) is not necessary in order to satisfy (9.6). More precisely, no contradiction arises by taking

$$\boldsymbol{F}_A = \frac{p}{2}\boldsymbol{k} + \lambda\boldsymbol{e},$$
$$\boldsymbol{F}_B = \frac{p}{2}\boldsymbol{k} - \lambda\boldsymbol{e}.$$

Such a choice allows in fact to satisfy the ideality assumption as well as the equilibrium condition.

As a matter of fact, the conclusion of the Authors is affected by a misunderstanding, in that they take condition (9.6) on the vector $\boldsymbol{F}^{(c)} \in T_{\boldsymbol{X}(t)}\mathcal{V}$ representing in $T_{\boldsymbol{X}(t)}\mathcal{V}$ the whole system of forces of constraints as if it were a condition on each of the applied vectors of the system. Thus, the example they give in [70] is to be simply meant as an occasion to stress that the ideality condition (9.6) does not mean that the devices realizing the constraints are frictionless at each contact point, but something less: in the considered case, simply that the action line of the resultant of the system $\{\boldsymbol{F}_A^{(c)}, \boldsymbol{F}_B^{(c)}\}$ contains the centre of σ.

Therefore, the true interest of the example we are discussing seems to consist in that it shows a sort of unadequacy of the frictionless physical scheme in describing the considered device, which is likely to cannot be considered really frictionless at each of the points A and B. This seems to be due to the fact that the deformations occurring at the contact points (which are in fact contact areas) cannot be neglected, as they probably produce a sort of groove of the ellipsoid in σ, so that a rotation of σ around the normal to the vertical plane containing A and B should be not free, but should encounter an actual resistance. This is in agreement with our experience and physical intuition, and contradicts the very definition of a frictionless constraint.

It will be now quite spontaneous to ask what will happen when at least one of assumptions (i) and (ii) is given up or changed in some way. In this connection, two recent contributions seem to deserve quotation: G. D. Blyumin [69] and J. G. Papastavridis [73] treat the case in which the constraints depend on time, and — even more generally — on the velocity (*nonholonomic* constraints).

9.2 - The statement of PVV in the case of unilateral constraints.

Up to now, we have not taken at all on consideration the possible presence of constraints described by conditions of the form $(9.3)_2$ (*unilateral constraints*). We want now to consider these latter in addition to bilateral ones. To this aim, denoting by $\mathcal{U}$ the set of the points of $\mathcal{V}$ that satisfy system $(9.3)_2$, assume that $\mathring{\mathcal{U}}$ is nonempty and connected. Then, for any $\boldsymbol{X} \in \mathring{\mathcal{U}}$, all the considerations developed in the foregoing Subsection obviously retain their validity. But what can be stated when $\boldsymbol{X} \in \partial\mathcal{U}$? Then, of course, it is still equation (9.5) which describes the motions of $\mathcal{X}$, but condition (9.6) on the forces of constraints needs to be suitably reformulated. To understand how to get such a reformulation, it will be useful to split the vector $\boldsymbol{F}^{(c)}$ in two terms, the former, $\boldsymbol{F}_\nu^{(c)}$, normal to $\mathcal{V}$ at $\boldsymbol{X}$, which must be quite arbitrary to prevent the system to leave the manifold $\mathcal{V}$; the latter, $\boldsymbol{F}_\tau^{(c)}$, belonging to the tangent space $T_{\boldsymbol{X}}\mathcal{V}$, which must prevent $\mathcal{X}$ to cross $\partial\mathcal{U}$. In order to perform this task, it has to be normal to $\partial\mathcal{U}$ and directed towards $\mathring{\mathcal{U}}$. We shall denote by $\mathcal{N}_{\boldsymbol{X}}^{+}$ the subset of $T_{\boldsymbol{X}}\mathcal{V}$ whose elements satisfy these two conditions. Therefore, the ideality condition is now expressed by the requirement

$$\boldsymbol{F}_{\tau}^{(c)} \in \mathcal{N}_{\boldsymbol{X}}^{+}.$$

But in the present case the expression of such a condition in terms of virtual powers is suggested by cleverness reasons, in that it allows a very clear understanding of the way of work of the forces of constraints, and makes the deduction of its consequences more direct. Accordingly, let us denote by $T_{\boldsymbol{X}}^{+}\mathcal{V}$ the subset of $T_{\boldsymbol{X}}\mathcal{V}$ whose elements are directed towards $\overset{\circ}{\mathcal{U}}$. The vectors of this set represent the velocities allowed to $\mathcal{X}$ by the constraints to which it is subjected, so that they identify in the present context what we have called virtual velocities. In the light of this new notation, the above ideality condition is equivalent to requiring that

$$W^{(c)}(\boldsymbol{V}) \geq 0 \qquad\qquad \forall \boldsymbol{V} \in T_{\boldsymbol{X}}^{+}\mathcal{V}.$$

From a purely formal viewpoint, internal configurations and boundary configurations may be treated in quite the same way, by requiring

$$W^{(c)}(\boldsymbol{V}) \geq 0 \qquad\qquad \forall \boldsymbol{V} \in \mathcal{W}_{\boldsymbol{X}}, \tag{9.17}$$

where $\mathcal{W}_{\boldsymbol{X}}$ is to be meant as $T_{\boldsymbol{X}}^{+}\mathcal{V}$, when $\boldsymbol{X} \in \partial\mathcal{U}$, and as the whole $T_{\boldsymbol{X}}\mathcal{V}$ when $\boldsymbol{X} \in \overset{\circ}{\mathcal{U}}$. Indeed, in this last case, condition (9.17) implies (9.11) in view of the fact that $\boldsymbol{V} \in T_{\boldsymbol{X}}\mathcal{V}$ yields $-\boldsymbol{V} \in T_{\boldsymbol{X}}\mathcal{V}$.

Therefore, by repeating step by step the line of reasoning adopted in the previous Subsection, we are able to state in the following form the

Fundamental Problem of the Dynamics of Systems subjected to both bilateral and unilateral constraints. *To find a couple* $(\boldsymbol{X}(t), \boldsymbol{F}^{(c)}(t))$ *such that, for all* t *in a suitable interval* $I \subseteq \mathbb{R}$, $\boldsymbol{X}(t) \in \mathcal{U}$, $\boldsymbol{F}^{(c)}$ *satisfies condition* (9.17) *at* $\boldsymbol{X}(t)$ *and, finally, equation* (9.5) *is satisfied.*

Such a problem will be completely solved when we shall have found a motion $\boldsymbol{X}(t)$ contained in $\mathcal{U}$ and satisfying, for all $t \in I$, the *Symbolic Relation of Dynamics*

$$W^{(m)}(\boldsymbol{V}) + W^{(a)}(\boldsymbol{V}) \leq 0, \qquad\qquad \forall \boldsymbol{V} \in \mathcal{W}_{\boldsymbol{X}(t)}. \tag{9.18}$$

In analogy to what has been done in connection with systems subjected to only bilateral constraints, we may again reformulate the Fundamental Problem of the Dynamics of Systems subjected to both bilateral and unilateral constraints by disregarding the forces of constraints, namely: *to find a function* $\boldsymbol{X}(t)$ *such that, for all* $t \in I \subseteq \mathbb{R}$, $\boldsymbol{X}(t) \in \mathcal{U}$ *and inequality* (9.18) *is satisfied.*

We may also define the rest solutions and, accordingly, the equilibrium positions in exactly the same way as we have done in the previous Subsection. Accordingly, we can restate PVV as follows

Theorem of Virtual Velocities. *Let* $\mathcal{X}$ *be any material system consisting of* K *mass points* $p_1, \ldots, p_K$ *and* H *rigid bodies* $\mathcal{B}_1, \mathcal{B}_2, \ldots, \mathcal{B}_H$*, subjected to holonomic and time-independent constraints* (9.3). *A necessary and sufficient condition in order that relation* (9.18) *have only the rest solution* (9.13) *corresponding to the initial conditions* (9.14) *is that*

$$W^{(a)}(\boldsymbol{X}^*, \boldsymbol{0}, t; \boldsymbol{V}) \leq 0, \qquad \forall \boldsymbol{V} \in \mathcal{W}_{\boldsymbol{X}^*}, \quad \forall t \geq t_0. \tag{9.19}$$

From the beginning of the present Century, this problem has been tackled, in a form more or less similar to the one we have just outlined, by several Authors (though not so many as one could have expected). It is almost impossible to start if not quoting Tullio Levi-Civita & Ugo Amaldi [49] who, in their celebrated wide-ranging treatise on Rational Mechanics, give only a hint to the proof. They however essentially deal with systems of material points, and appeal to the *law of incipient motion*, whose application in turn requires that the resultant of all the forces acting on the system (including the unknown forces of constraints) is nonzero at the initial instant (or, less restrictively, that it has a well defined limit direction as $t \to t_0^+$).

In more recent years, the problem has been re-examined from different viewpoints by Carlo Cattaneo [54] and Francesco Sbrana [56] (see also [53,57]) by making use of a method of energy jointly with the assumptions that the forces of constraints violate at each instant the ideality condition; more precisely, these forces are required to satisfy a reversed ideality condition. Rather recently Marziano Marziani published a paper [72] which has the merit of pointing out what really should be meant as a proof of PVV in the case of unilateral constraints, by explicitly setting the problem as a uniqueness problem for a differential system (though he also confines ourself to systems of points). Unfortunately, his attempt of proof seems to be affected by an oversight.

9.3 - The proof of PVV.

This Subsection is devoted to the presentation of the main results of this paper, that are collected in two propositions, which will tell us that the Theorem of Virtual Velocities for systems subjected to unilateral as well as bilateral constraints, according to the statement we have given in the previous Subsection, holds in a number of important cases.

Let us start by observing that it is almost obvious that for a position $\boldsymbol{X}^* \in \mathring{\mathcal{U}}$ condition (9.19) becomes (9.15), and the study of equilibrium may be carried out in exactly the same way as if the unilateral constraints were absent. Let us now consider the case of a configuration $\boldsymbol{X}^* \in \partial\mathcal{U}$. Also in this case, the necessity of condition (9.19) for the equilibrium at the position $\boldsymbol{X}^*$ is easily acknowledged from relation (9.18) itself. Let us then turn to the problem of proving (or disproving) sufficiency.

To this aim, let us start with remarking that, if $\boldsymbol{X}^* \in \partial\mathcal{U}$, then it must belong to the intersection of a number $\ell \leq s \leq n$ of surfaces

$$\mathcal{S}_\beta = \{\boldsymbol{X} \in \mathcal{V} \mid g_\beta(\boldsymbol{X}) = 0\}.$$

Without loss of generality, we shall assume $\ell = s$, since otherwise, by virtue of the continuity of the motion, we could always consider the system $\mathcal{X}$ to be subjected only to ℓ unilateral constraints.

At this stage, under well-known regularity assumptions on the $(n-1)$-dimensional submanifolds $\mathcal{S}_\beta$, it is possible to choose a system $\mathbf{q}$ of local coordinates on $\mathcal{V}$ in such a way that, in a neighborhood U of $\boldsymbol{X}^*$, $\mathcal{S}_\beta$ has equation $q^\beta = 0$, and relations $(9.3)_2$ take the form

$$q^\beta \geq 0. \tag{9.20}$$

Let us denote by $\mathbf{v} \equiv (v^1, \ldots, v^n)$ the n-tuple of components of $\boldsymbol{V}$ in the local basis associated with the above chosen coordinates. Equation (9.18) takes the form

$$\left[-\frac{\mathrm{d}}{\mathrm{d}t}\frac{\partial T}{\partial \dot{q}^h} + \frac{\partial T}{\partial q^h} + Q_h(\mathbf{q}, \dot{\mathbf{q}}, t)\right] v^h \leq 0,$$

where, by our choice of coordinates, it must be

$$v^\beta \geq 0$$

for any t such that $\boldsymbol{X}(t) \in \mathcal{S}_\beta$.

Thus, inequality (9.18) turns out to be equivalent to the system

$$\begin{aligned} \frac{\mathrm{d}}{\mathrm{d}t}\frac{\partial T}{\partial \dot{q}^\alpha} - \frac{\partial T}{\partial q^\alpha} &\geq Q_\alpha(\mathbf{q}, \dot{\mathbf{q}}, t), \\ \frac{\mathrm{d}}{\mathrm{d}t}\frac{\partial T}{\partial \dot{q}^H} - \frac{\partial T}{\partial q^H} &= Q_H(\mathbf{q}, \dot{\mathbf{q}}, t), \end{aligned} \tag{9.21}$$

where we have implicitly agreed, as we shall always do in the sequel, that greek indexes always range on $\{1, 2, \ldots, s\}$, latin capital indexes always range on $\{s+1, s+2, \ldots, n\}$, while only latin small indexes range on the whole $\{1, 2, \ldots, n\}$. It is to be carefully noted that each of inequalities $(9.21)_1$ can be satisfied as a strict inequality when and only when the corresponding coordinate is zero.

In view of our aims, it will be convenient to express at once system (9.21) in the form in which we shall use it in all what follows. First we exploit the expression of the kinetic energy

$$T = \frac{1}{2} a_{hk}(\mathbf{q}) \dot{q}^h \dot{q}^k,$$

where $(a_{hk}(\mathbf{q}))$ is a C^1-smooth positive definite symmetric matrix function of the coordinates. Next, we note that the above expression of T implies system (9.21) to have in fact the form

$$\begin{aligned} a_{\alpha k} \ddot{q}^k &\geq Q_\alpha(\mathbf{q}, \dot{\mathbf{q}}, t) - \frac{1}{2}\left(\frac{\partial a_{\alpha i}}{\partial q^j} + \frac{\partial a_{\alpha j}}{\partial q^i} - \frac{\partial a_{ij}}{\partial q^\alpha}\right) \dot{q}^i \dot{q}^j, \\ a_{Hk} \ddot{q}^k &= Q_H(\mathbf{q}, \dot{\mathbf{q}}, t) - \frac{1}{2}\left(\frac{\partial a_{Hi}}{\partial q^j} + \frac{\partial a_{Hj}}{\partial q^i} - \frac{\partial a_{ij}}{\partial q^H}\right) \dot{q}^i \dot{q}^j, \end{aligned} \tag{9.22}$$

so that, setting

$$Y_h(\mathbf{q}, \dot{\mathbf{q}}, \ddot{\mathbf{q}}, t) = Q_h(\mathbf{q}, \dot{\mathbf{q}}, t) - \frac{1}{2}\left(\frac{\partial a_{hi}}{\partial q^j} + \frac{\partial a_{hj}}{\partial q^i} - \frac{\partial a_{ij}}{\partial q^h}\right) \dot{q}^i \dot{q}^j - [a_{hk}(\mathbf{q}) - a^*_{hk}]\ddot{q}^k,$$

where

$$a^*_{hk} = a_{hk}(\mathbf{q}^*),$$

we can put it in the simple form

$$\begin{aligned} a^*_{\alpha k} \ddot{q}^k &\geq Y_\alpha(\mathbf{q}, \dot{\mathbf{q}}, \ddot{\mathbf{q}}, t), \\ a^*_{Hk} \ddot{q}^k &= Y_H(\mathbf{q}, \dot{\mathbf{q}}, \ddot{\mathbf{q}}, t), \end{aligned} \tag{9.23}$$

to which we shall always refer in the sequel.

Assume now that the components Q_h of the active forces are uniformly Lipschitz continuous with respect to the variables $\mathbf{q}$ and $\dot{\mathbf{q}}$, *i. e.*[1]

$$|Q_h(\mathbf{q}_1, \dot{\mathbf{q}}_1, t) - Q_h(\mathbf{q}_2, \dot{\mathbf{q}}_2, t)| \leq c\,(|\mathbf{q}_1 - \mathbf{q}_2| + |\dot{\mathbf{q}}_1 - \dot{\mathbf{q}}_2|)\,. \tag{9.24}$$

It is important to note that then the terms at left-hand sides of system (9.23), though explicitly depending on the second derivatives of the unknown functions, nevertheless turn out to be uniformly Lipschitz continuous at the point $(\mathbf{q}^*, \mathbf{0})$ with respect to the sole variables $\mathbf{q}$ and $\dot{\mathbf{q}}$. To be convinced of this, recalling the continuity of the partial derivatives of a_{hk}, we may use the Lagrange mean value theorem to get

$$\left|(a_{hk}(\mathbf{q}) - a^*_{hk})\,\ddot{q}^k\right| \leq \left|\frac{\partial a_{hk}}{\partial q^i}(\bar{\mathbf{q}})\right| |\ddot{q}^k||q^i - q^{*i}|, \quad \text{(no sum over } k\text{)}$$

for a suitable value $\bar{\mathbf{q}}$. Now, if we localize to a compact set of couples $(\mathbf{q}, \ddot{\mathbf{q}})$, we find that the coefficients of $|q^i - q^{*i}|$ may be majorized by a suitable positive constant, so that we finally find

$$\sum_{k=1}^{n} \left|(a_{hk}(\mathbf{q}) - a^*_{hk})\,\ddot{q}^k\right| \leq c \sum_{i=1}^{n} |q^i - q^{*i}|. \tag{9.25}$$

A similar procedure allows us to prove that, when $\mathbf{q}$, $\dot{\mathbf{q}}$ range in a suitable compact set, it results

$$\left|\left(\frac{\partial a_{hi}}{\partial q^j} + \frac{\partial a_{hj}}{\partial q^i} - \frac{\partial a_{ij}}{\partial q^h}\right)\dot{q}^i \dot{q}^j\right| \leq c \sum_{h=1}^{n} |\dot{q}^h|.$$

Collecting the obtained results we finally find

$$|Y_h(\mathbf{q}, \dot{\mathbf{q}}, \ddot{\mathbf{q}}, t) - Y_h(\mathbf{q}^*, \mathbf{0}, \mathbf{0}, t)| \leq c \sum_{h=1}^{n} \left(|q^h - q^{*h}| + |\dot{q}^h|\right), \tag{9.26}$$

what we needed to show.

---

[1] From now on c will denote a generic positive constant, independent of time, whose numerical value is unessential for our purposes and may change from line to line.

It is also important to point out that, in view of our choice of coordinates, condition (9.19) turns out to be equivalent to the system

$$
\begin{aligned}
&Q_\alpha(\mathbf{q}^*, \mathbf{0}, t) \leq 0, \\
&Q_H(\mathbf{q}^*, \mathbf{0}, t) = 0.
\end{aligned}
\tag{9.27}
$$

It is now clear that, once conditions (9.27) are satisfied, then the function (9.13) is certainly a solution to system (9.21), so that a proof of sufficiency of condition (9.19) to the equilibrium at $\boldsymbol{X}^*$, is to be obtained by showing the uniqueness of the rest solution (9.13) under condition (9.19). To this aim, in all what follows, we shall assume, *per absurdum*, that a nonzero solution $\mathbf{q}(t)$ to system (9.21) exists in an open interval $I = [t_0, b)$, where it may also be $b = +\infty$.

In order to prove our theorems, we need a preliminary lemma.

Lemma. *Let* $\mathbf{q}(t)$ *be a solution to system* (9.23) *in* I. *Then, for any* α *and for any* $t \in I$, *it results*

$$
a^*_{\alpha h}\ddot{q}^h(t)\phi(t) = Y_\alpha(\mathbf{q}(t), \dot{\mathbf{q}}(t), \ddot{\mathbf{q}}, t)\phi(t)
\tag{9.28}
$$

where ϕ *is any of the functions* q^α, $\dot{q}^\alpha$ *or* $\ddot{q}^\alpha$.

PROOF - Let α be arbitrarily fixed. For any $t \in I \setminus \{t_0\}$, three cases are possible: (*a*) $q^\alpha(t) > 0$, (*b*) $q^\alpha(t) = 0$ but a sequence $\{t_n\}$ exists that converges to t such that $q^\alpha(t_n) > 0$ for any $n \in \mathbb{N}$, and (*c*) $q^\alpha(t) = 0$ and a complete neighborhood $(t - \delta, t + \delta)$ exists in which q^α identically vanishes.

In the first case, the α-th of relations of system $(9.23)_1$ is satisfied as an equation, whence (9.28) trivially follows. In case (*b*), one has

$$
a^*_{\alpha h}\ddot{q}^h(t_n)\phi(t_n) = Y_\alpha(\mathbf{q}(t_n), \dot{\mathbf{q}}(t_n), \ddot{\mathbf{q}}(t_n), t_n)\phi(t_n), \quad \forall n \in \mathbb{N},
$$

so that, by continuity,

$$
\begin{aligned}
a^*_{\alpha h}\ddot{q}^h(t) - Y_\alpha(\mathbf{q}(t), \dot{\mathbf{q}}(t), \ddot{\mathbf{q}}(t), t) &= \\
&\lim_{n\to\infty} [a^*_{\alpha h}\ddot{q}^h(t_n) - Y_\alpha(\mathbf{q}(t_n), \dot{\mathbf{q}}(t_n), \ddot{\mathbf{q}}(t_n), t_n)] = 0,
\end{aligned}
$$

and (9.28) holds also in this case.

Finally, if an interval $(t - \delta, t + \delta)$ exists in which q^α identically vanishes, then it also results $\dot{q}^\alpha(t) = \ddot{q}^\alpha(t) = 0$, whence $\phi(t) = 0$ and (9.28) still holds true because both sides vanish.

The arbitrariness of the choice of α completes the proof of (9.28). □

Thus, we are in a position to prove the following

Theorem 9.1. *Assume that the components Q_h of active forces satisfy the Lipschitz condition (9.24) and one of the following assumptions*

(i) *it results*

$$Q_\alpha(\mathbf{q}^*, \mathbf{0}, t) < 0, \qquad \forall t \in [t_0, +\infty), \tag{9.29}$$

for some values of α and

$$Q_\alpha(\mathbf{q}^*, \mathbf{0}, t) = 0, \qquad \forall t \in [t_0, +\infty), \tag{9.30}$$

for the remaining values;

(ii) *the surfaces $\mathcal{S}_\beta$ are mutually orthogonal at $\boldsymbol{X}^*$ with respect to the inner product induced by the metrics expressed by the kinetic energy,*

to be met. Then the Theorem of Virtual Velocities holds in the whole class of C^2 solutions.

Proof in the case (i) - We start with remarking that

$$\ddot{q}^h(t_0) = 0, \qquad \forall h \in \{1, \ldots, n\}. \tag{9.31}$$

To this aim, let us first observe that, since $t = t_0$ is a minimum point for any function $q^\alpha(t)$, if $\ddot{q}^\alpha(t_0) \neq 0$, it should be $\ddot{q}^\alpha(t_0) > 0$. On the other hand, in virtue of the above Lemma and of the positive definitess of $(a^*_{\alpha k})$, we have

$$a^*_{hk}\ddot{q}^h\ddot{q}^k = Y_h\ddot{q}^h \geq 0, \qquad \forall t \geq t_0.$$

But, evaluating both sides of this equation at t_0, we find

$$a^*_{hk}\ddot{q}^h(t_0)\ddot{q}^k(t_0) = Q_h(\mathbf{q}^*, \mathbf{0}, t_0)\ddot{q}^h(t_0) \leq 0,$$

which at once entrains (9.31).

Next, let us take α such that (9.29) holds; if q^α were not identically zero in any interval $[t_0, t_0 + \delta]$, we should find a decreasing sequence $\{t_n\}$ converging to t_0, such that

$$a^*_{\alpha k}\ddot{q}^k(t_n) = Y_\alpha(\mathbf{q}(t_n), \dot{\mathbf{q}}(t_n), \ddot{\mathbf{q}}(t_n), t_n)$$

for any n. As a consequence

$$\begin{aligned}0 &= a^*_{\alpha k}\ddot{q}^k(t_0) = \lim_{n\to\infty} a^*_{\alpha k}\ddot{q}^k(t_n) = \\ &= \lim_{n\to\infty} Y_\alpha(\mathbf{q}(t_n), \dot{\mathbf{q}}(t_n), \dot{\mathbf{q}}(t_n), \ddot{\mathbf{q}}(t_n), t_n) = Q_\alpha(\mathbf{q}^*, \mathbf{0}, t_0) < 0,\end{aligned}$$

and the contradiction proves that $q^\alpha = 0$ in some right neighborhood J of t_0.

This stated, let us multiply both sides of each of relations (9.23) by the corresponding $\dot{q}^h$. Adding side by side the equations obtained by taking into account the above proven Lemma, and introducing the notation

$$T^*(t) = \frac{1}{2}a^*_{hk}\dot{q}^h(t)\dot{q}^k(t),$$

we find at once

$$\dot{T}^*(t) = Y_h(\mathbf{q}(t), \dot{\mathbf{q}}(t), \ddot{\mathbf{q}}(t), t)\dot{q}^h(t), \tag{9.32}$$

where, for any $t \in J$, the terms corresponding to those values of the index for which (9.29) is satisfied, identically vanish.

The proof of the uniqueness is now achieved by a standard argument. Indeed, integrating (9.32) on (t_0, t) $(t \in J)$, making use of the obvious inequality

$$\int_{t_0}^{t} |q^k(s) - q^{*k}|^2 \, \mathrm{d}s \leq (t - t_0)^2 \int_{t_0}^{t} |\dot{q}^k(s)|^2 \, \mathrm{d}s \tag{9.33}$$

and bearing in mind that $c_1 T^*(t) \leq \sum_h |\dot{q}^h(t)|^2 \leq c_2 T^*(t)$ for some suitable constants c_1 and c_2, we get

$$T^*(t) \leq c \int_{t_0}^{t} T^*(s) \, \mathrm{d}s.$$

Hence immediately follows that $\mathbf{q}(t) = \mathbf{q}^*$ in J. Finally, by simple iterating this reasoning, we cover the whole interval I and the theorem is proved. □

PROOF IN THE CASE (ii) - To start with, we remark that it is always possible to choose the coordinates q^h in such a way that $a^*_{HK} = \delta_{HK}$ and $a^*_{\alpha H} = 0$; the block $a^*_{\alpha\beta}$ is then completely determined by the requirement that the constraints are expressed by inequalities (9.20). In this connection, assumption

(ii) amounts to stating that it is instead possible to choose a coordinate system such that not only the relations expressing the constraints still have the form (9.20), but in addition

$$a^*_{\alpha\beta} = \delta_{\alpha\beta}.$$

Accordingly, under hypothesis (ii), system (9.23) takes the form

$$\begin{aligned} \ddot{q}_\alpha &\geq Y_\alpha(\mathbf{q}, \dot{\mathbf{q}}, \ddot{\mathbf{q}}, t), \\ \ddot{q}_H &= Y_H(\mathbf{q}, \dot{\mathbf{q}}, \ddot{\mathbf{q}}, t), \end{aligned} \tag{9.34}$$

where, of course, we don't need any more to make a distinction between contravariance and covariance indexes.

On the other hand, let f be any real function on $\mathbb{R}$, and set

$$f_+(t) = \frac{1}{2}(f(t) + |f(t)|), \qquad f_-(t) = \frac{1}{2}(f(t) - |f(t)|).$$

We want to remark that, if $a \in \mathbb{R}$ exists such that

$$\int_a^t f(s)\,\mathrm{d}s \geq 0, \qquad \forall t \in (a, +\infty),$$

since

$$\int_a^t f(s)\,\mathrm{d}s = \int_a^t f_+(s)\,\mathrm{d}s + \int_a^t f_-(s)\,\mathrm{d}s,$$

we have

$$\int_a^t |f_-(s)|\,\mathrm{d}s \leq \int_a^t f_+(s)\,\mathrm{d}s, \qquad \forall t \in (a, +\infty),$$

which in turn implies

$$\int_a^t |f(s)|\,\mathrm{d}s = \int_a^t f_+(s)\,\mathrm{d}s + \int_a^t |f_-(s)|\,\mathrm{d}s \leq 2\int_a^t f_+(s)\,\mathrm{d}s, \tag{9.35}$$

$\forall t \in (a, +\infty)$. In the same way, if $a \in \mathbb{R}$ exists such that

$$\int_a^t \left(\int_a^s f(\sigma)\,\mathrm{d}\sigma\right)\mathrm{d}s \geq 0, \qquad \forall t \in (a, +\infty),$$

then

$$\int_a^t \left(\int_a^s |f(\sigma)|\,\mathrm{d}\sigma\right)\mathrm{d}s \leq 2\int_a^t \left(\int_a^s f_+(\sigma)\,\mathrm{d}\sigma\right)\mathrm{d}s, \qquad \forall t \in (a, +\infty). \tag{9.36}$$

Next, consider system $(9.34)_2$. In view of (9.26) and $(9.27)_2$, taking into account that

$$Y_H(\mathbf{q}^*, \mathbf{0}, \mathbf{0}, t) = Q_H(\mathbf{q}^*, \mathbf{0}, t),$$

it implies

$$\begin{aligned} |\ddot{q}_H(t)| &= |Y_H(\mathbf{q}(t), \dot{\mathbf{q}}(t), \ddot{\mathbf{q}}(t), t)| \le \\ &\le c\left[\sum_K \left(|q_K(t) - q_K^*| + |\dot{q}_K(t)|\right) + \sum_\alpha \left(q_\alpha(t) + |\dot{q}_\alpha(t)|\right)\right]. \end{aligned}$$

Integrate now both sides of this last relation over $(t_0, s) \subset I$; it results

$$\begin{aligned} |\dot{q}_H(s)| \le c\Bigg[&\sum_K \left(\int_0^s |q_K(\sigma) - q_K^*| \, \mathrm{d}\sigma + \int_0^s |\dot{q}_K(\sigma)| \, \mathrm{d}\sigma\right) + \\ &+ \sum_\alpha \left(\int_{t_0}^s q_\alpha(\sigma) \, \mathrm{d}\sigma + \int_{t_0}^s |\dot{q}_\alpha(\sigma)| \, \mathrm{d}\sigma\right)\Bigg]. \end{aligned}$$

Taking into account (9.33) and (9.35) and adding side to side the relations thus obtained, we find

$$\sum_H |\dot{q}_H(t)| \le c\left(\sum_K \int_{t_0}^t |\dot{q}_K(s)| \, \mathrm{d}s + \sum_\alpha \int_{t_0}^t \dot{q}_{\alpha+}(s) \, \mathrm{d}s\right).$$

Hence, multiplying both sides by $\exp\{-ct\}$ a simple computation yields

$$\sum_H \int_{t_0}^t |\dot{q}_H(s)| \, \mathrm{d}s \le c \sum_\alpha \int_{t_0}^t \left(\int_{t_0}^s \dot{q}_{\alpha+}(\sigma) \, \mathrm{d}\sigma\right) \mathrm{d}s. \tag{9.37}$$

Estimate (9.37) also implies at once

$$\sum_H \int_{t_0}^t |q_H(s) - q_H^*| \, \mathrm{d}s \le c \sum_\alpha \int_{t_0}^t \left(\int_{t_0}^s \dot{q}_{\alpha+}(\sigma) \, \mathrm{d}\sigma\right) \mathrm{d}s. \tag{9.38}$$

We observe, by the way, that estimates (9.37) and (9.38), besides their value as tools for the next steps of the proof, is also intrinsicly interesting, in that it tells us that — as is readily seen — no motion is possible to the system $\mathcal{X}$ on the intersection of the constraints.

As the last preliminary result to the proof of our statement, we want to show that, for any solution $\mathbf{q}(t)$ to system (9.34),

$$\ddot{q}_{\alpha+}(t) = \left[Y_\alpha(\mathbf{q}(t), \dot{\mathbf{q}}(t), \ddot{\mathbf{q}}(t), t)\right]_+. \tag{9.39}$$

Indeed, once α and t have been fixed, the same three cases are again possible as in the proof of the above proven Lemma. And since the proof of (9.38) in cases (a) and (b) appeals to the same continuity arguments as that of (9.28), we confine ourselves to outline the proof only in case (c).

In this case, $\ddot{q}_\alpha(t)$ is obviously zero, while — according to the α-th of inequalities $(9.34)_1$ —

$$Y_\alpha(\mathbf{q}(t), \dot{\mathbf{q}}(t), \ddot{\mathbf{q}}(t), t) \le 0,$$

so that the right-hand side of (9.39) is in turn zero. Thus we have proved what we needed.

Now, we are in a position to prove that conditions (9.17) are sufficient to assure the rest of $\mathcal{X}$ at $\mathbf{q}^*$ when the constraints are assumed to satisfy condition (ii). In view of (9.39), taking into account (9.27), we have indeed

$$\begin{aligned}
\ddot{q}_{\alpha+}(t) &\le \left[Y_\alpha(\mathbf{q}(t), \dot{\mathbf{q}}(t), \ddot{\mathbf{q}}(t), t) - Q_\alpha(\mathbf{q}^*, \mathbf{0}, t) + Q_\alpha(\mathbf{q}^*, \mathbf{0}, t)\right]_+ \le \\
&\le \left[Y_\alpha(\mathbf{q}(t), \dot{\mathbf{q}}(t), \ddot{\mathbf{q}}(t), t) - Q_\alpha(\mathbf{q}^*, \mathbf{0}, t)\right]_+ + \left[Q_\alpha(\mathbf{q}^*, \mathbf{0}, t)\right]_+ \le \\
&\le \left[Y_\alpha(\mathbf{q}(t), \dot{\mathbf{q}}(t), \ddot{\mathbf{q}}(t), t) - Q_\alpha(\mathbf{q}^*, \mathbf{0}, t)\right]_+ .
\end{aligned}$$

Integrating over $(t_0, t) \subset I$, and taking into account the Lipschitz continuity of Y_α as well as inequalities (9.35), (9.37) and (9.38), it follows

$$\int_{t_0}^t \ddot{q}_{\alpha+}(s)\,\mathrm{d}s \le c \sum_\alpha \left(\int_{t_0}^t q_\alpha(s)\,\mathrm{d}s + \int_{t_0}^t \dot{q}_{\alpha+}(s)\,\mathrm{d}s \right), \tag{9.40}$$

But now, for any α, and for any $t \in I$,

$$q_\alpha(t) \le 2 \int_{t_0}^t \dot{q}_{\alpha+}(s)\,\mathrm{d}s, \qquad \dot{q}_{\alpha+}(t) \le \int_{t_0}^t \ddot{q}_{\alpha+}(s)\,\mathrm{d}s,$$

so that, from (9.40), we have

$$\int_{t_0}^{t} \ddot{q}_{\alpha+}(s)\,\mathrm{d}s \leq c \sum_{\alpha} \int_{t_0}^{t} \left(\int_{t_0}^{s} \ddot{q}_{\alpha+}(\sigma)\,\mathrm{d}\sigma \right) \mathrm{d}s.$$

Hence the desired result follows at once. □

Remark 9.1 - It deserves to be stressed that the result under assumption (i) is of the greatest relevance from an historical viewpoint, in that it covers in particular the case in which the active force is purely positional and is directed towards the region of $\mathcal{V}$ which is forbidden to the system $\mathcal{X}$ by the constraints. As a matter of fact, if we restrict ourselves to consider only one unilateral constraint, this delivers a rigorous proof of the Principle of Torricelli about heavy bodies.

Remark 9.2 - The assumption (i) of the above theorem is trivially satisfied when the active forces do not depend on time, so that the Theorem of Virtual Velocities turns out to hold true in the natural class of C^2 motions, with no additional conditions on forces further than Lipschitz continuity.

Remark 9.3 - We want to point out that, when $s = 1$, assumption (ii) looses its meaning, so that also in such a case the theorem must be understood as proved without any additional restriction (of course, apart from the standard Lipschitz continuity).

Remark 9.4 - Assumption (ii), according to which the constraints are all orthogonal at the position $\boldsymbol{X}^*$ or, equivalently, the matrix $(a^*_{\alpha\beta})$ is diagonal, is made mainly for the sake of simplicity. As a matter of fact, by suitably modifying the proof, and at the cost of more lengthy and involved — but not difficult — calculations, we would be able to prove our statement under the more general assumption that, for any α,

$$\sum_{\beta \neq \alpha} |a^*_{\alpha\beta}| < a^*_{\alpha\alpha}.$$

Now, it is readily seen that this condition is trivially met when $s = 2$, so that in this last case no assumption on the geometric features of the constraints is needed, and the Theorem of Virtual Velocities turns out to be proved in full generality.

Theorem 9.1 shows that PVV is in fact a rigorously provable theorem in the whole natural class of C^2 motions, provided some suitable additional assumptions are made on the forces or on the constraints. As we shall see in the sequel, such added requirements seem — at least as far as we are now aware — to be almost forced by the fact that there are no restrictions on the behaviour of nonconstant solutions whose existence is allowed *per absurdum* in any right neighborhood of t_0. Thus, also according to the logical line which seems to have been adopted in the proofs given *e. g.* in [20, 37, 49], one can feel to be allowed to try to avoid any additional conditions on forces and constraints by suitably confining the proof to a proper subclass of C^2. Indeed, the following theorem holds.

Theorem 9.2. *Assume that the components* Q_h *of active forces satisfy the Lipschitz condition* (9.24). *Then the Theorem of Virtual Velocities holds in the whole class* $P \subset C^2$ *of functions* $\mathbf{q}(t)$ *such that*

$$\int_{t_0}^{t}\left(\int_{t_0}^{s} Q_\alpha(\mathbf{q}^*,\mathbf{0},\sigma)\dot{q}^\alpha(\sigma)\,\mathrm{d}\sigma\right)\mathrm{d}s \leq 0, \qquad \forall t \in I. \tag{9.41}$$

PROOF - Setting $\phi = \dot{q}^\alpha$ in (9.28), repeating the steps of the proof of the Theorem 9.1(i) and making use of (9.41), we arrive at

$$\int_{t_0}^{t} T^*(s)\,\mathrm{d}s \leq c\int_{t_0}^{t}\left(\int_{t_0}^{s} T^*(\sigma)\,\mathrm{d}\sigma\right)\mathrm{d}s,$$

whence the result easily follows. □

Remark 9.5 - It is worth observing that condition (9.41) can be replaced by the following one

$$\int_{t_0}^{t} Q_\alpha(\mathbf{q}^*,\mathbf{0},\sigma)\ddot{q}^\alpha(s)\,\mathrm{d}s \leq 0, \qquad \forall t \in I.$$

Condition (9.41) could appear somehow artificial. But, on the other hand, one may be easily convinced that it is certainly satisfied by any function $\mathbf{q}(t)$ such that any component q^α is not decreasing in the time interval I. In our opinion, this is not a minor remark, as it allows a discussion — which will be carried out at the end of the paper — of the previous attempts to get the full proof of PVV. Nevertheless, we have chosen to assume (9.41) rather than the condition that $\dot{q}^\alpha(t) \geq 0$ in I, since this last one would have excluded a whole class of possible solutions.

To make this clear, let us introduce, for any C^2 solution $\mathbf{q}(t)$ to system (9.34) and for any $t \in I$, the set

$$K_\alpha(t) = \{s \in [t_0, t] \mid q^\alpha(s) = 0\}.$$

We agree to identify as a *crazy* solution to system (9.34) any solution $\mathbf{q}(t)$ for which at least one value of α exists such that, for any t, $K_\alpha(t)$ is the join of a sequence of open disjoint intervals clustering at $t = t_0$: this last condition may be expressed by stating that, for some α, there are two sequences $\{t'_n\}$ and $\{t''_n\}$, converging to t_0, with $t'_{n+1} < t''_{n+1} < t'_n < t''_n$ and such that

$$t \in \bigcup_{n\in\mathbb{N}} [t'_n, t''_n] \implies q^\alpha(t) = 0,$$
$$t \in \bigcup_{n\in\mathbb{N}} (t''_{n+1}, t'_n) \implies q^\alpha(t) > 0.$$

It is then easy to see that the assumption $\dot{q}^\alpha \geq 0$ would have led to take not on consideration among the solutions to system (9.34) the crazy ones.

We now turn our attention to the class P' of C^2 solutions to system (9.34) for which one $t^* \in I$ exists such that, for any α, $K_\alpha(t^*)$ is a set of isolated points (this set must be necessarily countable because, were it finite, we should go back to the previous case). These motions are not crazy solutions according to the above definition, but they deserve to be treated separately, as they turn out to be not so easy to treat as we would desire and believe. In fact, the following theorem holds.

Theorem 9.3. *Assume that the functions a_{hk} are of class C^2 and the components Q_h of active forces have the form*

$$Q_h = Q'_h(\mathbf{q}, t) + A_{hk}(\mathbf{q}, \dot{\mathbf{q}}, t)(q^k - q^{*k}) + B_{hk}(\mathbf{q}, \dot{\mathbf{q}}, t)\dot{q}^k, \tag{9.42}$$

where the functions A_{hk} and B_{hk} are assumed to be respectively continuous and continuously differentiable with respect to all of their arguments, and Q'_h satisfies the Lipschitz condition (9.24). Then the Theorem of Virtual Velocities holds in the whole class P'.

PROOF - In the class P', relations (9.34) are all satisfied as equations so that, in virtue of (9.42), they take the form

$$a^*_{hk}\ddot{q}^k = Q'_h(\mathbf{q},t) + A_{hk}(\mathbf{q},\dot{\mathbf{q}},t)(q^k - q^{*k}) + B_{hk}(\mathbf{q},\dot{\mathbf{q}},t)\dot{q}^k + \\ + \Gamma_{hij}(\mathbf{q})\dot{q}^i\dot{q}^j - [a_{hk}(\mathbf{q}) - a^*_{hk}]\ddot{q}^k, \tag{9.43}$$

where

$$\Gamma_{hij} = -\frac{1}{2}\left(\frac{\partial a_{hi}}{\partial q^j} + \frac{\partial a_{hj}}{\partial q^i} - \frac{\partial a_{ij}}{\partial q^h}\right)$$

Integrating (9.43) twice on time, we get

$$\begin{aligned} a^*_{hk}(q^k - q^{*k}) = & \int_{t_0}^t \left(\int_{t_0}^s [Q'_h(\mathbf{q},\sigma) - Q'_h(\mathbf{q}^*,\sigma)]\, \mathrm{d}\sigma\right) \mathrm{d}s + \\ & + \int_{t_0}^t \left(\int_{t_0}^s \left[\Gamma_{hij}\dot{q}^i\dot{q}^j + A_{hk}(q^k - q^{*k}) + B_{hk}\dot{q}^k\right] \mathrm{d}\sigma\right) \mathrm{d}s + \\ & - \int_{t_0}^t \left(\int_{t_0}^s [a_{hk}(\mathbf{q}) - a^*_{hk}]\,\ddot{q}^k \mathrm{d}\sigma\right) \mathrm{d}s + \\ & + \int_{t_0}^t \left(\int_{t_0}^s Q'_h(\mathbf{q}^*,\sigma)\mathrm{d}\sigma\right) \mathrm{d}s. \end{aligned}$$

Hence, integrating by parts, multiplying both sides by $(q^h - q^{*h})$ and summing over h, we have

$$\begin{aligned} a^*_{hk}(q^h - q^{*h})(q^k - q^{*k}) = & (q^h - q^{*h}) \int_{t_0}^t \left(\int_{t_0}^s [Q'_h(\mathbf{q},\sigma) - Q'_h(\mathbf{q}^*,\sigma)]\, \mathrm{d}\sigma\right) \mathrm{d}s + \\ & + (q^h - q^{*h}) \int_{t_0}^t \left(\Gamma_{hik}\dot{q}^i + B_{hk}\right)(q^k - q^{*k})\mathrm{d}s + \\ & - (q^h - q^{*h}) \int_{t_0}^t \left[\int_{t_0}^s \left(\frac{\mathrm{d}}{\mathrm{d}t}(\Gamma_{hik}\dot{q}^i + B_{hk}) - A_{hk}\right)(q^k - q^{*k})\mathrm{d}\sigma\right] \mathrm{d}s + \\ & - (q^h - q^{*h}) \int_{t_0}^t \left(\int_{t_0}^s [a_{hk}(\mathbf{q}) - a^*_{hk}]\,\ddot{q}^k \mathrm{d}\sigma\right) \mathrm{d}s + \\ & + (q^h - q^{*h}) \int_{t_0}^t \left(\int_{t_0}^s Q'_h(\mathbf{q}^*,\sigma)\mathrm{d}\sigma\right) \mathrm{d}s. \end{aligned}$$

By taking into account our hypoteses of regularity on a_{hk}, A_{hk} and B_{hk}, the Lipschitz continuity of Q'_h and (9.27), we have

$$\sum_k |q^k - q^{*k}|^2 \leq c\left(\sum_k |q^k - q^{*k}|\right) \int_{t_0}^t \sum_k |q^k - q^{*k}| \, \mathrm{d}s.$$

Since, in virtue of the arithmetic–geometric mean inequality and the Schwartz inequality we have, for any positive ξ,

$$\left(\sum_k |q^k - q^{*k}|\right) \int_{t_0}^t \sum_k |q^k - q^{*k}| \, \mathrm{d}s \leq$$

$$\leq \xi \left(\sum_k |q^k - q^{*k}|\right)^2 + \frac{c}{\xi} \int_{t_0}^t \sum_k |q^k - q^{*k}|^2 \, \mathrm{d}s.$$

Then, by choosing properly ξ, we get

$$\sum_k |q^k - q^{*k}|^2 \leq c \int_{t_0}^t \sum_k |q^k - q^{*k}|^2 \, \mathrm{d}s.$$

Hence, the desired result follows at once. □

Finally, we want to draw from the above theorems some concluding considerations. We trust to have been able to show how the Principle of Virtual Velocities can be plunged in a purely newtonian context, and how, in such a context, it can be given the *status* of a theorem. Nevertheless, the results here presented seem to suggest that not only the proof, but even a rigorous statement of such a theorem would need the nature of the system (including the obstacles constraining it, the active forces exerted on it, and the motions to be taken into account) to be specified. This means that, further than the list of points and rigid bodies composing the system, one has to fix the features of the obstacles and the assumptions on the active forces to be taken into account. Similarly, as it always happens when tackling a uniqueness problem, one has also to identify the class of solutions. This problem was not of course confined to the case of unilateral constraints, but was actually to be tackled also in the case in which only bilateral constraints are imposed to the system. In this last case, however, the problem seemed to be not worthy to be set explicitly, in that PVV turned out to be provable as a theorem for forces belonging to the whole class of Lipschitz continuous functions, which seems to be the widest class in which an existence and uniqueness theorem for a system of differential equations can be proved, and for all solutions belonging to C^2, which is in turn the widest class in which the Lagrange equations make sense. For systems subjected to unilateral constraints, instead, all the previous discussion seems to witness that PVV should be more correctly stated as follows: *let $\mathfrak{X}$ be a material system belonging to a class $\mathfrak{F}$. Then, condition* (9.19) *is necessary and sufficient in order that relation* (9.18) *have in a class $\mathfrak{S}$ only the rest solution* (9.13) *corresponding to the initial conditions* (9.14).

Keeping in mind this interpretation, we at once realize that Theorems 9.1 to 9.3 are in fact particular cases of this last statement. The cases considered in Theorem 9.1 both deal with a class $\mathfrak{S}$ of solutions that coincides with the whole of C^2, but while the former bounds the choice of active forces, and circumscribes $\mathfrak{F}$ as the subset of systems subjected to uniformly Lipschitz continuous force fields satisfying conditions (9.29)-(9.30) and to any number of time-independent ideal holonomic constraints, the latter allows instead to assign arbitrarily the forces in the widest class we are accustomed to take them when proving uniqueness theorems for systems of differential equations, but bounds the choice of the constraints. In Theorem 9.2, $\mathfrak{F}$ is again the whole class of systems for which the force field satisfies the Lipschitz condition (9.24), for all possible time-indepenent ideal holonomic constraints, but $\mathfrak{S} = P \subset C^2$. Finally, as far as Theorem 9.3 is concerned, we are left free to assign the constraints as we can desire, but either forces either solutions must be taken into proper subclasses of the natural ones.

In view of these remarks, we feel allowed to state that, though the above results could appear as mathematically not complete to those who would have expected or desired that PVV be proved in the natural classes of all Lipschitz continuous active forces and of all C^2 solutions, the problem of proving or disproving PVV, as it has been set from its very historical development, may be considered as completely solved from a conceptual viewpoint. As a matter of fact, the great mathematicians who first stated and tried to prove PVV, could not but have in mind purely positional forces, as they did not know forces acting at a distance different from weight, and, according to an intuitive conception of what a natural motion should be, solutions not exhibiting pathological behaviours around t_0. More precisely, in connection with such a background of physical intuition, when in the early XXth Century such important mathematicians as Appell [20], Marcolongo [28], Routh [37] and, above all, Levi-Civita and Amaldi [49], attempted to give a proof of the sufficiency of condition (9.19) to the equilibrium of a system subjected to unilateral constraints, they made use of the explicit, though expressed in a purely qualitative and intuitive language, assumption that for any given nonzero solution $\mathbf{q}(t)$ to system (9.21), the limit

$$\lim_{t \to t_0^+} \frac{\dot{q}^h}{\sqrt{\sum_k (\dot{q}^k)^2}} = \ell_h$$

not only exist but, what is more, be nonnegative for any h and positive for at least one h. Thus, in the light of Remark 9.5, the problem of proving PVV in the terms it was originally set for historical reasons, may be considered to have been here completely solved. On the other hand, when shifting the problem from the historically physical plane, to the general mathematical one, it would be expected that PVV be provable for only Lipschitz continuous forces and in the whole class of C^2 solutions. Since such a proof is lacking, one could suspect that a counterexample could be found. But, in this connection, Theorems 9.1(ii) and 9.3, that could seem to add nothing physically and historically so meaningful as Theorems 9.1(i) and 9.2, are extremely instructive, as they show how hard would be the task of finding such a counterexample.

Acknowledgements. This work was partially supported by grants from MURST (Ministry for University and Scientific and Technological Research), and italian CNR (National Research Council), Gruppo Nazionale per la Fisica Matematica.

We wish to express our deep gratitude to our friend and colleague Remigio Russo, who — during the preparation of the present paper — never let us lack his friendly support and his inspiring advice, without which this paper would have been probably impossible.

We are also greatly indebted to the Department of Mathematics and Applications of the University "Federico II" of Naples, in the person of its Director Professor Domenico Olanda, who set at our disposal all the ancient books, among the ones kept in the rich Historical Library of the Department, we needed to consult in order to achieve a sufficiently detailed picture of the evolution of PVV in the last centuries. Finally, we want to acknowledge the friendly solicitude with which Mr Guglielmo Avallone has given us concrete help in the research of the volumes.

References.

[1] D'ALEMBERT, J.-L.: *Traité de Dynamique*, I ed. 1758. Reprinted by Gauthier-Villars, Paris 1921.

[2] LAGRANGE, J. L.: *Mécanique Analytique*, Courcier, (I ed. 1788, II ed.1811).

[3] FOURIER, C.: Mémoire sur la Statique contenant la démonstration du principle des vîtesses virtuelles et la théorie des moments, *Journal de l'Ecole Politechnique*, **5** (1798), 20–60.

[4] AMPÈRE, A. M.: Démonstration générale du Principe des Vîtesses Virtuelles dégagée de la considération des infiniment petits, *Journal de l'Ecole Politechnique*, **13** (1806), 247–269.

[5] POISSON, S. D.: *Traité de Mécanique.* Bachelier, (1833).

[6] NAVIER, M.: *Resumé des Leçons de Mécanique*, Carilian-Goeury, (1841).

[7] MOSSOTTI, O. F.: *Lezioni Elementari di Fisica Matematica*, Piatti, (1843).

[8] CORIOLIS, G.: *Traité de la Mécanique des Corps Solides*, Carilian-Goeury, (1844).

[9] POINSOT, L.: *Éléments de Statique*, Bachelier, (1848).

[10] JULLIEN, P. M.: *Problèmes de Mécanique Rationelle*, Bachelier, (1855).

[11] ZANNOTTI, M.: *Elementi di Meccanica Razionale*, Raimondi, (1857).

[12] DEL GROSSO, R.: *Elementi di Meccanica*, Tipografia Militare, (1862).

[13] DUHAMEL, M.: *Cours de Mécanique*, Bachelier, (1862).

[14] VENTUROLI, G.: *Elementi di Meccanica e d'Idraulica*, Starita, (1862)

[15] BATTAGLINI, G.: *Trattato Elementare sulla Meccanica Razionale*, Pellerano, (1873).

[16] STURM, C.: *Cours de Mécanique*, Gauthier-Villars, (1875).

[17] MACH, E.: *Die Mechanik in ihrer historisch-kritisch dargestellt*, 1ª ed. (1883), 8ª ed. (1921).

[18] LAURENT, H.: *Traité de Mécanique Rationelle*, Gauthier-Villars, (1889).

[19] GILBERT, P.: *Cours de Mécanique Analitique*, Gauthier-Villars, (1891).

[20] APPELL, P.: *Traité de Mécanique Rationelle*, Gauthier-Villars, (1893).

[21] CASTELLANO, F.: *Lezioni di Meccanica Razionale*, Candeletti, (1894).

[22] VAILATI, G.: Del concetto di centro di gravità nella statica di Archimede, *Atti della Reale Accademia delle Scienze di Torino*, 32 (1897) (Reprinted in *Scritti*, Firenze 1911, 79–90).

[23] VAILATI, G.: Il principio dei lavori virtuali da Aristotele a Erone d'Alessandria, *Atti della Reale Accademia delle Scienze di Torino*, 32 (1897) (Reprinted in *Scritti*, Firenze 1911, 91–106).

[24] VAILATI, G.: Di una dimostrazione del principio della leva, attribuita ad Euclide, *Bolletino di Storia e Bibliografia Matematica*, (1897) (Reprinted in *Scritti*, Firenze 1911, 115–117).

[25] SIACCI, F.: *Lezioni di Meccanica Razionale*, R. Accad. Sci., (1898).

[26] FORMENTI, C.: *Lezioni di Meccanica Razionale*, Marelli, (1900).

[27] CALDARERA, F.: *Corso di Meccanica Razionale*, Tipografia Matematica, Palermo (1901)

[28] MARCOLONGO, R.: *Lezioni di Meccanica Razionale*, D'Amico, (1901).

[29] RUFFINI, F. P.: *Sinossi delle Lezioni di Meccanica Razionale*, (1901).

[30] VAILATI, G.: La dimostrazione del principio della leva data da Archimede nel Libro Primo sull'equilibrio delle figure piane, *Atti del Congresso Internazionale di Scienze storiche, Roma*, 12 (1903) (Reprinted in *Scritti*, Firenze 1911, 497–502).

[31] MORERA, G.: *Lezioni di Meccanica Razionale*, Paris, (1904).

[32] DUHEM, P.: *Les Origines de la Statique*, (1905).

[33] VAILATI, G.: La scoperta della condizione d'equilibrio d'un grave scorrevole lungo un piano inclinato, *Bollettino di Storia e Bibliografia matematica* (Reprinted in *Scritti*, Firenze 1911, 834–841).

[34] VAILATI, G.: A proposito di una recente pubblicazione sulla storia della Statica, *Nuovo Cimento*, **15** (1908) (Reprinted in *Scritti*, Firenze 1911, 844–846).

[35] VAILATI, G.: Sul posto da assegnare al principio dei lavori virtuali in un'esposizione elementare della Statica, *Nuovo Cimento*, **15** (1908) (Reprinted in *Scritti*, Firenze 1911, 862–869).

[36] JOUGUET, E.: *Lectures de Mécanique*, Gauthier-Villars, (1908).

[37] ROUTH, E. J.: *A Tratise on Analytical Statics*, Cambridge Un. Press, (1909).

[38] MASSAU, J.: *Leçons de Mécanique Rationnelle*, Association des Ingenieurs, (1911).

[39] HAMEL, G.: *Elementare Mechanik*, Druck und Verlag, (1912).

[40] DELASSUS, E.: *Leçons sur la Dinamique des Systemes Materiels*, Hermann, (1913).

[41] Lecornu, L.: *Cours de Mécanique*, Gauthier-Villars, (1914).

[42] Maggi, G.: *Elementi di Statica e Teoria dei Vettori Applicati*, Spoerri, (1917).

[43] Meurice, L.: *Cours de Mécanique Analytique*, Pholien, (1920).

[44] d'Adhemar, R.: *Statique cinématique*, Gauthier-Villars, (1923).

[45] Bouny, F.: *Leçons de Mécanique Rationnelle*, Blanchard, (1924).

[46] Bisconcini, G.: *Esercizi e Complementi di Meccanica Razionale*, Libreria Editrice Politecnica, (1927).

[47] Colonnetti, G.: *I fondamenti della Statica*, UTET, (1927).

[48] Painlevé, P., Platrier, C.: *Cours de Mécanique*, Gauthier-Villars, (1929).

[49] Levi Civita, T., Amaldi, U.: *Lezioni di Meccanica Razionale*, Zanichelli, (1929).

[50] Finzi, B.: Equilibrio, *Rend. Sem. Mat. Fis. Milano*, **16** (1942), 16–47.

[51] Platier, C.: Sur un postulat de la statique et sur une extension de la mecanique newtonienne, *C. R. Acad. Scie. Paris*, **214** (1942), 973–975.

[52] Nadile, A.: Influenza dei vincoli anolonomi sullo spostamento di equilibrio di un sistema, *Riv. Mat. Univ. Parma*, **1** (1950), 393–399.

[53] Sbrana, F.: Sul teorema di unicità per le equazioni differenziali della meccanica, *Boll. Un. Mat. Ital.*, **8** (1953), 123–127.

[54] Cattaneo, C.: Sulla sufficienza del principio dei lavori virtuali all'equilibrio di un generico sistema materiale, *Univ. Roma Ist. Naz. Alta Mat. Rend. Mat. e Appl.*, **14** (1954), 209–220.

[55] Dugas, R.: *Histoire de la Mécanique*, Griffon, (1955).

[56] Sbrana, F.: Sulle condizioni sufficienti per l'equilibrio di un sistema materiale, dedotte mediante il principio dei lavori virtuali, *Boll. Un. Mat. Ital.*, **11** (1956), 123–125.

[57] Sbrana, F.: Su una questione di statica, *Boll. Un. Mat. Ital.*, **11** (1956), 588–589.

[58] Arrighi, G.: I fondamenti della statica in una trattazione logico-deduttiva, *Boll. Un. Mat. Ital.*, **12** (1957), 679–688.

[59] Clagett, M.: *The science of mechanics in the middle age*, University of Wisconsin Press, (1959).

[60] Paoluzi, G.: Sul contenuto fisico del principio dei lavori virtuali, *Boll. Un. Mat. Ital.*, **15** (1960), 122–127.

[61] Valcovici, V.: The new form of the principle of virtual displacement, *Mathematica (Cluj)*, **3** (1961), 371–386.

[62] Noll, W.: La Mécanique classique basée sur un axiome d'objectivité, In *La méthode axiomatique dans la mécanique classique et nouvelle*, Colloques internationales, Paris (1959), Gauthier-Villars (1963), 47–56.

[63] Mattioli, E.: Critiche e proposte concernenti l'esposizione del principio dei lavori virtuali, *Matematiche (Catania)*, **20** (1965), 64–86.

[64] Noll, W.: The foundations of Mechanics, In *Non linear continuum theories*, C.I.M.E. lectures (1965). Cremonese (1966), 159–200.

[65] Truesdell, C.: *Essays in the History of Mechanics*, Springer-Verlag, (1968).

[66] Fusco, G.: Sul principio dei lavori virtuali e sul teorema del lavoro nel caso dei vincoli dipendenti dal tempo, *Rend. Mat. Appl.*, **7** (1974), 85–96.

[67] Truesdell, C.: *Introduction à la mécanique rationelle des milieux continus*, Masson, (1974).

[68] Chobanov, G., Chobanov, I.: A proposition of pure mechanics or proof of a corollary from the definition of equilibrium of systems of forces usually called the principle of virtual work, *Annuaire Univ. Sofia Fac. Math. Mec.*, **71** (1976/77), 229–251.

[69] Blyumin, G.: On the principle of virtual displacements, *Mec. Solids*, **17** (1982), 19–24.

[70] Chobanov, G., Chobanov, I.: Sapienti Sat, *Annuaire Univ. Sofia Fac. Math. Mec.*, **77** (1983), 21–25.

[71] Chobanov, I.: On the principle of virtual work, *Annuaire Univ. Sofia Fac. Math. Mec.*, **78** (1984), 267–284.

[72] Marziani, M.: Sulla sufficienza della relazione di D'Alembert-Lagrange in meccanica classica, *Rev. Roumaine Math. Pures Appl.*, **31** (1986), 151–157.

[73] Papastavridis, J.: On the sufficiency of the principle of virtual work for mechanical equilibrium: a critical reexamination, *Trans. ASME Ser. E J. Appl. Mech.*, **56** (1989), 704–707.

[74] Drago, A., Capriglione, M.: Lo stato logico del principio dei lavori virtuali, *Preprint del Dipartimento di Matematica e Applicazioni dell'Università di Napoli*, 14 (1994).

[75] Carbonaro, B., Russo, R., Starita, G.: *Meccanica*, Aracne (in press).

On the Steady, Translational Self-Propelled Motion of a Symmetric Body in a Navier-Stokes Fluid

Giovanni P. Galdi

Contents

1. Introduction

A body $\mathcal{B}$ moving in an infinite viscous fluid $\mathcal{F}$ undergoes a *self-propelled motion* if the net total force and torque, external to $\mathcal{B}$ and $\mathcal{F}$, acting on $\mathcal{B}$ are identically zero. Typical examples of self-propelled motions can be those performed by rockets, submarines, fishes, microorganisms, etc. This kind of movement is contrasted to that where $\mathcal{B}$ moves just because of nonzero net external actions. We shall call this latter a *towed motion* of $\mathcal{B}$. A characteristic example of towed motion is the fall of $\mathcal{B}$ in the air, under the action of gravity. In general, unlike the towed motion, a self-propelled motion is generated by a suitable nonzero distribution of velocity at its boundary.

In this paper we shall assume that $\mathcal{B}$ is symmetric around a unit direction e_1, say, and consider steady, translational self-propelled motion of $\mathcal{B}$ along e_1. By this we mean that $\mathcal{B}$ moves in $\mathcal{F}$ by purely translational motion, with constant velocity $-\xi \neq 0$, parallel to e_1, and that the motion of $\mathcal{F}$, as seen by an observer attached to $\mathcal{B}$, is independent of time. Such a motion may occur, for example, because of a nonzero momentum flux across portion of the boundary of $\mathcal{B}$ (as in a rocket), or because $\mathcal{B}$ moves tangentially portions of its boundary (as by belts).

In mathematical terms, denoting by Ω the region exterior to $\mathcal{B}$ occupied by $\mathcal{F}$, the problem under consideration leads to the following set of nondimensional equations[1]

$$\left.\begin{aligned} \Delta v &= \lambda v \cdot \nabla v + \nabla p \\ \operatorname{div} v &= 0 \end{aligned}\right\} \text{ in } \Omega$$
$$v = v_* \quad \text{on } \partial\Omega \equiv \partial\mathcal{B} \tag{1.1}$$
$$\lim_{|x|\to\infty} v(x) = \xi$$

together with the conditions

$$\int_{\partial\Omega} [T(v,p)\cdot n - \lambda(v-\xi)v\cdot n] = 0 \tag{1.2}$$

$$\int_{\partial\Omega} [x \times T(v,p)\cdot n - \lambda x \times (v-\xi)v\cdot n] = 0. \tag{1.3}$$

[1] We suppose, for simplicity, that no body force is acting on $\mathcal{F}$.

The quantities $v = v(x)$ and $p = p(x)$ represent velocity field and pressure field associated to each particle of $\mathcal{F}$, as seen by an observer attached to $\mathcal{B}$. Moreover, λ is a dimensionless (Reynolds) number which can be viewed as the inverse of the kinematical viscosity coefficient, and $T = T(v,p)$ is the stress tensor whose components are given by

$$T_{ij}(v,p) = \frac{\partial v_i}{\partial x_j} + \frac{\partial v_j}{\partial x_i} - p\,\delta_{ij}.$$

Finally, (1.2) and (1.3), respectively, express the requirement that the total external force and torque exerted on $\mathcal{B}$ are zero.

Despite its great physical relevance, the mathematical literature relating to this type of problem is not particularly rich. Seemingly, the first contribution to the problem is found in the book of Birkhoff and Zarantonello [2], where a formal asymptotic expression is derived, according to which the velocity field of a steady two-dimensional flow past a self-propelled body moving with velocity $-\xi$ decreases with the distance much faster than the velocity field of the flow past a body towed with the same velocity $-\xi$. Analogous considerations for the three-dimensional problem have been developed by Finn [3]. A more detailed analysis in this direction has been performed much later by Pukhnachev [16]. Similar properties, but in a slightly different context, have also been studied recently by Kozono and Sohr [11], and Kozono, Sohr and Yamazaki [12]. The first attempt to furnish a solution to $(1.1)_{1,2,4}$, (1.2), (1.3) for a given $\xi \neq 0$ is due to Sennitskii [20], [21] who, by the method of matched asymptotic expansion, has constructed, for sufficiently small values of λ, an approximate solution in the case when $\mathcal{B}$ is a cylinder or a sphere, under different prescriptions of boundary velocity.[1] The solvability of $(1.1)_{1,2,4}$, (1.2), for arbitrary $\mathcal{B}$, has been investigated and solved by Pukhnachev [17], [18] within the Stokes approximation, obtained by setting $\lambda = 0$ in $(1.1)_1$, (1.2). However, to our knowledge, no general and rigorous well-posedness theory is known for the full nonlinear Navier-Stokes problem.[2]

In the present paper we shall assume that $\mathcal{B}$ is symmetric around the x_1-axis. This allows us to restrict our attention to the class $\mathcal{P}$ of solutions v, p to

---

[1] See also [22] for a dynamical counterpart of these problems.

[2] For somewhat related questions in bounded domains, *cf.* Sauer [19].

(1.1), (1.2), (1.3) satisfying the following parity conditions:

$$
\begin{aligned}
&v_1(x_1,x_2,x_3) = v_1(x_1,-x_2,x_3) = v_1(x_1,x_2,-x_3)\\
&v_2(x_1,x_2,x_3) = -v_2(x_1,-x_2,x_3) = v_2(x_1,x_2,-x_3)\\
&v_3(x_1,x_2,x_3) = v_3(x_1,-x_2,x_3) = -v_3(x_1,x_2,-x_3)\\
&p(x_1,x_2,x_3) = p(x_1,-x_2,x_3) = p(x_1,x_2,-x_3).
\end{aligned}
\tag{1.4}
$$

Taking into account that the unit normal $n = (n_1, n_2, n_3)$ to $\partial\mathcal{B}$ satisfies

$$
\begin{aligned}
&n_1(x_1,x_2,x_3) = n_1(x_1,-x_2,x_3) = n_1(x_1,x_2,-x_3)\\
&n_2(x_1,x_2,x_3) = -n_2(x_1,-x_2,x_3) = n_2(x_1,x_2,-x_3)\\
&n_3(x_1,x_2,x_3) = n_3(x_1,-x_2,x_3) = -n_3(x_1,x_2,-x_3),
\end{aligned}
$$

it is easy to see that if $v, p \in \mathcal{P}$, and ξ is directed along x_1, then condition (1.3) is automatically satisfied. So, for a symmetric body, we need to consider only (1.1) and (1.2). In this respect, we shall be concerned with the resolutions of the following two problems of physical interest related to (1.1)–(1.2). A first one (Problem A), where the velocity v_* at the boundary of the body is prescribed in the class $\mathcal{P}$ and one has to find v, p and $\xi \neq 0$ solving (1.1)–(1.2). A second one (Problem B), where the velocity of the body $\xi \neq 0$ is prescribed along the direction of symmetry x_1 and one has to find v, p satisfying $(1.1)_{1,2,4}$–(1.2). Roughly speaking, Problem A investigates the way in which one should prescribe boundary velocities that can propel $\mathcal{B}$, whereas Problem B studies in which way we can propel $\mathcal{B}$ with a given translational velocity. It is not difficult to show that, in general, Problem A does not admit a solution for *all* prescribed (sufficiently regular) v_*; see Section 7. This means that only certain distributions of velocity at the boundary of $\mathcal{B}$ can propel $\mathcal{B}$ with a nonzero translational velocity. Likewise, it is also simple to see that Problem B admits an *infinite* number of solutions corresponding to the same ξ; see Section 8. This implies, in particular, that there is an infinite choice of boundary velocities that make $\mathcal{B}$ move with the same translational velocity. One of the objectives of this work is to characterize a class of boundary velocities for which Problems A and B admit *one and only one* solution. In this respect, we shall show that there exists a one-dimensional subspace $\mathcal{T}(\mathcal{B})$ of the space $L^2(\partial\Omega)$ with the following properties (see (5.15)). $\mathcal{T}(\mathcal{B})$ is generated by a vector $g \in L^2(\partial\Omega)$

which depends only on the geometric properties of $\mathcal{B}$ such as size or shape. In particular, it is independent of the orientation of $\mathcal{B}$ and on the fluid property. If $\mathcal{B}$ is a ball, g is proportional to the unit vector e_1. We shall call $\mathcal{T}(\mathcal{B})$ the *thrust space.* Furthermore, denote by $\mathbb{P}$ the orthogonal projection of $L^2(\partial\Omega)$ onto $\mathcal{T}(\mathcal{B})$, by $\gamma(v)$ the trace of v at $\partial\Omega$ and by $\|\cdot\|_{\mathcal{T}}$ the norm in $\mathcal{T}(\mathcal{B})$. Then, given v_* (regular enough and in the class $\mathcal{P}$) with $\mathbb{P}(v_*) \neq 0$, Problem A admits one and only one corresponding solution, for sufficiently small λ (depending on v_*). Moreover,

$$\|\mathcal{P}(v_*)\|_{\mathcal{T}} \leq c_1|\xi| \leq c_2\|\mathcal{P}(v_*)\|_{\mathcal{T}},$$

with $c_i = c_i(\mathcal{B})$, $i = 1, 2$; see Sections 6, 7. Conversely, given $\xi \neq 0$ in the direction x_1, for λ small enough (depending on ξ) there exists one and only one corresponding solution to Problem B with $\gamma(v) \in \mathcal{T}(\mathcal{B})$ and such that

$$|\xi| \leq c_3\|\gamma(v)\|_{\mathcal{T}} \leq c_4|\xi|$$

with $c_i = c_i(\mathcal{B})$, $i = 3, 4$; see Section 8. For Problem B, we can consider also the cases when either the normal or the tangential component of v at $\partial\Omega$ is prescribed. We shall call Problem B_n the first problem and Problem B_τ the second one. In such cases one can show results completely analogous to those mentioned for Problem B, with the thrust space $\mathcal{T}(\mathcal{B})$ replaced, accordingly, by suitable one-dimensional thrust spaces $\mathcal{T}_\tau(\mathcal{B})$ and $\mathcal{T}_n(\mathcal{B})$, respectively (see (5.17), (5.16)). Of course, several other interesting variants of Problem B can be considered, and this will be the object of a future research.

These results have several remarkable consequences. Let g be the element of $L^2(\Omega)$ generating $\mathcal{T}(\mathcal{B})$. For $w \in \mathcal{T}(\mathcal{B})$, we set

$$\tilde{G} = \tilde{G}(w) = \int_{\partial\Omega} w \cdot g.$$

We shall call $G = \tilde{G}e_1$ *thrust vector.* Then, our results imply that every steady, translational self-propelled motion with velocity $-\xi$ in the direction of e_1 is (for small λ) in a one-to-one correspondence with a suitable thrust vector G representative of the uniquely determined boundary velocity in the thrust space associated to the given ξ. It then arises quite naturally the question of the relation between the thrust vector G and the force vector F needed to tow $\mathcal{B}$ with the same velocity $-\xi$. Notice that, in view of the symmetry of the flow, F is directed along e_1. We shall show (see Section 9) that, for small values of λ, the vectors G and F are one-to-one related and that, moreover, $F = -G + O(\lambda^{1/2})$. Since $F \cdot \xi$ is always non-positive, the "–" sign in this latter relation is suggestive of the action-reaction principle.

Another consequence of our results concerns the characterization of self-propelled solutions that are *potential-like.* Actually, it is at once verified that for any given $\xi \neq 0$ in the direction x_1, the pair $v = \nabla\Phi, p = \frac{1}{2}(\nabla\Phi)^2$, with Φ harmonic function approaching $\xi \cdot x$ at large distance is a solution to Problem B. Now, by what we have proved, the only self-propelled solution corresponding to ξ — in the sense specified before — will be potential-like whenever $\gamma(\nabla\Phi) \in \mathcal{T}(\mathcal{B})$. We prove that this is indeed the case if $\mathcal{B}$ is a ball. We also show that, for $\mathcal{B}$ a ball, the only self-propelled solution with $\gamma(v) \cdot n = 0$ and $(\gamma(v) \times n) \times n \in \mathcal{T}_\tau(\mathcal{B})$, or $(\gamma(v) \times n) \times n = 0$ and $\gamma(v) \cdot n \in \mathcal{T}_n(\mathcal{B})$, is potential-like. Perhaps, results of this type continue to hold if $\mathcal{B}$ has some more general symmetry properties, but we were not able to prove it. This remains, therefore, an interesting open question.

This work represents a first step toward the resolution of other problems of physical interest like, for example, whether any of the steady self-propelled solutions we find is stable or whether it can be obtained as a limit of unsteady solutions. Concerning this latter problem, we recall that the question of attainability of steady motions of a towed body had a complete answer only recently in the work of Galdi, Heywood and Shibata [7]. The case when the body has no symmetry will be the object of a forthcoming. paper. The paper is organized as follows. In Section 2 we give our notation and show certain results concerning functions with finite Dirichlet integral. In Section 3, we study linearized versions of (1.1) of the Oseen and Stokes type, while in Section 4 we derive some properties of solutions to the full nonlinear problem (1.1). Section 5 is devoted to the study of Problems A and B (and variants of Problem B) within the Stokes approximation, obtained by setting $\lambda = 0$ in (1.1) and in the self-propelling condition (1.2). These results contain, as a particular case, those of [17], [18] and are of fundamental importance in the investigation of the nonlinear Problems A and B. This latter is performed in Sections 6,7 and 8. Finally, in Section 9, the relation between the steady, translational motion of a self-propelled body $\mathcal{B}$ and the corresponding steady towed motion is analyzed.

2. Notation and Preliminary Results

We begin with some notation.

$\mathbb{N}$ denotes the set of all non-negative natural numbers.

$\mathbb{R}^3$ is the three-dimensional Euclidean space and (e_1, e_2, e_3) the canonical orthonormal basis.

We denote by Ω the exterior of a closed bounded connected set (the body) $\mathcal{B}$, with $\mathcal{B}$ symmetric around the x_1 axis. Unless the contrary is explicitly stated, we shall assume Ω sufficiently regular, for instance, of class $C^{2,\lambda}$, $\lambda \in (0,1)$. We set $\delta = \operatorname{diam} \mathcal{B}$ and, for $R > r > \delta$, we put

$$\begin{aligned} \Omega_r &= \{x \in \Omega : \; |x| < r\} \\ \Omega^r &= \{x \in \Omega : \; r < |x|\} \\ \Omega_{r,R} &= \{x \in \Omega : \; r < |x| < R\} \end{aligned}$$

where the origin of coordinates is taken in the interior of $\mathcal{B}$.

For $a > 0$ we indicate by B_a the open ball of radius a centered at the origin.

For $\beta = (\beta_1, \beta_2, \beta_3)$, $\beta_i \geq 0$, we set

$$D^\beta = \frac{\partial^{|\beta|}}{\partial x_1^{\beta_1} \partial x_2^{\beta_2} \partial x_3^{\beta_3}}, \quad |\beta| = \beta_1 + \beta_2 + \beta_3.$$

If $u = \{u_i\}$ is a vector function, by $D(u) = \{D_{ij}(u)\}$ we denote the symmetric part of $\nabla u = \left\{ \dfrac{\partial u_i}{\partial x_j} \right\}$, that is

$$D_{ij}(u) = \frac{1}{2} \left(\frac{\partial u_i}{\partial x_j} + \frac{\partial u_j}{\partial x_i} \right)$$

For a domain $A \subseteq \mathbb{R}^3$ and $k \in \mathbb{N}$, $C^k(\bar{A})$ denotes the Banach space of functions u for which $D^\beta u$ is bounded and uniformly continuous in A, for all $0 \leq |\beta| \leq k$. The norm in $C^k(\bar{A})$ is given by

$$\|u\|_{C^k(A)} \equiv \max_{0 \leq |\beta| \leq k} \sup_{\Omega} |D^\beta u|.$$

$C_0^k(A)$ is the subset of $C^k(\bar{A})$ constituted by functions of compact support in A. As customary, we set $C_0^\infty(A) = \bigcap_{k\in\mathbb{N}} C_0^k(A)$ and denote by $C_0^k(\bar{A})$ the class of restrictions to A of functions from $C_0^\infty(\mathbb{R}^3)$.

Furthermore, $W^{m,q}(A)$, m a non-negative integer, $q \in [1,\infty]$, is the Sobolev space of order (m,q) on A, endowed with the norm[1]

$$\|u\|_{m,q,A} = \left(\sum_{|\beta|=0}^{m} \int_A |D^\beta u|^q\right)^{1/q} \tag{2.1}$$

The subscript A will be omitted if no confusion arises[2]. $W_0^{m,q}(A)$ is the completion of $C_0^\infty(A)$ in the norm (2.1). We have $W^{0,q}(A) = W_0^{0,q}(A) = L^q(A)$ (the Lebesgue space) and set $\|\cdot\|_{0,q,A} \equiv \|\cdot\|_{q,A}$.

The dual space of $W_0^{m,q}(A)$ is indicated by $W^{-m,q'}(A)$, $1/q' = 1 - 1/q$, and its norm by $\|\cdot\|_{-m,q',A}$. Furthermore, for sufficiently smooth A, by $W^{m-1/q,q}(\partial A)$ we denote the trace space on ∂A of functions in $W^{m,q}(A)$. The corresponding norm is denoted by $\|\cdot\|_{m-1/q,q,\partial A}$. The trace of u at $\partial\Omega$ will be often denoted by $\gamma(u)$.

By $D^{m,q}(A)$, $m \geq 1$, $1 < q < \infty$, we indicate the homogeneous Sobolev space of order (m,q) on A, [23], [5], that is, the class of functions u that are (Lebesgue) locally integrable in A and with $D^\beta u \in L^q(A)$, $|\beta| = m$. For $u \in D^{m,q}(A)$, we set

$$|u|_{m,q,A} = \left(\sum_{|\beta|=m} \int_A |D^\beta u|^q\right)^{1/q},$$

where, again, the subscript A is removed if no confusion arises.

Finally, we shall say that a vector function u is in the class $\mathcal{P}$ if its components (u_1, u_2, u_3) verify the parity conditions $(1.4)_{1,2,3}$.

We begin to recall a result describing the asymptotic behavior of functions from $D^{1,2}(\Omega)$.

---

[1] All functions we shall consider are with values in $\mathbb{R}^3$.

[2] Unless their use clarifies the context, we shall omit also the infinitesimal volume and surface elements in the integrals.

Lemma 2.1. *Let $u \in D^{1,2}(\Omega)$. Denote by (r, ω) a system of spherical coordinates with the origin O, and let S_1 be the unit sphere centered at O. Then, there exists a uniquely determined $\bar{u} \in \mathbb{R}^3$ such that*

$$\lim_{r\to\infty} \int_{S_1} |u(r,\omega) - \bar{u}|^2 d\omega = 0$$

and, if Ω is locally lipschitzian, there exists $C = C(\Omega)$ such that

$$\|u - \bar{u}\|_6 \leq C|u|_{1,2}.$$

If, moreover, $u \in \mathcal{P}$, then $\bar{u} = \mu e_1$, for some $\mu \in \mathbb{R}$.

PROOF - The proof of the first two properties is well-known and is due to [15] and [8] (see also [5], Theorem II.51, Lemma II.5.2). To show the second part, we notice that, in view of $(1.4)_2$, u_2 satisfies $u_2(x_1, 0, x_3) = 0$. We denote by $\tilde{u}_2$ the restriction of u_2 to the half space $x_2 > 0$. Let $\psi(x) \in C^\infty(\bar{\Omega})$ be one in a neighbourhood of $\partial\Omega$ and zero for all large $|x|$. and let us denote by $\tilde{\tilde{u}}_2$ the extension to $\mathbb{R}^3$ of the function $\psi\tilde{u}_2$ by setting $\tilde{u}_2(x) = 0$ for $x_2 < 0$. Clearly, $\tilde{\tilde{u}}_2 \in D^{1,2}(\mathbb{R}^3)$ and, by the first part of the lemma, there exists $\tilde{u}_2 \in \mathbb{R}$ such that

$$\lim_{r\to\infty} \int_{S_1} |\tilde{\tilde{u}}_2(r,\omega) - \tilde{u}_2|^2 \mathrm{d}\omega = 0.$$

Since $\tilde{\tilde{u}}_2$ is identically zero for $x_2 < 0$, we deduce $\tilde{u}_2 = 0$. Therefore, setting $S_1^+ = S_1 \cap \{x_2 > 0\}$, we obtain

$$\lim_{r\to\infty} \int_{S_1^+} |u_2(r,\omega)|^2 \mathrm{d}\omega = 0.$$

On the other hand, we have also

$$\lim_{r\to\infty} \int_{S_1^+} |u_2(r,\omega) - \bar{u}_2|^2 \mathrm{d}\omega = 0$$

and so $\bar{u}_2 = 0$. Likewise, we show $\bar{u}_3 = 0$ and the proof of the lemma is completed. □

We shall next establish a density property for a suitable subspace of $D^{1,2}(\Omega)$. Let $\mathcal{C}(\Omega)$ denote the class of solenoidal vector functions φ enjoying the following properties:

(i) $\varphi \in C_0^\infty(\bar{\Omega}) \cap \mathcal{P}$;
(ii) $\varphi = 0$ in a neighborhood of $\partial\Omega$;
(iii) There exist $\bar{\varphi} \in \mathbb{R}$ and $a_\varphi > 0$ such that $\varphi(x) = \bar{\varphi} e_1$, for all $|x| \geq a_\varphi$.

By $\dot{\mathcal{H}}(\Omega)$ we indicate the completion of $\mathcal{C}(\Omega)$ with respect to $|\cdot|_{1,2}$. Let

$$\mathcal{H}(\Omega) = \{u \in D^{1,2}(\Omega) \cap \mathcal{P} : \ u = 0 \text{ at } \partial\Omega; \ \operatorname{div} u = 0 \text{ in } \Omega.\} \tag{2.2}$$

The following characterization holds.

Lemma 2.2. $\dot{\mathcal{H}}(\Omega) = \mathcal{H}(\Omega)$.

PROOF - The Poincaré inequality applied to φ furnishes

$$\|\varphi\|_{2,\Omega_R} \leq C(R)|\varphi|_{1,2,\Omega_R}, \quad R > \delta,$$

and so, by the trace theorem we obtain $\dot{\mathcal{H}}(\Omega) \subset \mathcal{H}(\Omega)$. Thus, we have only to show that for any $u \in \mathcal{H}(\Omega)$ and $\varepsilon > 0$ there exists $\varphi_\varepsilon \in \mathcal{C}(\Omega)$ such that

$$|u - \varphi_\varepsilon|_{1,2} < \varepsilon. \tag{2.3}$$

Let $\bar{u}$ be the uniquely determined vector associated to u by Lemma 2.1. If $\bar{u} = 0$, the result follows from [5], Theorem II.6.1 and Lemma III.5.1. If $\bar{u} \neq 0$, we may take, without loss, $\bar{u}$ in the e_1 direction. Set

$$U = \bar{u} - \Delta(\zeta b) + \nabla[\operatorname{div}(\zeta b)],$$

where $\zeta = \zeta(|x|)$ is an arbitrary function from $C_0^\infty(\bar{\Omega})$ that is one near $\partial\Omega$ and zero far from $\partial\Omega$, while $b = \frac{1}{2}\bar{u}x_2^2$. The function $v = u - U$ is solenoidal, has a finite Dirichlet integral, belongs to $\mathcal{P}$ and vanishes at $\partial\Omega$ and at infinity in the sense of Lemma 2.1. By known methods ([5], Theorem II.6.1, Lemma III.5.1), it follows that for any $\varepsilon > 0$ there exists a solenoidal function $\psi_\varepsilon \in C_0^\infty(\Omega) \cap \mathcal{P}$ satisfying

$$|v - \psi_\varepsilon|_{1,2} < \varepsilon.$$

Inequality (2.3) then follows by taking $\varphi_\varepsilon = \psi_\varepsilon + U$. □

Taking into account Lemma 2.2, the proof of the next result becomes entirely analogous to that of Lemma VII.2.1 of [5] and therefore it will be omitted.

Lemma 2.3. *There exists a denumerable set of functions $\{\varphi_k\}$ whose linear hull is dense in $\mathcal{H}(\Omega)$ and has the following properties*

(i) $\varphi_k \in \mathcal{C}(\Omega) \cap \mathcal{P}$, *for all* $k \in \mathbb{N}$;

(ii) $\int_\Omega \nabla\varphi_k : \nabla\varphi_j = \delta_{kj}$, *for all* $k, j \in \mathbb{N}$;

(iii) Given $\varphi \in \mathcal{C}(\Omega) \cap \mathcal{P}$ *and* $\varepsilon > 0$, *there exist* $m = m(\varepsilon) \in \mathbb{N}$ *and* $\beta_1, \ldots \beta_m \in \mathbb{R}$ *such that*

$$\|\varphi - \sum_{i=1}^{m} \beta_i \varphi_i\|_{C^1(\Omega)} < \varepsilon.$$

We also have

Lemma 2.4. *Let* $u \in \mathcal{H}(\Omega)$. *Then*

$$|u|_{1,2}^2 = 2\|D(u)\|_2^2. \tag{2.4}$$

Proof - Using the identity

$$\Delta w = 2 \operatorname{div} D(w), \quad (\operatorname{div} w = 0)$$

one immediately verifies the validity of (2.4) for all $u \in \mathcal{C}(\Omega)$. Thus, in view of Lemma 2.2, (2.4) continues to hold for functions $u \in \mathcal{H}(\Omega)$. □

Lemma 2.5. *Let* $u \in \mathcal{H}(\Omega)$ *and let* $\bar{u}$ *be the uniquely determined vector associated to* u *by Lemma 2.1. Then,*

$$|\bar{u}|^2 \leq \frac{1}{4\pi K} |u|_{1,2}^2 \tag{2.5}$$

where K *is the capacity of* $\mathcal{B}$.

Proof - Inequality (2.5) holds for $u \in \mathcal{C}(\Omega)$ (see [26], Lemma 1). Then, by Lemma 2.2, it continues to hold for all $u \in \mathcal{H}(\Omega)$. □

3. On Some Linearized Boundary-Value Problems

In this section we shall collect some results related to linearized versions of the Stokes and Oseen type related to the equation (1.1).

We shall say that a solution u, p to any of these linearized problems is in $\mathcal{P}$ if and only if they satisfy the parity condition (1.4).

For $u_0 \neq 0$, we indicate by E, Q the *Oseen fundamental solution* defined by

$$\begin{aligned} E_{ij}(x) &= \left(\delta_{ij}\Delta - \frac{\partial^2}{\partial y_i \partial y_j}\right)\Phi(x) \\ Q_j(x) &= \frac{1}{4\pi}\frac{x_j}{|x|^3}, \end{aligned} \tag{3.1}$$

where

$$\Phi(x) = -\frac{1}{8\pi\lambda}\int_0^{\frac{1}{2}(|u_0||x| - x\cdot u_0)} \frac{1-e^{-\tau}}{\tau} d\tau.$$

For $|u_0| \to 0$, the tensor field E reduces to the following one

$$U_{ij}(x) = -\frac{1}{8\pi}\left(\frac{\delta_{ij}}{|x|} + \frac{x_i x_j}{|x|^3}\right). \tag{3.2}$$

The pair U, Q is the *Stokes fundamental solution.* We recall some of the uniform estimates and of the summability properties for E in the region $\mathcal{A} = \{|x| > a > 0\}$, those of U and Q being obvious. We have, see *e.g.* [5], §VII.2,

$$\begin{gathered} |E(x)| \leq \frac{c_1}{|x|}, \qquad |\nabla E(x)| \leq \frac{c_1}{|x|^{3/2}}, \quad x \in \mathcal{A}, \\ E \in L^s(\mathcal{A}), \quad \nabla E \in L^r(\mathcal{A}), \quad \text{for all } s > 2,\ r > 4/3. \end{gathered} \tag{3.3}$$

We also recall the following property of the tensor $E(x; u_0)$

$$E(x; \sigma u_0) = \sigma E(\sigma x; u_0), \quad \sigma \in \mathbb{R}. \tag{3.4}$$

We have the following general result concerning the existence of solutions in the class $\mathcal{P}$.

Lemma 3.1. *Let $u_0 = me_1$, $m \in \mathbb{R}$, and let F and u_* be a second-order tensor field and a vector field, respectively, such that*

$$\operatorname{div} F, u_* \in \mathcal{P}.$$

Then the solution u, p to the problem

$$(3.5)\qquad \left.\begin{aligned} \Delta u + u_0\cdot\nabla u &= \operatorname{div} F + \nabla p \\ \operatorname{div} u &= 0 \end{aligned}\right\} \text{ in } \Omega$$
$$u = u_* \quad \text{on } \partial\Omega$$
$$\lim_{|x|\to\infty} u(x) = 0,$$

is in the class $\mathcal{P}$.

PROOF - In view of the symmetry of $\mathcal{B}$, of the parity properties of u_* and $\operatorname{div} F$, and of the fact that u_0 if it is not zero is directed along e_1, we find that the fields $\tilde{u}, \tilde{p}$, with

$$\begin{aligned}
\tilde{u}_1 &= \frac{1}{4}\left(u_1(x_1,x_2,x_3) + u_1(x_1,x_2,-x_3) + u_1(x_1,-x_2,x_3) + u_1(x_1,-x_2,-x_3)\right)\\
\tilde{u}_2 &= \frac{1}{4}\left(u_2(x_1,x_2,x_3) + u_2(x_1,x_2,-x_3) - u_2(x_1,-x_2,x_3) - u_2(x_1,-x_2,-x_3)\right)\\
\tilde{u}_3 &= \frac{1}{4}\left(u_3(x_1,x_2,x_3) - u_3(x_1,x_2,-x_3) + u_3(x_1,-x_2,x_3) - u_3(x_1,-x_2,-x_3)\right)\\
\tilde{p}_1 &= \frac{1}{4}\left(p(x_1,x_2,x_3) + p(x_1,x_2,-x_3) + p(x_1,-x_2,x_3) + p(x_1,-x_2,-x_3)\right),
\end{aligned}$$

are in the class $\mathcal{P}$ and satisfy (3.5). By uniqueness, they are the only solution, and the lemma is proved. □

The following lemma is obtained as a corollary to Theorems V.4.1, V.5.1 (in the case $u_0 = 0$) and Theorems VII.7.1, VII.7.2 (in the case $u_0 \neq 0$) of [5], and to Lemma 3.2.

Lemma 3.2. *Let $u_0 = m e_1$, $m \in \mathbb{R}$, and let F and u_* be a second-order tensor field and a vector field, respectively, such that*

$$\operatorname{div} F \in L^q(\Omega), \quad u_* \in W^{2-1/q,q}(\partial\Omega), \quad 1 < q < 3/2.$$

Then, problem (3.5) admits one and only one solution u, p such that

$$\begin{gathered} u \in L^{2q/(2-q)}(\Omega) \cap D^{1,4q/(4-q)}(\Omega) \cap D^{1,3q/(3-q)}(\Omega) \cap D^{2,q}(\Omega) \\ p \in L^{3q/(3-q)}(\Omega) \cap D^{1,q}(\Omega). \end{gathered}$$

This solution satisfies the following estimate

$$\|u_0 \cdot \nabla u\|_q + |u_0|^{\frac{1}{2}}\|u\|_{2q/(2-q)} + |u_0|^{\frac{1}{4}}|u|_{1,4q/(4-q)} + |u|_{1,3q/(3-q)} + \|u\|_{3q/(3-2q)} \\ + |u|_{2,q} + \|p\|_{3q/(3-q)} + |p|_{1,q} \le c_1 \left(\| \operatorname{div} F\|_q + \|u_*\|_{2-1/q,q,\partial\Omega}\right),$$

where the positive constant c_1 depends on q and u_0. However, if $|u_0| \le B$, for some positive B, then c_1 depends only q and B. Moreover, if $F \in L^2(\Omega)$, it follows that

$$u \in L^4(\Omega) \cap D^{1,2}(\Omega),\ \ p \in L^2(\Omega),$$

and there holds

$$|u_0|^{\frac{1}{4}}\|u\|_4 + |u|_{1,2} + \|p\|_2 \le c_2 \left(\|F\|_2 + \|u_*\|_{1/2,2,\partial\Omega}\right),$$

with c_2 independent of u_0. Furthermore, if $F = u_0 \equiv 0$, the following asymptotic representations hold as $|x| \to \infty$

$$\begin{aligned} u_l &= -A_k U_{kl}(x) + O(\nabla U) \\ p &= -A_k Q_k(x) + O(\nabla Q) \end{aligned} \tag{3.6}$$

where U, Q is the Stokes fundamental tensor, and

$$A_k \equiv \int_{\partial\Omega} T_{kl}(u,p) n_l.$$

Finally, if $\operatorname{div} F, v_* \in \mathcal{P}$ then $u, p \in \mathcal{P}$.

We have also

Lemma 3.3. *Let F satisfy the following condition*

$$\sup_{x\in\Omega} |F(x)(1+|x|^2)| \equiv \langle F \rangle < \infty.$$

Moreover, assume that

$$u_* \in W^{1-1/r,r}(\partial\Omega),\quad r > 3.$$

Then, for any $u_0 \neq 0$ there exists one and only one solution to (3.5) such that

$$\sup_{x\in\Omega} |u(x)(1+|x|)| < \infty,\quad u \in D^{1,s}(\Omega),\quad \text{all } s \in (3/2, r]$$

and the following estimate holds

$$\sup_{x\in\Omega}|u(1+|x|)|+|u|_{1,s}+|p|_s\le c\left(\langle F\rangle+\|u_*\|_{1-1/r,r(\partial\Omega)}\right) \tag{3.7}$$

where the constant c depends only on Ω, s, r and B, whenever $|u_0|\le B$. In particular, if $\operatorname{div} F, u_*\in\mathcal{P}$, *then* $u,p\in\mathcal{P}$.

PROOF - We split the solution as $u=u_1+u_2$, $p=p_1+p_2$, where

$$\left.\begin{aligned}\Delta u_1+u_0\cdot\nabla u_1&=\nabla p_1\\ \operatorname{div} u_1&=0\end{aligned}\right\}\ \text{in } \Omega \tag{3.8}$$
$$u_1=u_* \ \text{ on } \partial\Omega$$
$$\lim_{|x|\to\infty}u_1(x)=0,$$

and

$$\left.\begin{aligned}\Delta u_2+u_0\cdot\nabla u_2&=\operatorname{div} F+\nabla p_2\\ \operatorname{div} u_2&=0\end{aligned}\right\}\ \text{in } \Omega \tag{3.9}$$
$$u_2=0 \ \text{ on } \partial\Omega$$
$$\lim_{|x|\to\infty}u_2(x)=0,$$

From Theorem VII.7.2 of [5] we know that problem (3.8) admits a unique solution $u_1\in\bigcap_{r\ge s>3/2}D^{1,s}(\Omega)$, $p_1\in\bigcap_{r\ge s>3/2}L^s(\Omega)$, such that

$$|u_1|_{1,s}+\|p_1\|_s\le c\|u_*\|_{1-1/r,r(\partial\Omega)},\quad \text{all } s\in(3/2,r], \tag{3.10}$$

where $c=c(\Omega,s,r,B)$. Moreover, denoting by Σ the surface of a ball of radius $\rho>2\delta$, we have the following representation for u_1 [5], Theorem VII.6.2

$$(u_1)_j=\int_\Sigma\big[u_{*i}(y)T_{il}(w_j,Q_j)(x-y)-E_{ij}T_{il}(v,p)(y)$$
$$+u_{*i}(y)E_{ij}(x-y)(u_0)_l\big]n_l\,d\Sigma_y$$

where $w_j=(E_{1j},E_{2j},E_{3j})$. Thus, setting

$$\mathcal{D}=\int_\Sigma\left(|T(v,p)|+|u_*|\right),$$

and assuming $|u_0| \le B$, we find

$$|u_1(x)| \le c\mathcal{D}(1+B)\left\{\sup_{y\in\Omega_\rho}|E(x-y;\sigma e)| + \sup_{y\in\Omega_\rho}\left[|Q(x-y)| + \nabla_x E(x-y;\sigma e)|\right]\right\}$$

where $u_0 = \sigma e$ with e unit vector. Taking into account that by (3.4) $E(\xi;\sigma e) = \sigma E(\sigma\xi; e)$, from the previous inequality we deduce

$$|u_1(x)| \le c\mathcal{D}(1+B)\left\{|\sigma| \sup_{|z|\le|\sigma|\rho}|E(\sigma x - z; e)|\right.$$
$$\left. +|\sigma| \sup_{|z|\le|\sigma|\rho}\left[|Q(\sigma x - z)| + \nabla_{\sigma x}E(\sigma x - z; e)|\right]\right\}.$$

Now, for any $x \in \Omega$ with $|x| \ge 2\rho$, and $|z| \le |\sigma|\rho$ we have

$$|\sigma x - z| \ge \frac{1}{2}|\sigma x| \ge |\sigma|\rho$$

and so from (3.3) and (3.1) we obtain

$$|u_1(x)| \le c\mathcal{D}(1+B)|x|^{-1}, \quad \text{for } |x| \ge 2\rho, \tag{3.11}$$

where the constant c is independent of σ. From the well-known estimates for the Stokes problem in bounded domains we also have [5], Theorem IV.5.3

$$\|u_1\|_{1,r,\Omega_{2\rho}} \le c\left((1+B)\|u_1\|_{r,\Omega_{3\rho}} + \|p_1\|_{-1,r,\Omega_{3\rho}} + \|u_*\|_{1-1/r,r(\partial\Omega)}\right).$$

Thus, from (3.10) and the Sobolev embedding theorem, we find

$$\sup_{\Omega_{2\rho}}|u_1(x)| \le c(1+B)\|u_*\|_{1-1/r,r(\partial\Omega)}$$

which, in conjunction with (3.11), gives

$$|u_1(x)| \le c(1+B)(|x|+1)^{-1}\left[\mathcal{D} + \|u_*\|_{1-1/r,r(\partial\Omega)}\right]. \tag{3.12}$$

However, from the trace theorem we have

$$\mathcal{D} \le \|u_1\|_{2,t,\Omega_{\rho,2\rho}}, \quad \text{any } t > 1, \tag{3.13}$$

and, again from the interior estimates for the Stokes problem, and (3.10)

$$\|u_1\|_{2,t,\Omega_{\rho,2\rho}} \leq c\left(|u_1|_{1,s,\Omega_{\rho/2,3\rho}} + \|p_1\|_{s,\Omega_{\rho/2,3\rho}}\right) \leq c\|u_*\|_{1-1/r,r(\partial\Omega)}.$$

Therefore, from this inequality, (3.12) and (3.13), and recalling Lemmas 2.1 and 3.4 we conclude

$$|u_1(x)| \leq c(|x|+1)^{-1}\|u_*\|_{1-1/r,r(\partial\Omega)}. \tag{3.14}$$

Let us now estimate the solution u_2, p_2. From Theorem VII.7.2 of [5] we have

$$|u_2|_{1,s} + \|p_2\|_s \leq c\langle F\rangle \tag{3.15}$$

where the constant c depends on Ω, s and B. Moreover, we have the following representation for u_2

$$(u_2)_i(x) = \int_\Omega D_l G_{ij}(x,y;u_0)F_{lj}(y)\mathrm{d}y \tag{3.16}$$

with G Green's tensor for the (first) Oseen problem in Ω, corresponding to u_0. From [3], Theorem 3.1, we know that

$$|x|\int_\Omega |D_l G_{ij}(x,y;u_0)|\,|y|^{-2}\mathrm{d}y \leq H$$

with $H = H(\Omega, B)$. Thus, from this estimate and (3.16) we conclude

$$|u_2(x)| \leq c(|x|+1)^{-1}\langle F\rangle. \tag{3.17}$$

The lemma is then a consequence of (3.10), (3.14), (3.15) and (3.17), and of Lemma 3.1. □

In the next lemma we consider the solution to a suitable Stokes problem in Ω, which will play an important role throughout this paper.

Lemma 3.4. *Let H, P be the solution to the following problem*

$$\left.\begin{aligned}\Delta H &= \nabla P\\ \operatorname{div} H &= 0\end{aligned}\right\}\ \text{in } \Omega \tag{3.18}$$
$$H = e_1 \quad \text{on } \partial\Omega$$
$$\lim_{|x|\to\infty} H(x) = 0,$$

and set

$$g_i = T_{il}(H,P)n_l, \quad i = 1,2,3, \tag{3.19}$$

with n unit outer normal to $\partial\Omega$. Then,

$$\Lambda \equiv \int_{\partial\Omega} g = m e_1; \quad m \neq 0.$$

Moreover, any of the following quantities

$$A = \int_{\partial\Omega} g^2, \quad B = \int_{\partial\Omega} (g\cdot n)^2, \quad \Gamma = \int_{\partial\Omega} [(g\times n)\times n]^2$$

is not identically zero.

PROOF - Since, by Lemma 3.1, it is $H, P \in \mathcal{P}$, we easily obtain $\Lambda = m e_1$. Multiplying the first equation in (3.18) by $H - e_1$ and integrating by parts over Ω, we find

$$-e_1\cdot\Lambda = 2\int_{\Omega} |D(H)|^2,$$

where, we recall, $D(H)$ is the symmetric part of ∇H. Thus, if $\Lambda \equiv 0$ we deduce $D(H) \equiv 0$. However, clearly, $H \in \mathcal{H}(\Omega)$ (see (2.2)), and so, by Lemma 2.4, we deduce H=const., which in turn, by $(3.18)_4$ gives $H \equiv 0$, that is, $e_1 = 0$ which is a contradiction. By the same token, one has $A \neq 0$. To prove that also B and Γ are nonzero, we need an intermediate result. Specifically, we shall show that every solution to (3.18) satisfies

$$n\cdot D(H)\cdot n = 0 \ \text{ at } \partial\Omega. \tag{3.20}$$

We pick an arbitrary $\bar{x} \in \partial\Omega$ and introduce a local system of cartesian coordinates (y_1, y_2, y_3) with the origin at $\bar{x}$ and y_3 directed along n. Moreover, we denote by $y_3 = \omega(y_1, y_2)$ the equation of the portion of the boundary in a neighborhood I of $\bar{x}$. Clearly,

$$\left.\frac{\partial\omega}{\partial y_i}\right|_{y=0} = 0. \tag{3.21}$$

We next observe that, since $n \cdot D(H) \cdot n$ and $\operatorname{div} H$ are invariant by an orthogonal transformation, we must have

$$n \cdot D(H) \cdot n = n_3^2 \frac{\partial H_3}{\partial y_3} = -n_3^2 \left(\frac{\partial H_1}{\partial y_1} + \frac{\partial H_2}{\partial y_2}\right), \quad y \in I, \tag{3.22}$$

where we have also used condition $(3.18)_2$. Moreover, by $(3.18)_3$, we obtain

$$\alpha_k = H_k(y_1, y_2, \omega(y_2, y_3)), \quad k = 1, 2, 3 \quad y \in I, \tag{3.23}$$

and so, differentiating this expression and using (3.21) we find

$$0 = \frac{\partial H_k}{\partial y_l} + \frac{\partial H_k}{\partial y_3}\frac{\partial\omega}{\partial y_l} = \frac{\partial H_k}{\partial y_l}, \quad l, k = 1, 2, \quad y = 0.$$

Therefore, from (3.22) we conclude $n \cdot D(H) \cdot n = 0$ at $x = \bar{x}$, which, by the arbitrariness of $\bar{x}$, implies (3.20). We are now ready to show that also B and Γ are nonzero. Actually, from the condition $B = 0$ and (3.21) we derive that $P = 0$ at $\partial\Omega$ and, since P is harmonic, from Lemma 3.2 we conclude $P \equiv 0$ in Ω. From the asymptotic representation for P given in $(3.6)_2$ we then infer

$$0 = Q_k \int_{\partial\Omega} T_{kl}(H, P) n_l + O\left(\frac{1}{|x|^3}\right), \quad \text{for all large } |x|. \tag{3.24}$$

It is easy to show that this relation implies

$$\Lambda_k = 0, \quad k = 1, 2, 3. \tag{3.25}$$

In fact, recalling the definition of Q we have

$$0 = m_1 + m_2 \frac{x_2}{x_1} + m_3 \frac{x_3}{x_1} + \frac{|x|^3}{x_1} O\left(\frac{1}{|x|^3}\right),$$

and so choosing, for instance, $x_1 = x_3^2 + x_2^2$, we find $m_1 = 0$. Similarly, we prove $m_2 = m_3 = 0$ and (3.25) follows. Once (3.25) has been established, by what we already proved, we recover that B is nonzero. Let us next consider the quantity Γ. With the same meaning for (y_1, y_2, y_3) and $\bar{x}$ as before, the condition $\Gamma = 0$ furnishes

$$\left.\begin{array}{l} \dfrac{\partial H_2}{\partial y_3} + \dfrac{\partial H_3}{\partial y_2} = 0 \\ \dfrac{\partial H_1}{\partial y_3} + \dfrac{\partial H_3}{\partial y_1} = 0 \end{array}\right. \qquad \text{at } y = 0.$$

Thus, in view of (3.21) and (3.23), from this relation we find

$$\frac{\partial H_2}{\partial y_3} = \frac{\partial H_1}{\partial y_3} = 0 \ \text{ at } y = 0.$$

Since H is solenoidal, this latter relation implies

$$\frac{\partial^2 H_3}{\partial y_3^2} = 0 \quad \text{at } y = 0. \tag{3.26}$$

Moreover, again from the solenoidality of H and by (3.23) we also have

$$\frac{\partial H_3}{\partial y_3} = 0 \quad \text{at } y = 0. \tag{3.27}$$

Thus from the identity

$$\frac{\partial^2 H_3}{\partial y_i^2} = -2\frac{\partial^2 H_3}{\partial y_i \partial y_3}\frac{\partial \omega}{\partial y_i} - \frac{\partial^2 H_3}{\partial y_3^2}\left(\frac{\partial \omega}{\partial y_i}\right)^2 - \frac{\partial H_3}{\partial y_3}\frac{\partial^2 \omega}{\partial y_i^2},$$

and (3.26), (3.27) we obtain

$$\Delta H_3 = 0 \ \text{ at } y = 0.$$

Therefore, from $(3.18)_1$, we conclude $\partial p/\partial y_3|_{y=0} = 0$ and, by the arbitrariness of $\bar{x}$,

$$\frac{\partial p}{\partial n} = 0 \ \text{ at } \partial\Omega.$$

However, since p is harmonic and satisfies $(3.6)_2$, from this latter condition we find $p = 0$. On the other hand, from the condition $\Gamma = 0$ and (3.20) we also have $D(H) \cdot n = 0$ at $\partial\Omega$ which implies $T(H, P) \cdot n = 0$ at $\partial\Omega$. As a consequence, we obtain $A = 0$ and we conclude that also Γ is nonzero. The lemma is completely proved. □

Remark 3.1 - The function g, introduced in the previous lemma, depends *only* on the geometric properties of the body $\mathcal{B}$ such as size or shape. Moreover, as a consequence of Lemma 3.1, $g \in \mathcal{P}$. In some cases, one can explicitly calculate g. For example, if $\mathcal{B}$ is the unit ball, the solution H, P is well known (see *e.g.* [10], p.163) and we have

$$g = -\frac{3}{2}e_1. \tag{3.28}$$

4. Estimates for Solutions to the Nonlinear Problem

The objective of this section is to furnish certain estimates for solutions to (1.1) whose velocity gradient is in $L^2(\Omega)$. We shall consider both cases $\xi = 0$ and $\xi \neq 0$. In this latter case, our results differ from known ones, see *e.g.* [6] Chapter IX, in that the constants involved are independent of the parameters ξ and λ, for sufficiently small λ.

We shall first address the case $\xi = 0$. The following theorem is due to [6], Theorems IX.9.1 and IX.9.2.

Theorem 4.1. *Let v, p be a solution to (1.1), with $v \in D^{1,2}(\Omega)$, corresponding to $v_* \in W^{1-1/r,r}(\partial\Omega)$, $r > 3$, and to $\xi = 0$. Assume, further, that v satisfies the following energy inequality*

$$2\int_\Omega |D(v)|^2 \leq \int_{\partial\Omega} [v_* \cdot T(v,p) \cdot n - \frac{\lambda}{2}v_*^2 v_* \cdot n].$$

There exists $C = C(\Omega, r) > 0$ such that if $\lambda \|v_*\|_{1-1/r,r(\partial\Omega)} < C$, then

$$(1 + |x|)v \in L^\infty(\Omega), \quad v \in D^{1,r}(\Omega), \quad p \in L^r(\Omega), \tag{4.1}$$

and the following estimate holds

$$\sup_{x\in\Omega} |v(1 + |x|)| + |v|_{1,r} + \|p\|_r \leq c\|v_*\|_{1-1/r,r(\partial\Omega)}, \tag{4.2}$$

with $c = c(\Omega, r)$.

We shall next consider the case $\xi \neq 0$. We begin with a preliminary key result.

Lemma 4.1. *Assume $\xi \neq 0$ and $v_* \in W^{2-1/q_0,q_0}(\partial\Omega)$, for some $q_0 > 3$. Let $q \in (1, 3/2)$, $s \in (3/2, 3q/(3-q))$. Then, there exists $\lambda_0 = \lambda_0(\Omega, q, s, q_0) > 0$ such that if*

$$\lambda(\|v_*\|_{2-1/q_0,q_0(\partial\Omega)} + |\xi|) \le \lambda_0, \tag{4.3}$$

problem (1.1) has at least one corresponding solution w, π such that

$$(w - \xi) \in L^{2q/(2-q)}(\Omega) \cap D^{1,4q/(4-q)}(\Omega) \cap D^{1,s}(\Omega) \cap D^{2,q}(\Omega)$$
$$\pi \in L^{3q/(3-q)}(\Omega) \cap D^{1,q}(\Omega).$$

Moreover, $\|(w - \xi)(1 + |x|)\|_\infty < \infty$ and the following estimate holds

$$\begin{aligned} &\|(w - \xi)(1 + |x|)\|_\infty + |w|_{1,s} + \lambda\|\xi \cdot \nabla w\|_q + (\lambda|\xi|)^{1/2}\|w - \xi\|_{2q/(2-q)} \\ &\quad + (\lambda|\xi|)^{1/4}|w|_{1,4q/(4-q)} + |w|_{2,q} + \|p\|_{3q/(3-q)} + |p|_{1,q} \\ &\le c(\|v_*\|_{2-1/q_0,q_0(\partial\Omega)} + |\xi|), \end{aligned} \tag{4.4}$$

with $c = c(\Omega, q, s, q_0)$.

PROOF - Setting $u = w - \xi$, from (1.1) we find that u satisfies the following boundary value problem

$$\left.\begin{aligned} \Delta u - \lambda\xi \cdot \nabla u = \lambda u \cdot \nabla u + \nabla\pi \\ \operatorname{div} u = 0 \end{aligned}\right\} \text{ in } \Omega$$
$$u = u_* \equiv v_* - \xi \quad \text{on } \partial\Omega \tag{4.5}$$
$$\lim_{|x|\to\infty} u(x) = 0.$$

A solution to (4.5) is determined by the contraction mapping theorem as follows. Let

$$\begin{aligned} \|u\|_X \equiv &\|u(1 + |x|)\|_\infty + |u|_{1,s} + \lambda\|\xi \cdot \nabla u\|_q + (\lambda|\xi|)^{1/2}\|u\|_{2q/(2-q)} \\ &+ (\lambda|\xi|)^{1/4}|u|_{1,4q/(4-q)} + |u|_{2,q} \end{aligned} \tag{4.6}$$

and let

$$X = \left\{u \in L^1_{loc}(\Omega) : \|u\|_X < \infty\right\}, \quad X_\delta = \left\{u \in L^1_{loc}(\Omega) : \|u\|_X \le \delta\right\}.$$

Clearly, for any λ, ξ and $q \in (1,2)$, X is a Banach space endowed with the norm (4.6) and X_δ is a closed subset of X. Consider the operator

$$L : \phi \in X_\delta \longrightarrow u$$

where u solves the problem

$$\text{(4.7)} \qquad \left.\begin{aligned} \Delta u - \lambda\xi\cdot\nabla u = \lambda\phi\cdot\nabla\phi + \nabla\pi \\ \operatorname{div} u = 0 \end{aligned}\right\} \text{ in } \Omega \qquad \begin{aligned} u = u_* \quad \text{on } \partial\Omega \\ \lim_{|x|\to\infty} u(x) = 0. \end{aligned}$$

By the trace theorem, for all $r > 3$,

$$W^{1-1/r,r}(\partial\Omega) \subset W^{2-1/q_0,q_0}(\partial\Omega),$$

continuously. Thus, in view of Lemma 3.3, we have that there exists a unique solution to (4.7) such that

$$\text{(4.8)} \qquad \|u(1+|x|)\|_\infty + |u|_{1,s} \le c(\lambda\|\phi(1+|x|)\|_\infty^2 + \|u_*\|_{2-1/q_0,q_0(\partial\Omega)}),$$

for all $s > 3/2$. Moreover, by Lemma 3.2, the solution u verifies also the estimate

$$\text{(4.9)} \qquad \begin{aligned} \lambda\|\xi\cdot\nabla u\|_q + (\lambda|\xi|)^{1/2}\|u\|_{2q/(2-q)} + (\lambda|\xi|)^{1/4}|u|_{1,4q/(4-q)} + |u|_{2,q} \\ \le c(\lambda\|\phi\cdot\nabla\phi\|_q + \|u_*\|_{2-1/q_0,q_0(\partial\Omega)}), \end{aligned}$$

with $q \in (1, 3/2)$. The constant c entering estimates (4.8), (4.9) depends only on Ω, q, s, q_0 and an upper bound for $\lambda|\xi|$. Since

$$\begin{aligned} \|\phi\cdot\nabla\phi\|_q \le \|\phi\|_{sq/(s-q)}\|\nabla\phi\|_s \\ \|\phi\|_{sq/(s-q)} \le c\|\phi(1+|x|)\|_\infty, \quad s \in (3/2, 3q/(3-q)), \end{aligned}$$

from (4.8), (4.9) and (4.6), we conclude

$$\|u\|_X \le c\left(\lambda\|\phi\|_X^2 + \|u_*\|_{2-1/q_0,q_0(\partial\Omega)}\right),$$

where c depends only on Ω, q and an upper bound for $\lambda|\xi|$. Now, for $\phi \in X_\delta$ we have

$$\|u\|_X \le c\left(\lambda\delta^2 + \|u_*\|_{2-1/q_0,q_0(\partial\Omega)}\right),$$

and so, taking

$$\delta = 2c\|u_*\|_{2-1/q_0,q_0(\partial\Omega)},$$

we find

$$\|u\|_X \le \delta\left(\lambda c\delta + 1/2\right). \tag{4.10}$$

Existence of solution to (4.5) (and hence to (4.4)) in the class X then follows by choosing

$$\lambda \le \frac{1}{4c^2\left(\|v_*\|_{2-1/q_0,q_0(\partial\Omega)} + |\xi|\right)} \le \frac{1}{2c\delta}.$$

Moreover, the solution u verifies also

$$\|u\|_X \le c\delta \le c\left(\|v_*\|_{2-1/q_0,q_0(\partial\Omega)} + |\xi|\right),$$

and the lemma is completely proved. □

The next result, due to Finn [3] and Babenko [1] (see also Galdi [6], Theorems IX.8.1, IX.8.2, IX.8.3), concerns the asymptotic behavior of solutions to (1.1) with v having a finite Dirichlet integral.

Lemma 4.2. *Let v, p be a solution to (1.1) with $v \in D^{1,2}(\Omega)$, corresponding to $\xi \ne 0$. Then, for all sufficiently large $|x|$, v, p admit the following representations:*

$$\begin{aligned} v(x) &= \xi + \mathcal{M}\cdot E(x) + \mathcal{V}(x),\\ D_k v(x) &= \mathcal{M}\cdot D_k E(x) + \mathcal{D}_k(x), \quad k = 1,2,3,\\ p(x) &= \mathcal{M}_1\cdot Q(x) + \mathcal{P}(x), \end{aligned}$$

where E, Q is the Oseen fundamental solution. Furthermore,

$$\begin{aligned} \mathcal{M} &= -\int_{\partial\Omega}[T(v,p)\cdot n - \lambda\,(v-\xi)\,v\cdot n],\\ \mathcal{M}_1 &= -\int_{\partial\Omega}[T(v,p)\cdot n - \lambda(v-\xi)(v+\xi)\cdot n], \end{aligned}$$

and $\mathcal{V}(x)$, $\mathcal{D}_k(x)$, and $\mathcal{P}(x)$ satisfy the estimates

$$\mathcal{V}(x) = O(|x|^{-3/2+\varepsilon}), \quad \mathcal{D}_k(x) = O(|x|^{-2+\varepsilon}), \quad \varepsilon > 0, \quad k = 1,2,3,$$
$$\mathcal{P}(x) = O(|x|^{-2}).$$

We are now in a position to give the following result.

Theorem 4.2. *Let v, p be a solution to (1.1), with $v \in D^{1,2}(\Omega)$, corresponding to $\xi \neq 0$ and $v_* \in W^{2-1/q_0,q_0}(\partial\Omega)$, $q_0 > 3$. Furthermore, let $q \in (1, 3/2)$, $s \in (3/2, 3q/(3-q))$. Then, there exists a positive constant $\lambda_1 = \lambda_1(\Omega, q, s, q_0)$ such that, if*

$$\lambda(\|v_*\|_{2-1/q_0,q_0(\partial\Omega)} + |\xi|) \leq \lambda_1,$$

we have

$$(v - \xi) \in L^{2q/(2-q)}(\Omega) \cap D^{1,4q/(4-q)}(\Omega) \cap D^{1,s}(\Omega) \cap D^{2,q}(\Omega)$$
$$p \in L^{3q/(3-q)}(\Omega) \cap D^{1,q}(\Omega).$$

Moreover, $\|(v - \xi)(1 + |x|)\|_\infty < \infty$ and the following estimate holds

$$\begin{aligned} &\|(v-\xi)(1+|x|)\|_\infty + |v|_{1,s} + \lambda\|\xi \cdot \nabla v\|_q + (\lambda|\xi|)^{1/2}\|v - \xi\|_{2q/(2-q)} \\ &\quad + (\lambda|\xi|)^{1/4}|v|_{1,4q/(4-q)} + |v|_{2,q} + \|p\|_{3q/(3-q)} + |p|_{1,q} \\ &\leq c(\|v_*\|_{2-1/q_0,q_0(\partial\Omega)} + |\xi|), \end{aligned} \tag{4.11}$$

with $c = c(\Omega, q, s, q_0)$.

Proof - The proof will be obtained by uniqueness. Setting $v = u_1 + \xi$ and $w = u + \xi$, with w the solution determined in Lemma 4.1, we shall show that $u = u_1$. The function $z = u_1 - u$ satisfies

$$\left.\begin{aligned} \Delta z - \lambda\xi \cdot \nabla z &= \lambda\left(z \cdot \nabla z + u \cdot \nabla z + z \cdot \nabla u\right) + \nabla\tau \\ \operatorname{div} z &= 0 \end{aligned}\right\} \text{ in } \Omega$$

$$z = 0 \text{ on } \partial\Omega$$

$$\lim_{|x|\to\infty} z(x) = 0.$$

Multiplying the first equation by z, integrating by parts over Ω and using Lemma 4.2, we find

$$\int_\Omega |\nabla z|^2 = \lambda \int_\Omega z \cdot \nabla z \cdot u.$$

Using (4.8) in this relation furnishes, for λ satisfying (4.3),

$$\int_\Omega |\nabla z|^2 \leq \lambda c(\|v_*\|_{2-1/q_0,q_0(\partial\Omega)} + |\xi|) \left(\int_\Omega \frac{|z|^2}{1+|x|^2}\right)^{1/2} \left(\int_\Omega |\nabla z|^2\right)^{1/2},$$

with $c = c(\Omega, q, s, q_0)$. The result then follows from this relation and from the well-known inequality

$$\int_\Omega \frac{|u|^2}{(1+|x|)^2} \leq 4 \int_\Omega |\nabla u|^2, \qquad u \in D_0^{1,2}(\Omega). \tag{4.12}$$

□

5. The Stokes Approximation of Steady Self-Propelled Motion

If we take $\lambda = 0$ into equations (1.1), (1.2) we get the following equations

$$\left.\begin{aligned} \Delta v_0 &= \nabla p_0 \\ \operatorname{div} v_0 &= 0 \end{aligned}\right\} \text{ in } \Omega$$

$$v_0 = v_* \text{ on } \partial\Omega \tag{5.1}$$

$$\lim_{|x|\to\infty} v_0(x) = \xi_0$$

$$\int_{\partial\Omega} T(v_0, p_0) \cdot n = 0.$$

Whenever $\xi_0 = me_1$, $m \neq 0$, and $v_* \in \mathcal{P}$, these equations describe the steady, translational motion of a body $\mathcal{B}$, symmetric around e_1, and moving with velocity $-\xi_0$ in a viscous fluid, within the Stokes approximation. The aim of this section is to study the solvability of (5.1) in the class $\mathcal{P}$ under different prescriptions of data. Specifically, we shall consider the following two problems, which are the linear counterpart of Problems A and B mentioned in the Introduction.

Problem A$_0$. Given $v_* \in \mathcal{P}$, find a solution v_0, p_0, ξ_0 to (5.1), with $v_0, p_0 \in \mathcal{P}$, $\xi_0 \neq 0$, and investigate its uniqueness.

Problem B$_0$. Given $\xi_0 = me_1$, $m \neq 0$, find a solution $v_0, p_0 \in \mathcal{P}$ to $(5.1)_{1,2,4,5}$, and investigate its uniqueness.

It is clear that the solvability of Problem A_0 requires v_* to be given in a suitable class of data. For instance, if $\mathcal{B}$ is a ball, and v_* is a uniform, radial distribution of velocity, that is, $v_{*i} = v_0 x_i$, $i = 1, 2, 3$, $v_0 \in \mathbb{R}$, then, as expected on the basis of physical intuition, there are no corresponding solutions $v, p \in \mathcal{P}$ to (5.1) with $\xi_0 \neq 0$; see the remarks after Lemma 5.1.

On the other hand, it is easy to see that Problem B_0 admits, in general, an infinite number of solutions corresponding to the same $\xi_0 \neq 0$. Actually, we may take $v_0 = \nabla\Phi, p_0 = C$ =const, with Φ *any* harmonic function approaching $\xi_0 \cdot x$ at large distances. Sometimes, based on physical motivations, one could impose certain restrictions on the velocity field at the boundary. For example, one may require that it has a prescribed normal or tangential component. However, also in these cases, the problem admits, in general, more than one solution corresponding to the same $\xi_0 \neq 0$. For example, if $\mathcal{B}$ is a ball and v_0, p_0 is a solution to (5.1) corresponding to a given $\xi_0 \neq 0$ prescribed $(v_* \times n) \times n$ at the boundary, $v_0 + u, p_0 + \pi$ is still a solution to the same problem, with u, π solution corresponding to any uniform, radial distribution of velocity at the boundary.

In view of these considerations, it arises natural the question of the search of the spaces $\mathcal{T}$ of boundary values v_*, for which both Problems A and B admit *one and only one* solution. The spaces $\mathcal{T}$ will be called *thrust spaces.* The reason for this nomenclature is that every $v_* \in \mathcal{T}$ generates a "thrust" to move the body at a certain uniquely determined nonzero velocity ξ_0 and that, conversely, for any nonzero velocity ξ_0 there is one and only one solution v_0, p_0 to $(5.1)_{1,2,3,5}$ with $\gamma(v_0) \equiv v_0|_{\partial\Omega} \in \mathcal{T}$ which furnishes the suitable "thrust".

In this section we shall show that there exists a one-dimensional subspace $\mathcal{T}(\mathcal{B})$ of the space $L^2(\partial\Omega)$ with the following properties (see (5.15)). Denote by $\mathbb{P}$ the orthogonal projection of $L^2(\partial\Omega)$ onto $\mathcal{T}(\mathcal{B})$. Then for any $v_*\mathcal{P}$ (sufficiently regular) with $\mathbb{P}(v_*) \neq 0$, Problem A_0 admits one and only one corresponding solution. Conversely, given $\xi_0 = me_1$, with $m \neq 0$, there exists one and only one corresponding solution to Problem B_0 with $\gamma(v) \in \mathcal{T}(\mathcal{B})$. For this latter problem, we can prescribe also the normal or the tangential component of v_0 at $\partial\Omega$. In such cases the thrust space $\mathcal{T}(\mathcal{B})$ will be replaced, accordingly, by suitable one-dimensional spaces $\mathcal{T}_\tau(\mathcal{B})$ and $\mathcal{T}_n(\mathcal{B})$, respectively (see (5.17), (5.16)). It should be emphasized that all these spaces depend only on the geometric properties of the body $\mathcal{B}$ such as size or shape. In particular, they are independent of the orientation of $\mathcal{B}$ and on the fluid property. Another important property of $\mathcal{T}(\mathcal{B})$ is the following one. Let $G \in \mathbb{R}^3$ be the uniquely determined vector corresponding to a given velocity of the body $-\xi_0 \neq 0$, and representative of the function $\mathbb{P}(v_*) \in \mathcal{T}(\mathcal{B})$. We shall call G the *thrust vector*, see (5.12). Moreover, let $F \in \mathbb{R}^3$ be the net force that we have to apply to $\mathcal{B}$ to tow it at the same velocity $-\xi_0$. Then, $F = -G$. Since $F \cdot \xi \leq 0$, the "–" sign in this latter relation is suggestive of the action-reaction principle.

We begin to prove the following

Theorem 5.1. *Let v_0, p_0, ξ_0, v_* be a solution to $(5.1)_{1,2,3,4}$ with v_0, p_0 and v_* in the class $\mathcal{P}$. Suppose $v_0 \in W^{2,r}(\Omega_R)$, some $r > 1$, all $R > \delta$. Then, the self-propelling condition $(5.1)_5$ is equivalent to the following one*

$$\int_{\partial\Omega} v_* \cdot g = \xi_0 \cdot \int_{\partial\Omega} g, \tag{5.2}$$

where the vector g, is defined in Lemma 3.3. Assume, further, that

$$v_* \in W^{2-1/q_0,q_0}(\partial\Omega),$$

for some $q_0 > 3$. Then, for all $s > 1$ and $q \in (1, q_0]$, we have

$$\begin{aligned} (v_0 - \xi_0) \in D^{1,s}(\Omega) \cap D^{2,q}(\Omega), \quad & \sup_{x\in\Omega} |(v_0 - \xi_0)(1 + |x|^2)| < \infty \\ p_0 \in D^{1,q}(\Omega), \quad & \sup_{x\in\Omega} |p_0(1 + |x|^3)| < \infty \end{aligned} \tag{5.3}$$

and the following estimate holds

$$\begin{aligned} \|(v_0 - \xi_0)(1 + |x|^2)\|_\infty + \|p_0(1 + |x|^3)\|_\infty + |v_0|_{1,s} \\ + |v_0|_{2,q} + |p_0|_{1,q} \leq c\|v_* - \xi_0\|_{2-1/q_0,q_0(\partial\Omega)} \end{aligned} \tag{5.4}$$

with $c = c(\Omega, q, s, q_0)$.

Proof - By well-known regularity results, we deduce

$$v_0 \in W^{2,r}(\Omega_R) \cap C^\infty(\Omega), \quad p_0 \in W^{1,r}(\Omega_R) \cap C^\infty(\Omega).$$

Therefore, multiplying $(5.1)_1$ by H, integrating by parts over Ω, and using Lemma 3.2, we find

$$e_1 \cdot \int_{\partial\Omega} T(v_0, p_0) \cdot n = 2 \int_{\Omega} D(H) : D(v_0). \tag{5.5}$$

Likewise, multiplying $(3.18)_1$ by $v_0 - \xi_0$ and integrating by parts over Ω, we obtain

$$\int_{\partial\Omega} (v_* - \xi_0) \cdot g = 2 \int_{\Omega} D(H) : D(v_0). \tag{5.6}$$

Thus, (5.5) and (5.6) imply

$$\int_{\partial\Omega} (v_* - \xi_0) \cdot g = e_i \cdot \int_{\partial\Omega} T(v_0, p_0) \cdot n.$$

Taking into account that for $v_0, p_0 \in \mathcal{P}$ it is

$$\int_{\partial\Omega} T(v_0, p_0) \cdot n = \kappa e_1, \quad \kappa \neq 0,$$

the first part of the lemma follows. The summability properties stated in (5.3) as well as the estimate

$$|v_0|_{1,s} + |v_0|_{2,q} + |p_0|_{1,q} \leq c \|v_* - \xi_0\|_{2-1/q_0, q_0(\partial\Omega)} \tag{5.7}$$

are a consequence of the results of §6 of [9] (see also §§V.4, V.6 of [5]). To complete the proof of the lemma, we have then to show the following inequalities

$$\begin{aligned} &\|(v_0 - \xi_0)(1 + |x|^2)\|_\infty \leq c \|v_* - \xi_0\|_{2-1/q_0, q_0(\partial\Omega)} \\ &\|p_0(1 + |x|^3)\|_\infty \leq c \|v_* - \xi_0\|_{2-1/q_0, q_0(\partial\Omega)} \end{aligned} \tag{5.8}$$

Set $w = v_0 - \xi_0$. The following representation holds [5], Theorem V.3.2

$$w_j(x) = \int_{\partial\Omega} \{U_{ij}(x-y) T_{il}(w, p_0)(y) - w_i(y) T_{il}(u_j, Q_j)(x-y) n_l(y)\} \, d\sigma_y$$

where $u_j = (U_{1j}, U_{2j}, U_{3j})$, and (U, Q) is the Stokes fundamental solution. Because of $(5.1)_5$, we have

$$\begin{aligned} w_j(x) = &\int_{\partial\Omega} [U_{ij}(x-y) - U_{ij}(x)] \, T_{il}(w, p_0)(y) d\sigma_y \\ &- \int_{\partial\Omega} w_i(y) T_{il}(u_j, Q_j)(x-y) n_l(y) d\sigma_y. \end{aligned}$$

Therefore, from the asymptotic properties of (U, Q), we find

$$\|w(1+|x|^2)\|_{\infty,\Omega^{2\delta}} \le c \int_{\partial\Omega} (|T(w,p_0)\cdot n| + |w|)\,. \tag{5.9}$$

However, from the trace theorem and estimates for the Stokes problem near the boundary, we find for $1 < r < q$

$$\int_{\partial\Omega} (|T(w,p_0)\cdot n| + |w|) \le c(\|w_0\|_{2,r,\Omega_{2\delta}} + \|p_0\|_{1,r,\Omega_{2\delta}} + \|v_* - \xi_0\|_{2-1/q_0,q_0(\partial\Omega)}).$$

Thus, from (5.7), we deduce

$$\int_{\partial\Omega} (|T(w,p_0)\cdot n| + |w|) \le c\|v_* - \xi_0\|_{2-1/q_0,q_0(\partial\Omega)},$$

which, once replaced into (5.9), furnishes

$$\|w(1+|x|^2)\|_{\infty,\Omega^{2\delta}} \le c\|v_* - \xi_0\|_{2-1/q_0,q_0(\partial\Omega)}. \tag{5.10}$$

Inequality $(5.8)_1$ becomes a consequence of (5.10), (5.7) and of the embedding theorems. To show $(5.8)_2$, we use the following representation for p_0 [5], Theorem V.3.2,

$$p_0(x) = \int_{\partial\Omega} \left\{ Q_j(x-y)T_{il}(w,p_0)(y) - 2w_i(y)\frac{\partial Q_l(x-y)}{\partial x_i} n_l(y) \right\} \mathrm{d}\sigma_y.$$

In view of $(5.1)_5$, we may write

$$\begin{aligned} p_0(x) = \int_{\partial\Omega} \Big\{ & [Q_j(x-y) - Q_j(x)]\, T_{il}(w,p_0)(y) \\ & - 2w_i(y)\frac{\partial Q_l(x-y)}{\partial x_i} n_l(y) \Big\} \mathrm{d}\sigma_y. \end{aligned}$$

Using this formula along with the asymptotic properties of Q, we may proceed as in the proof of $(5.8)_1$, to show also the validity of inequality $(5.8)_2$. □

We shall now derive several important consequences of Theorem 5.1. We begin to notice that, since the vector Λ is not identically zero (Lemma 3.4), condition (5.2) implies that a steady flow past the self-propelled body $\mathcal{B}$ ($\xi_0 \neq 0$) can occur if and only if the boundary value v_* of the solution satisfies the condition

$$\int_{\partial\Omega} v_* \cdot g \neq 0, \tag{5.11}$$

or, in other words, if the orthogonal projection of v_* along the subspace of $L^2(\partial\Omega)$ generated by g is not zero. For example, if $\mathcal{B}$ is the ball of unit radius centered at the origin and v_* is a uniform, radial distribution of velocity, that is, $v_{*i} = \tilde{v}_0 x_i$, $i = 1, 2, 3$, $\tilde{v}_0 \in \mathbb{R}$, in view of (3.28) we find that

$$\int_{\partial\Omega} v_* \cdot g = \tilde{v}_0 \int_{\partial\Omega} x_1 = 0,$$

and therefore this distribution of velocity at the boundary can not generate (as expected) any self-propelled motion.

Let us denote by G the following vector

$$G = \left(\int_{\partial\Omega} v_* \cdot g \right) e_1. \tag{5.12}$$

A steady flow past the self-propelled body $\mathcal{B}$ moving with velocity $-\xi_0$ can take place if and only if $G \neq 0$. G is the *thrust vector.* We shall establish a characterization of the vector G. To this end, consider the motion of the body $\mathcal{B}$ with the same velocity $-\xi_0$, but under the assumption that it is towed by an external force F. As is known, [10], §5-3, F is directed along ξ_0, that is, along e_1. Moreover, denoting by u, π the corresponding velocity and pressure fields of the fluid, we have

$$\left.\begin{aligned} \Delta u &= \nabla \pi \\ \operatorname{div} u &= 0 \end{aligned}\right\} \text{ in } \Omega \qquad u = 0 \text{ on } \partial\Omega \qquad \lim_{|x|\to\infty} u(x) = \xi_0 \tag{5.13}$$

and

$$\int_{\partial\Omega} T(u,\pi)\cdot n = F. \tag{5.14}$$

The following theorem establishes the relationship between F and G.

Theorem 5.2. $F = -G$.

PROOF - Multiplying (5.13) by H and integrating by parts over Ω

$$e_1 \cdot \int_{\partial\Omega} T(u,\pi)\cdot n = 2\int_{\Omega} D(H) : D(u).$$

Likewise, multiplying $(3.18)_1$ by $u - \xi_0$ and integrating by parts over Ω, we obtain

$$-\xi_0 \cdot \int_{\partial\Omega} g = 2\int_{\Omega} D(H) : D(u).$$

From these two equations and (5.14), we then obtain

$$F = -\xi_0 \cdot \int_{\partial\Omega} g.$$

The result then follows from this relation and (5.2), (5.12). □

The main consequence of Theorem 5.1 is that it allows us to give unique solvability for Problem A_0 and Problem B_0. To prove this, we introduce the following one-dimensional *thrust spaces*

$$\mathcal{T} = \mathcal{T}(\mathcal{B}) = \left\{u \in L^2(\partial\Omega) \,:\, u = \alpha g,\ \alpha \in \mathbb{R}\right\}, \tag{5.15}$$

$$\mathcal{T}_n = \mathcal{T}_n(\mathcal{B}) = \left\{u \in L^2(\partial\Omega) \,:\, u = \alpha (g\cdot n)n,\ \alpha \in \mathbb{R}\right\}, \tag{5.16}$$

$$\mathcal{T}_\tau = \mathcal{T}_\tau(\mathcal{B}) = \left\{u \in L^2(\partial\Omega) \,:\, u = \alpha (g\times n)\times n,\ \alpha \in \mathbb{R}\right\}. \tag{5.17}$$

We shall denote by $\mathbb{P}$, $\mathbb{P}_n$ and $\mathbb{P}_\tau$ the orthogonal projection of $L^2(\partial\Omega)$ onto $\mathcal{T}(\mathcal{B})$, $\mathcal{T}_n(\mathcal{B})$ and $\mathcal{T}_\tau(\mathcal{B})$, respectively. For $w = \alpha g \in \mathcal{T}(\mathcal{B})$, we set

$$\|w\|_{\mathcal{T}} = |\alpha|. \tag{5.18}$$

Likewise, for $w = \beta(g \cdot n)n \in \mathcal{T}_n(\mathcal{B})$, and $z = \sigma(g \times n) \times n \in \mathcal{T}_\tau(\mathcal{B})$ we set

$$
\begin{aligned}
\|w\|_{\mathcal{T}_n} &= |\beta|, \\
\|z\|_{\mathcal{T}_\tau} &= |\sigma|,
\end{aligned}
\tag{5.19}
$$

respectively.

Remark 5.1 - It is clear that for w in any of the spaces $\mathcal{T}(\partial\Omega)$, $\mathcal{T}_n(\mathcal{B})$, $\mathcal{T}_\tau(\mathcal{B})$, the corresponding norms (5.18), (5.19), are all equivalent to $\|w\|_{2-1/q,q(\partial\Omega)}$, $q > 1$. Moreover, denoting by G the corresponding thrust vector, that is, (5.12) with v_* in any of the spaces (5.15)–(5.16), we have that the norms (5.18), (5.19) are proportional to $|G|$.

The following theorem proves the unique solvability for Problem A_0.

Theorem 5.3. *Given $v_* \in W^{2-1/q_0,q_0}(\partial\Omega) \cap \mathcal{P}$, $q_0 > 3$, with $\mathbb{P}(v_*) \neq 0$, there exists one and only one solution v_0, p_0, ξ_0, $\xi_0 \neq 0$, to (5.1) with $v_0, p_0 \in \mathcal{P}$. This solution satisfies (5.3), for all $s > 1$ and $q \in (1, q_0]$, and the following estimate*

$$
\begin{aligned}
|\xi_0| + \|(v_0 - \xi_0)(1+|x|^2)\|_\infty + \|p_0(1+|x|^3)\|_\infty + |v_0|_{1,s} + |v_0|_{2,q} + |p_0|_{1,q} \\
\leq c\|v_*\|_{2-1/q_0,q_0(\partial\Omega)}.
\end{aligned}
$$

Proof - Given v_* with the mentioned property, since the vector Λ is nonzero and directed along e_1 (see Lemmas 1.1 and 3.4), we obtain a uniquely determined $\xi_0 = me_1$, $m \neq 0$ such that

$$
\xi_0 \cdot \int_{\partial\Omega} g = \int_{\partial\Omega} v_* \cdot g.
$$

Moreover,

$$
\|\mathbb{P}(v_*)\|_{\mathcal{T}} \leq c_1|\xi_0| \leq c_2\|\mathbb{P}(v_*)\|_{\mathcal{T}}.
\tag{5.20}
$$

The theorem then follows from this inequality, Lemma 3.1, Theorem 5.1, Remark 5.1 and known existence results for the Stokes problem in exterior domains, see [5] Theorem V.4.2. □

Our next objective is solvability of Problem B_0. We shall be concerned with the cases when the solutions we are looking for, have boundary velocity which either have no prescription or have a prescribed normal or tangential component. These latter conditions are motivated by physical interest. We may consider other possibilities like, for example, prescribing the velocity field on a proper subset of the boundary. However, we shall not treat this situation here, which will be the object of future work.

Theorem 5.4. *Let $\xi_0 = me_1$ be given with $m \neq 0$. Then there exists one and only one solution to $(5.1)_{1,2,3,5}$ with $\gamma(v_0) \equiv v_0|_{\partial\Omega} \in \mathcal{T}(\mathcal{B})$. This solution is in the class $\mathcal{P}$, and satisfies (5.3) for all $s, q > 1$ and the estimate*

$$\begin{aligned} \|\gamma(v_0)\|_{\mathcal{T}} + \|(v_0 - \xi_0)(1+|x|^2)\|_\infty + \|p_0(1+|x|^3)\|_\infty \\ + |v_0|_{1,s} + |v_0|_{2,q} + |p_0|_{1,q} \leq c|\xi_0|. \end{aligned} \tag{5.21}$$

Moreover, assume that either of the following conditions is met

$$\begin{aligned} &(i)\ \ \gamma(v_0)\cdot n = \psi_1 \ \text{ at } \ \partial\Omega, \\ &(ii)\ \ (\gamma(v_0)\times n)\times n = \psi_2 \ \text{at } \partial\Omega, \end{aligned}$$

where ψ_1 and ψ_2 are prescribed scalar and vector function at $\partial\Omega$, respectively, with $\psi_1 n, \psi_2 \in \mathcal{P}$ and

$$\psi_k \in W^{2-1/q_0,q_0}(\partial\Omega), \quad q_0 > 3, \quad k = 1,2.$$

Then, there exists one and only one solution to $(5.1)_{1,2,3,5}$-(i) and to $(5.1)_{1,2,3,5}$-(ii), with $(\gamma(v_0)\times n)\times n \in \mathcal{T}_\tau(\mathcal{B})$ (in case (i)) and $(\gamma(v_0)\cdot n)n \in \mathcal{T}_n(\mathcal{B})$ (in case (ii)). The corresponding solutions are in the class $\mathcal{P}$, satisfy (5.3), for all $s > 1$ and $q \in (1, q_0]$, and the following estimates

$$\begin{aligned} &\|(\gamma(v_0)\times n)\times n\|_{\mathcal{T}_\tau(\mathcal{B})} + \|(v_0 - \xi_0)(1+|x|^2)\|_\infty + \|p_0(1+|x|^3)\|_\infty \\ &\qquad + |v_0|_{1,s} + |v_0|_{2,q} + |p_0|_{1,q} \leq c(|\xi_0| + \|\psi_1\|_{2-1/q_0,q_0(\partial\Omega)}) \\ &\|(\gamma(v_0)\cdot n)n\|_{\mathcal{T}_n(\mathcal{B})} + \|(v_0 - \xi_0)(1+|x|^2)\|_\infty + \|p_0(1+|x|^3)\|_\infty \\ &\qquad + |v_0|_{1,s} + |v_0|_{2,q} + |p_0|_{1,q} \leq c(|\xi_0| + \|\psi_2\|_{2-1/q_0,q_0(\partial\Omega)}) \end{aligned} \tag{5.22}$$

in case (i) and in case (ii), respectively.

PROOF - Since the quantity A is nonzero (Lemma 3.4) we have that, for any $\xi_0 \neq 0$, there exists one and only one $v_* \in \mathcal{T}(\partial\Omega)$ satisfying (5.2). Moreover

$$|\xi_0| \leq c_1\|v_*\|_{\mathcal{T}} \leq c_2|\xi_0|. \tag{5.23}$$

Since $v_* \in W^{2-1/q_0,q_0}(\partial\Omega)$ for all $q_0 > 1$, by known methods, we may construct a solution v_0, p_0 to $(5.1)_{1,2,3,4}$ corresponding to these ξ_0 and v_* and with $v_0 \in D^{2,q}(\Omega)$, all $q > 1$. By Theorem 5.1, this solution satisfies $(5.1)_5$, (5.3), (5.4) for all $s, q > 1$, and, by Remark 5.1 and (5.23), it verifies (5.21). The solution is also unique in the class of those solutions having boundary data in $\mathcal{T}(\mathcal{B})$. In fact, denoting by u, π any other solution to $(5.1)_{1,2,4,5}$, by Theorem 5.1 we have

$$\int_{\partial\Omega} (v_* - u_*) \cdot g = 0,$$

that is, again because A in nonzero, $v_* = u_*$ at $\partial\Omega$. Thus, $(v_0 - u, p_0 - \pi)$ satisfies $(5.1)_{1,2,3,4}$ with $v_* = \xi_0 = 0$ and we conclude $v_0 = u$, $\nabla(p_0 - \pi) = 0$. Next, assume that v_0 satisfies condition (i). Then, we look for a solution w to the problem

$$\int_{\partial\Omega} w \cdot [(g \times n) \times n] = -\int_{\partial\Omega} \psi_1 g \cdot n + \int_{\partial\Omega} \xi_0 \cdot g, \quad w \in \mathcal{T}_\tau(\mathcal{B}). \tag{5.24}$$

Since the quantity B is nonzero (Lemma 3.4), this equation is uniquely solvable and, moreover

$$\|w\|_{\mathcal{T}_\tau} \leq c\left(|\xi_0| + \|\psi_1\|_{2-1/q,q(\partial\Omega)}\right).$$

We then set $v_* = w + \psi_1 n$ and find a solution to $(5.1)_{1,2,3,4}$ with $v_0 \in D^{2,q}(\Omega)$, $1 < q \leq q_0$. Since $(g \times n) \times n \in \mathcal{P}$ it follows that this solution is in $\mathcal{P}$. Further, in view of (5.24), Theorem 5.1 and Remark 5.1, it satisfies $(5.1)_5$, (5.3), for all $s > 1$ and $q \in (1, q_0]$, and $(5.22)_1$. Since B is nonzero, reasoning as in the previous case, we show that this is the only solution to $(5.1)_{1,2,3,5}$, (i) with $(\gamma(v_0) \times n) \times n \in \mathcal{T}_\tau(\mathcal{B})$. The proof in the case (ii) is entirely analogous and, therefore, the theorem is completely proved. □

In the light of Theorem 5.4, we can give an explicit solution to Problem B_0, in the case when $\mathcal{B}$ is a ball of unit radius (say), and $\psi_1 = \psi_2 = 0$. In fact, we have

Theorem 5.5. *Let $\mathcal{B}$ be the ball of radius one centered at the origin and let $\xi_0 = Ve_1$, $V \neq 0$. Then the self-propelled solutions v_0, p_0 uniquely determined in Theorem 5.4 and corresponding to $\psi_1 = \psi_2 = 0$ are potential-like, that,* *is* $v_0 = \nabla\Phi$, *for suitable scalar harmonic functions* Φ, *and* p_0 =const. *The functions* Φ *are given by*

(a) $\Phi = Vx_1$ (if no prescription of velocity is given at $\partial\Omega$);

(b) $\Phi = Vx_1\left(1 + \dfrac{1}{2|x|^3}\right)$ (if $v_0 \cdot n = 0$ at $\partial\Omega$);

(c) $\Phi = Vx_1\left(1 - \dfrac{1}{|x|^2}\right)$ (if $(v_0 \times n) \times n = 0$ at $\partial\Omega$).

Proof - Taking into account that, from $(5.1)_1$

$$\int_{\partial\Omega} T(v_0, p_0) \cdot n = \lim_{R\to\infty} \int_{\partial B_R} T(v_0, p_0) \cdot n,$$

and that any harmonic function Φ in Ω, having bounded first derivatives satisfies

$$D^\sigma\Phi = O(|x|^{-3}), \ |\sigma| = 2, \ \text{ as } |x| \to \infty$$

we at once deduce that any potential-like velocity field satisfies to (5.1), with $v_* = \nabla\Phi|_{\partial\Omega}$. Moreover, we have also

$$\left.\frac{\partial\Phi}{\partial n}\right|_{\partial\Omega} = 0 \qquad \text{(in case (b))},$$
$$(\nabla\Phi \times n) \times n|_{\partial\Omega} = 0 \qquad \text{(in case (c))}.$$

Therefore, in view of Theorem 5.4, and (3.28), to show the result, we have only to check the following properties

$$\text{(i)} \quad \nabla\Phi|_{|x|=1} = \alpha \qquad \text{(in case (a))},$$
$$\text{(ii)} \quad (\nabla\Phi \times x) \times x|_{|x|=1} = \beta - (\beta \cdot x)x \qquad \text{(in case (b))},$$
$$\text{(iii)} \quad x \cdot \nabla\Phi|_{|x|=1} = (\gamma \cdot x)x \qquad \text{(in case (c))},$$

for some constant vectors α, β, γ directed along e_1. However, these properties are readily established with the choices

$$\alpha = Ve_1, \ \ \beta = \frac{3}{2}Ve_1, \ \ \gamma = 2Ve_1.$$

The theorem is completely proved. □

6. Steady Self-Propelled Motion of a Symmetric Body in a Navier-Stokes Fluid: Problem A. Uniqueness of Solutions

The objective of the second part of this paper is to investigate the *nonlinear* steady translational motion of a self-propelled body $\mathcal{B}$ and to analyze its relation with the corresponding towed body problem. Specifically, we shall be interested to the nonlinear version of Problems A_0 and B_0, already solved for the linear case in Section 5.

In this and the next section we shall show unique solvability of the following

Problem A: Given $v_* \in \mathcal{P}$ in a suitable space, find $v, p \in \mathcal{P}$ and $\xi = me_1$, $m \neq 0$ such that

$$
\begin{aligned}
&\left.\begin{aligned}\Delta v &= \lambda v \cdot \nabla v + \nabla p\\ \operatorname{div} v &= 0\end{aligned}\right\} \text{ in } \Omega\\
&v = v_* \ \text{ on } \partial\Omega\\
&\lim_{|x|\to\infty} v(x) = \xi\\
&\int_{\partial\Omega} [T(v,p)\cdot n - \lambda v_* \cdot n(v_* - \xi)] = 0.
\end{aligned} \tag{6.1}
$$

In the present section, we shall treat the uniqueness of solutions to this problem, postponing the proof of their existence until section 7.

To this end, let us begin to put (6.1) in a different but equivalent form. Multiplying $(6.1)_1$ by H, where H is defined in (3.18), and integrating by parts over Ω, we find

$$
\begin{aligned}
e_1 \cdot \int_{\partial\Omega} &[T(v,p)\cdot n - \lambda v_* \cdot n(v_* - \xi)] =\\
&= \int_\Omega D(v) : D(H) - \lambda \int_\Omega (v-\xi)\cdot\nabla H \cdot (v-\xi) - \lambda\xi \cdot \int_\Omega \nabla H \cdot (v - \xi).
\end{aligned}
$$

Likewise, multiplying $(3.18)_1$ by $v - \xi$ and integrating by parts over Ω we find

$$
\int_{\partial\Omega} (v_* - \xi)\cdot g = \int_\Omega D(v) : D(H),
$$

where the vector g is defined in (3.19). Therefore, recalling that in the class of solutions belonging to $\mathcal{P}$ the left-hand side of equation $(6.1)_5$ is directed along e_1, the self-propelling condition $(6.1)_5$ becomes

$$\int_{\partial\Omega}(v_* - \xi)\cdot g = \lambda \int_{\Omega}(v-\xi)\cdot\nabla H\cdot(v-\xi) + \lambda\xi\cdot\int_{\Omega}\nabla H\cdot(v-\xi). \tag{6.2}$$

Next, let $v_* \in W^{2-1/q_0,q_0}(\partial\Omega)$, $q_0 > 3$, be any boundary function in the class $\mathcal{P}$ such that $\mathbb{P}(v_*) \neq 0$, and denote by v_0, p_0, ξ_0, $\xi_0 \neq 0$, the uniquely determined corresponding solution to the Stokes approximation of (6.1), see Theorem 5.3. Writing

$$v = v_0 + u + \mu, \quad p = p_0 + \pi, \quad \xi = \xi_0 + \mu,$$

from $(6.1)_{1,2,3,4}$ we deduce that u, π, μ satisfy the following equations

$$\begin{aligned} &\left.\begin{aligned} \Delta u + \lambda\xi\cdot\nabla u &= \lambda\,\mathrm{div}\,F + \nabla\pi \\ \mathrm{div}\,u &= 0 \end{aligned}\right\} \text{ in } \Omega \\ &u = -\mu \ \text{ on } \partial\Omega \\ &\lim_{|x|\to\infty} u(x) = 0 \\ &F := v_0\otimes(v_0-\xi_0) + (v_0-\xi_0)\otimes u \\ &\qquad + u\otimes(v_0-\xi_0) + u\otimes u + \mu\otimes(v_0-\xi_0), \end{aligned} \tag{6.3}$$

while (6.2) becomes

$$\mu\cdot\int_{\partial\Omega} g = \lambda\int_{\Omega} F : \nabla H + \lambda\xi\cdot\int_{\Omega}\nabla H\cdot u. \tag{6.4}$$

Thus, the uniqueness of solutions to Problem A, corresponding to a given v_* is equivalent to show the same property for problem (6.3), (6.4) for a given v_0.

Having established this equivalence, we shall now proceed to prove the uniqueness for problem (6.3), (6.4). We need some preliminary results.

Lemma 6.1. *Let v, p, ξ be a solution to (6.1) with $v, p \in \mathcal{P}$, corresponding to*

$$v_* \in W^{2-1/q_0,q_0}(\partial\Omega)\cap\mathcal{P}, \quad q_0 > 3.$$

Assume that $\mathbb{P}(v_*) \neq 0$ *and that* $v \in D^{1,2}(\Omega)$. *There exist constants* $C_i = C_i(\Omega, q_0) > 0$, $i = 1, 2$, *such that if* $\lambda \|v_*\|_{2-1/q_0, q_0(\partial\Omega)} < C_1$, *then* $|\xi| \leq C_2 \|v_*\|_{2-1/q_0, q_0(\partial\Omega)}$.

PROOF - From Lemma 2.5, we know that

$$|\mu| \leq c|u|_{1,2}, \tag{6.5}$$

which, by Theorem 5.3, in particular implies that

$$|\xi| \leq c(|u|_{1,2} + \|v_*\|_{2-1/q_0, q_0(\partial\Omega)}). \tag{6.6}$$

We need to give an estimate of the Dirichlet integral of u. Multiplying $(6.3)_1$ by u and integrating by parts over Ω, in view of the asymptotic properties of u, p and v_0 we find that

$$\begin{aligned} 2\int_\Omega |D(u)|^2 = & -\mu \cdot \int_{\partial\Omega} T(u,p)\cdot n + \lambda \int_\Omega v_0 \cdot \nabla u \cdot (v_0 - \xi_0) \\ & + \lambda \int_\Omega u \cdot \nabla u \cdot (v_0 - \xi_0) + \lambda\mu \cdot \int_\Omega \nabla u \cdot (v_0 - \xi_0). \end{aligned} \tag{6.7}$$

Since $v \in \mathcal{H}(\Omega)$, by Lemma 2.4 we find

$$2\int_\Omega |D(u)|^2 = \int_\Omega |\nabla u|^2 \tag{6.8}$$

and, moreover, by $(6.1)_5$,

$$\int_{\partial\Omega} T(u,p)\cdot n = \lambda \int_\Omega (v_* - \xi) v_* \cdot n \equiv \lambda \mathcal{Q}.$$

Thus, (6.7) becomes

$$\begin{aligned} \int_\Omega |\nabla u|^2 = & -\lambda\mu \cdot \mathcal{Q} + \lambda \int_\Omega v_0 \cdot \nabla u \cdot (v_0 - \xi_0) \\ & + \lambda \int_\Omega u \cdot \nabla u \cdot (v_0 - \xi_0) + \lambda\mu \cdot \int_\Omega \nabla u \cdot (v_0 - \xi_0). \end{aligned} \tag{6.9}$$

Now, from Theorem 5.3, the Hölder inequality and the inequality (4.12), it follows that

(6.10)

$$\left|\int_\Omega v_0 \cdot \nabla u \cdot (v_0 - \xi_0)\right| \le \sup_{x\in\Omega} |v_0(x)||u|_{1,2}\|v_0 - \xi_0\|_2$$

$$\begin{aligned}\left|\int_\Omega u \cdot \nabla u \cdot (v_0 - \xi_0)\right| &\le \sup_{x\in\Omega} |(1+|x|)(v_0(x) - \xi_0)||u|_{1,2}\|u/(|x|+1)\|_2 \\ &\le 2 \sup_{x\in\Omega} |(1+|x|)(v_0(x) - \xi_0)||u|_{1,2}^2.\end{aligned}$$

Moreover, using (6.5), we also find that

$$\left|\mu \cdot \int_\Omega \nabla u \cdot (v_0 - \xi_0)\right| \le |\mu|\|v_0 - \xi_0\|_2|u|_{1,2} \le c\|v_0 - \xi_0\|_2|u|_{1,2}^2. \tag{6.11}$$

Since by Theorem 5.3 we have

$$\sup_{x\in\Omega} |(1+|x|)(v_0(x) - \xi_0)| + \sup_{x\in\Omega} |v_0(x)| + \|v_0 - \xi_0\|_2 \le c\|v_*\|_{2-1/q_0,q_0(\partial\Omega)}, \tag{6.12}$$

(6.9)–(6.11) furnish

$$\int_\Omega |\nabla u|^2 \le -\lambda\mu \cdot \mathcal{Q} + \lambda c\|v_*\|_{2-1/q_0,q_0(\partial\Omega)} \left(\|v_*\|_{2-1/q_0,q_0(\partial\Omega)}|u|_{1,2} + |u|_{1,2}^2\right).$$

Therefore, there exists a constant $C = C(\Omega, q) > 0$ such that if

$$\lambda\|v_*\|_{2-1/q_0,q_0(\partial\Omega)} < C$$

we find

$$\int_\Omega |\nabla u|^2 \le c\|v_*\|_{2-1/q_0,q_0(\partial\Omega)}(\lambda|\mu||\xi| + |u|_{1,2}).$$

Using inequality (6.5) in this latter, we deduce

$$|u|_{1,2} \le c\|v_*\|_{2-1/q_0,q_0(\partial\Omega)}(1 + \lambda|\xi|) \tag{6.13}$$

and the lemma follows from (6.13), (6.6), by taking $\lambda\|v_*\|_{2-1/q_0,q_0(\partial\Omega)}$ less than a suitable constant depending on Ω and q_0. □

Lemma 6.2. *Let the assumption of Lemma 6.1 be satisfied. There exist constants $C_i = C_i(\Omega, q_0) > 0$, $i = 1, 2, 3$ such that if*

$$\lambda \|v_*\|_{2-1/q_0,q_0(\partial\Omega)} < C_1 \min\left\{1, \frac{\|\mathbb{P}(v_*)\|_{\mathcal{T}}^2}{\|v_*\|_{2-1/q_0,q_0(\partial\Omega)}^2}\right\} \tag{6.14}$$

then

$$C_2\|\mathbb{P}(v_*)\|_{\mathcal{T}} \le |\xi| \le C_3\|\mathbb{P}(v_*)\|_{\mathcal{T}}. \tag{6.15}$$

Proof - We estimate the right-hand side of (6.4). From (6.12), (6.13), (6.5) and Sobolev and Hölder inequalities we find

$$\begin{aligned}
\left|\int_\Omega v_0 \cdot \nabla H \cdot (v_0 - \xi_0)\right| &\le \sup_{x\in\Omega} |v_0(x)| \|v_0 - \xi_0\|_2 |H|_{1,2} \\
&\le c\|v_*\|_{2-1/q_0,q_0(\partial\Omega)}^2 \\
\left|\int_\Omega (v_0 - \xi_0) \cdot \nabla H \cdot u\right| &\le \|v_0 - \xi_0\|_3 |H|_{1,2} \|u\|_6 \\
&\le c\|v_*\|_{2-1/q_0,q_0(\partial\Omega)}^2 \\
\left|\int_\Omega u \cdot \nabla H \cdot (v_0 - \xi_0)\right| &\le c\|v_*\|_{2-1/q_0,q_0(\partial\Omega)}^2 \\
\left|\int_\Omega \mu \cdot \nabla H \cdot (v_0 - \xi_0)\right| &\le |\mu| \|v_0 - \xi_0\|_2 |H|_{1,2} \le c\|v_*\|_{2-1/q_0,q_0(\partial\Omega)}^2.
\end{aligned} \tag{6.16}$$

From Theorem 4.2, Lemma 6.1, (6.5) and (6.13) we infer that, under the stated assumptions,

$$\begin{aligned}
(\lambda|\xi|)^{1/2}\|u\|_{2q/(2-q)} + \|u(1+|x|)\|_\infty &\le c(\|v_*\|_{2-1/q_0,q_0(\partial\Omega)} + |\mu|) \\
&\le c\|v_*\|_{2-1/q_0,q_0(\partial\Omega)}.
\end{aligned} \tag{6.17}$$

Therefore,

$$\begin{aligned}
\left|\int_\Omega u \cdot \nabla H \cdot u\right| &\le c\|u\|_4^2 \le c\|v_*\|_{2-1/q_0,q_0(\partial\Omega)}^2 \\
\lambda\left|\xi \cdot \int_\Omega \nabla H \cdot u\right| &\le c\lambda^{1/2}|\xi|^{1/2}\|v_*\|_{2-1/q_0,q_0(\partial\Omega)} \\
&\le c\lambda^{1/2}\|v_*\|_{2-1/q_0,q_0(\partial\Omega)}^{3/2}.
\end{aligned} \tag{6.18}$$

From (6.4), (6.16), (6.18) and from the nonsingularity of the matrix Λ (see Lemma 3.5) we thus obtain

$$|\mu| \leq c\|v_*\|_{2-1/q_0,q_0(\partial\Omega)} \left(\lambda^{1/2}\|v_*\|^{1/2}_{2-1/q_0,q_0(\partial\Omega)} + \lambda\|v_*\|_{2-1/q_0,q_0(\partial\Omega)}\right).$$

In view of the assumptions made, from this relation we find

$$\begin{aligned} |\xi| &\geq |\xi_0| - c\lambda^{1/2}\|v_*\|^{3/2}_{2-1/q_0,q_0(\partial\Omega)} \\ |\xi| &\leq |\xi_0| + c\lambda^{1/2}\|v_*\|^{3/2}_{2-1/q_0,q_0(\partial\Omega)} \end{aligned}$$

and the lemma follows from these inequalities and (5.20). □

We are now in a position to prove the uniqueness of solutions to Problem A.

Theorem 6.1. *Let $\mathcal{S}$ be the class of solutions $\{v, p, \xi\}$ with $v, p \in \mathcal{P}$ to (6.1) corresponding to a given $v_* \in W^{2-1/q_0,q_0}(\partial\Omega) \cap \mathcal{P}$, $q_0 > 3$, with $\mathbb{P}(v_*) \neq 0$. Assume also $v \in D^{1,2}(\Omega)$. Then, there exists a positive constant $C = C(\Omega, q_0)$ such that if λ satisfies (6.14), $\mathcal{S}$ is constituted by at most one element.*

Proof - Let v_1, p_1, ξ_1 be another solution to (6.1) corresponding to the same v_*. We write

$$\begin{gathered} u = v - \xi, \quad u_1 = v_1 - \xi_1, \quad \mu = \xi - \xi_1 \\ U = u - u_1, \quad \pi = p - p_1 \end{gathered}$$

and obtain

$$\tag{6.19} \left.\begin{aligned} \Delta U - \lambda\xi\cdot\nabla U &= \lambda\left(\mu\cdot\nabla u_1 + U\cdot\nabla u + u_1\cdot\nabla U\right) + \nabla\pi \\ \operatorname{div} U &= 0 \end{aligned}\right\} \text{ in } \Omega \\ U = -\mu \text{ on } \partial\Omega \\ \lim_{|x|\to\infty} U(x) = 0$$

Moreover, recalling that u_1 satisfies (6.2), we find that

$$\tag{6.20} \mu\cdot\int_{\partial\Omega} g = \lambda\int_\Omega U\cdot\nabla H\cdot u + \lambda\int_\Omega u_1\cdot\nabla H\cdot U + \lambda\xi\cdot\int_\Omega \nabla U\cdot H + \lambda\mu\cdot\int_\Omega \nabla H\cdot u_1.$$

Applying Lemma 3.2 to (6.19) and using the assumptions, we find for $q \in (1,3/2)$

$$\begin{aligned}
&\lambda\|\xi\cdot\nabla U\|_q + (\lambda|\xi|)^{1/2}\|U\|_{2q/(2-q)} \\
(6.21)\qquad &\qquad + (\lambda|\xi|)^{1/4}|U|_{1,4q/(4-q)} + |U|_{1,3q/(3-q)} \\
&\le c\lambda\left(|\mu||u_1|_{1,q} + \|U\|_{2q/(2-q)}|u|_{1,2} + \|u_1\|_4|U|_{1,4q/(4-q)} + \frac{|\mu|}{\lambda}\right).
\end{aligned}$$

From Theorem 4.2 and Lemma 6.1, we have

$$\|u_1\|_4 + |u|_{1,2} \le c\|v_*\|_{2-1/q_0,q_0(\partial\Omega)},$$

and, using Lemma 6.2, we also have for $q \in (4/3, 3/2)$

$$|u_1|_{1,q} \le c(\lambda\|\mathbb{P}(v_*)\|_{\mathcal{T}})^{-1/4}\|v_*\|_{2-1/q_0,q_0(\partial\Omega)}.$$

Thus, from (6.21) and (6.15) we recover the following inequality

$$\begin{aligned}
&\lambda\|\xi\cdot\nabla U\|_q + (\lambda\|\mathbb{P}(v_*)\|_{\mathcal{T}})^{1/2}\|U\|_{2q/(2-q)} \\
(6.22)\qquad &\qquad + (\lambda\|\mathbb{P}(v_*)\|_{\mathcal{T}})^{1/4}|U|_{1,4q/(4-q)} + |U|_{1,3q/(3-q)} \\
&\le c\lambda\Big[|\mu|(\lambda\|\mathbb{P}(v_*)\|_{\mathcal{T}})^{-1/4}\|v_*\|_{2-1/q_0,q_0(\partial\Omega)} \\
&\qquad + \|v_*\|_{2-1/q_0,q_0(\partial\Omega)}\left(\|U\|_{2q/(2-q)} + |U|_{1,4q/(4-q)}\right) + |\mu|/\lambda\Big].
\end{aligned}$$

Moreover, from the Hölder inequality, we also obtain

$$\begin{aligned}
&\left|\int_\Omega U\cdot\nabla H\cdot u\right| + \left|\int_\Omega u_1\cdot\nabla H\cdot U\right| \\
&\qquad \le \|U\|_{2q/(2-q)}|H|_{1,2}\left(\|u_1\|_{q/(q-1)} + \|u\|_{q/(q-1)}\right)
\end{aligned}$$

and, since by Theorem 4.2 and Lemma 6.1, for $q < 3/2$ it is

$$\begin{aligned}
\|u_1\|_{q/(q-1)} + \|u\|_{q/(q-1)} &\le c\left(\|u_1(1+|x|)\|_\infty + \|u(1+|x|)\|_\infty\right) \\
&\le c\|v_*\|_{2-1/q_0,q_0(\partial\Omega)},
\end{aligned}$$

we obtain

$$(6.23)\qquad \left|\int_\Omega U\cdot\nabla H\cdot u\right| + \left|\int_\Omega u_1\cdot\nabla H\cdot U\right| \le c\|U\|_{2q/(2-q)}\|v_*\|_{2-1/q_0,q_0(\partial\Omega)}$$

Also, again from Theorem 4.2 and Lemma 6.2, for $s \in (2,3)$ we find

$$\lambda \left| \mu \cdot \int_\Omega \nabla H \cdot u_1 \right| \leq c\lambda |\mu| \|u\|_s |H|_{1,s/(s-1)} \tag{6.24}$$
$$\leq c|\mu| \lambda^{1/2} \|\mathbb{P}(v_*)\|_{\mathcal{T}}^{-1/2} \|v_*\|_{2-1/q_0,q_0(\partial\Omega)}.$$

Finally, for $q < q_1 < 3/2$ we have

$$\left| \int_\Omega \xi \cdot \nabla U \cdot H \right| \leq \|\xi \cdot \nabla U\|_{q_1} \|H\|_{q_1/(q_1-1)} \leq C \|\xi \cdot \nabla U\|_{q_1},$$

and, by the convexity inequality,

$$\|\xi \cdot \nabla U\|_{q_1} \leq \|\xi \cdot \nabla U\|_q^\theta \|\xi \cdot \nabla U\|_{3q/(3-q)}^{1-\theta}, \quad \theta \in (0,1).$$

Thus, by Lemma 6.1 and Young's inequality we deduce

$$\lambda \left| \int_\Omega \xi \cdot \nabla U \cdot H \right| \leq c(\lambda|\xi|)^{1-\theta} \left(\lambda^\theta \|\xi \cdot \nabla U\|_q^\theta |U|_{1,3q/(3-q)}^{1-\theta} \right) \tag{6.25}$$
$$\leq c(\lambda \|v_*\|_{2-1/q_0,q_0(\partial\Omega)})^{1-\theta} \left(\lambda \|\xi \cdot \nabla U\|_q + |U|_{1,3q/(3-q)} \right).$$

Thus, recalling that, by Lemma 2.1, $\mu = m_1 e_1$, for some $m_1 \in \mathbb{R}$, and that, by Lemma 3.4, $\int_{\partial\Omega} g = m e_1$ for some $m \neq 0$, collecting (6.23)–(6.25) and using (6.20), we find that there exists a constant $C = C(\Omega, q_0) > 0$ such that if (6.14) holds with $C_1 = C$, then

$$|\mu| \leq c[\lambda \|v_*\|_{2-1/q_0,q_0(\partial\Omega)} \|U\|_{2q/(2-q)}$$
$$+ (\lambda \|v_*\|_{2-1/q_0,q_0(\partial\Omega)})^{1-\theta} \left(\lambda \|\xi \cdot \nabla U\|_q + |U|_{1,3q/(3-q)} \right)].$$

Replacing this inequality into (6.22), it is immediate to show that there exists a positive constant C_1 depending only on Ω and q_0 such that if (6.14) is satisfied, we then get

$$(\lambda \|\mathbb{P}(v_*)\|_{\mathcal{T}})^{1/2} \|U\|_{2q/(2-q)} + (\lambda \|\mathbb{P}(v_*)\|_{\mathcal{T}})^{1/4} |U|_{1,4q/(4-q)} \leq 0,$$

from which uniqueness follows at once. The theorem is completely proved. □

Remark 6.1 - The theorem just proved can be extended to show uniqueness in a class of solutions satisfying (1.1)–(1.3) but not necessarily belonging to the class $\mathcal{P}$. This implies, in particular, that in the case of symmetric bodies, the symmetric solution is the only one possible, for small Reynolds number.

7. Steady Self-Propelled Motion of a Body in a Navier-Stokes Fluid: Problem A. Existence of Solutions

In this section we shall prove existence of solutions to Problem A. As we may expect from the linearized theory developed in section 5, not every boundary data $v_* \in \mathcal{P}$ will necessarily produce a self-propelled motion, *i.e.*, $\xi \neq 0$. In fact, if we take Φ such that

$$\Delta\Phi = 0 \;\; \text{in } \Omega$$
$$\lim_{|x|\to\infty} \Phi(x) = 0$$

we at once recognize that the pair $v = \nabla\Phi$, $p = \frac{1}{2}(\nabla\Phi)^2$, satisfies (6.1) with $\xi = 0$ and $v_* = \nabla\Phi\,|_{\partial\Omega}$.[1] We shall show that a nonlinear self-propelled motion does occur whenever v_* has a nonzero component in the thrust space $\mathcal{T}(\mathcal{B})$ and λ is suitably restricted.

We begin to give a weak formulation of Problem A. This will be done in the spirit of [26].

Let φ be an arbitrary element from $\mathcal{C}(\Omega)$ (see Section 2). Multiplying, formally, both sides of $(1.1)_1$ by $\varphi - \bar{\varphi}$ and integrating by parts, we obtain

$$-\bar{\varphi}\cdot\int_{\partial\Omega}[T(v,p)\cdot n - \lambda v\cdot n(v-\xi)] = 2\int_\Omega D(v) : D(\varphi) - \lambda\int_\Omega v\cdot\nabla\varphi\cdot(v-\xi).$$

[1] Clearly, the pair $(\nabla\Phi, \frac{1}{2}(\nabla\Phi)^2)$ verifies $(6.1)_{1,2,4}$. Moreover, since, for any $R > \delta$,

$$\int_{\partial\Omega}(T(v,p)\cdot n - \lambda(v-\xi)v\cdot n) = \int_{\partial B_R}(T(v,p)\cdot n - \lambda(v-\xi)v\cdot n),$$

taking into account that $D^\sigma\Phi(x) = O(|x|^{-1-|\sigma|})$, $|\sigma| = 1,2$, as $|x| \to \infty$, we deduce that also condition $(6.1)_5$ is satisfied.

If we impose the self-propelling condition (1.2), the preceding relation reduces to

$$2\int_\Omega D(v) : D(\varphi) - \lambda \int_\Omega v \cdot \nabla\varphi \cdot (v - \xi) = 0, \quad \text{for all } \varphi \in \mathcal{C}(\Omega). \tag{7.1}$$

We are thus led to the following definition. A vector field v is a *weak solution* to Problem A, if and only if

(i) $v \in D^{1,2}(\Omega)$;
(ii) $v = v_*$ at $\partial\Omega$ (in the trace sense);
(iii) $\operatorname{div} v = 0$ in Ω;
(iv) v satisfies (7.1), where ξ is the uniquely determined vector associated to v by Lemma 2.1.

To show the existence of weak solutions, we need a preliminary result concerning a suitable solenoidal extension of v_*.

Lemma 7.1. *Let $v_* \in W^{1/2,2}(\partial\Omega) \cap \mathcal{P}$, and let*

$$\Phi = \int_{\partial\Omega} v_* \cdot n.$$

Then, for any $\varepsilon > 0$ there exists a solenoidal extension $V = V(\varepsilon)$ of v_* to Ω such that, for some $R > \delta$ and all $q \in (1, \infty)$, $r \in (3/2, \infty)$:
(i) *$V \in W^{1,2}(\Omega_R) \cap D^{1,q}(\Omega^R) \cap \mathcal{P}$;*
(ii) *$V \in L^r(\Omega^R)$. Furthermore, for all $u \in \mathcal{C}(\Omega)$, it holds that*

$$\left| \int_\Omega u \cdot \nabla u \cdot V \right| \le (\varepsilon + C|\Phi|)\, |u|_{1,2}^2, \tag{7.2}$$

where $C = C(\Omega)$.

PROOF - With the origin of coordinates in the interior of $\mathcal{B}$, we set

$$\sigma(x) = \frac{1}{4\pi} \nabla \left(\frac{1}{|x|} \right).$$

Clearly,

$$\int_{\partial\Omega} \sigma \cdot n = 1. \tag{7.3}$$

Let

$$v_1(x) = v_*(x) - \Phi\sigma(x), \quad x \in \partial\Omega.$$

Then, by (7.3),

$$\int_{\partial\Omega} v_1 \cdot n = 0.$$

Thus, along the same lines of proof of Lemma III.6.2 of [6], for any $\varepsilon > 0$ we may find a (Hopf) solenoidal extension $V_1 = V_1(x;\varepsilon) \in \mathcal{P}$ of v_1 to Ω, such that
(a) $V_1 \in W^{1,2}(\Omega_R)$, $V_1(x;\varepsilon) = 0$ for all $|x| \geq R$;
(b) For all $u \in \mathcal{C}(\Omega)$,

$$\left|\int_\Omega u \cdot \nabla u \cdot V_1\right| \leq \varepsilon |u|_{1,2}^2.$$

Set

$$V = V_1 + \Phi\sigma.$$

Obviously, V is a solenoidal extension of v_* satisfying conditions (i) and (ii). Moreover,

$$\left|\int_\Omega u \cdot \nabla u \cdot \sigma\right| \leq \left|\int_\Omega (u - \bar{u}) \cdot \nabla u \cdot \sigma\right| + \left|\bar{u} \cdot \int_\Omega \nabla u \cdot \sigma\right|,$$

where $\bar{u}$ is the constant value of u in a neighborhood of infinity. By Lemmas 2.1 and 2.5, and the summability properties of σ, we find

$$\left|\int_\Omega (u - \bar{u}) \cdot \nabla u \cdot \sigma\right| \leq c\|u - \bar{u}\|_6 |u|_{1,2} \leq c|u|_{1,2}^2$$

$$\left|\bar{u} \cdot \int_\Omega \nabla u \cdot \sigma\right| \leq c|\bar{u}||u|_{1,2} \leq c|u|_{1,2}^2,$$

and the lemma follows from these latter relations and (b). □

The following existence result holds.

Theorem 7.1. *Let $v_* \in W^{1/2,2}(\partial\Omega) \cap \mathcal{P}$. Then, there exists a positive constant $C = C(\Omega)$ such that if $\lambda|\Phi| < C$, Problem A admits at least one weak solution $v \in \mathcal{P}$. Moreover, if $v_* \in W^{2-1/\bar{q},\bar{q}}(\partial\Omega)$ for some $\bar{q} \geq 3/2$, then this solution satisfies the energy inequality:*

$$(7.4) \qquad 2\int_\Omega |D(v)|^2 \leq \int_{\partial\Omega} [(v_* - \xi) \cdot T(v,p) \cdot n - \frac{\lambda}{2}(v_* - \xi)^2 v_* \cdot n]$$

for some $p \in W^{1,\bar{q}}(\Omega_R)$*, all* $R > \delta$*.*

PROOF - The proof follows standard arguments [6], Theorem IX.4.1. Let $\{\varphi_k\}$ be the orthonormal set introduced in Lemma 3.4. We look for an "approximating" solution $v_m = u_m + V$, $m \in \mathbb{N}$, where V is the solenoidal extension of Lemma 7.1 and u_m is defined by

$$u_m = \sum_{i=1}^{m} c_{im}\varphi_i,$$

with c_{im} satisfying

$$\begin{aligned} 2\int_\Omega & D(u_m) : D(\varphi_k) \\ &= \lambda \int_\Omega [u_m \cdot \nabla\varphi_k \cdot (u_m - \xi_m) + V \cdot \nabla\varphi_k \cdot (u_m - \xi_m) \\ &+ u_m \cdot \nabla\varphi_k \cdot V + V \cdot \nabla\varphi_k \cdot V] - 2\int_\Omega D(V) : D(\varphi_k), \end{aligned} \tag{7.5}$$

and where ξ_m is the constant value of u_m in a neighborhood of infinity. To show the existence of a solution c_{im} for all $m \in \mathbb{N}$, it is enough to prove a uniform bound on the Dirichlet norm of u_m, see, *e.g.*, [6], Lemma VIII.3.2. To this end, multiplying both sides of (7.5) by c_{km} and summing over k, we obtain

$$2\|D(u_m)\|_2^2 = \lambda \int_\Omega [u_m \cdot \nabla u_m \cdot V + V \cdot \nabla u_m \cdot V] - 2\int_\Omega D(u_m) : D(V). \tag{7.6}$$

Employing the Schwarz inequality in this relation along with Lemmas 2.4 and 7.1, we derive

$$|u_m|_{1,2} \le \lambda(\varepsilon + c|\Phi|)|u_m|_{1,2} + \mathsf{B}(V, \lambda) \tag{7.7}$$

where $\mathsf{B}(V, \lambda)$ depends only on V and λ. Thus, choosing ε sufficiently small and requiring $c\lambda|\Phi| < 1$, we obtain the desired bound on u_m. Estimate (7.7) and Poincaré's inequality imply also the existence of $u \in \mathcal{H}(\Omega)$ such that (along a subsequence again denoted by $\{u_m\}$)

$$\begin{aligned} \nabla u_m &\longrightarrow \nabla u, \quad \text{weakly in } L^2(\Omega) \\ u_m &\longrightarrow u, \quad \text{strongly in } L^q(\Omega_R), \text{ for all } q \in [2, 6) \text{ and } R > \delta. \end{aligned} \tag{7.8}$$

Also, by Lemmas 2.5 and 2.1, there is $\xi \in \mathbb{R}^3$ such that

$$\begin{aligned} &\xi_m \longrightarrow \xi \\ &\|u-\xi\|_6 \le c|u|_{1,2}. \end{aligned} \tag{7.9}$$

In view of all above properties, we may pass to the limit $m \to \infty$ in (7.5) for fixed k, and use standard arguments to show

$$\begin{aligned} 2\int_\Omega & D(u) : D(\varphi_k) \\ &= \lambda \int_\Omega [u\cdot\nabla\varphi_k\cdot(u-\xi) + V\cdot\nabla\varphi_k\cdot(u-\xi) \\ &+ u\cdot\nabla\varphi_k\cdot V + V\cdot\nabla\varphi_k V] - 2\int_\Omega D(V) : D(\varphi_k). \end{aligned} \tag{7.10}$$

However, from Lemma 2.3 we know that every $\varphi \in \mathcal{C}(\Omega)$ can be approximated in $C^1(\bar{\Omega})$ by linear combinations of the functions φ_k. Therefore, using this fact and the properties of u, we may replace φ_k by φ in (7.10), thus showing that the field $v \equiv u + V$ is a weak solution to Problem A. Also, from known regularity results, we have $v \in W^{2,q}(\Omega_R)\cap C^\infty(\Omega)$, all $R > \delta$, and, in addition, we may find a suitable pressure field $p \in L^3(\Omega)\cap W^{1,q}(\Omega_R)\cap C^\infty(\Omega)$, all $R > \delta$, such that $(6.1)_{1,2}$ holds; see [6] Remark IX.1.3 and Theorem IX.1.1. To prove the theorem completely, we have to show the validity of the energy inequality. Now, if $\xi \neq 0$, it is known that v, p obeys the energy *equality*, that is, (7.4) with the equality sign, [6], Theorem IX.5.1. If $\xi = 0$, we argue as follows. From $(7.8)_1$ and Lemma 7.1 we find

$$\begin{aligned} &|u|_{1,2}^2 \le \liminf m \to \infty\, |u_m|_{1,2}^2 \\ &\lim_{m\to\infty}\left(\int_\Omega V\cdot\nabla u_m\cdot V - 2\int_\Omega D(u_m) : D(V)\right) \\ &\quad = \int_\Omega V\cdot\nabla u\cdot V - 2\int_\Omega D(u) : D(V). \end{aligned} \tag{7.11}$$

Moreover, using again (7.8), (7.9) and reasoning as in [6], eq. (IX.4.34), we show

$$\lim_{m\to\infty}\left|\int_\Omega u_m\cdot\nabla u_m\cdot V - \int_\Omega u\cdot\nabla u\cdot V\right| = 0. \tag{7.12}$$

By (7.6), (7.11) and (7.12) we obtain

$$2\int_\Omega |D(u)|^2 \le \lambda \int_\Omega [u\cdot\nabla u\cdot V + V\cdot\nabla u\cdot V] - 2\int_\Omega D(u):D(V). \tag{7.13}$$

Writing $u = v - V$ in (7.13) and making the obvious simplifications we find

$$2\int_\Omega |D(v)|^2 - 2\int_\Omega D(v):D(V) \le \lambda \int_\Omega v\cdot\nabla(v-V)\cdot V. \tag{7.14}$$

Next, multiplying $(6.1)_1$ by V and using the asymptotic properties of v, p and V we can prove that

$$2\int_\Omega D(v):D(V) = \int_{\partial\Omega} v_*\cdot T(v,p)\cdot n - \lambda\int_\Omega v\cdot\nabla v\cdot V.$$

Replacing this latter relation in (7.14) we thus deduce

$$2\int_\Omega |D(v)|^2 \le \int_{\partial\Omega} v_*\cdot T(v,p)\cdot n - \lambda\int_\Omega v\cdot\nabla V\cdot V.$$

Integrating by parts the last term on the right-hand side of this inequality shows (7.4) and the proof of the theorem is complete. □

The result just proved does not ensure $\xi \ne 0$, that is, it does not ensure that the body $\mathcal{B}$ moves. As we already noticed, this is, in fact, not surprising, in that we made no assumption, other than certain regularity, on the boundary data v_*. Actually, even in the Stokes approximation, we know that $\mathcal{B}$ can move if v_* has a nonzero component on the thrust space $\mathcal{T}(\mathcal{B})$. In the next theorem we show that this result continues to hold also for the fully nonlinear Navier-Stokes equations, provided λ is suitably restricted.

Theorem 7.2. *Let the assumptions of Theorem 7.1 be satisfied. Suppose, in addition, that $\mathbb{P}(v_*) \ne 0$, where $\mathbb{P}$ is the projection operator of $L^2(\partial\Omega)$ onto $\mathcal{T}(\mathcal{B})$; see section 5. Then, there exists $C = C(\Omega, \bar{q}) > 0$ such that if*

$$\lambda\|v_*\|_{2-1/\bar{q},\bar{q}(\partial\Omega)} < C\min\left\{1, \frac{\|\mathbb{P}(v_*)\|_{\mathcal{T}}}{\|v_*\|_{2-1/\bar{q},\bar{q}(\partial\Omega)}}\right\}, \tag{7.15}$$

the value at infinity ξ of the weak solution v determined in Theorem 7.1 is nonzero.

PROOF - Assume, by contradiction, $\xi = 0$. From Theorem 4.1, we know that, under the stated assumptions, v, p satisfy (4.1). Thus, by using the same procedure leading to (6.2), we find

$$\int_{\partial\Omega} v_* \cdot g = -\lambda \int_\Omega v \cdot \nabla H \cdot v. \tag{7.16}$$

Recalling that $\nabla H \in L^{s'}(\Omega)$ for all $s' > 3/2$, from (7.16) we obtain

$$\|\mathbb{P}(v_*)\|_{\mathcal{T}} \leq \lambda c \|v\|_{2s}^2.$$

Using this inequality and (4.2) we infer

$$\|\mathbb{P}(v_*)\|_{\mathcal{T}} \leq \lambda c \|v_*\|_{2-1/\bar{q},\bar{q}(\partial\Omega)}^2,$$

from which the theorem follows. □

Taking into account that

$$\|\mathbb{P}(v_*)\|_{\mathcal{T}} \leq c \|v_*\|_{2-1/q_0,q_0(\partial\Omega)}$$
$$\|v_*\|_{2-1/\bar{q},\bar{q}(\partial\Omega)} \leq c \|v_*\|_{2-1/q_0,q_0(\partial\Omega)}, \quad \bar{q} \leq q_0,$$

from Lemma 6.2, Theorems 4.2, 7.1 and 7.2, and well-known regularity results we have the following

Theorem 7.3. *Let $v_* \in W^{2-1/q_0,q_0}(\Omega) \cap \mathcal{P}$, $q_0 > 3$, with $\mathbb{P}(v_*) \neq 0$. Then, there exists $C = C(\Omega, q_0)$ such that if*

$$\lambda \|v_*\|_{2-1/q_0,q_0(\partial\Omega)} < C \min\left\{1, \frac{\|\mathbb{P}(v_*)\|_{\mathcal{T}}^2}{\|v_*\|_{2-1/q_0,q_0(\partial\Omega)}^2}\right\},$$

Problem A admits at least one solution v, p, ξ such that $v, p \in C^\infty(\Omega) \cap \mathcal{P}$, and for $q \in (1, 3/2)$ and $s \in (3/2, 3q/(3-q))$,

$$(v - \xi) \in L^{2q/(2-q)}(\Omega) \cap D^{1,4q/(4-q)}(\Omega) \cap D^{1,s}(\Omega) \cap D^{2,q}(\Omega).$$
$$p \in L^{3q/(3-q)}(\Omega) \cap D^{1,q}(\Omega).$$

Moreover, $\|(v-\xi)(1+|x|)\|_\infty < \infty$ *and the following estimates hold*

$$
\begin{aligned}
&\|(v-\xi)(1+|x|)\|_\infty + |v|_{1,s} + \lambda\|\xi\cdot\nabla v\|_q + (\lambda|\xi|)^{1/2}\|v-\xi\|_{2q/(2-q)} \\
&\qquad + (\lambda|\xi|)^{1/4}|v|_{1,4q/(4-q)} + |v|_{2,q} + \|p\|_{3q/(3-q)} + |p|_{1,q} \\
&\quad \le c_1\|v_*\|_{2-1/q_0,q_0(\partial\Omega)} \\
&c_2\|\mathbb{P}(v_*)\|_{\mathcal{T}} \le |\xi| \le c_3\|\mathbb{P}(v_*)\|_{\mathcal{T}}.
\end{aligned}
\tag{7.17}
$$

with $c_i = c_i(\Omega, q, s, q_0)$, $i = 1, 2$.

8. Steady Self-Propelled Motion of a Body in a Navier-Stokes Fluid: Problem B. Existence and Uniqueness of Solutions

In this section we shall investigate the unique solvability of the following

Problem B: Given $\xi = me_1$, $m \neq 0$, find $v, p \in \mathcal{P}$ such that

$$
\begin{aligned}
&\left.\begin{aligned}\Delta v &= \lambda v\cdot\nabla v + \nabla p\\ \operatorname{div} v &= 0\end{aligned}\right\}\ \text{in } \Omega\\
&\lim_{|x|\to\infty} v(x) = \xi\\
&\int_{\partial\Omega}[T(v,p)\cdot n - \lambda v_*\cdot n(v_*-\xi)] = 0.
\end{aligned}
\tag{8.1}
$$

As in the linear approximation, we may consider also the case when the normal or the tangential component of v at $\partial\Omega$ is prescribed, that is,

$$v\cdot n = \psi_1, \quad \text{at } \partial\Omega, \tag{8.2}$$

or

$$(v\times n)\times n = \psi_2, \quad \text{at } \partial\Omega, \tag{8.3}$$

with ψ_1, ψ_2 given functions satisfying the same parity conditions as in Theorem 5.4. In this situation, we have to solve for (8.1)-(8.2) or for (8.1)-(8.3), respectively. We shall call Problem B_n the first problem and Problem B_τ the second one. Of course, several other interesting variants of Problem B can be considered, and this will be the object of a future research.

Here, we shall treat unique solvability of Problem B in full details, limiting ourselves to state the analogous results for Problems B_n and B_τ, since they can be obtained by an entirely similar procedure.

Before proving our results, we wish to notice that Problem B (or any of its variants B_n, B_τ) admits an infinite number of solutions corresponding to the same ξ. Actually, it is easy to show that $v = \nabla\Phi, p = \frac{1}{2}(\nabla\Phi)^2$, with Φ *any* harmonic function in the class $\mathcal{P}$ approaching $\xi \cdot x$ at large distance is a solution to Problem B. Therefore, in order to preserve uniqueness, we should impose some other restrictions on the class of solutions. We shall show that for any $\xi \neq 0$, and λ suitably restricted, there exists one and only one solution v, p to Problem B with boundary trace $\gamma(v)$ belonging to $\mathcal{T}(\mathcal{B})$ and such that

$$\|\gamma(v)\|_{\mathcal{T}} \leq c|\xi|, \tag{8.4}$$

with $c = c(\Omega)$. Condition (8.4) is very significant from the physical point of view, in that it expresses the continuous dependence of the thrust vector (see section 5) on the prescribed translational velocity of $\mathcal{B}$.

To solve Problem B, we shall put it into an equivalent form. For the prescribed $\xi \neq 0$, we denote by v_0, p_0 the corresponding solution to the linearized Stokes approximation given in Theorem 5.4. Setting

$$v = u + v_0, \quad p = \pi + p_0, \tag{8.5}$$

and proceeding as at the beginning of section 6 (see (6.19), (6.20)) we find that $(8.1)_{1,2,3}$ is equivalent to

$$\left.\begin{aligned} \Delta u + \lambda\xi \cdot \nabla u &= \lambda \operatorname{div} F + \nabla\pi \\ \operatorname{div} u &= 0 \end{aligned}\right\} \text{ in } \Omega \tag{8.6}$$
$$\lim_{|x|\to\infty} u(x) = 0$$

while the self-propelling condition $(8.1)_4$ becomes

$$\int_{\partial\Omega} u \cdot g = \lambda \int_\Omega F : \nabla H + \lambda\xi \cdot \int_\Omega \nabla H \cdot u. \tag{8.7}$$

In (8.6), (8.7) we set

$$F := v_0 \otimes (v_0 - \xi) + (v_0 - \xi) \otimes u + u \otimes (v_0 - \xi) + u \otimes u, \tag{8.8}$$

while the vector g is defined in (3.19).

Existence to (8.6)–(8.8) will be proved by the use of the following successive approximation scheme. We set $u^{(0)} = \pi^{(0)} = \mu^{(0)} = 0$ and, for $n \geq 1$,

$$\left.\begin{aligned} \Delta u^{(n)} + \lambda \xi \cdot \nabla u^{(n)} &= \lambda \operatorname{div} F^{(n-1)} + \nabla \pi^{(n)} \\ \operatorname{div} u^{(n)} &= 0 \end{aligned}\right\} \text{ in } \Omega$$
$$u^{(n)} = \mu^{(n)} g \quad \text{on } \partial\Omega \tag{8.9}$$
$$\lim_{|x|\to\infty} u^{(n)}(x) = 0$$

and

$$\mu^{(n)} \int_{\partial\Omega} g^2 = \lambda \int_\Omega F^{(n-1)} : \nabla H + \lambda \xi \cdot \int_\Omega \nabla H \cdot u^{(n-1)}, \tag{8.10}$$

where $\mu^{(n)}$, all $n \in \mathbb{N}$, is a number to be determined and

$$F^{(n)} := v_0 \otimes (v_0 - \xi) + (v_0 - \xi) \otimes u^{(n)} + u^{(n)} \otimes (v_0 - \xi) + u^{(n)} \otimes u^{(n)}. \tag{8.11}$$

Notice that, for all $n \in \mathbb{N}$, the trace of $u^{(n)}$ belongs to the thrust space $\mathcal{T}(\mathcal{B})$. For $q \in (1, 3/2)$ we put

$$\langle\!\langle u \rangle\!\rangle_{\lambda,q} := (\lambda|\xi|)^{1/2} \|u\|_{2q/(2-q)} + (\lambda|\xi|)^{1/4} \|u\|_4 + \|u\|_{3q/(3-2q)} + |u|_{2,q} + |u|_{1,2}.$$

From Lemma 3.2 applied to (8.9), we obtain

$$\langle\!\langle u^{(n)} \rangle\!\rangle_{\lambda,q} + |\pi^{(n)}|_{1,q} \leq c\lambda \left(\| \operatorname{div} F^{(n-1)} \|_q + \|F^{(n-1)}\|_4 + |\mu^{(n)}|/\lambda \right). \tag{8.12}$$

Using the Hölder and Sobolev inequalities along with (5.21), we readily deduce

$$\begin{aligned} \| \operatorname{div} F^{(n-1)} \|_q &\leq c(\|u^{(n-1)}\|_{2q/(2-q)} |u^{(n-1)}|_{1,2} \\ &\qquad + |\xi| |u^{(n-1)}|_{1,2} + |\xi| \|u\|_{3q/(3-2q)} + |\xi|^2) \\ &\leq c \left[(\lambda|\xi|)^{-1/2} \langle\!\langle u^{(n-1)} \rangle\!\rangle^2_{\lambda,q} + |\xi| \langle\!\langle u^{(n-1)} \rangle\!\rangle_{\lambda,q} + |\xi|^2 \right] \\ \|F^{(n-1)}\|_4 &\leq c \left(\|u^{(n-1)}\|_4^2 + |\xi| |u^{(n-1)}|_{1,2} + |\xi|^2 \right) \\ &\leq c \left[(\lambda|\xi|)^{-1/2} \langle\!\langle u^{(n-1)} \rangle\!\rangle^2_{\lambda,q} + |\xi| \langle\!\langle u^{(n-1)} \rangle\!\rangle_{\lambda,q} + |\xi|^2 \right]. \end{aligned} \tag{8.13}$$

Replacing (8.13) into (8.12), we obtain

$$\begin{aligned}&\langle\!\langle u^{(n)}\rangle\!\rangle_{\lambda,q}+|\pi^{(n)}|_{1,q}\\ &\le C_1\left(\lambda^{1/2}|\xi|^{-1/2}\langle\!\langle u^{(n-1)}\rangle\!\rangle^2_{\lambda,q}+\lambda|\xi|\langle\!\langle u^{(n-1)}\rangle\!\rangle_{\lambda,q}+\lambda|\xi|^2+|\mu^{(n)}|\right),\end{aligned}\tag{8.14}$$

where $C_1=C_1(\Omega,q)$. Furthermore, recalling that $\nabla H\in L^{s'}(\Omega)$, all $s'>3/2$, by the Hölder inequality and (5.21) we deduce

$$\begin{aligned}&\left|\int_\Omega F^{(n-1)}:\nabla H\right|+\left|\xi\cdot\int_\Omega\nabla H\cdot u^{(n-1)}\right|\\ &\le c\left((\lambda|\xi|)^{-1/2}\langle\!\langle u^{(n-1)}\rangle\!\rangle^2_{\lambda,q}+|\xi|\langle\!\langle u^{(n-1)}\rangle\!\rangle_{\lambda,q}+|\xi|^2+|\xi||H|_{1,s'}\|u^{(n-1)}\|_s\right),\end{aligned}$$

Assume $1<q<6/5$, and choose $s'=2q/(3q-2)$. We then find

$$\begin{aligned}&\left|\int_\Omega F^{(n-1)}:\nabla H\right|+\left|\xi\cdot\int_\Omega\nabla H\cdot u^{(n-1)}\right|\\ &\le c\left((\lambda|\xi|)^{-1/2}\langle\!\langle u^{(n-1)}\rangle\!\rangle^2_{\lambda,q}+|\xi|\langle\!\langle u^{(n-1)}\rangle\!\rangle_{\lambda,q}+\lambda^{-1/2}|\xi|^{1/2}\langle\!\langle u^{(n-1)}\rangle\!\rangle_{\lambda,q}+|\xi|^2\right).\end{aligned}$$

Using this latter inequality into (8.10), and recalling that the quantity A is nonzero (see Lemma 3.4), we infer for $\lambda|\xi|\le c$

$$|\mu^{(n)}|\le C_2\left(\lambda^{1/2}|\xi|^{-1/2}\langle\!\langle u^{(n-1)}\rangle\!\rangle^2_{\lambda,q}+\lambda^{1/2}|\xi|^{1/2}\langle\!\langle u^{(n-1)}\rangle\!\rangle_{\lambda,q}+\lambda|\xi|^2\right),\tag{8.15}$$

where $C_2=C_2(\Omega,q)$. Our next goal is to show a uniform bound for $u^{(n)}$ and $\mu^{(n)}$. From (8.15) and (8.14) with $n=1$ we deduce

$$\begin{gathered}|\mu^{(1)}|\le C_2\lambda|\xi|^2\\ \langle\!\langle u^{(1)}\rangle\!\rangle_{\lambda,q}+|\pi^{(1)}|_{1,q}\le C_1(1+C_2)\lambda|\xi|^2\equiv C_3\lambda|\xi|^2.\end{gathered}$$

We want to show that

$$\left.\begin{gathered}|\mu^{(n)}|\le 2C_2\lambda|\xi|^2\\ \langle\!\langle u^{(n)}\rangle\!\rangle_{\lambda,q}+|\pi^{(n)}|_{1,q}\le 2C_3\lambda|\xi|^2\end{gathered}\right\}\quad\text{for all } n\in\mathbb{N},\tag{8.16}$$

for $\lambda|\xi|$ sufficiently small. We argue by induction. Assuming that (8.16) holds for $n-1$, from (8.15) we immediately deduce

$$|\mu^{(n)}|\le C_2\lambda|\xi|^2\left(4C_3^2\lambda^{3/2}|\xi|^{3/2}+2C_3\lambda^{1/2}|\xi|^{1/2}+1\right),$$

which shows $(8.16)_1$, for $\lambda|\xi|$ less than a suitable constant depending only on Ω and q. Employing $(8.16)_1$ into (8.14) we then find

$$\langle\!\langle u^{(n)}\rangle\!\rangle_{\lambda,q} \leq C_1\lambda|\xi|^2\left(4C_3^2\lambda^{3/2}|\xi|^{3/2}+4C_3\lambda|\xi|+(1+2C_2)\right),$$

which proves $(8.16)_2$, for $\lambda|\xi|$ suitably small. Once (8.16) has been established, it is easy to show the convergence of $u^{(n)}, \pi^{(n)}$ and μ^n in suitable norms. Actually, setting $w^{(n)} = u^{(n)} - u^{(n-1)}$, from (8.8) and $(8.16)_2$ we obtain

$$\begin{aligned}
\|\operatorname{div}(F^{(n-1)}-F^{(n-2)})\|_q \leq c\big(&\|u^{(n-2)}\|_{2q/(2-q)}|w^{(n-1)}|_{1,2}\\
&+\|w^{(n-1)}\|_{2q/(2-q)}|u^{(n-1)}|_{1,2}\\
&+\|v_0-\xi\|_{2q/(2-q)}|w^{(n-1)}|_{1,2}\\
&+\|w^{(n-1)}\|_{2q/(2-q)}|v_0|_{1,2}\big)\\
\leq c&\left(\lambda^{1/2}|\xi|^{3/2}+|\xi|+\lambda^{-1/2}|\xi|^{1/2}\right)\langle\!\langle w^{(n-1)}\rangle\!\rangle_{\lambda,q}\\
\|F^{(n-1)}-F^{(n-2)}\|_2 \leq c\big(&(\|u^{(n-1)}\|_4+\|u^{(n-2)}\|_4)\|w^{(n-1)}\|_4\\
&+\|v_0-\xi\|_3\|w^{(n-1)}\|_6\big)\\
\leq c&\left(\lambda^{1/2}|\xi|^{3/2}+|\xi|\right)\langle\!\langle w^{(n-1)}\rangle\!\rangle_{\lambda,q}.
\end{aligned}$$

Thus, from Lemma 3.2 and $\lambda|\xi|$ less than a suitable constant depending only on Ω and q, we conclude

$$\langle\!\langle w^{(n)}\rangle\!\rangle_{\lambda,q} \leq c\left(\lambda^{1/2}|\xi|^{1/2}\langle\!\langle w^{(n-1)}\rangle\!\rangle_{\lambda,q}+|M^{(n)}|\right), \tag{8.17}$$

with $M^{(n)} = \mu^{(n)} - \mu^{(n-1)}$. Moreover, from (8.10), by an argument similar to that leading to (8.15), we obtain for $\lambda|\xi|$ small enough,

$$|M^{(n)}| \leq c\lambda^{1/2}|\xi|^{1/2}\langle\!\langle w^{(n-1)}\rangle\!\rangle_{\lambda,q}, \tag{8.18}$$

which, once replaced into (8.17), furnishes

$$\langle\!\langle w^{(n)}\rangle\!\rangle_{\lambda,q} \leq c\lambda^{1/2}|\xi|^{1/2}\langle\!\langle w^{(n-1)}\rangle\!\rangle_{\lambda,q}.$$

This inequality implies that, for $\lambda|\xi|$ smaller than a suitable constant depending on Ω and q only, $u^{(n)}$ is Cauchy in the norm $\langle\!\langle\cdot\rangle\!\rangle_{\lambda,q}$ and that, by (8.18), $M^{(n)}$ is Cauchy too. It is at once verified that, denoting by u and μ the limit of

$\{u^{(n)}\}$ and $\{\mu^{(n)}\}$, respectively, u verifies (8.6), (8.7), for a suitable π, and that $u = \mu_i g$ at $\partial\Omega$. By (8.16), we also have

$$(\lambda|\xi|)^{1/2}\|u\|_{2q/(2-q)} + (\lambda|\xi|)^{1/4}\|u\|_4 + \|u\|_{3q/(3-2q)} \\ + |u|_{2,q} + |u|_{1,2} + |\pi|_{1,q} \le c\lambda|\xi|^2 \tag{8.19}$$

and

$$\|\gamma(u)\|_{\mathcal{T}} \le c\lambda|\xi|^2. \tag{8.20}$$

Recalling (8.5), from what we have shown so far, Theorems 4.2 and 5.4, (8.19), (8.20), and well-known regularity results we have the following

Theorem 8.1. *Let $\xi = me_1$, $m \neq 0$, be given and let $1 < q < 6/5$. Then, there exists $C = C(\Omega, q) > 0$, such that if $\lambda|\xi| \le C$, Problem B admits at least one solution $v, p \in \mathcal{P}$ with $\gamma(v) \in \mathcal{T}(\Omega)$ and such that $v, p \in C^\infty(\Omega)$,*

$$(v-\xi) \in L^{2q/(2-q)}(\Omega) \cap D^{1,4q/(4-q)}(\Omega) \cap D^{1,2}(\Omega) \cap D^{2,q}(\Omega), \\ p \in L^{3q/(3-q)}(\Omega) \cap D^{1,q}(\Omega).$$

Moreover, $\|(v-\xi)(1+|x|)\|_\infty < \infty$ and the following estimates hold

$$\|(v-\xi)(1+|x|)\|_\infty + |v|_{1,2} + \lambda\|\xi\cdot\nabla v\|_q + (\lambda|\xi|)^{1/2}\|v-\xi\|_{2q/(2-q)} \\ + (\lambda|\xi|)^{1/4}|v|_{1,4q/(4-q)} + |v|_{2,q} + \|p\|_{3q/(3-q)} + |p|_{1,q} \le c_1|\xi|, \\ |\xi| \le c_2\|\gamma(v)\|_{\mathcal{T}} \le c_3|\xi| \tag{8.21}$$

with $c_i = c_i(\Omega, q)$, $i = 1, 2, 3$.

PROOF - To prove the result completely, we have to show the following inequality

$$|\xi| \le c\|\gamma(v)\|_{\mathcal{T}}. \tag{8.22}$$

Since the matrix A is nonsingular (see Lemma 3.4), from (5.6) (with $v_* = \gamma(v)$), we find

$$|\xi| \le c\left(\|\gamma(v)\|_{\mathcal{T}} + |v|_{1,2}\right),$$

and (8.22) follows from $(8.21)_1$. □

Our next objective is to investigate uniqueness for Problem B. In this respect, we have the following result.

Theorem 8.2. *Let $\mathcal{S}_\xi$ be the class of solutions $v, p \in \mathcal{P}$ to (8.1) corresponding to a given $\xi = me_1$, $m \neq 0$, such that*
(i) $v \in D^{1,2}(\Omega)$;
(ii) $\gamma(v) \in \mathcal{T}(\mathcal{B})$;
(iii) $\|\gamma(v)\|_{\mathcal{T}} \leq C_0|\xi|$ *for some* $C_0 > 0$.
Then, there exists $C = C(\Omega, C_0) > 0$ such that if $\lambda|\xi| < C$, $\mathcal{S}_\xi$ is constituted by at most one element.

PROOF - Let v, p and u, p_1 be two elements of $\mathcal{S}_\xi$ and let

$$U = v - u, \quad \pi = p - p_1.$$

From (8.1) and (6.2) we obtain

$$\left.\begin{aligned} \Delta U - \lambda\xi \cdot \nabla U &= \lambda\left[U \cdot \nabla v + (u - \xi) \cdot \nabla U\right] + \nabla \pi \\ \operatorname{div} U &= 0 \end{aligned}\right\} \text{ in } \Omega \qquad (8.23)$$
$$\lim_{|x| \to \infty} U(x) = 0$$

and

$$\int_{\partial\Omega} U_* \cdot g = \lambda \int_\Omega \left[(v - \xi) \cdot \nabla H \cdot U + U \cdot \nabla H \cdot (u - \xi)\right] + \lambda\xi \cdot \int_\Omega \nabla H \cdot U, \qquad (8.24)$$

where U_* is the trace of U at $\partial\Omega$. Set

$$\langle U \rangle_{\lambda,q} \equiv (\lambda|\xi|)^{1/2}\|U\|_{2q/(2-q)} + \|U\|_{3q/(3-2q)} + |U|_{1,2}.$$

Applying Lemma 3.2 to (8.23), and using the Hölder inequality, Theorem 4.2, Remark 5.1, and the assumptions (i)-(iii), we find

$$\begin{aligned} \langle U \rangle_{\lambda,q} &\leq c(\lambda\|U \cdot \nabla v + (u - \xi) \cdot \nabla U\|_q + \|U_*\|_{\mathcal{T}}) \\ &\leq c\left(\lambda\|U\|_{2q/(2-q)}|u|_{1,2} + \lambda\|v - \xi\|_{2q/(2-q)}|U|_{1,2} + \|U_*\|_{\mathcal{T}}\right) \\ &\leq c\left(\lambda^{1/2}|\xi|^{1/2}\langle U \rangle_{\lambda,q} + \|U_*\|_{\mathcal{T}}\right). \end{aligned} \qquad (8.25)$$

Furthermore, from (8.24) we obtain

$$\left|\int_{\partial\Omega} U_* \cdot g\right| \leq \lambda |H|_{1,6q/(13q-12)} \|U\|_{3q/(3-2q)} (\|u-\xi\|_{2q/(2-q)} + \|v-\xi\|_{2q/(2-q)}) + \lambda|\xi||H|_{1,2q/(3q-2)}\|U\|_{2q/(2-q)}. \tag{8.26}$$

Recalling that $H \in D^{1,r}(\Omega)$ for all $r > 3/2$, we choose $q \in (12/9)$ and obtain from (8.26) the following inequality

$$\|U_*\|_{\mathcal{T}} \leq c\lambda^{1/2}|\xi|^{1/2}\langle U\rangle_{\lambda,q}. \tag{8.27}$$

Replacing (8.27) into (8.25), and taking $\lambda|\xi|$ less than a suitable constant depending only on Ω and C_0, we prove uniqueness. □

Remark 8.1 - Theorem 8.1 ensures that for any $\xi \neq 0$, in the direction e_1, the class $\mathcal{S}_\xi$ defined in Theorem 8.2 is not empty.

Theorems 8.1 and 8.2 admits of a straightforward extension to the case when either the normal or the tangential component of v is prescribed at the boundary, according to (8.2), (8.3). In fact, concerning existence, one looks again for solutions of the form (8.6) where, this time, v_0, p_0 is the solution to the linearized Stokes problem given in Theorem 5.4 (i) (in case (8.2)) or (ii) (in case (8.3)). The construction of the fields u, π uses an approximating scheme of the type (8.9), (8.10) where, this time,

$$\begin{aligned} u^{(n)}|_{\partial\Omega} &= \mu^{(n)}(g \times n) \times n \quad \text{in case (8.2)} \\ u^{(n)}|_{\partial\Omega} &= \mu^{(n)}(g \cdot n)n \quad \text{in case (8.3)}, \end{aligned}$$

and the $\mu^{(n)}$'s are determined from an equation analogous to (8.10) with its left-hand side replaced by

$$\mu^{(n)} \int_{\partial\Omega} [(g \times n) \times n]^2 \quad \text{in case (8.2)}$$

$$\mu^{(n)} \int_{\partial\Omega} (g \cdot n)^2 \quad \text{in case (8.3)}.$$

Concerning uniqueness, the proof is completely analogous to that given in Theorem 8.2, provided in the assumptions (ii) and (iii) we replace $\mathcal{T}(\mathcal{B})$ with $\mathcal{T}_\tau(\mathcal{B})$ (in case (8.2)) and with $\mathcal{T}_n(\mathcal{B})$ (in case (8.3)).

We thus have the following results concerning Problems B_n and B_τ, respectively

Theorem 8.3. *Let $\xi = me_1$, $m \neq 0$ and $\psi_1 \in W^{2-1/q_0,q_0}(\partial\Omega)$, $q_0 > 3$, be given with $\psi_1 n \in \mathcal{P}$. There exists $C_1 = C_1(\Omega, q_0) > 0$ such that if $\lambda(|\xi| + \|\psi_1\|_{2-1/q_0,q_0(\partial\Omega)}) < C_1$, problem (8.1)-(8.2) admits at least one solution $v, p \in \mathcal{P}$, with $(\gamma(v) \times n) \times n \in \mathcal{T}_\tau(\Omega)$ and such that $v, p \in C^\infty(\Omega)$,*

$$(v - \xi) \in L^{2q/(2-q)}(\Omega) \cap D^{1,4q/(4-q)}(\Omega) \cap D^{1,2}(\Omega) \cap D^{2,q}(\Omega)$$
$$p \in L^{3q/(3-q)}(\Omega) \cap D^{1,q}(\Omega).$$

Moreover, $\|(v - \xi)(1 + |x|)\|_\infty < \infty$ and the following estimates hold

$$\begin{aligned}&\|(v - \xi)(1 + |x|)\|_\infty + |v|_{1,2} + \lambda\|\xi \cdot \nabla v\|_q + (\lambda|\xi|)^{1/2}\|v - \xi\|_{2q/(2-q)} \\ &\quad + (\lambda|\xi|)^{1/4}|v|_{1,4q/(4-q)} + |v|_{2,q} + \|p\|_{3q/(3-q)} + |p|_{1,q} \\ &\qquad \leq c_1(|\xi| + \|\psi_1\|_{2-1/q_0,q_0(\partial\Omega)}) \\ &|\xi| + \|\psi_1\|_{2-1/q_0,q_0(\partial\Omega)} \leq c_2\|(\gamma(v) \times n) \times n\|_{\mathcal{T}_\tau} \leq c_3(|\xi| + \|\psi_1\|_{2-1/q_0,q_0(\partial\Omega)}).\end{aligned}$$

with $c_i = c_i(\Omega, q)$, $i = 1, 2, 3$. Moreover, this solution is unique in the class of solutions u, π such that
(i) $u \in D^{1,2}(\Omega)$,
(ii) $(\gamma(u) \times n) \times n \in \mathcal{T}_\tau(\mathcal{B})$
(iii) $\|(\gamma(u) \times n) \times n\|_{\mathcal{T}_\tau} \leq c_3(|\xi| + \|\psi_1\|_{2-1/q_0,q_0(\partial\Omega)})$.

Theorem 8.4. *Let $\xi = me_1$, $m \neq 0$ and $\psi_2 \in W^{2-1/q_0,q_0}(\partial\Omega)$, $q_0 > 3$, be given with $\psi_2 \in \mathcal{P}$. There exists $C_2 = C_2(\Omega, q_0) > 0$ such that if $\lambda(|\xi| + \|\psi_2\|_{2-1/q_0,q_0(\partial\Omega)}) < C_2$, problem (8.1)-(8.3) admits at least one solution $v, p \in \mathcal{P}$, with $\gamma(v) \cdot n \in \mathcal{T}_n(\Omega)$ and such that $v, p \in C^\infty(\Omega)$,*

$$(v - \xi) \in L^{2q/(2-q)}(\Omega) \cap D^{1,4q/(4-q)}(\Omega) \cap D^{1,2}(\Omega) \cap D^{2,q}(\Omega)$$
$$p \in L^{3q/(3-q)}(\Omega) \cap D^{1,q}(\Omega).$$

Moreover, $\|(v - \xi)(1 + |x|)\|_\infty < \infty$ and the following estimates hold

$$\begin{aligned}&\|(v - \xi)(1 + |x|)\|_\infty + |v|_{1,2} + \lambda\|\xi \cdot \nabla v\|_q + (\lambda|\xi|)^{1/2}\|v - \xi\|_{2q/(2-q)} \\ &\quad + (\lambda|\xi|)^{1/4}|v|_{1,4q/(4-q)} + |v|_{2,q} + \|p\|_{3q/(3-q)} + |p|_{1,q} \\ &\qquad \leq c_1(|\xi| + \|\psi_2\|_{2-1/q_0,q_0(\partial\Omega)}) \\ &|\xi| + \|\psi_2\|_{2-1/q_0,q_0(\partial\Omega)} \leq c_2\|\gamma(v) \cdot n\|_{\mathcal{T}_n} \leq c_3(|\xi| + \|\psi_2\|_{2-1/q_0,q_0(\partial\Omega)}).\end{aligned}$$

with $c_i = c_i(\Omega, q)$, $i = 1, 2, 3$. *Moreover, this solution is unique in the class of solutions* u, π *such that*

(i) $u \in D^{1,2}(\Omega)$,

(ii) $\gamma(u) \cdot n \in \mathcal{T}_n(\mathcal{B})$

(iii) $\|\gamma(u) \cdot n\|_{\mathcal{T}_n} \leq c_3(|\xi| + \|\psi_2\|_{2-1/q_0,q_0(\partial\Omega)})$.

In the light of Theorems 8.3 and 8.4, we can give an explicit solution to Problem B, in the case when $\mathcal{B}$ is a ball of unit radius (say), and $\psi_1 = \psi_2 = 0$. The proof is essentially the same as that given for the linearized case in Theorem 5.5, and, therefore, it will be omitted.

Theorem 8.5. *Let* $\mathcal{B}$ *be the ball of radius one centered at the origin and let* $\xi = Ve_1$, $V > 0$. *Then there exists* $C = C(\Omega) > 0$ *such that if* $\lambda V < C$, *the self-propelled solutions* v, p *uniquely determined in Theorems 8.1-8.5 and corresponding to* V *and to* $\psi_1 = \psi_2 = 0$ *are potential-like, that, is* $v = \nabla\Phi$, $p = \frac{1}{2}(\nabla\Phi)^2$, *for suitable scalar harmonic functions* Φ. *The functions* Φ *are given by*

(a) $\Phi = Vx_1$ *(if no prescription of velocity is given at* $\partial\Omega$*);*

(b) $\Phi = Vx_1\left(1 + \frac{1}{2|x|^3}\right)$ *(if* $v_0 \cdot n = 0$ *at* $\partial\Omega$*);*

(c) $\Phi = Vx_1\left(1 - \frac{1}{|x|^2}\right)$ *(if* $(v_0 \times n) \times n = 0$ *at* $\partial\Omega$*).*

9. On the Relation Between Steady Towed Motion and Steady Self-Propelled Motion

Our goal is to give a nonlinear counterpart of the results established for the Stokes approximation in Theorem 5.2. To this end, we need to derive some information concerning the steady flow of a Navier-Stokes fluid past a towed body $\mathcal{B}$. We recall that, if $\mathcal{B}$ is towed by a given force F with a constant velocity $-\xi$ $(\neq 0)$, and the motion of the fluid is seen by an observer attached to the body, the relevant equations are given by

$$(9.1)\qquad \left.\begin{aligned} \Delta v &= \lambda v \cdot \nabla v + \nabla p \\ \operatorname{div} v &= 0 \end{aligned}\right\} \text{ in } \Omega$$
$$v = 0 \quad \text{on } \partial\Omega$$
$$\lim_{|x|\to\infty} v(x) = \xi$$
$$F = \int_{\partial\Omega} T(v,p)\cdot n.$$

If ξ is prescribed, this is the "classical" exterior problem for the steady-state Navier-Stokes equations, and it is well known that for any $\lambda \geq 0$ it admits at least one solution and that this solution is uniquely determined for $\lambda|\xi| \leq \tilde{\lambda}$, with $\tilde{\lambda} = \tilde{\lambda}(\Omega)$, [13], [3], [4], [1], [6]. As a consequence, also F is uniquely determined for $\lambda|\xi| \leq \tilde{\lambda}$. In particular, if $\mathcal{B}$ is symmetric around the direction e_1 of ξ, then also F is directed along e_1. Conversely, if F is prescribed along e_1 and v, p and $\xi \neq 0$ are unknown, existence of solutions to (9.1) in the class $\mathcal{P}$, for all $\lambda \geq 0$ can be obtained as a corollary to the results proved by Weinberger in [26]. Our first concern here is to show uniqueness of solutions to (9.1) in the class $\mathcal{P}$, namely, that for any given F in the direction e_1 there is at most one solution v, p, ξ, with $v, p \in \mathcal{P}$, at least for small values of $\lambda|F|$. As a consequence, for the towed body problem, we obtain a one-to-one correspondence between the force F and the velocity of the body $-\xi$, for λ not too large. This result will allow us to set a suitable one-to-one map between F and the thrust vector G which generates the self-propelled motion of $\mathcal{B}$ with the same velocity $-\xi$. Moreover, we shall show that $F = -G + O(\lambda^{1/2})$, as $\lambda \to 0$. These results will be achieved through several intermediate steps.

Lemma 9.1. *Let v, p, ξ be a solution to* (9.1) *with $v, p \in \mathcal{P}$ corresponding to a given $F = F_1 e_1$, and with $v \in D^{1,2}(\Omega)$. Then, condition* $(9.1)_5$ *is equivalent to the following one*

$$(9.2)\qquad \xi \cdot \int_{\partial\Omega} g = -F_1 - \lambda \int_\Omega u \cdot \nabla H \cdot u + \lambda \xi \cdot \int_\Omega \nabla u \cdot H,$$

where $u = v - \xi$ and g, H are defined in (3.19), (3.18), *respectively.*

Proof - Multiply $(9.1)_1$ by H, integrate by parts over Ω and use Lemmas 3.2 and 4.2 to obtain

$$F_1 = \int_\Omega T(u,p) : D(H) - \lambda \int_\Omega u \cdot \nabla H \cdot u + \lambda \xi \cdot \int_\Omega \nabla u \cdot H.$$

By the same token, multiplying $(3.18)_1$ by u and integrating by parts over Ω, we find

$$-\xi \cdot \int_{\partial\Omega} T(H,P) = \int_{\Omega} T(u,p) : D(H)$$

and the result follows by subtracting side by side these two last displayed equations □

Lemma 9.2. *Let the assumptions of the previous lemma be satisfied. Then,*

$$C_1|\xi|^2 \leq \int_{\Omega} |\nabla v|^2 = F \cdot \xi, \tag{9.3}$$

with $C_1 = C_1(\Omega) > 0$. Moreover, there exists a positive constant $C_2 = C_2(\Omega)$ such that, if $\lambda|F| < C_2$, then

$$|\xi| \geq C_3|F|. \tag{9.4}$$

with $C_3 = C_3(\Omega) > 0$.

Proof - We multiply both sides of (9.1) by $u = v - \xi$ and integrate by parts on Ω. Taking into account the asymptotic properties of u and p (see Lemma 4.2)

$$2\int_{\Omega} |D(v)|^2 = F \cdot \xi.$$

Since

$$2\int_{\Omega} |D(v)|^2 = \int_{\Omega} |\nabla v|^2,$$

see Lemma 2.5, relation (9.3) follows from these last two equations and from Lemma 2.1. To show the second part, we observe that from Theorem 4.2 and (9.3), there exists $C = C(\Omega, q) > 0$ such that if $\lambda|F| < C$, the solution v obeys (4.11). Then, recalling the summability properties of H (Lemma 3.2), we find

$$\lambda\left|\int_{\Omega} u \cdot \nabla H \cdot u\right| \leq c\|u\|_4^2 \leq c\lambda|\xi|^2 \leq c\lambda|F|^2 \tag{9.5}$$

Furthermore, by the convexity inequality, for all $q_1 \in (q, 3/2)$ we have

$$\|\xi \cdot \nabla u\|_{q_1} \leq \|\xi \cdot \nabla u\|_q^{\theta} \|\xi \cdot \nabla u\|_{3q/(3-q)}^{(1-\theta)}, \quad \theta \in (0,1)$$

Thus, in view of the Sobolev-like inequality

$$|u|_{1,3q/(3-q)} \le |u|_{2,q}, \tag{9.6}$$

see [5], Theorem II.5.1, again from (4.11), Lemma 3.2, and Young's inequality it follows that

$$\begin{aligned} \lambda\left|\xi\cdot\int_\Omega \nabla u\cdot H\right| &\le c\lambda^{(1-\theta)}|\xi|^{(1-\theta)}\left(\lambda^\theta\|\xi\cdot\nabla u\|_q|u|_{2,q}^{(1-\theta)}\right) \\ &\le c\lambda^{(1-\theta)}|F|^{(1-\theta)}\left(\lambda\|\xi\cdot\nabla u\|_q+|u|_{2,q}\right) \\ &\le c\lambda^{(1-\theta)}|F|^{(2-\theta)}. \end{aligned} \tag{9.7}$$

Therefore, from (9.2), (9.5) and (9.7) we conclude

$$|\xi| \ge c|F|(1-\lambda|F|-\lambda^{(1-\theta)}|F|^{(1-\theta)})$$

and the lemma is proved. □

From this lemma and Theorem 4.2 we deduce

Lemma 9.3. *Let v be as in Lemma 9.1. Then, there exists a positive constant $C=C(\Omega)$ such that, if $\lambda|F|<C$, the following estimate holds*

$$\begin{aligned} &\|(v-\xi)(1+|x|)\|_\infty+\lambda\|\xi\cdot\nabla v\|_q+(\lambda|\xi|)^{1/2}\|v-\xi\|_{2q/(2-q)} \\ &\quad+(\lambda|\xi|)^{1/4}|v|_{1,4q/(4-q)}+|v|_{2,q}+\|p\|_{3q/(3-q)}+|p|_{1,q}\le c|F|, \end{aligned} \tag{9.8}$$

for all $q\in(1,3/2)$ and with a constant c depending only on q and Ω.

We are now in a position to show the following result.

Theorem 9.1 (Uniqueness for the towed body problem). *Let $\mathcal{D}_F$ be the class of solutions $\{v,p,\xi\}$ to (9.1) with $v,p\in\mathcal{P}$, corresponding to a given $F=F_1e_1$. Assume $v\in D^{1,2}(\Omega)$. Then, there exists a constant $C=C(\Omega)$ such that if $\lambda|F|<C$, $\mathcal{D}_F$ is constituted by at most one element.*

Proof - If $F=0$, the theorem follows from Lemma 8.1. We shall thus assume $F\neq 0$. Let $\{v_1,p_1,\xi\}$, $\{v_2,p_2,\mu\}$ be two elements in $\mathcal{D}$. Setting $v_1=u_1+\xi$, $v_2=u_2+\mu$ and

$$U=u_1-u_2,\quad p=p_1-p_2,\quad \Xi=\xi-\mu,$$

from (9.1), (9.2) we have

$$\Xi \cdot \int_{\partial\Omega} g = \lambda S, \tag{9.9}$$

with

$$S = -\int_\Omega U \cdot \nabla H \cdot u_1 + \int_\Omega u_2 \cdot \nabla H \cdot U + \xi \cdot \int_\Omega \nabla U \cdot H - \Xi \cdot \int_\Omega \nabla H \cdot u_2, \tag{9.10}$$

and

$$\begin{aligned} &\left.\begin{aligned} \Delta U - \lambda\xi \cdot \nabla U &= \lambda\left(\Xi \cdot \nabla u_2 + U \cdot \nabla u_1 + u_2 \cdot \nabla U\right) + \nabla p \\ \operatorname{div} U &= 0 \end{aligned}\right\} \text{ in } \Omega \\ &U = -\Xi \ \text{ on } \partial\Omega \\ &\lim_{|x|\to\infty} U(x) = 0 \end{aligned} \tag{9.11}$$

From Lemma 8.2 we know that $u_2 \in D^{1,s}(\Omega)$ for all $s > 4/3$. Therefore, from Lemma 3.2 applied to (9.11), (9.4), and (9.6) we obtain for all $s \in (4/3, 3/2)$

$$\begin{aligned} \lambda\|\xi \cdot \nabla U\|_s &+ (\lambda|F|)^{1/2}\|U\|_{2s/(2-s)} \\ &+ (\lambda|F|)^{1/4}|U|_{1,4s/(4-s)} + |U|_{1,3s/(3-s)} \\ &\le c\lambda\left(|\Xi|\,|u_2|_{1,s} + \|U\|_{2s/(2-s)}|u_1|_{1,2} + \|u_1\|_4|U|_{1,4s/(4-s)} + \frac{|\Xi|}{\lambda}\right) \end{aligned} \tag{9.12}$$

with a constant c depending on Ω, s and an upper bound for $\lambda|F|$. From Lemma 8.3 and (9.6), for all $s \in (4/3, 3/2)$ it follows that

$$|u_1|_{1,2} + \|u_1\|_4 + (\lambda|F|)^{1/4}|u_2|_{1,s} \le c|F|.$$

Using this inequality in (9.12), we obtain, in particular, that there exists $C > 0$ depending on q and Ω such that, if $\lambda|F| < C$, the following inequality holds

$$\lambda\|\xi \cdot \nabla U\|_s + (\lambda|F|)^{1/2}\|U\|_{2s/(2-s)} + |U|_{1,3s/(3-s)} \le c|\Xi|, \tag{9.13}$$

with c independent of F. By the Hölder inequality and the summability properties of H, we deduce

$$\begin{aligned} \left|\int_\Omega U \cdot \nabla H \cdot u_1\right| &\le c\|U\|_{2s/(2-s)}\|u_1\|_{s/(s-1)} \\ \left|\int_\Omega u_2 \cdot \nabla H \cdot U\right| &\le c\|U\|_{2s/(2-s)}\|u_2\|_{s/(s-1)}. \end{aligned}$$

Since $s/(s-1) > 3$, from Lemma 8.3 it follows that

$$\|u_1\|_{s/(s-1)} + \|u_2\|_{s/(s-1)} \le c|F|$$

and we deduce

$$\left|\int_\Omega U \cdot \nabla H \cdot u_1\right| + \left|\int_\Omega u_2 \cdot \nabla H \cdot U\right| \le c|F| \|U\|_{2s/(2-s)}. \tag{9.14}$$

Next, we observe that for all $s < s_1 < 3/2$ we have

$$\left|\int_\Omega \xi \cdot \nabla U \cdot H\right| \le \|\xi \cdot \nabla U\|_{s_1} \|H\|_{s_1/(s_1-1)} \le C\|\xi \cdot \nabla U\|_{s_1},$$

and, by the convexity inequality,

$$\|\xi \cdot \nabla U\|_{s_1} \le \|\xi \cdot \nabla U\|_s^\theta \|\xi \cdot \nabla U\|_{3s/(3-s)}^{1-\theta}.$$

Therefore, from Lemma 8.1 and Young's inequality we obtain

$$\lambda \left|\int_\Omega \xi \cdot \nabla U \cdot H\right| \le c(\lambda|F|)^{1-\theta} \left(\lambda\|\xi \cdot \nabla U\|_s + |U|_{1,3s/(3-s)}\right). \tag{9.15}$$

Finally, from Lemma 8.3 for any $r \in (2,3)$ it follows that

$$\lambda \left|\int_\Omega \nabla H \cdot u_1\right| \le \lambda \|\nabla H\|_{r/(r-1)} \|u_1\|_r \le c(\lambda|F|)^{1/2}. \tag{9.16}$$

Replacing (9.14)–(9.16) into (9.9), (9.10), we conclude for $\lambda|F|$ sufficiently small

$$|\Xi| \le c\left[\lambda|F| \|U\|_{2s/(2-s)} + (\lambda|F|)^{1-\theta} \left(\lambda\|\xi \cdot \nabla U\|_s + |U|_{1,3s/(3-s)}\right)\right], \tag{9.17}$$

with c depending only on Ω (for a fixed s). Combining (9.13) and (9.17) we deduce the existence of a positive $C = C(\Omega)$ such that, if $\lambda|F| < C$, then

$$\lambda\|\xi \cdot \nabla U\|_s + (\lambda|F|)^{1/2} \|U\|_{2s/(2-s)} + |U|_{1,3s/(3-s)} \le 0$$

from which uniqueness follows. The theorem is completely proved. □

Remark 9.1. - Concerning the theorem just proved, the same kind of consideration made in Remark 6.1 applies.

We are now in a position to show the main result of this section. To this end, for $w \in \mathcal{T}(\mathcal{B})$, we set

$$G = G(w) = \left(\int_\Omega w \cdot g\right) e_1.$$

G is a thrust vector (see section 5). We shall say that a body $\mathcal{B}$, moving at constant velocity $-\xi$, is *self-propelled by the thrust vector* G, if $G = G(v_*)$, where $v_* \in \mathcal{T}(\mathcal{B})$ is the trace at $\partial\Omega$ of the velocity field v associated to a steady solution corresponding to ξ, in the sense of Theorems 7.3 and 8.1.

Theorem 9.2. *There exists a positive constant* $\lambda_0 = \lambda_0(\mathcal{B})$ *for which the following properties hold. Let the force* F *be given with* $|F| \le \lambda_0/\lambda$ *and let* $-\xi$ *be the corresponding velocity with which* F *tows* $\mathcal{B}$ *(see [26] and Theorem 9.1). Then, there is a uniquely determined thrust vector* G *by which* $\mathcal{B}$ *is self-propelled with the same velocity* $-\xi$. *Moreover,*

$$F = -G + \mathcal{F}, \tag{9.18}$$

where

$$|\mathcal{F}| \le c_1 \lambda^{1/2} |F|^{3/2} (1 + \lambda^{1/2} |F|^{1/2}), \tag{9.19}$$

and $c_1 = c_1(\mathcal{B})$. *Conversely, there exists a positive constant* $\lambda_1 = \lambda_1(\mathcal{B})$ *for which the following properties hold. Let the thrust vector* G *be given with* $|G| \le \lambda_1/\lambda$ *and let* $-\xi$ *be the corresponding velocity with which* $\mathcal{B}$ *is self-propelled by* G *(see Theorems 6.1 and 7.3). Then, there is a uniquely determined force* F *which tows* $\mathcal{B}$ *with the same velocity* $-\xi$. *Moreover,*

$$F = -G + \mathcal{G}, \tag{9.20}$$

where

$$|\mathcal{G}| \le c_1 \lambda^{1/2} |G|^{3/2} (1 + \lambda^{1/2} |G|^{1/2}) \tag{9.21}$$

and $c_2 = c_2(\mathcal{B})$.

PROOF - From Theorem 9.1 and [26], we know that for $|F| \leq C_1/\lambda$, $C_1 = C_1(\mathcal{B})$, there exists a unique solution v, p, ξ to (9.1). In particular, by (9.3), we have

$$|\xi| \leq C_2|F|, \tag{9.22}$$

which in turn implies $\lambda|\xi| \leq C_1C_2$. By taking $\lambda|F|$ less than a constant smaller than C_1, if necessary, we can meet the condition $\lambda|\xi| \leq C$, where C is the constant appearing in the assumption of Theorem 8.1. Therefore, from that theorem and Theorem 8.2 (see also Remark 8.1), we deduce the existence of a unique thrust vector $G = G(\gamma(v))$, with v, p unique solution associated to ξ. By $(8.21)_2$, and (9.22) we have

$$|G| \leq c|F|,$$

where $c = c(\mathcal{B})$. Moreover, denoting by u, π the steady-state solution corresponding to the towed body problem and by v, p that corresponding to the self-propelled body, from (9.1) and (6.2), we find

$$\begin{aligned} F_i = & -G_i + \lambda \int_\Omega (v-u) \cdot \nabla H \cdot (v-\xi) \\ & \qquad -\lambda \int_\Omega (u-\xi) \cdot \nabla H \cdot (u-v) - \lambda\xi \cdot \int_\Omega \nabla H \cdot (u-v) \\ \equiv & -G_i + \mathcal{F}. \end{aligned} \tag{9.23}$$

From Lemma 9.3, Theorem 8.1 and (9.22), we find

$$\begin{aligned} \left| \int_\Omega (v-u) \cdot \nabla H \cdot (v-\xi) \right| & \leq |H|_{1,2} \|v-\xi\|_4 \left(\|v-\xi\|_4 + \|u-\xi\|_4 \right) \\ & \leq c\|(v-\xi)(1+|x|)\|_\infty \left[\|(v-\xi)(1+|x|)\|_\infty \right. \\ & \qquad \left. + \|(u-\xi)(1+|x|)\|_\infty \right] \\ & \leq c|\xi| \left(|\xi| + |F| \right) \leq c|F|^2. \end{aligned} \tag{9.24}$$

Likewise,

$$\left| \int_\Omega (v-u) \cdot \nabla H \cdot (v-\xi) \right| \leq c|F|^2. \tag{9.25}$$

Moreover, by the same token, for $q \in (1, 6/5)$,

$$\begin{aligned}\left|\int_\Omega \nabla H \cdot (u-v)\right| &\le c\left(\|u-\xi\|_{2q/(2-q)} + \|v-\xi\|_{2q/(2-q)}\right)\\ &\le c(\lambda|\xi|)^{-1/2}(|F|+|\xi|)\\ &\le c(\lambda|\xi|)^{-1/2}|F|.\end{aligned} \tag{9.26}$$

Collecting (9.24)–(9.26), we obtain (9.19), and the first part of the theorem is proved. To show the second part, from Theorems 6.1 and 7.3, we know that for $|G| \le C_1/\lambda$, $C_1 = C_1(\mathcal{B})$, there exists a unique solution v, p, ξ to (6.1).[1] In particular, by $(7.17)_2$, we have

$$|\xi| \le C_2|G|, \tag{9.27}$$

which in turn implies $\lambda|\xi| \le C_1C_2$. By taking $\lambda|G|$ less than a constant smaller than C_1, if necessary, we can meet the assumptions of well-known uniqueness theorems for the "classical" exterior Navier-Stokes problem; see, *e.g.* [6], Theorem IX.5.3, from this result we then deduce the existence of a unique force F which tows $\mathcal{B}$ with velocity ξ. Furthermore, by (9.27) and (9.3) we have also

$$|F| \le c|G|,$$

where $c = c(\mathcal{B})$. To show the estimate for $\mathcal{G}$ we start with identity (9.23) and argue as in the proof of (9.19), using, this time (9.27), Lemma 8.3 and Theorems 6.1 and 7.3. □

Acknowledgments. I am indebted to A. M. Robertson for bringing to my attention the potential-like self-propelled solutions. I am also indebted to A. V. Kazhikov and Y. Shibata for the many stimulating conversations we had about uniqueness for Problem B, during my stay at the University of Tsukuba, in December 1996. I am glad to take this opportunity to thank Y. Shibata for his invitation. Furthermore, I wish to thank C. G. Simader for his kind invitation to visit the University of Bayreuth in May 1997, and for the time he spent discussing with me the possibility of characterizing the potential-like self-propelled solutions. I owe special thanks to H. Sohr for the interest he showed in this work, and for the endless conversations we had in Bucke and Paderborn in May 1997. This paper was completed while I was visiting the Department of Mathematics at the University of Pittsburgh. I wish to thank my colleagues for warm hospitality and, in particular, J. Chadam, W. Layton and B. McLeod.

---

[1] Recall that for $w \in \mathcal{T}(\mathcal{B})$, the norm $\|w\|_{\mathcal{T}}$ is equivalent to $\|w\|_{2-1/q,q(\partial\Omega)}$, $q > 1$, and that, moreover, $\|w\|_{\mathcal{T}} = \delta|G(w)|$, $\delta > 0$; see Remark 5.1.

References.

[1] BABENKO, K. I.: On Stationary Solutions of the Problem of Flow Past a Body of a Viscous Incompressible Fluid, *Math. USSR-Sb.*, **20** (1973), 1-25.

[2] BIRKHOFF G. & ZARANTONELLO, E.H.: *Jets, Wakes, and Cavities*, Academic Press (1957).

[3] FINN, R.: On the Exterior Stationary Problem for the Navier-Stokes Equations, and Associated Perturbation Problems, *Arch. Rational Mech. Anal.*, **19** (1965), 363-406.

[4] FUJITA, H.: On the Existence and Regularity of the Steady-State Solutions of the Navier-Stokes Equation, *J. Fac. Sci. Univ. Tokyo Sect. IA Math.*, **9** (1961), 59-102.

[5] GALDI, G. P.: *An Introduction to the Mathematical Theory of the Navier-Stokes Equations: Linearized Steady Problems*, Springer Tracts in Natural Philosophy, Vol. 38 (1994), Springer-Verlag.

[6] GALDI, G. P.: *An Introduction to the Mathematical Theory of the Navier-Stokes Equations: Nonlinear Steady Problems*, Springer Tracts in Natural Philosophy, Vol. 39 (1994), Springer-Verlag.

[7] GALDI, G. P., HEYWOOD, J. G. & SHIBATA, Y.: On the Global Existence and Convergence to Steady State of Navier-Stokes Flow Past an Obstacle that is Started from the Rest, *Arch. Rational Mech. Anal.*, in press.

[8] GALDI, G. P., AND MAREMONTI, P.: Monotonic Decreasing and Asymptotic Behavior of the Kinetic Energy for Weak Solutions of the Navier-Stokes Equations in Exterior Domains, *Arch. Rational Mech. Anal.* **94** (1986), 253-266.

[9] GALDI, G. P., & SIMADER, C. G.: Existence, Uniqueness and L^q-Estimates for the Stokes Problem in an Exterior Domain, *Arch. Rational Mech. Anal.*, **112** (1990), 291-318.

[10] HAPPEL, V. & BRENNER, H.: *Low Reynolds Number Hydrodynamics* (1965), Prentice Hall.

[11] KOZONO, H. & SOHR, H.: On Stationary Navier-Stokes Equations in Unbounded Domains, *Ricerche Mat.*, **42** (1993), 69-86.

[12] KOZONO, H., SOHR, H. & YAMAZAKI, M.: Representation Formula, Net Force and Energy Relation to the Stationary Navier-Stokes Equations in 3-Dimensional Exterior Domains, *Kyushu J. Math.*, **51** (1997), 239-260.

[13] LADYZHENSKAYA, O.A.: Investigation of the Navier- Stokes Equation for a Stationary Flow of an Incompressible Fluid, *Uspekhi Mat. Nauk* (3) **14** (1959), 75-97 (in Russian).

[14] LERAY, J.: Étude de Diverses Équations Intégrales non Linéaires et de Quelques Problèmes que Pose l'Hydrodynamique, *J. Math. Pures Appl.* **12** (1933), 1-82.

[15] PAYNE, L. E. & WEINBERGER, H. F.: Note on a Lemma of Finn and Gilbarg, *Acta Math.*, **98** (1957), 297-299.

[16] PUKHNACHEV, V. V.: Asymptotics of a Velocity Field at Considerable Distances From a Self Propelled Body, *J. Appl. Mech. Tech. Phys.*, **30** (1989), 52-60.

[17] PUKHNACHEV, V. V.: Stokes Approximation in a Problem of the Flow Around a Self-Propelled Body, *Boundary Value Problems in Mathematical Physics*, Naukova Dumka, Kiev (1990), 65-73 (in Russian).

[18] PUKHNACHEV, V. V.: The Problem of Momentumless Flow for the Navier-Stokes Equations, *Springer Lecture Notes in Mathematics*, **1431** (1990), Springer-Verlag, 87-94.

[19] SAUER, N.: The Steady State Navier-Stokes Equations for Incompressible Flows with Rotating Boundary, *Proc. Roy. Soc. Edinburgh Sect. A*, **110** (1972), 93-99.

[20] SENNITSKII, V. L.: Liquid Flow Around a Self-Propelled Body, *J. Appl. Mech. Tech. Phys.*, **3** (1978), 15-27.

[21] SENNITSKII, V. L.: An Example of Axisymmetric Fluid Flow Around a Self-Propelled Body, *J. Appl. Mech. Tech. Phys.*, **25** (1984), 526-530.

[22] SENNITSKII, V. L.: Self-Propulsion of a Body in a Fluid, *J. Appl. Mech. Tech. Phys.*, **31** (1990), 266-272.

[23] SIMADER, C. G. & SOHR, H.: *The Dirichlet Problem for the Laplacian in Bounded and Unbounded Domains*, Pitman Research Notes in Mathematics, Vol. 460 (1997).

[24] WEINBERGER, H. F.: Variational Properties of Steady fall in Stokes Flow, *J. Fluid Mech.*, **52** (1972), 321-344.

[25] WEINBERGER, H. F.: Variational Principles for a Body Falling in Steady Stokes Flow, *Proc. Symp. on Continuum Mechanics and Related Problems of Analysis*, **2** (1974), Mecniereba, 330-339.

[26] WEINBERGER, H. F.: On the Steady Fall of a Body in a Navier-Stokes Fluid, *Proc. Sympos. Pure Math.*, **23** (1973), 421-440.

Current address of the author:
Department of Mathematics and Statistics
301 Thackeray Hall
University of Pittsburgh
Pittsburgh 15260, PA - U.S.A.

On Existence and Uniqueness of Classical Solutions to the Stationary Navier-Stokes Equations and to the Traction Problem of Linear Elastostatics

Paolo Maremonti and Remigio Russo

Contents

1. Introduction

The basic mathematical problem of steady viscous hydrodynamics consists in finding a *classical solution* $(\boldsymbol{u}(\boldsymbol{x}), \pi(\boldsymbol{x})) \in [C^2(\Omega) \cap C(\overline{\Omega})] \times C^1(\Omega)$ to the Navier-Stokes equations

$$\begin{aligned} \nu \Delta \boldsymbol{u} + \boldsymbol{f} &= \nabla \pi + (\nabla \boldsymbol{u})\boldsymbol{u} \\ \operatorname{div} \boldsymbol{u} &= 0 \end{aligned} \qquad \text{in } \Omega\,, \tag{1.1}$$

where Ω is an open connected subset of $\mathbb{R}^3$ such that the velocity field $\boldsymbol{u}(\boldsymbol{x})$ assumes a prescribed value $\boldsymbol{a}(\boldsymbol{x})$ on the boundary $\partial\Omega$ of Ω. In physical terms, the surface velocity field $\boldsymbol{a}(\boldsymbol{x})$ of a vessel being assigned, one wants to know the steady motion of an incompressible viscous fluid contained in it and subjected to a volume force field $\boldsymbol{f}(\boldsymbol{x})$. Since the pioneering works by T. Boggio [2], L. Lichtenstein [32], F. K. G. Odqvist [40] and J. Leray [31], this problem has been the subject of a long series of researches devoted to establish, in particular, the minimal regularity conditions on data Ω, $\boldsymbol{f}$ and $\boldsymbol{a}$, assuring the solvability of the problem, under the (necessary) assumption, if Ω is bounded, that *the total flux of the velocity field throughout the boundary does vanish*:

$$\int_{\partial\Omega} \boldsymbol{a} \cdot \boldsymbol{n} \, \mathrm{d}\sigma = 0\,, \tag{1.2}$$

(where $\boldsymbol{n}$ stands for the outward unit normal to $\partial\Omega$), at need under suitable hypotheses on the magnitude of the kinematical viscosity ν. If $\mathbb{R}^3 \setminus \overline{\Omega}$ has $m+1$ connected components Ω_i $(i = 0, 1, 2, \dots, m)$, then condition (1.2) reads

$$\sum_{i=0}^{m} \int_{\partial\Omega_i} \boldsymbol{a} \cdot \boldsymbol{n} \, \mathrm{d}\sigma = \sum_{i=0}^{m} \Phi_i = 0\,. \tag{1.3}$$

In the class of solutions *with finite energy*, *i. e.* those solutions such that

$$\int_{\Omega} (\nabla \boldsymbol{u})^2 \, \mathrm{d}v < +\infty\,,$$

the natural formulation of the problem is the one called *variational* or *weak*, for which it is necessary that the surface kinetic field $\boldsymbol{a}$ belong to the trace space

$W^{\frac{1}{2},2}(\Omega)$. In this context, the most general result known today (cf., *e.g.*, [16]) assures that, if Ω is of class C^2 and

$$(1.4)\qquad \boldsymbol{f} \in W^{1,2}(\Omega) \cap W^{1,p}_{\text{loc}}(\Omega)\,, \qquad \boldsymbol{a} \in W^{1-\frac{1}{p},p}(\partial\Omega)\,,$$

with $p > 3$ and

$$(1.5)\qquad \sum_{i=0}^{m} c_i|\Phi_i| < \nu,$$

where the c_i's positive constants depend on Ω, then the Navier-Stokes equations have a solution. Moreover, it is unique provided $\boldsymbol{f}$ and $\boldsymbol{a}$ are *sufficiently small* and/or ν *is sufficiently large.* We observe that instead of $\boldsymbol{f}$ belonging to $W^{1,p}_{\text{loc}}(\Omega)$, we could require $\boldsymbol{f}$ to be Hölder continuous [30]. Furthermore, (1.5) may be replaced by the condition that the boundary datum $\boldsymbol{a}$ be *sufficiently small* [16].

A natural formulation of the problem of finding the steady motion of an incompressible viscous fluid, could assume the only continuity of the boundary datum, without *a priori* requiring that the solution have a square summable gradient in Ω. On the other hand, from a mathematical viewpoint, assumption $(1.4)_2$ is certainly redundant for the research of solutions in the class $[C^2(\Omega) \cap C(\overline{\Omega})] \times C^1(\Omega)$. Of course, this approach involves the use of different techniques from the ones usually adopted in variational problems. The *maximum modulus theorem* turned out — in connection with other, essentially linear, boundary value problems — to be an appropriate tool to treat this kind of questions (cf. [8],[14], [37], [38]).

In some recent papers [35], [34] the maximum modulus theorem has been proved for Stokes' system in bounded domains, in two and three dimensions respectively (see also [27, 28, 33]). This theorem assures that a solution $(\boldsymbol{u}(\boldsymbol{x}), \pi(\boldsymbol{x})) \in [C^2(\Omega) \cap C(\overline{\Omega})] \times C^1(\Omega)$ to Stokes' system (which is nothing else than the Navier-Stokes system where the nonlinear term is suppressed) exists corresponding to a datum $\boldsymbol{a} \in C(\partial\Omega)$ satifying condition (1.2), and such that

$$(1.6)\qquad \max_{\overline{\Omega}} |\boldsymbol{u}| \le c \max_{\partial\Omega} |\boldsymbol{a}|\,,$$

where the positive constant c is independent of $\boldsymbol{u}$ and $\boldsymbol{a}$.

In the current paper, just starting with the results of [34], we shall tackle, among others, the problem of existence and uniqueness of solutions to the boundary value problem associated with the three dimensional Navier-Stokes system in bounded domains in its classical terms, *i.e.* in the class $[C^2(\Omega) \cap C(\overline{\Omega})] \times C^1(\Omega)$, under the assumption that the boundary datum be only continuous on $\partial\Omega$. To this aim, we shall have first to complete the study of the solutions to Stokes' problem, showing that it has at most one solution in $[C^2(\Omega) \cap C(\overline{\Omega})] \times C^1(\Omega)$, which in turn assures that *every solution to this problem satisfies* (1.6). This established, we shall be in a position to prove that the steady-state Navier-Stokes system has a unique classical solution if $\boldsymbol{a}$ is continuous on $\partial\Omega$, (1.2) is satisfied, the viscosities are large and the usual "smallness" requirements of data or fluxes are met.

Another problem of great interest for applications concerns the determination of equilibrium configurations of a linearly elastic body loaded on the boundary, and is known as the traction problem of linear elastostatics. Since the second half of XIXth Century, it has been object of several researches (cf. [19], References) among which we may recall the basic ones by A. Korn [26] and G. Fichera [13], concerning homogeneous and isotropic bodies. As far as inhomogeneous bodies are concerned, we refer the reader to the monographies [15] and [29]. In the general case, one proves that, if the force $\boldsymbol{s}$ on the boundary satisfies suitable summability conditions, then there exists a unique variational solution $\boldsymbol{u}$ with a finite energy integral (cf. [12]), *i.e*

$$\int_\Omega (\hat{\nabla}\boldsymbol{u})^2 \mathrm{d}v < +\infty\,,$$

where $\hat{\nabla}\boldsymbol{u}$ denotes the symmetric part of the deformation gradient. Such a solution belongs to $C^2(\Omega) \cap C^1(\overline{\Omega})$, provided $\boldsymbol{s}$ and the elasticity tensor $\mathbf{C}$ are sufficiently regular. Nevertheless, the classical formulation of the problem only assumes $\boldsymbol{s}$ to be continuous. As a consequence, the corresponding solution to the traction problem should be looked for in the space of vector fields belonging to $C^2(\Omega) \cap C(\overline{\Omega})$, whose *conormal derivative* $\mathbf{C}(\nabla\boldsymbol{u})\boldsymbol{n}$ is continuous in $\overline{\Omega}$.

In this paper, with the aid of the maximum modulus theorem for Stokes' system, we shall also study the existence and the uniqueness of classical solutions to the traction problem of three–dimensional linear elastostatics in bounded and exterior domains, and in the half space. More precisely, dealing with a homogeneous and isotropic elastic body, we shall first observe that, *in a neighborhood* $\Omega(\delta)$ *of* $\partial\Omega$, $\mathbf{C}(\nabla \boldsymbol{u})\boldsymbol{n}$ obeys a system of Stokes' type, then we shall prove, by means of (1.6), that

$$\max_{\overline{\Omega}(\delta)} |\mathbf{C}(\nabla \boldsymbol{u})\boldsymbol{n}| \leq c \max_{\partial\Omega} |\boldsymbol{s}| \,. \tag{1.7}$$

Finally, by using (1.7) and well-known estimates inside Ω on the derivatives of $\boldsymbol{u}$, we shall obtain existence and uniqueness of classical solutions to the traction problem for linearly elastic bodies that turn out to be isotropic *near to the boundary*, under the only hypothesis of continuity on $\boldsymbol{s}$.

The matter is organized as follows. In Section 2, we list the main notation and the preliminary results we use in the sequel; in Section 3, we describe both the variational and classical formulations for either Stokes' system, either the Navier-Stokes one, and in the fourth Section we show, by means of a counterexample similar to a celebrated one by J. Hadamard [20] for the Dirichlet principle, that the two formulations are quite different; in Section 5, we prove the uniqueness of classical solutions to Stokes' problem both in bounded and exterior domains, while in the sixth Section we give the maximum modulus theorem for the classical solutions of Stokes' problem in exterior domains and in the half-space; in Section 7, we prove an existence and uniqueness theorem for solutions to the boundary value problem associated with the steady-state Navier-Stokes system in bounded domains, provided the boundary datum is continuous. Finally, in the eighth and last Section, we derive a maximum modulus theorem for the traction problem of linear elastostatics, by virtue of which, assuming that the traction boundary is continuous, we are able to prove existence and uniqueness theorems of classical solutions for such a problem in bounded and exterior domains, and in the half-space.

2. Notation and Preliminary Results

Light face letters indicate scalars, bold face lower case letters different from $\boldsymbol{o}$, $\boldsymbol{x}$, $\boldsymbol{y}$ and $\boldsymbol{\xi}$ denote vectors (in $\mathbb{R}^n$) ($n = 2, 3$), while $\boldsymbol{o}$ denotes the origin of a reference frame of $\mathbb{R}^n$ and $\boldsymbol{x}, \boldsymbol{y}, \boldsymbol{\xi}$ generic points of $\mathbb{R}^n$; bold face upper case letters stand for second order tensors (linear transformations from $\mathbb{R}^n$ into $\mathbb{R}^n$); we set $\boldsymbol{r} = \boldsymbol{r}(\boldsymbol{x}) = \boldsymbol{x} - \boldsymbol{o}$, $r = r(\boldsymbol{x}) = |\boldsymbol{x} - \boldsymbol{o}|$ and $\boldsymbol{e}_r = r^{-1}\boldsymbol{r}, \forall\, \boldsymbol{x} \neq \boldsymbol{o}$. Lin [resp. Sym] stands for the whole set of second order [resp. symmetric second order] tensors; $\operatorname{tr} \boldsymbol{A}$ is the scalar A_{ii} and $\boldsymbol{A} \cdot \boldsymbol{B} = \operatorname{tr} \boldsymbol{A}\boldsymbol{B}^{\mathrm{T}}$, where A_{ij} are the components of $\boldsymbol{A}$ in the reference frame $\{\boldsymbol{o}, \boldsymbol{e}_i\}$ $(i = 1, \dots, n)$, $\boldsymbol{B}^{\mathrm{T}}$ denotes the *transpose* of $\boldsymbol{B}$ and the summation convention over repeated indexes is used.

Unless otherwise stated, Ω will denote an open connected set of $\mathbb{R}^n$ of class C^2 and Ω_i $(i = 0, 1, \dots, m)$ stand for the connected components of $\mathbb{R}^n \setminus \overline{\Omega}$; in particular $\Omega_0 = \mathbb{R}^n \setminus (\overline{\Omega} \cup (\cup_{i=1}^m \Omega_i))$. The diameter of Ω is denoted by $\mathrm{d}(\Omega)$ and its measure by $\mathfrak{m}(\Omega)$; $\partial\Omega$ is the boundary of Ω and $\boldsymbol{\xi}$ its generic point; the region $\mathbb{R}^n \setminus \overline{\Omega}$ is called an *exterior domain*; in this case, as is always possible, we assume that $\boldsymbol{o} \in \mathbb{R}^n \setminus \overline{\Omega}$. From now on we only consider bounded domains, exterior domains and the half–space $\mathbb{R}^3_+ = \{\boldsymbol{x} \,:\, x_3 > 0\}$. We denote by $S_R(\boldsymbol{x}_o)$ the ball of radius R centered at $\boldsymbol{x}_o$ and we set $S_R = S_R(\boldsymbol{o})$, $T_R = S_{2R} \setminus S_R$, $S_R^+ = S_R \cap \overline{\mathbb{R}}^3_+$. We write $\Omega' \subset\subset \Omega$ to mean that $\overline{\Omega}' \subset \Omega$.

Let $\boldsymbol{\varphi}$ be a vector field on Ω. As customary, we denote by $\nabla\boldsymbol{\varphi}$ the second-order tensor with components $(\nabla\boldsymbol{\varphi})_{ij} = \varphi_{i,j}$, where φ_i are the components of $\boldsymbol{\varphi}$ in $\{\boldsymbol{o}; \boldsymbol{e}_i\}$ and the comma stands for partial differentiation with respect to the x_j coordinate; $\hat{\nabla}\boldsymbol{\varphi}$ and $\tilde{\nabla}\boldsymbol{\varphi}$ are the symmetric and skew parts of $\nabla\boldsymbol{\varphi}$ respectively; $\operatorname{div} \boldsymbol{\varphi}$ is the scalar $\varphi_{i,i}$ and $\nabla \times \boldsymbol{\varphi}$, $\Delta\boldsymbol{\varphi}$ are the vectors with components $(\varphi_{3,2} - \varphi_{2,3}, \varphi_{1,3} - \varphi_{3,1}, \varphi_{2,1} - \varphi_{1,2})$ if $(n = 3)$ and $\varphi_{i,jj}$ respectively. Let φ be a function on Ω and $\beta = (\beta_1, \dots, \beta_n) \in \mathbb{N}^n$ a multi–index, where $\mathbb{N}$ denotes the set of all natural numbers. By $D^\beta\varphi$ we mean the derivative $\partial^{|\beta|}\varphi/\partial x_1^{\beta_1} \dots \partial x_n^{\beta_n}$, with $|\beta| = \beta_1 + \ldots + \beta_n$. $C^k(\Omega)$ is the whole set of functions which are differentiable in Ω up to the order $k \in \mathbb{N}$ inclusive. We set $C^0(\Omega) = C(\Omega)$. $C^k(\overline{\Omega})$ is the set of function φ for which $D^\beta\varphi$ is bounded and uniformly continuous in Ω, for all $0 \le |\beta| \le k$. $C^k(\overline{\Omega})$ is a Banach space with respect to the norm

$$\|\varphi\|_{C^k(\overline{\Omega})} = \max_{0 \le |\beta| \le k} \sup_{\Omega} |D^\beta\varphi|.$$

We set $C^\infty(\Omega) = \cap_{k=0}^\infty C^k(\Omega)$. $C_0^k(\Omega)$ is the set of all C^k functions having a compact support in Ω. We set $C_0^0(\Omega) = C_0(\Omega)$ and $C_0^\infty(\Omega) = \cap_{k=0}^\infty C_0^k(\Omega)$. $C^{k,\alpha}(\overline{\Omega})$ $(\alpha \in (0,1])$ is the subset of $C^k(\overline{\Omega})$ of all functions whose derivatives up to the k–th order inclusive are Hölder continuous in Ω (Lipschitz continuous if $\alpha = 1$), *i. e.*

$$[\varphi]_{k,\alpha} = \max_{0\le|\beta|\le k} \sup_{\boldsymbol{x},\boldsymbol{y}\in\Omega,\boldsymbol{x}\neq\boldsymbol{y}} \frac{|D^\beta\varphi(\boldsymbol{x}) - D^\beta\varphi(\boldsymbol{y})|}{|\boldsymbol{x}-\boldsymbol{y}|^\alpha} < +\infty.$$

$C^{k,\alpha}(\overline{\Omega})$ is a Banach space with respect to the norm

$$\|\varphi\|_{C^{k,\alpha}(\overline{\Omega})} = \|\varphi\|_{C^k(\overline{\Omega})} + [\varphi]_{k,\alpha}.$$

$C^{k,\alpha}(\Omega)$ is the set of all function φ such that $\varphi \in C^{k,\alpha}(\overline{\Omega}'), \forall\,\Omega' \subset\subset \Omega$. $L^p(\Omega)$ ($p \ge 1$) is the Banach space of all measurable functions φ on Ω such that

$$\|\varphi\|^p_{L^p(\Omega)} = \int_\Omega |\varphi|^p \mathrm{d}v < +\infty.$$

$L^\infty(\Omega)$ is the Banach space of all measurable functions φ on Ω such that

$$\|\varphi\|_{L^\infty(\Omega)} = \operatorname{ess\,sup}|\varphi| < +\infty.$$

$W^{m,p}(\Omega)$ is the space of all functions φ such that $D^\beta\varphi \in L^p(\Omega)$, for all $0 \le |\beta| \le m$. $W^{m,p}(\Omega)$ is a Banach space with respect to the norm

$$\|\varphi\|_{W^{m,p}(\Omega)} = \left(\sum_{|\beta|=0}^{m} \|D^\beta\varphi\|^p_{L^p(\Omega)}\right)^{\frac{1}{p}}. \tag{2.1}$$

$W_0^{m,p}(\Omega)$ is the completion of $C_0^\infty(\Omega)$ with respect to the norm (2.1). $L^p(\partial\Omega)$ is the set of all measurable functions on $\partial\Omega$ such that the norm $\|\varphi\|_{L^p(\partial\Omega)}$ is finite. $W^{1-\frac{1}{p},p}(\partial\Omega)$ is the trace space of functions in $W^{1,p}(\Omega)$. It is a Banach space with respect to the norm

$$\|\varphi\|_{W^{1-\frac{1}{p},p}(\partial\Omega)} = \|\varphi\|_{L^p(\partial\Omega)} + \left(\int_\Omega\int_\Omega \frac{|\varphi(\boldsymbol{x}) - \varphi(\boldsymbol{y})|^p}{|\boldsymbol{x}-\boldsymbol{y}|^{n-2+p}} \mathrm{d}\sigma_x \mathrm{d}\sigma_y\right)^{\frac{1}{p}}.$$

From now on, for $1 \le p \le \infty$, we set

$$p' = \frac{p}{p-1} \quad (p' = 1, \text{ if } p = \infty).$$

$W_0^{-m,p}(\Omega)$ is the completion of the space $L^p(\Omega)$, with respect to the norm

$$\|\varphi\|_{W_0^{-m,p}(\Omega)} = \sup_{\|v\|_{W_0^{m,p'}(\Omega)}=1} \left| \int_\Omega \varphi v \, dv \right| .$$

The space $W_0^{-m,p}(\Omega)$ is isomorphic to the (strong) dual of $W_0^{m,p'}(\Omega)$ (cf., *e.g.*, [39]).

Let Ω be bounded. $L^{p,\lambda}(\Omega)$, with $p \geq 1$ and $\lambda \in [0, n]$, denotes the Morrey space, *i.e.* the Banach space of all functions $\varphi \in L^p(\Omega)$ such that

$$\|\varphi\|^p_{L^{p,\lambda}(\Omega)} = \sup_{x_o \in \Omega, \rho > 0} \rho^{-\lambda} \int_{\Omega \cap S_\rho(x_o)} |\varphi|^p dv < +\infty.$$

Of course, $L^{p,0}(\Omega) = L^p(\Omega)$. Moreover, $L^{p,n}(\Omega)$ is isomorphic to $L^\infty(\Omega)$ (cf., *e.g.*, [18]).

Let $\varphi \in L^1(\mathcal{A})$ with $\mathcal{A}$ measurable bounded subset of $\mathbb{R}^n$. We set

$$\varphi_{\mathcal{A}} = \frac{1}{\mathfrak{m}(\mathcal{A})} \int_{\mathcal{A}} \varphi \, d\mathcal{A}.$$

$\mathcal{L}^{p,\lambda}(\Omega)$, with $p \geq 1$ and $\lambda \in [0, n+p]$, denotes the Campanato space, *i.e.* the space of all functions $\varphi \in L^p(\Omega)$ such that

$$[\![\varphi]\!]^p_{p,\lambda} = \sup_{x_o \in \Omega, \rho > 0} \rho^{-\lambda} \int_{\Omega \cap S_\rho(x_o)} |\varphi - \varphi_{\Omega \cap S_\rho(x_o)}|^p dv < +\infty.$$

$\mathcal{L}^{p,\lambda}(\Omega)$ is a Banach space with respect to the norm

$$\|\varphi\|_{\mathcal{L}^{p,\lambda}(\Omega)} = \|\varphi\|_{L^p(\Omega)} + [\![\varphi]\!]_{p,\lambda}.$$

The following results hold true (cf., *e.g.*, [7], [18])

$$\mathcal{L}^{p,\lambda}(\Omega) \simeq L^{p,\lambda}(\Omega), \quad \lambda \in [0, n),$$

$$\mathcal{L}^{p,n}(\Omega) \simeq \mathcal{L}^{q,n}, \ \forall p, q \geq 1,$$

$$\text{if } \lambda \in (n, n+p] \text{ then } \mathcal{L}^{p,\lambda}(\Omega) \simeq C^{0,\alpha}(\overline{\Omega}), \quad \alpha = \frac{\lambda - n}{p},$$

where the simbol $\mathcal{P} \simeq \mathcal{Q}$ means that the space $\mathcal{P}$ and $\mathcal{Q}$ are isomorphic.

From now on, if χ is a vector (or tensor) field in Ω, we write $\chi \in \mathcal{V}(\Omega)$, where $\mathcal{V}(\Omega)$ is a linear space of functions defined almost everywhere in Ω, to mean that all the components of χ belong to $\mathcal{V}(\Omega)$. Also by $\mathcal{V}_{\text{loc}}(\Omega)$ we mean the set of all fields χ such that $\chi \in \mathcal{V}(\Omega'), \forall \Omega' \subset\subset \Omega$. Let $\mathcal{C}(\Omega) = \{\varphi \in C_0^\infty(\Omega) : \operatorname{div} \varphi = 0\}$. $J^p(\Omega)$ and $J^{1,p}(\Omega)$ stand for the completion of $\mathcal{C}(\Omega)$ with respect to the norms of $L^p(\Omega)$ and $W^{1,p}(\Omega)$ respectively. If Ω is an exterior domain, $\mathcal{J}(\Omega)$ denotes the completion of $\mathcal{C}(\Omega)$ with respect to the seminorm $\|\nabla\varphi\|_{L^2(\Omega)}$.

By the symbol $\mathfrak{R}$ we mean the whole set of (infinitesimal) rigid displacement fields, *i.e.* the fields $\boldsymbol{w}$ defined by

$$\boldsymbol{w}(\boldsymbol{x}) = \boldsymbol{a} + \boldsymbol{W}\boldsymbol{r}(\boldsymbol{x}) = \boldsymbol{a} + \boldsymbol{\omega} \times \boldsymbol{r}(\boldsymbol{x}).$$

with $\boldsymbol{a}$, $\boldsymbol{b}$ constant vectors, $\boldsymbol{W}$ constant second order skew tensors and $\boldsymbol{\omega}$ axial vector of $\boldsymbol{W}$.

Now, we collect the main preliminary results we shall need in the sequel. The symbol c will denote a positive constant whose value is unessential for our purposes; the numerical value of c may change from line to line and in the same line it may be, *e.g.*, $2c \leq c$. When we find it suitable to specify the dependence of c from some quantities, say $\Xi, \Phi, \ldots$, we write $c(\Xi, \Phi, \ldots)$. Also, in order to avoid to crowd the paper with a lot of constants which make the inequalities we consider dimensionally equivalent, we shall often use a unique constant c. For example, we write

$$\alpha \leq c(\beta + \gamma + \theta + \xi + \ldots\ldots)$$

instead of

$$\alpha \leq c_1\beta + c_2\gamma + c_3\xi + c_4\theta + \ldots\ldots,$$

even if $\beta, \gamma, \xi, \theta, \ldots.$ have different dimensions. Of course, if somebody does not agree to this formal simplification, he can always assume that the quantities we consider and the partial differential systems we study have been put in a dimensionless form.

Lemma 2.1. *Let $f \in W_0^{m,p}(\Omega)$, $p \in (1, +\infty)$. Then, the equation*

$$\operatorname{div} \varphi = f \quad \text{in } \Omega \tag{2.2}$$

admits a solution $\varphi \in W_0^{m+1,p}(\Omega)$ *such that*

$$\|\varphi\|_{W_0^{m+1,p}(\Omega)} \le c\|f\|_{W_0^{m,p}(\Omega)}.$$

Of course, in virtue of Sobolev's imbedding Theorem (cf., *e.g.*, [1]), the solution φ to system (2.2), whose existence is guaranteed by Lemma 2.1, must be understood in a variational sense if $(m+1)p \le n$ and in the classical one if $m(p+1) > n$. A proof of Lemma 2.1 can be found in [16, Theorem 3.2, Chap. III].

Remark 2.1 – Let $f \in W_0^{1,2}(\Omega)$ and let φ be a solution to equation (2.2) satisfying the estimate

$$\|\nabla\nabla\varphi\|_{L^2(\Omega)} \le c(\Omega)\|f\|_{W_0^{1,2}(\Omega)}.$$

By making use of the Poincaré inequality (cf. (2.6) below), we can majorize the right hand side of the above inequality as follows

$$\|\nabla\nabla\varphi\|_{L^2(\Omega)} \le c(\Omega)\|\nabla f\|_{L^2(\Omega)}. \tag{2.3}$$

By a rescaling argument, it is not difficult to see that the constant $c(\Omega)$ in (2.3) is invariant under translations, orthogonal transformations and dilatations, so that, in particular, if $\Omega = S_R(\boldsymbol{x}_o)$, then it is independent of R and $\boldsymbol{x}_o$.

Lemma 2.2. *Let* Ω *be bounded and let* $\varphi \in W^{1,p}(\Omega)$. *If* $\nabla\varphi \in L^{p,\lambda}(\Omega)$, *then*

$$\|\varphi\|_{\mathcal{L}^{p,\lambda+p}(\Omega)} \le c\left\{\|\nabla\varphi\|_{L^{p,\lambda}(\Omega)} + \|\varphi\|_{W^{1,p}(\Omega)}\right\}.$$

Of course, if $\lambda > n-p$, then φ is Hölder continuous. Lemma 2.2 is proved in [5] (see also [18], p. 113).

Lemma 2.3. *Let* Ω *be bounded and* $\varphi \in W^{1,2}(\Omega)$. *Then*

$$\|\varphi - \varphi_\Omega\|_{L^2(\Omega)} \le c_1(\Omega)\|\nabla\varphi\|_{L^2(\Omega)} \quad \textit{Poincaré's inequality,} \tag{2.4}$$

$$\|\nabla\varphi - (\tilde{\nabla}\varphi)_\Omega\|_{L^2(\Omega)} \le c_2(\Omega)\|\hat{\nabla}\varphi\|_{L^2(\Omega)} \quad \textit{Korn's inequality.} \tag{2.5}$$

Moreover, if φ vanishes on a subset Σ of $\partial\Omega$ such that $\mathfrak{m}(\Sigma) > 0$, then (2.4), (2.5) *specialize in*

$$\|\varphi\|_{L^2(\Omega)} \le c_1(\Omega)\|\nabla\varphi\|_{L^2(\Omega)}, \tag{2.6}$$

$$\|\nabla\varphi\|_{L^2(\Omega)} \le c_2(\Omega)\|\hat{\nabla}\varphi\|_{L^2(\Omega)}. \tag{2.7}$$

Finally, if $\varphi \in W_0^{1,2}(\Omega)$ and Ω is a three–dimensional domain star–shaped with respect to $\boldsymbol{o}$, then

$$\|r^{-1}\varphi\|_{L^2(\Omega)} \le 2\|\nabla\varphi\|_{L^2(\Omega)}. \tag{2.8}$$

Remark 2.2 – Inequalities (2.4)–(2.5) are well known. A proof of (2.4), (2.5) can be found in [18] and [12] respectively. We shall be mainly concerned with the case in which Ω is a the ball S_R, the half–ball S_R^+ and the shell T_R. In this case $c_1(\Omega) = k_1 R$ and k_1, c_2 are independent of R. If $\varphi \in W_0^{1,2}(\Omega)$, then in (2.6), (2.7) $c_1(\Omega) = \mathrm{d}(\Omega)$ and $c_2 = \sqrt{2}$. Finally, if $\Omega = S_R^+$ and $\varphi = \mathbf{0}$ in the set $\{\boldsymbol{x} \in \partial S_R^+ : r(\boldsymbol{x}) = R\}$, then in (2.6) $c_1 = k_1 R$ and k_1, c_2 are independent of R.

Observe that in (2.4) we can replace φ_Ω by $\varphi_{\partial\Omega}$.

Lemma 2.4. *Let Ω be an exterior domain of $\mathbb{R}^3$ and let $\varphi \in L^2_{\rm loc}(\Omega)$. If $\nabla\varphi \in L^2(\Omega)$, then there exists a constant vector φ_0 such that*

$$\begin{aligned} \|r^{-1}(\varphi - \varphi_0)\|_{L^2(\mathbb{R}^3\setminus S_R)} &\le 2\|\nabla\varphi\|_{L^2(\mathbb{R}^3\setminus S_R)},\\ \|\varphi - \varphi_0\|_{L^6(\Omega)} &\le c\|\nabla\varphi\|_{L^2(\Omega)}, \end{aligned} \tag{2.9}$$

where $S_R \supset \partial\Omega$.

If $\hat{\nabla}\varphi \in L^2(\Omega)$, then there exists a constant skew tensor $\boldsymbol{W}_\varphi$ such that

$$\|\nabla\varphi - \boldsymbol{W}_\varphi\|_{L^2(\Omega)} \le c\|\hat{\nabla}\varphi\|_{L^2(\Omega)}. \tag{2.10}$$

Inequalities (2.9) are well–known (cf.,*e.g.*, [16]), while (2.10) is the extension of Korn's inequality (2.5) to exterior domains. As far as we are aware, it has been first proved in [24]. Here we propose a simple proof of (2.10).

From (2.5) we have

$$\|\nabla\varphi - (\tilde{\nabla}\varphi)_{S_R}\|_{L^2(S_R)} \le c\|\hat{\nabla}\varphi\|_{L^2(\mathbb{R}^n)}, \quad \forall R > 0. \tag{2.11}$$

with c independent of R (see Remark 2.1). Integrating the inequality

$$|(\tilde{\nabla}\varphi)_{S_R} - (\tilde{\nabla}\varphi)_{S_\rho}|^2 \le 2\left[\nabla\varphi - (\tilde{\nabla}\varphi)_{S_\rho}\right]^2 + 2\left[\nabla\varphi - (\tilde{\nabla}\varphi)_{S_R}\right]^2,$$

over S_ρ, where $0 < \rho < R$, we get

$$|(\tilde{\nabla}\varphi)_{S_R} - (\tilde{\nabla}\varphi)_{S_\rho}|^2 \le c\rho^{-n}\|\hat{\nabla}\varphi\|^2_{L^2(\mathbb{R}^n)}.$$

Hence it follows that $(\tilde{\nabla}\varphi)_{S_\rho}$ converges to a skew tensor $\boldsymbol{W}_\varphi$ as $\rho \to +\infty$. Therefore, letting $R \to \infty$ in (2.11), we have (2.10).

Starting from the Korn inequality in $\mathbb{R}^3$ it is not difficult to get (2.10) for an exterior domain Ω (see [25]). Moreover, since our proof of (2.10) is based on the invariance under dilatation of the constant c_2 in (2.5), we see that (2.10) holds also for the half–space, or, more generally, for a cone.

It is worth noting that inequality $(2.9)_2$ in $\mathbb{R}^3$ can be proved by making use of the same technique employed to get (2.10) and $\varphi_0 = \lim_{R\to\infty}\varphi_{S_R}$, by only noting that the constant c in the Sobolev inequality

$$\|\varphi - \varphi_{S_R}\|_{L^6(S_R)} \le c\|\nabla\varphi\|_{L^2(S_R)}$$

is invariant under dilatations. Finally, from Sobolev's inequality in $\mathbb{R}^3$ it is not difficult to obtain we can obtain $(2.9)_2$.

If $\hat{\nabla}\varphi \in L^2(\Omega)$, we set

$$\boldsymbol{w}_\varphi = \varphi_0 + \boldsymbol{W}_\varphi \boldsymbol{r}. \tag{2.12}$$

Lemma 2.5. *Let f be a nonnegative and nondecreasing function in $(0, d]$ such that*

$$f(\rho) \le c\left[\left(\frac{\rho}{R}\right)^\gamma + \epsilon\right] f(R) + hR^\eta, \quad \forall \rho < R \le d\,,$$

for some positive constants c, h, γ and η with $\eta < \gamma$. A constant constant ϵ_0 exists such that, if $\epsilon < \epsilon_0$, then

$$f(\rho) \le c\left(\frac{\rho}{R}\right)^\eta f(R) + h\rho^\eta, \quad \forall \rho < R \le d\,.$$

Lemma 2.5 is due to S. Campanato (see also [17], p.179).

Lemma 2.6. *Let f be a nonnegative and nondecreasing function in $[\bar{R}, +\infty)$ such that*

$$f(\rho) \leq \left[k\left(\frac{\rho}{R}\right)^3 + \epsilon\right] f(R), \quad \forall R \geq \rho > \bar{R},$$

with k and ϵ positive constants.

$$\epsilon < \left[\frac{\alpha}{3k}\right]^{\frac{\alpha}{3-\alpha}} \left(1 - \frac{\alpha}{3}\right),$$

then

$$f(\rho) \leq c\left(\frac{\rho}{R}\right)^{\alpha} f(R), \quad \forall R \geq \rho > \bar{R}.$$

Lemma 2.6 is proved in [22], [36].

Let

$$\Omega^{\epsilon} = \{\boldsymbol{x} \in \Omega \,:\, \mathrm{dist}(\boldsymbol{x}, \partial\Omega) < \epsilon\}, \quad \epsilon \in (0, \bar{\epsilon}),$$

with $\bar{\epsilon}$ such that $\partial\Omega_i^{\epsilon} \cap \partial\Omega_j^{\epsilon} = \varnothing, \forall\, i \neq j = 0, 1, \ldots, m$.

Lemma 2.7. *Let $\gamma(\epsilon) = \exp[-1/\epsilon]$. Then, for any $\epsilon \in (0, \bar{\epsilon})$, there exists a function $\psi_{\epsilon}(\boldsymbol{x}) \in C^{\infty}(\Omega \setminus \Omega^{\epsilon})$ such that the following properties are satisfied*

(i) $|\psi_{\epsilon}(\boldsymbol{x})| \leq 1, \ \forall\, \boldsymbol{x} \in \Omega \setminus \Omega^{\epsilon}$;

(ii) $\psi_{\epsilon}(\boldsymbol{x}) = 1, \ \forall\, \boldsymbol{x} : \mathrm{dist}(\boldsymbol{x}, \partial\Omega) < \frac{1}{2}\gamma^2(\epsilon)$;

(iii) $\psi_{\epsilon}(\boldsymbol{x}) = 0, \ \forall\, \boldsymbol{x} : \mathrm{dist}(\boldsymbol{x}, \partial\Omega) \geq 2\gamma(\epsilon)$;

(iv) $\mathrm{dist}(\boldsymbol{x}, \partial\Omega)|\nabla\psi_{\epsilon}(\boldsymbol{x})| \leq \epsilon, \ \forall \boldsymbol{x} \in \Omega \setminus \Omega^{\epsilon}$.

Lemma 2.8. *Let $\tilde{d}(\boldsymbol{x}) = (\mathrm{dist}(\boldsymbol{x}, \partial\Omega))^{-1}$ and $p \in (1, +\infty)$. Then, the following inequality holds*

$$\|\tilde{d}\varphi\|_{L^p(\Omega)} \leq c(\Omega)\|\nabla\varphi\|_{L^p(\Omega)}, \quad \forall \varphi \in W_0^{1,p}(\Omega).$$

Lemmas 2.7 and 2.8 are proved in [16].

Lemma 2.9. *Let Ω be a bounded domain of $\mathbb{R}^3$ and let $\boldsymbol{\rho}$, $\boldsymbol{\mu}$ two assigned vectors. Then there exists a unique rigid diplacement $\boldsymbol{w} = \boldsymbol{a} + \boldsymbol{\omega} \times (\boldsymbol{x} - \boldsymbol{x}_c)$, defined by*

$$\mathfrak{m}(\partial\Omega)\boldsymbol{a} = \boldsymbol{\rho}, \quad \boldsymbol{\omega} = \overset{-1}{\boldsymbol{I}}\boldsymbol{\mu},$$

where $\boldsymbol{x}_c$ is the centroid of $\partial\Omega$ and $\boldsymbol{I}$ is the centroidal inertial tensor of $\partial\Omega$, such that

$$\int_{\partial\Omega} \boldsymbol{w}\,\mathrm{da} = \boldsymbol{\rho}, \quad \int_{\partial\Omega} (\boldsymbol{x}-\boldsymbol{x}_c)\times\boldsymbol{w}\,\mathrm{da} = \boldsymbol{\mu}. \tag{2.13}$$

Lemma 2.9 is proved in [19, p. 185].

Let $\boldsymbol{s}$ be a continuous vector field on $\partial\Omega$ and let

$$\boldsymbol{\rho} = \int_{\partial\Omega} \boldsymbol{s}\,\mathrm{da}, \quad \boldsymbol{\mu} = \int_{\partial\Omega} (\boldsymbol{x}-\boldsymbol{x}_c)\times\boldsymbol{s}\,\mathrm{da}.$$

In the sequel we shall set

$$\boldsymbol{s}^* = \boldsymbol{s} - \boldsymbol{w}, \tag{2.14}$$

where $\boldsymbol{w} \in \mathfrak{R}$ is defined by (2.13). Of course the field $\boldsymbol{s}^*$ is equilibrated, *i. e.*

$$\boldsymbol{s}^*_{\partial\Omega} = \boldsymbol{0}, \quad (\boldsymbol{r}\times\boldsymbol{s}^*)_{\partial\Omega} = \boldsymbol{0}.$$

3. The Boundary Value Problem for Stokes and Navier–Stokes Problems

Unless otherwise stated, from now on we assume that Ω is an open connected set of $\mathbb{R}^3$ of class C^2.

As is well known, in the linear approximation the stationary motions of an incompressible fluid, subjected to a body force field $\boldsymbol{f}$, in a bounded region Ω of $\mathbb{R}^3$ are governed by the Stokes system

$$\begin{aligned} \Delta\boldsymbol{u} + \boldsymbol{f} &= \nabla\pi \\ \operatorname{div}\boldsymbol{u} &= 0 \end{aligned} \qquad \text{in } \Omega, \tag{3.1}$$

where $\boldsymbol{u}$ is the *kinetic field* and π the *hydrostatic pressure field.*

Let $\boldsymbol{n}$ denote the outward unit normal to $\partial\Omega$ and let $\boldsymbol{a}$ be a field on $\partial\Omega$ which satisfies the *zero flow condition*

$$\int_{\partial\Omega} \boldsymbol{a}\cdot\boldsymbol{n}\,\mathrm{d}\sigma = 0. \tag{3.2}$$

If $\boldsymbol{f} \in C(\Omega)$ and $\boldsymbol{a} \in C(\partial\Omega)$, then the *classical boundary value problem* associated with system (3.1) consists in finding a couple $(\boldsymbol{u}, \pi) \in [C^2(\Omega) \cap C(\overline{\Omega})] \times C^1(\Omega)$ satisfying (3.1) and the *boundary condition*

$$\boldsymbol{u} = \boldsymbol{a} \qquad \text{on } \partial\Omega. \tag{3.3}$$

From now on, such a solution will be called *classical.*

Let $p \in (1, \infty)$ and $\boldsymbol{f} \in W_0^{-1,p}(\Omega)$. The *variational formulation* of system (3.1) is to find a field $\boldsymbol{u} \in J^{1,p}_{\text{loc}}(\Omega)$ such that

$$\int_\Omega \nabla\boldsymbol{\varphi} \cdot \nabla\boldsymbol{u}\, dv = \langle \boldsymbol{f}, \boldsymbol{\varphi} \rangle, \quad \forall \boldsymbol{\varphi} \in \mathcal{C}(\Omega), \tag{3.4}$$

where $\langle \boldsymbol{f}, \boldsymbol{\varphi} \rangle$ denotes the value of the functional $\boldsymbol{f}$ at $\boldsymbol{\varphi}$. A solution to equation (3.4) is known as a *variational solution* to system (3.1).

Let

$$\boldsymbol{a} \in W^{1-\frac{1}{p},p}(\partial\Omega) \tag{3.5}$$

and consider a *solenoidal extension* of $\boldsymbol{a}$, *i.e.* a field $\hat{\boldsymbol{a}} \in J^{1,p}(\Omega)$ such that $\boldsymbol{a} = \hat{\boldsymbol{a}}$ on $\partial\Omega$ in the *trace sense.*

Let Ω be bounded and $\boldsymbol{a}$ satisfy (3.2). The *variational boundary value problem* associated with system (3.1) in bounded domains is to find a field $\boldsymbol{v} \in J^{1,p}(\Omega)$ such that the field $\boldsymbol{v} + \hat{\boldsymbol{a}}$ satisfies equation (3.4).

Let Ω be an exterior domain. In such a case condition (3.2) is no longer required and we have to append to (3.3) the *condition at infinity*

$$\lim_{r(x)\to\infty} \boldsymbol{u}(\boldsymbol{x}) = \boldsymbol{0}. \tag{3.6}$$

Let $\boldsymbol{f} \in \mathcal{J}^{-1}(\Omega)$, $\boldsymbol{a} \in W^{\frac{1}{2},2}(\partial\Omega)$. A variational solution to system (3.1), (3.3), (3.6) is a field $\boldsymbol{u} \in \mathcal{J}(\Omega)$ such that $\boldsymbol{v} + \hat{\boldsymbol{a}}$ meets (3.4). Of course, condition (3.6) is to be pointwise satisfied for classical solutions to system (3.1), (3.3) and in a generalized sense for variational solutions. For the sake of simplicity, we confined ourselves, as far as exterior domains are concerned, to state the variational formulation only in the space $W^{1,2}(\Omega)$. More general variational formulations for the Stokes problem in exterior domains can be found in [16].

If the above problems admit unique solutions in the functional classes where they have been formulated, then a (pointwise or integral) property p involving some subsets $\mathfrak{I}$ of the class of solutions becomes a property to be satisfied by any solution belonging to the natural class. In particular, if p is an inequality involving data and solutions, then it becomes an *a priori estimate.*

The following existence, uniqueness and regularization theorem about variational solution to the Stokes system is now a classical result [9, 47, 48] (see also [16] vol. I, p. 225).

Theorem 3.1. *If Ω is bounded, $\boldsymbol{a} \in W^{1-\frac{1}{p},p}(\partial\Omega)$ satisfies (3.2) and $\boldsymbol{f} \in W_0^{-1,p}(\Omega)$, then there exists a unique variational solution $\boldsymbol{u} \in J^{1,p}(\Omega)$ to system (3.1), (3.3) and an associated pressure field $\pi \in L^p(\Omega)$ such that*

$$\|\boldsymbol{u}\|_{W^{1,p}(\Omega)} + \|\pi\|_{L^p(\Omega)} \le c\left\{\|f\|_{W_0^{-1,p}(\Omega)} + \|\boldsymbol{a}\|_{W^{1-\frac{1}{p},p}(\partial\Omega)}\right\}. \tag{3.7}$$

Moreover, if Ω is of class C^{m+2} $(m \ge 0)$ and

$$\boldsymbol{f} \in W^{m,p}(\Omega), \quad \boldsymbol{a} \in W^{m+2-\frac{1}{p},p}(\partial\Omega),$$

then

$$\boldsymbol{u} \in W^{m+2,p}(\Omega), \quad p \in W^{m+1,p}(\Omega)$$

and

$$\|\boldsymbol{u}\|_{W^{m+2,p}(\Omega)} + \|\pi\|_{W^{m+1,p}(\Omega)} \le c\left\{\|f\|_{W^{m,p}(\Omega)} + \|\boldsymbol{a}\|_{W^{m+2-\frac{1}{p},p}(\partial\Omega)}\right\}, \tag{3.8}$$

so that if $p > 3$ and $m \ge 1$, the variational solution is a classical one.

If Ω is an exterior domain, $\boldsymbol{f} \in \mathfrak{J}^{-1}(\Omega)$ and $\boldsymbol{a} \in W^{\frac{1}{2},2}(\partial\Omega)$, then there exists a unique variational solution $\boldsymbol{u} \in \mathfrak{J}(\Omega)$ to system (3.1), (3.3), (3.6) and an associated pressure field $\pi \in L^6(\Omega)$ such that

$$\|\nabla\boldsymbol{u}\|_{L^2(\Omega)} + \|\pi\|_{L^6(\Omega)} \le c\left\{\|\boldsymbol{f}\|_{\mathfrak{J}^{-1}(\Omega)} + \|\boldsymbol{a}\|_{W^{\frac{1}{2},2}(\partial\Omega)}\right\}.$$

Moreover, if $\boldsymbol{f} \in L^2(\Omega) \cap W^{2,2}_{\mathrm{loc}}(\Omega)$ and $\boldsymbol{a} \in W^{\frac{3}{2},2}(\partial\Omega)$ the above variational solution is a classical one.

Of course, the pressure π in system (3.1) is determined to within a constant. However, we can always normalize it by requiring that $\pi_\Omega = 0$, if Ω is bounded, and $\pi_0 = 0$, if Ω is an exterior domain, where π_0 is the constant appearing in $(2.9)_2$.

In the sequel we shall repeatedly consider the solutions to the following Skokes system

$$\begin{aligned} \Delta \boldsymbol{u} &= \nabla \pi \\ \operatorname{div} \boldsymbol{u} &= 0 \end{aligned} \quad \text{in } \Omega, \tag{3.9}$$

Now, as rigorously formulated, the mathematical steady problem of incompressible viscous fluid dynamics consists in finding a couple $(\boldsymbol{u}, \pi)$ on Ω satisfying the *Navier–Stokes equations*

$$\begin{aligned} \nu \Delta \boldsymbol{u} + \boldsymbol{f} &= \nabla \pi + (\nabla \boldsymbol{u})\boldsymbol{u} \\ \operatorname{div} \boldsymbol{u} &= 0 \end{aligned} \quad \text{in } \Omega, \tag{3.10}$$

where $\nu(> 0)$ is the kinematical viscosity.

A variational solution to system (3.10) is a field $\boldsymbol{u} \in J^{1,2}_{\text{loc}}(\Omega)$ which satisfies the integral equation

$$\nu \int_\Omega \nabla \boldsymbol{\varphi} \cdot \nabla \boldsymbol{u} \, dv = \int_\Omega \boldsymbol{\varphi} \cdot \boldsymbol{f} \, dv - \int_\Omega \boldsymbol{\varphi} \cdot (\nabla \boldsymbol{u})\boldsymbol{u} \, dv, \quad \forall \boldsymbol{\varphi} \in \mathcal{C}. \tag{3.11}$$

In a quite analogous way to what has been made for the Stokes system, we can state the classical and variational boundary value problems associated with system (3.10) in a bounded domains Ω. Then, the classical boundary value problem for system (3.10) is to find a solution $(\boldsymbol{u}, \pi) \in [C^2(\Omega) \cap C(\overline{\Omega})] \times C^1(\Omega)$ to (3.10) which meets condition (3.3) pointwise , with $\boldsymbol{a}$ satisfying (3.2). Also a variational solution to system (3.10), (3.3) is a field $\boldsymbol{u} \in J^{1,2}(\Omega)$ such that $\boldsymbol{u} + \hat{\boldsymbol{a}}$ satisfies equation (3.11), with $\hat{\boldsymbol{a}}$ solenoidal extension of $\boldsymbol{a}$. Existence and uniqueness theorems of variational solutions to Navier–Stokes' system can be found in [16, 30, 49].

4. Nonequivalence between Classical and Variational formulations

It seems now quite natural to set the question of comparing the boundary value problems as defined according to the classical and the variational formulation given in the previous Section. Such a question, which was posed for the first time with regard to harmonic functions having a finite Dirichlet integral, and goes back to the formulation of the so-called *Dirichlet principle* (cf. *e.g.*, [10], Chap. I), found in this framework an answer expressed by a counter-example due to J. Hadamard, which, suitably rephrased, we shall adapt to Stokes' problem and extend to the class of solutions whose gradients belong to L^p $(p > 1)$.

The fact that the two problems are not related, may be argued from the following simple considerations of analytical character. Denoting by $\boldsymbol{u}$ *the unique solution* of the classical problem corresponding to datum $\boldsymbol{a} \in C(\partial\Omega) \setminus W^{1-\frac{1}{p},p}(\partial\Omega)$, if $\boldsymbol{u}$ were also a variational solution, then it should have a p-summable gradient, for some $p > 1$, so that, in virtue of the trace theorem [cf., *e g.*, [1]), $\boldsymbol{a}$, further than being continuous, should also belong to the space $W^{1-\frac{1}{p},p}(\partial\Omega)$, what is in contradiction with the minimal assumptions made on $\boldsymbol{a}$. On the other hand, it is quite evident that, chosen $\boldsymbol{a} \in W^{1-\frac{1}{p},p}(\partial\Omega)$, with $p \in [1,3]$, *the unique variational solution* $\boldsymbol{u}$ corresponding to $\boldsymbol{a}$ is not necessarily the classical solution.

As far as the first remark is concerned, following [20] (cf. also [10], p. 9), let us consider the Dirichlet problem in the unit disk $\mathfrak{D}$ centered at $\boldsymbol{o}$

$$\begin{aligned} \Delta u &= 0 \quad \text{in } \mathfrak{D}, \\ u &= a \quad \text{on } \partial\mathfrak{D}. \end{aligned} \tag{4.1}$$

with $\boldsymbol{a}$ expressed by the sum of the Fourier series

$$a(\theta) = \frac{a_0}{2} + \sum_{m=1}^{\infty} \left[a_m \cos(m\theta) + b_m \sin(m\theta)\right],$$

where (r, θ) is a polar coordinate system in S_1. A solution to problem (4.1) is furnished by the following Fourier series:

$$u(r,\theta) = \frac{a_0}{2} + \sum_{m=1}^{\infty} r^m \left[a_m \cos(m\theta) + b_m \sin(m\theta)\right],$$

or by the Poisson integral

$$u(r,\theta)=\frac{1}{2\pi}\int_0^{2\pi}\frac{a(\theta)(1-r^2)}{1-2r\cos(\alpha-\theta)+r^2}\mathrm{d}\alpha.$$

Chosen

$$a(\theta)=\sum_{m=1}^{\infty}\frac{\sin(m!\theta)}{m^2},$$

the solution of system (4.1) is given by

$$u(r,\theta)=\sum_{m=1}^{\infty} r^{m!}\,\frac{\sin(m!\theta)}{m^2}.$$

It is easily verified that the function u belongs to $C^2(\mathcal{D})\cap C(\overline{\mathcal{D}})$, but $\nabla u\notin L^2(\mathcal{D})$, so that u is not a variational solution of problem (4.1). On the other side, if one considers the cylinder

$$\varGamma=\left\{\boldsymbol{x}=(r,\theta,z)\in\mathbb{R}^3\,:\,(r,\theta)\in\mathcal{D},\,z\in\mathbb{R}\right\},$$

it is obvious that the couple $(\boldsymbol{u},\pi)$, with

$$\boldsymbol{u}=(0,0,u),\qquad \pi=\text{const}.$$

is a solution of Stokes' system (3.9) in $\varGamma$ of class $C^2(\varGamma)\cap C(\overline{\varGamma})$, corresponding to the boundary datum $\boldsymbol{a}=(0,0,a)$.

Let now Ω be the unit ball centered at $\boldsymbol{o}$. It is quite evident that a classical solution of Stokes' system (3.9) in Ω is just furnished by the couple $(\boldsymbol{u},\pi)\in[C^2(\Omega)\cap C(\overline{\Omega})]\times C^1(\Omega)$. It corresponds to the boundary datum

$$\boldsymbol{a}=(r,\theta,z)=\left(0,0,\sum_{m=1}^{\infty}\frac{(1-z^2)^{\frac{m!}{2}}}{m^2}\sin(m!\theta)\right).$$

We shall prove in the next Section that it is unique in the class $[C^2(\Omega)\cap C(\overline{\Omega})]\times C^1(\Omega)$.

We remark that $\boldsymbol{u}$ is indefinitely differentiable in Ω and, since the series expressing it is uniformly convergent together with the series of the first derivatives, one has

$$\nabla\boldsymbol{u}=\sum_{j=1}^{\infty}\frac{j!}{j^2}r^{j!-1}\left[\sin(j!\theta)\boldsymbol{e}_r+\cos(j!\theta)\boldsymbol{e}_\theta\right].$$

Hence, one can deduce at once that $\nabla \boldsymbol{u} \in L^1(\Omega)$. Let us now prove that $\nabla \boldsymbol{u} \notin L^p(\Omega)$, $\forall\, p > 1$, by showing that its radial component has not a summable p-th power. To achieve this goal, let us consider the sequence

$$\varphi_m = \sum_{j=1}^{m} \frac{j!}{j^2} r^{j!-1} \sin(j!\theta)$$

and observe that

$$|\varphi_m| \le \sum_{j=1}^{m} \frac{j!}{j^2} r^{j!-1} = \psi_n \le \psi = \sum_{j=1}^{\infty} \frac{j!}{j^2} r^{j!-1}.$$

Since ψ_n is nonnegative, monotonic and equi-bounded in $L^1(\Omega)$, one has

$$\lim_{m\to\infty} \psi_n = \psi, \qquad \lim_{m\to\infty} \int_\Omega \psi_n \mathrm{d}v = \int_\Omega \psi\, \mathrm{d}v.$$

Recall now that

$$\|\varphi\|_{L^p(\Omega)} = \sup_{v \in L^{p'}(\Omega)} \|v\|^{-1}_{L^{p'}(\Omega)} \left| \int_\Omega v\varphi\, \mathrm{d}v \right|.$$

Hence

$$\|\varphi\|_{L^p(\Omega)} \ge \|v_\mu\|^{-1}_{L^{p'}(\Omega)} \left| \int_\Omega v_\mu \varphi\, \mathrm{d}v \right|,$$

where, for any $\mu \in \mathbb{N}$, we have set

$$v_\mu = \sum_{j=1}^{\mu} \frac{(j!)^{\frac{1}{p'}}}{j^2} r^{(j!-1)/p'} \sin(j!\theta),$$

so that

$$\|v_\mu\|_{L^{p'}(\Omega)} \le \sum_{j=1}^{\infty} \frac{1}{j^2}, \ \forall\, \mu \in \mathbb{N}.$$

In a quite analogous way as for the function φ, we can prove that

$$v_\mu \varphi = \lim_{m\to\infty} v_\mu \varphi_m \quad \text{e} \quad \lim_{m\to\infty} \int_\Omega v_\mu \varphi_m \mathrm{d}v = \int_\Omega v_\mu \varphi\, \mathrm{d}v.$$

As a consequence,

$$\|v_\mu\|^{-1}_{L^{p'}(\Omega)}\int_\Omega v_\mu\varphi\,\mathrm{d}v=\|v_\mu\|^{-1}_{L^{p'}(\Omega)}\lim_{m\to\infty}\int_\Omega v_\mu\varphi_m\mathrm{d}v.$$

Since

$$\int_0^{2\pi}\sin^2(j!\theta)\mathrm{d}\theta=\pi,\ \forall\, j,\qquad \int_0^{2\pi}\sin(j!\theta)\sin(h!\theta)\mathrm{d}\theta=0,\ \forall\, j\neq h,$$

$\forall\, m\geq\mu$, one has

$$\begin{aligned}\int_\Omega v_\mu\varphi_m\mathrm{d}v&=\sum_{j=1}^{\mu}\frac{(j!)^{1+1/p'}}{j^4}\int_0^1\mathrm{d}r\int_0^{2\pi}r^{j!(1+1/p')-1/p'}\sin^2(j!\theta)\mathrm{d}\theta\\&\geq\sum_j^{\mu}\frac{(j!)^{1+1/p'}}{1/p+j!(1+1/p')\,j^4}\frac{\pi}{2}\geq\frac{\pi}{2}\sum_j^{\mu}\frac{(j!)^{1/p'}}{j^4}.\end{aligned}$$

Hence

$$\lim_{m\to\infty}\int_\Omega v_\mu\varphi_m\mathrm{d}v\geq\frac{\pi}{2}\sum_{j=1}^{\mu}\frac{(j!)^{1/p'}}{j^4}$$

and from the above relations it follows that

$$\|\varphi\|_{L^p(\Omega)}\geq\frac{\pi}{2}\sum_{j=1}^{\mu}\frac{(j!)^{1/p'}}{j^4},$$

which in turn, since μ may be arbitrarily chosen, implies $\varphi\notin L^p(\Omega)$, that is the desired conclusion.

5. Uniqueness of classical solutions to the Stokes problem

The purpose of this Section is to show that the boundary value problem associated with the Stokes system admits at most one classical solution $(\boldsymbol{u}(\boldsymbol{x}),\pi(\boldsymbol{x}))$ in the class $(C^2(\Omega)\cap C(\overline{\Omega}))\times C^1(\Omega)$. To this end we need three preliminary lemmas.

Lemma 5.1. *Let $g(t)$ be a C^1 function in the interval $(0,a]$ and assume that*

$$\lim_{t\to0^+}[t^\alpha g'(t)]=0,\tag{5.1}$$

for some $\alpha > 1$*. Then*

$$\lim_{t\to 0+}\left[t^{\alpha-1}g(t)\right] = 0.$$

PROOF - In virtue of (5.1), we have that the for any positive ϵ

$$-\frac{\epsilon}{t^{\alpha}} < g'(t) < \frac{\epsilon}{t^{\alpha}}, \quad \forall t \in (0,\bar{t}),$$

for some positive $\bar{t}(\epsilon)$. Hence, integrating over (t,t_0) with $t_0 < \bar{t}$, it follows that

$$-\frac{\epsilon}{1-\alpha}\left(\frac{1}{t_0^{\alpha-1}} - \frac{1}{t^{1-\alpha}}\right) < g(t_0) - g(t) < \frac{\epsilon}{1-\alpha}\left(\frac{1}{t_0^{\alpha-1}} - \frac{1}{t^{\alpha-1}}\right).$$

Therefore .

$$-\frac{\epsilon}{\alpha-1}\left[1-\left(\frac{t}{t_0}\right)^{\alpha-1}\right] < t^{\alpha-1}\left[g(t)-g(t_0)\right] < \frac{\epsilon}{\alpha-1}\left[1-\left(\frac{t}{t_0}\right)^{\alpha-1}\right].$$

so that

$$-\frac{\epsilon}{\alpha-1} < \lim_{t\to 0}\left[t^{\alpha-1}g(t)\right] < \frac{\epsilon}{\alpha-1}.$$

Hence, since ϵ is an arbitrary positive number, the desired result follows at once. □

In Lemma 5.1 we confined ourselves to consider the case $\alpha > 1$. However, it is easy to prove that the lemma holds for any $\alpha \neq 1$.

Lemma 5.2. *Let* φ *be a biharmonic function, i.e. a solution to the equation*

$$\Delta_2\varphi = \varphi_{,iijj} = 0.$$

Then

$$\varphi(\boldsymbol{x}) = \frac{3}{2\pi R^3}\int_{S_R(\boldsymbol{x})}\varphi(\boldsymbol{y})\left[5 - \frac{6|\boldsymbol{y}-\boldsymbol{x}|}{R}\right]\mathrm{d}v_{\boldsymbol{y}}, \tag{5.2}$$

for any $\boldsymbol{x} \in \Omega$ *and for any* R *such that* $R < \operatorname{dist}(\boldsymbol{x},\partial\Omega)$.

Lemma 5.2 is proved in [46].

Let

$$T(u,\pi) = -\pi \mathbf{1} + 2\mu\hat{\nabla} u$$

be the stress tensor associated with a classical solution to system (3.1), where $\mathbf{1}$ and μ denote the unit tensor and the viscosity coefficient respectively.

Lemma 5.3. *Let (u,π) be a classical solution to system (3.9), with $u = \mathbf{0}$ on $\partial\Omega$. Let ξ be a point of $\partial\Omega$ and let $l(\xi)$ be a unit vector such that $l(\xi)\cdot n(\xi) \geq \alpha_0 > 0$ and $\xi - tl(\xi) \in \Omega$, for any $t \in [0,d)$. Then,*

$$\begin{aligned} &\lim_{t\to 0} t\pi(\xi - tl(\xi)) = 0, \\ &\lim_{t\to 0} t\nabla u(\xi - tl(\xi)) = \mathbf{0}, \end{aligned} \tag{5.3}$$

uniformly in $\xi \in \partial\Omega$, so that $\lim_{t\to 0} tT(u(\xi - tl(\xi))), \pi(\xi - tl(\xi)) = \mathbf{0}$, uniformly in $\xi \in \partial\Omega$.

Proof - Following [34], fix a direction $l(\xi)$ (see figure). Let

$$0 < \alpha_0 \leq \cos\theta = l(\xi)\cdot n(\xi), \quad z = \xi - \zeta n(\xi),$$

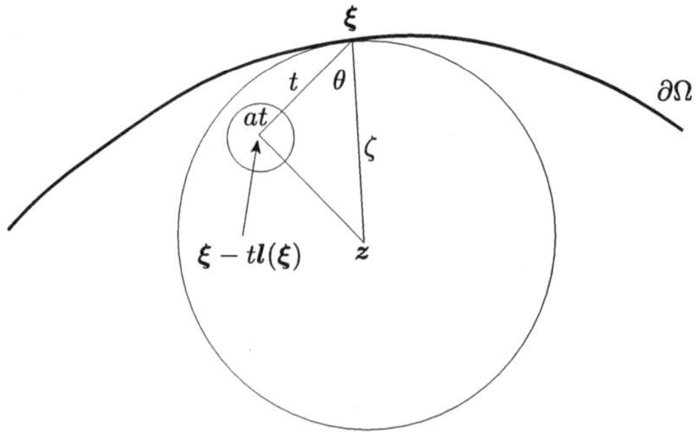

with $\zeta > 0$ such that the ball $S_\zeta(z)$ is contained on Ω and tangent to $\partial\Omega$ at ξ. Let t be a positive number such that the point

$$\eta(t) = \xi - tl(\xi) \in S_\zeta(z).$$

The ball $S_{at}(\boldsymbol{\eta}(t))$, with

$$a \in (0, \cos\theta), \quad t \in \left(0, \zeta\big(\cos\theta - \frac{a\sin\theta}{\sqrt{1-a^2}}\big)\right],$$

is contained in $S_\zeta(\boldsymbol{z})$. Indeed, to be convinced of this, it is sufficient to consider the function

$$\zeta - (t^2 + \zeta^2 - 2t\zeta\cos\theta)^{\frac{1}{2}} - at,$$

which represents the distance of $S_{at}(\boldsymbol{\eta}(t))$ from $\partial S_\zeta(\boldsymbol{z})$, and to note that it vanishes at $t = 0$, its first derivative is positive at $t = 0$ with $a \in (0, \cos\theta)$ and assumes its maximum value at

$$\bar{t} = \zeta\left(\cos\theta - \frac{a\sin\theta}{\sqrt{1-a^2}}\right).$$

Let $\boldsymbol{h}$ be the harmonic function in $S_{at}(\boldsymbol{\eta}(t))$ which assumes the value $\tilde{\boldsymbol{u}} = \boldsymbol{u}$ at $\partial S_{at}(\boldsymbol{\eta}(t))$. Of course, the function $\boldsymbol{b} = \boldsymbol{u} - \boldsymbol{h}$ is biharmonic in $S_{at}(\boldsymbol{\eta}(t))$ and vanishes at $\partial S_{at}(\boldsymbol{\eta}(t))$. Then, from (5.2), integrating by parts, it follows that

$$\boldsymbol{b}_{,k}(\boldsymbol{x})_{x=\eta(t)} = -\frac{9}{\pi a^4 t^4}\int_{S_{at}(\eta(t))} \frac{\boldsymbol{b}(\boldsymbol{y})(y_k - \eta_k(t))}{|\boldsymbol{y} - \boldsymbol{\eta}(t)|} dv. \tag{5.4}$$

Since $\Delta\boldsymbol{b} = \Delta\boldsymbol{u}$, by iterating (5.4), we have that

$$\begin{aligned} |\Delta\boldsymbol{u}|_{x=\eta(t)} &= \left[\frac{c(a)}{t^4}\max_{S_{at}(\eta(t))}|\boldsymbol{b}|\right]\int_{S_{at}(\eta(t))}\frac{1}{|\boldsymbol{y} - \boldsymbol{\eta}(t)|}dv \\ &\le \frac{1}{t^2}c\max_{S_{at}(\eta(t))}|\boldsymbol{b}|. \end{aligned} \tag{5.5}$$

Also

$$\begin{aligned} \max_{S_{at}(\eta(t))}|\boldsymbol{b}| &\le \max_{S_{at}(\eta(t))}|\boldsymbol{h}(\boldsymbol{x}) - \boldsymbol{u}(\boldsymbol{\xi})| + \max_{S_{at}(\eta(t))}|\boldsymbol{u}(\boldsymbol{x}) - \boldsymbol{u}(\boldsymbol{\xi})| \\ &\le \max_{|y-\eta(t)|=at}|\tilde{\boldsymbol{u}}(\boldsymbol{y}) - \boldsymbol{u}(\boldsymbol{\xi})| + \max_{S_{at}(\eta(t))}|\boldsymbol{u}(\boldsymbol{x}) - \boldsymbol{u}(\boldsymbol{\xi})|. \end{aligned} \tag{5.6}$$

Then, taking into account the uniform continuity of $\boldsymbol{u}$, (5.5) and (5.6) imply that

$$\lim_{t\to 0}\left[t^2\Delta\boldsymbol{u}(\boldsymbol{\eta}(t))\right] = \boldsymbol{0}, \tag{5.7}$$

uniformly with respect to $\boldsymbol{\xi} \in \partial\Omega$.

As far as the pressure field is concerned, we first observe that (3.1) and (5.7) yield

$$\lim_{t\to 0}\left[t^2\nabla\pi(\boldsymbol{\eta}(t))\right] = \mathbf{0}, \tag{5.8}$$

uniformly with respect to $\boldsymbol{\xi}$. Then, (5.8) yields

$$\lim_{t\to 0}\left[t^2\boldsymbol{l}(\boldsymbol{\xi})\cdot\nabla\pi(\boldsymbol{\eta}(t))\right] = \lim_{t\to 0}\left[t^2\frac{\mathrm{d}}{\mathrm{d}t}\pi(\boldsymbol{\eta}(t))\right] = 0.$$

Therefore, by taking into account Lemma 5.1, we get $(5.3)_1$.

To complete the proof of Lemma 5.3, we should prove $(5.3)_2$. Since the technique to be used to get this result is quite similar to that employed to derive (5.5), we refer to [34], where this approach has been introduced. □

We are now in a position to prove the following *uniqueness theorem.*

Theorem 5.1. *Let Ω be a bounded or an exterior domain. Then, the boundary value problem associated with the Stokes system admits at most one classical solution in $[C^2(\Omega)\cap C(\overline{\Omega})]\times C^1(\Omega)$.*

PROOF - Assume first that Ω is a bounded domain. Let $\boldsymbol{b}\in C_0(\Omega)$ and denote by $(\boldsymbol{\varphi},\varpi)\in W^{2,p}(\Omega)\times W^{1,p}(\Omega)$ $(p>3)$ the unique variational solution to the system (cf. Theorem 3.1)

$$\begin{aligned} \Delta\boldsymbol{\varphi}+\boldsymbol{b} &= \nabla\varpi && \text{in } \Omega,\\ \operatorname{div}\boldsymbol{\varphi} &= 0 && \text{in } \Omega,\\ \boldsymbol{\varphi} &= \mathbf{0} && \text{on } \partial\Omega. \end{aligned} \tag{5.9}$$

Multiply system $(5.9)_1$ scalarly by a solution $\boldsymbol{u}\in[C^2(\Omega)\cap C(\overline{\Omega})]\times C^1(\Omega)$ to the homogeneous Stokes system

$$\begin{aligned} \Delta\boldsymbol{u} &= \nabla\pi && \text{in } \Omega,\\ \operatorname{div}\boldsymbol{u} &= 0 && \text{in } \Omega,\\ \boldsymbol{u} &= \mathbf{0} && \text{on } \partial\Omega. \end{aligned} \tag{5.10}$$

Then, integrating by parts over

$$\Omega_m = \left\{ \boldsymbol{x} \in \Omega \,:\, \operatorname{dist}(\boldsymbol{x}, \partial\Omega) \geq \frac{1}{m},\ m \in \mathbb{N} \right\}, \tag{5.11}$$

we have

$$\int_{\Omega_m} \boldsymbol{u} \cdot \boldsymbol{b} \, \mathrm{d}v = -\int_{\partial\Omega_m} \boldsymbol{u} \cdot \boldsymbol{T}(\boldsymbol{\varphi}, \varpi)\boldsymbol{n} \, \mathrm{d}\sigma + \int_{\partial\Omega_m} \boldsymbol{\varphi} \cdot \boldsymbol{T}(\boldsymbol{u}, \pi)\boldsymbol{n} \, \mathrm{d}\sigma. \tag{5.12}$$

Recall that, in virtue of Sobolev's imbedding theorem,

$$(\boldsymbol{\varphi}, \varpi) \in C^1(\overline{\Omega}) \times C(\overline{\Omega})$$

so that

$$|\boldsymbol{\varphi}(\boldsymbol{x})| \leq c|\boldsymbol{x} - \boldsymbol{\xi}|, \quad \forall\, (\boldsymbol{x}, \boldsymbol{\xi}) \in \Omega \times \partial\Omega \,:\, \boldsymbol{x} + \lambda(\boldsymbol{\xi} - \boldsymbol{x}) \in \Omega, \forall \lambda \in [0,1]. \tag{5.13}$$

Hence, in virtue of the continuity of $\boldsymbol{u}$ and $\boldsymbol{T}(\boldsymbol{\varphi}, \varpi)$ in $\overline{\Omega}$, it follows that

$$\lim_{m\to\infty} \int_{\partial\Omega_m} \boldsymbol{u} \cdot \boldsymbol{T}(\boldsymbol{\varphi}, \varpi)\boldsymbol{n} \, \mathrm{d}\sigma = 0.$$

Now, taking into account (5.13), from Lemma 5.3 we have that

$$\lim_{m\to\infty} \int_{\partial\Omega_m} \boldsymbol{\varphi} \cdot \boldsymbol{T}(\boldsymbol{u}, \pi)\boldsymbol{n} \, \mathrm{d}\sigma = 0.$$

so that

$$\int_{\Omega} \boldsymbol{u} \cdot \boldsymbol{b} \, \mathrm{d}v = 0, \quad \forall \boldsymbol{b} \in C_0(\Omega).$$

Hence the desired result follows at once.

Let Ω be an exterior domain. We have to show that, if $(\boldsymbol{u}, \pi)$ is a classical solution to system (5.10) satisfying the condition at infinity

$$\lim_{r(\boldsymbol{x})\to\infty} \boldsymbol{u}(\boldsymbol{x}) = \boldsymbol{0}, \tag{5.14}$$

then $\boldsymbol{u} \equiv \boldsymbol{0}$. To this end, let $\boldsymbol{v}$ be the variational solution to system (3.9) in Ω_R, with $R \gg \operatorname{diam}(\mathbb{R}^3 \setminus \Omega)$, corresponding to the boundary conditions

$$\boldsymbol{v} = \boldsymbol{0} \qquad \text{on } \partial\Omega,$$

$$\boldsymbol{v} = \boldsymbol{u} \qquad \text{on } \partial S_R.$$

In virtue of the just proved uniqueness of classical solutions to Stokes' system in bounded domains, we see that $\boldsymbol{u} \equiv \boldsymbol{v}$ so that $\nabla\boldsymbol{u} \in L^2(\Omega_R)$. On the other hand, $\boldsymbol{u}$ is biharmonic in Ω and infinitesimal at infinity so that by classical results (cf, *e.g.*, [42]) we have that $\nabla\boldsymbol{u} = O(r^{-2})$ at large spatial distance. As a consequence, $\nabla\boldsymbol{u} \in L^2(\Omega)$ and $\boldsymbol{u}$ is a variational solution to system (5.10), (5.14). Finally, on appealing to the uniqueness of variational solutions (cf. Theorem 3.1), we conclude that $\boldsymbol{u} \equiv \boldsymbol{0}$. □

Remark 5.1 – It is worth noting that the uniqueness problem of classical solutions to the Stokes problem has been approached by means of very different arguments in the plane case and in the three dimensional case, or, more generally, for any $n > 2$. Indeed, in the two–dimensional case the question is reduced to the well–known uniqueness problem of classical solutions to the Dirichlet problem associated with the biharmonic equation (cf., *e.g.*, [37]). For the sake of completeness we propose a simple and direct proof of uniqueness of classical solutions to the Stokes problem for bounded plane domains. Denote by $\psi(x, y)$ the *stream function* associated with the homogeneous Stokes system. Of course, since

$$u_x = \frac{\partial \psi}{\partial y}, \quad u_y = -\frac{\partial \psi}{\partial x},$$

ψ turns out to be a solution of class $C^4(\Omega) \cap C^1(\overline{\Omega})$ to the problem

$$\begin{aligned} \Delta_2 \psi = 0 \quad & \text{in } \Omega, \\ \psi = c_i \quad & \text{on } \partial\Omega, \\ \boldsymbol{n} \cdot \nabla \psi = 0 \quad & \text{in } \partial\Omega, \end{aligned} \tag{5.15}$$

where c_i are $m + 1$ constants.

Denote by $\overline{\psi} \in W^{2,p}(\Omega)$ a variational solution to system (5.15) (cf., *e.g.*, [49]). Since $\overline{\psi} \in C^4(\Omega) \cap C^1(\overline{\Omega})$, the maximum modulus theorem by C. Miranda [37] assures that $\psi = \overline{\psi}$. Then $D^2\psi \in L^p(\Omega)$ so that $\nabla \boldsymbol{u} \in L^p(\Omega)$. Hence the desired result follows from the uniqueness theorem about variational solutions (Theorem 3.1).

6. The maximum Modulus Theorem in exterior domain and the half–space

The aim of this Section is to prove the *maximum modulus theorem* for classical solutions to system (3.1), (3.3), (3.6) in exterior domains. To this end we have to recall some results in form of lemmas [1] .

[1] We have been informed of a proof of the maximum modulus theorem, presented by prof. W. Varnhorn at the *International Conference on Applied Analysis* (Lisbon – february 26 to march 1, 1997), which will appear in a paper joinly written by him and prof. G.P. Galdi.

Lemma 6.1. *Let Ω be bounded and let $\boldsymbol{a} \in C(\partial\Omega)$ satisfy (3.2). Then, there exists a unique classical solution $(\boldsymbol{u}, \pi)$ to system (3.9), (3.3) such that*

$$\|\boldsymbol{u}\|_{C(\overline{\Omega})} \le c\|\boldsymbol{a}\|_{C(\partial\Omega)}, \tag{6.1}$$

where c is a positive constant independent of $\boldsymbol{u}$ and $\boldsymbol{a}$.

The existence of a classical solution satisfying (6.1) has been proved in [34]. Of course, in virtue of Theorem 5.1, this solution is unique in $[C^2(\Omega) \cap C(\overline{\Omega})] \times C^1(\Omega)$.

Lemma 6.2. *Let $(\boldsymbol{u}, \pi) \in W^{1,2}(\Omega)$ be a variational solution to system (3.9). Then, $\forall\, \boldsymbol{x}_o \in \Omega$, $\forall R < \frac{1}{2}\mathrm{dist}\,(\boldsymbol{x}_o, \partial\Omega)$,*

$$\int_{S_R(\boldsymbol{x}_o)} (\nabla \boldsymbol{u})^2 \mathrm{d}v \le \frac{c}{R^2} \int_{S_{2R}(\boldsymbol{x}_o)} \boldsymbol{u}^2 \mathrm{d}v, \tag{6.2}$$

where c is a positive constant independent of $\boldsymbol{u}$ and invariant under dilation, rotation and translation. In particular, since any derivative of $(\boldsymbol{u}, \pi)$ is a solution to system (3.9), we have

$$\|D^\beta \boldsymbol{u}\|^2_{L^2(S_R(\boldsymbol{x}_o))} \le \frac{c}{R^{2k}} \|\boldsymbol{u}\|^2_{L^2(S_{(k+1)R}(\boldsymbol{x}_o))}. \tag{6.3}$$

for any multi–index β and for any radius R such that $|\beta| = k$ and $R < \frac{1}{k+1}\mathrm{dist}(\boldsymbol{x}_o, \partial\Omega)$.

Proof - Let $\eta \in C_0^\infty(S_{2R}(\boldsymbol{x}_o))$ be a cut–off function in $S_{2R}(\boldsymbol{x}_o)$ such that

$$\eta(\boldsymbol{x}) = 1, \forall\, \boldsymbol{x} \in S_R(\boldsymbol{x}_o), \quad |\nabla \eta| \le \frac{c}{R}, \quad |\nabla\nabla\eta| \le \frac{c}{R^2},$$

where the constants c are independent of R and $\boldsymbol{x}_o$. In virtue of Lemma 2.1, equation (2.2) admits a solution $\boldsymbol{\psi} \in W_0^{2,2}(S_{2R}(\boldsymbol{x}_o))$ corresponding to $f = -\boldsymbol{u} \cdot \nabla \eta^2$. Then, setting $\boldsymbol{\varphi} = \eta^2 \boldsymbol{u} + \boldsymbol{\psi}$ in (3.4), written with $\boldsymbol{f} = \boldsymbol{0}$ and $\Omega = S_{2R}(\boldsymbol{x}_o)$, we have that

$$\begin{aligned} \int_{S_{2R}(\boldsymbol{x}_o)} (\eta \nabla \boldsymbol{u})^2 \mathrm{d}v = & \int_{S_{2R}(\boldsymbol{x}_o)} \boldsymbol{u} \cdot \Delta \boldsymbol{\psi}\, \mathrm{d}v \\ & + 2 \int_{S_{2R}(\boldsymbol{x}_o)} \left[\eta \Delta \eta + (\nabla \eta)^2\right] \boldsymbol{u}^2 \mathrm{d}v. \end{aligned} \tag{6.4}$$

In virtue of the arithmetic–geometric mean inequality, we have

$$\left|\int_{S_{2R}(\boldsymbol{x}_0)} \boldsymbol{u}\cdot\Delta\boldsymbol{\psi}\,dv\right| \le \frac{1}{\xi R^2}\|\boldsymbol{u}\|^2_{L^2(S_{2R}(\boldsymbol{x}_0))} + \xi R^2\|\Delta\boldsymbol{\psi}\|^2_{L^2(S_{2R}(\boldsymbol{x}_0))}, \tag{6.5}$$

for any $\xi > 0$. On the other hand, from (2.3), by making use of the inequality $(\alpha+\beta+\gamma)^2 \le 3(\alpha^2+\beta^2+\gamma^2)$, it follows that

$$\begin{aligned}\|\Delta\boldsymbol{\psi}\|^2_{L^2(S_{2R}(\boldsymbol{x}_0))} &\le c\|\nabla(\boldsymbol{u}\cdot\nabla\eta^2)\|^2_{L^2(S_{2R}(\boldsymbol{x}_0))} \le c\|\eta(\nabla\boldsymbol{u})\nabla\eta\|^2_{L^2(S_{2R}(\boldsymbol{x}_0))}\\ &\quad + \|(\nabla\eta)^2\boldsymbol{u}\|^2_{L^2(S_{2R}(\boldsymbol{x}_0))} + \|\eta(\nabla\nabla\eta)\boldsymbol{u}\|^2_{L^2(S_{2R}(\boldsymbol{x}_0))}\\ &\le \frac{c}{R^4}\left\{\|\boldsymbol{u}\|^2_{L^2(S_{2R}(\boldsymbol{x}_0))} + R^2\|\eta\nabla\boldsymbol{u}\|^2_{L^2(S_{2R}(\boldsymbol{x}_0))}\right\},\end{aligned} \tag{6.6}$$

where the constants c are independent of R and $\boldsymbol{x}_o$ (see Remark 2.1). Finally, (6.2) follows from (6.4), (6.5) and (6.6), by choosing properly ξ and taking into account the properties of the function η. □

Relation (6.2) is known as *Caccioppoli's inequality*. For elliptic systems of the Stokes type it has been proved in [17]. Following the argument lines of [17] we have reproduced the proof for Stokes's system because of its simplicity.

Lemma 6.3. *Let Ω be an exterior domain and let $\boldsymbol{u}$ be a classical solution to system (3.9). Then, for any $p > 3$,*

$$\|\boldsymbol{u}\|_{L^p(\Omega)} \le c\|\boldsymbol{u}\|_{C(\partial\Omega)}, \tag{6.7}$$

where c is a positive constant independent of $\boldsymbol{u}$.

Lemma 6.3 is proved in [35] (lemma 4.1).

We are now in a position to prove the maximum modulus theorem for the Stokes system in exterior domains.

Theorem 6.1. *Let Ω be an exterior domain and let $\boldsymbol{a} \in C(\partial\Omega)$. Then, there exists a unique classical solution to the system*

$$\begin{aligned}\Delta\boldsymbol{u} &= \nabla\pi \quad \text{in } \Omega,\\ \operatorname{div}\boldsymbol{u} &= 0 \quad \text{in } \Omega,\\ \boldsymbol{u} &= \boldsymbol{a} \quad \text{on } \partial\Omega,\\ \lim_{r(\boldsymbol{x})\to\infty}\boldsymbol{u}(\boldsymbol{x}) &= \boldsymbol{0},\end{aligned} \tag{6.8}$$

such that

$$\|\boldsymbol{u}\|_{C^k(\overline{\Omega}_\delta)} \le c(k,\delta)\|\boldsymbol{a}\|_{C(\partial\Omega)}, \tag{6.9}$$

where $\Omega_\delta = \{\boldsymbol{x} \in \Omega : \operatorname{dist}(\boldsymbol{x}, \partial\Omega) > \delta\}$ *and* $c(\delta) \to +\infty$ *as* $\delta \to 0^+$. *Moreover*

$$\|\boldsymbol{u}\|_{C(\overline{\Omega})} \le c\|\boldsymbol{a}\|_{C(\partial\Omega)}. \tag{6.10}$$

PROOF - Assume first that $\boldsymbol{a} \in C^1(\partial\Omega)$. Then, in virtue of Theorem 3.1, system (6.8) admits a unique variational solution $(\boldsymbol{u}, \pi)$ which belongs to $C^\infty(\Omega)\times C^\infty(\Omega)$.

By making use of Sobolev's imbedding theorem and Caccioppoli's inequality (6.1) one proves the *Campanato inequality* [6]

$$\|\boldsymbol{u}\|^2_{L^2(S_\rho(\boldsymbol{x}))} \le c\left(\frac{\rho}{R}\right)^3 \|\boldsymbol{u}\|^2_{L^2(S_R(\boldsymbol{x}))}, \quad \forall\, \rho < R < \delta, \tag{6.11}$$

where the constant c is independent of $\boldsymbol{x}$, ρ and R. Bearing in mind that the spaces $L^{2,3}$ and L^∞ are isomorphic, choosing $R = \delta/2$ and by applying the Schwarz–Hölder inequality at the right hand side of (6.11), we have

$$|\boldsymbol{u}(\boldsymbol{x})|^2 \le c\delta^{-\frac{6}{p}}\|\boldsymbol{u}\|^2_{L^p(S_\delta(\boldsymbol{x}))},$$

for any $p > 3$. Hence, in virtue of (6.7), it follows that

$$\|\boldsymbol{u}\|_{C(\overline{\Omega}_\delta)} \le c\delta^{-\frac{3}{p}}\|\boldsymbol{a}\|_{C(\partial\Omega)}.$$

Finally, since any derivatives of $(\boldsymbol{u}, \pi)$ is a solution to system $(6.8)_{1,2}$, we obtain inequality (6.9) by repeating the above reasoning and making use of (6.3), (6.11).

Let $S_{R^*} \supset \partial\Omega$, with R^* sufficiently large, and let $(\boldsymbol{v}, \varpi)$ be the classical solution to the Stokes system

$$\begin{aligned} \Delta \boldsymbol{v} &= \nabla\pi && \text{in } S_{R^*}\cap\Omega,\\ \operatorname{div}\boldsymbol{v} &= 0 && \text{in } S_{R^*}\cap\Omega,\\ \boldsymbol{v} &= \boldsymbol{a} && \text{on } \partial\Omega,\\ \boldsymbol{v} &= \boldsymbol{u} && \text{on } \partial\Omega_{R^*}. \end{aligned}$$

Since $\boldsymbol{u}$ is continuous on ∂S_{R^*}, in virtue of Lemma 6.1, $\boldsymbol{v}$ satisfies the estimate

$$\|\boldsymbol{v}\|_{C(\overline{S}_{R^*}\cap\overline{\Omega})} \leq c\left\{\|\boldsymbol{u}\|_{C(\partial S_{R^*})} + \|\boldsymbol{a}\|_{C(\partial\Omega)}\right\}.$$

Hence, taking into account (6.9), it follows that

$$\|\boldsymbol{v}\|_{C(\overline{S}_{R^*}\cap\overline{\Omega})} \leq c\|\boldsymbol{a}\|_{C(\partial\Omega)}.$$

On appealing to Theorem 5.1, we see that $\boldsymbol{u} = \boldsymbol{v}$ in Ω_{R^*} so that

$$\|\boldsymbol{u}\|_{C(\overline{S}_{R^*}\cap\overline{\Omega})} \leq c\|\boldsymbol{a}\|_{C(\partial\Omega)}. \tag{6.12}$$

then, coupling (6.9) with (6.12) we have (6.10). Observe, by the way, that the constant c in (6.10) is independent of the regularity hypothesis made on $\boldsymbol{a}$.

Assume now $\boldsymbol{a} \in C(\partial\Omega)$. Then there exists a sequence $\{\boldsymbol{a}_n\}_{n\in\mathbb{N}}$, with $\{\boldsymbol{a}_n\} \in C^1(\partial\Omega)$, which converges to $\boldsymbol{a}$ in $C(\partial\Omega)$. Denote by $\{(\boldsymbol{u}_n, \pi_n)\}_{n\in\mathbb{N}}$ the sequence of classical solutions to system (6.8) corresponding to the boundary data $\{\boldsymbol{a}_n\}_{n\in\mathbb{N}}$. Then, from (6.9), (6.10) we get

$$\begin{aligned}\|\boldsymbol{u}_n - \boldsymbol{u}_m\|_{C(\overline{\Omega})} &\leq c\|\boldsymbol{a}_n - \boldsymbol{a}_m\|_{C(\partial\Omega)},\\ \|\boldsymbol{u}_n - \boldsymbol{u}_m\|_{C^2(\overline{\Omega}')} &\leq c(\Omega', \Omega)\|\boldsymbol{a}_n - \boldsymbol{a}_m\|_{C(\partial\Omega)}, \quad \forall\,\Omega' \subset\subset \Omega,\end{aligned}$$

and, taking into account $(6.8)_1$,

$$\|\nabla\pi_n - \nabla\pi_m\|_{C(\overline{\Omega}')} \leq c(\Omega', \Omega)\|\boldsymbol{a}_n - \boldsymbol{a}_m\|_{C(\partial\Omega)},$$

so that $(\boldsymbol{u}_n, \pi_n)$ is a Cauchy sequence in $[C^2(\Omega)\cap C(\overline{\Omega})]\times C^1(\Omega)$ which converges to the desired classical solution $(\boldsymbol{u}, \pi)$. Finally, $(\boldsymbol{u}, \pi)$ is unique in virtue of Theorem 5.1. □

Assume now Ω to be the half–space $\mathbb{R}^3_+$, $\boldsymbol{f} \equiv \boldsymbol{0}$ and $\boldsymbol{a} \in L^\infty(\mathbb{R}^2) \cap C(\mathbb{R}^2)$, and set $\boldsymbol{x}' = (x_1, x_2, 0)$ Then, system (3.1), (3.3) admits the classical solution [40] (cf. [16] vol. I, p.192)

$$\begin{aligned}\boldsymbol{u}(\boldsymbol{x}) &= \frac{3x_3}{2\pi}\int_{\mathbb{R}^2}\frac{[\boldsymbol{a}(\boldsymbol{y}')\cdot(\boldsymbol{x}-\boldsymbol{y}')](\boldsymbol{x}-\boldsymbol{y}')}{|\boldsymbol{x}-\boldsymbol{y}'|^5}\mathrm{d}\sigma_{\boldsymbol{y}'},\\ \pi(\boldsymbol{x}) &= -\frac{x_3}{\pi}\frac{\partial}{\partial x_j}\int_{\mathbb{R}^2}\frac{a_j(\boldsymbol{y}')}{|\boldsymbol{x}-\boldsymbol{y}'|^3}\mathrm{d}\sigma_{\boldsymbol{y}'},\end{aligned} \tag{6.13}$$

Observe that this solution is unique in the class (cf., *e.g*, [23])

$$\mathfrak{I} = \left\{ \boldsymbol{u} \in C^2(\Omega) \cap C(\overline{\Omega}) \, : \, \lim_{r(\boldsymbol{x})\to\infty} \frac{\boldsymbol{u}(\boldsymbol{x})}{r(\boldsymbol{x})} = \boldsymbol{0} \right\}.$$

From (6.13) we have

$$\boldsymbol{u}^2(\boldsymbol{x}) \le \frac{3x_3}{2\pi} \|\boldsymbol{a}\|_{L^\infty(\mathbb{R}^2)} |\boldsymbol{u}(\boldsymbol{x})| \int_{\mathbb{R}^3} \frac{1}{|\boldsymbol{x}-\boldsymbol{y}'|^3} \mathrm{d}\sigma_{\boldsymbol{y}'}.$$

Hence, computing the integral, it follows that

$$|\boldsymbol{u}(\boldsymbol{x})| \le 3\|\boldsymbol{a}\|_{L^\infty(\mathbb{R}^2)}, \qquad \forall \boldsymbol{x} \in \overline{\mathbb{R}}^3_+. \tag{6.14}$$

Estimate (6.14) allows us to prove the following

Theorem 6.2. *Let Ω be the half–space $\mathbb{R}^3_+$. If*

$$\lim_{r(\boldsymbol{y}')\to\infty} \boldsymbol{a}(\boldsymbol{y}') = \boldsymbol{0}, \tag{6.15}$$

then system (3.9)*, admits a unique classical solution $\boldsymbol{u} \in \mathfrak{I}$ and*

$$\begin{aligned} &\lim_{r(\boldsymbol{x})\to\infty} \boldsymbol{u}(\boldsymbol{x}) = \boldsymbol{0}, \\ &\max_{\overline{\mathbb{R}}^3} |\boldsymbol{u}| \le 3 \max_{\mathbb{R}^2} |\boldsymbol{a}|. \end{aligned} \tag{6.16}$$

Proof - Consider the sequence

$$\boldsymbol{a}_n(\boldsymbol{y}') = \boldsymbol{a}(\boldsymbol{y}') \left(\frac{1}{r(\boldsymbol{y}')+1} \right)^{\frac{1}{n}}$$

which uniformly converges to $\boldsymbol{a}(\boldsymbol{y}')$ in $\mathbb{R}^2$. Indeed, taking into account (6.15), we have that $|\boldsymbol{a}(\boldsymbol{y}')| < \epsilon$, $\forall \boldsymbol{y}' : r(\boldsymbol{y}') > R_\epsilon$, so that, $\forall n > [R_\epsilon/2\epsilon] + 1$,

$$|\boldsymbol{a}_n(\boldsymbol{y}') - \boldsymbol{a}(\boldsymbol{y}')| \le \begin{cases} 2\epsilon & r(\boldsymbol{y}') > R_\epsilon, \\ 1 - \left(\frac{1}{r(\boldsymbol{y}')+1} \right)^{\frac{1}{n}} < \frac{1}{n} < 2\epsilon & r(\boldsymbol{y}') \le R_\epsilon. \end{cases}$$

Let $\{(\boldsymbol{u}_n(\boldsymbol{x}), \pi(\boldsymbol{x}))\}_{n\in\mathbb{N}}$ be the sequence of classical solution corresponding to the data sequence $\{\boldsymbol{a}_n(\boldsymbol{y}')\}_{n\in\mathbb{N}}$. In virtue of $(6.13)_1$ and the construction of the sequence $\{\boldsymbol{a}_n\}_{n\in\mathbb{N}}$, we have that

$$|\boldsymbol{u}_n(\boldsymbol{x})| \le c\, [r(\boldsymbol{x})]^{-\frac{1}{n}}. \tag{6.17}$$

Indeed

$$|\boldsymbol{u}_n(\boldsymbol{x})| \le c \left\{ \int_{\{y' : r(y') \le r(x)/2\}} \frac{x_3}{(\boldsymbol{x}-\boldsymbol{y}')^3} \left(\frac{1}{r(\boldsymbol{y}')+1}\right)^{\frac{1}{n}} \mathrm{d}\sigma_{\boldsymbol{y}'}, \right.$$

$$\left. + \int_{\{y' : r(y') \ge r(x)/2\}} \frac{x_3}{(\boldsymbol{x}-\boldsymbol{y}')^3} \left(\frac{1}{r(\boldsymbol{y}')+1}\right)^{\frac{1}{n}} \mathrm{d}\sigma_{\boldsymbol{y}'} \right\} = I_1 + I_2.$$

Since, for any couple $(\boldsymbol{x}, \boldsymbol{y}')$ such that $r(\boldsymbol{y}') < r(\boldsymbol{x})/2$, $|\boldsymbol{x}-\boldsymbol{y}'| = r^2(\boldsymbol{x}) + r^2(\boldsymbol{y}') - 2(\boldsymbol{x}-\boldsymbol{o})\cdot(\boldsymbol{y}'-\boldsymbol{o}) \ge [r(\boldsymbol{x}) - r(\boldsymbol{y}')]^2 \ge r^2(\boldsymbol{x})/4$, we see that

$$I_1 \le \frac{c x_3}{r^3(\boldsymbol{x})} \int_{\{y' : r(y') \le r(x)/2\}} \left(\frac{1}{r(\boldsymbol{y}')+1}\right)^{\frac{1}{n}} \mathrm{d}\sigma_{\boldsymbol{y}'} \le c\,[r(\boldsymbol{x})]^{-\frac{1}{n}},$$

$$I_2 \le c \left(\frac{1}{r(\boldsymbol{x})+1}\right)^{\frac{1}{n}} \int_{\{y' : r(y') \ge r(x)/2\}} \frac{x_3}{(\boldsymbol{x}-\boldsymbol{y}')^3} \mathrm{d}\sigma_{\boldsymbol{y}'} \le c\,[r(\boldsymbol{x})]^{-\frac{1}{n}}.$$

Hence (6.17) follows.

Now, by (6.14) and the linearity of the Stokes system we have that

$$\max_{\overline{\mathbb{R}}^3} |\boldsymbol{u}_n - \boldsymbol{u}_m| \le 3 \max_{\mathbb{R}^2} |\boldsymbol{a}_n - \boldsymbol{a}_m|,$$

$$\|\boldsymbol{u}_n - \boldsymbol{u}_m\|_{C^2(\overline{\Omega}')} \le c(\Omega') \max_{\mathbb{R}^2} |\boldsymbol{a}_n - \boldsymbol{a}_m|,$$

$$\|\nabla\pi_n - \nabla\pi_m\|_{C(\overline{\Omega}')} \le c(\Omega') \max_{\mathbb{R}^2} |\boldsymbol{a}_n - \boldsymbol{a}_m|,$$

for any $\Omega' \subset\subset \mathbb{R}^3_+$, so that $(\boldsymbol{u}_n, \pi_n)$ converges in $[L^\infty(\mathbb{R}^3_+) \cap C^2(\mathbb{R}^3_+) \cap C(\overline{\mathbb{R}}^3_+)] \times C^1(\mathbb{R}^3)$ to a classical solution to Stokes'problem which, in virtue of the uniqueness theorem, is expressed by (6.13). To complete the proof we have only to show that $\boldsymbol{u}$ tends to zero at large spatial distance. To this end observe that

$$|\boldsymbol{u}(\boldsymbol{x})| \le |\boldsymbol{u}_n(\boldsymbol{x}) - \boldsymbol{u}(\boldsymbol{x})| + |\boldsymbol{u}_n(\boldsymbol{x})|.$$

Hence, taking into account (6.17) and bearing in mind that $|\boldsymbol{u}_n(\boldsymbol{x}) - \boldsymbol{u}(\boldsymbol{x})|$ uniformly converges to zero, we get

$$|\boldsymbol{u}(\boldsymbol{x})| \le c\left[\epsilon + (r(\boldsymbol{x}))^{-\frac{1}{n}}\right] \le 2\epsilon,$$

at large spatial distance and, as a consequence, $(6.16)_1$. Finally, $(6.16)_2$ immediately follows from (6.14). □

Remark 6.1 – A relevant question concerning the maximum modulus theorem for the Stokes system is related to the knowledge of the costant c in (6.1) or at least a lower and upper bound for it. In [27, 35] it is proved by means of some counter-examples that c cannot be equal to 1. As far as the ball is concerned, in a recent paper [29] W. Kratz showed that

$$c \in \begin{cases} (2, \sqrt{5}) & n = 2, \\ [n, n(n+1)/2) & n > 2. \end{cases}$$

If Ω is *star–shaped* with respect to a point, say $\boldsymbol{o}$, then the constant c in (6.1) is invariant under dilatations. Indeed, assume that

$$\Omega = \{\boldsymbol{x} : \boldsymbol{x} = R\boldsymbol{y},\ \boldsymbol{y} \in \Omega^*\}$$

and denote by $(\boldsymbol{u}(\boldsymbol{x}), \pi(\boldsymbol{x}))$ the classical solution to system (3.9), (3.3). Then, the couple

$$\boldsymbol{v}(\boldsymbol{y}) = \boldsymbol{u}(R\boldsymbol{y}), \quad \varpi(\boldsymbol{y}) = \pi(R\boldsymbol{y})$$

is a solution to the system

$$\begin{aligned} \Delta \boldsymbol{v} &= \nabla \varpi \quad && \text{in } \Omega^*, \\ \operatorname{div} \boldsymbol{v} &= \boldsymbol{0} && \text{in } \Omega^*, \\ \boldsymbol{v} &= \boldsymbol{b} && \text{on } \partial\Omega^*, \end{aligned}$$

where $\boldsymbol{b}(\boldsymbol{y}) = \boldsymbol{a}(R\boldsymbol{y})$. Then, from Lemma 6.1 we get

$$\|\boldsymbol{u}\|_{C(\overline{\Omega})} = \|\boldsymbol{v}\|_{C(\overline{\Omega}^*)} \leq c\|\boldsymbol{b}\|_{C(\partial\Omega^*)} = c\|\boldsymbol{a}\|_{C(\partial\Omega)},$$

where, of course, the constant c is independent of R.

Let Ω be a domain of $\mathbb{R}^n$. A classical result about subharmonic functions, *i.e.* solutions to the inequality

$$\Delta u \geq 0 \quad \text{in } \Omega,$$

assures that, if $u \in C^2(\Omega) \cap C(\overline{\Omega})$, then

$$\|u\|_{C(\overline{\Omega})} \leq \|u\|_{C(\partial\Omega)}.$$

This inequality is known as *the maximum principle.*

Let $\boldsymbol{u} \in C^2(\Omega) \cap C(\overline{\Omega})$ be a solution to the harmonic system

$$\Delta \boldsymbol{u} = \boldsymbol{0} \quad \text{in } \Omega. \tag{6.18}$$

Since $\Delta \boldsymbol{u}^2 = 2(\nabla \boldsymbol{u})^2$, we have that $\boldsymbol{u}^2$ is subharmonic so that from the maximum principle it follows that

$$\|\boldsymbol{u}\|_{C(\overline{\Omega})} \leq \|\boldsymbol{u}\|_{C(\partial\Omega)}. \tag{6.19}$$

Of course, by repeating the above argument we see that, if u is an harmonic function, then $|u|$ obeys the maximum principle.

We can ask ourselves whether the point $\boldsymbol{\xi}$ where $|\boldsymbol{u}|$ attains its maximum in $\overline{\Omega}$ is the maximum point for the absolute values of the components u_i of $\boldsymbol{u}$. The following counter–example shows that, in general, this is not true. For the sake of simplicity we consider the case $n = 2$.

Consider system (6.18) in the unit disk centered at $\boldsymbol{o}$ with the boundary condition

$$\begin{aligned} a_1(\boldsymbol{\xi}) &= \xi_1^2(1 - \xi_2), \\ a_2(\boldsymbol{\xi}) &= \xi_1(1 - \xi_2)^2. \end{aligned}$$

In the polar coordinate system with center $\boldsymbol{o}$ we have

$$\begin{aligned} a_1(\boldsymbol{\xi}) &= a_1(\theta) = (1 - \sin\theta)\cos^2\theta, \\ a_2(\boldsymbol{\xi}) &= a_2(\theta) = (1 - \sin\theta)^2\cos\theta, \end{aligned}$$

with $\theta \in [0, 2\pi]$. A simple computation shows that $a_1(\theta)$ attains its maximum value in two points, say $\hat{\theta}_1$ and $\tilde{\theta}_1$, such that $\sin\hat{\theta}_1 = \sin\tilde{\theta}_1 = -1/3$, while $|a_2(\theta)|$ attains its maximum value in two points $\hat{\theta}_2$, $\tilde{\theta}_2$ such that $\sin\hat{\theta}_2 = \sin\tilde{\theta}_2 = -2/3$ and

$$\max_{[0,2\pi]} |a_1(\theta)| = \frac{32}{27}, \qquad \max_{[0,2\pi]} |a_2(\theta)| = \left(\frac{5}{3}\right)^{\frac{3}{2}}.$$

On the other hand the quantity $m(\theta) = (a_1^2(\theta) + a_2^2(\theta))^{1/2}$ attains its maximum value at the points $\hat{\theta}$ and $\tilde{\theta}$ such that $m(\hat{\theta}) = m(\tilde{\theta}) = 4(2/\sqrt{5})^5$ and by a direct computation we see that

$$m(\hat{\theta}) = m(\tilde{\theta}) < (a_1^2(\theta) + a_2^2(\theta))^{1/2}.$$

As an immediate consequence of the above counter–example we have that (6.19) does not follow from the maximum principle holding for the absolute values of its components. Moreover, observe that the above counter–example shows that it is the very character of the system, and more precisely the link between the kinetic and pressure fields, rather than its vector form, what implies a constant c necessarily greater than 1 in (6.1).

Remark 6.2 - The maximum modulus theorem for the Stokes system and so the existence of a classical solution, has been proved in [34] under the hypothesis that the domain Ω has a boundary of class $C^{1,\alpha}$. On the other hand, Theorem 5.1 requires Ω to be of class C^2. It has been observed in [34, Remark 6.1] that if one can estimate the value of the constant c for a domain Ω in (6.1), then uniqueness of classical solutions holds provided Ω is of class $C^{1,\alpha}$. We aim at showing now that the foregoing conclusion holds, provided the domain Ω is star shaped with respect to a point, say $\boldsymbol{o}$. To this end, denote by $(\boldsymbol{u}, \pi)$ a solution to system (5.10) and observe that (5.11) defines a sequence of $C^{1,\alpha}$ domains. Since $\boldsymbol{u} \in C^2(\Omega)$ the sequence $\hat{\boldsymbol{u}}_m$ defined by

$$\hat{\boldsymbol{u}}_m(\boldsymbol{x}) = \boldsymbol{u}(\boldsymbol{x}), \quad \forall \boldsymbol{x} \in \partial\Omega_m$$

belongs to $W^{\frac{1}{2},2}(\partial\Omega)$. Then, in virtue of Theorem 3.1, there exists a unique variational solution $(\boldsymbol{u}_m, \pi_m)$ to system (5.10) in Ω_m corresponding to the boundary datum $\hat{\boldsymbol{u}}_m$. On the other hand, the couple $(\boldsymbol{u}, \pi)$, restricted to Ω_m, is a variational solution to system (5.10) corresponding to $\hat{\boldsymbol{u}}_m$, so that, by Theorem 3.1, $\boldsymbol{u}_m = \boldsymbol{u}$ in Ω_m. Consider now the sequence of classical solutions $(\bar{\boldsymbol{u}}_m, \bar{\pi}_m)$ corresponding to $\hat{\boldsymbol{u}}_m$ and satisfying (6.1), whose existence is guaranteed by lemma 6.1. Of course, $\bar{\boldsymbol{u}}$ is a variational solution too, so that $\bar{\boldsymbol{u}}_m = \boldsymbol{u}_m$ and

$$\|\boldsymbol{u}_m\|_{C(\overline{\Omega}_m)} \leq c\|\hat{\boldsymbol{u}}_m\|_{C(\partial\Omega_m)}. \tag{6.20}$$

Since Ω is star shaped, the constant c is invariant by dilation so that it is independent of m. On the other hand, in virtue of the continuity of $\boldsymbol{u}$ in $\overline{\Omega}$, we have that

$$\lim_{m\to\infty} |\hat{\boldsymbol{u}}_m(\boldsymbol{x})| = \boldsymbol{0}, \tag{6.21}$$

uniformly in $\boldsymbol{x}$. Finally, letting $m \to \infty$ in (6.20) and taking into account (6.21), we arrive at the desired conclusion.

7. Existence and Uniqueness of Classical Steady-State Solutions to the Navier-Stokes Equations

An open problem in the theory of stationary viscous hydrodynamics is to prove existence and uniqueness of a classical solution to system (3.10), (3.3), provided the *natural compatibility condition* (1.3) is satisfied, without requiring that any flux Φ_i in (1.3) vanishes. We refer to the monographies [16] and [30] for a deep analysis of the problem and further details. The aim of this Section is just to show that the stationary problem to the Navier Stokes system admits a unique classical solution, provided the viscositity is *sufficiently large* and the data $(\boldsymbol{a}, \boldsymbol{f})$ are *sufficiently small* in a suitable sense (cf. $(\mathrm{h})_1$ and $(\mathrm{h})_2$ in Theorem 7.1). Indeed, the following theorem holds true.

Theorem 7.1. *Let Ω be bounded, let $\boldsymbol{f} \in W^{1,p}(\Omega)$, with $p > 3$, and let $\boldsymbol{a} \in C(\partial\Omega)$ satisfy (3.2). If one of the following conditions*

$$(h_1), \qquad \|\boldsymbol{a}\|_{C(\partial\Omega)} \leq \eta_1$$

$$(h_2) \qquad \sum_{i=0}^{m} |\Phi_i| \leq \eta_2$$

is satisfied (for some sufficiently small positive constants η_1 and η_2), then system (3.10), (3.3) has at least a classical solution $\boldsymbol{u}$. Moreover, it is unique in $C^2(\Omega) \cap C(\overline{\Omega})$, provided

$$\nu > \mathrm{d}(\Omega)\|\boldsymbol{u}\|_{C(\overline{\Omega})}. \tag{7.1}$$

In order to prove Theorem 7.1 we need the following two lemmas. The first one gives an *extension* of the datum $\boldsymbol{a}$ in Ω in such a way that we can separate the contribution of the flux from the value of $\boldsymbol{a}$. To this aim we follow an idea by G.P. Galdi [16].

Lemma 7.1. *Let $\boldsymbol{a} \in C(\partial\Omega)$ satisfy (1.3). Then, there exists a field $\boldsymbol{\alpha} \in C^2(\Omega) \cap C(\overline{\Omega})$, with $\boldsymbol{\alpha} = \boldsymbol{a}$ on $\partial\Omega$,*

$$\boldsymbol{\alpha}(\boldsymbol{x}) = \nabla \times \boldsymbol{q}(\boldsymbol{x}) + \boldsymbol{\mu}(\boldsymbol{x}), \quad \forall \boldsymbol{x} \in \Omega, \tag{7.2}$$

where the fields $\boldsymbol{q}$ *and* $\boldsymbol{\mu}$ *are such that* $\boldsymbol{\mu}, \boldsymbol{q}, \nabla\times\boldsymbol{q} \in C^2(\Omega)\cap C(\overline{\Omega})$ *and*

$$
\begin{aligned}
&\|\boldsymbol{q}\|_{C(\overline{\Omega})} + \|\nabla\times\boldsymbol{q}\|_{C(\overline{\Omega})} + \|\nabla\boldsymbol{q}\|_{L^p(\Omega)} \le c\|\boldsymbol{a}\|_{C(\partial\Omega)}, \quad \forall p>1,\\
&\|\nabla\boldsymbol{\mu}\|_{L^p(\Omega)} + \|\boldsymbol{\mu}\|_{C(\overline{\Omega})} \le c\sum_{i=0}^{m}|\Phi_i|, \quad \forall p>1,
\end{aligned} \tag{7.3}
$$

with

$$\Phi_i = \int_{\Omega_i} \boldsymbol{a}\cdot\boldsymbol{n}\,\mathrm{d}\sigma, \quad i=0,1,\dots,m.$$

Moreover, there exists a function ϖ *in* Ω *such that* $(\boldsymbol{\alpha},\varpi)$ *is a classical solution to system* (3.9), (3.2), (3.3). *Finally, if* $\boldsymbol{a}\in C^1(\partial\Omega)$, *then* $\nabla\boldsymbol{\alpha}, \varpi \in L^p(\Omega)$, *for any* $p>1$.

PROOF - Let

$$
\boldsymbol{a}_i = \begin{cases} \boldsymbol{a}(\boldsymbol{\xi}) - [\boldsymbol{a}\cdot\boldsymbol{n}]_{\partial\Omega_i}\boldsymbol{n} & \boldsymbol{\xi}\in\partial\Omega_i,\\[1em] \boldsymbol{0} & \boldsymbol{\xi}\in\partial\Omega\setminus\partial\Omega_i. \end{cases}
$$

Denote by $(\boldsymbol{\alpha}_i,\varpi_i)$ the solution to system (3.9), (3.2), (3.3) in Ω corresponding to the boundary datum $\boldsymbol{a}_i$, by $(\tilde{\boldsymbol{\alpha}}_i,\tilde{\varpi}_i)$ $(i=1,\dots,m)$ the solution to system (3.9), (3.2), (3.3) in Ω_i which corresponds to the boundary datum $\boldsymbol{a}_i$ and, finally, by $(\tilde{\boldsymbol{\alpha}}_0,\tilde{\varpi}_0)$ the solution to system (3.9), (3.2), (3.3) in $[\mathbb{R}^3\setminus(\Omega\cup(\cup_{i=1}^m\overline{\Omega}_i))]\cap S_R$ $(S_R\supset\overline{\Omega})$ with boundary datum $\boldsymbol{a}_0$ at $\partial\Omega_0$ and zero on ∂S_R. The existence of the above solutions is guaranteed by the maximum modulus theorem (cf. Lemma 6.1). Also, they satisfy the estimate (6.1).

Let

$$
\hat{\boldsymbol{\alpha}}_i(\boldsymbol{x}) = \begin{cases} \boldsymbol{\alpha}_i & \boldsymbol{x}\in\Omega,\\ \boldsymbol{0} & \boldsymbol{x}\in\overline{\Omega}_j,\ i\neq j,\\ \tilde{\boldsymbol{\alpha}}_i(\boldsymbol{x}) & \boldsymbol{x}\in\overline{\Omega}_i,\ i=1,\dots,m,\\ \tilde{\boldsymbol{\alpha}}_0(\boldsymbol{x}) & \boldsymbol{x}\in[\mathbb{R}^3\setminus(\Omega\cup(\cup_{i=1}^m\overline{\Omega}_i))]\cap S_R,\ i=0. \end{cases}
$$

and set

$$\tilde{\boldsymbol{\alpha}}(\boldsymbol{x}) = \sum_{i=0}^{m}\hat{\boldsymbol{\alpha}}_i(\boldsymbol{x}), \quad \tilde{\varpi} = \sum_{i=0}^{m}\varpi_i(\boldsymbol{x}).$$

Of course, the couple $(\tilde{\boldsymbol{\alpha}}, \tilde{\varpi})$ is the classical solution to system (3.9), (3.2), (3.3) in Ω corresponding to the boundary datum $\boldsymbol{a} - [\boldsymbol{a}\cdot\boldsymbol{n}]_{\partial\Omega}\boldsymbol{n}$ and, setting $\tilde{\boldsymbol{\alpha}} = \mathbf{0}$ outside S_R, we see that $\tilde{\boldsymbol{\alpha}} \in C(\mathbb{R}^3)$, $\operatorname{div}\tilde{\boldsymbol{\alpha}} = 0$ almost everywhere in $\mathbb{R}^3$.

Let $\boldsymbol{q}(\boldsymbol{x}) = \nabla \times \boldsymbol{e}(\boldsymbol{x})$, with

$$\boldsymbol{e}(\boldsymbol{x}) = -\int_{\mathbb{R}^3} \mathcal{E}(\boldsymbol{x}-\boldsymbol{y})\tilde{\boldsymbol{\alpha}}(\boldsymbol{y})\mathrm{d}v_{\boldsymbol{y}},$$

where

$$\mathcal{E}(\boldsymbol{x},\boldsymbol{y}) = \frac{1}{4\pi}\frac{1}{|\boldsymbol{x}-\boldsymbol{y}|}.$$

A simple computation shows that $\tilde{\boldsymbol{\alpha}} = \nabla\times\nabla\times\boldsymbol{e}$ so that $|\boldsymbol{q}(\boldsymbol{x})|$ and $|\nabla\times\boldsymbol{e}(\boldsymbol{x})|$ can be majorized by the maximum of $|\boldsymbol{a}(\boldsymbol{x})|$ on $\partial\Omega$. Hence, since the Calderon–Zygmund theorem assures that the L^p–norm of second derivatives of $\boldsymbol{e}$ can be estimated in terms of a constant times the L^p–norm of $\tilde{\boldsymbol{\alpha}}$, $(7.3)_1$ follows.

Let $(\boldsymbol{\mu}, \zeta)$ be the classical solution to system (3.9), (3.2), (3.3) corresponding to the boundary datum $[\boldsymbol{a}\cdot\boldsymbol{n}]_{\partial\Omega_i}\boldsymbol{n}$, $(i = 0, 1, \ldots, m)$. The existence of this solution is guaranteed by Theorem 3.1. Then, the field $\nabla\times\boldsymbol{q}+\boldsymbol{\mu}$ gives the desired extension. Estimate $(7.3)_2$ follows from Theorem 3.1. □

Lemma 7.2. *Let $\boldsymbol{a} \in C(\partial\Omega)$ satisfy (1.3) and, for any $\epsilon \in (0,\bar{\epsilon})$, consider the cut–off function ψ_ϵ constructed in Lemma 2.7. Then there exists a solenoidal field $\boldsymbol{\vartheta}_\epsilon = \nabla\times(\psi_\epsilon\boldsymbol{q}) + \boldsymbol{\mu} \in C^2(\Omega)\cap C(\overline{\Omega})\cap W^{1,p}_{\mathrm{loc}}(\Omega)$, for any $p > 1$, such that $\boldsymbol{\vartheta}_\epsilon = \boldsymbol{a}$ on $\partial\Omega$, and the following estimates hold*

$$\begin{aligned}(7.4)\qquad &\left|\int_\Omega \boldsymbol{\vartheta}_\epsilon\cdot(\nabla\boldsymbol{u})\boldsymbol{u}\mathrm{d}v\right| \le \\ &\le c\left\{\epsilon\|\boldsymbol{a}\|_{C(\partial\Omega)} + \sum_{i=0}^m |\Phi_i|\right\}\|\nabla\boldsymbol{u}\|^2_{L^2(\Omega)}, \forall\,\boldsymbol{u}\in W^{1,2}_0(\Omega), \\ &\|\boldsymbol{\vartheta}_\epsilon\|_{C(\overline{\Omega})} \le c(\epsilon)\|\boldsymbol{a}\|_{C(\partial\Omega)}.\end{aligned}$$

Finally, if $\boldsymbol{a}\in C^1(\partial\Omega)$, then $\nabla\boldsymbol{\vartheta}_\epsilon \in L^p(\Omega)$, for any $\epsilon\in(0,\bar{\epsilon})$.

Proof – Consider the decomposition (7.2) and set

$$\boldsymbol{\vartheta}_\epsilon = \nabla\times(\psi_\epsilon\boldsymbol{q}) + \boldsymbol{\mu},$$

It evident that $\boldsymbol{\vartheta}_\epsilon \in C^2(\Omega) \cap C(\overline{\Omega}) \cap W^{1,p}_{\text{loc}}(\Omega)$, $\operatorname{div} \boldsymbol{\vartheta}_\epsilon = 0$, $\boldsymbol{\vartheta}_\epsilon = \boldsymbol{a}$ at $\partial\Omega$ and $\boldsymbol{\vartheta}_\epsilon$ satisfies $(7.4)_2$. In order to get inequality $(7.4)_1$ we use the generalized Hölder inequality as well as (7.3), Lemmas 2.7, 2.8, Sobolev's inequality and the properties of the function ψ_ϵ:

$$\begin{aligned}\left|\int_\Omega \boldsymbol{\vartheta}_\epsilon \cdot (\nabla \boldsymbol{u})\boldsymbol{u} \mathrm{d}v\right| &= \left|\int_\Omega \boldsymbol{u} \cdot (\nabla \boldsymbol{u})\left(\psi_\epsilon \nabla \times \boldsymbol{q} + \nabla \psi_\epsilon \times \boldsymbol{q} + \boldsymbol{\mu}\right) \mathrm{d}v\right| \\ &\leq \|\boldsymbol{u}\|_{L^6(\Omega)} \|\nabla \boldsymbol{u}\|_{L^2(\Omega)} \|\psi_\epsilon \nabla \times \boldsymbol{q}\|_{L^3(\Omega)} \\ &+ \epsilon \|\boldsymbol{q}\|_{C(\overline{\Omega})} \|\tilde{d}\boldsymbol{u}\|_{L^2(\Omega)} \|\nabla \boldsymbol{u}\|_{L^2(\Omega)} \\ &+ \|\boldsymbol{\mu}\|_{C(\overline{\Omega})} \|\boldsymbol{u}\|_{L^2(\Omega)} \|\nabla \boldsymbol{u}\|_{L^2(\Omega)} \\ &\leq c\Big(\epsilon \|\boldsymbol{a}\|_{C(\partial\Omega)} + \sum_{i=0}^m |\Phi_i|\Big) \|\nabla \boldsymbol{u}\|^2_{L^2(\Omega)}. \qquad \square\end{aligned}$$

We are now in a position to prove Theorem 7.1.

Proof of Theorem 7.1 – Assume first that $\boldsymbol{a} \in C^1(\partial\Omega)$. Let us determine a solution to system (3.10), (3.2), (3.3) having the form $\boldsymbol{v}(\boldsymbol{x}) = \boldsymbol{u}_\epsilon(\boldsymbol{x}) + \boldsymbol{\vartheta}_\epsilon(\boldsymbol{x})$, where $\boldsymbol{\vartheta}_\epsilon$ is the field constructed in Lemma 7.2. and $\boldsymbol{u}_\epsilon \in J^{1,2}(\Omega) \cap C(\overline{\Omega})$ is the solution to

$$\begin{aligned}&\int_\Omega [\nu \nabla \boldsymbol{\varphi} \cdot \nabla \boldsymbol{u}_\epsilon + \boldsymbol{\varphi} \cdot (\nabla \boldsymbol{u}_\epsilon)\boldsymbol{u}_\epsilon + \boldsymbol{\varphi} \cdot (\nabla \boldsymbol{\vartheta}_\epsilon)\boldsymbol{u}_\epsilon + \boldsymbol{\varphi} \cdot (\nabla \boldsymbol{u}_\epsilon)\boldsymbol{\vartheta}_\epsilon] \mathrm{d}v \\ &\qquad = \int_\Omega [\boldsymbol{\varphi} \cdot \boldsymbol{f} - \nu \nabla \boldsymbol{\varphi} \cdot \nabla \boldsymbol{\vartheta}_\epsilon + \boldsymbol{\vartheta}_\epsilon \cdot (\nabla \boldsymbol{\varphi})\boldsymbol{\vartheta}_\epsilon] \mathrm{d}v, \quad \forall \boldsymbol{\varphi} \in J^{1,2}(\Omega).\end{aligned} \tag{7.5}$$

Set

$$E = \|\boldsymbol{f}\|_{W_0^{-1,2}(\Omega)} + c(\epsilon)\left(\|\boldsymbol{a}\|_{C(\partial\Omega)} + \|\boldsymbol{a}\|^2_{C(\partial\Omega)}\right).$$

The crucial point in establishing the existence of a solution $\boldsymbol{u}_\epsilon$ to equation (7.5) is to prove the following *energy inequality*

$$(\nu - \eta)\|\nabla \boldsymbol{u}_\epsilon\|_{L^2(\Omega)} \leq E, \tag{7.6}$$

for some $\eta \in (0, \nu)$ depending on ϵ. By making use of (7.6) and of well-known techniques (cf. [16], [30]), one can prove the existence of a solution $\boldsymbol{u}_\epsilon$ to equation (7.6), so we confine ourselves to prove the validity of inequality (7.5) under our assumptions.

From now on, for the sake of formal simplicity, we omit to specify the symbol ϵ and recall its value only when we use inequality (7.4).

Replace $\boldsymbol{\varphi}$ in (7.5) with the field $\boldsymbol{u} \in J^{1,2}(\Omega)$. Then, an integration by parts yields

$$\begin{aligned}\nu \int_{\Omega} (\nabla \boldsymbol{u})^2 \mathrm{d}v &= -\int_{\Omega} \boldsymbol{\vartheta} \cdot (\nabla \boldsymbol{u}) \boldsymbol{u} \, \mathrm{d}v + \int_{\Omega} \boldsymbol{u} \cdot \boldsymbol{f} \, \mathrm{d}v \\ &+ \int_{\Omega} \boldsymbol{\vartheta} \cdot (\nabla \boldsymbol{u}) \boldsymbol{\vartheta} \, \mathrm{d}v - \nu \int_{\Omega} \nabla \boldsymbol{\vartheta} \cdot \nabla \boldsymbol{u} = \sum_{i=1}^{4} I_i. \end{aligned} \tag{7.7}$$

From Lemma 7.2 it follows that

$$|I_1| \le c \left(\epsilon \|\boldsymbol{a}\|_{C(\partial\Omega)} + \sum_{i=0}^{m} |\Phi_i| \right) \|\nabla \boldsymbol{u}\|^2_{L^2(\Omega)}.$$

Hence, taking into account hypothesis (h_2) and choosing ϵ sufficiently small, we have

$$|I_1| \le \eta \|\nabla \boldsymbol{u}\|^2_{L^2(\Omega)}, \tag{7.8}$$

for some $\eta < \nu$. As far as I_2 and I_3 are concerned, we get

$$|I_2| \le \|\boldsymbol{f}\|_{W_0^{-1,2}(\Omega)} \|\nabla \boldsymbol{u}\|_{L^2(\Omega)},$$

and

$$|I_3| \le \|\boldsymbol{\vartheta}\|_{L^4(\Omega)} \|\nabla \boldsymbol{u}\|^2_{L^2(\Omega)} \le c(\epsilon) \|\boldsymbol{a}\|^2_{C(\partial\Omega)} \|\nabla \boldsymbol{u}\|_{L^2(\Omega)},$$

where $(7.4)_2$ has been used. Therefore we obtain

$$|I_2 + I_3| \le \left(\|\boldsymbol{f}\|_{W_0^{-1,2}(\Omega)} + c(\epsilon) \|\boldsymbol{a}\|^2_{C(\partial\Omega)} \right) \|\nabla \boldsymbol{u}\|_{L^2(\Omega)}. \tag{7.9}$$

Note that, actually, I_4 makes sense under hypothesis $\boldsymbol{a} \in C^1(\partial\Omega)$ which, in virtue of Lemma 7.2, assures that $\nabla \boldsymbol{\vartheta} \in L^2(\Omega)$. Our aim is just to estimate I_4 by only requiring that $\boldsymbol{a} \in C(\partial\Omega)$. Let us start with observing that from Lemma 7.2 and decomposition (7.2) we get

$$\begin{aligned}\nabla \boldsymbol{\vartheta}(\boldsymbol{x}) &= \nabla[\psi(\boldsymbol{x}) \nabla \times \boldsymbol{q}(\boldsymbol{x}) + \nabla \psi(\boldsymbol{x}) \times \boldsymbol{q}(\boldsymbol{x})] + \nabla \boldsymbol{\mu}(\boldsymbol{x}) \\ &= \nabla \psi(\boldsymbol{x}) \otimes \nabla \times \boldsymbol{q}(\boldsymbol{x}) + \psi(\boldsymbol{x}) \nabla(\nabla \times \boldsymbol{q}(\boldsymbol{x})) \\ &+ \nabla(\nabla \psi(\boldsymbol{x}) \times \boldsymbol{q}(\boldsymbol{x})) + \nabla \boldsymbol{\mu}(\boldsymbol{x}) \\ &= \nabla \psi(\boldsymbol{x}) \otimes \nabla \times \boldsymbol{q}(\boldsymbol{x}) + \nabla(\nabla \psi(\boldsymbol{x}) \times \boldsymbol{q}(\boldsymbol{x})) \\ &+ (1 - \psi(\boldsymbol{x})) \nabla \boldsymbol{\mu}(\boldsymbol{x}) + \psi(\boldsymbol{x}) \nabla \tilde{\boldsymbol{\alpha}}(\boldsymbol{x}). \end{aligned} \tag{7.10}$$

Recall now that $(\tilde{\boldsymbol{\alpha}}, \tilde{\varpi})$ is a classical solution to system (3.9), (3.2), (3.3). Then, an integration by parts yields

$$\int_\Omega \nabla \boldsymbol{h} \cdot \nabla \tilde{\boldsymbol{\alpha}} \, \mathrm{d}v - \int_\Omega \tilde{\varpi} \operatorname{div} \boldsymbol{h} \, \mathrm{d}v = 0, \quad \forall \, \boldsymbol{h} \in C_0^\infty(\Omega). \tag{7.11}$$

Since $\nabla \tilde{\boldsymbol{\alpha}}, \tilde{\varpi} \in L^2(\Omega)$ by a density argument we realize that (7.11) holds for any $\boldsymbol{h} \in W_0^{1,2}(\Omega)$. Then, setting $\boldsymbol{h} = \psi \boldsymbol{u}$ in (7.11), a simple computation gives

$$\int_\Omega \psi \nabla \tilde{\boldsymbol{\alpha}} \cdot \nabla \boldsymbol{u} \, \mathrm{d}v = - \int_\Omega \boldsymbol{u} \cdot (\nabla \tilde{\boldsymbol{\alpha}}) \nabla \psi \, \mathrm{d}v + \int_\Omega \tilde{\varpi} \boldsymbol{u} \cdot \nabla \psi \, \mathrm{d}v. \tag{7.12}$$

Therefore, from (7.10), (7.12) we have

$$\begin{aligned} |I_4| \leq \nu \Big\{ & \int_\Omega \Big[|D^2 \psi| |\boldsymbol{q}| |\nabla \boldsymbol{u}| + 3 |\nabla \psi| |\nabla \boldsymbol{q}| |\nabla \boldsymbol{u}| \Big] \mathrm{d}v \\ & + \int_\Omega \Big[|\nabla \psi| (|\nabla \tilde{\boldsymbol{\alpha}}| + \tilde{\varpi}|) |\boldsymbol{u}| + (1 - \psi) |\nabla \boldsymbol{\mu}| |\nabla \boldsymbol{u}| \Big] \mathrm{d}v \Big\}. \end{aligned}$$

Since

$$\operatorname{supp} \nabla \psi \subset \left\{ \boldsymbol{x} \in \Omega \, : \, \operatorname{dist}(\boldsymbol{x}, \partial\Omega) \in \left(\frac{\gamma^2(\epsilon)}{2}, 2\gamma(\epsilon) \right) \right\},$$

$$\operatorname{supp}(1 - \psi) \subset \left\{ \boldsymbol{x} \in \Omega \, : \, \operatorname{dist}(\boldsymbol{x}, \partial\Omega) > \frac{\gamma^2(\epsilon)}{2} \right\},$$

in virtue of the interior regularity inside Ω of the fields in (7.10), and from inequality (7.3), we get

$$\begin{aligned} (1 - \psi(\boldsymbol{x})) |\nabla \boldsymbol{\mu}| \leq c \|\boldsymbol{a}\|_{C(\partial\Omega)}, & \quad \forall \, \boldsymbol{x} : \operatorname{dist}(\boldsymbol{x}, \partial\Omega) > \frac{\gamma^2(\epsilon)}{2}, \\ |\nabla \psi(\boldsymbol{x})| (|\nabla \tilde{\boldsymbol{\alpha}}(\boldsymbol{x})| + |\tilde{\varpi}(\boldsymbol{x})|) \leq c(\epsilon) \|\boldsymbol{a}\|_{C(\partial\Omega)}, & \quad \forall \, \boldsymbol{x} \in \operatorname{supp} \nabla \psi, \\ |D^2 \psi(\boldsymbol{x})| |\boldsymbol{q}(\boldsymbol{x})| \leq c(\epsilon) \|\boldsymbol{a}\|_{C(\partial\Omega)}, & \quad \forall \, \boldsymbol{x} \in \operatorname{supp} \nabla \psi. \end{aligned}$$

Then, making use of Schwarz–Hölder and Poincaré inequalities and taking into account $(7.4)_1$, we have, $\forall p > 1$,

$$
\begin{aligned}
\int_\Omega |D^2\psi||\boldsymbol{q}||\nabla \boldsymbol{u}|\mathrm{d}v &\le c(\epsilon)\|\boldsymbol{a}\|_{C(\partial\Omega)}\|\nabla \boldsymbol{u}\|_{L^p(\Omega)},\\
\int_\Omega |\nabla\psi||\nabla \boldsymbol{q}||\nabla \boldsymbol{u}|\mathrm{d}v &\le c(\epsilon)\|\nabla \boldsymbol{q}\|_{L^{p'}(\Omega)}\|\nabla \boldsymbol{u}\|_{L^p(\Omega)}\\
&\le c(\epsilon)\|\boldsymbol{a}\|_{C(\partial\Omega)}\|\nabla \boldsymbol{u}\|_{L^p(\Omega)}\\
\int_\Omega |\nabla\psi|(|\nabla\tilde{\boldsymbol{\alpha}}| + |\tilde{\varpi}|)|\boldsymbol{u}|\mathrm{d}v &\le c(\epsilon)\|\boldsymbol{a}\|_{C(\partial\Omega)}\|\nabla \boldsymbol{u}\|_{L^p(\Omega)},\\
\int_\Omega (1-\psi)|\nabla\boldsymbol{\mu}||\nabla \boldsymbol{u}|\mathrm{d}v &\le c\left(\sum_{i=0}^m |\Phi_i|\right)\|\nabla \boldsymbol{u}\|_{L^p(\Omega)}.
\end{aligned}
\tag{7.13}
$$

Hence, choosing $p = 2$, it follows that

$$
|I_4| \le \left(c(\epsilon)\nu\|\boldsymbol{a}\|_{C(\partial\Omega)} + c\sum_{i=0}^m |\Phi_i|\right)\|\nabla \boldsymbol{u}\|_{L^2(\Omega)}. \tag{7.14}
$$

Putting together (7.8), (7.9) and (7.14) we obtain (7.6). Observe that from inequality (7.13) we deduce that I_4 can be estimated without requiring that $\boldsymbol{a} \in C^1(\partial\Omega)$.

As already said, inequality (7.6) is sufficient to prove the existence of a solution $\boldsymbol{u} \in J^{1,2}(\Omega)$ to equation (7.5). We now show that $\nabla\boldsymbol{u} \in L^p(\Omega)$, $\forall p > 1$. To this end, we first prove that $\nabla\boldsymbol{u} \in L^3(\Omega)$. To do this we follow a standard argument (cf., *e.g.*, [16]). Consider the linear functional

$$
\begin{aligned}
\boldsymbol{b}[\boldsymbol{\varphi}] &= \int_\Omega \boldsymbol{\varphi}\cdot[\nabla(\boldsymbol{u}+\boldsymbol{\vartheta})](\boldsymbol{u}+\boldsymbol{\vartheta})\mathrm{d}v\\
&\quad + \nu\int_\Omega \nabla\boldsymbol{\vartheta}\cdot\nabla\boldsymbol{\varphi}\,\mathrm{d}v - \int_\Omega \boldsymbol{\varphi}\cdot\boldsymbol{f}\,\mathrm{d}v, \quad \forall\boldsymbol{\varphi}\in W_0^{1,\frac{3}{2}}(\Omega).
\end{aligned}
\tag{7.15}
$$

In virtue of relations (7.10), (7.12) and estimate (7.13), making use of

Schwarz–Hölder and Poincaré inequalities, we get

$$
\begin{aligned}
|\boldsymbol{b}[\boldsymbol{\varphi}]| \leq & \int_\Omega |\boldsymbol{\varphi}\cdot[\nabla(\boldsymbol{u}+\boldsymbol{\vartheta})](\boldsymbol{u}+\boldsymbol{\vartheta})|\mathrm{d}v + \nu\left\{\int_\Omega (1-\psi)|\nabla\boldsymbol{\varphi}\cdot\nabla\boldsymbol{\mu}|\mathrm{d}v\right. \\
& + \int_\Omega |\boldsymbol{\varphi}\cdot(\nabla\tilde{\boldsymbol{\alpha}})\nabla\psi|\mathrm{d}v + \int_\Omega |\tilde{\varpi}\boldsymbol{\varphi}\cdot\nabla\psi|\mathrm{d}v \\
& \left. + c\int_\Omega |\nabla\psi||\nabla\boldsymbol{\varphi}||\nabla\boldsymbol{q}|\mathrm{d}v + c\int_\Omega |D^2\psi||\nabla\boldsymbol{\varphi}||\boldsymbol{q}|\mathrm{d}v\right\} + \int_\Omega |\boldsymbol{\varphi}\cdot\boldsymbol{f}|\mathrm{d}v \\
\leq & \left\{\|\boldsymbol{u}+\boldsymbol{\vartheta}\|^2_{L^6(\Omega)} + \nu\left(c(\epsilon)\|\boldsymbol{a}\|_{C(\partial\Omega)} + c\sum_{i=1}^m |\Phi_i|\right)\right. \\
& \left. + \|\boldsymbol{f}\|_{W_0^{-1,3}(\Omega)}\right\}\|\nabla\boldsymbol{\varphi}\|_{L^{\frac{3}{2}}(\Omega)}.
\end{aligned}
$$

Hence, by taking into account that by Sobolev's inequality, (7.4) and (7.6)

$$
\|\boldsymbol{u}+\boldsymbol{\vartheta}\|^2_{L^6(\Omega)} \leq c\left\{\|\boldsymbol{\vartheta}\|^2_{C(\overline{\Omega})} + \|\nabla\boldsymbol{u}\|^2_{L^2(\Omega)}\right\} \leq c(\epsilon)\|\boldsymbol{a}\|^2_{C(\partial\Omega)} + c(\nu-\eta)^{-2}E^2,
$$

it follows that

$$
\begin{aligned}
\|\boldsymbol{b}\|_{W_0^{-1,3}(\Omega)} \leq & \, c(\nu-\eta)^{-2}E^2 + c(\epsilon)\|\boldsymbol{a}\|^2_{C(\partial\Omega)} \\
& + \nu\left(c(\epsilon)\|\boldsymbol{a}\|_{C(\partial\Omega)} + c\sum_{i=0}^m |\Phi_i|\right) + \|\boldsymbol{f}\|_{W_0^{-1,3}(\Omega)} = M(\boldsymbol{f},\boldsymbol{a}).
\end{aligned} \tag{7.16}
$$

Set

$$
\boldsymbol{b}(\boldsymbol{x}) = \operatorname{div}\left[(\boldsymbol{u}+\boldsymbol{\theta})\otimes(\boldsymbol{u}+\boldsymbol{\theta}) - \nu\nabla\boldsymbol{\theta}\right] - \boldsymbol{f}
$$

and note that

$$
\boldsymbol{b}[\boldsymbol{\varphi}] = \int_\Omega \boldsymbol{\varphi}\cdot\boldsymbol{b}\,\mathrm{d}v, \quad \forall\boldsymbol{\varphi}\in W_0^{1,\frac{3}{2}}(\Omega).
$$

Hence by (7.16) $\boldsymbol{b}\in W_0^{-1,3}(\Omega)$.

By Theorem 3.1, Stokes' system admits a unique variational solution $\boldsymbol{v}\in W^{1,3}(\Omega)$ corresponding to body force $\boldsymbol{b}$ and zero boundary data. Of course, $\nabla\boldsymbol{v}\in L^2(\Omega)$. Since $\boldsymbol{u}$ is a solution to the same Stokes problem and, in virtue of (7.6), $\nabla\boldsymbol{u}\in L^2(\Omega)$, by appealing to the uniqueness of variational solutions, we have that $\boldsymbol{u}\equiv\boldsymbol{v}$ so that $\nabla\boldsymbol{u}\in L^3(\Omega)$. Hence, bearing in mind (3.7) and (7.16) we have

$$
\|\nabla\boldsymbol{u}\|_{L^3(\Omega)} \leq c\|\boldsymbol{b}\|_{W_0^{-1,3}(\Omega)} \leq cM(\boldsymbol{f},\boldsymbol{a}), \tag{7.17}
$$

which, by taking into account Sobolev's imbedding theorem, yields

$$\|\boldsymbol{u}\|_{L^p(\Omega)} \le M(\boldsymbol{f},\boldsymbol{a}), \quad \forall p \in (1,+\infty). \tag{7.18}$$

Next, by making use of (7.18), let us modify the estimate concerning the functional $\boldsymbol{b}[\varphi]$ and (7.16) as follows

$$\begin{aligned}
|\boldsymbol{b}[\varphi]| &\le \Big\{ \|\boldsymbol{u}+\boldsymbol{\vartheta}\|^2_{L^{2p}(\Omega)} + \nu \Big(c(\epsilon)\|\boldsymbol{a}\|_{C(\partial\Omega)} + c\sum_{i=1}^m |\Phi_i| \Big) \\
&\quad + \|\boldsymbol{f}\|_{W_0^{-1,p}(\Omega)} \Big\} \|\nabla\varphi\|_{L^{\frac{p}{p-1}}(\Omega)} \\
&\le \Big\{ cM^2(\boldsymbol{f},\boldsymbol{a}) + \nu \Big(c(\epsilon)\|\boldsymbol{a}\|_{C(\partial\Omega)} + c\sum_{i=1}^m |\Phi_i| \Big) \\
&\quad + \|\boldsymbol{f}\|_{W_0^{-1,p}(\Omega)} \Big\} \|\nabla\varphi\|_{L^{\frac{p}{p-1}}(\Omega)},
\end{aligned}$$

for any $p > 3$. Hence

$$\|\boldsymbol{b}\|_{W_0^{-1,p}(\Omega)} \le M_1(\boldsymbol{f},\boldsymbol{a}),$$

where we have set

$$M_1(\boldsymbol{f},\boldsymbol{a}) = cM^2(\boldsymbol{f},\boldsymbol{a}) + \nu \Big(c(\epsilon)\|\boldsymbol{a}\|_{C(\partial\Omega)} + c\sum_{i=1}^m |\Phi_i| \Big) \|\boldsymbol{f}\|_{W_0^{-1,p}(\Omega)}.$$

Repeating the reasoning we used in proving (7.17), we see that

$$\|\nabla \boldsymbol{u}\|_{L^p(\Omega)} \le cM_1(\boldsymbol{f},\boldsymbol{a}), \quad \forall p > 3. \tag{7.19}$$

Therefore, in virtue of Sobolev's imbedding theorem, we have

$$\|\boldsymbol{u}\|_{C(\overline{\Omega})} \le cM_1(\boldsymbol{f},\boldsymbol{a}). \tag{7.20}$$

Note now that in the *energy inequality* (7.6) as well as in (7.18) the constants c and η depend on ϵ but do not depend on the on C^1 regularity of the boundary datum $\boldsymbol{a}$. We only used the smoothness of $\boldsymbol{a}$ to write (7.5) and to deduce (7.11). However, in view of the properties of the *extension* $\boldsymbol{\vartheta}$, the smootheness hypothesis on $\boldsymbol{a}$ may be relaxed to deduce (7.4), (7.11) as follows.

Assume that $\boldsymbol{a} \in C(\partial\Omega)$ satisfies (3.2). Then, there exists a sequence

$$\{\boldsymbol{a}_n(\boldsymbol{x})\}_{n\in\mathbb{N}},\ \boldsymbol{a}_n \in C^1(\partial\Omega), \qquad \int_\Omega \boldsymbol{a}_n \cdot \boldsymbol{n}\, d\sigma = 0.$$

which converges in $C(\partial\Omega)$ to $\boldsymbol{a}$. In virtue of Lemma 7.1, we can find a sequence of *extensions* $\boldsymbol{\alpha}_n \in C(\overline{\Omega}) \cap W^{1,p}(\Omega)$

$$\boldsymbol{\alpha}_n = \nabla \times \boldsymbol{q}_n + \boldsymbol{\mu}_n$$

and a sequence of associated *pressure fields* $\varpi_n \in L^p(\Omega)$ such that $(\boldsymbol{\alpha}_n, \varpi_n)$ are classical solutions to the Stokes system, and

$$\begin{aligned} \|\boldsymbol{q}_n - \boldsymbol{q}_m\|_{C(\overline{\Omega})} + \|\nabla \times (\boldsymbol{q}_n - \boldsymbol{q}_m)\|_{C(\overline{\Omega})} &\le c\|\boldsymbol{a}_n - \boldsymbol{a}_m\|_{C(\partial\Omega)}, \\ \|\nabla(\boldsymbol{q}_n - \boldsymbol{q}_m)\|_{L^p(\Omega)} &\le c\|\boldsymbol{a}_n - \boldsymbol{a}_m\|_{C(\partial\Omega)},\ \forall p > 1, \\ \|\nabla(\boldsymbol{\mu}_m - \boldsymbol{\mu}_m)\|_{L^p\Omega)} + \|\boldsymbol{\mu}_m - \boldsymbol{\mu}_m\|_{C(\overline{\Omega})} &\le \\ &\le c\sum_{i=0}^{m} \left| \int_{\partial\Omega_i} (\boldsymbol{a}_n - \boldsymbol{a}_m) \cdot \boldsymbol{n}\, d\sigma \right|. \end{aligned} \tag{7.21}$$

From (7.21) it follows that $(\boldsymbol{q}_n, \nabla \times \boldsymbol{q}_n, \boldsymbol{\mu}_n)$ and $(\nabla\boldsymbol{q}_n, \nabla\boldsymbol{\mu}_n)$ are Cauchy sequences in $C(\overline{\Omega})$ and $L^p(\Omega)$ respectively. Then, they converge to the fields $\boldsymbol{q}, \boldsymbol{\mu} \in C(\overline{\Omega})$, with $\nabla \times \boldsymbol{q} \in C(\overline{\Omega})$ and $\nabla\boldsymbol{q}, \nabla\boldsymbol{\mu} \in L^p(\Omega), \forall p > 1$. Of course, $\boldsymbol{\alpha}_n$ is also a Cauchy sequence in $C(\overline{\Omega})$ and its limit $\boldsymbol{\alpha}$ has the form (7.2), with $\nabla\boldsymbol{q}$ and $\nabla\boldsymbol{\mu} \in L^p(\Omega)$. Moreover, ϖ_n converges in $C(\Omega) \cap L^p_{\text{loc}}(\Omega)$ to a *pressure field* ϖ. For the linearity of system (3.1), (3.3), we have that $(\boldsymbol{\alpha}, \varpi)$ is a classical solution to the Stokes system (3.9) in Ω.

In virtue of Lemma 7.2, we find a sequence of extensions $\boldsymbol{\vartheta}_n \in C(\overline{\Omega}) \cap W^{1,p}(\Omega)$ which converges to a limit $\boldsymbol{\vartheta} \in C(\overline{\Omega}) \cap W^{1,p}_{\text{loc}}(\Omega)$, for any $p > 1$. Then we construct a sequence of variational solutions $\{\boldsymbol{u}_n\}_{n\in\mathbb{N}} \in C(\overline{\Omega}) \cap J^{1,2}(\Omega)$ which satisfy the energy inequality (7.6) and estimate (7.19), (7.20) uniformly in n. Since, according to (7.6), $\{\boldsymbol{u}_n\}_{n\in\mathbb{N}}$ is (uniformly) bounded in $J^{1,2}(\Omega)$, in virtue of Rellich compacteness theorem, there exists a subsequence, again labelled $\boldsymbol{u}_n$, which strongly converges in $L^2(\Omega)$ to a field $\boldsymbol{u}$. Let us prove that

$\{\boldsymbol{u}_n\}_{n\in\mathbb{N}}$ converges to $\boldsymbol{u}$ in $C(\overline{\Omega})$. To this end, set

$$\begin{aligned}
\boldsymbol{u}_{n,m} &= \boldsymbol{u}_n - \boldsymbol{u}_m, \quad \boldsymbol{q}_{n,m} = \boldsymbol{q}_n - \boldsymbol{q}_m,\\
\boldsymbol{\vartheta}_{n,m} &= \boldsymbol{\vartheta}_n - \boldsymbol{\vartheta}_m, \quad \varpi_{n,m} = \varpi_n - \varpi_m, \quad \boldsymbol{\alpha}_{n,m} = \boldsymbol{\alpha}_n - \boldsymbol{\alpha}_m.\\
\boldsymbol{\chi}_{n,m} &= (\nabla\boldsymbol{u}_{n,m})\boldsymbol{u}_{n,m} + (\nabla\boldsymbol{u}_{n,m})\boldsymbol{u}_n + (\nabla\boldsymbol{u}_n)\boldsymbol{u}_{n,m}\\
&\quad + (\nabla\boldsymbol{\vartheta}_{n,m})\boldsymbol{\vartheta}_{n,m} + (\nabla\boldsymbol{\vartheta}_{n,m})\boldsymbol{\vartheta}_n + (\nabla\boldsymbol{\vartheta}_n)\boldsymbol{\vartheta}_{n,m}\\
&\quad + (\nabla\boldsymbol{\vartheta}_n)\boldsymbol{u}_{n,m} + (\nabla\boldsymbol{\vartheta}_{n,m})\boldsymbol{u}_m + (\nabla\boldsymbol{u}_n)\boldsymbol{\vartheta}_{n,m} + (\nabla\boldsymbol{u}_{n,m})\boldsymbol{\vartheta}_m\\
&\quad + \nu\,\mathrm{div}[(1-\psi)\nabla\boldsymbol{\mu}_{n,m} + \nabla\psi\otimes\nabla\times\boldsymbol{q}_{n,m} + \nabla(\nabla\psi\times\boldsymbol{q}_{n,m})\\
&\quad + \psi\nabla\boldsymbol{\alpha}_{n,m}]
\end{aligned}$$

and note that in virtue of (7.5) and (7.10), $\boldsymbol{u}_{n,m}$ must satisfy the equation

$$\nu\int_\Omega \nabla\boldsymbol{\varphi}\cdot\nabla\boldsymbol{u}_{n,m}\mathrm{d}v = -\int_\Omega \boldsymbol{\varphi}\cdot\boldsymbol{\chi}_{n,m}\mathrm{d}v, \quad \forall\boldsymbol{\varphi}\in J^{1,p'}(\Omega),$$

for any $p > 3$. By making use of the divergence theorem, (7.12) and the Schwarz–Hölder inequality, we have

$$\begin{aligned}
\left|\int_\Omega \boldsymbol{\varphi}\cdot\boldsymbol{\chi}_{n,m}\mathrm{d}v\right| \le \Big\{&\|\boldsymbol{u}_{n,m}\|^2_{L^{2p}(\Omega)} + 2\|\boldsymbol{u}_{n,m}\|_{L^{2p}(\Omega)}\|\boldsymbol{u}_n\|_{L^{2p}(\Omega)}\\
&+ \|\boldsymbol{\vartheta}_{n,m}\|^2_{L^{2p}(\Omega)} + 2\|\boldsymbol{\vartheta}_{n,m}\|_{L^{2p}(\Omega)}\|\boldsymbol{\vartheta}_n\|_{L^{2p}(\Omega)}\\
&+ \|\boldsymbol{\vartheta}_n + \boldsymbol{\vartheta}_m\|_{L^{2p}(\Omega)}\|\boldsymbol{u}_{n,m}\|_{L^{2p}(\Omega)}\\
&+ \|\boldsymbol{u}_n + \boldsymbol{u}_m\|_{L^{2p}(\Omega)}\|\boldsymbol{\vartheta}_{n,m}\|_{L^{2p}(\Omega)}\\
&+ \nu\Big[\|\nabla\psi\|_{L^{2p}(\Omega)}(\|\nabla\boldsymbol{\alpha}_{n,m}\|_{L^{2p}(\mathrm{supp}\nabla\psi)} + \|\varpi_{n,m}\|_{L^{2p}(\mathrm{supp}\nabla\psi)})\\
&+ \|1-\psi\|_{L^{2p}(\Omega)}\|\nabla\boldsymbol{\mu}_{n,m}\|_{L^{2p}(\Omega)}\\
&+ 3\|\nabla\psi\|_{L^{2p}(\Omega)}\|\nabla\boldsymbol{q}_{n,m}\|_{L^{2p}(\Omega)}\\
&+ \|D^2\psi\|_{L^{2p}(\Omega)}\|\boldsymbol{q}_{n,m}\|_{L^{2p}(\Omega)}\Big]\Big\}\|\nabla\boldsymbol{\varphi}\|_{L^{p'}(\Omega)}.
\end{aligned}$$

Then, calling $\mathcal{F}(\boldsymbol{u}_{n,m},\boldsymbol{\vartheta}_{n,m},\boldsymbol{\mu}_{n,m},\boldsymbol{q}_{n,m},\boldsymbol{\alpha}_{n,m},\varpi_{n,m})\|\nabla\boldsymbol{\varphi}\|_{L^{p'}(\Omega)}$ the right hand side of the above inequality, we get

$$\|\boldsymbol{\chi}_{n,m}\|_{W_0^{-1,p}(\Omega)} \le \mathcal{F}(\boldsymbol{u}_{n,m},\boldsymbol{\vartheta}_{n,m},\boldsymbol{\mu}_{n,m},\boldsymbol{q}_{n,m},\boldsymbol{\alpha}_{n,m},\varpi_{n,m}). \tag{7.22}$$

Taking into account the convexity theorem for the spaces $L^r(\Omega)$ (cf. [39]):

$$\|\boldsymbol{u}_{n,m}\|_{L^{2p}(\Omega)} \le \|\boldsymbol{u}_{n,m}\|^{1/p'}_{L^\infty(\Omega)}\|\boldsymbol{u}_{n,m}\|^{1/p}_{L^2(\Omega)} \le [M_1(\boldsymbol{f},\boldsymbol{a})]^{1/p'}\|\boldsymbol{u}_{n,m}\|^{1/p}_{L^2(\Omega)},$$

we have that $\{\boldsymbol{u}_n\}_{n\in\mathbb{N}}$ strongly converges in $L^{2p}(\Omega)$. Then, from (7.21) and (7.22) we have that $\{\boldsymbol{\chi}_n\}_{n\in\mathbb{N}}$ is a Cauchy sequence in $W_0^{-1,p}(\Omega)$. Then, in virtue of Theorem 3.1, we have that

$$\|\nabla(\boldsymbol{u}_n - \boldsymbol{u}_m)\|_{L^p(\Omega)} \leq \|\boldsymbol{\chi}_{n,m}\|_{W_0^{-1,p}(\Omega)}. \tag{7.23}$$

From (7.23), by choosing $p > 3$ and making use of Sobolev's imbedding theorem, it follows that

$$\|\boldsymbol{u}_n - \boldsymbol{u}_m\|_{C(\overline{\Omega})} \leq c\|\boldsymbol{\chi}_{n,m}\|_{W_0^{-1,p}(\Omega)}$$

so that $\{\boldsymbol{u}_n\}_{n\in\mathbb{N}}$ converges in $C(\overline{\Omega})$ and, taking into account inequality (7.20), we see that the limit $\boldsymbol{u}(\boldsymbol{x})$ satisfies the estimate

$$\|\boldsymbol{u}\|_{C(\overline{\Omega})} \leq cM_1(\boldsymbol{f}, \boldsymbol{a}).$$

Now, relations (7.5), (7.10) and (7.12) imply that $\boldsymbol{u}(\boldsymbol{x})$ is a solution to the integral equation

$$\begin{aligned}\int_\Omega \{\nu\nabla\boldsymbol{\varphi}\cdot\nabla\boldsymbol{u} + \boldsymbol{\varphi}\cdot[\nabla(\boldsymbol{u}+\boldsymbol{\vartheta})]\boldsymbol{u} + \boldsymbol{\varphi}\cdot(\nabla\boldsymbol{u})\boldsymbol{\vartheta}\}\mathrm{d}v &= \int_\Omega \boldsymbol{\varphi}\cdot\boldsymbol{f}\,\mathrm{d}v \\ &- \nu[\nabla(\nabla\psi\times\boldsymbol{q}) + \nabla\psi\otimes\nabla\times\boldsymbol{q} + (1-\psi)\nabla\boldsymbol{\mu}]\cdot\nabla\boldsymbol{\varphi}\}\mathrm{d}v \\ &- \nu\int_\Omega[\boldsymbol{\varphi}\cdot(\nabla\boldsymbol{\alpha})\nabla\psi - \varpi\boldsymbol{\varphi}\cdot\nabla\psi]\mathrm{d}v + \int_\Omega \boldsymbol{\vartheta}\cdot(\nabla\boldsymbol{\varphi})\boldsymbol{\vartheta}\mathrm{d}v,\ \forall\boldsymbol{\varphi}\in\mathcal{C}(\Omega).\end{aligned}$$

Taking into account (7.10), (7.11), we get

$$\begin{aligned}\int_\Omega [\nu\nabla\boldsymbol{\varphi}\cdot\nabla\boldsymbol{u} + \boldsymbol{\varphi}\cdot[\nabla(\boldsymbol{u}+\boldsymbol{\vartheta})]\boldsymbol{u} + \boldsymbol{\varphi}\cdot(\nabla\boldsymbol{u})\boldsymbol{\vartheta}]\mathrm{d}v &= \int_\Omega \boldsymbol{\varphi}\cdot\boldsymbol{f}\,\mathrm{d}v \\ &+ \int_\Omega[\boldsymbol{\vartheta}(\nabla\boldsymbol{\varphi})\boldsymbol{\vartheta} - \nu\nabla\boldsymbol{\varphi}\cdot\nabla\boldsymbol{\vartheta}]\mathrm{d}v, \quad \forall\boldsymbol{\varphi}\in\mathcal{C}(\Omega).\end{aligned}$$

Hence, setting $\boldsymbol{v} = \boldsymbol{u} + \boldsymbol{\vartheta}$, it follows that

$$\nu\int_\Omega \nabla\boldsymbol{\varphi}\cdot\nabla\boldsymbol{v}\,\mathrm{d}v = \int_\Omega[\boldsymbol{\varphi}\cdot\boldsymbol{f} - \boldsymbol{v}\cdot(\nabla\boldsymbol{\varphi})\boldsymbol{v}]\mathrm{d}v, \quad \forall\boldsymbol{\varphi}\in\mathcal{C},$$

with $\boldsymbol{v}\in C(\overline{\Omega})\cap W^{1,p}_{\mathrm{loc}}(\Omega)$. Then, by means of well–known regularitation techniques (cf, *e.g.*, [16], [30]), we can show that $\boldsymbol{v}\in C^2(\Omega)$ as well as the existence of a pressure field in $C^1(\Omega)$. As a consequence, the existence of a classical solution to the boundary value problem for the stationary Navier–Stokes system is completely proved under hypothesis (h_2). The proof of Theorem 8.1 under hypothesis (h_1) is very similar to the foregoing one and, therefore, it will be omitted. However, we aim at pointing out that in this case some simplifications are possible. For example, the extension $\boldsymbol{\vartheta}$ may be chosen to be the solution to the Stokes system (3.9), (3.2), (3.3). Also, the cut–off function ψ is no longer necessary because the smallness of the right hand side of (7.4) is assured by the hypothesis (h_1) on the boundary data.

To complete the proof of Theorem 7.1, we have to show that the classical solution we have just found is unique in $C^2(\Omega)\cap C(\overline{\Omega})$. To this end, denote by $(\boldsymbol{u}_1,\pi_1)$ and $(\boldsymbol{u}_2,\pi_2)$ two classical solutions to the stationary Navier–Stokes system corresponding to the same body force field and boundary data. Thus, the couple $(\boldsymbol{u}=\boldsymbol{u}_1-\boldsymbol{u}_2, \pi=\pi_1-\pi_2)$ is a solution to the Stokes problem

$$\begin{aligned} &\nu\Delta\boldsymbol{u} = \nabla\pi + (\nabla\boldsymbol{u}_1)\boldsymbol{u} + (\nabla\boldsymbol{u})\boldsymbol{u}_2 = \boldsymbol{\psi}(\boldsymbol{u},\boldsymbol{u}_1,\boldsymbol{u}_2) && \text{in } \Omega,\\ &\operatorname{div}\boldsymbol{u} = 0 && \text{in } \Omega,\\ &\boldsymbol{u} = \boldsymbol{0} && \text{on } \partial\Omega. \end{aligned} \tag{7.24}$$

Then, for any $\boldsymbol{\varphi}\in\mathcal{C}(\Omega)$, we have

$$\begin{aligned} \left|\int_\Omega \boldsymbol{\varphi}\cdot\boldsymbol{\psi}(\boldsymbol{u},\boldsymbol{u}_1,\boldsymbol{u}_2)\mathrm{d}v\right| &= \left|\int_\Omega [\boldsymbol{u}_1\cdot(\nabla\boldsymbol{\varphi})\boldsymbol{u} + \boldsymbol{u}\cdot(\nabla\boldsymbol{\varphi})\boldsymbol{u}_2]\,\mathrm{d}v\right| \\ &\le \|\boldsymbol{u}\|_{C(\overline{\Omega})}\left(\|\boldsymbol{u}_1\|_{C(\overline{\Omega})} + \|\boldsymbol{u}_2\|_{C(\overline{\Omega})}\right)\|\nabla\boldsymbol{\varphi}\|_{L^1(\Omega)} \le c\|\nabla\boldsymbol{\varphi}\|_{L^p(\Omega)} \end{aligned}$$

so that $\boldsymbol{\psi}\in W_0^{-1,p}(\Omega)$, $\forall p>1$. Then, in virtue of Theorem 3.1, system (7.24) adimts a unique variational solution $(\hat{\boldsymbol{u}},\hat{\pi})\in J^{1,p}(\Omega)\times L^p(\Omega), p>3$. Since $\nabla\boldsymbol{\psi}\in L^p(\Omega')$, $\forall\,\Omega'\subset\subset\Omega$, we have that $\hat{\boldsymbol{u}}\in C^2(\Omega)\cap C(\overline{\Omega})$. Therefore, the field $\boldsymbol{v}=\boldsymbol{u}-\hat{\boldsymbol{u}}$ belongs to $C^2(\Omega)\cap C(\overline{\Omega})$ and, in virtue of the uniqueness theorem about classical solutions to the Stokes system, we have that $\boldsymbol{u}=\hat{\boldsymbol{u}}$ so that $\boldsymbol{u}\in J^{1,2}(\Omega)$.

Next, multiply (7.24) scalarly by $\boldsymbol{u}$ and integrate over Ω. Then we have

$$\nu\|\nabla\boldsymbol{u}\|^2_{L^2(\Omega)} = \int_\Omega \boldsymbol{u}\cdot(\nabla\boldsymbol{u})\boldsymbol{u}_1\mathrm{d}v.$$

Hence, by making use of the Schwarz inequality and Poincaré inequality, it follows that

$$\nu\|\nabla \boldsymbol{u}\|^2_{L^2(\Omega)} \le \|\boldsymbol{u}_1\|_{C(\overline{\Omega})}\|\boldsymbol{u}\|_{L^2(\Omega)}\|\nabla \boldsymbol{u}\|_{L^2(\Omega)} \le \mathrm{d}(\Omega)\|\boldsymbol{u}_1\|_{C(\overline{\Omega})}\|\nabla \boldsymbol{u}\|^2_{L^2(\Omega)}$$

and, as a consequence,

$$\left[\nu - \mathrm{d}(\Omega)\|\boldsymbol{u}_1\|_{C(\overline{\Omega})}\right]\|\nabla \boldsymbol{u}\|^2_{L^2(\Omega)} \le 0.$$

Hence the desired result follows at once. □

8. Existence and uniqueness of classical solution to the traction problem of linear elastostatics

In this section we consider the traction problem of linear elastostatics and we look for the regularity conditions on the data, elasticity coefficients and traction field $\boldsymbol{s}$ on the boundary, assuring existence and uniqueness of a classical solution for bounded domains as well as exterior domains and the half–space. In particular, by making use of the maximum modulus theorem for the Stokes system, we are able to prove that the traction problem of linear elastostatics admits a unique classical solution provided $\boldsymbol{s}$ is only continuous and the body is *isotropic near to the boundary*. For the sake of completeness we start by stating the traction boundary value problem of linear elastostatics.

Let $\mathcal{B}$ be a linearly elastic body we identify with the open connected set Ω of $\mathbb{R}^3$ it occupies in an assigned reference configuration. Let $\mathbf{C}_x$ be the *elasticity tensor* of $\mathcal{B}$, *i.e.* a map from $\overline{\Omega} \times \mathrm{Lin}$ into Sym, linear in Lin, such that $\mathbf{C}_x(\boldsymbol{W}) = \mathbf{0}$, for any skew $\boldsymbol{W}$. We assume that $\mathbf{C}_x$ is bounded, continuous in $\overline{\Omega}$ and positive definite, *i.e.*

$$\mu_p \boldsymbol{A}^2 \le \boldsymbol{A} \cdot \mathbf{C}_x(\boldsymbol{A}) \le \mu_m \boldsymbol{A}^2, \quad \forall\, \boldsymbol{A} \in \mathrm{Sym}, \tag{8.1}$$

for some positive constants μ_m and μ_p. For the sake of simplicity, when no confusion may arise, we set $\mathbf{C}_x = \mathbf{C}$. Also, $\mathbf{C}$ is symmetric iff

$$\boldsymbol{A} \cdot \mathbf{C}(\boldsymbol{B}) = \boldsymbol{B} \cdot \mathbf{C}(\boldsymbol{A}), \quad \forall\, \boldsymbol{A}, \boldsymbol{B}.$$

Assume that $\mathcal{B}$ is body force free and subjected to a surface traction field $\boldsymbol{s}$. Then, the *equilibrium configurations* $\chi(\Omega) = \{\boldsymbol{x}+\boldsymbol{u}(\boldsymbol{x}),\ \boldsymbol{x} \in \Omega\}$ are given by the solutions $\boldsymbol{u}(\boldsymbol{x})$ (displacement fields) to the traction boundary value problem

$$\begin{aligned} \operatorname{div} \boldsymbol{S}(\boldsymbol{u}) &= \boldsymbol{0} && \text{in } \Omega, \\ \boldsymbol{S}(\boldsymbol{u}) &= \mathbf{C}(\nabla \boldsymbol{u}) && \text{in } \Omega, \\ \mathbf{C}(\nabla \boldsymbol{u})\boldsymbol{n} &= \boldsymbol{s} && \text{on } \partial\Omega, \end{aligned} \tag{8.2}$$

where the *stress tensor* $\boldsymbol{S}(\boldsymbol{u})$ gives the internal force distribution in the deformed configuration $\chi(\mathcal{B})$ and $(8.2)_2$ is the *Hooke law*. In components system (8.2) reads

$$\begin{aligned} \partial_j(C_{ijhk}\partial_k u_h) &= 0 && \text{in } \Omega, \\ n_j C_{ijhk}\partial_k u_h &= s_i && \text{on } \partial\Omega. \end{aligned}$$

If $\mathcal{B}$ is isotropic, then $(8.2)_2$ takes the form

$$\boldsymbol{S}(\boldsymbol{u}) = \frac{\beta}{1+\nu}\left[\hat{\nabla}\boldsymbol{u} + \frac{\nu}{1-2\nu}(\operatorname{div}\boldsymbol{u})\mathbf{1}\right], \tag{8.3}$$

where the constants $\nu = \nu(\boldsymbol{x})$ and $\beta = \beta(\boldsymbol{x})$ are respectively the *Poisson ratio* and the *Young modulus*. In this case system (8.2) becomes

$$\begin{aligned} \Delta\boldsymbol{u} + \frac{1}{1-2\nu}\nabla\operatorname{div}\boldsymbol{u} &= \boldsymbol{0} \quad \text{in } \Omega, \\ \frac{\beta}{1+\nu}\left[(\hat{\nabla}\boldsymbol{u})\boldsymbol{n} + \frac{\nu}{1-2\nu}(\operatorname{div}\boldsymbol{u})\boldsymbol{n}\right] &= \boldsymbol{s} \quad \text{on } \partial\Omega. \end{aligned} \tag{8.4}$$

If $\mathcal{B}$ is also homogeneous, then ν and β are independent of $\boldsymbol{x}$. Observe that hypothesis (8.1) implies that $\beta > 0$ and $\nu \in (-1, 1/2)$.

Denote by $\boldsymbol{n}(\boldsymbol{\xi})$ the outward unit normal at $\boldsymbol{\xi} \in \partial\Omega$ and by $\boldsymbol{\sigma}$ a continuous field on $\partial\Omega$. Let

$$\mathfrak{C} = \left\{\boldsymbol{u} \in C^2(\Omega) \cap C(\overline{\Omega}) : \lim_{t\to 0^+}\,[\boldsymbol{S}(\boldsymbol{u}(\boldsymbol{\xi} - t\boldsymbol{n}(\boldsymbol{\xi})))\boldsymbol{n}(\boldsymbol{\xi})] = \boldsymbol{\sigma}(\boldsymbol{\xi}),\ \forall\,\boldsymbol{\xi} \in \partial\Omega\right\}.$$

If $\mathbf{C} \in C^1(\Omega)$ and $\boldsymbol{s}$ is continuous on $\partial\Omega$, a classical solution to system (8.2) is a field $\boldsymbol{u} \in \mathfrak{C}$ which satisfies (8.2) pointwise and such that $\boldsymbol{s} = \boldsymbol{\sigma}$ at $\partial\Omega$.

• Bounded Domains – Let Ω be bounded and let $\boldsymbol{s}$ be equilibrated, *i.e.*

$$\int_{\partial\Omega} \boldsymbol{s}\,\mathrm{d}\sigma = \mathbf{0}, \quad \int_{\partial\Omega} \boldsymbol{r} \times \boldsymbol{s}\,\mathrm{d}\sigma = \mathbf{0}.$$

Observe that system (8.2) is satisfied by any field $\boldsymbol{w} \in \mathfrak{R}$. Then, to avoid arbitrariness of rigid displacements we append to system (8.2) the requirement

$$\boldsymbol{u}_{\mathcal{B}} = \mathbf{0}, \qquad (\tilde{\nabla}\boldsymbol{u})_{\mathcal{B}} = \mathbf{0}.$$

Let $\boldsymbol{s} \in L^{\frac{4}{3}}(\partial\Omega)$ and let

$$H(\Omega) = \left\{\boldsymbol{\varphi} \in W^{1,2}(\Omega) : \boldsymbol{\varphi}_\Omega = \mathbf{0}, \;\; (\tilde{\nabla}\boldsymbol{\varphi})_\Omega = \mathbf{0}\right\}.$$

Note that, in virtue of inequalities (2.4)–(2.5), $H(\Omega)$ is a Hilbert space equipped with the scalar product $(\boldsymbol{u}, \boldsymbol{\varphi}) = \int_\Omega \hat{\nabla}\boldsymbol{u} \cdot \hat{\nabla}\boldsymbol{\varphi}\,\mathrm{d}v$.

A variational solution to system (8.2) is a field $\boldsymbol{u} \in H(\Omega)$ such that

$$\int_\Omega \nabla\boldsymbol{\varphi} \cdot \mathsf{C}(\nabla\boldsymbol{u})\mathrm{d}v = \int_{\partial\Omega} \boldsymbol{\varphi} \cdot \boldsymbol{s}\,\mathrm{d}\sigma, \quad \forall\, \boldsymbol{\varphi} \in H(\Omega). \tag{8.5}$$

Of course, a classical solution to the traction problem is a variational solution too.

Let us prove now, for the sake of completeness, the following existence, uniqueness and regularization theorem of variational solutions.

Theorem 8.1. *Let $\boldsymbol{s} \in L^p(\partial\Omega)$, with $p \geq 4/3$. Then, there exists a unique variational solution $\boldsymbol{u}$ to system (8.2) and*

$$\|\nabla\boldsymbol{u}\|_{L^{2,\lambda}(\Omega)} \leq c\|\boldsymbol{s}\|_{L^p(\partial\Omega)}, \tag{8.6}$$

with

$$\lambda = 3 - \frac{4}{p} \in [0, 3),$$

so that if $p = 2$, then $\boldsymbol{u} \in L^q(\Omega)$, for any $q \in [1, +\infty)$ and, if $p > 2$, then $\boldsymbol{u} \in C^{0,\alpha}(\overline{\Omega})$, with $\alpha = 1 - 2/p$ and

$$\|\boldsymbol{u}\|_{C^{0,\alpha}(\overline{\Omega})} \leq c\|\boldsymbol{s}\|_{L^p(\partial\Omega)}. \tag{8.7}$$

Moreover, if $\boldsymbol{s} \in L^\infty(\partial\Omega)$, *then* $\boldsymbol{u} \in C^{0,\alpha}(\overline{\Omega})$ *for any* $\alpha \in (0,1)$ *and*

$$\|\boldsymbol{u}\|_{C^{0,\alpha}(\overline{\Omega})} \le c\|\boldsymbol{s}\|_{L^\infty(\partial\Omega)}. \tag{8.8}$$

If $\mathbf{C} \in C^{k,\alpha}(\Omega)$ $(k = 0,1)$, *then*

$$\|\boldsymbol{u}\|_{C^{k+1,\alpha}(\overline{\Omega}')} \le c(\Omega', \Omega)\|\boldsymbol{s}\|_{L^{\frac{4}{3}}(\partial\Omega)}, \tag{8.9}$$

for any $\Omega' \subset\subset \Omega$. *Moreover, if* $\mathbf{C} \in C^{0,\alpha}(\overline{\Omega})$ *and* $\boldsymbol{s} \in C^{0,\alpha}(\partial\Omega)$, *then*

$$\|\boldsymbol{u}\|_{C^{1,\alpha}(\overline{\Omega})} \le c\|\boldsymbol{s}\|_{C^{0,\alpha}(\partial\Omega)}. \tag{8.10}$$

Finally, if $\mathbf{C} \in C^{1,\alpha}(\Omega) \cap C^{0,\alpha}(\overline{\Omega})$ *and* $\boldsymbol{s} \in C^{0,\alpha}(\partial\Omega)$, *then* $\boldsymbol{u} \in C^{2,\alpha}(\Omega) \cap C^{1,\alpha}(\overline{\Omega})$.

PROOF - The existence and uniqueness of a variational solution to system (8.2) is achieved by a standard technique (see, *e.g.*, [4], [12]). For the sake of completeness, here we reproduce the main steps of the proof.

In virtue of hypothesis (8.1), the left hand side of (8.5) defines a coercive bilinear form on $H(\Omega)$. On the other hand, by the Schwarz–Hölder inequality, the trace theorem and (2.4)–(2.5), we have

$$\left|\int_{\partial\Omega} \boldsymbol{\varphi} \cdot \boldsymbol{s}\, d\sigma\right| \le \|\boldsymbol{\varphi}\|_{L^4(\partial\Omega)}\|\boldsymbol{s}\|_{L^{\frac{4}{3}}(\partial\Omega)} \le c\|\boldsymbol{\varphi}\|_{H(\Omega)}\|\boldsymbol{s}\|_{L^{\frac{4}{3}}(\partial\Omega)}.$$

Hence by the Lax–Milgram lemma it follows that (8.5) admits a unique solution in $H(\Omega)$ and, taking into account (2.4)–(2.5),

$$\|\boldsymbol{u}\|_{W^{1,2}(\Omega)} \le c\|\boldsymbol{s}\|_{L^{\frac{4}{3}}(\partial\Omega)}. \tag{8.11}$$

Let us prove inequality (8.6) *near to the boundary*. To this end, by the regularity of $\partial\Omega$, for any $\tilde{\boldsymbol{x}} \in \partial\Omega$ there exists a diffeomorfism τ of class C^2 from S_1^+ into a neighbourhood $\mathcal{U} \cap \overline{\Omega}$ of $\tilde{\boldsymbol{x}}$, with $\tau(\boldsymbol{o}) = \tilde{\boldsymbol{x}}$, which transforms system (8.2) in $\mathcal{U} \cap \overline{\Omega}$ in an equivalent system in S_1^+. For the sake of simplicity we denote the transformed system by the same symbols as system (8.2). We follow a technique developed by S. Campanato [6] (see also [17] and [18]).

Set

$$\varGamma_R=\left\{\boldsymbol{x}\in\partial S_R^+\,:\,r(\boldsymbol{x})=R\right\},\quad \varSigma_R=\left\{\boldsymbol{x}\in\partial S_R^+\,:\,x_3=0\right\},$$

and consider the Hilbert space

$$H_{\varGamma_R}(S_R^+)=\{\boldsymbol{\varphi}\in W^{1,2}(S_R^+)\,:\,\boldsymbol{\varphi}=\mathbf{0}\text{ on }\varGamma_R\}\quad(R\le 1).$$

Write the variational solution to system (8.2) $\boldsymbol{u}$ in S_R^+ as $\boldsymbol{u}=\boldsymbol{u}_1+\boldsymbol{u}_2$, where $\boldsymbol{u}_1$ is a solution to the system

$$\begin{aligned}&\int_{S_R^+}\nabla\boldsymbol{\varphi}\cdot\mathbf{C}_0(\nabla\boldsymbol{u}_1)\mathrm{d}v=\mathbf{0},\quad\forall\boldsymbol{\varphi}\in H_{\varGamma_R}(S_R^+),\\&\qquad\qquad \boldsymbol{u}_1-\boldsymbol{u}\in H_{\varGamma_R}(S_R^+),\end{aligned}\tag{8.12}$$

where $\mathbf{C}_0$ is the elasticity tensor at the point $\boldsymbol{o}$. By a standard argument (cf, *e.g.*, [251) we see that system (8.12) admits a unique solution $\boldsymbol{u}_1$ in $H_{\varGamma_R}(S_R^+)$. Also, $\boldsymbol{u}_1$ satisfies the following Campanato's inequalities (cf. [7, 45])

$$\begin{aligned}\|\hat\nabla\boldsymbol{u}_1\|^2_{L^2(S_\rho^+)}&\le c\left(\frac{\rho}{R}\right)^3\|\hat\nabla\boldsymbol{u}_1\|^2_{L^2(S_R^+)},\\\|\nabla\boldsymbol{u}_1-(\nabla\boldsymbol{u}_1)_{S_\rho^+}\|^2_{L^2(S_\rho^+)}&\le c\left(\frac{\rho}{R}\right)^5\|\nabla\boldsymbol{u}_1-(\nabla\boldsymbol{u}_1)_{S_R^+}\|^2_{L^2(S_R^+)},\end{aligned}\tag{8.13}$$

for any $\rho\in(0,R]$. Of course, the field $\boldsymbol{u}_2\in H_{\varGamma_R}(S_R^+)$ is a solution to the integral equation

$$\begin{aligned}\int_{S_R^+}\nabla\boldsymbol{\varphi}\cdot\mathbf{C}_0(\nabla\boldsymbol{u}_2)\mathrm{d}v=&\int_{S_R^+}\nabla\boldsymbol{\varphi}\cdot(\mathbf{C}_0-\mathbf{C})(\nabla\boldsymbol{u})\mathrm{d}v\\&+\int_{\varSigma_R}\boldsymbol{\varphi}\cdot\boldsymbol{s}\,\mathrm{d}\sigma,\qquad\forall\boldsymbol{\varphi}\in H_{\varGamma_R}(S_R^+).\end{aligned}\tag{8.14}$$

Choosing $\boldsymbol{\varphi}=\boldsymbol{u}_2$ in (8.14) and using (8.1), the Schwarz–Hölder inequality, the trace theorem and (2.6)–(2.7), we get

$$\begin{aligned}\mu_p\|\hat\nabla\boldsymbol{u}_2\|^2_{L^2(S_R^+)}&\le\omega(R)\|\hat\nabla\boldsymbol{u}\|_{L^2(S_R^+)}\|\hat\nabla\boldsymbol{u}_2\|_{L^2(S_R^+)}+\|\boldsymbol{u}_2\|_{L^4(\varSigma_R)}\|\boldsymbol{s}\|_{L^{\frac43}(\varSigma_R)}\\&\le\omega(R)\|\hat\nabla\boldsymbol{u}\|_{L^2(S_R^+)}\|\hat\nabla\boldsymbol{u}_2\|_{L^2(S_R^+)}+c_3\|\nabla\boldsymbol{u}_2\|_{L^2(S_R^+)}\|\boldsymbol{s}\|_{L^{\frac43}(\varSigma_R)}\\&\le c\|\hat\nabla\boldsymbol{u}_2\|_{L^2(S_R^+)}\left\{\omega(R)\|\hat\nabla\boldsymbol{u}\|_{L^2(S_R^+)}+R^{\frac{3p-4}{2p}}\|\boldsymbol{s}\|_{L^p(\partial\Omega)}\right\},\end{aligned}$$

where the constant c_3 is independent of R and

$$\omega(R) = \max_{|x-y|\le R} |\mathbf{C}_x - \mathbf{C}_y|.$$

Hence, by making use of the inequality $(|a|+|b|)^2 \le 2(a^2+b^2)$, it follows that

$$\|\hat\nabla \boldsymbol{u}_2\|^2_{L^2(S_R^+)} \le c\left\{\omega^2(R)\|\hat\nabla \boldsymbol{u}\|^2_{L^2(S_R^+)} + R^{\frac{3p-4}{p}}\|\boldsymbol{s}\|^2_{L^p(\partial\Omega)}\right\}. \tag{8.15}$$

Since $(\hat\nabla \boldsymbol{u})^2 \le 2(\hat\nabla \boldsymbol{u}_1)^2 + 2(\hat\nabla \boldsymbol{u}_2)^2$ and $(\hat\nabla \boldsymbol{u}_1)^2 \le 2(\hat\nabla \boldsymbol{u})^2 + 2(\hat\nabla \boldsymbol{u}_2)^2$, from $(8.13)_1$ and (8.15) we have

$$\begin{aligned}
\|\hat\nabla \boldsymbol{u}\|^2_{L^2(S_\rho^+)} &\le 2\left\{\|\hat\nabla \boldsymbol{u}_1\|^2_{L^2(S_\rho^+)} + \|\hat\nabla \boldsymbol{u}_2\|^2_{L^2(S_\rho^+)}\right\}\\
&\le c\left\{\left(\frac{\rho}{R}\right)^3\|\hat\nabla \boldsymbol{u}_1\|^2_{L^2(S_R^+)} + \omega^2(R)\|\hat\nabla \boldsymbol{u}\|^2_{L^2(S_R^+)} + R^{\frac{3p-4}{p}}\|\boldsymbol{s}\|^2_{L^p(\partial\Omega)}\right\}\\
&\le c\left\{\left[\left(\frac{\rho}{R}\right)^3 + \omega^2(R)\right]\|\hat\nabla \boldsymbol{u}\|^2_{L^2(S_R^+)} + R^{\frac{3p-4}{p}}\|\boldsymbol{s}\|^2_{L^p(\partial\Omega)}\right\}.
\end{aligned}$$

Hence, in virtue of Lemma 2.5 and (8.11), we get

$$\|\hat\nabla \boldsymbol{u}\|^2_{L^2(S_\rho^+)} \le c\left(\frac{\rho}{R}\right)^{\frac{3p-4}{p}}\|\boldsymbol{s}\|^2_{L^p(\partial\Omega)}. \tag{8.16}$$

By repeating the above arguments in any half–ball $S_R^+(\boldsymbol{x}_o)$, with $\boldsymbol{x}_o \in \Sigma_1$ and $R < \operatorname{dist}(\boldsymbol{x}_o, \Gamma_1)$, we immediately realize that (8.16) holds in $S_\rho^+(\boldsymbol{x}_o)$, for all $\rho < R$. On the other hand, since (8.16) also holds for any ball contained in Ω (cf., *e.g.*, [7]), by a standard covering argument, we get

$$\|\hat\nabla \boldsymbol{u}\|_{L^{2,\lambda}(\Omega)} \le c\|\boldsymbol{s}\|_{L^p(\partial\Omega)}. \tag{8.17}$$

Let $\mathcal{I}$ be either a ball $S_\rho(\boldsymbol{x}_o)$ or a half–ball $S_\rho^+(\boldsymbol{x}_o)$. Then, bearing in mind that

$$\|\nabla \boldsymbol{u} - (\nabla \boldsymbol{u})_{\mathcal{I}}\|^2_{L^2(\mathcal{I})} \le \|\nabla \boldsymbol{u} - \boldsymbol{A}\|^2_{L^2(\mathcal{I})}, \quad \forall \boldsymbol{A},$$

from Korn's inequality (2.5) we have

$$\|\nabla \boldsymbol{u} - (\nabla \boldsymbol{u})_{\mathcal{I}}\|^2_{L^2(\mathcal{I})} \le \|\nabla \boldsymbol{u} - (\tilde\nabla \boldsymbol{u})_{\mathcal{I}}\|^2_{L^2(\mathcal{I})} \le c\|\hat\nabla \boldsymbol{u}\|^2_{L^2(\mathcal{I})},$$

where c is independent of $\boldsymbol{x}_o$ and ρ. Hence, by taking into account (8.17), it follows that $\nabla \boldsymbol{u} \in \mathcal{L}^{2,\lambda}(\Omega)$ and

$$[\![\nabla \boldsymbol{u}]\!]_{2,\lambda} \leq c\|\hat{\nabla}\boldsymbol{u}\|_{L^{2,\lambda}(\Omega)}. \tag{8.18}$$

Since $L^{2,\lambda}(\Omega)$ and $\mathcal{L}^{2,\lambda}(\Omega)$ are isomorphic for $\lambda \in [0,3)$, we see that

$$\|\nabla \boldsymbol{u}\|_{L^{2,\lambda}(\Omega)} \leq c\|\nabla \boldsymbol{u}\|_{L^2(\Omega)} + [\![\nabla \boldsymbol{u}]\!]_{2,\lambda}.$$

Hence, taking into account (8.17), (8.18) and (8.11), we have (8.6). If $p = 2$, from inequalities (2.4)–(2.5) and (8.6) we have

$$\begin{aligned}
\|\boldsymbol{u} - \boldsymbol{u}_{S_R^+}\|^2_{L^2(S_R^+)} &\leq \|\boldsymbol{u} - \boldsymbol{a} - (\tilde{\nabla}\boldsymbol{u})_{S_R^+}\boldsymbol{r}\|^2_{L^2(S_R^+)} \\
&\leq cR^2\|\nabla \boldsymbol{u} - (\tilde{\nabla}\boldsymbol{u})_{S_R^+}\|^2_{L^2(S_R^+)} \\
&\leq cR^2\|\hat{\nabla}\boldsymbol{u}\|^2_{L^2(S_R^+)} \leq cR^3\|\boldsymbol{s}\|^2_{L^2(\partial\Omega)}.
\end{aligned}$$

where $\boldsymbol{a} = (\boldsymbol{u} - (\tilde{\nabla}\boldsymbol{u})_{S_R^+}\boldsymbol{r})_{S_R^+}$. Hence it follows that $\boldsymbol{u} \in \mathcal{L}^{2,3}(\Omega)$ so that $\boldsymbol{u} \in L^q(\Omega)$, for any $q \geq 1$.

Of course, (8.7), (8.8) are a consequence of (8.6) and Lemma 2.2.

If $\boldsymbol{s} \in L^\infty(\partial\Omega)$, then letting $p \to \infty$ in (8.15) yields

$$\|\hat{\nabla}\boldsymbol{u}_2\|^2_{L^2(S_R^+)} \leq c\left\{\omega^2(R)\|\hat{\nabla}\boldsymbol{u}\|^2_{L^2(S_R^+)} + R^3\|\boldsymbol{s}\|^2_{L^\infty(\partial\Omega)}\right\}.$$

Then, by proceeding as we made in the proof of (8.17), (8.18) we get (8.8).

The estimate (8.9) is a consequence of well–known interior estimates (cf., *e.g.*, [7]) and of (8.11).

Assume now that $\mathsf{C} \in C^{0,\alpha}(\overline{\Omega})$, $\boldsymbol{s} \in C^{0,\alpha}(\partial\Omega)$ and consider system (8.2) in the half–ball S_R^+. Let $\boldsymbol{A}$ be a solution to the (algebraic) linear system

$$\mathsf{C}(\boldsymbol{A})e_3 = \boldsymbol{s}_o,$$

where $\boldsymbol{s}_o = \boldsymbol{s}(\boldsymbol{o})$. Split $\boldsymbol{u}$ in S_R^+ as $\boldsymbol{u}_1 + \boldsymbol{u}_2$, where $\boldsymbol{u}_1$ and $\boldsymbol{u}_2$ are the solutions to the systems

$$\begin{gathered}
\int_{S_R^+} \nabla\boldsymbol{\varphi}\cdot \mathsf{C}_0(\nabla \boldsymbol{u}_1)\mathrm{d}v = \int_{S_R^+} \nabla\boldsymbol{\varphi}\cdot \mathsf{C}_0(\boldsymbol{A})\mathrm{d}v, \quad \forall\boldsymbol{\varphi} \in H_{\Gamma_R}(S_R^+), \\
\boldsymbol{u}_1 - \boldsymbol{u} \in H_{\Gamma_R}(S_R^+),
\end{gathered}$$

and

$$\int_{S_R^+} \nabla\varphi\cdot\mathbf{C}_0(\nabla \boldsymbol{u}_2)\mathrm{d}v = \int_{S_R^+} \nabla\varphi\cdot(\mathbf{C}_0 - \mathbf{C})(\nabla\boldsymbol{u})\mathrm{d}v + \int_{\Sigma_R} \boldsymbol{\varphi}\cdot(\boldsymbol{s}-\boldsymbol{s}_o)\mathrm{d}\sigma, \qquad \forall\boldsymbol{\varphi}\in H_{\Gamma_R}(S_R^+),$$

respectively.

The field $\boldsymbol{u}_1$ satisfies inequality $(8.13)_2$ (cf. [17], p. 206). On the other hand, setting $\boldsymbol{\varphi}=\boldsymbol{u}_2$ in the last integral equation, in virtue of the hypotheses made on $\mathbf{C}$ and $\boldsymbol{s}$, using (8.1), Schwarz's inequality, the trace theorem and (2.7), we have that

$$\begin{aligned}
&\mu_p\|\hat{\nabla}\boldsymbol{u}_2\|^2_{L^2(S_R^+)} \le \\
&\quad \le \|\boldsymbol{u}_2\|_{L^2(\Sigma_R)}\|\boldsymbol{s}-\boldsymbol{s}_o\|_{L^2(\Sigma_R)} + cR^\alpha\|\hat{\nabla}\boldsymbol{u}\|_{L^2(S_R^+)}\|\hat{\nabla}\boldsymbol{u}_2\|_{L^2(S_R^+)}\\
&\quad \le cR^\alpha\Big\{R\|\boldsymbol{u}_2\|_{L^2(\Sigma_R)}\|\boldsymbol{s}\|_{C^{0,\alpha}(\partial\Sigma_R)} + \|\hat{\nabla}\boldsymbol{u}\|_{L^2(S_R^+)}\|\hat{\nabla}\boldsymbol{u}_2\|_{L^2(S_R^+)}\Big\}\\
&\quad \le cR^\alpha\Big\{R^{\frac{3}{2}}\|\nabla\boldsymbol{u}_2\|_{L^2(S_R^+)}\|\boldsymbol{s}\|_{C^{0,\alpha}(\partial\Omega)} + \|\hat{\nabla}\boldsymbol{u}\|_{L^2(S_R^+)}\|\hat{\nabla}\boldsymbol{u}_2\|_{L^2(S_R^+)}\Big\}\\
&\quad \le cR^\alpha\|\hat{\nabla}\boldsymbol{u}_2\|_{L^2(S_R^+)}\Big\{R^{\frac{3}{2}}\|\boldsymbol{s}\|_{C^{0,\alpha}(\partial\Omega)} + \|\hat{\nabla}\boldsymbol{u}\|_{L^2(S_R^+)}\Big\}.
\end{aligned}$$

Hence, by taking into account that, in virtue of (8.6),

$$\|\hat{\nabla}\boldsymbol{u}\|^2_{L^2(S_R^+)} \le cR^{3-\epsilon}\|\boldsymbol{s}\|^2_{L^\infty(\partial\Omega)},$$

for any positive ϵ, it follows that

$$\|\hat{\nabla}\boldsymbol{u}_2\|^2_{L^2(S_R^+)} \le cR^{3+2\alpha-\epsilon}\|\boldsymbol{s}\|^2_{C^{0,\alpha}(\partial\Omega)}. \tag{8.19}$$

Then, putting together $(8.13)_2$ and (8.19), and repeating the steps in the proof of (8.16), we have

$$\|\nabla\boldsymbol{u} - (\nabla\boldsymbol{u})_{S_\rho^+}\|^2_{L^2(S_\rho^+)} \le c\left\{\left(\frac{\rho}{R}\right)^5 + R^{3+2\alpha-\epsilon}\|\boldsymbol{s}\|^2_{C^{0,\alpha}(\partial\Omega)}\right\}. \tag{8.20}$$

Of course, (8.20) holds for any half–ball $S_\rho(\boldsymbol{x}_o)$, with $\boldsymbol{x}_o\in\Sigma_1$ and $\rho<R<\operatorname{dist}(\boldsymbol{x}_o,\Gamma_1)$. Therefore, from (8.20), by taking into account Lemma 2.5, it follows that $\nabla\boldsymbol{u}$ is bounded and

$$\|\nabla\boldsymbol{u}\|_{L^\infty(\Omega)} \le c\|\boldsymbol{s}\|_{C^{0,\alpha}(\partial\Omega)},$$

so that

$$\|\nabla \boldsymbol{u} - (\nabla \boldsymbol{u})_{S_\rho^+}\|^2_{L^2(S_\rho^+)} \leq c\left\{\left(\frac{\rho}{R}\right)^5 + R^{3+2\alpha}\|\boldsymbol{s}\|^2_{C^{0,\alpha}(\partial\Omega)}\right\},$$

which yields (8.10). Finally (8.9) and (8.10) imply $\boldsymbol{u} \in C^{2,\alpha}(\Omega) \cap C^{1,\alpha}(\overline{\Omega})$ so that, in particular, $\boldsymbol{u}$ is a classical solution to system (8.2). □

Of course, in virtue of Theorem 8.1, system (8.2) admits at most one classical solution.

It is worth noting that, in order to prove the first part of Theorem 3.1 [resp. (8.10)], it is sufficient to assume Ω of class C^1 [resp. $C^{1,\alpha}$].

Remark 8.1 – If $\mathbf{C} \in C^{0,\alpha}(\overline{\Omega})$ and $\boldsymbol{s} \in L^\infty(\partial\Omega)$, then $\nabla \boldsymbol{u} \in \mathcal{L}^{2,3}(\Omega)$ so that $\nabla \boldsymbol{u} \in L^p(\Omega)$, for any $p \in [1, +\infty)$. Indeed, by repeating the steps in the proof of (8.20), we have

$$\|\hat{\nabla} \boldsymbol{u}_2\|^2_{L^2(S_R^+)} \leq cR^3\|\boldsymbol{s}\|^2_{L^\infty(\partial\Omega)}.$$

Hence, in virtue of $(8.13)_2$, (8.11), it follows that

$$\|\nabla \boldsymbol{u} - (\nabla \boldsymbol{u})_{S_\rho^+}\|^2_{L^2(S_\rho^+)} \leq c\left\{\left(\frac{\rho}{R}\right)^5 \|\nabla \boldsymbol{u} - (\nabla \boldsymbol{u})_{S_R^+}\|^2_{L^2(S_R^+)} + R^3\|\boldsymbol{s}\|_{L^\infty(\partial\Omega)}\right\},$$

which implies the desired result, taking into account Lemma 2.5.

Remark 8.2 – Relation (8.7) can be regarded as a maximum modulus theorem for the displacement field $\boldsymbol{u}$ in terms of the traction field on the boundary. We aim at showing that from (8.7) we can deduce a relation between the L^1–norm of a solution $\boldsymbol{u} \in \partial\Omega$ to the problem

$$\begin{aligned} \operatorname{div} \mathbf{C}(\nabla \boldsymbol{u}) + \boldsymbol{b} &= \mathbf{0} \quad \text{in } \Omega, \\ \mathbf{C}(\nabla \boldsymbol{u})\boldsymbol{n} &= \mathbf{0} \quad \text{in } \partial\Omega \end{aligned} \tag{8.21}$$

and the L^1–norm of $\boldsymbol{b}$ in Ω, where $\boldsymbol{b}$ stands for a body force field.

Let

$$\tilde{H}(\Omega) = \left\{\boldsymbol{u} \in W^{1,2}(\Omega) \,:\, \boldsymbol{u}_{\partial\Omega} = \mathbf{0} \text{ and } (\tilde{\nabla}\boldsymbol{u})_\Omega = \mathbf{0}\right\},$$

and let $\boldsymbol{b} \in L^{\frac{6}{5}}$, with $\boldsymbol{b}_\Omega = \mathbf{0}$. A variational solution to system (8.21) is a field $\boldsymbol{u} \in \tilde{H}(\Omega)$ such that

$$\int_\Omega \nabla\boldsymbol{\varphi} \cdot \mathbf{C}(\nabla \boldsymbol{u}) \mathrm{d}v = \int_\Omega \boldsymbol{\varphi} \cdot \boldsymbol{b}\, \mathrm{d}v, \quad \forall \boldsymbol{\varphi} \in \tilde{H}(\Omega). \tag{8.22}$$

By a stardard technique (cf., *e.g.*, [5], [12]), it is not difficult to show that system (8.21) admits a unique variational solution $\boldsymbol{u} \in \tilde{H}(\Omega)$.

Let $\boldsymbol{s} \in L^\infty(\partial\Omega)$ and, let $\boldsymbol{v} \in \tilde{H}(\Omega)$ be the variational solution to the system

$$\begin{aligned} \operatorname{div} \mathbf{C}^{\mathrm{T}}(\nabla \boldsymbol{v}) &= \mathbf{0} && \text{in } \Omega, \\ \mathbf{C}^{\mathrm{T}}(\nabla \boldsymbol{v})\boldsymbol{n} &= \boldsymbol{s}^* && \text{on } \partial\Omega, \end{aligned}$$

where $\mathbf{C}^{\mathrm{T}}$ is the fourth order tensor defined by

$$\boldsymbol{A} \cdot \mathbf{C}^{\mathrm{T}}(\boldsymbol{B}) = \boldsymbol{B} \cdot \mathbf{C}(\boldsymbol{A}), \quad \forall\, \boldsymbol{A}, \boldsymbol{B},$$

and $\boldsymbol{s}^*$ is the field defined by (2.14). Then, since $\boldsymbol{v}$ is permissible as a *test field* in (8.22), from (8.5) it follows that

$$\int_\Omega \boldsymbol{v} \cdot \boldsymbol{b}\, \mathrm{d}v = \int_\Omega \nabla \boldsymbol{v} \cdot \mathbf{C}(\nabla \boldsymbol{u}) \mathrm{d}v = \int_\Omega \nabla \boldsymbol{u} \cdot \mathbf{C}^{\mathrm{T}}(\nabla \boldsymbol{v}) \mathrm{d}v = \int_{\partial\Omega} \boldsymbol{u} \cdot \boldsymbol{s}\, \mathrm{d}\sigma. \tag{8.23}$$

Taking into account that $\|\boldsymbol{s}^*\|_{L^\infty(\partial\Omega)} \le c\|\boldsymbol{s}\|_{L^\infty(\partial\Omega)}$, (8.23) yields

$$\begin{aligned} \left| \int_{\partial\Omega} \boldsymbol{u} \cdot \boldsymbol{s} \mathrm{d}\sigma \right| &\le \|\boldsymbol{v}\|_{C(\overline{\Omega})} \|\boldsymbol{b}\|_{L^1(\Omega)} \le c\|\boldsymbol{s}^*\|_{L^\infty(\Omega)} \|\boldsymbol{b}\|_{L^1(\Omega)} \\ &\le c\|\boldsymbol{s}\|_{L^\infty(\partial\Omega)} \|\boldsymbol{b}\|_{L^1(\Omega)}. \end{aligned}$$

Hence, in virtue of a well–known result of functional analysis (cf., *e.g.*, [39]), it follows that

$$\|\boldsymbol{u}\|_{L^1(\partial\Omega)} \le c\|\boldsymbol{b}\|_{L^1(\Omega)}.$$

From (8.3) and $(8.4)_1$ it follows that $\boldsymbol{S}$ satisfies the *Beltrami equation* (cf., *e.g.*, [19], p. 92)

$$\Delta \boldsymbol{S} + \frac{1}{1+\nu} \nabla\nabla(\operatorname{tr} \boldsymbol{S}) = \mathbf{0}. \tag{8.24}$$

Let

$$\Omega(2\delta) = \{\boldsymbol{x} \in \Omega : \operatorname{dist}(\boldsymbol{x}, \partial\Omega) < 2\delta\} \tag{8.25}$$

and choose δ so small that, for any couple of different points $\boldsymbol{\xi}_1, \boldsymbol{\xi}_2 \in \partial\Omega$, $\{\boldsymbol{\xi}_1 - t\boldsymbol{n}(\boldsymbol{\xi}_1)\}$ and $\{\boldsymbol{\xi}_2 - t\boldsymbol{n}(\boldsymbol{\xi}_2)\}$, $t \in [0, \delta)$, are disjoint, where $\boldsymbol{n}(\boldsymbol{\xi}_i)$ $(i = 1, 2)$ denotes the outward unit normal to $\partial\Omega$ at $\boldsymbol{\xi}_i$. Of course, in $\Omega(2\delta)$ we can define the function $\boldsymbol{n}(\boldsymbol{x})$ which is equal to $\boldsymbol{n}(\boldsymbol{\xi})$ on $\{\boldsymbol{\xi} - t\boldsymbol{n}(\boldsymbol{\xi})\}$ $(t \in [0, \delta))$.

Theorem 8.2. *Let Ω be of class C^3, let $\mathbf{C} \in C^{1,\alpha}(\Omega) \cap C^{0,\alpha}(\overline{\Omega})$, $\boldsymbol{s} \in C(\partial\Omega)$ and assume that $\mathcal{B}$ is isotropic near to the boundary. Then, the traction problem of linear elastostatics admits a unique classical solution $\boldsymbol{u}$. Moreover $\boldsymbol{u}$ satisfies (8.7), (8.8) and*

$$\|\boldsymbol{S}(\boldsymbol{u})\boldsymbol{n}\|_{C(\overline{\Omega}(\delta))} \le c\|\boldsymbol{s}\|_{C(\partial\Omega)}. \tag{8.26}$$

PROOF - Assume first that $\mathcal{B}$ is homogeneous and isotropic and $\boldsymbol{s} \in C^1(\partial\Omega)$. Then, in virtue of theorem 8.1, system (8.2) admits a unique solution $\boldsymbol{u} \in C^{2,\alpha}(\Omega) \cap C^{1,\alpha}(\overline{\Omega})$.

Let $\kappa(\boldsymbol{x}) \in C^\infty(\mathbb{R}^3)$ be a cut–off function equal to 1 in $\Omega(\delta)$ and vanishing outside $\Omega(2\delta)$, where $\Omega(\delta)$ is defined by (8.25) and set $\boldsymbol{\tau}(\boldsymbol{x}) = \kappa(\boldsymbol{x})\boldsymbol{n}(\boldsymbol{x})$.

Multiply system (8.24) scalarly by $\boldsymbol{\tau}$. Then, setting

$$\boldsymbol{v} = \boldsymbol{S}\boldsymbol{\tau}, \quad \pi = -\frac{1}{1+\nu}\left[\boldsymbol{\tau}\cdot\nabla(\operatorname{tr}\boldsymbol{S})\right], \quad \psi = \boldsymbol{S}\cdot\nabla\boldsymbol{\tau},$$

$$\boldsymbol{f} = -\operatorname{div}\left[2\boldsymbol{S}^{\mathrm{T}}\nabla\boldsymbol{\tau} + \frac{1}{1+\nu}(\operatorname{tr}\boldsymbol{S})\nabla\boldsymbol{\tau}\right] + \boldsymbol{S}\Delta\boldsymbol{\tau} + \frac{1}{1+\nu}(\operatorname{tr}\boldsymbol{S})\nabla(\operatorname{div}\boldsymbol{\tau}),$$

a simple computation shows that $(\boldsymbol{v}, \pi)$ satisfies the Stokes system

$$\begin{aligned} \Delta\boldsymbol{v} + \boldsymbol{f} &= \nabla\pi && \text{in } \Omega,\\ \operatorname{div}\boldsymbol{v} &= \psi && \text{in } \Omega,\\ \boldsymbol{v} &= \boldsymbol{s} && \text{on } \partial\Omega. \end{aligned} \tag{8.27}$$

Let $\boldsymbol{v}_1$ and $\boldsymbol{v}_2$ be the unique classical solutions to the systems

$$\begin{aligned} \Delta\boldsymbol{v}_1 &= \nabla\pi_1 && \text{in } \Omega,\\ \operatorname{div}\boldsymbol{v}_1 &= \psi_\Omega && \text{in } \Omega,\\ \boldsymbol{v}_1 &= \boldsymbol{s} && \text{on } \partial\Omega, \end{aligned} \tag{8.28}$$

$$(8.29)\qquad \begin{aligned} \Delta \boldsymbol{v}_2 + \boldsymbol{f} &= \nabla \pi_2 && \text{in } \Omega, \\ \operatorname{div} \boldsymbol{v}_2 &= \psi - \psi_\Omega && \text{in } \Omega, \\ \boldsymbol{v}_2 &= \boldsymbol{0} && \text{on } \partial\Omega. \end{aligned}$$

Observe that the field $\boldsymbol{z} = \boldsymbol{v}_1 - \frac{1}{3}\psi_\Omega \boldsymbol{r}$ is a solution to system (3.9) corresponding to the boundary datum $\boldsymbol{s} - \frac{1}{3}\psi_\Omega \boldsymbol{r}$. Then, for Lemma 6.1 and (8.11), we have

$$(8.30)\qquad \|\boldsymbol{v}_1\|_{C(\overline{\Omega})} \le c\{\|\boldsymbol{s}\|_{C(\partial\Omega)} + \|\psi\|_{L^2(\Omega)}\} \le c\|\boldsymbol{s}\|_{C(\partial\Omega)} \,.$$

Since $\boldsymbol{S} \in L^{2,\lambda}(\Omega)$ ($\lambda \in (0,3)$), by reproducing the technique employed to prove Theorem 1.3 in [17, p.198] and taking into account (8.11), we see that

$$\|\nabla \boldsymbol{v}_2\|_{L^{2,\lambda}(\Omega)} \le c\|\boldsymbol{s}\|_{C(\partial\Omega)},$$

whence by Lemma 2.2 it follows that

$$(8.31)\qquad \|\boldsymbol{v}_2\|_{C(\overline{\Omega})} \le c\|\boldsymbol{s}\|_{C(\partial\Omega)}.$$

Since by Theorem 5.1 $\boldsymbol{v} = \boldsymbol{v}_1 + \boldsymbol{v}_2$, putting together (8.30) and (8.31) we get

$$\|\boldsymbol{v}\|_{C(\overline{\Omega})} \le \|\boldsymbol{v}_1\|_{C(\overline{\Omega})} + \|\boldsymbol{v}_2\|_{C(\overline{\Omega})} \le c\|\boldsymbol{s}\|_{C(\partial\Omega)}.$$

Hence, by taking into account the properties of the function κ, (8.26) follows at once.

Next, assume that $\boldsymbol{s} \in C(\partial\Omega)$, let $\{\boldsymbol{s}_n\}_{n\in\mathbb{N}}$ be a sequence of fields in $C^1(\partial\Omega)$ which converges to $\boldsymbol{s}$ in $C(\partial\Omega)$. Bearing in ming the definition (2.14) of $\boldsymbol{s}_n^*$, it is not difficut to realize that the sequence $\{\boldsymbol{s}_n^*\}_{n\in\mathbb{N}}$ converges to $\boldsymbol{s}$. Denote by $\boldsymbol{u}_n$ the solution to system (8.4) corresponding to $\boldsymbol{s}_n^*$. Since $\|\boldsymbol{s}_n^* - \boldsymbol{s}_m^*\|_{C(\partial\Omega)} \le c\|\boldsymbol{s}_n - \boldsymbol{s}_m\|_{C(\partial\Omega)}$, in virtue of (8.8) and (8.9), we see that

$$\begin{aligned} &\|\boldsymbol{u}_n - \boldsymbol{u}_m\|_{C(\overline{\Omega})} \le c\|\boldsymbol{s}_n - \boldsymbol{s}_m\|_{C(\partial\Omega)}, \\ &\|\boldsymbol{u}_n - \boldsymbol{u}_m\|_{C^2(\overline{\Omega}')} \le c\|\boldsymbol{s}_n - \boldsymbol{s}_m\|_{C(\partial\Omega)}, \quad \forall\, \Omega' \subset\subset \Omega, \end{aligned}$$

Hence it follows that the sequence $\{\boldsymbol{u}_n\}_{n\in\mathbb{N}}$ converges in $C^2(\Omega) \cap C(\overline{\Omega})$ to a solution $\boldsymbol{u} \in C^2(\Omega) \cap C(\overline{\Omega})$ to system $(8.4)_1$. Moreover, since by (8.26)

$$\|\boldsymbol{S}(\boldsymbol{u}_n - \boldsymbol{u}_m)\boldsymbol{n}\|_{C(\overline{\Omega}(\delta))} \le c\|\boldsymbol{s}_n - \boldsymbol{s}_m\|_{C(\partial\Omega)},$$

we have that $\boldsymbol{u}$ satisfies $(8.4)_3$ so that it turns out to be a classical solution to system (8.2). Finally, Theorem 8.1 assures that $\boldsymbol{u}$ is unique in the class $\mathfrak{C}$.

Assume now that $\mathcal{B}$ is *isotropic near to the boundary*, *i.e*, there exists a positive δ such that $\boldsymbol{S}$ has the form (8.3) in $\Omega(\delta)$. Let $\boldsymbol{s} \in C^1(\partial\Omega)$ and let $\boldsymbol{u}$ be the classical solution to system (8.2). Since Ω is of class C^3, in order to estimate the solution, we can use a standard covering argument to infer that system (8.2) can be safety considered in the half–ball S_R^+ $(R \leq 1)$

$$
\begin{aligned}
\operatorname{div} \mathbf{C}(\nabla \boldsymbol{u}) &= \mathbf{0} \quad \text{in } S_R^+,\\
\mathbf{C}(\nabla \boldsymbol{u})\boldsymbol{n} &= \boldsymbol{s} \quad \text{on } \partial S_R^+.
\end{aligned}
\tag{8.32}
$$

Following [18, p. 384], consider a cut–off function $\theta \in C^\infty(S_R)$ equal to 1 in $S_{\frac{1}{2}}$ and let $\mathcal{S} \subset S_1^+$ be a regular domain containing $\operatorname{supp}\theta \cap S_1^+$. For any $R < 1$ set $\eta(\boldsymbol{x}) = \theta(R\boldsymbol{x})$ and $\mathcal{S}_R = \{R\boldsymbol{x} : \boldsymbol{x} \in \mathcal{S}\}$.

Let $\boldsymbol{v} = \eta\boldsymbol{u}$. Then, from (8.32) it follows that $\boldsymbol{v}$ is a solution to the system

$$
\begin{aligned}
\operatorname{div} \mathbf{C}(\nabla \boldsymbol{v}) + \boldsymbol{\chi} &= \mathbf{0} \quad \text{in } \mathcal{S}_R,\\
\mathbf{C}(\nabla \boldsymbol{v})\boldsymbol{n} &= \mathbf{0} \quad \text{on } \Lambda_R,\\
\mathbf{C}(\nabla \boldsymbol{v})\boldsymbol{n} &= \boldsymbol{\gamma} \quad \text{on } \hat{\Sigma}_R,
\end{aligned}
$$

where $\hat{\Sigma}_R = \Sigma_R \cap \overline{\mathcal{S}}_R$, $\Lambda_R = \partial\mathcal{S} \setminus \hat{\Sigma}_R$ and

$$
\begin{aligned}
\chi_i &= -C_{ijhk}\partial_k u_h \partial_j \eta - \partial_j(C_{ijhk} u_h \partial_k \eta),\\
\boldsymbol{\gamma} &= \eta\boldsymbol{s} + \mathbf{C}(\boldsymbol{u} \otimes \nabla\eta)\boldsymbol{n}.
\end{aligned}
\tag{8.33}
$$

It is not difficult to realize that $\hat{\nabla}\boldsymbol{v} = \hat{\nabla}\boldsymbol{v}_1 + \hat{\nabla}\boldsymbol{v}_2$, where $\boldsymbol{v}_1$ and $\boldsymbol{v}_2$ are the solutions (within a rigid displacement) to the systems

$$
\begin{aligned}
\operatorname{div} \mathbf{C}_o(\nabla \boldsymbol{v}_1) + \boldsymbol{\chi} &= \mathbf{0} \quad \text{in } \mathcal{S}_R,\\
\mathbf{C}_o(\nabla \boldsymbol{v}_1)\boldsymbol{n} &= \mathbf{0} \quad \text{on } \Lambda_R,\\
\mathbf{C}_0(\nabla \boldsymbol{v}_1)\boldsymbol{n} &= \boldsymbol{\gamma} \quad \text{on } \hat{\Sigma}_R
\end{aligned}
$$

and

$$
\begin{aligned}
\operatorname{div} \mathbf{C}_0(\nabla \boldsymbol{v}_2) - \operatorname{div}(\mathbf{C}_0 - \mathbf{C})(\nabla \boldsymbol{v}) &= \mathbf{0} && \text{in } \mathcal{S}_R,\\
\mathbf{C}_0(\nabla \boldsymbol{v}_2)\boldsymbol{n} &= (\mathbf{C}_0 - \mathbf{C})(\nabla \boldsymbol{v})\boldsymbol{n} && \text{on } \partial\mathcal{S}_R,
\end{aligned}
$$

respectively, where $\mathbf{C}_0$ is the elasticity tensor at $\boldsymbol{o}$. Since $\boldsymbol{S}_o = \mathbf{C}_o(\nabla \boldsymbol{v}_1)$ satisfies the following *Beltrami equation* (cf., *e.g.*, [19], p. 92)

$$\Delta \boldsymbol{S}_o + \frac{1}{1+\nu}\nabla\nabla \operatorname{tr} \boldsymbol{S}_o + 2\hat{\nabla}\boldsymbol{\chi} + \frac{\nu}{1-\nu}(\operatorname{div} \boldsymbol{\chi})\mathbf{1} = \mathbf{0},$$

we see that the field $\boldsymbol{S}_o\boldsymbol{\tau}$ is a solution to system (8.27), where, of course, in the expression of the functions $\boldsymbol{f}$ and ψ we have to take into account the derivatives of the field $\boldsymbol{\chi}$. Then, repeating the steps in the proof of (8.31) and making use of Theorem 8.1 we have that

$$\|\mathbf{C}_o(\nabla \boldsymbol{v}_1)\boldsymbol{n}\|^2_{L^2(\tau(\Omega(\delta))\cap \mathcal{S}_R)} \le cR^3\|\boldsymbol{s}\|_{C(\partial\Omega)}. \tag{8.34}$$

An integration by parts and the use of the Schwarz inequality yield

$$\|\hat{\nabla}\boldsymbol{v}_2\|^2_{L^2(\mathcal{S}_R)} \le c\left(\max_{\mathcal{S}_R}|\mathbf{C}-\mathbf{C}_o|\right)\|\hat{\nabla}\boldsymbol{v}\|_{L^2(\mathcal{S}_R)}\|\hat{\nabla}\boldsymbol{v}_2\|_{L^2(\mathcal{S}_R)},$$

whence, bearing in mind that $\mathbf{C} \in C^{0,\alpha}(\overline{\Omega})$, it follows that

$$\|\hat{\nabla}\boldsymbol{v}_2\|^2_{L^2(\mathcal{S}_R)} \le cR^\alpha\|\hat{\nabla}\boldsymbol{v}\|^2_{L^2(\mathcal{S}_R)}.$$

Hence, taking into account that by (8.17),

$$\|\hat{\nabla}\boldsymbol{v}\|^2_{L^2(\mathcal{S}_R)} \le cR^{3-\epsilon}\|\boldsymbol{s}\|_{C(\partial\Omega)}, \tag{8.35}$$

for any positive ϵ, it follows that

$$\|\hat{\nabla}\boldsymbol{v}_2\|^2_{L^2(\mathcal{S}_R)} \le cR^3\|\boldsymbol{s}\|_{C(\partial\Omega)}. \tag{8.36}$$

Since

$$\begin{aligned}\mathbf{C}(\nabla\boldsymbol{v})\boldsymbol{n} &= (\mathbf{C}-\mathbf{C}_o)(\nabla\boldsymbol{v})\boldsymbol{n} + \mathbf{C}_o(\nabla\boldsymbol{v})\boldsymbol{n}\\ &= (\mathbf{C}-\mathbf{C}_o)(\nabla\boldsymbol{v})\boldsymbol{n} + \mathbf{C}_o(\nabla\boldsymbol{v}_1) + \mathbf{C}_o(\nabla\boldsymbol{v}_2),\end{aligned}$$

from (8.34), (8.35) and (8.36) we have that

$$\begin{aligned}\|\mathbf{C}(\nabla\boldsymbol{v})\boldsymbol{n}\|^2_{L^2(\tau(\Omega_\delta)\cap\mathcal{S}_R)} &\le c\left\{R^\alpha\|\hat{\nabla}\boldsymbol{v}\|^2_{L^2(\mathcal{S}_R)} + R^3\|\boldsymbol{s}\|_{C(\partial\Omega)}\right\}\\ &\le cR^3\|\boldsymbol{s}\|_{C(\partial\Omega)}.\end{aligned} \tag{8.37}$$

Since (8.37) holds evidently for any $\boldsymbol{x}_0 \in \Sigma_1$ and for all R less that a suitable R_0, bearing in mind that $\boldsymbol{u} = \boldsymbol{v}$ in $\mathcal{S}_{1/2}$, by a covering argument we have (8.26). Finally, the existence and uniqueness of a classical solution is proved by the standard argument outlined after relation (8.31). □

Of course, it is very important to know the best value of the constant c in (8.26) or at least a lower and an upper bound for it. In general, not much is know about this constant. Nevertheless, in some particular but interesting problems we can obtain some numerical values for c. To this end we refer the reader to the papers [21, 52].

• EXTERIOR DOMAINS – Let

$$\mathfrak{A} = \left\{ \boldsymbol{\varphi} \in L^2_{\text{loc}}(\Omega) \, : \, \hat{\nabla}\boldsymbol{\varphi} \in L^2(\Omega), \, \boldsymbol{w}_{\varphi} = \boldsymbol{0} \right\},$$

where the rigid displacement $\boldsymbol{w}_{\varphi}$ is given by (2.12). Note that, in virtue of $(2.9)_2$–(2.10), $\mathfrak{A}$ is equivalent to the Hilbert space equipped with the scalar product $(\boldsymbol{u}, \boldsymbol{\varphi}) = \int_{\Omega} \nabla \boldsymbol{u} \cdot \nabla \boldsymbol{\varphi} \, dv$. Also, it is worth noting that if $\boldsymbol{\varphi} \in \mathfrak{A}$, then $\boldsymbol{\varphi}$ and $\tilde{\nabla}\boldsymbol{\varphi}$ tend to zero at large spatial distance, at least in a weak sense.

A variational solution to system (8.2) in Ω is a field $\boldsymbol{u} \in \mathfrak{A}$ such that

$$\int_{\Omega} \nabla \boldsymbol{\varphi} \cdot \mathbf{C}(\nabla \boldsymbol{v}) dv = \int_{\partial\Omega} \boldsymbol{\varphi} \cdot \boldsymbol{s} \, d\sigma, \quad \forall \boldsymbol{\varphi} \in \mathfrak{A}. \tag{8.38}$$

Of course, a classical solution to the traction problem which belongs to the space $\mathfrak{A}$ is also a variational solution.

Theorem 8.3. *Let $\boldsymbol{s} \in L^{\infty}(\partial\Omega)$. Then system (8.2) admits a unique variational solution $\boldsymbol{u} \in C^{0,\alpha}(\overline{\Omega})$ and*

$$\|\boldsymbol{u}\|_{\mathfrak{A}} \leq c \|\boldsymbol{s}\|_{L^{\infty}(\partial\Omega)}, \tag{8.39}$$

$$\|\boldsymbol{u}\|_{C^{0,\alpha}(\overline{\Omega} \cap \overline{S}_{\hat{R}})} \leq c(\alpha, \hat{R}) \|\boldsymbol{s}\|_{L^{\infty}(\partial\Omega)}, \quad \forall \alpha \in (0,1), \, \forall \hat{R} > \mathrm{d}(\mathbb{R}^3 \setminus \Omega). \tag{8.40}$$

Moreover, if $\mathbf{C} \in C^{0,\alpha}(\overline{\Omega}_{\delta}) \cap C^{1,\alpha}(\Omega)$ and $\boldsymbol{s} \in C^{0,\alpha}(\partial\Omega)$, then $\boldsymbol{u} \in C^{2,\alpha}(\Omega) \cap C^{1,\alpha}(\overline{\Omega}_{\delta})$ satisfies (8.9) and locally (8.10). Finally, if Ω is of class C^3, $\mathbf{C} \in C^{0,\alpha}(\overline{\Omega}_{\delta}) \cap C^{1,\alpha}(\Omega)$, $\boldsymbol{s} \in C(\partial\Omega)$ and $\mathcal{B}$ is isotropic near to $\partial\Omega$, then system (8.2) admits a unique classical solution $\boldsymbol{u} \in \mathfrak{A}$ and $\boldsymbol{u}$ satisfies (8.26).

PROOF - Using (2.9)–$(2.10)_2$, the trace theorem and the Schwarz–Hölder inequality, we have

$$\left| \int_{\partial\Omega} \boldsymbol{\varphi} \cdot \boldsymbol{s} \, da \right| \leq \|\boldsymbol{\varphi}\|_{L^4(\partial\Omega)} \|\boldsymbol{s}\|_{L^{\frac{4}{3}}(\partial\Omega)} \leq c(\tilde{R}) \|\boldsymbol{\varphi}\|_{W^{1,2}(\Omega_{\tilde{R}})} \|\boldsymbol{s}\|_{L^{\frac{4}{3}}(\partial\Omega)}$$
$$\leq c \|\boldsymbol{\varphi}\|_{\mathfrak{A}} \|\boldsymbol{s}\|_{L^{\frac{4}{3}}(\partial\Omega)},$$

where $\tilde{R} \gg \mathrm{d}(\mathbb{R}^3 \setminus \Omega)$. Then, taking into account hypothesis (8.1), the existence and uniqueness of a variational solution satisfying (8.39) follows from the Lax–Milgram lemma. Finally, the regularity properties of $\boldsymbol{u}$ and the existence of a classical solution to system (8.2) under the only hypothesis of continuity of $\boldsymbol{s}$ are achieved by repeating the steps in the proof of Theorems 8.1, 8.2. □

Next theorem is concerned with the uniqueness of solution $\boldsymbol{u}$, whose existence has been proved in Theorem 8.3, in some function classes characterized by suitable behaviours at large spatial distance. To avoid repetitions, from now on uniqueness will be understood to within rigid displacements.

Theorem 8.4. *Assume that* $\mathbf{C} \in C^{1,\alpha}(\Omega) \cap C^{\alpha}(\overline{\Omega})$ *and either* $\boldsymbol{s} \in C^{0,\alpha}(\partial\Omega)$ *or* $\mathcal{B}$ *is isotropic near to the boundary and* $\boldsymbol{s} \in C(\partial\Omega)$. *Let* $\boldsymbol{u} \in \mathfrak{A}$ *be the classical solution to system* (8.2). *Then* $\boldsymbol{u}$ *is unique in*

$$\mathfrak{C}_1 = \left\{ \varphi \in \mathfrak{C} : \varphi - \boldsymbol{w} = o(r^{\frac{-1+\gamma}{2}}) \quad \text{or} \quad \hat{\nabla}\varphi = o(r^{\frac{-3+\gamma}{2}}) \right\},$$

for some $\boldsymbol{w} \in \mathfrak{R}$, *where*

$$\gamma = \begin{cases} \frac{1}{2}\left(\frac{\mu_p}{c\mu_m}\right)^{\frac{1}{2}} & \text{if } \mathbf{C} \text{ is symmetric,} \\ \frac{\mu_p}{2c\mu_m} & \text{otherwise,} \end{cases}$$

with c *the product of the Poincaré and Korn constants* k *and* c_2 *in* (2.4)–(2.5) *for the spherical shell (see Remark 2.2).*

If there exists a constant elasticity tensor $\mathbf{C}_\infty$ *such that*

$$\exists\, \mu_0 > 0 : \quad \boldsymbol{a} \cdot \mathbf{C}(\boldsymbol{a} \otimes \boldsymbol{b})\boldsymbol{b} \geq \mu_0 \boldsymbol{a}^2 \boldsymbol{b}^2, \quad \forall\, \boldsymbol{a}, \boldsymbol{b} \tag{8.41}$$

and

$$\exists\, \omega,\, R_0 > 0 : \quad |\mathbf{C} - \mathbf{C}_\infty| \leq \omega\mu_0 \quad \text{in } \mathbb{R}^3 \setminus S_{R_0}, \tag{8.42}$$

then $\boldsymbol{u}$ *is unique in*

$$\mathfrak{C}_2 = \left\{ \varphi \in \mathfrak{C} : \varphi - \boldsymbol{w} = o(r^{\frac{-1+\alpha}{2}}) \quad \text{or} \quad \hat{\nabla}\boldsymbol{u} = o(r^{\frac{-3+\alpha}{2}}) \right\},$$

where $\alpha \in (0,3)$ *satisfies the inequality*

$$4\omega^2 < \left(\frac{\alpha}{36\tilde{c}}\right)^{\frac{\alpha}{\alpha-3}} \left(1-\frac{\alpha}{3}\right). \tag{8.43}$$

and $\tilde{c}$ *is the constant appearing in the Campanato inequality* $(8.13)_1$ *for the solutions to the system* $\operatorname{div} \mathbf{C}_\infty(\nabla \boldsymbol{u}) = \mathbf{0}$.

If

$$\lim_{r\to\infty} \mathbf{C}_x = \mathbf{C}_\infty,$$

then $\boldsymbol{u}$ *is unique in*

$$\mathfrak{C}_3 = \left\{\varphi \in \mathfrak{C} : \varphi - \boldsymbol{w} = o(r^{1-\epsilon}) \quad or \quad \hat{\nabla}\boldsymbol{u} = o(r^{-\epsilon})\right\},$$

for some positive ϵ. *Finally, if* $\mathbf{C}$ *is constant, then* $\boldsymbol{u}$ *is unique in*

$$\mathfrak{C}_4 = \left\{\varphi \in \mathfrak{C} : \varphi - \boldsymbol{w} = o(r) \quad or \quad \hat{\nabla}\boldsymbol{u} = o(r)\right\}.$$

PROOF - Let $\boldsymbol{u}$ be a classical solution to system (8.2) corresponding to $\boldsymbol{s} = \mathbf{0}$. Of course, for (8.39), in order to prove uniqueness it is sufficient to show that $\boldsymbol{u} \in \mathfrak{A}$.

Let us prove that $\boldsymbol{u}$ satisfies the following *Caccioppoli inequality*.

$$\|\hat{\nabla}\boldsymbol{u}\|_{L^2(\Omega_R)} \le cR^{-1}\|\boldsymbol{u}-\boldsymbol{w}\|_{L^2(T_R)}, \tag{8.44}$$

for any $R \gg \mathrm{d}(\mathbb{R}^3 \setminus \Omega)$ and for any $\boldsymbol{w} \in \mathfrak{R}$. To this end, let g be a smooth cut–off function in $\mathbb{R}^3$ vanishing outside S_{2R}, equal to 1 in S_R and such that $|\nabla g| \le cR^{-1}$. Then an integration by parts and the use of (8.1) yield

$$\mu_p \int_\Omega (g\hat{\nabla}\boldsymbol{u})^2 \mathrm{d}v \le -2\int_\Omega g\boldsymbol{u}\cdot \mathbf{C}(\nabla\boldsymbol{u})\nabla g\, \mathrm{d}v.$$

Hence, by making use of the inequality

$$2|g\boldsymbol{u}\cdot\mathbf{C}(\nabla\boldsymbol{u})\nabla g| \le c\left[\xi(g\hat{\nabla}\boldsymbol{u})^2 + \xi^{-1}(\nabla g)^2\boldsymbol{u}^2\right], \quad \forall \xi > 0, \tag{8.45}$$

if ξ is properly choosen, it follows that

$$\int_\Omega (g\hat{\nabla}\boldsymbol{u})^2 \mathrm{d}v \le c\int_\Omega (\nabla g)^2\boldsymbol{u}^2 \mathrm{d}v.$$

which implies (8.44), when the properties of the function g and the fact that $\boldsymbol{u}-\boldsymbol{w}$ is a solution to system (8.2) are taken into account.

Note that, by choosing

$$\boldsymbol{w}=\boldsymbol{u}_{T_R}+(\tilde{\nabla}\boldsymbol{u})_{T_R}\boldsymbol{r}, \tag{8.46}$$

and making use of inequalities (2.4)–(2.5), from (8.4) it follows that

$$\|\hat{\nabla}\boldsymbol{u}\|_{L^2(\Omega_R)}\le c\|\hat{\nabla}\boldsymbol{u}\|_{L^2(T_R)}, \tag{8.47}$$

Let $\mathbf{C}$ be symmetric, assume $\boldsymbol{u}\in\mathfrak{C}_1$ and consider the cut–off function

$$g(\boldsymbol{x})=\begin{cases}0 & \boldsymbol{x}\notin S_{2R},\\ 1 & \boldsymbol{x}\in S_R,\\ R^{-1}(2R-r(\boldsymbol{x})) & \boldsymbol{x}\in T_R.\end{cases}$$

Set $\varepsilon(\boldsymbol{A})=\boldsymbol{A}\cdot\mathbf{C}(\boldsymbol{A})$. Then, integrating by parts, we get

$$\int_\Omega g\varepsilon(\nabla\boldsymbol{u})\mathrm{d}v=R^{-1}\int_{T_R}(\boldsymbol{u}-\boldsymbol{w})\cdot\mathbf{C}(\nabla\boldsymbol{u})\boldsymbol{e}_r\mathrm{d}v. \tag{8.48}$$

Let $\boldsymbol{w}$ be given by (8.46). Then, in virtue of the symmetry of $\mathbf{C}$, (8.1) and of inequalities (2.4)–(2.5), we have

$$\begin{aligned}\Big|\int_{T_R}(\boldsymbol{u}-\boldsymbol{w})\cdot\mathbf{C}(\nabla\boldsymbol{u})\boldsymbol{e}_r\mathrm{d}v\Big| &\le\Big\{\int_{T_R}\varepsilon((\boldsymbol{u}-\boldsymbol{w})\otimes\boldsymbol{e}_r)\mathrm{d}v\int_{T_R}\varepsilon(\nabla\boldsymbol{u})\mathrm{d}v\Big\}^{\frac12}\\ &\le\Big\{c\mu_m\int_{T_R}(\hat{\nabla}\boldsymbol{u})^2\mathrm{d}v\int_{T_R}\varepsilon(\nabla\boldsymbol{u})\mathrm{d}v\Big\}^{\frac12}\le\gamma^{-1}\int_{T_R}\varepsilon(\nabla\boldsymbol{u})\mathrm{d}v.\end{aligned} \tag{8.49}$$

Set

$$f(R)=\int_\Omega g\varepsilon(\nabla\boldsymbol{u})\mathrm{d}v.$$

Since by the basic calculus

$$f'(R)=R^{-2}\int_{T_R}\varepsilon(\nabla\boldsymbol{u})r(\boldsymbol{x})\mathrm{d}v,$$

from (8.48), (8.49) it follows that

$$f(R)\le\gamma^{-1}Rf'(R). \tag{8.50}$$

Integrating (8.50) over (ρ, R) yields

$$\int_{\Omega} g(\rho)\varepsilon(\nabla\boldsymbol{u})\mathrm{d}v \leq \left(\frac{\rho}{R}\right)^{\gamma} \int_{\Omega} g(R)\varepsilon(\nabla\boldsymbol{u})\mathrm{d}v.$$

Hence, taking into account (8.1) and the properties of the function g, we get

$$\int_{\Omega\cap S_\rho} (\hat{\nabla}\boldsymbol{u})^2\mathrm{d}v \leq c\left(\frac{\rho}{R}\right)^{\gamma} \int_{\Omega\cap S_R} (\hat{\nabla}\boldsymbol{u})^2\mathrm{d}v. \tag{8.51}$$

for any $\rho \in (0, R/2)$. It is a simple matter to show that (8.51) also holds for any $\rho \in [R/2, R)$. Now, coupling (8.51) with (8.44) and (8.46) respectively, we have

$$\begin{aligned}
&\int_{\Omega\cap S_\rho} (\hat{\nabla}\boldsymbol{u})^2\mathrm{d}v \leq c\frac{\rho^{\gamma}}{R^{\gamma+2}} \int_{T_R} (\boldsymbol{u}-\boldsymbol{w})^2\mathrm{d}v,\\
&\int_{\Omega\cap S_\rho} (\hat{\nabla}\boldsymbol{u})^2\mathrm{d}v \leq c\left(\frac{\rho}{R}\right)^{\gamma} \int_{T_R} (\hat{\nabla}\boldsymbol{u})^2\mathrm{d}v.
\end{aligned}$$

Hence, letting $R \to \infty$ and bearing in mind that $\boldsymbol{u} \in \mathfrak{C}_1$, the desired result follows. The proof of uniqueness in the class $\mathfrak{C}_1$, with a general elasticity tensor C is quite analogous to the previous one, so it is omitted.

Let C satisfy (8.41), (8.42) and $\boldsymbol{u} \in \mathfrak{C}_2$. Let $\eta(\boldsymbol{x}) \in C^{\infty}(\mathbb{R}^3)$ be a cut–off function vanishing in S_{R^*} and equal to 1 outside S_{2R^*}, with $R^* \gg \mathrm{d}(\mathbb{R}^3 \setminus \Omega)$. Then, the field $\boldsymbol{v} = \eta\boldsymbol{u}$ is a classical solution to the system

$$\operatorname{div}\mathsf{C}(\nabla\boldsymbol{v}) + \boldsymbol{\psi} = \mathbf{0} \quad \text{in } \mathbb{R}^3. \tag{8.52}$$

where the field $\boldsymbol{\psi}$ is given by $(8.33)_1$ and vanishes outside T_{R^*}.

Let us show that $\boldsymbol{v}$ satisfies the following *Caccioppoli inequalities*

$$\begin{aligned}
&\|\hat{\nabla}\boldsymbol{v}\|^2_{L^2(S_R)} \leq c\left\{R^{-2}\|\boldsymbol{u}-\boldsymbol{w}\|^2_{L^2(T_R)} + \|r\boldsymbol{\psi}\|^2_{L^2(\mathbb{R}^3)}\right\},\\
&\|\hat{\nabla}\boldsymbol{v}\|^2_{L^2(S_R)} \leq c\left\{\|\hat{\nabla}\boldsymbol{u}\|^2_{L^2(T_R)} + \|r\boldsymbol{\psi}\|^2_{L^2(\mathbb{R}^3)}\right\},
\end{aligned} \tag{8.53}$$

for any $R > 2R^*$ and for any $\boldsymbol{w} \in \mathfrak{R}$. To this end, let g be the smooth cut–off function employed to prove (8.44). Then an integration by parts and the use of (8.1) yield

$$\mu_p \int_{\mathbb{R}^3} (g\hat{\nabla}\boldsymbol{v})^2\mathrm{d}v \leq -2\int_{\mathbb{R}^3} g\boldsymbol{v}\cdot\mathsf{C}(\nabla\boldsymbol{v})\nabla g\,\mathrm{d}v + \int_{\mathbb{R}^3} g^2\boldsymbol{v}\cdot\boldsymbol{\psi}\,\mathrm{d}v.$$

Now, since

$$g^2|\boldsymbol{v}\cdot\boldsymbol{\psi}| \le g^2\left[\xi r^{-2}\boldsymbol{v}^2+\xi^{-1}(r\boldsymbol{\psi})^2\right], \quad \forall \xi>0,$$

we have

$$\begin{aligned}\left|\int_{\mathbb{R}^3} g^2\boldsymbol{v}\cdot\boldsymbol{\psi}\,\mathrm{d}v\right| &\le c\left\{\xi\|gr^{-1}\boldsymbol{v}\|^2_{L^2(\mathbb{R}^3)}+\xi^{-1}\|r\boldsymbol{\psi}\|^2_{L^2(\mathbb{R}^3)}\right\}\\ &\le c\left\{\xi\|\nabla(g\boldsymbol{v})\|^2_{L^2(\mathbb{R}^3)}+\xi^{-1}\|r\boldsymbol{\psi}\|_{L^2(\mathbb{R}^3)}\right\}\\ &\le c\left\{\xi\|\hat{\nabla}(g\boldsymbol{v})\|^2_{L^2(\mathbb{R}^3)}+\xi^{-1}\|r\boldsymbol{\psi}\|_{L^2(\mathbb{R}^3)}\right\}\\ &\le c\left\{\xi\|g\hat{\nabla}\boldsymbol{v}\|^2_{L^2(\mathbb{R}^3)}+\xi\|\nabla g\otimes\boldsymbol{v}\|^2_{L^2(\mathbb{R}^3)}+\xi^{-1}\|r\boldsymbol{\psi}\|^2_{L^2(\mathbb{R}^3)}\right\},\end{aligned}$$

where $(2.9)_1$ and (2.10) have been used. By choosing properly ξ and taking into account (8.45), together with the properties of the function g and the fact that $\boldsymbol{v}-\boldsymbol{w}$ is a solution to system (8.52), we get inequality $(8.53)_1$. Finally, $(8.53)_2$ follows from $(8.53)_1$, (2.4) and (2.5) once $\boldsymbol{w}$ is properly chosen.

Of course, system (8.52) can be written

$$\operatorname{div}\mathbf{C}_\infty(\nabla\boldsymbol{v})-\operatorname{div}(\mathbf{C}_\infty-\mathbf{C})(\nabla\boldsymbol{v})+\boldsymbol{\psi}=\mathbf{0} \quad \text{in } \mathbb{R}^3.$$

Let $\boldsymbol{v}_1$ and $\boldsymbol{v}_2$ be the solutions to the systems

$$\begin{aligned}\operatorname{div}\mathbf{C}_\infty(\nabla\boldsymbol{v}_1)&=\mathbf{0} \quad \text{in } S_R,\\ \boldsymbol{v}_1&=\boldsymbol{v} \quad \text{on } \partial S_R,\end{aligned}$$

$$\begin{aligned}\operatorname{div}\mathbf{C}_\infty(\nabla\boldsymbol{v}_2)+\operatorname{div}\left[\mathbf{C}-\mathbf{C}_\infty\right](\nabla\boldsymbol{v})+\boldsymbol{\psi}&=\mathbf{0} \quad \text{in } S_R,\\ \boldsymbol{v}_2&=\mathbf{0} \quad \text{on } \partial S_R,\end{aligned}$$

respectively. Integrating by parts, making use of (8.41), of the Van Hove inequality (cf. *e.g.*, [19], p.105)

$$\int_{S_R}\nabla\boldsymbol{v}_2\cdot\mathbf{C}_\infty(\nabla\boldsymbol{v}_2)\mathrm{d}v \ge \mu_0\int_{S_R}\nabla\boldsymbol{v}_2\mathrm{d}v,$$

of Schwarz's inequality and of (8.42), (2.7)–(2.8) (see Remark 2.2), we have

$$\begin{aligned}\mu_0\|\hat{\nabla}\boldsymbol{v}_2\|^2_{L^2(S_R)} &\le \int_{S_R}\nabla\boldsymbol{v}_2\cdot(\mathbf{C}-\mathbf{C}_\infty)(\nabla\boldsymbol{v})\mathrm{d}v+\int_{S_R}\boldsymbol{v}_2\cdot\boldsymbol{\psi}\,\mathrm{d}v\\ &\le \omega\mu_0\|\hat{\nabla}\boldsymbol{v}_2\|_{L^2(S_R)}\|\hat{\nabla}\boldsymbol{v}\|_{L^2(S_R)}+\|r^{-1}\boldsymbol{v}_2\|_{L^2(S_R)}\|r\boldsymbol{\psi}\|_{L^2(\mathbb{R}^3)}\\ &\le \mu_0\left\{\omega\|\hat{\nabla}\boldsymbol{v}\|_{L^2(S_R)}+2\sqrt{2}\mu_0^{-1}\|r\boldsymbol{\psi}\|_{L^2(\mathbb{R}^3)}\right\}\|\hat{\nabla}\boldsymbol{v}_2\|_{L^2(S_R)}.\end{aligned}$$

Hence

$$\|\hat{\nabla}\boldsymbol{v}_2\|^2_{L^2(S_R)} \le 2\omega^2\|\hat{\nabla}\boldsymbol{v}\|^2_{L^2(S_R)} + M, \tag{8.54}$$

where

$$M = 8\mu_0^{-2}\|r\boldsymbol{\psi}\|^2_{L^2(\mathbb{R}^3)}.$$

Moreover, $\boldsymbol{v}_1$ satisfies Campanato's inequality $(8.13)_1$ (with $\boldsymbol{x}_o = \boldsymbol{o}$).

Assume $\|\hat{\nabla}\boldsymbol{v}\|_{L^2(\mathbb{R}^3)} > 0$. Since $\hat{\nabla}\boldsymbol{v} = \hat{\nabla}\boldsymbol{v}_1 + \hat{\nabla}\boldsymbol{v}_2$, by $(8.13)_1$, (8.54) the usual computation yields

$$\begin{aligned}
\|\hat{\nabla}\boldsymbol{v}\|^2_{L^2(S_\rho)} &\le 2\|\hat{\nabla}\boldsymbol{v}_1\|^2_{L^2(S_\rho)} + 2\|\hat{\nabla}\boldsymbol{v}_2\|^2_{L^2(S_\rho)}\\
&\le 2\tilde{c}\left(\frac{\rho}{R}\right)^3\|\hat{\nabla}\boldsymbol{v}_1\|^2_{L^2(S_R)} + 4\omega^2\|\hat{\nabla}\boldsymbol{v}\|^2_{L^2(S_R)} + 2M\\
&\le \left\{4\tilde{c}(1+2\omega^2)\left(\frac{\rho}{R}\right)^3 + 4\omega^2 + M_1\|\hat{\nabla}\boldsymbol{v}\|^{-2}_{L^2(\mathbb{R}^3)}\right\}\|\hat{\nabla}\boldsymbol{v}\|^2_{L^2(S_R)},
\end{aligned} \tag{8.55}$$

where $M_1 = 2M(1+2\tilde{c})$.

We claim that $\hat{\nabla}\boldsymbol{v} \in L^2(\mathbb{R}^3)$. Indeed, if *per absurdum* $\hat{\nabla}\boldsymbol{v} \notin L^2(\mathbb{R}^3)$, in virtue of (8.43), we could choose a positive R_1 such that

$$\epsilon = 4\omega^2 + M_1\|\hat{\nabla}\boldsymbol{v}\|^{-2}_{L^2(S_R)} < \left(\frac{\alpha}{36\tilde{c}}\right)^{\frac{\alpha}{\alpha-3}}\left(1-\frac{\alpha}{3}\right), \quad \forall R > R_1,$$

so that (8.55) yields

$$\|\hat{\nabla}\boldsymbol{v}\|_{L^2(S_\rho)} \le \left[12\tilde{c}(\rho/R)^3 + \epsilon\right]\|\hat{\nabla}\boldsymbol{v}\|_{L^2(S_R)}, \quad \forall R > R_1. \tag{8.56}$$

Then, in virtue of Lemma 2.6, (8.56) implies

$$\|\hat{\nabla}\boldsymbol{v}\|_{L^2(S_\rho)} \le c\left(\frac{\rho}{R}\right)^\alpha\|\hat{\nabla}\boldsymbol{v}\|_{L^2(S_R)}.$$

Hence, by taking into account *Caccioppoli's inequalities* (8.53), it follows that

$$\begin{aligned}
\|\hat{\nabla}\boldsymbol{v}\|_{L^2(S_\rho)} &\le c\left\{\frac{\rho^\alpha}{R^{\alpha+2}}\|\boldsymbol{u}-\boldsymbol{w}\|^2_{L^2(T_R)} + \|r\boldsymbol{\psi}\|^2_{L^2(\mathbb{R}^3)}\right\},\\
\|\hat{\nabla}\boldsymbol{v}\|_{L^2(S_\rho)} &\le c\left\{\left(\frac{\rho}{R}\right)^\alpha\|\hat{\nabla}\boldsymbol{u}\|^2_{L^2(T_R)} + \|r\boldsymbol{\psi}\|^2_{L^2(\mathbb{R}^3)}\right\}.
\end{aligned} \tag{8.57}$$

Letting $R \to +\infty$ in (8.57) and taking into account that $\boldsymbol{u} \in \mathfrak{C}_2$, we have $\hat{\nabla}\boldsymbol{v} \in L^2(\mathbb{R}^3)$. Therefore, since this contradicts the *extra assumption* $\hat{\nabla}\boldsymbol{v} \notin L^2(\mathbb{R}^3)$, we conclude that $\hat{\nabla}\boldsymbol{v} \in L^2(\mathbb{R}^3)$ so that $\hat{\nabla}\boldsymbol{u} \in L^2(\mathcal{B})$.

The technique just used to prove uniqueness in the class $\mathfrak{C}_2$ has been introduced by M. Meier [36] to obtain Liouville theorems for nondiagonal elliptic systems.

If $\mathbf{C}$ converges at infinity, then (8.42) if satisfied by any positive number ω, for some $R_0(\omega)$. Hence uniqueness in the class $\mathfrak{C}_3$ easily follows.

Let $\mathbf{C}$ be constant and let $\boldsymbol{v}_1$ and $\boldsymbol{v}_2$ be the solutions to the systems

$$\begin{aligned} \operatorname{div}\mathbf{C}(\nabla \boldsymbol{v}_1) = \mathbf{0} \quad & \text{in } S_R, \\ \boldsymbol{v}_1 = \boldsymbol{v} \quad & \text{on } \partial S_R, \end{aligned}$$

$$\begin{aligned} \operatorname{div}\mathbf{C}(\nabla \boldsymbol{v}_2) + \boldsymbol{\psi} = \mathbf{0} \quad & \text{in } S_R, \\ \boldsymbol{v}_2 = \mathbf{0} \quad & \text{on } \partial S_R, \end{aligned}$$

respectively. An integration by parts and the use of (8.1), of Schwarz's inequality and of (2.7)-(2.8), gives

$$\begin{aligned} \|\hat{\nabla}\boldsymbol{v}_2\|^2_{L^2(S_R)} &\le c\left|\int_{S_R} \boldsymbol{v}_2 \cdot \boldsymbol{\psi}\,\mathrm{d}v\right| \le c\|r^{-1}\boldsymbol{v}_2\|_{L^2(S_R)}\|r\boldsymbol{\psi}\|^2_{L^2(\mathbb{R}^3)} \\ &\le c\|\hat{\nabla}\boldsymbol{v}_2\|_{L^2(S_R)}\|r\boldsymbol{\psi}\|_{L^2(\mathbb{R}^3)}. \end{aligned}$$

Hence

$$\|\hat{\nabla}\boldsymbol{v}_2\|^2_{L^2(S_R)} \le c\|r\boldsymbol{\psi}\|^2_{L^2(\mathbb{R}^3)}. \tag{8.58}$$

Taking into account that $\boldsymbol{v} = \boldsymbol{v}_1 + \boldsymbol{v}_2$ and $\boldsymbol{v}_1$, $\boldsymbol{v}_2$ satisfy $(8.13)_1$, (8.58) we arrive at

$$\|\hat{\nabla}\boldsymbol{v}\|^2_{L^2(S_\rho)} \le c\left\{\left(\frac{\rho}{R}\right)^3 \|\hat{\nabla}\boldsymbol{v}\|^2_{L^2(S_R)} + \|r\boldsymbol{\psi}\|_{L^2(\mathbb{R}^3)}\right\}.$$

Hence uniqueness in the class $\mathfrak{C}_4$ follows by repeating the usual arguments. □

It is worth noting that the above uniqueness theorem also holds for variational solutions to System (8.2).

TWO COUNTER–EXAMPLES – We aim at showing that the uniqueness theorem 8.4 is *sharp* for homogeneous bodies and *sufficiently strong* for inhomogeneous bodies. To this end, for the linearity of the problem, it is sufficient to exhibit nontrivial solutions to system (8.2) with $\boldsymbol{s} = \mathbf{0}$.

- *Homogeneous bodies* – Let $\nu = 0$ and $\Omega = \mathbb{R}^3 \setminus S_1$. Then, a simple computation shows that system (8.4) admits the classical solution

$$\boldsymbol{u}(\boldsymbol{x}) = \left(2r + \frac{1}{r^2}\right)\boldsymbol{e}_r.$$

Since $\boldsymbol{S}(\boldsymbol{u})\boldsymbol{n}$ vanishes on ∂S_1, we conclude that uniqueness does not hold in the class

$$\{\varphi \in \mathfrak{C} : \varphi - \boldsymbol{w} = O(r) \quad \text{or} \quad \hat{\nabla}\varphi = O(1)\}.$$

- *Inhomogeneous bodies* – Let C^* be the *elasticity tensor* defined by

$$\mathsf{C}^*(\boldsymbol{L}) = (\boldsymbol{A} \otimes \boldsymbol{A})\boldsymbol{L} + 2\mu\,\mathrm{sym}\boldsymbol{L},$$

where μ is a positive constant, $\mathrm{sym}\boldsymbol{L}$ stands for the symmetric part of $\boldsymbol{L}$ and

$$\boldsymbol{A} = \mathbf{1} + 3\boldsymbol{e}_r \otimes \boldsymbol{e}_r.$$

Observe that $\mathsf{C}^* \in L^\infty(\mathbb{R}^3) \cap C^\infty(\mathbb{R}^3 \setminus \{\boldsymbol{o}\})$.

Since

$$\boldsymbol{L} \cdot \mathsf{C}^*(\boldsymbol{L}) = (\boldsymbol{A} \cdot \boldsymbol{L})^2 + 2\mu\,\mathrm{sym}\boldsymbol{L}^2, \quad \forall \boldsymbol{L},$$

we see that C^* is positive definite. Also

$$\mu_p = 2\mu, \quad \mu_m = 16 + 2\mu.$$

By a simple computation (cf. [11]) we acknowledge that the system

$$\mathrm{div}\,\mathsf{C}^*(\nabla\boldsymbol{u}) = \mathrm{div}[\boldsymbol{A} \otimes \boldsymbol{A}](\nabla\boldsymbol{u}) + \mu(\nabla\boldsymbol{u} + \nabla\,\mathrm{div}\,\boldsymbol{u}) = \mathbf{0} \tag{8.59}$$

admits the solutions

$$\boldsymbol{u}(\boldsymbol{x}) = \left[\beta_1 r^{\alpha_1+1}(\boldsymbol{x}) + \beta_2 r^{\alpha_2+1}(\boldsymbol{x})\right] \boldsymbol{e}_r, \quad \forall\, \beta_1, \beta_2 \in \mathbb{R},$$

where

$$\alpha_1 = \frac{3}{2}\left[\sqrt{\frac{\mu}{8+\mu}} - 1\right] > -\frac{3}{2},$$
$$\alpha_2 = -\frac{3}{2}\left[\sqrt{\frac{\mu}{8+\mu}} + 1\right] < -\frac{3}{2}.$$

By choosing properly β_1 and β_2, we construct a classical solution to system (8.59) such that $\boldsymbol{S}(\boldsymbol{u})\boldsymbol{n} = \boldsymbol{0}$ on ∂S_1. Then, we have that system (8.59) admits a non trivial solution in $\mathbb{R}^3 \setminus S_1$ whose traction field vanishes on ∂S_1 in the class

$$\left\{\boldsymbol{\varphi} \in \mathfrak{C} \,:\, \boldsymbol{\varphi} = O\Big(r^{\frac{-1}{2}+\frac{3}{2}\sqrt{\frac{\mu_p}{\mu_m}}}\Big) \text{ or } \hat{\nabla}\boldsymbol{\varphi} = O\Big(r^{\frac{-3}{2}+\frac{3}{2}\sqrt{\frac{\mu_p}{\mu_m}}}\Big)\right\}.$$

Observe that $\nabla \boldsymbol{u} \notin L^2(\Omega)$ and, for any $p > 2$, we can find a positive μ such that $\nabla \boldsymbol{u} \in L^p(\Omega)$. Hence it follows that, in general, the traction problem of linear elastostatics in exterior domains is not uniquely solvable in the space

$$\left\{\boldsymbol{\varphi} \in L^2_{\mathrm{loc}}(\Omega) \,:\, \hat{\nabla}\boldsymbol{\varphi} \in L^p(\Omega),\ \boldsymbol{w}_{\boldsymbol{\varphi}} = \boldsymbol{0}\right\},$$

where $p \in (2, +\infty)$. Therefore, we can say that the space $\mathfrak{A}$ is the natural setting in which we have to formulate the traction problem of linear elastostatics in exterior domains.

The above counter–example [44] to uniqueness of solutions to System (8.2) in exterior domains is a minor modification of a famous one by E. De Giorgi [11] in the theory of regularization of weak solutions to elliptic systems. An interpretation of De Giorgi's counter–example in elasticity is given in [43].

It is of some interest to detect wether uniqueness holds in the class

$$\hat{\mathfrak{A}} = \left\{\boldsymbol{\varphi} \in \mathfrak{C} \,:\, \boldsymbol{\varphi} = o\Big(r^{-\frac{1}{2}+\frac{3}{2}\sqrt{\frac{\mu_p}{\mu_m}}}\Big) \text{ or } \hat{\nabla}\boldsymbol{\varphi} = o\Big(r^{-\frac{3}{2}+\frac{3}{2}\sqrt{\frac{\mu_p}{\mu_m}}}\Big)\right\}.$$

As far as we are aware, the above problem is open. We only remark that the uniqueness class $\mathfrak{C}_1$ is *close* to the class $\hat{\mathfrak{A}}$.

Remark 8.3 – Assume that $\mathcal{B}$ is homogeneous and $\boldsymbol{s} \in C^{0,\alpha}(\partial\Omega)$. We aim at showing that the *natural* traction problem in an exterior domain Ω is to find a classical solution to system (8.2) which satisfies the condition at infinity

$$\lim_{r\to\infty} \hat{\nabla}\boldsymbol{u} = \boldsymbol{A}, \tag{8.60}$$

where $\boldsymbol{A}$ is an assigned symmetric second–order constant tensor.

Denote by $\eta(\boldsymbol{x}) \in C^{\infty}(\mathbb{R}^3)$ a cut–off function which vanishes in $S_{\tilde{R}}$ and is equal to 1 outside $S_{2\tilde{R}}$ ($\tilde{R} \gg \mathrm{d}(\mathbb{R}^3 \setminus \Omega)$). Let $\boldsymbol{\xi}$ be the vector field with components

$$\xi_i = C_{ijhk}A_{hk}\partial_j\eta + C_{ijhk}A_{hl}x_l\partial_{hj}\eta.$$

Note that $\boldsymbol{\xi}$ vanishes outside the shell $T_{\tilde{R}}$.

A variational solution to system (8.2), (8.60) is a field $\boldsymbol{v} \in \mathfrak{A}$ such that

$$\int_\Omega \nabla\boldsymbol{\varphi}\cdot\mathbf{C}(\nabla\boldsymbol{v})\mathrm{d}v = \int_{\partial\Omega}\boldsymbol{\varphi}\cdot\boldsymbol{s}\,\mathrm{d}\sigma + \int_\Omega \boldsymbol{\varphi}\cdot\boldsymbol{\xi}\,\mathrm{d}v, \quad \forall\boldsymbol{\varphi}\in\mathfrak{A}. \tag{8.61}$$

Since

$$\left|\int_\Omega \boldsymbol{\varphi}\cdot\boldsymbol{\xi}\,\mathrm{d}v\right| \le \|\boldsymbol{\varphi}\|_{L^6(\Omega)}\|\boldsymbol{\xi}\|_{L^{\frac{6}{5}}(\mathbb{R}^3)} \le \|\boldsymbol{\varphi}\|_{\mathfrak{A}}\|\boldsymbol{\xi}\|_{L^{\frac{6}{5}}(\mathbb{R}^3)},$$

by a standard argument we have that equation (8.61) admits a unique solution in $\mathfrak{A}$. Also, by repeating the steps of the proof of Theorem 8.3, we see that $\boldsymbol{u} = \boldsymbol{v} + \eta\boldsymbol{A}\boldsymbol{r}$ is a classical solution to system (8.2). Moreover, if $\boldsymbol{x}_o$ is a point of a shell T_R ($R > 2\tilde{R}$), from Campanato's and Caccioppoli's inequalities we have

$$\|\hat{\nabla}\boldsymbol{u} - \boldsymbol{A}\|^2_{L^2(S_\rho(\boldsymbol{x}_o))} \le c\left(\frac{\rho}{\zeta}\right)^3\|\hat{\nabla}\boldsymbol{v}\|^2_{L^2(S_\zeta(\boldsymbol{x}_o))} \le \frac{\rho^3}{\zeta^5}\|\boldsymbol{v}-\boldsymbol{w}\|^2_{L^2(S_{2\zeta}(\boldsymbol{x}_o))},$$

for any $\rho \le \zeta < \frac{1}{2}\mathrm{dist}(\boldsymbol{x}_o, T_R)$ and for any $\boldsymbol{w} \in \mathfrak{R}$. Hence, for a proper choice of $\boldsymbol{w}$, by making use of inequalities (2.4)–(2.5), we have

$$|\hat{\nabla}\boldsymbol{u}(\boldsymbol{x}_o) - \boldsymbol{A}| \le c\|\hat{\nabla}\boldsymbol{v}\|_{L^2(T_R)}. \tag{8.62}$$

Letting $R \to \infty$ (and so $r(\boldsymbol{x}_o) \to \infty$) in (8.62) and taking into account that $\hat{\nabla}\boldsymbol{v} \in \mathfrak{A}$, we see that $\boldsymbol{u}$ satisfies also condition (8.60). Then, taking into account

Theorem 8.4, we can state that system (8.2), (8.60) admits a unique classical solution $\boldsymbol{u}$ modulo a rigid displacement and

$$\|\hat{\nabla}\boldsymbol{u}\|_{L^\infty(\Omega)} \leq c\left\{\|\boldsymbol{s}\|_{C^{0,\alpha}(\partial\Omega)} + |\boldsymbol{A}|\right\}.$$

Finally, if $\mathcal{B}$ is isotropic and homogeneous and $\boldsymbol{s} \in C(\partial\Omega)$, we conclude that system (8.2), (8.60) admits a unique classical solution $\boldsymbol{u}$ and

$$\|\boldsymbol{S}(\boldsymbol{u})\boldsymbol{n}\|_{C(\overline{\Omega}_\delta)} + \|\hat{\nabla}\boldsymbol{u}\|_{L^\infty(\mathbb{R}^3\setminus S_R)} \leq c(R)\left\{\|\boldsymbol{s}\|_{C(\partial\Omega)} + |\boldsymbol{A}|\right\} \quad (R > \mathrm{d}(\mathbb{R}^3 \setminus \Omega)).$$

• THE HALF–SPACE – Assume Ω to be the half–space $\mathbb{R}^3_+ = \{\boldsymbol{x} : x_3 > 0\}$. The traction problem in the elastic half–space is known as *the Boussinesq–Cerruti problem.*

If $\mathcal{B}$ is homogeneous and isotropic and $\boldsymbol{s} \in C_0(\partial\Omega)$, then system (8.2) admits a classical solution $\boldsymbol{u}$ given by J. Boussinesq [3] (cf. also [51], p. 667). Moreover, it is unique in the class (cf., *e.g.*, [23])

$$\mathfrak{L} = \{\boldsymbol{v} \in \mathfrak{C} : \lim_{r(\boldsymbol{x})\to\infty} \hat{\nabla}\boldsymbol{v} = \boldsymbol{0}\}.$$

Since, in virtue of (8.24), the couple $(\boldsymbol{S}(\boldsymbol{u})\boldsymbol{e}_3, \partial_3(\operatorname{tr}\boldsymbol{S}(\boldsymbol{u})))$ is a classical solution to Stokes' system (3.9), (3.3) corresponding to $\boldsymbol{a} = \boldsymbol{s}$, from Theorem 6.2 we have

$$\max_{\overline{\mathbb{R}}^3} |\boldsymbol{S}(\boldsymbol{u})\boldsymbol{e}_3| \leq 3 \max_{\mathbb{R}^2} |\boldsymbol{s}|. \tag{8.63}$$

As far as we are aware, the remark that $\boldsymbol{S}(\boldsymbol{u})\boldsymbol{e}_3$ is a solution to Beltrami's equation is due to M.J. Turteltaub and E. Sternberg [50].

If $\boldsymbol{s}$ is continuous on $\partial\mathbb{R}^3_+$ and vanishes at infinity, we can find a sequence in $C_0(\partial\mathbb{R}^3_+)$ which converges uniformly to $\boldsymbol{s}$. Then, reasoning as we made in Theorem (8.3) and making use of interior estimates and (8.63), we have the following

Theorem 8.5. *Let Ω be the half–space $\mathbb{R}^3_+$ and let $\mathcal{B}$ be homogeneous and isotropic. If $\boldsymbol{s}$ is continuous on $\partial\mathbb{R}^3_+$ and vanishes at infinity, then system* (8.2)

admits a classical solution which is unique in the function class $\mathfrak{L}$ and satisfies (8.63).

Acknowledgments. Work partially supported by grants from MURST (Ministry for University and Scientific and Technological Research), and italian CNR (National Research Council), Gruppo Nazionale per la Fisica Matematica.

References.

[1] ADAMS, R.A.: *Sobolev spaces*, Academic Press, New York (1975).

[2] BOGGIO, T.: Sul moto stazionario di una sfera in un liquido viscoso, *Rend. Circ. Mat. Palermo*, **30** (1910), 65–81.

[3] BOUSSINESQ, J.: *Application des potentiels a l'étude de l'équilibre e des mouvements des solides élastiques*, Gautier–Villard, Paris (1885).

[4] CAMPANATO, S.: Sui problemi al contorno per sistemi di equazioni differenziali lineari del tipo dell'elasticità, I, II, *Ann. Scuola Norm. Sup. Pisa* (III), **13**, (1959); 223–258, 275–302.

[5] CAMPANATO, S.: Proprietà di inclusione in spazi di Morrey, *Ricerche Mat.*, **12** (1963), 67–86.

[6] CAMPANATO, S.: Equazioni ellittiche del secondo ordine e spazi $\mathcal{L}^{2,\lambda}$, *Ann. Mat. Pura Appl.*, **69** (1965), 321–380.

[7] CAMPANATO, S.: *Sistemi ellittici in forma divergenza. Regolarità all'interno*, Quaderni Scuola Norm. Sup. Pisa (1980).

[8] CANFORA, A.: Teorema del massimo modulo e teorema di esistenza per il problema di Dirichlet relativo ai sistemi fortemente ellittici, *Ricerche Mat.*, **15** (1964), 249–294.

[9] CATTABRIGA, L.: Su un problema al contorno relativo al sistema di equazioni di Stokes, *Rend. Sem. Mat. Padova*, **31** (1961), 308–340.

[10] Courant, R.: *Dirichlet's principle, conformal mapping and minimal surfaces*, Interscience, New York (1950).

[11] De Giorgi, E.: Un esempio di estremali discontinue per un problema variazionale di tipo ellittico, *Boll. Un. Mat. Ital.*, **4** (1968), 134–137.

[12] Duvaut, G. and Lions, J.L.: *Sur les inéquations en mécanique et en physique*, Dunod, Paris (1972).

[13] Fichera, G.: Sull'esistenza e sul calcolo delle soluzioni dei problemi al contorno, relativi all'equilibrio di un corpo elastico, *Ann. Scuola Norm. Sup. Pisa* (III), **4** (1950), 35–99.

[14] Fichera, G.: Il teorema del massimo modulo per l'equazione dell'elastostatica, *Arch. Rational Mech. Anal.*, **7**, 373–387, 1961.

[15] Fichera, G.: Existence theorems in linear elasticity, in *Handbuch der Physik* (ed. C. Truesdell) vol. VIa/2, Springer–Verlag, Berlin–Heidelberg–New York (1971).

[16] Galdi, G.P.: *An introduction to the mathematical theory of the Navier–Stokes equations*, vol. I, II, Springer Tracts Nat.l Philos. (ed. C. Truesdell) vol. 38, 39, Springer–Verlag, Berlin–Heidelberg–New York (1994).

[17] Giaquinta, M. and Modica, G.: Nonlinear systems of the type of the stationary Navier–Stokes system, *J. Reine U. Angew. Math.* **330** (1992), 173–214.

[18] Giusti, E.: *Metodi diretti nel calcolo delle variazioni*, Unione Matematica Italiana (1994).

[19] Gurtin, M.E.: The linear theory of elasticity, in *Handbuch der Physik* (ed. C. Truesdell) vol. VIa/2, Springer–Verlag, Berlin–Heidelberg–New York (1971).

[20] Hadamard, J.: Sur le principle de Dirichlet, *Bull. Soc. Math. France*, **24** (1906), 135–138.

[21] Horgan, C.O.: Maximum principle and bounds on stress concentration factors in the torsion of grooved shaft of revolution, *J. Elasticity*, **12** (1982) 281–291.

[22] Kadleč, J. and Nečas, J.: Sulla regolarità delle soluzioni di equazioni ellittiche negli spazi $H^{k,\lambda}$, *Ann. Scuola Norm. Sup. Pisa* (IV), **21** (1979), 527–545.

[23] Knops, R.J. and Payne L.E.: *Uniqueness theorems in linear elasticity*, Springer Tracts Nat. Philos. (ed.B. Coleman) vol. 19, Springer–Verlag, Berlin–Heidelberg–New York (1971).

[24] Kondratiev, V.A. and Oleinik, O.A.: Asymptotic properties of solutions of the elasticity system, in: *Proceedings of international conference on applications of multiple scaling in mechanics* (P.G. Ciarlet and E. Sanchez–Palencia) Eds, Masson, Paris (1987), 188-205.

[25] Kondratiev, V.A. and Oleinik, O.A.: Boundary–value problems for the system of elasticity theory in unbounded domains. Korn's inequality, *Russian Math. Surveys*, **43**, 65–119, 1988.

[26] Korn, A.: Solution générale du problème d'équilibre dans la théorie de l'elasticité, dans le cas où les efforts sont donnés à la surface, *Ann. Fac. Sci. Toulouse Math.*, **10** (1908), 165–269.

[27] Kratz, W.: On the maximum modulus theorem for Stokes function, *App. Anal.*, **58** (1995), 293–302.

[28] Kratz, W.: The maximum modulus theorem for the Stokes system in a ball, *Math. Z.* 1996 (in press).

[29] Kupradze, V.D., Gegelia, T.G, Basheleishvili, M.O. and Burchuladze, T.V.: *Three–dimensional problems of the mathematical theory of elasticity and thermoelasticity*, Series in Applied Mathematics and Mechanics, **23** (ed.V.D. Kupradze), North–Holland Pub. Co., Amsterdam–New York–Oxford (1979).

[30] Ladyzhenskaia, O.A.: *The Mathematical theory of viscous incompressible fluid*, Gordon and Breach, New York–London–Paris (1969).

[31] Leray, J.: Etude de diverses équations intégrales non linéaires et de quelques problèmes que pose l'hydrodynamique, *J. Math. Pures Appl.*, **12** (1933), 1–82.

[32] Lichtenstein, L.: Über einige existenzeprobleme der hydrodynamik, *Math. Z.*, **28** (1928), 387–415.

[33] Maremonti, P.: On the Stokes flows: the maximum modulus theorem, in *7th Conference on Waves and Stability in Continuous Media*, (S. Rionero and T. Ruggeri Eds.), Series on Advances in Mathematics fo Applied Sciences, **23**, 258-264, World Scientific, Singapore (1994).

[34] Maremonti, P.: On the Stokes equations: the maximum modulus Theorem, submitted for publication.

[35] Maremonti, P. Russo, R.: On the maximum modulus theorem for the Stokes system, *Ann. Scuola Norm. Sup. Pisa* (IV), **30** (1994), 630–643.

[36] MEIER, M.: Liouville theorems for nondiagonal elliptic systems in arbitrary dimensions, *Math. Z.*, **176** (1981), 207–228.

[37] MIRANDA, C.: Formule di maggiorazione e teorema di esistenza per le funzioni biarmoniche in due variabili, *Gior. Mat. Battaglini*, **78** (1948), 97–118.

[38] MIRANDA, C.: Teorema del massimo modulo e teorema di esistenza e di unicità per il problema di Dirichlet relativo alle equazioni ellittiche in due variabili, *Ann. Mat. Pura Appl.*, **46** (1958), 265–312.

[39] MIRANDA, C.: *Istituzioni di analisi funzionale lineare*, Unione Matematica Italiana, Oderisi Gubbio Editrice (1978).

[40] ODQVIST, F.K.G.: Über die randwertaufgaben der hydrodynamik zäher flüssigkeiten, *Math. Z.*, **32** (1930), 329–375.

[41] PAYNE, L.E. AND WEINBERGER, H.: On Korn's inequality, *Arch. Rational Mech. Anal.*, **8** (1961), 89–98.

[42] PICONE, M.: Nuovi indirizzi di ricerca nella teoria e nel calcolo delle soluzioni di talune equazioni lineari alle derivate parziali della fisica–matematica, *Ann. Scuola Norm. Sup. Pisa* (II), **5** (1936), 213–288.

[43] PODIO GUIDUGLI, P.: De Giorgi's counterexample in elasticity, *Quart. Appl. Math.*, **34** (1977), 411–419.

[44] RUSSO, R.: An extension of the basic theorems of linear elastostatics to exterior domains, *Ann. Univ. Ferrara* (VII), **34** (1988), 101-119.

[45] RUSSO, R.: On the traction problem in linear elastostatics, *J. Elasticity*, **27** (1992), 57–68.

[46] SIMADER, C.G.: Mean value formulas, Weyl's lemma and Liouville theorems for Δ^2 and Stokes' system, *Resultate Math.*, **22** (1992) 761–780.

[47] SOLONNIKOV, V.A.: On the estimates of the tensor Green's function for some boundary–value problems, *Dokl. Akad. Nauk SSSR*, **130**, (1960) 988–991; english trans. in *Soviet Math. Dokl.*, **1** (1960), 128–131.

[48] SOLONNIKOV, V.A.: General boundary value problems for Douglis–Niremberg elliptic systems II, *Trudy Mat. Inst. Steklov*, **92** (1966), 233–297; english trans. in *Proc. Steklov Inst. Math.*, **92** (1966) 212–272.

[49] TEMAM, R.: *Navier–Stokes equations*, North–Holland Pub. Co., Amsterdam–New York–Tokyo (1977).

[50] TURTELTAUB, M.J. AND STERNBERG, E.: Elastostatic uniqueness in the half–space, *Arch. Rational Mech. Anal.*, **24** (1967), 233–242.

[51] VILLAGGIO, P., Maximum modulus theorem for the elastic half–space, *Riv. Mat. Univ. Parma*, **5** (1979): 663–672.

[52] WHEELER, L.T.: Maximum principle in classical elasticity, in *Mathematical problems in elasticity* (ed. R. RUSSO), Series on Advances in Mathematics for Applied Sciences, **38**, 157–185, World Scientific, Singapore (1996).

Steady flows of barotropic viscous fluids

Mariarosaria Padula

Contents

1. Introduction

The equations governing the flow of viscous compressible fluids are, with no doubt, of basic interest within the context of the modern fluid-dynamical theory. Such equations can be considered as a generalization of the "incompressible" Navier–Stokes system. More precisely, equations governing motions of viscous compressible fluids were derived for the first time by S. D. Poisson (1831) [81], but only after the basic work of G.G. Stokes (1845) [94], they have been set in a more precise axiomatic thermodynamical context. The barotropy assumption represents a typical approximation which renders the problem mathematically more affordable. Nowadays, there is yet neither a satisfactory physical justification of such approximation neither a complete mathematical theory.

The objective of this article is to develop the theory of viscous barotropic flows as a rigorous mathematical science. Precisely, we shall investigate such properties of the fluid flows as the validity of the mathematical model of barotropic fluids, together with the existence, uniqueness, regularity, and asymptotic behaviour in space for steady state solutions.

Over the last ten years, a great interest has been devoted to the study of the mathematical theory of steady-state Poisson–Stokes equations, and several results have been reached for general domains. However, several crucial basic questions still remain unsolved. We wish to give here a landscape of this subject as complete as possible, pointing out that the mathematical difficulties of the problem depend on the region Ω in which the flow occurs.

The first scientific question we pursue is the mathematical modeling of viscous compressible fluids resulting in the Poisson-Stokes equations. In other words, we analyze the approximations which have to be required on the thermodynamical process.

Next, we distinguish between Ω: bounded; exterior to a bounded region; with unbounded boundaries. In all cases, we add suitable boundary and side conditions, we outline the difficulties which each problem presents, noticing that the problems, as they usually stand, can be ill-posed, and, finally, we direct our attention to those fundamental questions that still have no answer. In particular, for each kind of domain, we show, through counterexamples, some pathological behaviours of the classical well-posedness problem. Then, the analysis of such paradoxical solutions leads us to determine the appropriate boundary and side conditions, which bring to the correct well-posedness of the problem.

In general, we renounce to give detailed proofs of theorems, in order to stress only the main physical and mathematical difficulties one encounters.

In the main part of the article (Section 3), we develop the mathematical theory of viscous barotropic fluids in bounded domains. Here, we analyze first the correctness of the boundary value problem one is supposed to solve, then for isothermal flows occurring in a bounded region we propose a new iterative procedure for the proof of an existence and uniqueness theorem. Here, we consider several kinds of bounded domains, beginning with the classical rigid container, where we prescribe adherence conditions, then considering the star atmosphere where stress free boundaries, conditions appear more appropriate, ending with a bounded portion of an unbounded domain, where for numerical reasons the boundedness of the domain is required and therefore artificial boundaries seem needed to be introduced. In the last case, on artificial boundary it is auspicable to not disturb the real motion: in this paper we devote particular attention on this problem. Still for bounded domains, we analyze the case of isothermal fluids where the potential forces can be arbitrarily large. The section ends with a survey of early results and the method of proof there employed. Finally, we juxtapose the possibility of interior regularity of steady viscous compressible flows, to the possibility of interior discontinuity for the density.

Because of the novelty of our approach and the extension of the subject, we must limit our proofs, even in the case of rigid boundaries, to a short outline of the main tools employied. The iterative procedure we are proposing has major advantages: it is in the line of the proofs usually adopted for incompressible fluids, it looks as the natural one suggested by the equations, no modifications in the scheme are needed for different boundary conditions, it appears the most efficient for numerical computations. For each of the other above described problems, we either give rough drafts of proof of an existence theorem or just point out the main questions which remain to be solved. The last part of the second section ends with a brief review of the previous results, and with some comments on the regularity of the solutions in rigid domains.

For unbounded domains some limit conditions should be added, and these will depend on the kind of domain in which the flow occurs. Therefore, we are led to distinguish between domains exterior to a compact region $\mathcal{B}_0$ and domains with unbounded boundary.

If the fluid fills an exterior region, the first existence proofs of steady flows have been given in [45], [46], [75]. Successively, in [58], always in exterior domains, it was proved existence, uniqueness and regularity of steady flows of a viscous, isothermal gas, at least for sufficiently small data, see also [76]. These flows possess good summability properties, say the velocity and the variation of density to a constant state, and their derivatives as well, are in suitable Lebesgue spaces. In the sequel, in [59], [60] are studied the asymptotic properties of the velocity and density fields, in particular, the wake region is exhibited for obstacles which are moving with a constant translational speed.

When the fluid fills regions with a non-compact boundary, one should distinguish between domains having bounded cross sections, which are unbounded only in one direction, also called "pipes", and those having unbounded cross section, also known as "diverging channels": in this last class are included the half space and the aperture flow. Only few results can be quoted in this field, see, *e.g.*, [63], [78]. For domains with a non-compact boundary we derive new "energy estimates" and further "a priori" estimates, which will depend on the number of the directions which go to infinity. We also prove that the classical formulation, proposed by Leray in tubes for incompressible steady flows [32], sometimes gives contradictory results.

The plan of the paper is the following. After the introductory physical Section 2, we divide the remaining part of the paper into three sections, each of which takes into account a different geometry of the domain filled by the gas: bounded, exterior, with a non-compact boundary. In each section, we shall follow a common line. First, we propose the classical boundary and side conditions one would usually prescribe on the kinetic field and on the density. Therefore, we warn the reader to use them with care, by providing some pathological situation for the rest state. Precisely, in each chapter, we exhibit a representative and illustrative ill-posed problem. The anomalous situation, furnishes the key to gain a proper understanding of the properties of flow of a viscous compressible gas. This leads us in the position to set correctly the well-posedness question, and hopefully to solve it, at least for one prescribed large class of flows, corresponding to small forces. Next, we show that such limit conditions, for small external data, solve the classical existence and uniqueness problems.

As a matter of fact, in order to solve the well posedness problem for large external data, we are led, in a very natural way, to change the classical formulation of the problem, proposed in next chapters.

2. The Poisson-Stokes equations of viscous barotropics fluids

2.1 - An introduction to heat conducting fluids.

As is well known, a good mechanical model which results quite appropriate to describe the mathematical properties of a barotropic gas has been furnished, for the first time, in an axiomatically clear and satisfactory way, by Poisson [81], and Stokes [94]. Precisely, the indefinite equations governing the flow of a continuum medium are derived from the balance laws for the density, the linear momentum, and the energy [1] :

$$\begin{aligned} &\frac{\partial \rho}{\partial t} + \nabla \cdot (\rho \boldsymbol{v}) = 0, \\ &\rho \frac{\mathrm{d}\boldsymbol{v}}{\mathrm{d}t} = \nabla \cdot \boldsymbol{T} + \rho \boldsymbol{f} + \boldsymbol{b}, \qquad (2.1) \\ &\rho \frac{\mathrm{d}\epsilon}{\mathrm{d}t} = \boldsymbol{T} : \boldsymbol{D} - \nabla \cdot \boldsymbol{q} + r. \end{aligned}$$

Here the thermodynamical state of the fluid is given by the density $\rho(x,t)$, the velocity $\boldsymbol{v}(x,t)$, and the temperature $\theta(x,t)$. Furthermore, ϵ is the internal energy, $\boldsymbol{D}$ is the velocity deformation tensor, and $\boldsymbol{f}$, $\boldsymbol{b}$ are the external body forces respectively per unit mass and volume, r the heat source per unit volume. Finally, $\mathrm{d}/\mathrm{d}t = \partial/\partial t + \boldsymbol{v} \cdot \nabla$ is the material time derivative. Notice that the volume force $\boldsymbol{b}$ takes into account either mechanical effects due

[1] Light face letters and bold–face lower-case letters denote scalars and vectors (in $\mathbb{R}^n$, $n = 2, 3$), respectively; x and y generic points of $\mathbb{R}^n$, $\boldsymbol{r}(x)$ is the vector position of the point x and the operators ∇, $\nabla\cdot$, $\nabla\times$ and Δ have their usual meaning; $\boldsymbol{v} \cdot \nabla \boldsymbol{v}$ is the vector with components $v_i \partial_i v_j$ and $\boldsymbol{T} : \boldsymbol{D}$ is the scalar $T_{ij} D_{ij}$, where $\boldsymbol{T}$ and $\boldsymbol{D}$ are two second-order tensors (in $\mathbb{R}^n$). Other notation we shall use, will be specified when it will be introduced for the first time.

to non-homogeneous boundary data, or electromagnetic effects. Finally, in a isotropic viscous fluid the stress tensor $\boldsymbol{T}$, and the heat flux $\boldsymbol{q}$, are given in first approximation by the Newton-Cauchy-Poisson law and by Fourier's law, respectively,

$$\begin{aligned} \boldsymbol{T} &= (-p + \lambda \nabla \cdot \boldsymbol{v})\boldsymbol{I} + 2\mu \boldsymbol{D}, \\ \boldsymbol{q} &= -\chi \nabla \theta, \end{aligned} \tag{2.2}$$

where p is the pressure, λ, μ denote the bulk and shear viscosities respectively, χ is the thermal condictivity and $\boldsymbol{I}$ is the unit second–order tensor.

The fundamental question which a "pure" fluid dynamicist would like to solve is the following classical mechanical problem:

Given the external sources $\boldsymbol{f}$, $\boldsymbol{b}$, r, and the stress tensor $\boldsymbol{T}$, the heat flux $\boldsymbol{q}$ and the internal energy ϵ as functionals of the thermodynamical state (the response of the material), to determine the density, velocity, and temperature fields.

The pourpose of this paper is to study homogeneous viscous fluids under some particular constitutive assumptions and under small applied external forces.

2.2 - Some properties of homogeneous viscous fluids.

In what follows we shall make use of some of the concepts of classical thermodynamics, [97], [98]. A fluid is *homogeneous* if there exists a caloric state equation of the type

$$\epsilon = \epsilon(\eta, \rho), \tag{2.3}$$

where ϵ, and η are the internal energy and the entropy, per unit mass, respectively.

For such fluids, the pressure p, the temperature θ, and the specific heats are given by

$$p = \rho^2 \left(\frac{\partial \epsilon}{\partial \rho}\right)_\eta, \quad \theta = \left(\frac{\partial \epsilon}{\partial \eta}\right)_\rho, \quad c_p := \theta \left(\frac{\partial \eta}{\partial \theta}\right)_p, \quad c_v := \theta \left(\frac{\partial \eta}{\partial \theta}\right)_\rho. \tag{2.4}$$

Moreover, *Carnot's law*

$$c_p - c_v = R_*,$$

holds, with R_* the universal constant of gases ($R_* = 2.870\times10^3 cm^2/(sec^2 degC)$ for dry air). We also define the adiabatic (constant) exponent $\gamma = (c_p/c_v)$. Recall that, for most gases, γ varies between 1 and 5/3, the value $\gamma = 1.4$ describes the air at moderate temperature.

Let us say few words on the thermal state equation for the pressure,

$$p = p(\rho, \theta), \qquad p = p(\rho, \eta)$$

also said *caloric equation.* The *coefficient of thermal expansion* is given by

$$\alpha_\theta := -\frac{1}{\rho}\left(\frac{\partial \rho}{\partial \theta}\right)_p .$$

A fluid is *piezotropic* if the internal energy is a functional of the form

$$\epsilon = H(\eta) + Y(\rho),$$

for such fluids (2.4) yields

$$p = \rho^2 Y'(\rho), \quad \theta = H'(\eta). \tag{2.5}$$

Therefore a fluid is *piezotropic* if and only if $\gamma = 1$ or, equivalently, $\alpha_\theta = 0$ [97].

If the effect of viscosity and heat conduction are neglected, we define the local real sound speed at $V_s(x,t)$ by, cf. [14], sect.35,

$$V_s^2(x,t) := \left(\frac{\partial p}{\partial \rho}(x,t)\right)_\eta . \tag{2.6}$$

We find it convenient to consider a *perfect gas* whose molecules exert no force on each other except at collision and have a negligible volume. It seems likely that, under normal conditions, real gases have properties which approximate closely those of the hypothetical perfect gas, and observation shows this to be tha case. Indeed, some empirical laws, such as Boyle's and Charles' laws, can be deduced as properties of perfect gases. By choosing ρ and θ as state variables, the *equation of state of a perfect gas* is given by

$$p = R_* \theta \rho. \tag{2.7}$$

Under these assumptions, it can be proved, [14], sect. 4, p. 8, that the internal energy is a function of the temperature only. This fact simpiflies some of the general expressions for specific heat. Indeed, for such special case of a *perfect gas with constant specific heats* we obtain explicit expressions for ϵ, and η, *i.e.*

$$\epsilon = c_v \theta, \quad \eta = c_v \log(p\rho^{-\gamma}).$$

As a consequence, under the more strict assumption of an isentropic change of state, it is $p = k\rho^\gamma$, with k constant, whence (2.6) yields the Laplace-Poisson formula

$$V_s^2(x,t) := \frac{\gamma p}{\rho}(x,t).$$

In liquids such formula doesn't hold at all. For example, many liquids can be approximated with equations of state of the special type $p \equiv (\rho - \rho_0)^\delta$. Hence, (2.6) yields $V_s^2 = (p\delta/(\rho - \rho_0))$, and $\gamma = 1$! For liquids the ratio between the two specific heats, has the expression

$$\gamma - 1 = \frac{\theta \alpha_\theta^2 V_0^2}{c_p}.$$

Now c_v, c_p, like ϵ, are functions of θ alone, and the equation of state for the internal energy ϵ,

$$\epsilon := \int c_v \, \mathrm{d}\theta; \qquad \eta := \int \frac{1}{\theta} \mathrm{d}\epsilon - \int \frac{p}{\theta} \mathrm{d}\frac{1}{\rho} = \int \frac{c_v}{\theta} \mathrm{d}\theta - R_* \ln \rho. \tag{2.8}$$

As observed above, to the equations of state (2.8) are, frequently, added further constraints. Precisely, if one puts the kinematical constraint of isocoricity, one shall deal with liquids, also said incompressible fluids, while, if one puts constraints on the thermodynamical process then one can reach barotropic fluids. We recall that a gas is *barotropic* if the constitutive equation of the pressure can be expressed as a function of the density only, namely if

$$p = p(\rho).$$

In such a case, thermodynamics will influence the mechanical behavior of the gas only indirectly through the density ρ. As a prototype of barotropic gases we quote gases which undergo to isothermal or isentropic processes (more concrete cases are those where the entropy is negligible). Precisely, the following definitions can be given:[1]

(a) A thermodynamical process is *isothermal* if the temperature is constant along the path lines of the material particles $d\theta/dt = 0$. Indeed for isothermal processes, it follows directly from the assumption of perfect gases, that the pressure is linear in ρ. Notice, also, that such processes occur in thermal equilibrium.

(b) A thermodynamical process is *isentropic* if the entropy is constant along the path lines of the material particles $d\eta/dt = 0$. Notice that, for isentropic processes, and for constant specific heat, we can eliminate the temperature in the law of ideal gases by using $(2.4)_2$. We thus obtain

$$p = k\rho^\gamma, \quad \gamma > 1, \quad k = e^{\eta/c_v}.$$

Isentropic processes are realized in absence of sources and fluxes of entropy, that is in adiabatic situations.

2.3 - Unbounded domains and vanishing density.

Unbounded domains and vanishing density, as well, are some mathematical abstractions and can present pathological behavior. One peculiar aspect which arises at once is the very different behavior between isothermal and isentropic fluids when density is supposed to vanish at some point. Precisely, from $(2.8)_2$ we deduce that, for constant values of the temperature, the entropy tends to infinity when density tends to zero; while for constant entropy, and specific heats, from $(2.8)_2$ divided by c_v

$$R_*\theta = \exp[\eta/c_v]\rho^{\gamma-1},$$

[1] It is costumary to use the words isothermal or isentropic, to denote processes with spatially and temporally uniform temperature or entropy, respectively, [14], [97]. From the above definitions this last case occurs only when initially the temperature or the entropy, are respectively uniform. Another useful term, not yet generally adopted, is homentropic, meaning the entropy η is to be uniform over the fluid (η can be varying in time).

and the temperature tends to zero when the density vanishes. This reflects the physical fact that in absence of matter the absolute temperature should reach the zero. Thus if we want to study equilibrium configurations of a star in the vacuum, the most natural idea is that the gas cannot be subjected to isothermal processes and we are led to study only isentropic gases, cf., *e.g.*, [9], [44], [51]. However, concerning the entropy, it is not clear what should happen at infinity. In fact, global existence results for polytropic gases filling unbounded intervals of the real line $\mathbb{R}$, with stress free boundary conditions, are given with entropy which can become infinite for isothermal gases, see [21], [44], [67], [74].

2.4 - Departures from the perfect gas laws.

As a typical example of departure from the perfect gas laws occurs at large densities and is due to changes in the structure of the molecules. The expression for p can then be written as

$$p = \frac{R_* \rho \theta}{1 - b\rho} - a\rho^2.$$

Here, a is a constant for a given gas which depends on the intermolecular forces, while the first term at right hand side represents the flux of normal momentum per unit of area. This is the *van der Waals' equation* and is the best known to take into account the imperfections of real gases. For air the empirical values of a and b are about $3 \times 10^{-3}(p_0/\rho_0^2)$ and $3 \times 10^{-3}/\rho_0$, where p_0, ρ_0 refer to standard conditions.

Moreover, for fluids in more than one phase the behavior of the pressure changes, precisely, the transition water-vapor is governed by the van der Waals equation

$$p := \frac{R_* a \rho \theta}{b^2(1 - b\rho)}$$

where b is a term responsible of the volume reduction because the molecules occupy an effective volume, and a represents an influence on the pressure due to intermolecular attraction (proportional to ρ^2), [102]. As natural, the correct solution must satisfy the following conditions

$$\rho < b, \qquad p > 0, \qquad \frac{\partial p}{\partial \rho}(x,t) > 0;$$

therefore, the sound speed can be defined only for densities which are greather than a fixed value. More rigorously, for fluids in phase-transition it should be considered in the stress tensor also a function of $\nabla\rho$, [98] sect. 124. Recent papers are devoted to the mathematical treatment of this subject, [29]. They consider the more stringent constitutive conditions

$$\begin{gathered} p(\rho*) \geq p(\rho), \ \text{if}\, 0 < \rho* < \rho; \qquad p(\rho*) \leq p(\rho), \ \text{if}\, 0 < \rho < \rho*, \\ \epsilon \to 0, \quad p/\rho \to 0, \quad \theta \to 0, \quad V_s \to 0, \quad \text{as}\ \rho \to 0. \end{gathered} \tag{2.9}$$

Another departure from the perfect gas relation occurs at very high temperatures when some collision are so violent that polyatomic molecules may dissociated into their constituent atoms. In this case, the equation of state for the pressure is still formally written $p = k\rho\theta$, but, k is now a function of temperature and density.

2.5 - The Poisson–Stokes equations of motion.

In the Stokes axiomatics [94], it is required that the stress tensor in a fluid at rest is everywhere isotropic, namely $\boldsymbol{T} = -p\boldsymbol{I}$, thus only normal stresses act. However, during the motion the fluid is supposed to satisfy the linear Stokes law $(2.2)_1$, and the Clausius Duhem inequality implies

$$\mu \geq 0, \qquad n\lambda + 2\mu \geq 0,$$

where $n = 1, 2, 3$ is the dimension of the space.

We shall always assume λ, μ, to be constants. Moreover, as concerns the pressure, we shall mainly adopt the following thermodynamical law

$$p = k\rho^\gamma, \quad \gamma \geq 1.$$

In such a way, the number of the indefinite equations of motion equals that of the unknowns ρ, $\boldsymbol{v}$.

For gases in unbounded regions, the density might vanish at infinity: this can happen only under suitable hypotheses on the other thermodynamical variables, cf. [14] sect. 2, ch. 1, p. 6.

We deduce, then, the following indefinite Poisson–Stokes equations[1]

[1] System (2.10) is also known as *compressible Navier–Stokes equations*.

$$
(2.10) \qquad \begin{aligned}
&\frac{\partial \rho}{\partial t} + \nabla \cdot (\rho \boldsymbol{v}) = 0, \\
&\rho \frac{\mathrm{d}\boldsymbol{v}}{\mathrm{d}t} = -\nabla p + \mu \Delta \boldsymbol{v} + (\lambda + \mu) \nabla \nabla \cdot \boldsymbol{v} + \rho \boldsymbol{f} + \boldsymbol{b}, \\
&p = p(\rho).
\end{aligned}
$$

Clearly, the Poisson–Stokes system represents a mathematical idealization of a physical sistuation. Moreover, equations $(2.10)_{1,2}$ are not sufficient to determine the full thermodynamical state of the system (there is missing the energy balance equation). However, system (2.10) is selfconsistent, and allows to determine the mechanical state of the system once only the mechanical forces are prescribed. This reflects the physical fact that, under the above hypotheses, the thermodynamics doesn't influence the mechanical behaviour of the fluid.

2.6 - Concluding remarks.

This section just ends with the differential equations governing the flow of common fluids. Therefore, we may conclude that *we have now a fairly reliable and understandable set of laws on which a study of motion of fluids can be based* [5]. Actually, a mathematician could claim that the main goal has been reached. However, such point of view is quite inappropriate for a fluid dynamicist. Indeed, (2.10) hide several difficulties from both mathematical and physical point of wiev, due to the complexity of the physical processes which involve many different mechanical and thermal interactions. An essential part of our study is the capability to deduce from the equations correct predictions in any given situation. This objective will be reached through a correct formulation of the well-posedness problem. Therefore, an accurate prediction should demand simultaneously a clear physical expectation of the phenomenon at hand, and a deep mathematical knowledge of the governing equations. Say, the pure scientist should understand how to set mathematically a question in order to receive a reasonable answer from the equations.

Likewise the set of governing equations is much too complicated for a direct mathematical approach. Because of the complexity of the subject, we shall limit ourselves to study only steady motions.

3. Statement of the problem and open questions in bounded domains

3.1 - Position of the problem. Some function spaces.

So far, in Section 2 we have deduced the indefinite equations governing motions of Newtonian fluids. These equations, in the steady situation, are expressed by

$$\begin{aligned} &\nabla \cdot (\rho \boldsymbol{v}) = 0, \\ &\rho \boldsymbol{v} \cdot \nabla \boldsymbol{v} = -\nabla p + \mu \triangle \boldsymbol{v} + (\lambda + \mu)\, \nabla(\nabla \cdot \boldsymbol{v}) + \rho \boldsymbol{f} + \boldsymbol{b}, \end{aligned} \tag{3.1}$$

where $\boldsymbol{f}$ and $\boldsymbol{b}$ are given. In order to study the well-posedness of (3.1), one must add suitable boundary and side conditions: here we wish investigate just which are the most appropriate ones.

As matter of fact, we notice that a steady flow represents a limit state (as $t \to \infty$) of a unsteady flow, thus it is an idealized situation. Therefore, it is natural to expect that, by varying the data, or by varying the boundary or side conditions, in some unspecified way, a steady flow becomes no more physically realizable, thus no more observable. This, sometime, is due to different factors:

i) it may happen that the added boundary or side conditions are not correct, then the steady flow doesn't exist;

ii) it may happen that the steady flow does exist, but it looses its stability.

For an interesting discussion of case i), we refer the reader to [14]. A clear sample of case ii) can be found in [37], [38] where the existence of steady solutions for the Navier–Stokes equations is proved in correspondence of large data. In that case, it is clear that steady solutions can be observed, as limiting states, only for small data. Actually, for large data, the non-steady solution is converging to a steady one.

However, for incompressible fluids it is a clear result that at least *the rest state is always stable, thus observable.* For compressible isentropic fluids, first of all, we show that even the rest doesn't exist if the data are too large (supersonic regions).

Indeed, the well-posedness problem for steady flows of viscous barotropic gases presents unexpected difficulties even when the flow occurs in a simply connected bounded region: in this line we remark that several questions still remain open. Below, we furnish an landscape of the boundary and side conditions which are more usually adopted in bounded domains. Next, in Subsection 3.4, we describe one problem which is physically ill-posed, then, in order to solve it, we propose a new formulation of the problem. In the next subsections, we solve the existence problem in the presence of small forces.

NOTATION – Let Ω be a domain of $\mathbb{R}^n$. As customary, $C^k(\Omega)$, with k natural number, stands for the space of all continuous functions on Ω, together with their derivatives up to the order k inclusive; $C_0^\infty(\Omega)$ is the space of all functions which belong to $C^k(\Omega)$, for any k, and have a compact support in Ω; $W^{m,q}(\Omega)$ (m nonnegative integer, $q \in [1, \infty]$) denotes the Sobolev space of order m, q on Ω, endowed with the usual norm

$$\|u\|_{m,q} = \left(\sum_{|\beta|=0}^{m} \int_\Omega |D^\beta u|^q \right)^{1/q},$$

where in the integral the differentiation element is omitted, and for $\beta = (\beta_1, \ldots, \beta_n)$, $\beta_i \geq 0$, we set

$$D^\beta = \frac{\partial^{|\beta|}}{\partial x_1^{\beta_1} \ldots \partial x_n^{\beta_n}}, \qquad |\beta| = \beta_1 + \ldots + \beta_n.$$

$W_0^{m,q}(\Omega)$ is the completion of $C_0^\infty(\Omega)$ with respect to the norm $\| \cdot \|_{m,q}$. We have $W^{0,q}(\Omega) = L^q(\Omega)$ and set $\| \cdot \|_{0,q} = \| \cdot \|_q$, $\| \cdot \| = \| \cdot \|_2$.

The dual space of $W_0^{m,q}(\Omega)$ is denoted by $W^{-m,q'}(\Omega)$, $1/q' = 1 - 1/q$, and its norm by $\|\cdot\|_{-m,q'}$. Furthermore, for sufficiently smooth Ω by $W^{m-1/q,q}(\partial\Omega)$ we indicate the trace space on $\partial\Omega$ of functions on $W^{m,q}(\Omega)$. The corresponding norm is denoted by $\| \cdot \|_{m-1/q,q,\partial\Omega}$. By $(\cdot,\cdot)$, $\langle \cdot,\cdot \rangle$ we indicate the inner product in L^2 and the duality between $W_0^{m,q}(\Omega)$ and $W_0^{-m,q'}(\Omega)$, respectively.

3.2 - Boundary and side conditions.

In this subsection, we discuss the possible boundary and side conditions which should be added to (3.1) in order to solve the well-posedness problem. On one side, the prescriptions on the density and kinetic field should be suggested by the physical instruments of measure. On the other side, in order to set correctly the physical problem, we seek a characterization of appropriate (may be idealized) boundary conditions: *the correct boundary conditions should ensure simultaneously the existence and the uniqueness of the solution for steady flows.* Possibly, we should be able also to prove the continuous dependence of the solution on the data.

As far as the density is concerned, we make the following obvious remarks, each leading to *side conditions on the density.*

(i) Let Ω be any (bounded or unbounded) domain. The density must be almost everywhere non-negative: $\rho \geq 0$.

(ii) Let Ω be any domain. In the absence of selfgravitational forces, the density must be bounded: $\rho \leq m$.

(iii) Let Ω be a bounded domain: the total mass of the fluid must be prescribed

$$\int_{\Omega} \rho = M.$$

As regard the *boundary conditions on the velocity* in bounded domains, let us notice what follows.

(1) *Impermeable walls.* Let the fluid fill a rigid container Ω bounded by an impermeable wall $\partial\Omega$. It is costumary, for a viscous gas, to identify the velocity of the particles of the fluid with that of the particles of the boundary $\partial\Omega$. However, since the problem is stationary, also Ω must be the same, as time is varying. This suggests that either Ω is of arbitrary shape and fixed, or Ω changes with time and has a particular symmetric geometry (it is either a section of a cylinder, or a sphere). Therefore, for Ω of arbitrary shape, the requirement

$$\boldsymbol{v}|_{\partial\Omega} = \boldsymbol{v}_*,$$

implies $\boldsymbol{v}_* = \mathbf{0}$. Moreover, if Ω has a particular shape, the condition that the walls are impermeable yields

$$\boldsymbol{v} \times \boldsymbol{n}|_{\partial\Omega} = \boldsymbol{v}_* \times \boldsymbol{n}, \quad \boldsymbol{v} \cdot \boldsymbol{n}|_{\partial\Omega} = 0,$$

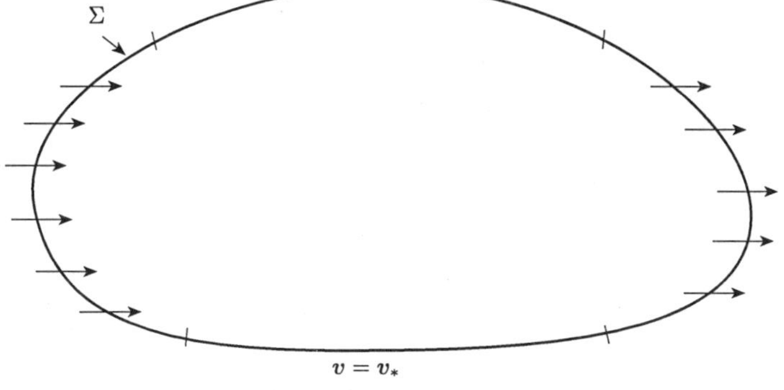

Figure 1.

where $\boldsymbol{n}$ is the outward unit normal and $\boldsymbol{v}_*$ is the velocity of the particles on the boundary (necessarily it will be $\boldsymbol{v}_* \cdot \boldsymbol{n} = 0$).

(2) *Rigid porous walls.* Let the fluid fill a bounded rigid container Ω, with porous walls $\partial\Omega$. In this case, it doesn't happen any more that the velocity of the particles at the boundary is orthogonal to $\boldsymbol{n}$. Therefore, we are led to change point of view. For example [86], one can fix the linear momentum at the boundary. However, it is not clear how to measure it. Notice that, in general, the momentum of the fluid's particles differs from that of the particles at the boundary: however, for permeable walls, at the points where the fluid is entering, it is possible to prescribe the (nonzero) momentum at boundaries. If one prescribes

$$\boldsymbol{v}|_{\partial\Omega} = \boldsymbol{v}_*, \quad \rho|_\Sigma = \rho_*, \tag{3.2}$$

where Σ is the part of the boundary through which the fluid is entering (see figure 1), that is where $\boldsymbol{v} \cdot \boldsymbol{n} < 0$, it is possible at least to solve the uniqueness problem for unsteady flows, [83], [84], [86]. Notice that ρ_* can have also discontinuities. In the sequel we shall adopt equations (3.2) at the boundary. Integrating the continuity equation over Ω, and employing the Gauss lemma, one deduces the following condition

$$\int_{\partial\Omega} (\rho \boldsymbol{v}_*)(x) \cdot \boldsymbol{n} = \int_{\partial\Omega - \Sigma} (\rho \boldsymbol{v}_*)(x) \cdot \boldsymbol{n} + \int_\Sigma (\rho_* \boldsymbol{v}_*)(x) \cdot \boldsymbol{n} = 0$$

where ρ itself is unknown on the part of the boundary $\partial\Omega - \Sigma$ where the fluid is leaving. Despite what happens for incompressible fluids, the above condition is not a compatibility condition, because the solution, once one proves it exists, will authomatically satisfy it. Recently, in [12], [13], [30], [31], [42], it has been studied the problem of existence and uniqueness of steady flows for model equations and for compressible flows in particular two-dimensional domains, assuming that the entering flow has discontinuous density.

(3) *Free surfaces.* On a given[1] free surface $\mathcal{S}$ at ambient pressure π, the stress vector must be continuous. Therefore, in the absence of surface tension, on $\mathcal{S}$ we require

$$\begin{aligned} &\boldsymbol{n} \cdot \nabla \boldsymbol{v} \cdot \boldsymbol{\tau} + \boldsymbol{\tau} \cdot \nabla \boldsymbol{v} \cdot \boldsymbol{n} = 0, \\ &-\pi = -p + \lambda \nabla \cdot \boldsymbol{v} + 2\mu \boldsymbol{n} \cdot \frac{\partial \boldsymbol{v}}{\partial n}, \quad \boldsymbol{v} \cdot \boldsymbol{n} = 0, \end{aligned} \tag{3.3}$$

where $\boldsymbol{\tau}$ is a unit tangent vector at $\partial\Omega$ and $\partial \boldsymbol{v}/\partial n$ denotes the derivative of $\boldsymbol{v}$ along $\boldsymbol{n}$.

(4) *Artificial Boundary Conditions.* Sometimes, flows occur in very large domains while the phenomenon of interest is focused in a ("small") region very distant from the boundaries of the real domain and therefore, the affect of distant boundaries will not effect such a motion. Therefore, unbounded domains are introduced in order to stress the fact that the phenomenon of interest should be free of the effects of distant boundaries. However, in order to solve numerically the problem, the domain is reduced again to a bounded one, and on the geometrical exterior surface one must fix some boundary conditions, also called *artificial* boundary conditions. In this regard, several boundary conditions have been proposed [25], [27], [50]. Here, we analyze the well-posedness only in the particular case of an aperture domain, where prescriptions on pressure drops or on net flux are involved. Here, we adopt the *do nothing* boundary conditions proposed in [27], in the case of incompressible fluids. These conditions have the characteristic to leave functions on the artificial side of Ω as free as possible. Precisely, on the boundary we set

$$\begin{aligned} &(\lambda + 2\mu)\frac{\partial \boldsymbol{v}}{\partial n} \cdot \boldsymbol{n} - k\rho \Big|_{\Sigma_\pm} = c_\pm, \qquad \frac{\partial(\boldsymbol{v} \cdot \boldsymbol{\tau})}{\partial n}\Big|_{\Sigma} = 0, \\ &\boldsymbol{v}|_{\partial\Omega - \Sigma} = \boldsymbol{0}, \quad \int_\Omega \rho = M, \end{aligned} \tag{3.4}$$

[1] The free surface must be given because we are in a steady situation.

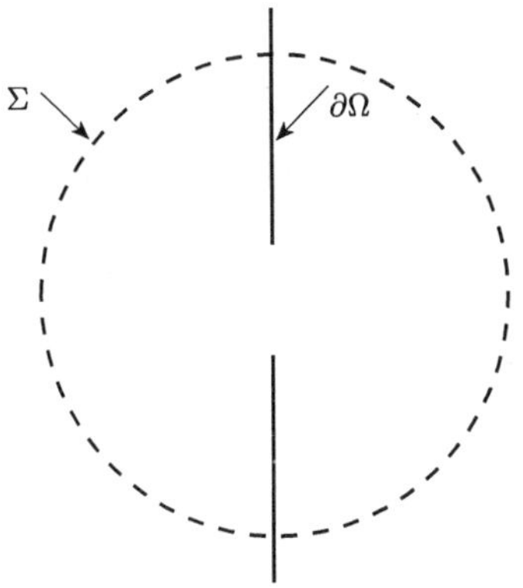

Figure 2.

where Σ denotes the part of the boundary where the in or out flow occurs (artificial boundary), M is the total mass (see figure 2) and $C_{\pm}$ are constants. Moreover, setting the z-axis orthogonal to $\partial\Omega$, we put $\Sigma_{\pm} = \{(x, y, z) \in \Sigma |\, z \neq 0\}$. In Subsection 3.8, for two-dimensional domains, we present the beginnings of a mathematical theory for these problems, in the form of theorems of existence, uniqueness, drawing attention on the difficulties one encounters.

We end this roundup of the boundary conditions, by noticing that we are far from having considered all situations in a bounded domains. For example, we have omitted the case of mixed boundary conditions, which appear, *e.g*, in the case of a container partially filled with the gas. Moreover, also non regular domains could be considered, *e.g.*, domains with corners [49], [64].

3.3 - Goals reached.

In Subsection 3.2, we have set several boundary conditions and commented their physical meaning and in Subsection 3.4 we discuss the possibility for a gas to be at rest and show how this situation is not well understood, either intuitively or mathematically. From Subsection 3.5 on, under the further assumption $\mu > 0$, $\lambda + 2\mu \geq 0$, which weakens the usual assumption on the bulk viscosity, we study the mathematical properties of (3.1) under the "isothermal" assumption that $p = k\rho$, where k is a constant. We start with assuming that the fluid under consideration adheres to the boundary of the region it occupies.

Thus the stationary problem is

$$\begin{aligned} &\nabla \cdot (\rho \boldsymbol{v}) = 0, \\ &\rho \boldsymbol{v} \cdot \nabla \boldsymbol{v} = -\nabla p + \mu \triangle \boldsymbol{v} + (\lambda + \mu) \nabla (\nabla \cdot \boldsymbol{v}) + \rho \boldsymbol{f} + \boldsymbol{b}, \\ &\boldsymbol{v}|_{\partial\Omega} = \boldsymbol{0}, \quad \int_\Omega \rho = \overline{\rho}|\Omega|, \end{aligned} \tag{3.5}$$

wherein the mean density $\overline{\rho} > 0$ is prescribed. Normalizing the density by dividing ρ by $\overline{\rho}$, we may take $\overline{\rho} = 1$.

Our main results are simplified proofs of the following small data existence and uniqueness theorems.

Theorem 3.1. *Let Ω be a bounded subdomain of $\mathbb{R}^n$, $n = 1, 2$, or 3, of class C^2. Let $\boldsymbol{f} \in L^q(\Omega)$, with $q > n$. Then, if $\|\boldsymbol{f}\|_q$ is sufficiently small, depending on n, Ω, q, k, μ, and λ, there exists a unique solution $\boldsymbol{v}, \rho$ of problem (3.5) with $\boldsymbol{v} \in W_0^{1,2}(\Omega) \cap W^{2,q}(\Omega)$ and $\rho \in W^{1,q}(\Omega)$.*

If more regularity is assumed on the force, an independent but entirely analogous method of proof, provides a correspondingly more regular solution. We show this by proving the following theorem.

Theorem 3.2. *Let Ω be a bounded subdomain of $\mathbb{R}^3$, of class C^3. Let $\boldsymbol{f} \in W^{1,2}(\Omega)$. Then, if $\|\boldsymbol{f}\|_{1,2}$ is sufficiently small, depending on Ω, k, μ, and λ, there exists a unique solution $\boldsymbol{v}, \rho$ of problem (3.5) with $\boldsymbol{v} \in W_0^{1,2}(\Omega) \cap W^{3,2}(\Omega)$ and $\rho \in W^{2,2}(\Omega)$.*

We next assume that the stress free boundary conditions (3.3) hold. Thus the stationary problem is

$$\begin{aligned} &\nabla \cdot (\rho \boldsymbol{v}) = 0, \\ &\rho \boldsymbol{v} \cdot \nabla \boldsymbol{v} = -\nabla p + \mu \triangle \boldsymbol{v} + (\lambda + \mu) \nabla (\nabla \cdot \boldsymbol{v}) + \rho \boldsymbol{f} + \boldsymbol{b}, \\ &\boldsymbol{\tau} \cdot \frac{\partial \boldsymbol{v}}{\partial n} + \boldsymbol{n} \cdot \frac{\partial \boldsymbol{v}}{\partial \tau}\Big|_{\partial\Omega} = 0, \\ &-\pi = -p + \lambda \nabla \cdot \boldsymbol{v} + 2\mu \boldsymbol{n} \cdot \frac{\partial \boldsymbol{v}}{\partial n}\Big|_{\partial\Omega}, \\ &\boldsymbol{v} \cdot \boldsymbol{n}|_{\partial\Omega} = 0, \quad \int_\Omega \rho = \overline{\rho}\,|\Omega|, \end{aligned} \tag{3.6}$$

wherein the mean density $\overline{\rho} > 0$ is prescribed. Normalizing the density by dividing ρ by $\overline{\rho}$, we may take $\overline{\rho} = 1$.

Our main results are sketches of proof of the following small data existence and uniqueness theorems.

Theorem 3.3. *Let Ω be a bounded subdomain of $\mathbb{R}^n$, $n = 1, 2$, or 3, of class C^2. Let $\boldsymbol{f} \in L^q(\Omega)$, with $q > n$. Then, if $\|\boldsymbol{f}\|_q$ is sufficiently small, depending on n, Ω, q, k, μ, and λ, there exists a unique solution $\boldsymbol{v}, \rho$ of problem (3.6) with $\boldsymbol{v} \in W^{2,q}(\Omega)$ and $\rho \in W^{1,q}(\Omega)$.*

If more regularity is assumed of the force, an independent but entirely analogous method of proof, using more elementary lemmas, provides a correspondingly more regular solution. We show this by proving the following theorem.

Theorem 3.4. *Let Ω be a bounded subdomain of $\mathbb{R}^3$, with the boundary of class C^3. Let $\boldsymbol{f} \in W^{1,2}(\Omega)$. Then, if $\|\boldsymbol{f}\|_{1,2}$ is sufficiently small, depending on Ω, k, μ, and λ, there exists a unique solution $\boldsymbol{v}, \rho$ of problem (3.6) with $\boldsymbol{v} \in W^{3,2}(\Omega)$ and $\rho \in W^{2,2}(\Omega)$.*

We remark that in all above theorems the density turns out to be continuous.

In Subsection 3.8, we make some considerations about existence when the potential forces are large and again we give only a sketch of proof.

We end this section by giving a survey of the previous results with the corresponding methods of proof. Then, we make some considerations about the possibility of regularization of a generalized solution.

3.4 - Mechanical equilibrium of a fluid.

The conditions for a fluid to be in equilibrium are quite complex, and they substantially depend on the nature of the fluid. In this section, we first establish the restrictions imposed by the equations on the forces. The well-posedness problem studied in this section is formulated as follows

$$(3.7)\qquad \begin{aligned} &\nabla \cdot (\rho \boldsymbol{v}) = 0, \\ &\rho \boldsymbol{v} \cdot \nabla \boldsymbol{v} = -\nabla p + \mu \Delta \boldsymbol{v} + (\lambda + \mu) \nabla(\nabla \cdot \boldsymbol{v}) + \rho \nabla U, \\ &\boldsymbol{v}|_{\partial\Omega} = \boldsymbol{0}, \qquad \int_\Omega \rho = \overline{\rho}\, |\Omega|, \end{aligned}$$

where ∇U is a potential force. Below, we list and discuss several properties of the rest for barotropic fluids. We end the section by recalling and commenting some pathological situations. In the sequel, if it is not explicitly remarked, we consider $\boldsymbol{b} = \mathbf{0}$.

- **Concerning the rest.**

As well known, the necessary and sufficient condition for the fluid to be in equilibrium is given by

$$\nabla p = \rho_s \boldsymbol{f}, \tag{3.8}$$

where ρ_s stands for the density distribution at the rest state ($\boldsymbol{v} = \mathbf{0}$). In (3.8) if we don't make any thermodynamical assumptions, the quantities ρ and p are two independent variables. Therefore, relation (3.8) states that the forces $\rho \boldsymbol{f}$, must be expressed as gradient of a scalar quantity. Indeed, for barotropic fluids, ρ is considered as an integrable factor, since introducing the enthalpy h we have, for $\boldsymbol{f} = \nabla U$,

$$\rho_s = h^{-1}(U), \quad \frac{\mathrm{d}h}{\mathrm{d}\rho} = \frac{1}{\rho}\frac{\mathrm{d}p}{\mathrm{d}\rho}, \tag{3.9}$$

and h^{-1} is its inverse function.

For barotropic viscous fluids, subjected to potential body forces $\boldsymbol{f} = \nabla U$, in a rigid fixed domain ($\boldsymbol{v}_* = \mathbf{0}$), in the class of solutions to (3.7), the following propositions hold true:

(1) the *only possible* solution belongs to the class of the rest solutions;

(2) for any potential force, it there always exists a density distribution (which could be not real) $\rho: \ x \in \Omega \ \longrightarrow \ \rho(x)$, solution of (3.8);

(3) there exists a positive constant a, such that, for any $\|f\|_X < a$, where X is a suitable functional space, there exists a unique positive density;

(4) there exists a positive constant b, such that, for any $\|f\|_X < b$, where X is a suitable functional space, the positive density if exists is also unique.

Notice that if the vacuum is allowed, then uniqueness fails.

(1) - Assume, *per absurdum*, that there exists another solution $\boldsymbol{v} \neq \mathbf{0}$, ρ, to the system (3.7). Then we shall have

$$\begin{gathered} \nabla \cdot (\rho \boldsymbol{v}) = 0, \\ \rho \boldsymbol{v} \cdot \nabla \boldsymbol{v} = -\nabla p + \mu \Delta \boldsymbol{v} + (\lambda + \mu) \nabla \nabla \cdot \boldsymbol{v} + \rho \nabla U. \end{gathered} \tag{3.10}$$

Multiplying $(3.10)_2$ by $\boldsymbol{v}$ and integrating over Ω, taking into account of the solenoidality condition of $\rho\boldsymbol{v}$, and the zero boundary condition for $\boldsymbol{v}$, we deduce

$$\mu \int_\Omega \nabla\boldsymbol{v} : \nabla\boldsymbol{v} + (\lambda+\mu)\int_\Omega (\nabla\cdot\boldsymbol{v})^2 = 0, \tag{3.11}$$

which, together with the boundary conditions, implies $\boldsymbol{v} = \mathbf{0}$. Therefore, even for large potential forces, the only possible solution must belong to the class of the rest solutions $\boldsymbol{v} = \mathbf{0}$. The proof has been given in [68].

(2) - Indeed, the existence of the rest can be directly exhibited by integrating the system

$$0 = -\nabla p(\rho) + \rho\nabla U. \tag{3.12}$$

By using the enthalpy h, we recover

$$\rho_s = h^{-1}(U).$$

(3) - The proof of existence of a positive density is given in [6].

(4) - Let $\Omega \subseteq \mathbb{R}^3$. Assume, *per absurdum*, that there exist two density distributions ρ_0 and $\rho = \rho_0 + \sigma$, solutions to (3.12), having the same total mass M. Their difference will satisfy

$$0 = -\nabla[p(\rho) - p(\rho_0)] + \sigma\nabla U. \tag{3.13}$$

Now, we multiply (3.13) by a vector function $\boldsymbol{\varphi}$ solution of the problem ([22])

$$\begin{gathered} \nabla\cdot\boldsymbol{\varphi} = \sigma, \quad \boldsymbol{\varphi}|_{\partial\Omega} = 0, \\ \|\boldsymbol{\varphi}\|_{1,2} \le c_1\|\sigma\|_2. \end{gathered} \tag{3.14}$$

Notice that, since $\int_\Omega \sigma = 0$, the compatility condition for the problem (3.14) is verified. In this way, integrating over Ω, we obtain

$$\int_\Omega [p(\rho) - p(\rho_0)]\sigma = -\int_\Omega \sigma\boldsymbol{\varphi}\cdot\nabla U \le \|\nabla U\|_3\|\sigma\|_2\|\boldsymbol{\varphi}\|_6. \tag{3.15}$$

Notice that, by the Lagrange mean value theorem, it results

$$p(\rho) - p(\rho_s) = \left.\frac{\mathrm{d}p}{\mathrm{d}\rho}\right|_{\hat{\rho}} \sigma, \tag{3.16}$$

where $\hat{\rho}$ is a point between ρ_s and ρ. Employing the limit Sobolev inequality to increase the norm of φ at the right hand side of (3.15), and recalling $(3.14)_2$, we can increase φ with the L^2-norm of σ. Therefore, from (3.15) we deduce also that $\sigma = 0$ for small $\|\nabla U\|_q$, i.e. when

$$\min_{\Omega} \left.\frac{\mathrm{d}p}{\mathrm{d}\rho}\right|_{\hat{\rho}} - c_1 \|\nabla U\|_q > 0. \tag{3.17}$$

Then, for small forces, the rest is the *only physically reasonable* steady solution allowed! Of course, inequality (3.17) can be satisfied only when $\rho > 0$.

We shall now consider a particular case in which problem (3.7) is ill posed. This is performed through a deeper analysis of point (2). Actually, the example below, concerning an isentropic gas in a bounded domain, shows an inconsistency between the theory and the experiments.

We consider here an isentropic gas in a bounded domain.

- **Nonexistence of the rest state for an isentropic gas under large external forces ($\gamma > 1$).**

The example below is due to Beirao da Veiga, [6]. Let $\Omega = (0, d)$, $p = k\rho^\gamma$, $1 < \gamma$, $\boldsymbol{v}_* = \mathbf{0}$, $\boldsymbol{f} = f\boldsymbol{i}$, where f is a positive constant and $\boldsymbol{i}$ is the *direction* of the x–axis. Then the rest state is given by

$$\rho(x) = \left[c + \frac{f(\gamma - 1)}{k\gamma} x\right]^{1/(\gamma-1)}, \tag{3.18}$$

and solves the problem (3.7) with homogeneous boundary conditions. The constant c is fixed by the condition that the mass is given.

Now, the value of c can be easily computed, for the given domain Ω, by a direct integration of (3.18) over Ω, employing the condition of the fixed amount of gas M. In particular, if f is positive and sufficiently large, then the constant c can assume a negative value. Under these conditions, also the enthalpy vanishes at some point $\bar{x}$: thus, if we are searching for a flow which fills the whole of the container, for x larger than $\bar{x}$, the square bracket in (3.18) becomes negative and, consequently, the density may become complex. Notice that, if the length of the domain is fixed, the prescription of the total mass determines uniquely ρ.

Remark 3.1 – Integration becomes explicit for $\gamma = 2$. In this case, the condition on f is expressed by

$$\frac{4kM}{d^2} \leq f.$$

We thus claim that, for large forces, and for large d, solutions of (3.8) do exist, but with complex density. Therefore, such a mathematical solution doesn't represent any physical material distribution of mass. Moreover, if we allow the vacuum in the container, say Ω is no more fixed (for $\gamma = 2$ in Remark 3.1 this means that d is varying), then uniqueness for ρ fails also for small forces! In this direction, it is worth noticing the result in [43], examples 3.4, 3.5, where the authors exhibit infinitely many solutions with positive densities by changing the domain occupied by the gas, say allowing for cavities. With such a treatment, however, we are no more in the scheme of continuum, because vacuum is allowed. In order to avoid these pathological solutions, we first give a physical explanation of such paradoxical result, and then propose a different mathematical setting of the problem.

Let Ω be a circular cylindrical vertical rigid vessel of height d, filled with a viscous fluid of total mass M. In this case, we are dealing with the most realistic large constant force, say the gravity. Indeed, it is very natural that if we put in Ω a small quantity of heavy gas, it will fall at the bottom of the recipient. Actually, the gas will perform a nonsteady motion. However, there will be still a limit steady situation which can be described by dividing Ω into two parts: Ω_1 occupied by the fluid, and Ω_2 which is empty (see figure 3).

Remark 3.2 – We stress the fact that the fluid is not isothermal, say $\gamma \neq 1$, and that the domain is bounded. This example cannot be extended to isothermal fluids. Indeed, the most general situation was considered in [57], see also [54] for exterior domains, where it was shown that for $\gamma > 1$ the forces can be large provided the amount of matter is large enough. In [57] it was proved an even stronger result. Precisely, for isothermal fluids, it was shown an existence theorem of steady solutions, with positive density, assuming small non potential forces and large potential forces. The stability of such flows is proved in [47].

Remark 3.3 – Also worthy to be mentioned are the existence results [39], [40], [41], [55], [56], proved under the assumption of large forces. Notice that the above paradoxical solution satisfies all the hypotheses requested by the authors, therefore, to our opinion it is better either to look for solutions under stronger hypotheses on the forces, or to change the position of the basic problem, in order to find only physically reasonable solutions.

Below, we shall follow the second point of view and we propose a change of the "classical" formulation of the problem, in such a way that, at least for constant forces, in the one-dimensional case, we are able to find positive densities for all forces.

- **Change of the "classical formulation".**

First of all, let us notice that steady flows are asymptotical idealized situations. Now, since for small amount of gas the vacuum can appear, one should consider the problem of existence of a steady solution only in the part of the domain, Ω_1 say, which is expected to be occupied by the continuum. However, such a part of the domain is not known "a priori": indeed (see below), it depends on the amount M of the gas. Therefore, in our opinion, the correct way of setting mathematically the problem is to divide Ω into two parts: Ω_1 occupied by the fluid, Ω_2 occupied by the vacuum. In Ω_1 we set the usual problem

$$\begin{aligned} &\nabla \cdot (\rho \boldsymbol{v}) = 0, \\ &\rho \boldsymbol{v} \cdot \nabla \boldsymbol{v} = -\nabla p + \mu \Delta \boldsymbol{v} + (\lambda + \mu) \nabla \nabla \cdot \boldsymbol{v} + \rho \boldsymbol{f}. \end{aligned} \tag{3.19}$$

To (3.19) we append the usual boundary and side conditions

$$\begin{aligned} &\int_{\Omega_1} \rho = M, \\ &\boldsymbol{v}(x) = \boldsymbol{v}_*, \quad x \in \partial\Omega \cap \partial\Omega_1. \end{aligned} \tag{3.20}$$

The peculiarity of this problem is that the domain Ω_1 is unknown, and its boundary $\Sigma = \partial\Omega_1 \cap \partial\Omega_2$ is a stress free boundary. In order to understand what should be added, we now consider the balance of linear and angular momentum in Ω_2 for the vacuum. Since in Ω_2 there is no inertia, these balance equations state that the resultant of all external forces acting on Ω_2 must be zero. In other words, since there are no body forces acting on the vacuum, the only

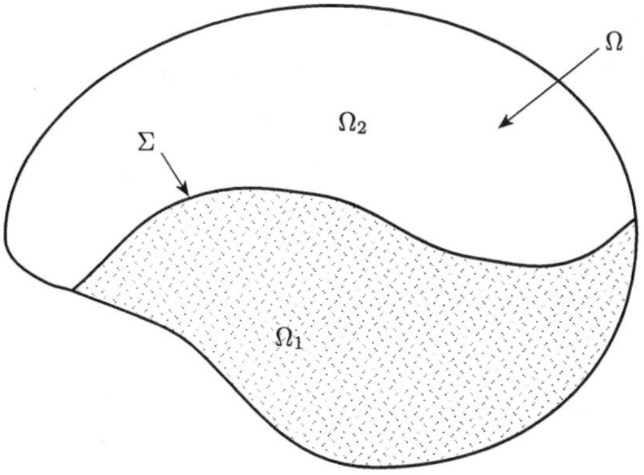

Figure 3.

nontrivial resultants are due to the stress and the momentum of the stress acting on the stress free boundary Σ (notice that $\partial\Omega_2 - \Sigma = \partial\Omega \cap \partial\Omega_2$ is rigid). Precisely, we shall have

$$(3.21) \qquad \begin{aligned} \mathbf{0} &= \int_\Sigma [\boldsymbol{T}(\boldsymbol{v},\rho)\cdot\boldsymbol{n} - \rho(\boldsymbol{v}\cdot\boldsymbol{n})\boldsymbol{v}], \\ \mathbf{0} &= \int_\Sigma [\boldsymbol{r}(y)\times\boldsymbol{T}(\boldsymbol{v},\rho)\cdot\boldsymbol{n} - \rho(\boldsymbol{v}\cdot\boldsymbol{n})\boldsymbol{r}(y)\times\boldsymbol{v}], \end{aligned}$$

where $\boldsymbol{T}(\boldsymbol{v},\rho)$ is the stress $(2.2)_1$, with $p = p(\rho)$. In (3.21) the velocity $\boldsymbol{v}$ and the density ρ are unknown, as well as also Σ. Therefore, the correct wellposedness question is formulated for equations (3.19), (3.20), (3.21). We propose this as an open problem.

Example 3.1. If we limit ourselves to find real solutions in the one dimensional case of the rest, and for constant forces, we can completely solve the problem. Indeed, we fix a coordinate system with the same origin as in the previous example, so that the domains $\Omega_1 = (d_1, d)$, $\Omega_2 = (0, d_1)$ will have as only unkown variable the depth, say d_1. The boundary Σ will reduce to the point of abscisse d_1. The only nontrivial balance equation will be that of the linear momentum. Noticing that for the rest $\boldsymbol{T} = -k\rho^\gamma \boldsymbol{I}$, (3.21) furnishes $\rho^\gamma(d_1) = 0$. Therefore, introducing such an information in (3.18), we have at once $\gamma kc = -(\gamma-1)fd_1$. The condition that the mass is given implies

$$\int_0^{d_1} \left(\frac{\gamma-1}{k\gamma} f(x-d_1)\right)^{(1/(\gamma-1))} = M$$

which furnishes the unknown d_1. With this construction, the density is always positive and real. The above phenomenon shows that, in order to find (for large forces) global existence theorems of steady flow of a viscous gas one should care of the constitutive equations and of the domain as well.

Remark 3.4 – Example 3.1 suggests that one might prescribe the shape of Σ as a one parameter family. In this way, one should find, as unknown related to Σ only one real number. The shape of Σ can be fixed as an equipotential surface, since we know the potential U.

In conclusion, the possibility $\rho = 0$ is to be excluded.

3.5 - Rigid boundary conditions: preliminary considerations.

The study performed in Subsection 3.4 furnishes a new reading key of the equations, which will lead to a new iterative procedure. Precisely, we look for solutions with strictly positive density. Since the intensity of the perturbation in the density is controlled by the external data, this implies that we are confining ourselves to consider only small external data.

We shall prove existence theorems for two kinds of bounding surfaces: *rigid surfaces* on which no slip occurs and *free surfaces* on which no tangential stresses act. Here, we choose a diachronic presentation, hence, we prove existence of steady flows first in bounded rigid domains.

The condition that no slip occurs on this surface implies that the velocity must assume the value of the particles of the boundary, say $\boldsymbol{v}_*$. Therefore, we are led to study the following steady Poisson–Stokes system

$$
\begin{aligned}
&\nabla \cdot (\rho \tilde{\boldsymbol{v}}) = 0, \\
&\rho \tilde{\boldsymbol{v}} \cdot \nabla \tilde{\boldsymbol{v}} = -\nabla p + \mu \Delta \tilde{\boldsymbol{v}} + (\lambda + \mu) \nabla (\nabla \cdot \tilde{\boldsymbol{v}}) + \rho \tilde{\boldsymbol{f}} + \tilde{\boldsymbol{b}}, \\
&\tilde{\boldsymbol{v}}|_{\partial\Omega} = \boldsymbol{v}_*, \qquad \int_\Omega \rho = M = \bar{\rho}|\Omega|.
\end{aligned}
\tag{3.22}
$$

Let us denote by $\boldsymbol{V}$ a regular extension of the boundary data $\boldsymbol{v}_*$. Let $\sigma = \rho - \bar{\rho}$ denote the perturbation in the density ρ, from the mean density $\bar{\rho}$. Normalizing the density by dividing ρ, p, μ, and λ by $\bar{\rho}$, and relabelling, we can assume that

$\bar{\rho} = 1$, so that $\sigma = \rho - 1$. Using the given decompositions for $\tilde{\boldsymbol{v}} = \boldsymbol{v} + \boldsymbol{V}$, and ρ, it is easy to see that system (3.22) assumes the equivalent form

$$\begin{gathered}\nabla \cdot \boldsymbol{v} = -\nabla \cdot (\sigma \boldsymbol{v}) - \nabla \cdot (\rho \boldsymbol{V}),\\ \rho \boldsymbol{v} \cdot \nabla \boldsymbol{v} = -\nabla p + \mu \Delta \boldsymbol{v} + (\lambda + \mu) \nabla \nabla \cdot \boldsymbol{v} + \rho \boldsymbol{f} + \boldsymbol{b},\\ \boldsymbol{v}|_{\partial\Omega} = \mathbf{0}, \quad \int_{\Omega} \sigma = 0,\end{gathered} \tag{3.23}$$

where $\boldsymbol{f} = \tilde{\boldsymbol{f}} + \tilde{\boldsymbol{v}} \cdot \nabla \boldsymbol{V} + \boldsymbol{V} \cdot \nabla \boldsymbol{v}, \quad \boldsymbol{b} = \tilde{\boldsymbol{b}} + \mu \Delta \boldsymbol{V} + (\lambda + \mu) \nabla \nabla \cdot \boldsymbol{V}$.

Let us start to describe the new iterative procedure. Given $\boldsymbol{w}$, τ, we first consider the following three linear systems.

STOKES SYSTEM

$$\begin{gathered}\nabla \cdot \boldsymbol{v} = g(\tau, \boldsymbol{w}),\\ -\mu \Delta \boldsymbol{v} - (\lambda + \mu) \nabla (\nabla \cdot \boldsymbol{v}) = -\nabla \pi + \boldsymbol{F}(\tau, \boldsymbol{w}),\\ \boldsymbol{v}|_{\partial\Omega} = \mathbf{0},\\ \boldsymbol{F}(\tau, \boldsymbol{w}) := (1 + \tau)(\boldsymbol{f} - \boldsymbol{w} \cdot \nabla \boldsymbol{w}) + \boldsymbol{b},\\ g(\tau, \boldsymbol{w}) := -\nabla \cdot (\tau \boldsymbol{w}), \quad g|_{\partial\Omega} = 0.\end{gathered} \tag{3.24}$$

POISSON SYSTEM

$$\begin{gathered}\Delta H = \nabla \cdot \boldsymbol{F}(\tau, \boldsymbol{w}),\\ \left.\frac{\partial H}{\partial n}\right|_{\partial\Omega} = \boldsymbol{n} \cdot [\mu(\Delta \boldsymbol{v} - \nabla(\nabla \cdot \boldsymbol{v})) + \boldsymbol{F}(\tau, \boldsymbol{w})]|_{\partial\Omega}, \quad \int_{\Omega} H = 0.\end{gathered} \tag{3.25}$$

STEADY TRANSPORT EQUATION

$$k\sigma + (\lambda + 2\mu) \nabla \cdot (\sigma \boldsymbol{v}) = H. \tag{3.26}$$

Notice that, since $\nabla \cdot \boldsymbol{v}|_{\partial\Omega} = 0$, $H = 0$, for regular solutions the condition

$$\int_{\partial\Omega} \nabla \cdot (\sigma \boldsymbol{v}) = 0. \tag{3.27}$$

also holds. In this way, we also impose the usual boundary and side conditions, on the velocity and density fields.

Our iterative scheme is formally justified in that, if it converges, say $\boldsymbol{w}, \tau \to \boldsymbol{v}, \sigma$, and if we set $\pi \equiv k\sigma$, then $\boldsymbol{v}, \sigma, \pi$ will satisfy (3.23). This follows easily if we prove that

$$H := k\sigma - (\lambda + 2\mu)\nabla \cdot \boldsymbol{v}. \tag{3.28}$$

To show that H satisfies (3.28), one may take (3.28) as the definition of H and then observe that the second of equations (3.24) can be rewritten, by using the vector identity $-\Delta \boldsymbol{v} = \nabla \times \nabla \times \boldsymbol{v} - \nabla\nabla \cdot \boldsymbol{v}$, as

$$\mu\nabla \times \nabla \times \boldsymbol{v} + \nabla H = \boldsymbol{F}. \tag{3.29}$$

This clearly implies that H, defined by (3.28), is the unique solution of the Neumann problem (3.25). In what follows, it is more convenient to regard (3.25) as the definition of H because H will be bounded using estimates for the Neumann problem, independently of estimates for π.

3.6 - An existence proof.

In this subsection, we shall construct a solution of (3.23) as the limit of a suitable sequence. Precisely, our iteration scheme is given by $\boldsymbol{v}_m, \sigma_m \to \boldsymbol{v}_{m+1}, \sigma_{m+1}$, beginning with $\boldsymbol{v}_0 = \boldsymbol{0}$, $\sigma_0 = 0$. Given $\boldsymbol{v}_m, \sigma_m$, we define g_m and $\boldsymbol{F}_m$ as functions of $\boldsymbol{v}_m$, σ_m, as done in $(3.24)_{4,5}$, and find $\boldsymbol{v}_{m+1}$ by solving the Stokes problem $(3.24)_{1,2,3}$ and then find an auxiliary function H_{m+1} by solving the Neumann problem $(3.25)_{1,2,3}$, and finally obtain σ_{m+1} by solving the transport equation (3.26).

- **Regularity lemmas.**

In the proof of the existence we shall make use of the following three lemmas which bound suitable norms of the solutions of the three simplified problems (3.24), (3.25), (3.26), in terms of suitable norms of the data.

Lemma 3.1. *In the steady Stokes problem (3.24), let* $g_m \in W^{1,q}(\Omega)$ *and* $\boldsymbol{F}_m \in L^q(\Omega)$. *Then there exists a unique solution* $\boldsymbol{v}_{m+1}, \pi_{m+1} \in W^{2,q}(\Omega) \cap W_0^{1,2}(\Omega) \times W^{1,q}(\Omega)$. *Moreover,*

$$\|\boldsymbol{v}_{m+1}\|_{2,q} \leq c(\|\boldsymbol{F}_m\|_q + \|g_m\|_{1,q}). \tag{3.30}$$

Lemma 3.2. *In the Neumann problem (3.25), let* $\boldsymbol{F}_m \in L^q(\Omega)$, *and* $\boldsymbol{v}_{m+1} \in W^{2,q}(\Omega)$. *Then there exists a unique solution* $H_{m+1} \in W^{1,q}(\Omega)$. *Moreover,*

$$\begin{aligned} \|H_{m+1}\|_{1,q} &\leq c(\|\boldsymbol{F}_m\|_q + \|g_m\|_{1,q}), \\ \|\Delta H_{m+1}\|_{-1,q} &\leq c\|\boldsymbol{F}_m\|_q. \end{aligned} \tag{3.31}$$

From (3.25) it follows that if $\boldsymbol{F}_m \in L^p(\Omega)$, then $\Delta H_{n+1} \in W^{-1,p}(\Omega)$. Indeed, since $(\Delta H_{m+1}, \phi) = (\nabla \cdot \boldsymbol{F}_m, \phi) = -(\boldsymbol{F}_m, \nabla\phi)$, for $\phi \in W_0^{1,p'}(\Omega)$, there holds

$$\|\Delta H_{m+1}\|_{-1,p} \equiv \sup_{\phi \in W_0^{1,p'}} \frac{|(\Delta H_{m+1}, \phi)|}{\|\phi\|_{1,p'}} = \sup_{\phi \in W_0^{1,p'}} \frac{(\boldsymbol{F}_m, \nabla\phi)}{\|\phi\|_{1,p'}} \leq \|\boldsymbol{F}_m\|_p .$$

Lemma 3.3. *In the steady transport equation (3.26), let* $H_{m+1} \in W^{1,q}(\Omega)$, *and* $\boldsymbol{v}_{m+1} \in W^{2,q}(\Omega)$, *with* $\boldsymbol{v}_{m+1} \cdot \boldsymbol{n}|_{\partial\Omega} = 0$ *and* $\|\boldsymbol{v}_{m+1}\|_{2,q} < c_0$. *Then, if* c_0 *is sufficiently small, there exists a unique solution* $\sigma_{m+1} \in W^{1,q}(\Omega)$. *Moreover,*

$$\begin{aligned} \|\sigma_{m+1}\|_{1,q} &\leq c(\|\boldsymbol{F}_m\|_q + \|g_m\|_{1,q}), \\ \|\Delta\nabla \cdot (\sigma_{m+1}\boldsymbol{v}_{m+1})\|_{-1,q} &\leq c(\|\boldsymbol{F}_m\|_q + (\|\boldsymbol{F}_m\|_q + \|g_m\|_{1,q})^2). \end{aligned} \tag{3.32}$$

- **Sketch of the existence proof.**

Here we prove the boundedness of the sequence $(\boldsymbol{v}_m, \rho_m)$ and its convergence. By Lemmas 3.1, 3.2, 3.3, estimates (3.30), (3.31), (3.32) are true. Moreover, for the steady transport equation (3.26), Lemma 3.3 furnishes also the following estimate

$$\|\nabla \cdot (\sigma_{m+1}\boldsymbol{v}_{m+1})\|_{1,q} \leq c\|\Delta H_{m+1}\|_{-1,q}. \tag{3.33}$$

Notice that in the last inequality, for $\nabla \cdot (\sigma_{m+1}\boldsymbol{v}_{m+1})$ we could increase the (negative) norm of its laplacian in $W^{-1,q}(\Omega)$ with its (positive) norm in $W^{1,q}(\Omega)$ because this quantity vanishes on the boundary. Let

$$\begin{gathered} \|\sigma_m\|_{1,q} + \|\boldsymbol{v}_m\|_{2,q} \leq \epsilon, \quad \|\nabla \cdot (\sigma_m\boldsymbol{v}_m)\|_{1,q} \leq \eta, \\ \|\boldsymbol{f}\|_q + \|\nabla \cdot \boldsymbol{v}\|_{1,q} \leq \delta. \end{gathered} \tag{3.34}$$

Substituting assumptions (3.34) in the definitions $(3.24)_{3,4}$, we get

$$\|\boldsymbol{F}_m\|_q \le (1+\eta)(\delta+\epsilon^2), \quad \|g_m\|_{1,q} \le \eta.$$

By replacing these informations into (3.30), (3.32) we obtain

$$\begin{aligned} \|\sigma_{m+1}\|_{1,q} + \|\boldsymbol{v}_{m+1}\|_{2,q} &\le c[(1+\eta)(\delta+\epsilon^2)+\eta], \\ \|\nabla\cdot(\sigma_{m+1}\boldsymbol{v}_{m+1})\|_{1,q} &\le c(1+\eta)(\delta+\epsilon^2). \end{aligned} \tag{3.35}$$

In order to recover, for $\boldsymbol{v}_{m+1}$, σ_{m+1}, the same estimate we assumed on $\boldsymbol{v}_m$ and σ_m it must be

$$c[(1+\eta)(\delta+\epsilon^2)+\eta] \le \epsilon, \quad c(1+\eta)(\delta+\epsilon^2) \le \eta. \tag{3.36}$$

These inequalities are compatible. Indeed, let us fix $\eta < \epsilon/(2c)$, then, for δ sufficiently small there exists an ϵ solution to the second degree inequality $4c\epsilon^2 - \epsilon + 4c\delta \le 0$.

Till now, we constructed a sequence $\boldsymbol{v}_m$, σ_m, bounded in $W^{2,q}(\Omega) \times W^{1,q}(\Omega)$, say

$$\|\boldsymbol{v}_m\|_{2,q} + \|\sigma_m\|_{1,q} \le R.$$

It remains to be proved that the whole sequence is convergent in $W^{2,q}(\Omega) \times W^{1,q}(\Omega)$. We observe that the difference $\boldsymbol{v}'_{m+1} := \boldsymbol{v}_{m+1} - \boldsymbol{v}_m$, $\pi'_{m+1} = \pi_{m+1} - \pi_m$, $\sigma'_{m+1} = \sigma_{m+1} - \sigma_m$, satisfies the system

$$\begin{aligned} & -\mu\Delta\boldsymbol{v}'_{m+1} - (\lambda+\mu)\boldsymbol{v}'_{m+1} = -\nabla\pi'_{m+1} + \boldsymbol{F}'_m, \\ & \nabla\cdot\boldsymbol{v}'_{m+1} = g'_m, \\ & -\Delta H'_{m+1} = -\nabla\cdot\boldsymbol{F}'_m, \\ & k\sigma'_{m+1} + (\lambda+2\mu)\nabla\cdot(\boldsymbol{v}_{m+1}\sigma'_{m+1}) = H'_{m+1} - (\lambda+2\mu)\nabla\cdot(\sigma_m\boldsymbol{v}'_{m+1}), \\ & \boldsymbol{v}'_{m+1}|_{\partial\Omega} = \boldsymbol{0}, \\ & \frac{\partial H'_{m+1}}{\partial n} = -\mu\boldsymbol{n}\cdot\nabla\times\nabla\times\boldsymbol{v}'_{m+1} + \boldsymbol{n}\cdot\boldsymbol{F}'_m, \end{aligned} \tag{3.37}$$

here we set

$$\boldsymbol{v}'_m := \boldsymbol{v}_m - \boldsymbol{v}_{m-1}, \qquad \sigma'_m = \sigma_m - \sigma_{m-1},$$
$$\boldsymbol{F}'_m := \sigma'_m\boldsymbol{f} - (1+\sigma_m)(\boldsymbol{v}_m\cdot\nabla\boldsymbol{v}'_m + \boldsymbol{v}'_m\cdot\nabla\boldsymbol{v}_{m-1}) - \sigma'_m\boldsymbol{v}_{m-1}\cdot\nabla\boldsymbol{v}_{m-1}$$
$$g'_m := -\nabla\cdot(\sigma'_m\boldsymbol{v}_m + \sigma_{m-1}\boldsymbol{v}'_m).$$

The problem of convergence is not so easy because at the right hand side of $(3.37)_4$ the last term looses its regularity. We therefore refer to [28] for a more detailed proof. Once the convergence of $(\boldsymbol{v}_m, \rho_m)$ has been proved, it is a standard argument to prove that the limit $(\boldsymbol{v}, \rho)$ satisfies the full system.

It is straightforward to show that

$$\|\boldsymbol{F}'_m\|_q \leq c(R)[\|\boldsymbol{v}'_m\|_{2,q} + \|\sigma'_m\|_{1,q}], \tag{3.38}$$

where $c(R)$ is a suitable constant, homogeneous function of R which can be taken arbitraly small, for R small. Below, by C we shall denote any other (maybe large) constant.

The convergence will be proved for sequences in $W^{3,2}(\Omega) \times W^{2,2}(\Omega)$. Actually, using Lemmas 3.1, 3.2, 3.3 we prove,

$$\|\boldsymbol{v}'_{m+1}\|_{1,q} + \|\sigma'_{m+1}\|_q \leq c(R)(\|\boldsymbol{v}'_m\|_{1,q} + \|\sigma'_m\|_q + \|\boldsymbol{v}'_{m-1}\|_{1,q} + \|\sigma'_{m-1}\|_q), \tag{3.39}$$

where $c(R)$ can be taken arbitrarily small. Therefore, for $c(R)$ sufficiently small, we obtain the convergence of the full sequence[1]. The theorem is then completely proved.

---

[1] Let us set

$$\xi_m := \|\nabla \boldsymbol{v}'_m\| + \|\sigma'_m\|.$$

Let $c(R) = \alpha < 1/2$ and rewrite (3.39) as

$$\xi_{m+1} \leq \alpha(\xi_m + \xi_{m-1}). \tag{I}$$

We proceed by induction, setting $m = 2h$ and assuming

$$\xi_{2h-1} < (2\alpha)^h \xi_0; \qquad \xi_{2h} < (2\alpha)^h \xi_0.$$

Then, (I) yields, for $m = 2h$, $m = 2h+1$

$$\begin{aligned} &\xi_{2h+1} < (2\alpha)^{h+1}\xi_0, \\ &\xi_{2h+2} < \alpha[(2\alpha)^{h+1}\xi_0 + (2\alpha)^h\xi_0] < (2\alpha)^{h+1}\xi_0, \end{aligned}$$

and we find satisfied the same hypotheses for the next step. Therefore, letting h to infinity we find that the whole sequence converges to zero.

- **Some remarks on the auxiliary regularity lemmas.**

We wish to make some remarks about Lemmas 3.1, 3.2 and 3.3. Precisely, we shall not prove Lemmas 3.1, 3.3 and we just limit ourselves to prove Lemma 3.2.

Since the Stokes problem has been widely discussed in several places, cf., *e.g*, [22], [33], we refer to these monographies for the proof of Lemma 3.1.

As regard Lemma 3.2, we start with the definition of weak solution to the Neumann problem.

Definition 3.1. *Let Ω be a bounded set of $\mathbb{R}^n$, $\boldsymbol{f} \in L^q(\Omega)$ and $\boldsymbol{v} \in W^{-1+1/q,q}(\partial\Omega)$, dual space of $W^{1-1/p,p}(\partial\Omega)$, $1/q + 1/p = 1$. We shall say that $H \in W^{1,q}(\Omega)$ is a weak solution of the Neumann problem*

$$(3.40)\qquad \begin{aligned} \Delta H &= \nabla \cdot \boldsymbol{F}, \\ \left.\frac{\partial H}{\partial n}\right|_{\partial\Omega} &= \{\boldsymbol{F}\cdot\boldsymbol{n} - \mu\boldsymbol{n}\cdot(\nabla\times\nabla\times\boldsymbol{v})\}|_{\partial\Omega} \end{aligned}$$

iff, $\forall\varphi \in W^{1,p}(\Omega)$, it satisfies the identity

$$(3.41)\qquad \begin{aligned} \mathcal{F}(\varphi) &:= \int_\Omega \nabla H\cdot\nabla\varphi\,\mathrm{d}x = \\ &= \int_\Omega \boldsymbol{F}\cdot\nabla\varphi\,\mathrm{d}x - \int_{\partial\Omega}\mu\boldsymbol{n}\cdot(\nabla\times\nabla\times\boldsymbol{v})\,\varphi\,\mathrm{d}\sigma, \qquad \int_\Omega H\mathrm{d}x = 0. \end{aligned}$$

As one can easily check by an integration by parts, solutions of (3.41) satisfy, $\forall\phi \in W^{1,p}(\Omega)$, also the identity

$$(3.42)\qquad \begin{aligned} &\int_\Omega \varphi\Delta H\,\mathrm{d}x = \\ &= \int_\Omega \varphi\nabla\cdot\boldsymbol{F}\,\mathrm{d}x - \int_{\partial\Omega}\left[\frac{\partial H}{\partial n} + \boldsymbol{n}\cdot\boldsymbol{F} - \mu\boldsymbol{n}\cdot(\nabla\times\nabla\times\boldsymbol{v})\right]\varphi\,\mathrm{d}\sigma. \end{aligned}$$

Therefore, the definition of weak solution is really an extension of the usual notion of classical solution to problem (3.40).

Let us prove the fundamental inequality

$$(3.43)\qquad \|\nabla H\|_q \le c\left(\|\boldsymbol{F}\|_q + \|D^2\boldsymbol{v}\|_{-1+1/q,q,\partial\Omega}\right).$$

Inequality (3.43) follows from (3.41) by taking the supremum of the absolute value of the left hand side in the ball $\|\nabla\phi\|_p = 1$, and applying Hölder inequality at the right hand side. Therefore, the linear functional $\mathcal{F}(\phi)$ is continuous in $W^{1,p}(\Omega)$. The existence now follows from a classical theorem on the unique representation of linear functionals on $W^{1,p}(\Omega)$ cf. [87].

Concerning Lemma 3.3, we consider in Ω the the following equation, which is symmetric positive in the sense of Friedrichs, also called steady transport equation,

$$k\sigma + (\lambda + 2\mu)\,\nabla\cdot(\sigma\boldsymbol{v}) = H. \tag{3.44}$$

with $\boldsymbol{v} \in W^{2,q}(\Omega) \cap W_0^{1,2}(\Omega)$, $H \in W^{1,q}(\Omega)$. Let $\|\boldsymbol{v}\|_{2,q} = \gamma_1$, where γ_1 is sufficiently small. Equation (3.44) is not of definite type since $\boldsymbol{v}$ can vanish, this leads to several complications, see *e.g.* [7], [16], [17], [65], [66]. In [28] Lemmas 3.3 has been proved in the details.

3.7 - Stress free boundaries: remarks on existence.

The proofs of Theorems 3.3, 3.4 are in the same line as those of Theorems 3.1 and 3.2, sketched in Subsection 3.6, so that we limit ourselves to discuss the differences between them. For different proofs, see [67], [76]. Taking $\boldsymbol{v}_0 = \boldsymbol{0}$, $\sigma_0 = 0$, we obtain an iterative scheme which consists of setting first

$$g_m = -\nabla\cdot(\sigma_m\boldsymbol{v}_m)\,, \qquad \boldsymbol{F}_m = -\,(1+\sigma_m)\,(\boldsymbol{v}_m\cdot\nabla\boldsymbol{v}_m - \boldsymbol{f})\,, \tag{3.45}$$

and then solving the Stokes problem

$$\begin{aligned} &\nabla\cdot\boldsymbol{v}_{m+1} = g_m,\\ &-\mu\Delta\boldsymbol{v}_{m+1} - (\lambda+2\mu)\nabla(\nabla\cdot\boldsymbol{v}_{m+1}) = -\nabla\pi_{m+1} + \boldsymbol{F}_m,\\ &\boldsymbol{v}_{m+1}\cdot\boldsymbol{n}|_{\partial\Omega} = 0, \qquad \left.\frac{\partial(\boldsymbol{v}_{m+1}\times\boldsymbol{n})}{\partial n}\right|_{\partial\Omega} = \boldsymbol{0}, \quad \int_\Omega \pi_{m+1} = 0. \end{aligned} \tag{3.46}$$

Next, we solve the following Neumann problem for H_{m+1}

$$\begin{aligned} &\Delta H_{m+1} = \nabla\cdot\boldsymbol{F}_m, \quad \int_\Omega H_{m+1} = 0\\ &\left.\frac{\partial H_{m+1}}{\partial n}\right|_{\partial\Omega} = \boldsymbol{n}\cdot(\boldsymbol{F}_m - \nabla\times\nabla\times\boldsymbol{v}_{m+1})\,|_{\partial\Omega}. \end{aligned} \tag{3.47}$$

Let us analyze only the term $\beta := -\boldsymbol{n} \cdot \nabla \times \nabla \times \boldsymbol{v}_{m+1}|_{\partial\Omega}$. Taken any point $\xi \in \partial\Omega$, we introduce a local orthonormal frame $y \equiv (y_1, y_2, y_3)$ at ξ, with y_1, y_2 in the tangent plane to $\partial\Omega$ at ξ, and with y_3 directed along the exterior normal to $\partial\Omega$ at ξ. Since β is invariant with respect to rotations of coordinate system, we can write it in the above frame y, with $y_3 =: \omega(y_1, y_2)$. Recall that

$$\boldsymbol{n} \equiv \left(-\frac{\partial\omega}{\partial y_1}, -\frac{\partial\omega}{\partial y_2}, 1\right), \quad \left.\frac{\partial\omega}{\partial y_\alpha}\right|_\xi = 0, \quad \alpha = 1, 2.$$

Furthermore, for any function u, vanishing on the boundary, we have

$$\text{(3.48)} \quad \begin{aligned} &\frac{\mathrm{d}u}{\mathrm{d}y_\alpha} = 0 \iff \frac{\partial u}{\partial y_\alpha} = -\frac{\partial u}{\partial y_3}\frac{\partial\omega}{\partial y_\alpha}, \\ &\frac{\partial^2 u}{\partial y_\alpha^2} = -\frac{\partial u}{\partial y_3}\frac{\partial^2\omega}{\partial y_\alpha^2}, \qquad \left.\frac{\partial u}{\partial y_\alpha}\right|_\xi = -\left.\frac{\partial u}{\partial y_3}\frac{\partial\omega}{\partial y_\alpha}\right|_\xi = 0 \end{aligned}$$

[34] p. 19. With a prime as index, $\boldsymbol{w}'(\xi)$ will denote the projection of the vector $\boldsymbol{w}(\xi)$ over the plane tangent to $\partial\Omega$ at ξ or, in other words, the component of $\boldsymbol{w}$ along the axis y_3 is taken to be zero. From the above positions, since $\frac{\partial\boldsymbol{n}}{\partial y_3} = \boldsymbol{0}$, it follows

$$\begin{aligned} -\boldsymbol{n} \cdot \nabla \times \nabla \times \boldsymbol{v}_{m+1}|_{\partial\Omega} &= [\Delta\boldsymbol{v}_{m+1} - \nabla(\nabla \cdot \boldsymbol{v}_{m+1})] \cdot \boldsymbol{n}|_{\partial\Omega} \\ &= \Big\{\nabla' \cdot [(\nabla'\boldsymbol{v}_{m+1}) \cdot \boldsymbol{n}] - \nabla'\boldsymbol{v}_{m+1} : \nabla'\boldsymbol{n} + \frac{\partial^2\boldsymbol{v}_{m+1}}{\partial y_3^2} \cdot \boldsymbol{n} \\ &\qquad - \frac{\partial}{\partial y_3}\Big(\nabla' \cdot \boldsymbol{v}'_{m+1} + \frac{\partial\boldsymbol{v}_{m+1}}{\partial y_3} \cdot \boldsymbol{n}\Big)\Big\}\Big|_{\partial\Omega} \\ &= \Big\{\nabla' \cdot [\nabla'(\boldsymbol{v}_{m+1} \cdot \boldsymbol{n})] - \nabla' \cdot [(\nabla'\boldsymbol{n}) \cdot \boldsymbol{v}_{m+1}] \\ &\qquad - \nabla'\boldsymbol{v}_{m+1} : \nabla'\boldsymbol{n} - \frac{\partial}{\partial y_3}\nabla' \cdot \boldsymbol{v}'_{m+1}\Big\}\Big|_{\partial\Omega}. \end{aligned}$$

We notice now that, on the boundary, $\boldsymbol{v}_{m+1} \cdot \boldsymbol{n} = 0$; therefore, by $(3.48)_2$, the first term turns out to be a function of only the first order derivatives of $\boldsymbol{v}_{m+1} \cdot \boldsymbol{n}$, the fourth term cancels with the last one. Finally, by noticing that $(3.46)_4$ means $\frac{\partial\boldsymbol{v}'_{m+1}}{\partial y_3} = \boldsymbol{0}$, we deduce that $\nabla' \cdot \left.\frac{\partial\boldsymbol{v}'_{m+1}}{\partial y_3}\right|_\xi = 0$. Thus, by changing the order of the derivatives, we infer that the fifth term in the above relation equals zero. Therefore, we have proved that

$$-\boldsymbol{n}\cdot\nabla\times\nabla\times\boldsymbol{v}_{m+1}|_{\partial\Omega}=-\nabla'\cdot[(\nabla'\boldsymbol{n})\cdot\boldsymbol{v}_{m+1}]-\nabla'\boldsymbol{v}_{m+1}:\nabla'\boldsymbol{n}-\frac{\partial\boldsymbol{v}_{m+1}}{\partial y_3}\cdot\boldsymbol{n}\Delta'\omega.$$

Hence, for H_{m+1} we obtain the following boundary condition

$$\frac{\partial H_{m+1}}{\partial y_3}=-\nabla'\cdot[(\nabla'\boldsymbol{n})\cdot\boldsymbol{v}_{m+1}]-\nabla'\boldsymbol{v}_{m+1}:\nabla'\boldsymbol{n}+\boldsymbol{F}_m\cdot\boldsymbol{n}.$$

Finally, in the usual way, we determine σ_{m+1} as the solution of the transport equation

$$k\sigma_{m+1}+(\lambda+2\mu)\,\nabla\cdot(\sigma_{m+1}\boldsymbol{v}_{m+1})=H_{m+1}. \tag{3.49}$$

The proof of existence will now follow, *mutatis mutandis*, the same lines developed in subections 3.5, 3.6, paying better attention to the Neumann problem (3.47). The complete proof can be found in [28].

3.8 - Artificial boundary conditions: inputs for an existence proof.

In this subsection, we assume that the artificial boundary conditions (3.4) hold. The region occupied by the fluid is a bounded domain Ω of $\mathbb{R}^3$. Thus the stationary problem is

$$\begin{aligned}
&\nabla\cdot(\rho\boldsymbol{v})=0,\\
&\rho\boldsymbol{v}\cdot\nabla\boldsymbol{v}=-\nabla p+\mu\Delta\boldsymbol{v}+(\lambda+\mu)\,\nabla(\nabla\cdot\boldsymbol{v})+\rho\boldsymbol{f}+\boldsymbol{b},\\
&(\lambda+2\mu)\frac{\partial\boldsymbol{v}}{\partial n}\cdot\boldsymbol{n}-k\rho\Big|_{\Sigma_\pm}=c_\pm \qquad \frac{\partial(\boldsymbol{v}\cdot\boldsymbol{\tau})}{\partial n}\Big|_{\Sigma}=0,\\
&\boldsymbol{v}|_{\partial\Omega-\Sigma}=\boldsymbol{0}\quad \int_\Omega\rho=M,\quad \int_\Omega\rho=\overline{\rho}\,|\Omega|\,,
\end{aligned} \tag{3.50}$$

where the mean density $\overline{\rho}>0$ is prescribed. Normalizing the density by dividing ρ by $\overline{\rho}$, we may take $\overline{\rho}=1$.

Our main object would be a proof of the following small data existence and uniqueness theorem.

Theorem 3.5. *Let Ω be a bounded subdomain of $\mathbb{R}^3$ of class C^2. Let $\boldsymbol{f} \in L^q(\Omega)$, with $q > n$. Then, if $\|\boldsymbol{f}\|_q$ is sufficiently small, depending on n, Ω, q, k, μ, and λ, there exists a unique solution $\boldsymbol{v}, \rho$ of problem (3.50) with $\boldsymbol{v} \in W^{1,2}(\Omega) \cap W^{2,q}(\Omega)$, $\boldsymbol{v} = \boldsymbol{0}$ on $\partial\Omega \setminus \Sigma$ and $\rho \in W^{1,q}(\Omega)$.*

A proof of the existence Theorem 3.5 is expected to be in the same line as that of above Theorems 3.1, 3.3. However, in this case the embedding theorems do not hold any more. Thus, we are no more able to give complete proofs, and we shall limit ourselves to furnish a description of some crucial points in the proof, and only for two dimensional plane artificial boundaries.

Assume that Ω is a two-dimensional domain, with flat rectangular boundary. We take $\boldsymbol{v}_0 = \boldsymbol{0}$, $\sigma_0 = 0$ and $\boldsymbol{f}|_{\partial\Omega} = \boldsymbol{0}$. Then, we obtain an iterative scheme which consists of first setting

$$g_m = -\nabla \cdot (\sigma_m \boldsymbol{v}_m), \qquad \boldsymbol{F}_m = -(1+\sigma_m)(\boldsymbol{v}_m \cdot \nabla \boldsymbol{v}_m - \boldsymbol{f}), \tag{3.51}$$

and then solving the Stokes problem

$$\begin{gathered} \nabla \cdot \boldsymbol{v}_{m+1} = g_m, \quad \int_\Omega g_m = 0, \\ -\mu \Delta \boldsymbol{v}_{m+1} - (\lambda + 2\mu)\nabla(\nabla \cdot \boldsymbol{v}_{m+1}) = -k\nabla\sigma_{m+1} + \boldsymbol{F}_m, \\ \left[(\lambda+2\mu)\frac{\partial \boldsymbol{v}_{m+1}}{\partial n} \cdot \boldsymbol{n} - k\sigma_{m+1}\right]_{\Sigma_\pm} = c_\pm, \qquad \left.\frac{\partial(\boldsymbol{v}_{m+1} \times \boldsymbol{n})}{\partial n}\right|_\Sigma = \boldsymbol{0}. \end{gathered} \tag{3.52}$$

Furthermore, H_{n+1} satisfies

$$\begin{gathered} \Delta H_{m+1} = \nabla \cdot \boldsymbol{F}_m, \quad \int_\Omega H_{m+1} = 0, \\ \left.\frac{\partial H_{m+1}}{\partial n}\right|_{\partial\Omega} = \boldsymbol{n} \cdot (\boldsymbol{F}_m - \mu \nabla \times \nabla \times \boldsymbol{v}_{m+1})|_{\partial\Omega} . \end{gathered} \tag{3.53}$$

Finally, we determine σ_{m+1} as the solution of the transport equation

$$k\sigma_{m+1} + (\lambda + 2\mu)\, \nabla \cdot (\sigma_{m+1} \boldsymbol{v}_{m+1}) = H_{m+1}. \tag{3.54}$$

- **Regularity lemmas.**

For the artificial boundary conditions the problem becomes a little more involved, because we have only conditions on the normal derivatives of the unknowns. In this case, it will be essential the following estimate which will be called the *solenoidality property*

$$\int_{\partial\Omega} |\boldsymbol{\varphi}\cdot\boldsymbol{n}|^q \leq c\int_{\Omega} |\boldsymbol{\varphi}|^q, \tag{3.55}$$

for all solenoidal functions. Therefore, following what has been done in [27], it should be possible to prove the lemma below.

Lemma 3.4. *In the steady Stokes problem* (3.52), *let* $g_m \in L^q(\Omega)$ *and* $\boldsymbol{F}_m \in W^{-1,q}(\Omega)$. *Then there exists a unique solution*

$$\boldsymbol{v}_{m+1}, \pi_{m+1} \in W^{1,q}(\Omega) \times L^q(\Omega).$$

Moreover,

$$\|\boldsymbol{v}_{m+1}\|_{1,q} \leq c(\|\boldsymbol{F}_m\|_{-1,q} + \|g_m\|_q). \tag{3.56}$$

Notice that

$$\begin{aligned}\|g_m\|_q \leq \|\nabla\cdot(\sigma_m \boldsymbol{v}_m)\|_q &\leq \|\sigma_m \nabla\cdot\boldsymbol{v}_m\|_q + \|\boldsymbol{v}_m\cdot\nabla\sigma_m\|_q,\\ &\leq c\|\sigma_m\|_{1,q}\|\boldsymbol{v}_m\|_{2,q}.\end{aligned}$$

This inequality tells us that $\|g_m\|_q$ is a non-linear term.

For the Neumann problem we assume, for the sake of simplicity, that $\boldsymbol{F}$ vanishes on the boundary. Next, mantaining the same notation introduced in this subsection 3.6, we notice that

$$\left.\frac{\partial H_{m+1}}{\partial n}\right|_{\partial\Omega} = -\mu\boldsymbol{n}\cdot\nabla\times\nabla\times\boldsymbol{v}_{m+1}|_{\partial\Omega} = \Delta'(\boldsymbol{v}_{m+1}\cdot\boldsymbol{n})|_{\partial\Omega}.$$

Let us denote by w_* the extension in Ω of $(\boldsymbol{v}_{m+1}\cdot\boldsymbol{n})$.

Lemma 3.5. *In the Neumann problem (3.53), let $\boldsymbol{F}_m \in L^q(\Omega)$, and $\boldsymbol{v}_{m+1} \in W^{2,q}(\Omega)$. Then there exists a unique solution $H_{m+1} \in W^{1,q}(\Omega)$. Moreover,*

$$\|H_{m+1}\|_{1,q} \le c(\|\boldsymbol{F}_m\|_q + \|w_*\|_{1,q}). \tag{3.57}$$

PROOF - Let us multiply $(3.53)_1$ by $\varphi \in W^{1,q'}(\Omega)$ and integrate over Ω, recalling that $\boldsymbol{F}$ vanishes at the boundary, we get

$$(\nabla H_{m+1}, \nabla\varphi) = \int_{\partial\Omega} \Delta' \boldsymbol{v}_{m+1} \cdot \boldsymbol{n}\varphi - (\boldsymbol{F}_m, \nabla\varphi). \tag{3.58}$$

Since $\partial\Omega$ is a closed surface, every smooth vector field satisfies $\int_{\partial\Omega} \nabla' \cdot \boldsymbol{f}' = 0$. Therefore, in particular,

$$\int_{\partial\Omega} \varphi\Delta' \boldsymbol{v}_{m+1} \cdot \boldsymbol{n} = -\int_{\partial\Omega} \nabla'\varphi \cdot (\nabla' \boldsymbol{v}_{m+1}) \cdot \boldsymbol{n} - \varphi\nabla'\boldsymbol{n} \cdot \nabla'\boldsymbol{v}.$$

Next, we take the supremum of the absolute value of the left hand side of (3.58) for φ varying in the subset $\mathcal{B}_1$ of $W^{1,q'}(\Omega)$ of functions having unitary norms, it delivers

$$\begin{aligned}\|\nabla H_{m+1}\|_q &= \sup_{\varphi\in\mathcal{B}_1} |(\nabla H_{m+1}, \nabla\varphi)| \le \sup_{\varphi\in\mathcal{B}_1} \left| \int_{\partial\Omega} \nabla'(\boldsymbol{v}_{m+1} \cdot \boldsymbol{n}) \cdot \nabla'\varphi \right| \\ &+ \sup_{\varphi\in\mathcal{B}_1} \left| \int_{\partial\Omega} [\nabla'\varphi \cdot (\nabla'\boldsymbol{n}) \cdot \boldsymbol{v}_{m+1} + \varphi\nabla'\boldsymbol{n} \cdot \nabla'\boldsymbol{v}] \right| \\ &+ \sup_{\varphi\in\mathcal{B}_1} |(\boldsymbol{F}_m, \nabla\varphi)| \le \|\nabla' \boldsymbol{v}_{m+1}\|_q + \|\boldsymbol{F}\|_q.\end{aligned} \tag{3.59}$$

In the above estimate we use now in essential way the solenoidality property. Indeed, since $\boldsymbol{\tau} = \boldsymbol{n} \times \boldsymbol{k}$, where $\boldsymbol{k}$ is the normal direction to the flow, for any smooth scalar field χ, we have $\nabla'\chi = \boldsymbol{\tau} \cdot \nabla\chi = \boldsymbol{n} \cdot \nabla\chi \times \boldsymbol{k}$. Notice that, in two dimensions, it is $\nabla\chi \times \boldsymbol{k} \equiv (\partial\chi/\partial n, -\partial\chi/\partial\tau, 0)$, where we have choosen $\boldsymbol{\tau}, \boldsymbol{n}$ as a basis in the plane of the flow: this has been possible because the boundary is flat. Now, it is almost trivial to verify that $\nabla\varphi \times \boldsymbol{k}$ is a solenoidal vector, and the solenoidal property can be applied to get

$$\|\nabla H_{m+1}\|_q \le \|\nabla' \boldsymbol{v}_{m+1}\|_q + \|\boldsymbol{F}_m\|_q. \tag{3.60}$$

The lemma is thus completely proved. □

For the steady transport equation, we have

Lemma 3.6. *In the steady transport equation* (3.54), *let* $H_{m+1} \in W^{1,q}(\Omega)$, *and* $\boldsymbol{v}_{m+1} \in W^{2,q}(\Omega)$, *with* $\boldsymbol{v}_{m+1} \cdot \boldsymbol{n}|_{\partial\Omega} = 0$ *and* $\|\boldsymbol{v}_{m+1}\|_{2,q} < c_0$. *Then, if* c_0 *is sufficiently small, there exists a unique solution* $\sigma_{m+1} \in W^{1,q}(\Omega)$. *Moreover,*

$$\|\sigma_{m+1}\|_{1,q} + \|\Delta\nabla \cdot (\sigma_{m+1}\boldsymbol{v}_{m+1})\|_{1,q} \leq c(\|\boldsymbol{F}_m\|_q + \|\nabla_T \boldsymbol{v}_{m+1}\|_q). \tag{3.61}$$

In Lemma 3.4 we showed that $\|\nabla' \boldsymbol{v}_{m+1}\|_q$ is estimated by only non-linear terms. Hence, Lemma 3.6 states that the same happens for the above norms of σ.

Finally, we have

Lemma 3.7. *In the steady Stokes problem* (3.52), *let* $g_m \in W^{1,q}(\Omega)$ *and* $\boldsymbol{F}_m \in L^q(\Omega)$. *Then there exists a unique solution* $\boldsymbol{v}_{m+1}, \pi_{m+1} \in W^{2,q}(\Omega) \times W^{1,q}(\Omega)$. *Moreover,*

$$\|\boldsymbol{v}_{m+1}\|_{2,q} \leq c(\|\boldsymbol{F}_m\|_q + \|g_m\|_{1,q}). \tag{3.62}$$

Some of the main tools of an existence theorem have been so established.

3.9 - Large potential forces: on the existence problem.

We notice that if the fluid is isothermal, say $\gamma = 1$, and the domain is bounded, the example of H. Beirao da Veiga does not work. Then it is natural to ask

Do generalized, physical solutions exist for large external forces, if $\gamma = 1$*?*

Indeed, the most general situation was considered in [57], where it was shown that the forces can be large provided the amount of matter is large enough. In order to state the existence theorem, we make the following assumptions.

Hypothesis (A)

$$\lim_{r\to\infty} \int_{\bar{\rho}}^{r} \frac{p'(s)}{s} ds = \infty, \quad \lim_{r\to 0} \int_{\bar{\rho}}^{r} \frac{p'(s)}{s} ds = \infty \tag{3.63}$$

where $\bar{\rho} := M/|\Omega|$, and $|\Omega|$ is the Lebesgue measure of Ω.

Hypothesis (B) – Condition $(3.63)_1$ and

$$\int_0^r \frac{p'(s)}{s} \mathrm{d}s < \infty,$$

are satisfied. Defining $\rho_c(x)$ as follows

$$\int_0^{\rho_c(x)} \frac{p'(s)}{s} \mathrm{d}s := -\phi(x) + \sup_{\overline{\Omega}} \phi,$$

we assume that

$$\int_\Omega \rho_c < M.$$

Theorem 3.6. *Let Ω be a bounded domain with a boundary of class C^4 and let either assumptions (A) or (B) be true. Then there exists a unique rest state $(\hat{\rho}, \mathbf{0})$ corresponding to external potential force ∇U, with $U \in C^3(\overline{\Omega})$, and a unique $\bar{U}$=const. such that*

$$\int_{\bar{\rho}(x)}^{\hat{\rho}} \frac{p'(s)}{s} \mathrm{d}s + U(x) = \bar{U}.$$

Thanks to the above theorem, it is then not too difficult to prove that a physical solution to (3.23), with $\boldsymbol{b} = \mathbf{0}$ and $\boldsymbol{v}_* = \mathbf{0}$, can be constructed, corresponding to arbitrary potential forces, provided the total mass is sufficiently great and the nonpotential forces, together with the boundary data, are sufficiently small.

- **A sketch of an existence proof.**

Below we shall prove Theorem 3.6 for isothermal gases, noticing that in this case hypotesis (A) is satisfied, and no condition on the total mass is now required.

First of all we shall assume $\boldsymbol{v}_* = \mathbf{0}$, $\boldsymbol{b} = \mathbf{0}$. Making use of the Helmholtz decomposition for the force $\boldsymbol{f}$, we can always write

$$\boldsymbol{f} = \boldsymbol{f}_1 + \nabla U, \quad \left.\frac{\partial U}{\partial n}\right|_{\partial\Omega} = \boldsymbol{f} \cdot \boldsymbol{n}|_{\partial\Omega}, \quad \nabla \cdot \boldsymbol{f}_1 = 0.$$

Now, due to the presence of a potential force, we introduce a basic density distribution at the rest, as follows

$$-k\nabla\rho_0 + \rho_0\nabla U = 0, \qquad \int_\Omega \rho_0 = M. \tag{3.64}$$

Notice that integration of (3.64) furnishes

$$\rho_0(x) = M\left(\int_\Omega \exp[U(y)/k]\mathrm{d}y\right)\exp[U(x)/k].$$

Therefore, for regular U, ρ_0 is everywhere positive. We can always write $\rho = \rho_0 + \sigma$, with $\int_\Omega \sigma = 0$, and from equation $(3.64)_1$ we find

$$-k\nabla\rho + \rho\nabla U = -k\nabla\sigma + \sigma\nabla U = -k\nabla\sigma + k\frac{\sigma}{\rho_0}\nabla\rho_0 = -k\rho_0\nabla\left(\frac{\sigma}{\rho_0}\right). \tag{3.65}$$

Using the given decomposition for ρ and (3.65), it is easy to see that system (3.23) assumes the equivalent form

$$\begin{aligned} &\nabla\cdot(\rho_0\boldsymbol{v}) = -\nabla\cdot(\sigma\boldsymbol{v}),\\ &\rho\boldsymbol{v}\cdot\nabla\boldsymbol{v} = -k\rho_0\nabla\left(\frac{\sigma}{\rho_0}\right) + \mu\Delta\boldsymbol{v} + (\lambda+\mu)\nabla(\nabla\cdot\boldsymbol{v}) + \rho\boldsymbol{f}_1,\\ &\boldsymbol{v}|_{\partial\Omega} = \boldsymbol{0}, \qquad \int_\Omega \sigma = 0, \end{aligned} \tag{3.66}$$

where $\int_{\partial\Omega}\boldsymbol{f}_1\cdot\boldsymbol{n} = 0$.

Given $\boldsymbol{w}$ and τ, we consider the following three linear systems.

Stokes System

$$\begin{aligned} &\nabla\cdot(\rho_0\boldsymbol{v}) = g(\tau,\boldsymbol{w}),\\ &-\mu\Delta\boldsymbol{v} - (\lambda+\mu)\nabla(\nabla\cdot\boldsymbol{v}) = -\rho_0\nabla\pi + \boldsymbol{F}(\tau,\boldsymbol{w}),\\ &\boldsymbol{v}|_{\partial\Omega} = \boldsymbol{0},\\ &\boldsymbol{F}(\tau,\boldsymbol{w}) := (\rho_0+\tau)\left(\boldsymbol{f}_1 - \boldsymbol{w}\cdot\nabla\boldsymbol{w}\right), \qquad \int_{\partial\Omega}\boldsymbol{F}\cdot\boldsymbol{n} = 0,\\ &g(\tau,\boldsymbol{w}) := -\nabla\cdot(\tau\boldsymbol{w}), \quad g|_{\partial\Omega} = 0. \end{aligned} \tag{3.67}$$

Poisson System

$$
(3.68)\qquad
\begin{aligned}
&\Delta H = \nabla \cdot \boldsymbol{F}(\tau, \boldsymbol{w}) + \nabla \cdot (\tau \nabla U), \qquad \int_\Omega H = H_0\\
&\frac{\partial H}{\partial n}\bigg|_{\partial\Omega} = \boldsymbol{n} \cdot \{\mu[\Delta \boldsymbol{v} - \nabla(\nabla \cdot \boldsymbol{v})] + \boldsymbol{F}(\tau, \boldsymbol{w}) + \tau \nabla U\}\big|_{\partial\Omega}.
\end{aligned}
$$

Steady Transport Equation

$$
(3.69)\qquad k\sigma + \frac{(\lambda + 2\mu)}{\rho_0} \nabla \cdot (\sigma \boldsymbol{v}) = H - \frac{(\lambda + 2\mu)}{\rho_0} \boldsymbol{v} \cdot \nabla \rho_0.
$$

Notice that, for a suitable value H_0, we can always take $\int_\Omega \sigma = 0$, furthermore, $(3.67)_{1,7}$ yields

$$
(3.70)\qquad \nabla \cdot (\sigma \boldsymbol{v})|_{\partial\Omega} = 0.
$$

In this way, we also impose the usual boundary and side conditions on the velocity and density fields. It is easy to check that substituting $\boldsymbol{w} = \boldsymbol{v}$ in (3.67)-(3.69), $\tau = \sigma$ one recovers the usual Poisson–Stokes system (3.66).

As in the previous Subsection 3.5, we shall construct a solution of (3.66) as the limit of a suitable sequence given by $\boldsymbol{v}_m, \sigma_m$, beginning with $\boldsymbol{v}_0 = 0$, $\sigma_0 = 0$. Given $\boldsymbol{v}_m, \sigma_m$, we define g_m and $\boldsymbol{F}_m$ in function of $\boldsymbol{v}_m$, σ_m as done in $(3.67)_{4,5}$ and find $\boldsymbol{v}_{m+1}$ by solving the Stokes problem $(3.67)_{1,2,3}$ and then find an auxiliary function H_{m+1} by solving the Neumann problem (3.68), and finally obtain σ_{m+1} by solving the transport equation (3.69).

We shall give here some sketch of proof of some auxiliary regularity Lemmas.

Lemma 3.8. *In the steady Stokes problem (3.67), let $g_m \in W^{1,q}(\Omega)$ and $\boldsymbol{F}_m \in L^q(\Omega)$. Then there exists a unique solution $\boldsymbol{v}_{m+1}, \pi_{m+1} \in W^{2,q}(\Omega) \cap W_0^{1,2}(\Omega) \times W^{1,q}(\Omega)$. Moreover,*

$$
(3.71)\qquad \|\boldsymbol{v}_{m+1}\|_{2,q} \le c(\|\boldsymbol{F}_m\|_q + \|g_m\|_{1,q}).
$$

Proof - Even though the estimates for the Stokes system are well known, system (3.67) is, we say, a "weighted" Stokes system. Precisely, Lemma 3.8

claims that the norm of $\boldsymbol{v}_{m+1}$ in $W^{1,q}(\Omega)$ is small provided only $(\|\boldsymbol{f}_m\|_q + \|g_m\|_{1,q})$ is small, in particular, the norm of ρ_0, linked to the potential force ∇U by (3.64), can be large.

The proof will be divided in two parts: in the first one we find an estimate for $\nabla \boldsymbol{v}_{m+1}$, π_{m+1} in $L^2(\Omega)$ in terms of the norms of $\boldsymbol{F}_m$ in $W^{-1,2}(\Omega)$ and of g_m in $L^2(\Omega)$ only. In the second part, we shall limit ourselves to write the classical known estimates for the solutions of a Stokes problem.

We outline, here, the first part of the proof. Let us multiply $(3.67)_2$ by $\boldsymbol{v}_{m+1}$ and integrate over Ω. Then, by an integration by parts, we get

$$\|\nabla \boldsymbol{v}_{m+1}\|^2 \le c\|\boldsymbol{F}_m\|_{-1,2}^2 + \int_\Omega g_m \pi_{m+1} \le c\, \|\boldsymbol{F}_m\|_{-1,2}^2 + \|g_m\|\|\pi_{m+1}\|. \tag{3.72}$$

Moreover, let us solve the following problem

$$\begin{gathered} \nabla \cdot (\rho_0 \boldsymbol{\varphi}) = \pi_{m+1}, \qquad \boldsymbol{\varphi}|_{\partial\Omega} = \boldsymbol{0}, \\ \|\boldsymbol{\varphi}\| \le c(\rho_0)\|\pi_{m+1}\|, \end{gathered} \tag{3.73}$$

where $c(\rho_0)$ can be large. Notice that (3.73) admits solutions because the compatibility condition of zero mean for π_{m+1} is satisfied. Thus, multiplying $(3.67)_2$ by $\boldsymbol{\varphi}$, againg integrating over Ω, integrating by parts, and isolating the term in π_{m+1}, we deduce

$$\|\pi_{m+1}\| \le c(\rho_0)(\|\nabla \boldsymbol{v}_{m+1}\| + \|\boldsymbol{F}_m\|_{-1,2}). \tag{3.74}$$

Substituting (3.74) into (3.72) we obtain the wanted estimate.

In the second part of the lemma, we study the classical Stokes system

$$\begin{aligned} &\nabla \cdot \boldsymbol{v}_{m+1} = \tilde{g}_m, \\ &-\mu \Delta \boldsymbol{v}_{m+1} - (\lambda + \mu)\nabla(\nabla \cdot \boldsymbol{v}_{m+1}) = -\nabla P_{m+1} + \tilde{\boldsymbol{F}}_m, \\ &\boldsymbol{v}_{m+1}|_{\partial\Omega} = \boldsymbol{0}, \\ &\tilde{g}_m := \frac{1}{\rho_0}[g(\sigma_m, \boldsymbol{v}_m) - \boldsymbol{v}_{m+1} \cdot \nabla \rho_0], \\ &P_{m+1} := \rho_0 \pi_{m+1}, \quad \tilde{\boldsymbol{F}}_m := \pi_{m+1} \nabla \rho_0 + \boldsymbol{F}(\sigma_m, \boldsymbol{v}_m). \end{aligned} \tag{3.75}$$

Since the force and the divergence of $\boldsymbol{v}_{m+1}$ in (3.75) contain only lower order terms of $\boldsymbol{v}_{m+1}$, and P_{m+1} and these have been estimated in terms of the norms of $\boldsymbol{F}_m$ in $W^{-1,2}(\Omega)$ and of g_m in $L^2(\Omega)$ only, the second part of theorem is quite standard. $\square$

For the Neumann problem, we have the following

Lemma 3.9. *In the Neumann problem* (3.68), *let* $\boldsymbol{F}_m \in L^q(\Omega)$, *and* $\boldsymbol{v}_{m+1} \in W^{2,q}(\Omega)$. *Then there exists a unique solution* $H_{m+1} \in W^{1,q}(\Omega)$. *Moreover,*

$$\begin{aligned} \|H_{m+1}\|_{1,q} &\le c(\|\boldsymbol{F}_m\|_q + \|g_m\|_{1,q}), \\ \|\Delta H_{m+1}\|_{-1,q} &\le c\|\boldsymbol{F}_m\|_q. \end{aligned} \tag{3.76}$$

PROOF - From (3.68) it follows that if $\boldsymbol{F}_m + \sigma_m \nabla U \in L^p(\Omega)$, then $\triangle H_{n+1} \in W^{-1,p}(\Omega)$ Indeed, since $(\triangle H_{m+1}, \varphi) = (\nabla \cdot \boldsymbol{f}_m, \varphi) = -(\boldsymbol{F}_m, \nabla\varphi)$, for $\varphi \in W_0^{1,p'}(\Omega)$,

$$\begin{aligned} \|\triangle H_{m+1}\|_{-1,p} \equiv \sup_{\varphi\in W_0^{1,p'}} \frac{|(\triangle H_{m+1}, \varphi)|}{\|\varphi\|_{1,p'}} = \sup_{\varphi\in W_0^{1,p'}} \frac{(\boldsymbol{F}_m + \sigma_m \nabla U, \nabla\varphi)}{\|\varphi\|_{1,p'}} \le \\ \le c\,(\|\boldsymbol{F}_m\|_p + \|\sigma_m \nabla U\|_p)\,. \end{aligned}$$

□

Lemma 3.10. *In the steady transport equation* (3.69), *let* $H_{m+1} \in W^{1,q}(\Omega)$, *and* $\boldsymbol{v}_{m+1} \in W^{2,q}(\Omega)$, *with* $\boldsymbol{v}_{m+1} \cdot \boldsymbol{n}|_{\partial\Omega} = 0$ *and* $\|\boldsymbol{v}_{m+1}\|_{2,q} < c_0$. *Then, if* c_0 *is sufficiently small, there exists a unique solution* $\sigma_{m+1} \in W^{1,q}(\Omega)$. *Moreover,*

$$\begin{aligned} \|\sigma_{m+1}\|_{1,q} &\le c(\|\boldsymbol{F}_m\|_q + \|g_m\|_{1,q}), \\ \|\Delta\nabla \cdot (\sigma_{m+1}\boldsymbol{v}_{m+1})\|_{-1,q} &\le c(\|\boldsymbol{F}_m\|_q + (\|\boldsymbol{F}_m\|_q + \|g_m\|_{1,q})^2). \end{aligned} \tag{3.77}$$

Finally, the boundedness, and the convergence of $\boldsymbol{v}_m$, σ_m is proved, without further difficulty, in the wake of the method outlined in Section 5.

- **Formulation of the problem.**

We are now ready to formulate the problem in bounded domains.

(1) For isentropic gases, $\gamma \neq 1$, there always exists a steady generalized solution (which is also regular) corresponding to large external forces, in which case it could be not physical;

(2) for isothermal gases ($\gamma = 1$) physical solutions corresponding to large potential, and small nonpotential, forces can always be constructed. In particular, we can be in supersonic regimes! However, there is no proof of existence in the general case.

We ask: *do generalized solutions exist for large external forces, if* $\gamma = 1$*?*

For isothermal gases ($\gamma = 1$) existence of generalized steady solution, corresponding to large external forces, is not known even in the one dimensional case. Specifically, let the external force be given by

$$\boldsymbol{F} := \rho \boldsymbol{f}.$$

In one dimension all $\boldsymbol{f}$ are potential forces, so that our theorem allows $\boldsymbol{f}$ to be large. Notice that for $\boldsymbol{b} \neq 0$ the problem is still open in one dimension.

3.10 - Previous results and regularity.

Here we are interested to analyze the mathematical structure of the Poisson-Stokes equations, even though the complete mathematical understanding of equations (3.23) has not yet been achieved. Some insight concerning the difficulties arising from these equations, may be obtained from the linearized form of these equations. More specifically, the linearization leads to different mathematical equations depending on the steady state around which it occurs. First of all, if the density is allowed to vanish at the boundary, the linearization becomes not possible. Moreover, if one linearizes around the rest $\boldsymbol{V} = 0$, with constant density $\rho = 1$, one obtains for the perturbation $\boldsymbol{v}$, σ

$$\begin{aligned} &\nabla \cdot \boldsymbol{v} = 0, \\ &-\mu \Delta \boldsymbol{v} - (\lambda + \mu) \nabla (\nabla \cdot \boldsymbol{v}) = -k_1 \nabla \sigma + \sigma \boldsymbol{f}, \end{aligned} \tag{3.78}$$

where $k_1 = (\mathrm{d}p/\mathrm{d}\rho)$ at $\rho = 1$, while, if one linearizes around a basic flow $\boldsymbol{V}$ with constant density $\rho = 1$, one gets

$$\begin{aligned} &\nabla \cdot \boldsymbol{v} + \boldsymbol{V} \cdot \nabla \sigma + \sigma \nabla \cdot \boldsymbol{V} = 0, \\ &-\mu \Delta \boldsymbol{v} - (\lambda + \mu) \nabla (\nabla \cdot \boldsymbol{v}) = \\ &\qquad -k_1 \nabla \sigma + \sigma \boldsymbol{f} - \boldsymbol{V} \cdot \nabla \boldsymbol{v} - \boldsymbol{v} \cdot \nabla \boldsymbol{V} - \sigma \boldsymbol{V} \cdot \nabla \boldsymbol{V}, \end{aligned} \tag{3.79}$$

In the above linearizations (3.78), (3.79), the main difference in the mathematical structure is played by the term $\boldsymbol{V} \cdot \nabla \sigma$ which changes the order of differentiation between the linearizations (3.78), (3.79) proposed.

In this section, we wish to reach two goals: first, we wish to comment the mathematical structure of the Poisson–Stokes equations. Next, for a rigid three-dimensional container, we provide a formal "a priori" estimate for an hypothetical solution $\boldsymbol{v}$, ρ in $W^{1,\infty}(\Omega)\times L^\infty(\Omega)$, which furnishes a bound for the gradient of the density in terms of the norm of the solution in $W^{1,\infty}(\Omega)\times L^\infty(\Omega)$ only. This let us to conjecture that the density can be regularized in a rigid, impermeable container.

We begin with a survey of mathematical results and of the previous methods proposed.

- **Earlier contributions.**

The study of the well-posedness problem for the system

$$
\begin{aligned}
&\nabla\cdot\boldsymbol{v} = -\nabla\cdot(\sigma\boldsymbol{v}),\\
&-\mu\nabla\times\nabla\times\boldsymbol{v}-(\lambda+2\mu)\nabla(\nabla\cdot\boldsymbol{v}) = -k\nabla\sigma+(1+\sigma)\,(\boldsymbol{f}-\boldsymbol{v}\cdot\nabla\boldsymbol{v})\,,\\
&\boldsymbol{v}|_{\partial\Omega}=\mathbf{0},\qquad \int_\Omega\sigma=0,
\end{aligned}
\tag{3.80}
$$

was started only in 1981, [68] where it was proved a uniqueness theorem of regular solutions, in case either $\Omega=\mathbb{R}^3$, or Ω bounded. Moreover, an existence theorem, true only under a condition on the viscosity coefficients, appeared the following year in [70]. Since then the theory has stimulated intense interest in many scientists and a large literature has been produced in these last ten years. It is enough to remark that all problems concerning existence and uniqueness in bounded and exterior two- or three-dimensional domains have already received the main answers. Here, we only recall the state of the art in this field by quoting the main results, and describing the mathematical difficulties hidden in the system.

Uniqueness theorems have been proved in [68], [70], [71], [72] in the case of Ω bounded, exterior to a bounded region or the whole of three-dimensional space. Next, in [69], [70], the first existence theorem were given for Ω bounded, under particular values of the viscosity coefficients, see also [73]. Some years later (1987) existence theorems for arbitrary viscosity coefficients in Ω bounded, have been proved in [99], [100] and in [6], [8]. Later, several extensions have been analysed in bounded domains, as the case of slip boundary conditions, or the extension to large potential forces, and to stress-free boundaries as well, [15], [47], [57], [80], [91].

In order to understand the mathematical structure of (3.80), we adopt a partial linearization around a constant state $\rho=1$, $\boldsymbol{v}=\mathbf{0}$, which mantains all the difficulties of the problem represented by terms containing the density. Therefore, we start with the system

$$
\begin{aligned}
&\nabla \cdot \boldsymbol{v} = -\nabla \cdot (\sigma \boldsymbol{v}), \\
&-\mu \nabla \times \nabla \times \boldsymbol{v} - (\lambda + 2\mu)\nabla(\nabla \cdot \boldsymbol{v}) = -k_1 \nabla \sigma + \boldsymbol{f}, \\
&\boldsymbol{v}|_{\partial\Omega} = \mathbf{0}, \quad \int_\Omega \sigma = 0.
\end{aligned} \tag{3.81}
$$

Apparent difficulties.

We make, now, the following remarks.

(A) One cannot apply the usual Nash-Moser *implicit function theorem*, due to the presence of the term $\boldsymbol{v} \cdot \nabla\sigma$ in $(3.81)_1$ which brings a loss of regularity.

(B) One could use a method of elliptic regularization, adding in $(3.81)_1$ the term $-\epsilon\Delta\sigma$. However, since system (3.81) is not elliptic in the sense of Agmon-Douglis-Niremberg (again due to the presence of $\boldsymbol{v} \cdot \nabla\sigma$!), the usual regularization procedures are not going to work.

The above remarks yield to the conclusion that a working existence method should be more refined and tightly connected to the structure of (3.81). We sketch below some previous methods of resolution not ordered in temporal sequence.

Methods employed.

Let us write (3.81) in the operatorial form

$$
\begin{aligned}
&\nabla \cdot [(1+\sigma)\boldsymbol{v}] = 0, \\
&L(\boldsymbol{v}) + k_1 \nabla\sigma = \boldsymbol{f},
\end{aligned} \tag{3.82}
$$

with obvious meaning of symbols. In (3.82), the operator L is not orthogonal to $\nabla\sigma$. We describe below several different alternative methods of resolution.

(I) Take the projection of $(3.82)_2$ in the space $J_\rho := \{\boldsymbol{u} \in L^2 : \nabla \cdot (\rho \boldsymbol{u}) = 0\}$, $\rho = 1+\sigma$ and $\boldsymbol{u} \cdot \boldsymbol{n} = 0$ in the sense of traces. Then, decompose L^2 as direct sum of J_ρ with $G_\rho := \{\boldsymbol{w} \in L^2 : \exists\phi \in W^{1,2}, \nabla\phi = \boldsymbol{w}\}$. This decomposition, which can be named *the weighted Helmholtz decomposition* was proposed by Prodi and developed in [20]. The method appears to be involved and does not bring anything new to older results.

(II) Change the variable velocity $\boldsymbol{v}$ in the variable momentum $\boldsymbol{w} = \rho\boldsymbol{v}$. It can be easily verified that (3.82), rewritten in the new variable, furnish a Stokes system with an additional solenoidal term in the force. Then, in the case of the whole space, if the external force has the additional regularity $\nabla \cdot \boldsymbol{f} \in L^q$, the proof is given very simple. In this case, the density has the same regularity as the velocity. However, it seems not possible to extend this method to domains with boundary. This method was developed in [75].

(III) If in $(3.82)_2$ one brings $\nabla\sigma$ at right hand side, then one can solve first such elliptic equation in the only unknown $\boldsymbol{v}$, by retaining σ as given. In this case, it is need to recover one suitable auxiliary equation for σ, which we call E$-\sigma$. This can be done only through a more detailed analysis of the full system. Such new equation for σ, was formulated for the first time in [69], [70], [73], as a steady transport equation, and then recovered again, by many authors, for example by [6] and [15], which followed different inspirations.

(1) Let us briefly recall how in [75] E$-\sigma$ was derived. Precisely, $(3.82)_2$ was considered as the first equation of the Stokes system

$$\begin{aligned} -\Delta \boldsymbol{v} &= -\nabla\pi + \boldsymbol{F}, \\ \nabla \cdot \boldsymbol{v} &= g, \end{aligned} \tag{3.83}$$

in the unknowns $\boldsymbol{v}$, π, with $\boldsymbol{F}$, g given. If one puts in (3.83)

$$\pi = k_1\sigma - (\lambda + \mu)\nabla \cdot \boldsymbol{v}, \quad g := \nabla \cdot (\sigma\boldsymbol{v}),$$

then recovers the starting equations. In this way, it becomes natural, once π is calculated from (3.83), to find σ from

$$k_1\sigma + (\lambda + \mu)\nabla \cdot (\sigma\boldsymbol{v}) = \pi. \tag{3.84}$$

With this procedure, an existence theorem is proved only under a smallness assumption on the ratio $(\lambda + \mu)/\mu$, which is not physically true in general (for benzene it can be 90).

(2) In [15] the finite elements method is used in the non-steady continuity equation,

$$\frac{\sigma(t+h) - \sigma(t)}{h} + \nabla(\sigma(t+h)\boldsymbol{v}) = g, \tag{3.85}$$

with h sufficiently small. In this way, by setting $\sigma(t) = \tau$ given, equation (3.85) becomes again a steady transport equation in the unknow $\sigma(t+h) = \sigma$. This scheme is proved to be convergent to a solution of the steady compressible equation (3.81).

(3) In [6] an equation for $\Delta\sigma$ is obtained by taking the divergence in $(3.82)_2$. The equation is the following

$$k_1\Delta\sigma + (\lambda + 2\mu)\Delta[\nabla \cdot (\sigma \boldsymbol{v})] = \Delta\pi + \nabla \cdot (\Delta \boldsymbol{F}). \tag{3.86}$$

Besides lower order terms, equation (3.86) differs from (3.82) for the coefficient of the leading term in which one more μ appears. It is just such correction that allows to prove existence without restrictions on the coefficients.

- **Generalized solutions.**

The formulation in Subsection 3.5, allows us to introduce the weak (or generalized) formulation of the steady compressible Poisson—Stokes system described by (3.23).

Definition 3.2. *Let Ω be a bounded domain of $\mathbb{R}^n$, $n \geq 2$. A field $\boldsymbol{v}, \rho : \Omega \to \mathbb{R}^n \times \mathbb{R}$ is called a weak (or generalised) solution to the Poisson–Stokes problem (3.23) if and only if*

(i) $\boldsymbol{v} \in W^{1,2}(\Omega)$, $\nabla \cdot \boldsymbol{v} \in L^s(\Omega)$,*with* $s > 2$, *if* $n = 2$, *and* $s > 6$, *if* $n = 3$;

(ii) $\rho \in L^s(\Omega)$, *with* $s > 2$, *if* $n = 2$, *and* $s > 6$, *if* $n = 3$;

(iii) $\boldsymbol{v}$ *satisfies the following generalized boundary conditions:*

$$\boldsymbol{v} \in W_0^{1,2}(\Omega), \qquad (\nabla \cdot \boldsymbol{v}, \nabla\phi) = -(\nabla T_{\nabla\cdot\boldsymbol{v}}, \phi), \quad \forall \phi \in C^\infty(\overline{\Omega}),$$

where $T_{\nabla\cdot\boldsymbol{v}}$ *is the distribution corresponding to* $\nabla \cdot \boldsymbol{v}$.

(iv) $\boldsymbol{v}$, $\rho = 1 + \sigma$ *obey the identities*

$$\begin{aligned} \mu(\nabla\boldsymbol{v}, \nabla\varphi) + (\lambda + \mu)(\nabla \cdot \boldsymbol{v}, \nabla \cdot \varphi) + (\rho\boldsymbol{v} \cdot \nabla\boldsymbol{v}, \varphi)& \\ = (h, \nabla \cdot (\rho\varphi)) + \langle \rho\boldsymbol{f}, \varphi\rangle&, \\ (\nabla \cdot \boldsymbol{v}, \psi) = -(\nabla \cdot (\sigma\boldsymbol{v}), \psi)&, \\ k(\sigma, \psi) + (\lambda + 2\mu)(\nabla \cdot (\sigma\boldsymbol{v}), \psi) = (H, \psi)&, \end{aligned} \tag{3.87}$$

where H is defined by (3.28), for all φ, $\psi \in C_0^\infty(\Omega)$, and $h := p'/\rho$ is the enthalpy.

We shall now prove that the generalized solutions do satisfy the energy identity. We give the proof for $n = 3$. To this end, we first observe that *(i)* implies $\sigma \boldsymbol{v} \cdot \nabla \boldsymbol{v} \in L^q$, $q > 6/5$. Therefore, by density argument we can substitute $\boldsymbol{\varphi} = \boldsymbol{v}$ in

$$\mu(\nabla \boldsymbol{v}, \nabla \boldsymbol{\varphi}) + (\lambda + \mu)(\nabla \cdot \boldsymbol{v}, \nabla \cdot \boldsymbol{\varphi}) + (\rho \boldsymbol{v} \cdot \nabla \boldsymbol{v}, \boldsymbol{\varphi}) = (h, \nabla \cdot (\rho \boldsymbol{\varphi})) + \langle \rho \boldsymbol{f}, \boldsymbol{\varphi} \rangle$$

and, using condition $(3.19)_1$ and the fact that $\boldsymbol{v}$ vanishes at the boundary, we obtain

$$\|\nabla \boldsymbol{v}\|^2 + (\lambda + \mu)\|\nabla \cdot \boldsymbol{v}\|^2 = \langle \rho \boldsymbol{f}, \boldsymbol{v} \rangle, \tag{3.88}$$

which is just the wanted energy equation. Notice that (3.88) *does not furnish any estimate on the density!* This makes the problem of compressible fluids difficult.

- **Regularity of generalized solutions.**

Since system (3.78) is not elliptic, it is of interest to ask whether a solution of this system can be discontinuous. One simplified and very discussed problem is constituted by the possibility that linearized equations have interior discontinuities. It has been proved, in two-space dimensions, in [31], and in [13] for a linearized simplified version, and then in [12] for the general case, that if the ambient flow $\boldsymbol{v}$ is almost uniform then discontinuities of the density are possible if one prescribes them at the points of the boundary where the flow is entering.

The main goal of these papers is to exhibit a discontinuous solution, in the particular case when the *ambient flow is a steady non-zero flow.* The boundary conditions require the specification of the density at that part of the boundary Σ, on which the ambient flow enters. The interior discontinuity in the solution arises from a jump in the specified density on Σ, and propagates to a jump in the density across the streamlines of the ambient flow field. The strenght of the discontinuity decreases as the viscosity increases, and decays as one moves along the stream line across the boundary.

Precisely, in [12], [30] the problem of existence in a bounded plane domain is studied, when non-zero velocities are prescribed on the boundary of Ω, and the density is prescribed on that part of the boundary corresponding to entering velocity. Furthermore, even though such a problem causes a weak singularity at the junction of incoming and outgoing flows, in [30] the authors prove existence in the Sobolev space $W^{2,q}(\Omega) \times W^{1,q}(\Omega)$, $2 < q < 3$ (q is greater than the dimension of the space).

However, if the boundary is rigid and impermeable, only zero boundary conditions on the velocity are imposed, so there is no inflow boundary on which to impose conditions on the density. In this case, with suitably regular data, it is possible to obtain continuous solutions, cf. [6], [73], [100].

Since generalized solutions can be subjected to regular forces, we ask: *Do generalized solutions become regular for regular external forces?*

This will be the object of this subsection. Precisely, we wish to prove that if it there exists a generalized solution $\boldsymbol{v}$, $\rho = 1 + \sigma$ in $W^{1,\infty}(\Omega) \times L^\infty(\Omega)$ of the steady Poissonr-Stokes equations, and if the norm $[\|\boldsymbol{v}\|_{1,\infty} + \|\sigma\|_\infty]$ is suitably small, then the solution is continuous and belongs to $W^{2,q}(\Omega) \times W^{1,q}(\Omega)$. However, we have not yet the complete proof and we limit ourselves to give a formal "a priori" estimate for $\boldsymbol{v}$, ρ in $W^{2,q}(\Omega) \times W^{1,q}(\Omega)$.

First of all, we assume that there exists a solution $\boldsymbol{v}$, $\rho = 1 + \sigma$ in $W^{1,\infty}(\Omega) \times L^\infty(\Omega)$ to the system

$$\begin{aligned} & -\mu\Delta\boldsymbol{v} - (\lambda+\mu)\nabla(\nabla\cdot\boldsymbol{v}) = -k\nabla\sigma + \boldsymbol{F}, \\ & \nabla\cdot\boldsymbol{v} = g, \\ & -\Delta H = -\nabla\cdot\boldsymbol{F}, \\ & k\sigma + (\lambda+2\mu)\nabla\cdot(\boldsymbol{v}\sigma) = H, \\ & \boldsymbol{v}|_{\partial\Omega} = \boldsymbol{0}, \end{aligned} \tag{3.89}$$

where

$$\begin{aligned} \boldsymbol{F} &:= -(1+\sigma)[\boldsymbol{v}\cdot\nabla\boldsymbol{v} - \boldsymbol{f}], \\ g &:= -\nabla\cdot(\sigma\boldsymbol{v}). \end{aligned}$$

Moreover, setting

$$\mathcal{R} := [\|\boldsymbol{v}\|_{1,\infty} + \|\sigma\|_\infty],$$

it is straightforward to show that

$$\|\boldsymbol{F}\|_q \le c(\mathcal{R})[\|\boldsymbol{v}\|_{1,q} + \|\sigma\|_q + \|\boldsymbol{f}\|_q], \tag{3.90}$$

where $c(\mathcal{R})$ is a suitable constant, homogeneous function of $\mathcal{R}$ which can be taken arbitraly small, for $\mathcal{R}$ small. Below, by C we shall denote any other (may be large) constant.

The regularization of our solution will be proved once we show that $\nabla\rho \in L^q$ for some $q > 1$. The procedure will follow two steps, in one we derive a formal a priori estimate for the L^q–norm of the gradient of density in terms of $\mathcal{R}$. In the second part we should justify such a procedure. Below, we furnish only the first part of the proof, which will be proved exactly in the same way as was proved the convergence of the sequence. Actually, we shall use Lemmas 3.1, 3.2, 3.3, for system (3.89). Precisely, we have

$$\begin{aligned}
\|\boldsymbol{v}\|_{2,q} &\le C(\|\boldsymbol{F}\|_q + \|g\|_{1,q}) \le c(\mathcal{R})[\|\boldsymbol{v}\|_{1,q} + \|\sigma\|_q + \|\boldsymbol{f}\|_q] + C\|g\|_{1,q},\\
\|H\|_{1,q} &\le C\ (\|\boldsymbol{F}\|_q + \|\boldsymbol{v}\|_{2,q}) \le c(\mathcal{R})[\|\boldsymbol{v}\|_{1,q} + \|\sigma\|_q + \|\boldsymbol{f}\|_q] + C\|g\|_{1,q},\\
\|\Delta H\|_{-1,q} &:= \sup_{v\in W_0^{1,q'}} \frac{|(\Delta H, v)|}{\|v\|_{1,q'}} = \sup_{v\in W_0^{1,q'}} \frac{|(\boldsymbol{F}, \nabla v)|}{\|v\|_{1,q'}},\\
&\le c\ \|\boldsymbol{F}\|_q \le c(\mathcal{R})[\|\boldsymbol{v}\|_{1,q} + \|\sigma\|_q + \|\boldsymbol{f}\|_q].
\end{aligned} \tag{3.91}$$

The term $\|\Delta H\|_{-1,q}$ in $(3.91)_3$ becomes arbitrarily small, for small $\mathcal{R}$. Now, repeating the same steps as in the previous subsection, it is not difficult to show that

$$\|\sigma\|_{1,q} \le C\|H\|_{1,q} + c(\mathcal{R})(\|\boldsymbol{v}\|_{2,q} + \|\sigma\|_{1,q}).$$

Therefore, for small $\mathcal{R}$, we get

$$\|\sigma\|_{1,q} \le c(\mathcal{R})[\|\boldsymbol{v}\|_{2,q} + \|\boldsymbol{f}\|_q] + C\|g\|_{1,q}. \tag{3.92}$$

Furthermore, we have

$$\begin{aligned}
\|\Delta\nabla\cdot(\sigma\boldsymbol{v})\|_{-1,q} &\le C\|\Delta H\|_{-1,q} + c(\mathcal{R})(\|\boldsymbol{v}\|_{2,q} + \|\sigma\|_{1,q})\\
&\le c(\mathcal{R})[\|\boldsymbol{v}\|_{2,q} + \|\sigma\|_{1,q} + \|\boldsymbol{f}\|_q].
\end{aligned} \tag{3.93}$$

Next, we notice that

$$(\lambda + 2\mu)g = (\lambda + 2\mu)\nabla\cdot(\boldsymbol{v}\sigma),$$

then, employing inequalities (3.91), (3.92), (3.93), and recalling that g vanishes on the boundary, we get

$$\|g\|_{1,q} \le C\|\Delta\nabla\cdot(\sigma \boldsymbol{v})\|_{-1,q} \le c(\mathcal{R})[\|\boldsymbol{v}\|_{2,q} + \|\sigma\|_{1,q} + \|\boldsymbol{f}\|_q]. \tag{3.94}$$

Substituting this last inequality into $(3.91)_1$, we deduce for the $W^{2,q}$–norm of $\boldsymbol{v}$, and for the $W^{1,q}$–norm of σ, the following estimate

$$\|\boldsymbol{v}\|_{2,q} + \|\sigma\|_{1,q} \le c(\mathcal{R})(\|\boldsymbol{v}\|_{2,q} + \|\sigma\|_{1,q} + \|\boldsymbol{f}\|_q). \tag{3.95}$$

Therefore, for $\mathcal{R}$ suitably small, we deduce formally the continuity of $\nabla \boldsymbol{v}$ and σ.

4. Statement of the Problem and Open Questions in Exterior Domains

4.1 - Position of the problem.

Let the fluid fill the exterior of a compact body $\mathcal{B}$; we must add boundary and side conditions and, again, we meet several unexpected difficulties. For this reason, in this section we shall be content to furnish only some boundary and side conditions, which can lead the problem to be solvable.

In order to understand the difficulties one encounters, it is better to start with recalling the so called *classical exterior problem* for the (incompressible) Navier–Stokes equations, set by Leray in 1933. It can be stated as

Problem 1 (incompressible fluids). Given $\boldsymbol{v}_\infty$, find a pair $\boldsymbol{v}$, p such that

$$\begin{gathered} \Delta \boldsymbol{v} = \boldsymbol{v}\cdot\nabla\boldsymbol{v} + \nabla p, \\ \nabla\cdot\boldsymbol{v} = 0, \\ \boldsymbol{v}|_{\partial\Omega} = \boldsymbol{v}_*|_{\partial\Omega}, \qquad \lim_{|x|\to\infty} \boldsymbol{v}(x) = \boldsymbol{v}_\infty. \end{gathered} \tag{4.1}$$

The correct formulation of the problem.

Problem 1 describes a steady flow of an incompressible fluid past a body $\mathcal{B}$, which moves with a constant velocity $\boldsymbol{v}_{\mathcal{B}} = -\boldsymbol{v}_\infty$. However, once we solve problem 1, in order to realize, effectively, such a steady flow, we must apply on $\mathcal{B}$ a system of external forces, equivalent to a resultant $\boldsymbol{R}$ and to a pair of moment $\boldsymbol{M}$ given by

$$
\begin{aligned}
\boldsymbol{R} &= \int_{\partial\Omega} [\boldsymbol{T}\cdot\boldsymbol{n} - (\boldsymbol{v}_* + \boldsymbol{v}_{\mathcal{B}})(\boldsymbol{v}_*\cdot\boldsymbol{n})], \\
\boldsymbol{M} + \boldsymbol{r}(x_G)\times\boldsymbol{R} &= \int_{\partial\Omega} [\boldsymbol{r}(y)\times\boldsymbol{T}\cdot\boldsymbol{n} - \boldsymbol{r}(y)\times(\boldsymbol{v}_* + \boldsymbol{v}_{\mathcal{B}})(\boldsymbol{v}_*\cdot\boldsymbol{n})].
\end{aligned}
\tag{4.2}
$$

Thus the *classical* problem 1 should be indeed, more precisely described as an *inverse problem*, cf. [23]. Therefore, in order to solve properly the problem, one should modify the usual well-posedness problem by solving the coupled system (4.1) (4.2). Actually, the fact that the limit conditions for a steady incompressible motion occurring at the exterior of a compact body require a more deep understanding, was firstly noticed and studied in [101]. However, only recently the correct boundary value problem is receiving some first partial answer, *e.g.*, in the case of a self-propelled body, see [23]. Therefore, in this article we shall be content to deal only with the formulation proposed by Leray for incompressible fluids, when the fluid fills the space exterior to a compact rigid body $\mathcal{B}$.

Boundary and side conditions

As concerns the density, we retain all what said at points (i), (ii) of Subsection 3.1, and we shall prove that the density at infinity cannot be 0 at least for isothermal gases.

Also for the velocity, assumptions (i), (ii), (iii) will continue to hold. We shall not study the case (iv) of free boundaries.

Let us consider domains exterior to the compact region $\mathcal{B}$. In this case the velocity and the density can go to infinity. Thus we add the following conditions at infinity:

$$\boldsymbol{v}(x)\to\boldsymbol{v}_\infty,\quad \rho(x)\to\rho_\infty(x),\quad \text{as}\quad |x|\to\infty.$$

Notice that, while the velocity field at infinity must be uniform, the density may be non-uniform at infinity, this depends only by external forces. For the sake of simplicity we take

$$\rho_\infty(x) = 1.$$

Moreover, in unbounded domains, besides the problems of existence and uniqueness, it is also very important, from both the mathematical and the physical points of wiev, to solve the so called problem of spatial stability. This last question consists in proving that, under certain regularity hypotheses on the external data, there is a control of the solution at infinity, say, the solution doesn't differ too much from its value at infinity after a fixed spatial distance from the boundary. This study is known as the study of the *asymptotic behavior* of the solution. For applications to compressible fluids see [59], [60].

4.2 - Mechanical equilibrium of a fluid.

The conditions for a fluid to be in equilibrium are quite complex, and they substantially depend on the nature of the fluid. In this section, we first comment a pathological situation which occurs for barotropic isothermal fluids, then we derive an "energy estimate" for a particular constitutive relation of the pressure.

We shall now consider some particular circumstances in which problem

$$
\begin{gathered}
\nabla \cdot \boldsymbol{v} = -\nabla \cdot (\sigma \boldsymbol{v}), \\
\rho \boldsymbol{v} \cdot \nabla \boldsymbol{v} = -\nabla p + \mu \Delta \boldsymbol{v} + (\lambda + \mu) \nabla \nabla \cdot \boldsymbol{v} + \rho \boldsymbol{f}, \\
\boldsymbol{v}|_{\partial\Omega} = \mathbf{0}, \\
\lim_{|x|\to\infty} \boldsymbol{v}(x) = \mathbf{0}, \qquad \lim_{|x|\to\infty} \rho(x) = \rho_\infty,
\end{gathered}
\tag{4.3}
$$

is ill posed. In order to give here an example of inconsistency between the theory and the experiments, we consider an isothermal gas in unbounded domains.

- **Non existence of the rest.**

We wish to prove here the following result:

nonexistence of the rest state for an isotermal gas under small external forces ($\gamma = 1$).

Here, we assume Ω either exterior to a compact region $\mathcal{B}$, or the whole of $\mathbb{R}^3$, the gas has finite total mass, the fluid is isothermal. Such a problem can represent a star in the vacuum, or the star's atmosphere around a compact core

$\mathcal{B}$. In [74], [75], it has been proved that, subject to suitably small "gravitational-like" forces $\boldsymbol{f}$, with $\boldsymbol{v}_* = \mathbf{0}$, the only possible steady solution is the vacuum

$$\boldsymbol{v} = \mathbf{0}, \quad \rho = 0.$$

Furthermore, this vacuum solution is also stable, [74]. Such result can be interpreted mathematically as a non-existence result of steady solutions for a rarefied gas, and, physically, as an attractivity of infinity, that is, the fluid evolves to infinity. An essential characteristic of such pathological solution is that, since the mean density of the gas, at infinity, becomes arbitrarily small (it is vanishing) the gas at infinity does not behave entirely as a continuum, and kinetic theory must be used.

We remark that the fluid must be isothermal and the domain unbounded, so that we are exactly in a situation which is the opposite of that considered at the beginning of this section.

Skecht of the proof.

Let Ω be an exterior domain. It is obvious that the zero solution $\rho = 0, \boldsymbol{v} = \mathbf{0}$ (vacuum), solves the Poisson–Stokes equations, for every body force and any domain. In the sequel, we prove the uniqueness of the zero solution under the action of suitably small body forces, in the following regularity class

$$\mathcal{R} := \{(\rho, \boldsymbol{v}) \in (L^3 \cap C^1) \times W_0^{1,2} \cap C^1) : \int_\Omega \rho \boldsymbol{v} \cdot \nabla[\ln \rho + (v^2/2)] = 0\}.$$

This regularity class allows integration by parts. We shall prove

Lemma 4.1. *Let $(\rho, \boldsymbol{v}) \in \mathcal{R}$, and the norm of $\boldsymbol{f}$ in L^3 be sufficiently small. Then it cannot exist any steady solution of an isothermal viscous gas.*

PROOF - The proof is given *per absurdum.* Let $(\rho, \boldsymbol{v})$ be any solution to (4.3). Multiply $(4.3)_2$ by $\boldsymbol{v}$, integrate over Ω and take into account the solenoidality condition of $\rho\boldsymbol{v}$, and the vanishing conditions on the boundary for $\boldsymbol{v}$; we thus deduce

$$c\|\nabla \boldsymbol{v}\| \leq c(\epsilon)\|\rho\|\|\boldsymbol{f}\|_3. \tag{4.4}$$

Let φ be a solution to system (3.14), where we set $\sigma = \rho$. Multiplying by φ equation $(4.3)_2$ and integrating over Ω, fot $p = k\rho$, it yields

$$k\|\rho\|^2 \le c(\|\nabla \boldsymbol{v}\|\|\rho\| + \|\boldsymbol{v}\|_\infty^2\|\rho\|^2 + \|\boldsymbol{f}\|_3\|\rho\|^2). \tag{4.5}$$

If $\|\boldsymbol{f}\|_3$ and $\|\boldsymbol{v}\|_\infty$ are sufficiently small, we have $\|\rho\| \le c\|\nabla \boldsymbol{v}\|$. Hence, substituting in (4.4), we obtain

$$\|\nabla \boldsymbol{v}\| \le c\|\boldsymbol{f}\|_3\|\nabla \boldsymbol{v}\|$$

which for $\|\boldsymbol{f}\|_3$ sufficiently small gives the contradiction. We stress the fact that, if $\gamma > 1$, Lemma 4.1 now does not hold. □

- **Energy estimates for $\boldsymbol{f} = \mathbf{0}$, $\boldsymbol{b} \neq \mathbf{0}$.**

Let us notice that if one considers also forces for unity of volume $\boldsymbol{b} \neq \mathbf{0}$, the functions $\rho = 0$, $\boldsymbol{v} = \mathbf{0}$ do not satisfy (4.5) any more.

Moreover, if $\boldsymbol{b} \neq \mathbf{0}$, an "a priori" estimate can be given for steady solutions of a viscous isentropic gas under large external forces in exterior domains, when $\gamma = 3$, see example 3.6, [77]. In this example, the body forces $\boldsymbol{b}(x)$ have a compact support. Let us deduce an "a priori" estimate for the steady solutions ρ, $\boldsymbol{v}$ having a sufficiently fast decay at infinity, to allow the integration by parts. Under this assumption, we multiply $(4.3)_2$ by $\boldsymbol{v}$ and integrate over Ω. This delivers

$$\begin{aligned} a\|\nabla \boldsymbol{v}\|^2 &\le \mu \int_\Omega \nabla \boldsymbol{v} : \nabla \boldsymbol{v} + (\lambda + \mu)\int_\Omega c(\nabla \cdot \boldsymbol{v})^2, \\ &\le \int_\Omega \left[-\rho \boldsymbol{v} \cdot \nabla(\frac{v^2}{2} + \frac{3}{2}\rho^2) + \boldsymbol{v} \cdot \boldsymbol{b} \right]. \end{aligned} \tag{4.6}$$

Since $\rho\boldsymbol{v}$ is a solenoidal field, which vanishes at infinity and on $\partial\Omega$, from (4.6) we easily obtain

$$\|\nabla \boldsymbol{v}\|^2 \le \|\boldsymbol{v}\|_6\|\boldsymbol{b}\|_{6/5} \le \epsilon\|\nabla \boldsymbol{v}\|^2 + c(\epsilon)\|\boldsymbol{b}\|_{6/5}^2$$

which furnishes the first a priori estimate

$$\|\nabla \boldsymbol{v}\| \le c\|\boldsymbol{b}\|_{6/5}. \tag{4.7}$$

In order to find an estimate for ρ, multiply $(4.3)_2$ by a solution φ to system (3.14), where we set[1] $\sigma = \rho^3$, and integrate over Ω. Since $\boldsymbol{v}$ vanishes on the boundary, integrating by parts, using Hölder and Sobolev inequalities, we obtain

$$\|\rho\|_6^6 := \int_\Omega \rho^6 \le c\|\nabla \boldsymbol{v}\|\|\nabla\varphi\| + \int_\Omega \rho|\boldsymbol{v}\cdot\nabla\varphi\cdot\boldsymbol{v}| + |\boldsymbol{b}||\varphi|. \tag{4.8}$$

Relation (4.8) furnishes the wanted a priori estimate for ρ. Actually, from (4.7), and (4.8) we have

$$\begin{aligned}\|\rho\|_6^6 &\le c\left(\|\boldsymbol{b}\|_{6/5}\|\rho\|_6^3 + \|\rho\|_6\|\boldsymbol{v}\|_6^2\|\nabla\varphi\| + \|\boldsymbol{b}\|_{6/5}\|\varphi\|_6\right)\\ &\le \epsilon\|\rho\|_6^6 + c(\epsilon)(\|\boldsymbol{b}\|_{6/5}^2 + \|\boldsymbol{b}\|_{6/5}^6).\end{aligned} \tag{4.9}$$

In (4.9) we used the limit Sobolev inequality $\|\boldsymbol{v}\|_6 \le c\|\nabla\boldsymbol{v}\|$. Notice that such a solution might loose its physical meaning if the density becomes negative.

The above example finds a nice agreement with the physical observation that in an isothermal fluid with vanishing density the entropy must tend to infinity, [14]. Therefore, it is our opinion that, in order to find global (for large forces) existence of steady flows of a viscous gas one should care simultaneously about the constitutive equations and the domain as well.

Conclusion: the possibility $\rho = 0$, *has to be excluded.*

4.3 - Existence in exterior domains: the main theorems.

As in case of bounded domain, we look for solutions with strictly positive density. Since the intensity of the perturbation in the density is controled by the external data, this implies that we are confining ourselves to consider only small external data.

We shall consider *non rotating rigid impermeable compact boundaries.* The condition that no slip occurs on such surfaces implies that the velocity must vanish at the boundary. Here, we shall limit ourselves to state the main existence theorems of steady flows in exterior domains, governed by the following

---

[1] Observe that, in this case, problem (3.14) is solvable without any compatibility condition (see [22])

system

$$
(4.10)\qquad
\begin{gathered}
\nabla\cdot(\rho\tilde{\boldsymbol{v}})=0,\\
\rho\tilde{\boldsymbol{v}}\cdot\nabla\tilde{\boldsymbol{v}}=-\nabla p+\mu\Delta\tilde{\boldsymbol{v}}+(\lambda+\mu)\nabla(\nabla\cdot\tilde{\boldsymbol{v}})+\rho\tilde{\boldsymbol{f}}+\tilde{\boldsymbol{b}},\\
\tilde{\boldsymbol{v}}|_{\partial\Omega}=\boldsymbol{0},\\
\lim_{|x|\to\infty}\rho=\rho_\infty,\qquad \lim_{|x|\to\infty}\boldsymbol{v}=\boldsymbol{v}_\infty,
\end{gathered}
$$

where the density $\rho_\infty>0$, and the velocity $\boldsymbol{v}_\infty$ are prescribed.

Let us denote by σ the pertubation to the value at infinity $\rho:=\rho_\infty$ of the density. Normalizing the density by dividing ρ by ρ_∞, we may take $\rho_\infty=1$. Therefore, after a rescaling of the variable, we can always write $\rho=1+\sigma$, $\tilde{\boldsymbol{v}}=\boldsymbol{v}_\infty+\boldsymbol{v}$; in this way system (4.10) will assume the equivalent form

$$
(4.11)\qquad
\begin{gathered}
\nabla\cdot\boldsymbol{v}=-\nabla\cdot(\sigma\tilde{\boldsymbol{v}}),\\
\boldsymbol{v}_\infty\cdot\nabla\boldsymbol{v}-\mu\Delta\boldsymbol{v}-(\lambda+\mu)\nabla(\nabla\cdot\boldsymbol{v})=\\
=-k\nabla\sigma+(1+\sigma)(\boldsymbol{f}-\boldsymbol{v}\cdot\nabla\boldsymbol{v})-\sigma\boldsymbol{v}_\infty\cdot\nabla\boldsymbol{v},\\
\boldsymbol{v}|_{\partial\Omega}=-\boldsymbol{v}_\infty;\quad \sigma\to0,\ \ \boldsymbol{v}\to\boldsymbol{0}\ \ \text{as } |x|\to\infty.
\end{gathered}
$$

The first fundamental contribution for Ω unbounded, by the use of a weighted approach in Hilbert spaces, is due to Matsumura and Nishida, 1989, [44], [45]. A completely different proof in L^q spaces was proposed in [75], however, its validity was confined to the whole space. A strong effort for the exterior problem was then made with the method of decomposition by Novotny' and the author in a series of papers, [24], [52], [58], [59], [60], [76], [77].

In [58], existence, uniqueness and regularity of steady flows have been proved for a viscous, ideal and isothermal gas, filling the threedimensional space exterior to a compact region $\mathcal{C}$, at least when the data $\boldsymbol{v}_\infty$, $\boldsymbol{f}$ are sufficiently small. These flows possess good summability properties, say, the velocity $\boldsymbol{v}$ and the variation of the density with respect to a constant state σ, with their first derivatives, are in suitable Lebesgue spaces. Moreover, in [58] only a uniform decay property has been proved for the velocity $\boldsymbol{v}(x)=O(1/|x|)$ when the obstacle is fixed.

In order to explain more precisely the results proved in [58], we must, now, introduce some functional spaces.

- $\hat{H}_0^{1,t}(\Omega) := \overline{C_0^\infty(\Omega)}^{|\cdot|_{1,t}}$, (the superposed bar means the completion with respect to the corresponding norm), is a Banach space with norm $|\cdot|_{1,t} := \|\nabla \cdot\|_t$. If $1 < t < 3$, then
$$\hat{H}_0^{1,t}(\Omega) = \{u : u \in L^{\frac{3t}{3-t}}(\Omega),\ \nabla u \in L^t(\Omega)\}$$
- $\mathcal{H}_0^{k,t}(\Omega) := \overline{C_0^\infty(\overline{\Omega})}^{\|\nabla\cdot\|_{k-1,t}} \cap \hat{H}_0^{1,t}(\Omega)$, $k = 1, 2\cdots$, is a Banach space with norm $\|\nabla \cdot\|_{k-1,t}$, $1 < t < +\infty$.
- $\hat{H}_\infty^{1,t}(\Omega) := \overline{C_0^\infty(\overline{\Omega})}^{|\cdot|_{1,t}}$,is a Banach space with norm $|\cdot|_{1,t} = \|\nabla \cdot\|_t$, $1 < t < +\infty$. If $t \geq 3$, then the elements of this space are equivalence classes $u + c$, $c \in \mathbb{R}$, $u \in L^t_{loc}(\Omega), \nabla u \in L^t(\Omega)$. If $1 < t < 3$, then
$$\hat{H}_\infty^{1,t}(\Omega) = \{u : u \in L^{\frac{3t}{3-t}}(\Omega),\ \nabla u \in L^t(\Omega)\}.$$

Similarly, $\hat{H}_\infty^{k,t}(\Omega) := \overline{C_0^\infty(\overline{\Omega})}^{|\cdot|_{k,t}}$, $k = 1, 2, \ldots$.

In [45] the following two existence and uniqueness theorems are proved, one for $\boldsymbol{v}_\infty = \mathbf{0}$ (Theorem 4.1), and one for $\boldsymbol{v}_\infty \neq \mathbf{0}$ (Theorem 4.2). Let us begin with assuming $\boldsymbol{v}_\infty = \mathbf{0}$.

Theorem 4.1. *Let $\Omega \in \mathcal{C}^{k+3}$, $k = 0, 1, 2, \ldots$, $p > 3$, $1 \leq q_1 < 3/2 < q_2 < 3$, and $\boldsymbol{f} \in W^{k,p}(\Omega)$, $|x|\boldsymbol{f} \in L^{q_1}(\Omega) \cap L^{q_2}(\Omega)$. Then, for any q, $3/2 < q \leq 2$, there exist positive constants γ_0, γ_1, (depending only on k, q,p, q_1, q_2, $\partial\Omega$), such that, if*
$$]\boldsymbol{f}[_{k,q,p} := \|\boldsymbol{f}\|_{k,p} + \||x|\boldsymbol{f}\|_{q_1} + \||x|\boldsymbol{f}\|_{q_2} \leq \gamma_1$$
then in the ball
$$\begin{aligned} B_{\gamma_0}^{k+2,q,p}(\Omega) := \{(\sigma, \boldsymbol{v}) :\ & \sigma \in W^{1,q}(\Omega) \cap W^{k,p}(\Omega),\ \boldsymbol{v} \in \mathcal{H}_0^{2,q}(\Omega) \cap \mathcal{H}_0^{k+2,p}(\Omega), \\ & \nabla \cdot \boldsymbol{v}|_{\partial\Omega} = 0,\ |x|\boldsymbol{v} \in L^\infty(\Omega),\ |x|\nabla \cdot \boldsymbol{v} \in L^q(\Omega) \cap L^p(\Omega), \\ & \|\sigma\|_{k+1,q,p} + \|\boldsymbol{v}\|_{k+2,q,p} := \|\sigma\|_{1,q} + \|\sigma\|_{k+1,p} + \|\boldsymbol{v}\|_{2,q} + \|\nabla \boldsymbol{v}\|_{k+1,p} \\ & + \|\,|x|\boldsymbol{v}\|_\infty + \|\,|x|\nabla \cdot \boldsymbol{v}\|_q + \|\,|x|\nabla \cdot \boldsymbol{v}\|_p \leq \gamma_0\} \end{aligned}$$
there exists just one solution $\sigma, \boldsymbol{v}$ of (4.11), with $\boldsymbol{v}_\infty = \mathbf{0}$, satisfying the estimate
$$\|\sigma\|_{k+1,q,p} + \|\boldsymbol{v}\|_{k+2,q,p} \leq c]\boldsymbol{f}[_{k,q,p}.$$

In Theorem 4.1 it is needed a prescribed decay rate on the external force $\boldsymbol{f}$; however, under such assumption, the existence of solutions with $\boldsymbol{v}$ decaying at infinity with order $|x|^{-1}$ is assured; such solutions are also known as physically reasonable solutions.

The next theorem guarantees existence for $\boldsymbol{v}_\infty \neq \mathbf{0}$.

Theorem 4.2. *Let Ω be of class C^{k+3}, $k = 0, 1, 2, \cdots$, $p > 3$, $1 < r < 6/5$, and $\boldsymbol{f} \in L^r(\Omega) \cap W^{k,p}(\Omega)$. Then, for any q, such that $p_r \le q \le 2$, $p_r = 3r/(3-r)$, there exists a positive constant κ_0, $\kappa_0 < 1$, depending only on k, q, p, r, $\partial\Omega$, and $|\boldsymbol{v}_\infty|$, such that, for any $|\boldsymbol{v}_\infty| < \kappa_0$, there exist positive constants γ_0, γ_1, depending only on k, q, p, r, $\partial\Omega$, and $|\boldsymbol{v}_\infty|$, which under the requirement*

$$]]\boldsymbol{f}[[_{k,p,r} := \|\boldsymbol{f}\|_{k,p} + \|\boldsymbol{f}\|_r \le \gamma_1$$

ensure that in the ball

$$\begin{aligned}\mathbb{B}^{k+2,q,p}_{\gamma_0}(\Omega) := \{(\sigma, \boldsymbol{v}) :\ & \sigma \in W^{1,q}(\Omega) \cap W^{k+1,p}(\Omega), \\ & \boldsymbol{v} \in \mathcal{H}^{2,q}_\infty(\Omega) \cap \mathcal{H}^{1,p}_\infty(\Omega) \cap L^{4q/(4-q)}(\Omega), \\ & \nabla \cdot \boldsymbol{v}|_{\partial\Omega} = 0, \\ & \|\sigma\|_{k+1,q,p} + \|\boldsymbol{v}\|_{k+2,q,p,\infty} := \|\sigma\|_{1,q} + \|\sigma\|_{k+1,p} \\ & + \|\boldsymbol{v}\|_{2,q} + \|\nabla \boldsymbol{v}\|_{k+1,p} + |\boldsymbol{v}_\infty|^{1/4} \|\boldsymbol{v}\|_{4q/(4-q)} \le \gamma_0\}\end{aligned}$$

there exists just a solution $\sigma, \boldsymbol{v}$ of (4.11), with $\boldsymbol{v}_\infty \neq \boldsymbol{0}$, satisfying the estimate

$$\|\sigma\|_{k+1,q,p} + \|\boldsymbol{v}\|_{k+2,q,p,\infty} \le c(]\boldsymbol{f}[_{k,p,r} + |\boldsymbol{v}_\infty|).$$

Theorem 4.2 proves existence of solutions weaker than those constructed in Theorem 4.1. Since no explicit decay at infinity on the external force is required in Theorem 4.2 we have a larger set of data; nevertheless, the solutions do not have any decay rate and, furthermore, the estimate on the solution is not uniform with respect to $\boldsymbol{v}_\infty$, even for small $\boldsymbol{v}_\infty$. Therefore, we cannot pass to the limit as $\boldsymbol{v}_\infty \to \boldsymbol{0}$, because the constants γ_0, γ_1 can go to zero. Under certain assumptions on the decay of the external forces, however, one can still obtain physically reasonable solutions also for $\boldsymbol{v}_\infty \neq \boldsymbol{0}$ (with decay rate of order $|x|^{-1}$ for the velocity at infinity), and uniform estimates for given norms of the solution, with respect to $\boldsymbol{v}_\infty$ when it goes to zero. Such problems are known as asymptotic properties of the solutions and have been investigated in [59], [60]. This constitutes the object of Subsection 4.5.

Before giving further properties of solutions in exterior domains, we deem it better to say few words on the decomposition method introduced in [45] to prove existence of steady solutions for a viscous barotropic gas in exterior domains.

4.4 - The method of decomposition.

Here, we give an heuristic approach of the decomposition method which provides an algorithm for constructing solutions of the linear system, (4.12) below, obtained by a suitable linearization of system (4.11), we refer to [58] for details.

To show existence for the non linear system (4.11), we need a "good" existence theorem for σ, $\boldsymbol{v}$, solutions of the linearized system

$$\begin{gathered} \nabla \cdot \boldsymbol{v} = \mathcal{G}(\tau, \boldsymbol{w}), \\ \boldsymbol{v}_\infty \cdot \nabla \boldsymbol{v} - \mu \Delta \boldsymbol{v} - (\lambda + \mu) \nabla (\nabla \cdot \boldsymbol{v}) = -k \nabla \sigma + \mathcal{F}(\tau, \boldsymbol{w}), \\ \boldsymbol{v}|_{\partial\Omega} = -\boldsymbol{v}_\infty; \quad \sigma \to 0, \ \boldsymbol{v} \to \boldsymbol{0} \ \text{ as } |x| \to \infty, \end{gathered} \tag{4.12}$$

where, τ, $\tilde{\boldsymbol{w}} = \boldsymbol{v}_\infty + \boldsymbol{w}$ are given, and we have set

$$\begin{gathered} \mathcal{G}(\tau, \boldsymbol{w}) := -\nabla \cdot (\tau \tilde{\boldsymbol{w}}), \\ \mathcal{F}(\tau, \boldsymbol{w}) := (1 + \tau)\,(\boldsymbol{f} - \boldsymbol{w} \cdot \nabla \boldsymbol{w}) - \tau \boldsymbol{w}_\infty \cdot \nabla \boldsymbol{w}. \end{gathered}$$

Indeed, the existence of solutions of the non linear problem (4.11) is proved by applying the contraction principle to the composite map

$$\mathcal{N} : \ (\tau, \boldsymbol{w}) \longrightarrow (\sigma, \boldsymbol{v}),$$

where σ, $\boldsymbol{v}$ is a solution of (4.12) corresponding to $\mathcal{F}(\tau, \boldsymbol{w})$, $\mathcal{G}(\tau, \boldsymbol{w})$. Therefore, the key problem is the resolution of (4.12): this will be achieved by the use of the decomposition method.

Precisely, let $\boldsymbol{v}$ be a solution of (4.12) in a suitable functional space, say $\mathcal{V}$. We look for its Helmholtz decomposition in $\mathcal{V}$, that is we look for the existence of two fields φ, $\boldsymbol{u}$, satisfying

$$\begin{gathered} \varphi \in L^q_{loc}(\Omega), \quad \nabla \varphi \in \mathcal{V}, \quad \left.\frac{\partial \varphi}{\partial n}\right|_{\partial\Omega} = -\boldsymbol{v}_\infty \cdot \boldsymbol{n} \\ \boldsymbol{u} \in \mathcal{V}, \quad \nabla \cdot \boldsymbol{u} = 0, \ \boldsymbol{u}|_{\partial\Omega} = -\boldsymbol{v}_\infty - \nabla \varphi|_{\partial\Omega} \end{gathered}$$

such that

$$\boldsymbol{v} = \boldsymbol{u} + \nabla \varphi. \tag{4.13}$$

After the Helmholtz decomposition (4.13), it is straightforward to deduce that $(\boldsymbol{u}, \sigma, \nabla\varphi)$, satisfy the following systems

$$
\begin{aligned}
-\mu\Delta \boldsymbol{u} + \boldsymbol{v}_\infty \cdot \nabla \boldsymbol{u} + \nabla p &= \mathcal{F}(\tau, \boldsymbol{w}), \\
\nabla \cdot \boldsymbol{u} &= 0, \\
\boldsymbol{u}|_{\partial\Omega} &= -\boldsymbol{v}_\infty - \nabla\varphi|_{\partial\Omega}, \\
\boldsymbol{u} \to \boldsymbol{0}, \quad p \to 0, &\quad \text{as } |x| \to \infty;
\end{aligned}
\tag{4.14}
$$

$$
\begin{aligned}
\sigma + (\lambda + 2\mu)\nabla \cdot [\sigma(\boldsymbol{w} + \boldsymbol{v}_\infty)] &= p - \boldsymbol{v}_\infty \cdot \nabla\varphi \\
\boldsymbol{w} + \boldsymbol{v}_\infty|_{\partial\Omega} = \boldsymbol{0}, \quad \sigma \to 0, &\quad \text{as } |x| \to \infty;
\end{aligned}
\tag{4.15}
$$

$$
\begin{aligned}
\Delta\varphi &= -\nabla \cdot [\tau(\boldsymbol{v}_\infty + \boldsymbol{w})], \\
\left.\frac{\partial\varphi}{\partial n}\right|_{\partial\Omega} &= -\boldsymbol{v}_\infty \cdot \boldsymbol{n} \\
\nabla\varphi \to \boldsymbol{0}, &\ \text{as } |x| \to \infty.
\end{aligned}
\tag{4.16}
$$

For the linearized systems (4.14), (4.15), (4.16), there hold existence theorems, cf. [10]. We are so led to define the linear map $\mathcal{L} : \tau \to \sigma$ in following way.

(1) For given τ, $\boldsymbol{w}$ we solve a Neumann problem (4.16) in the unknown φ;

(2) Once φ is known, we solve for given $\mathcal{F}$, $\mathcal{G}$, the nonhomogeneous Oseen (if $\boldsymbol{v}_\infty \neq \boldsymbol{0}$), or Stokes (if $\boldsymbol{v}_\infty = \boldsymbol{0}$) problem (4.14) in the unknowns $\boldsymbol{u}$, p;

(3) Given p, we solve the steady transport equation (4.15) in the unknown σ.

The proof of the existence of a fixed point for $\mathcal{L}$ furnishes the existence of a solution of the linear system (4.12).

As remarked in Subsection 3.10, also within this scheme, the main difficulties arise from the lack of regularity at right-hand side of the continuity equation $(4.11)_1$. To overcome this difficulty, we heavily utilize the properties of the transport equation which furnishes the same regularity for σ, and for $\nabla \cdot (\sigma\tilde{\boldsymbol{w}})$. In particular, we gain more regularity for a directional derivative of σ. Another pivot tool is the property $\nabla \cdot \boldsymbol{v} = 0$ on the boundary which, roughly speaking, provides more friction on the boundary, and therefore, it acts as a dissipative effect, and avoides interior discontinuities for the density.

4.5 - On the asymptotic behaviour of solutions in exterior domains.

Here, we investigate the asymptotic structure of isothermal flows [1] of compressible viscous fluids past a threedimensional body. From the physical point of view it is auspicated a uniform decay to zero for the above quantities, cf. [38]. We just mention some of the problems solved for incompressible fluids performing steady flows at the exterior of a moving obstacle, cf. [11], [18], [19], [22].

(1) the flow must exhibit an infinite wake extending in the direction of a prescribed velocity $\boldsymbol{v}_\infty$, if different from zero;

(2) according to the boundary layer, the flow is expected to be potential only in the vicinity of the obstacle, exponential decay for the vorticity is presumed.

In [59], [60] are studied the asymptotic properties of the kinetic and density fields of a compressible viscous fluid filling the threedimensional space exterior to a compact region $\mathcal{C}$.

In [59], the asymptotic properties of the kinetic and density fields of a compressible isothermal viscous fluid, filling the threedimensional space exterior to a fixed compact region $\mathcal{C}$, are investigated. Precisely, for small external data and for $\boldsymbol{v}_\infty = \mathbf{0}$, it has been proved the existence of a solution $\boldsymbol{v}$ and ρ which decays respectively to $\mathbf{0}$ and ρ_∞ at infinity, for the velocity field it is exhibited the same asymptotic structure as that of the fundamental Stokes tensor.

In [60] it is investigated the asymptotic structure of isothermal flows of compressible viscous fluids past a threedimensional body. The main goal reached is the existence of a wake region in the case when $\boldsymbol{v}_\infty \neq \mathbf{0}$, actually, they furnish the decay rate to $\boldsymbol{v}_\infty$ and ρ_∞ for $\boldsymbol{v}$ and ρ. For small external data, there exists a (unique) steady flow which exhibits the wake region, furthermore, the asymptotic structure of the velocity coincides with the asymptotic structure of the fundamental Oseen tensor.

---

[1] The results are valid also for the barotropic (i.e. in particular for isentropic) case. Then $\nabla\rho$ in equation $(4.10)_2$ is replaced by $\nabla\pi(\rho)$, where the pressure π is a scalar function, a restriction on $\mathbb{R}^1_+$ (positive real axis) of an analytic function on $\mathcal{C}_+$ (a complex half-plane containing $\mathbb{R}^1_+$).

These results can be interpreted by saying that, for small Reynolds numbers, the velocity of a isothermal gas at infinity behaves as that of an incompressible fluid. In other words, far from the obstacle an isothermal gas does not remember the compressibility.

Here, we first investigate the existence when $\boldsymbol{v}_\infty = 0$, see [59], by stating that the velocity and its gradient possess the asymptotic behaviour of the fundamental Stokes tensor. Then, we concentrate our attention on the existence of a wake region in the case when $\boldsymbol{v}_\infty \neq \mathbf{0}$.

In [58], it was proved existence, uniqueness and regularity of steady flows of a viscous, ideal and isothermal gas, at least when the data are sufficiently small. These flows possess good summability properties, say, the velocity and the variation of the density with respect to a constant state, and their derivatives as well, are in suitable Lebesgue spaces. Moreover, in [58], when the obstacle is fixed, it was proved only a uniform decay property for the velocity $\boldsymbol{v}(x) = O(1/|x|)$, not for the gradient of velocity: we call these solutions *physically reasonable solutions*[1]. In line with what formulated for incompressible fluids, also for compressible viscous fluids we can ask analoguos questions. Specifically,

(1) the kinetic field of a compressible fluid is expected to be potential only in the vicinity of the obstacle, while far from the obstacle it is expected to behave as that of an incompressible fluid;

(2) the decay properties for $\boldsymbol{v}$ are expected to be not better than those enjoyed by the analogous velocity Stokes tensor, i.e. $|x|^{-1}$ for the velocity and $|x|^{-2}$ for the gradient of velocity;

(3) The density is expected to decay to its prescribed constant value at infinity.

Here, we describe the asymptotic structure of isothermal flows of compressible viscous fluids past a fixed threedimensional body, with $v_\infty = \mathbf{0}$. Actually, Theorems 4.3, 4.4 show that, far from the obstacle an isothermal gas does not remember the compressibility.

The main goal of [59] is the following theorem[1]

---

[1] For the notion of *physically reasonable solutions* see [18], for incompressible fluids, and [58], for compressible fluids

[1] As is customary, B_{R_0} denotes the ball of radius R_0 centered at the origin of the coordinate system. Moreover, we set $\nabla^2 f = \nabla\nabla f$.

Theorem 4.3. *Let Ω be of class C^{k+3} and for some $R_0 > 0$ $\boldsymbol{f} \in W^{l,q}(\Omega) \cap W^{k,p}(\Omega)$, $\operatorname{supp} \boldsymbol{f} \in B_{R_0}$, with $p > 3$, $3/2 < q < 3$, $l = 1, \cdots, k$, $k = 2, 3, \cdots$. Then, there exist two positive constants γ_0, γ_1, dependent on l, k, p, q, $\partial\Omega$, R_0, such that, if*

$$]|\boldsymbol{f}|[_{k,q,p} := \|\boldsymbol{f}\|_{l,q} + \|\boldsymbol{f}\|_{k,p} < \gamma_1,$$

then in the ball

$$\begin{aligned}
B^{k+2,q,p}_{\gamma_0}(\Omega) := \{(\sigma, \boldsymbol{v}) :\ & \sigma \in W^{l+1\,q}(\Omega) \cap W^{k+1,p}(\Omega),\ \boldsymbol{v} = \boldsymbol{u} + \nabla\varphi, \\
& \boldsymbol{v} \in \mathcal{H}^{l+2,q}_0(\Omega) \cap \mathcal{H}^{k+1,p}_0(\Omega),\ \nabla\cdot\boldsymbol{v}|_{\partial\Omega} = 0, \\
& |x|^2\sigma \in L^\infty(\Omega),\ |x|\nabla\sigma \in L^q(\Omega), |x|\nabla\varphi \in L^\infty(\Omega), \\
& |x|^2\nabla^2\varphi \in W^{1,q}(\Omega),\ |x|\boldsymbol{u} \in L^\infty(\Omega),\ |x|^2\nabla\boldsymbol{u} \in L^\infty(\Omega) \\
& \|\!|\sigma|\!\|_{k+1,q,p} + \|\!|\boldsymbol{v}|\!\|_{k+2,q,p} := \|\sigma\|_{1,q} + \|\sigma\|_{k+1,p} + \|\boldsymbol{v}\|_{2,q} \\
& + \|\nabla\boldsymbol{v}\|_{k+1,p} + \||x|\nabla\cdot\boldsymbol{v}\|_q + \||x|\nabla\cdot\boldsymbol{v}\|_p + \||x|^2\sigma\|_\infty + \||x|\nabla\sigma\|_\infty \\
& + \||x|^2\nabla\sigma\|_r + \||x|\nabla\varphi\|_\infty + \||x|^2\nabla^2\varphi\|_{1,q} + \||x|\boldsymbol{u}\|_\infty + \||x|^2\nabla\boldsymbol{u}\|_\infty \le \gamma_0\}
\end{aligned}$$

there exists just a solution $\sigma, \boldsymbol{v}$ of (4.10), *with $\boldsymbol{v}_\infty = \boldsymbol{0}$, of* (4.11) *satisfying the estimate*

$$\|\!|\sigma|\!\|_{k+1,q,p} + \|\!|\boldsymbol{v}|\!\|_{k+2,q,p} \le c]|\boldsymbol{f}|[_{k,q,p}.$$

These results correspond to the physical expectations, in the sense that the velocity field and its gradient go to zero at infinity as the solutions of the Stokes problem, in other words, the inertia can be disregarded if compared with the viscosity effects. The decay rate for $\boldsymbol{v}$ resembles that of the Stokes fundamental tensor, therefore it can be considered optimal. Moreover, the decay rate to zero for the difference between the density and its constant value at infinity, σ, is faster than that proved for the velocity, but weaker than that enjoied by the volume variation. Actually, the decay rate to zero for the volume variation $\nabla\cdot\boldsymbol{v}$ is faster than that experienced by the other spatial derivatives of $\boldsymbol{v}$, and by σ (the fluid flow becomes essentially isochoric).

To achieve these results, in [59] the following tools have been used:

(1) The decomposition method (in incompressible and compressible part) for the velocity, introduced in [58], through which it is possible to split the Poisson–Stokes system, with Dirichlet data, into the (for the incompressible part of the kinetic field) Stokes system, with Dirichlet data, (for the density) the

transport equation, (for the compressible part of the kinetic field) the Poisson equation, with Neumann data.

(2) The integral representation formulas for Stokes and Laplace operators, due to Finn, see *e.g.*, [18], [19].

(3) The estimates of weakly singular integrals, some of them are due to Finn, one to Stein and Weiss, cf. [18], [19], [92], [93], and one to Novotny' and Padula [61].

(4) The decay estimates for steady transport equation, see [53], [58]. The validity of decomposition (4.13) was proved in [59].

For compressible fluids there exist steady solutions only for small forces. However, one can still ask, for a given steady solution corresponding to large external compact support forces, whether the solution decays to given values at infinity. A work providing an answer to such a question when $\boldsymbol{v}_\infty = \mathbf{0}$ is in preparation, where it is shown that any regular solution $(\boldsymbol{v}, \rho)$ such that

$$\begin{aligned} &\boldsymbol{v} \in C^2(\overline{\Omega}), \qquad \rho \in C^1(\overline{\Omega}), \qquad \rho > 0, \\ &\rho(x) \to 1, \quad \boldsymbol{v}(x) \equiv |x|^{-1} \qquad |x| \to \infty, \end{aligned}$$

satisfies

$$\nabla \boldsymbol{v} \equiv \ln|x||x|^{-2}, \qquad (\rho - 1) \equiv \ln|x||x|^{-2}, \qquad |x| \to \infty, \tag{4.17}$$

whatever the size of the external data, provided they either have compact support or are sufficiently rapidly decaying at infinity[1].

Let $\boldsymbol{v}_\infty$ have the direction of the first coordinate axis x_1, then, we set $\mathcal{S}(x) := |x| - x_1$.

Theorem 4.4 below, in the case of small external forces and small and non-zero $\boldsymbol{v}_\infty$, concerns the existence of solutions for which the velocity exhibits a wake region, say parabolic asymptotic structure. For such solutions, the kinetic

[1] The investigation of the decay of the vorticity (which is expected to be exponential outside the wake reagion) seems to be more complicated and represents still an open question.

field behaves exactly as the Oseen tensor at infinity. Precisely, for the velocity we prove that

$$\boldsymbol{v} \sim O(|x|^{-1}\mathcal{S}(x)^{-\epsilon}), \qquad \nabla \boldsymbol{v}(x) \sim O(|x|^{-3/2}\mathcal{S}(x)^{-(3/2)\epsilon})$$

for any ϵ less than one, where the symbol O have its usual meaning. Furthermore, for the density we show that

$$|x|^{1+\epsilon}\sigma \in W^{2,r}(\Omega), \qquad |x|^{1+\epsilon}\sigma,\ |x|^{1+\epsilon}\nabla\sigma,\ |x|^{2+\epsilon}\nabla\cdot\boldsymbol{v} \in L^\infty(\Omega)$$

for $r \leq 3/(1-\epsilon)$.

Theorem 4.4. *Let Ω be of class C^{k+3}, $\operatorname{supp}\boldsymbol{f} \in B_{R_0}$, for some $R_0 > 0$ and $\boldsymbol{f} \in L^{3q/3-q}(\Omega) \cap W^{l,q}(\Omega) \cap W^{k,p}(\Omega)$, with $l = 1, \cdots, k,\ k = 3, \cdots$ and*

$$\frac{3}{2} < q < 3, \quad p > 3, \quad \frac{1}{2} < \alpha \leq \beta < 1, \quad r > \frac{6}{1-\beta}.$$

Then, there exist two positive constants γ_0, γ_1, dependent on l, k, p, r, $\partial\Omega$, R_0, α, β, and independent of $\boldsymbol{v}_\infty$, such that, if

$$]|\boldsymbol{f}|[_{l,k,q,p,\infty} := \|\boldsymbol{f}\|_{l,q} + \|\boldsymbol{f}\|_{k,p} + |\boldsymbol{v}_\infty| < \gamma_1,$$

then in the ball

$$\begin{gathered}
B^{k+2,q,p}_{\gamma_0}(\Omega) := \{(\sigma,\boldsymbol{v}) :\ \sigma \in W^{l+1,q}(\Omega) \cap W^{k+1,p}(\Omega),\ \boldsymbol{v} = \boldsymbol{u} + \nabla\varphi,\\
\boldsymbol{v} \in \mathcal{H}^{l+2,q}_0(\Omega) \cap \mathcal{H}^{k+1,p}_0(\Omega),\ \nabla\cdot\boldsymbol{v}|_{\partial\Omega} = 0,\\
|x|^{1+\beta}\sigma \in W^{2,r}(\Omega),\ |x|^{2+\beta/2}(1+|\boldsymbol{v}_\infty|^{3\alpha/2}\mathcal{S}^{1/2}(x))\nabla\sigma \in L^r(\Omega),\\
|x|^{1+\beta}\nabla\varphi \in W^{2,r}(\Omega), |x|^{2+\beta/2}(1+|\boldsymbol{v}_\infty|^{3\alpha/2}\mathcal{S}^{1/2}(x))\nabla^2\varphi \in W^{1,r}(\Omega),\\
\boldsymbol{u} \in \hat{H}^{1,q}_\infty(\Omega) \cap \hat{H}^{1,p}_\infty(\Omega),\ \nabla\boldsymbol{u} \in W^{l+1,q}(\Omega) \cap W^{k+1,p}(\Omega),\\
|x|(1+|\boldsymbol{v}_\infty|^{\alpha}\mathcal{S}^{\alpha}(x))\boldsymbol{u} \in L^\infty(\Omega),\ |x|^{3/2}(1+|\boldsymbol{v}_\infty|^{3\alpha/2}\mathcal{S}^{3\alpha/2}(x))\nabla\boldsymbol{u} \in L^\infty(\Omega),\\
|x|^{1+\beta}\nabla^2\boldsymbol{u} \in L^\infty(\Omega),\\
\|\!|\sigma\|\!|_{k+1,q,p} + \|\!|\boldsymbol{v}\|\!|_{k+2,q,p} := \|\sigma\|_{l+1,q} + \|\sigma\|_{k+1,p} + \|\nabla\boldsymbol{v}\|_{l+1,q} + \|\nabla\boldsymbol{v}\|_{k+1,p}\\
+\||x|^{1+\beta}\sigma\|_{2,r} + \||x|^{2+\beta/2}(1+|\boldsymbol{v}_\infty|^{3\alpha/2}\mathcal{S}^{1/2}(x))\nabla\sigma)\|_r\\
+\||x|^{1+\beta}\nabla\varphi\|_{2,r} + \||x|^{2+\beta/2}(1+|\boldsymbol{v}_\infty|^{3\alpha/2}\mathcal{S}^{1/2}(x))\nabla^2\varphi\|_{1,r}\\
+\||x|(1+|\boldsymbol{v}_\infty|^{\alpha}\mathcal{S}^{\alpha}(x)\boldsymbol{u}\|_\infty + \||x|^{3/2}(1+|\boldsymbol{v}_\infty|^{3\alpha/2}\mathcal{S}^{3\alpha/2}(x))\nabla\boldsymbol{u}\|_\infty\\
+\||x|^{1+\beta}\nabla^2\boldsymbol{u}\|_r \leq \gamma_0\}
\end{gathered}$$

there exists just a solution σ, $\boldsymbol{v}$ *of* (4.11), *with* $\boldsymbol{v}_\infty \neq \mathbf{0}$, *satisfying the estimate*

$$\|\sigma\|_{k+1,q,p} + \|\boldsymbol{v}\|_{k+2,q,p} \leq c]|\boldsymbol{f}|[_{k,q,p}.$$

In particular, $\boldsymbol{v}$ *exhibits the wake region*

$$|x|(1+|\boldsymbol{v}_\infty|^\alpha \mathcal{S}^\alpha(x))\boldsymbol{v} \in L^\infty(\Omega), \quad |x|^{3/2}(1+|\boldsymbol{v}_\infty|^{3\alpha/2}\mathcal{S}^{3\alpha/2}(x))\nabla\boldsymbol{v} \in L^\infty(\Omega),$$

and

$$|x|^{1+\beta}\sigma \in L^\infty(\Omega).$$

These results correspond to the physical expectations in the sense, that the velocity field and its gradient go to zero at infinity as the solutions of the Oseen problem. In other words, the inertial term can be disregarded if compared with the viscosity terms. Moreover, the decay to a constant value for the density is uniform in all directions (the density is uniformly distributed), while the decay rate for the volume variation $\nabla \cdot \boldsymbol{v}$, still uniform, is faster than that given for the other spatial derivatives of $\boldsymbol{v}$ (the fluid flow becomes essentially isochoric). Moreover, the decay is almost optimal (recall that the decay of the velocity components of the Oseen tensor reads $|x|^{-2}$ outside the wake region and $|x|^{-1}$ inside it, the decay of its gradient $|x|^{-3}$ outside and $|x|^{-3/2}$ inside and the decay of the pressure components $|x|^{-2}$ throughout all directions).

Besides this, in [60] it is investigated a limit $\boldsymbol{v}_\infty \to \mathbf{0}$. We show that the limit density ρ_0 and the velocity $\boldsymbol{v}_0$ are physically reasonable solutions to the Poisson–Stokes equations with $\boldsymbol{v}_\infty = \mathbf{0}$.

The proof relies on the following techniques

(i) The method of decomposition introduced in [58], which splits the linearized Poisson–Stokes system into the Stokes equation (governing the incompressible part of the velocity), Neumann problem (governing the compressible part of the velocity field), and transport equation (governing the density).

(ii) Known results for the above auxiliary linear problems in exterior domains, cf. [22].

(iii) Integral representation formulas for Laplace and Oseen operators, due to Finn, Chang and Finn, cf. [10], [18].

(iv) Known estimates of weakly singular integrals with anisotropic weights and kernels, due to Finn, cf. also [19].

(v) Estimates with anisotropic weights (belonging to the Mouckenhoupt classes) of singular integrals (corresponding to the classes of multipliers), due to Kurtz and Wheeden [32].

(vi) Appropriate choice of norms (anisotropic in space), respecting the wake structure of solutions and rescaling properties (with respect to $\boldsymbol{v}_\infty$) of the Oseen tensor, [22].

In a paper in preparation, for arbitrary size of external data it a theorem is proved which guarantees a good asymptotic behavior for any regular solution σ, $\boldsymbol{v}$, furthermore, it is shown an implementing property of the solutions. Precisely, assume that $\sigma \in C^2(K)$, $\boldsymbol{v} \in C^3(K)$, for any compact $K \subset \Omega$, is a solution to (4.11) and

$$|\boldsymbol{v}| \sim O(|x|^{1+\gamma}); \quad |x|^{1+\epsilon}\sigma \in W^{1,r}(\Omega),\ |x|^{1+\delta}\nabla\sigma \in W^{1,r}(\Omega),\ |x|\nabla^3\sigma \in L^r(\Omega),$$

for suitable $0 < \epsilon < 1$, $1 \leq \delta < 2$ and $r \leq 3/(3-\epsilon)$. Then, the kinetic fields posses at infinity all properties of the Oseen tensor. However, this result is still in the progress.

5. Statement of the problem and open questions in domains with a non-compact boundary

5.1 - Position of the problem.

This section is devoted to the study of existence, uniqueness and asymptotic behaviour of a steady flow occurring in domains with a non-compact boundary. Precisely, we assume Ω to be unbounded in $\mathbb{R}^n$, $n = 2, 3$, with only two exits at infinity, Ω_i, $i = 1, 2$, i.e.,

$$\Omega = \Omega_1 \cup \Omega_2, \quad \Omega_1 \cap \Omega_2 = \varnothing.$$

We remind that these geometries are representative of a large class of problems in fluid-dynamics, [2], [3], [22], [33], [35], [63], [78], [88], [89], [90]. Moreover, a generalization to Ω with $h > 2$ exits could also be considered, however, since this field of research is at its sunset, we prefer omit it, in order to not obscure the line of the reasoning. In Ω_i, $i = 1, 2$, we introduce the coordinate system

$c_i = \{O, x_i, y_i, z_i\}$, with $O \in \partial\Omega_1 \cap \Omega_2$. In the sequel, when this will be no misleading, we shall omit the subscript index i. In this way, the domain $\Omega = \Omega_i$ will have the following analytical expression

$$\Omega = \{(x, y, z) \in \mathbb{R}^3 : \ x' := (x, y) \in S_z\}.$$

The cross section S_z is a smoothly varying, simply connected domain of $\mathbb{R}^2$. We shall suppose S_z star-shaped with respect to a circle $B_\delta \subset \mathbb{R}^2$ in the plane with $z = const.$. Then,

$$\partial S_z = \{(x, y) \in \mathbb{R}^2 : \ x = f(y, z) \text{ or } y = f(x, z)\}.$$

As limit situations, we recover:

(1) cylindrical pipes when $f(x, z) = f(x)$, or $f(y, z) = f(y)$, that is when the cross section is bounded;

(2) aperture domains when $f(y, 0) = f(y)$, or $f(x, 0) = f(x)$, and S_0 contains a ball of radius d said the radius of the aperture and $f(x, z) = f(y, z) = \infty$ for all other $z \neq 0$.

Notice that in pipes there is only one direction at infinity given by that of z, while for the aperture domains we have three independent directions at infinity given by x, y, z. In general, for given $f(z)$, with $\lim_{z\to\infty} f(z) = \infty$ we have two indipendent directions at infinity, say z, x, because it results $x < \sqrt{f(y, z)^2 - y^2}$ or $y < \sqrt{f(x, z)^2 - x^2}$.

Steady flows in channels have been largely studied for incompressible flows, see [22] for the literature. As we shall see below, the well-posedness for the Navier-Stokes steady equations in channels, admits the same formulation irrespective of the number of the directions at infinity.

The main goal of this chapter is to criticize the formulation of the well-posedness problem for viscous isothermal gases in channels. As matter of fact, we wish to show that, despite of what happens for incompressible fluids, formulation of well-posedness for compressible fluids, must be varying by varying the number of the directions at infinity. This will be achieved through the analisis of the two limit cases: pipes, aperture domains. Moreover, we shall not deal here with the general case, because there are not yet complete results in this direction.

Boundary and side conditions.

Concerning the boundary and side conditions, in line with Section 3, we make the following assumptions.

Let Ω be any (bounded or unbounded) domain. The density must be almost everywhere non-negative and in the absence of selfgravitational forces, the density must be bounded, and furthermore the fluid must adhere to $\partial\Omega$. We choose

$$m \leq \rho \leq M, \qquad \boldsymbol{v}|_{\partial\Omega} = \mathbf{0}.$$

For domains with a non-compact boundary, some limit condition will be added, and this will be considered below. We shall distinguish between domains which are unbounded only in one direction, say "pipes", channels with bounded cross section, or diverging channels: in this last class is included the half space and the aperture flow.

5.2 - "Well-posedness" problem in diverging channels for incompressible fluids.

Let us first briefly recall some now *classical formulations* of well-posedness question for incompressible fluids.

Owing the continuity of the mass, and assuming the adherence condition at the boundary, from

$$(5.1) \qquad \begin{cases} \nabla \cdot \boldsymbol{v} = 0, \\ \boldsymbol{v} \cdot \nabla \boldsymbol{v} = -\nabla p + \nu \Delta \boldsymbol{v} + \boldsymbol{f}, \\ \boldsymbol{v}|_{\partial\Omega} = \mathbf{0}, \end{cases}$$

($\nu := \mu/\rho$) we deduce the conservation of the mass flux, i.e.

$$(5.2) \qquad \phi(\boldsymbol{v}) = \int_{S_z} \boldsymbol{v} \cdot \boldsymbol{n} = \Phi,$$

where Φ is arbitrary constant.

- **Formulation of the well-posedness problem in pipes.**

Notice that, if we set $\boldsymbol{f} = \mathbf{0}$, it is possible to prove the existence of a non-zero stationary flow $(\boldsymbol{v}_\Phi, p_\Phi)$, function of the given flux Φ, which for a cylinder is known as the Hagen-Poiseuille flow. Furthermore, it has been proved that the pressure p_Φ at infinity is constant in x'. Therefore, it is reasonable to introduce the corresponding pressure drop p_*,

$$p_* := p_+ - p_-, \quad p_\pm := \lim_{z\to\pm\infty} p_\Phi(z).$$

The Hagen-Poiseuille flow (which corresponds to zero forces, and zero boundary data) shows that, in order to recover uniqueness for incompressible steady flows, besides the forces and the boundary data, one should prescribe further conditions. It is known, by now, that uniqueness is recovered by prescribing the flux Φ as an independent datum. Analogously, it is also possible to show that to any given pressure drop p_* there corresponds a unique, non-zero, stationary, incompressible flow $(\boldsymbol{v}_0, p_0)$, still coinciding with the Hagen-Poiseuille flow. For such a flow we can also compute the unique mass flux Φ associated to it.

In conclusion, in cylinders, for a compact support force $\boldsymbol{f} \neq \boldsymbol{0}$, it appears natural to study the well-posedness problem equivalently for one of the following two formulations:

(1) Given a net flux Φ, find a stationary solution of

$$(5.3) \qquad \begin{aligned} &\nabla\cdot\boldsymbol{v} = 0,\\ &\boldsymbol{v}\cdot\nabla\boldsymbol{v} = -\nabla p + \nu\Delta\boldsymbol{v} + \boldsymbol{f},\\ &\boldsymbol{v}|_{\partial\Omega} = \boldsymbol{0},\\ &\int_{S(z)} \boldsymbol{v}\cdot\boldsymbol{n} = \Phi, \qquad \lim_{|z|\to\infty} \boldsymbol{v}(x', z) = \boldsymbol{v}_\Phi(x'). \end{aligned}$$

(2) Given a pressure drop p_*, find a stationary solution of

$$(5.4) \qquad \begin{aligned} &\nabla\cdot\boldsymbol{v} = 0,\\ &\boldsymbol{v}\cdot\nabla\boldsymbol{v} = -\nabla p + \nu\Delta\boldsymbol{v} + \boldsymbol{f},\\ &\boldsymbol{v}|_{\partial\Omega} = \boldsymbol{0},\\ &p_* = \lim_{z\to\infty} p(z) - \lim_{z\to-\infty} p(z), \qquad \lim_{|z|\to\infty} \boldsymbol{v}(x', z) = \boldsymbol{v}_0(x'). \end{aligned}$$

The above formulation in pipes was proposed for the first time by Leray, see [33]. The main objectives proposed by the above formulations, are the proofs of

- Existence
- Uniqueness
- Asymptotic Behaviour at Large Distances.

For the solutions of (5.3) or (5.4) several objectives have been reached. However, the proof of the asymptotic decay of $\boldsymbol{v}$, till now, is known only for small forces.

- **Formulation of the well-posedness problem in diverging channels.**

The well-posedness for flows in diverging channels is recovered once one admits that $f(x,z) \to \infty$ or $f(y,z) \to \infty$, in particular if S_z is a circle we have

$$S_z = \{(x,y,z): \ \sqrt{x^2+y^2} < f(z)\}.$$

One case of interest is given when $f(z) = z^\alpha$. In general, it has been proved that the well-posedness can be formulated by the same two equivalent formulations as those (5.3), (5.4) described for flows occurring in pipes. Also in these geometries several results have been achieved. It is worthy to be noticed that the well-posedness theorems depend on the rate of growth at infinity of f, in particular, when $f(z) = z^\alpha$ the results heavily depend on α.

- **Formulation of the well-posedness problem in aperture domains.**

The formulation of the well-posedness problem in aperture domains was set by [26] in 1976, who studied existence and uniqueness for problem (5.4) and proved the equivalence between problems (5.3), (5.4).

The formulations of the above problems opened the way to a large series of papers in the *more general class of diverging channels.* We limit ourselves to quote only some of the early contributions: [2], [3], [26], [33], [35], [88], [89], [90].

- **Concluding remarks.**

Let us observe what follows.

(a) *The above formulation* **does not change** *by varying the cross section of the channel.*

(b) *Condition* $(5.3)_4$ *on the flux is not exactly a boundary condition. However, it is necessary for the uniqueness. Intuitively, condition* $(5.3)_4$ **furnishes a control** *on the velocity in the direction in which the domain is unbounded.*

(c) *Formulations* (5.3), (5.4) *are equivalent, in other words, one obtains uniqueness if one prescribes either the flux of mass or the pressure drop. It will be just such equivalence to be failing for compressible flows.*

Our chief interest is to analyze the mathematical properties of the solutions to the Poisson–Stokes equations in channels. As we shall see, in the aforesaid geometries, the mathematical theory is as yet incomplete, and even the correct formulation of the problem is unclear. Indeed, we wish to show how the above stated equivalence between (5.3) and (5.4) fails for compressible fluids. Therefore, we shall devote our attention only to the two limit cases of pipes, in Subsection 5.3, and of aperture damains, Subsection 5.4.

5.3 - "Well-posedness" problem in pipes.

Let us formulate, now, the well-posedness problem for viscous, isothermal gases, when Ω is a pipe. For the sake of simplicity, we shall consider only cylinders, i.e. three-dimensional tubes Ω with constant cross section S. The non compact lateral surface is denoted by $\partial\Omega$. More precisely, we consider domains Ω of the form

$$\Omega = \{x \equiv (x', z) : \; x' = (x, y) \in S, \; z \in (-\infty, \infty)\}, \qquad \partial\Omega = \partial S \times (-\infty, \infty),$$

where S is a bounded, simply connected domain in $\mathbb{R}^2$, with a smooth boundary ∂S. On $\partial\Omega$ we attach the adherence condition $\boldsymbol{v}|_{\partial\Omega} = \mathbf{0}$. Thus, the starting equations are

$$\begin{aligned} &\nabla \cdot (\rho \boldsymbol{v}) = 0, \\ &-\mu\Delta\boldsymbol{v} - (\lambda + \mu)\nabla \operatorname{div} \boldsymbol{v} = -k\nabla\rho + \rho\,(\boldsymbol{f} - \boldsymbol{v} \cdot \nabla\boldsymbol{v}), \\ &\boldsymbol{v}|_{\partial\Omega} = \mathbf{0}. \end{aligned} \tag{5.5}$$

Equation $(5.5)_1$ implies that the mass flux $\int_{S(z)} \rho\boldsymbol{v} \cdot \boldsymbol{n} = \Phi$, must be constant in z. Therefore, analogously to what is known for incompressible fluids, it seems natural to add to the boundary value problem (5.5) the side flux condition

$$\phi(\boldsymbol{v}) = \Phi = \text{const.} \tag{5.6}$$

In this section, we shall first recall a result [63] proving that problem (5.5), (5.6) is ill-posed and then we propose the correct analytical formulation of the problem.

- **Ill-posedness in channels with constant cross section.**

Let $\Omega_{t,T} := \{(x', z) \in \mathbb{R}^3 : x' \in S, \quad z \in (t, T)\}$, and denote by $|\Omega_{t,T}|$ the Lebesgue measure of $\Omega_{t,T}$. We consider the regularity class $\mathcal{H}$ consisting of those locally smooth solutions $\boldsymbol{v}$, ρ of problem (5.5) which satisfy:

(1) the density ρ is uniformly bounded from above and from below by positive constants

$$m \leq \rho(x) \leq M \qquad x \in \Omega \tag{5.7}$$

and its gradient up to the order l has uniformly bounded L^3-norms, over subsets of fixed lenght of the pipe, i.e.,

$$\int_{\Omega_{t,t+1}} |D^l \rho|^3 \mathrm{d}x \leq D; \tag{5.8}$$

(2) the velocity field $\boldsymbol{v}$ satisfies the following rate of growth condition when $z \to \infty$:

$$\int_{\Omega_{0,z}} |\nabla \boldsymbol{v}|^2 \mathrm{d}x \equiv o(|z|^3). \tag{5.9}$$

It has been proved in [63], that, provided $\boldsymbol{f} = \nabla U$, despite how large is the potential part ∇U, any solution $\boldsymbol{v}$, ρ in the class $\mathcal{H}$ satisfies the following properties

$$\nabla \rho,\ \nabla^2 \boldsymbol{v} \in L^2(\Omega); \qquad \|\boldsymbol{v}\|_{1,2,S_z} \to 0, \ \text{as } t \to \infty. \tag{5.10}$$

As a corollary of the above result we have the energy estimate in a pipe.

Theorem 5.1 (Energy identity in pipes). *Let $\boldsymbol{f} = \nabla U + \boldsymbol{f}_1$, $U \in L^\infty(\Omega)$, $\nabla U \in L^2(\Omega)$, and let $\boldsymbol{f}_1$ have a compact support, say, in $\Omega_{-1,1}$, then, in the class $\mathcal{H}$,*

$$E(\Omega) := \int_{-\infty}^{\infty} \{\mu \|\nabla \boldsymbol{v}\|^2_{S_\tau} + (\lambda + \mu)\|\nabla \cdot \boldsymbol{v}\|^2_{S_\tau}\}\, \mathrm{d}\tau = \int_\Omega \rho \boldsymbol{f} \cdot \boldsymbol{v}. \tag{5.11}$$

PROOF - From $(5.10)_2$ we deduce that

$$\lim_{z \to \pm\infty} \boldsymbol{v}(x', z) = \boldsymbol{0}.$$

Let us multiply $(5.5)_2$ by $\boldsymbol{v}$ and integrate over $\Omega_{-t,t}$, $t > 1$, after integrations by parts, we get

$$\begin{aligned} E(\Omega_{-t,t}) &:= \int_{-t}^{t} \{\mu \|\nabla \boldsymbol{v}\|_{S_\tau}^2 + (\lambda + \mu)\|\nabla \cdot \boldsymbol{v}\|_{S_\tau}^2\} \, d\tau = \\ &= \Sigma_t - \Sigma_{-t} + \int_{\Omega_{-t,t}} \rho \boldsymbol{f} \cdot \boldsymbol{v} \end{aligned}$$

with

$$\Sigma_t := \int_{S_t} \left\{ \mu \frac{\partial \boldsymbol{v}}{\partial z} \cdot \boldsymbol{v} + (\lambda + \mu)(\operatorname{div} \boldsymbol{v}) \boldsymbol{v} \cdot \boldsymbol{n} - \rho \frac{v^2}{2} \boldsymbol{v} \cdot \boldsymbol{n} \right\} - \int_{S_t} k (\ln \rho) \rho \boldsymbol{v} \cdot \boldsymbol{n}.$$

Taking the limit as $t \to \infty$, we know that Σ_t vanishes, and therefore, the energy identy (5.11) is easily obtained. □

CONSEQUENCES

(1) If $\boldsymbol{f} = \boldsymbol{0}$ then $\boldsymbol{v} = \boldsymbol{0}$, $\rho_* = 0$, where ρ_* is the density drop;

(2) If $\boldsymbol{f}$ has compact support, then $\lim_{z \to \pm\infty} \int_{S(z)} \rho \boldsymbol{v} \cdot \boldsymbol{n} = 0$, $\Phi = 0$ and ρ_* is uniquely determined by $\boldsymbol{f}$.

The energy identity suggests that the mass flux Φ is a dependent variable, despite what happened in the case of incompressible flows, where Φ could be prescribed independently of the external force. Therefore, we claim that the problem (5.5), (5.6) is ill-posed. This is one reason why, unlike the incompressible case, the question of establishing the existence of a flow subjected to a given flux, is still open. The result of [63] is in the line of the result in [78], where, in order to solve problem (5.5), (5.6), the authors had to add a further variable, which was interpreted as an unknown (control) force. Moreover, the boundary condition $(5.5)_3$ alone may be not enough to determine the flow uniquely, and similarly to what we did for motions in exterior domains, we must prescribe a velocity, and density fields at the exits. However, unlike the case of flows past a body, the kinetic field needs not to be uniform. In fact, if $\Phi \neq 0$, the velocity will be uniform if and only if the channel is diverging at infinity, [22] chap. VI.

Remark 5.1 – In the proof an important role is played by the Poincaré constant, which depends on the diameter h of S. The same proof continues to hold for domains in which $h(z) = z^\alpha$, and α is sufficiently small.

Remark 5.2 – This is not a uniqueness result! The energy identity doesn't provide a uniqueness result.

Remark 5.3 – The density will have, in general, two different constant limits at infinity. One can also prove that the density tends pointwise to such limits

$$\lim_{z\to\pm\infty} \rho(x,z) = \rho_\pm .$$

The two limits are arbitrary. If S is of constant measure, then it was proved that the density drop ρ_* is uniquely determined by $\boldsymbol{f}$. In particular, if $\boldsymbol{f} = \boldsymbol{0}$, then $\rho_* = 0$. Therefore, one value of the density at infinity must still be prescribed.

- **Correct formulation for problems in pipes**

The analysis performed allows us to propose as a correct formulation of the well-posedness problem for a compressible fluid in a pipe, the following one:

Given $\boldsymbol{f} = \boldsymbol{f}_1 + \nabla U$ — where $\boldsymbol{f}_1$ has a compact support — and $\rho_+ > 0$, to find a solution to the following boundary problem

$$\begin{aligned}
&-\mu\Delta\boldsymbol{v} - (\lambda+\mu)\nabla(\nabla\cdot\boldsymbol{v}) = -k\nabla\rho + \rho(\boldsymbol{f} - \boldsymbol{v}\cdot\nabla\boldsymbol{v}),\\
&\nabla\cdot(\rho\boldsymbol{v}) = 0,\\
&\boldsymbol{v}|_{\partial\Omega} = \boldsymbol{0},\\
&\frac{1}{S}\lim_{z\to+\infty}\int_{S(z)} \rho(x,z) = \rho_+, \qquad \lim_{|z|\to\infty} \boldsymbol{v}(x,z) = \boldsymbol{v}_0(x),
\end{aligned} \tag{5.12}$$

where $\boldsymbol{v}_0$, ρ_+ is the unique solution to (5.12) when $\boldsymbol{f}_1 = \boldsymbol{0}$.

Remark 5.4 – The problem of existence of steady flows when the mass flux through the boundary is not zero is an open problem. Till now, it is not known a solution in L^q spaces even in subsonic regime, *i.e.* for small forces.

An application of such case can be found in the problem of existence of steady flows in a pipe, with cylindrical ends.

(1) The existence problem was studied for the first time in [78]; however, since also the flux was required to be prescribed, the solution was constructed by adding into the equation a new term, say, an unknown control force.

(2) The well-posedness for the boundary value problem (5.12) is now studied in [79].

However, it is worth remarking that the general problem, say, without control forces, is still open.

3.10 - Channels with unbounded cross section.

In this section we wish to analyze the well-posedness problem for viscous, isothermal gases in aperture domains, and to discuss the possibility of giving two correct equivalent formulations for it. Precisely, we shall prove that the formulations in terms of pressure drop, and that in terms of the flux of mass do not lead to any contraddiction in the theory. The proof of the well-posedness, as well as the equivalence between the two formulations, are still in preparation.

- **Energy estimate in aperture domains.**

The equations governing the steady flows of a viscous isothermal gas are

$$
\begin{aligned}
&\nabla \cdot (\rho \boldsymbol{v}) = 0,\\
&-\mu\Delta \boldsymbol{v} - (\lambda+\mu)\nabla(\nabla\cdot \boldsymbol{v}) = -k\nabla\rho + \rho(\boldsymbol{f} - \boldsymbol{v}\cdot\nabla \boldsymbol{v}),\\
&\boldsymbol{v}|_{\partial\Omega} = \boldsymbol{0},\\
&\lim_{|x|\to\infty} \boldsymbol{v}(x) = \boldsymbol{0}, \qquad \lim_{z\to\pm\infty}\rho(z) = \rho_{\pm}.
\end{aligned}
\tag{5.13}
$$

Let $\mathbb{R}_+$ and $\mathbb{R}_-$ denote the sets of positive and negative numbers, respectively. We set

$$
\Omega_\pm = \left\{(x,y,z)\in\mathbb{R}^3 \,:\, (x,y)\in S_z,\ z\in\mathbb{R}_\pm\right\}
$$

$$
\Omega_{\pm,R} = (\Omega_\pm \cap B_R)\setminus B_1, \quad \Omega_1 = \Omega\cap B_1, \quad S_\pm = \partial B_1 \cap \Omega_\pm.
$$

Since we don't know any existence theorem for aperture flows, we shall make some initial considerations starting with solutions having the same behavior at infinity as that of the kinetic field ($\boldsymbol{v}$) and the pressure (see ρ) of an incompressible fluid subjected to a small flux Φ. We consider the class $\mathfrak{R}$ of regular solutions $\boldsymbol{v}$, ρ to system (5.13) such that $\nabla \boldsymbol{v} \in L^2$, $\boldsymbol{v} \in L^3(\Omega)$, and $\rho - \rho_\pm \in L^3(\Omega_\pm)$. $\mathfrak{R}$ furnishes a class of some heuristically reasonable decay properties of the flow as one moves away form the aperture.

Theorem 5.2 (Energy identity in aperture domains). *Let $\boldsymbol{f}$ have a compact support, say, in Ω_1. Then in the class*

$$0 < m \leq \rho \leq M, \quad |\nabla \rho| \leq m_1, \quad |\boldsymbol{v}| \leq b z^2,$$

the only possible kinetic field solving (5.13) must satisfy the energy identity

$$\int_\Omega [\mu \nabla \boldsymbol{v} : \nabla \boldsymbol{v} + (\lambda + \mu)(\nabla \cdot \boldsymbol{v})^2] \mathrm{d}x = -k\Phi \ln \left(\frac{\rho_+}{\rho_-} \right) + \int_\Omega \rho \boldsymbol{f} \cdot \boldsymbol{v} dx. \tag{5.14}$$

PROOF - Let us multiply $(5.13)_1$ by $\boldsymbol{v}$ and integrate over $\Omega_{\pm,R}$, and Ω_1. We get

$$\int_{\Omega_{\pm,R}} [\mu \nabla \boldsymbol{v} : \nabla \boldsymbol{v} + (\lambda + \mu)(\nabla \cdot \boldsymbol{v})^2] r^2 d\omega \mathrm{d}r =$$
$$= \Sigma_\pm(R) + b_\pm - k \int_{\Omega_{\pm,R}} \boldsymbol{v} \cdot \nabla \rho \, r^2 d\omega \mathrm{d}r,$$
$$\int_{\Omega_1} [\mu \nabla \boldsymbol{v} : \nabla \boldsymbol{v} + (\lambda + \mu)(\nabla \cdot \boldsymbol{v})^2] r^2 d\omega \mathrm{d}r =$$
$$= -b_+ - b_- + \int_{\Omega_1} \rho \boldsymbol{v} \cdot (-k \nabla \ln \rho + \boldsymbol{f}) \, r^2 d\omega \mathrm{d}r,$$

where

$$\Sigma_\pm(R) := R^2 \int_{S_\pm} \left\{ \mu \frac{\partial \boldsymbol{v}}{\partial R} \cdot \boldsymbol{v} + [(\lambda + \mu) \nabla \cdot \boldsymbol{v} - \rho(v^2/2)] \boldsymbol{v} \cdot \boldsymbol{n} \right\}_{|x|=R} \mathrm{d}\omega,$$
$$b_\pm := - \int_{S_\pm} \left\{ \mu \frac{\partial \boldsymbol{v}}{\partial r} \cdot \boldsymbol{v} + [(\lambda + \mu) \nabla \cdot \boldsymbol{v} - \rho(v^2/2)] \boldsymbol{v} \cdot \boldsymbol{n} \right\}_{|x|=1} \mathrm{d}\omega.$$

Employing the summability assumptions on $\boldsymbol{v}$ and ρ, we can easily deduce

$$\lim_{R \to \infty} R^2 \int_{S_\pm} \left\{ \mu \frac{\partial \boldsymbol{v}}{\partial R} \cdot \boldsymbol{v} + [(\lambda + \mu) \nabla \cdot \boldsymbol{v} - \rho(v^2/2)] \boldsymbol{v} \cdot \boldsymbol{n} \right\}_{|x|=R} \mathrm{d}\omega = 0.$$

In this way, in the limit $R \to \pm\infty$ we get

$$
(5.15)\qquad
\begin{aligned}
&\int_{\Omega_\pm} [\mu \nabla \boldsymbol{v} : \nabla \boldsymbol{v} + (\lambda+\mu)(\nabla \cdot \boldsymbol{v})^2] \mathrm{d}x = \\
&\qquad = +b_\pm - k \lim_{R\to\infty} \int_{\Omega_{\pm,R}} \boldsymbol{v} \cdot \nabla \rho \, r^2 d\omega \mathrm{d}r, \\
&\int_{\Omega_1} [\mu \nabla \boldsymbol{v} : \nabla \boldsymbol{v} + (\lambda+\mu)(\nabla \cdot \boldsymbol{v})^2] \mathrm{d}x = \\
&\qquad = -b_+ - b_- + \int_{\Omega_1} \rho \boldsymbol{v} \cdot (-k \nabla \ln \rho + \boldsymbol{f}) \, r^2 d\omega \mathrm{d}r.
\end{aligned}
$$

How to deal with the pressure term

Till now, we didn't change the term containing the pressure: this is just our purpose now. Indeed, it is the one which, essentially, makes the difference between compressible and incompressible fluids. For every volume V, taking into account the solenoidality of $\rho \boldsymbol{v}$, we have

$$
-\int_V \rho \boldsymbol{v} \cdot \nabla \ln \rho = -\int_{\partial V} \rho \boldsymbol{v} \cdot \boldsymbol{n} \ln \rho.
$$

We apply this formula to the integrals over $\Omega_\pm$, to get

$$
\begin{aligned}
&- \lim_{R\to\infty} \int_{\Omega_{\pm,R}} \rho \boldsymbol{v} \cdot \nabla \ln \rho \, r^2 \mathrm{d}\omega \mathrm{d}r = \\
&\qquad = - \lim_{R\to\infty} R^2 \int_{S_\pm} [\rho \boldsymbol{v} \cdot \boldsymbol{n} \ln \rho]_{|x|=R} \, \mathrm{d}\omega - \int_{S_\pm} [\rho \boldsymbol{v} \cdot \boldsymbol{n} \ln \rho]_{|x|=1} \, \mathrm{d}\omega \mathrm{d}r.
\end{aligned}
$$

Moreover, since $\rho - \rho_\pm \in L^3(\Omega_\pm)$ and $\boldsymbol{v} \in L^3(\Omega)$ we have

$$
\begin{aligned}
&\lim_{R\to\infty} R^2 \int_{S_+} [\rho \boldsymbol{v} \cdot \boldsymbol{n} \ln \rho]_{|x|=R} \, \mathrm{d}\omega = \Phi \ln \rho_+, \\
&\lim_{R\to\infty} R^2 \int_{S_-} [\rho \boldsymbol{v} \cdot \boldsymbol{n} \ln \rho]_{|x|=R} \, \mathrm{d}\omega = -\Phi \ln \rho_-.
\end{aligned}
$$

Therefore, we obtain

$$
(5.16)\qquad
\begin{aligned}
&- k \lim_{R\to\infty} \int_{\Omega_{\pm,R}} \boldsymbol{v} \cdot \nabla \rho \, r^2 \mathrm{d}\omega \mathrm{d}r = \\
&\qquad = -k(\pm\Phi) \ln \rho_\pm - k \int_{S_\pm} [\rho \boldsymbol{v} \cdot \boldsymbol{n} \ln \rho]_{|x|=1} \mathrm{d}\omega \mathrm{d}r, \\
&- k \int_{\Omega_1} \boldsymbol{v} \cdot \nabla \rho \, d\omega dr = k \int_{S_1} \rho \boldsymbol{v} \cdot \boldsymbol{n} \ln \rho \, d\omega dr.
\end{aligned}
$$

Thus, adding identities (5.15) to (5.16), we obtain (5.14). □

CONCLUSIONS

(1) The energy identity (5.14) has been deduced assuming $\boldsymbol{v} \to \mathbf{0}$ at infinity. From the energy identity (5.14) we cannot deduce any more that the mass flux Φ is zero,

(2) In order to get uniqueness it seems reasonable to prescribe either of the two conditions:

(A) The flux Φ through the aperture.
(B) The two limits at infinity for the density $\lim_{R\to\infty} \frac{1}{S_\pm} \int_{S_\pm} \rho(\omega, R) d\omega = \rho_\pm$.

- **Correct formulation for problems in aperture domains.**

(A) Given $\boldsymbol{f}$, $\rho_\pm > 0$, to find a solution to the following boundary problem

$$\begin{aligned} &\nabla \cdot (\rho \boldsymbol{v}) = 0, \\ &-\mu\Delta\boldsymbol{v} - (\lambda + \mu)\nabla(\nabla \cdot \boldsymbol{v}) = -k\nabla\rho + \rho\boldsymbol{f}, \\ &\boldsymbol{v}|_{\partial\Omega} = \mathbf{0}, \\ &\int_S \rho\boldsymbol{v} \cdot \boldsymbol{n} = \Phi, \quad \lim_{R\to\infty} \boldsymbol{v}(\omega, R) = \mathbf{0}. \end{aligned} \tag{5.17}$$

(B) Given $\boldsymbol{f}$, $\rho_\pm > 0$, to find a solution to the following boundary problem

$$\begin{aligned} &\nabla \cdot (\rho \boldsymbol{v}) = 0, \\ &-\mu\Delta\boldsymbol{v} - (\lambda + \mu)\nabla(\nabla \cdot \boldsymbol{v}) = -k\nabla\rho + \rho\boldsymbol{f}, \\ &\boldsymbol{v}|_{\partial\Omega} = \mathbf{0}, \\ &\lim_{R\to\infty} \frac{1}{S_\pm} \int_{S_\pm} \rho(\omega, R) d\omega = \rho_\pm, \quad \lim_{R\to\infty} \boldsymbol{v}(\omega, R) = \mathbf{0}. \end{aligned} \tag{5.18}$$

It is in course of preparation a paper with J. Heywood [28] concerning the resolution of the above boundary problem.

Moreover, in unbounded domains, besides the problems of existence and uniqueness, it is also very important, from both mathematical and physical point of wiev, to solve the so called problem of spatial stability. This last question consists in proving that, under certain regularity hypotheses on the external data, there is a control of the solution at infinity, say, the solution doesn't differ too much from its value at infinity after a fixed spatial distance from the boundary. This new kind of study is known as the study of the *asymptotic behaviour* of the solution.

Acknowledgements. The author wishes to express her gratitude to professors R. Russo and G. Starita for their carefull reading of the paper and their useful suggestions. The author is indebted with professor J. Heywood for the help he gave her, during his visit in Italy supported by GNFM of italian CNR, through several stimulating discussions and criticism. We also thank the MURST 40% and 60% contracts and the GNFM of italian CNR.

References.

[1] Adams, R.A.: *Sobolev Spaces*, Academic Press (1975).

[2] Amick, C. J.: Steady Solutions of the Navier–Stokes Equations in Unbounded Channels and Pipes, *Ann. Scuola Norm. Sup. Pisa Cl. Sci.* (4), **4** (1977), 473–513.

[3] Amick, C. J. & and Fraenkel, L. E.: Steady Solutions of the Navier–Stokes Equations Representing Plane Flow in Channels of Various Types, *Acta Math.* **144** (1980), 83–152.

[4] Babenko, K. I.: On stationary solutions of the problem of flow past a body of a viscous incompressible fluid, *Mat. Sb.*, **91** (133), **1** (1973), 1–25.

[5] Batchelor, G. K.: *An introduction to Fluid Dynamics*, Cambridge Univ. Press (1967).

[6] Beirao da Veiga, H.: An L^p-theory for the n-dimensional, stationary compressible Navier–Stokes equations and the incompressible limit for compressible fluids. The equilibrium solutions, *Comm. Math. Phys.*, **109** (1987), 229–248.

[7] Beirao da Veiga, H.: Existence results in Sobolev spaces for a stationary transport equation, *Ricerche Mat.*, vol. in honour of C. Miranda (1987).

[8] Boldrini, J. L.: Stationary spatially periodic compressible flows at high Mach number, *Rend. Sem. Mat. Univ. Padova*, **84** (1990), 201–215.

[9] Chandrashekar, S.: *An introduction to the study of stellar structure.* Dover Publ. inc. (1939).

[10] Chang, I. D. & Finn, R.: On the solutions of a class of equations in continuum mechanics with applications to the Stokes paradox, *Arch. Rational Mech. Anal.*, **7** (1961), 388–441.

[11] Clark, D. C.: The vorticity at infinity for solutions of the stationary Navier–Stokes equations in exterior domains, *Indiana Univ. Math. J.* **20** (1971), 633–654.

[12] Chen, X. & Xie, W.: Discontinuous solutions of steady state, viscous compressible Navier–Stokes equations, *J. Differential Equations*, **115** (1995), 99–119.

[13] Chen, S. E. & Kellogg, B.: An interior discontinuity of a non-linear elliptic-hyperbolic system, *SIAM J. Math. Anal.*, **22** (1991), 602-622.

[14] Courant, R. & Friedrichs, K.O.: *Supersonic flow and shock waves*, Interscience (1948).

[15] Farwig, R: Stationary solutions of the Navier–Stokes equations with slip boundary conditions, *Comm. Partial Differential Equations*, **14** (1989), 1579–1606.

[16] Fichera, G.: Sulle equazioni differenziali lineari ellittico paraboliche del secondo ordine, *Atti Acc. Naz. Lincei Mem. Cl. Sc. Fis. Mat. Nat. Sez. Ia (8)*, **5** (1956), 1–30.

[17] Fichera, G.: On a unified theory of boundary value problem for elliptic-parabolic equations ofl second order in boundary problems, *Differential Equations*, Univ. Wisconsin press (1960), 87–120.

[18] Finn, R.: On the exterior stationary problem for the Navier–Stokes equations and associated perturbation problems, *Arch. Rational Mech. Anal.*, **19** (1965), 363–406.

[19] Finn, R.: Estimates at infinity for stationary solutions of the Navier–Stokes equations, *Bull. Math. Soc. Sci. Math. Phys. R.P. Roumaine* **3** (53) (1959).

[20] FUJITA YASHIMA, H.: Existence et regularité de la solution des equations de Navier–Stokes compressible stationaires, *Scuola Normale Superiore di Pisa*, preprint 1986.

[21] FUJITA YASHIMA, H., NOVOTNY, A. & PADULA, M.: Equation monodimensionnelle d'un gas visqueux et calorifere avec des conditions initiales moins restrictives, *Ricerche Mat.*, **42** (1993), 199–248.

[22] GALDI, G. P.: *An introduction to the mathematical theory of the Navier Stokes equations*, I. II. Springer Tracts in Natural Philosophy (1993).

[23] GALDI, G. P.: On the steady, translational self-propelled motion of a symmetric body in a Navier–Stokes fluid, *Quaderni Mat.*, **1** (1997), 97–169.

[24] GALDI, G. P., NOVOTNY, A. & PADULA, M.: On the twodimensional steady-state problem of a viscous gas in an exterior domain, *Pacific J. of Math.*, **179** (1997), 65–100.

[25] GRESHO, P.M.: Some current CDF issues relevant to the incompressible Navier–Stokes equations, *Comput. Methods Appl. Mech. Eng.*, **87** (1991), 201–252.

[26] HEYWOOD, J. G: On Uniqueness Questions in the Theory of Viscous Flow, *Acta Math.*, **136** (1976), 61–102.

[27] HEYWOOD, J.G., RANNACHER, R. & TUREK, S.: Artificial boundaries and flux and pressure conditions for incompressible Navier–Stokes equations, *Internat. J. Numer. Methods in Fluids* **22** (1996), 325–352.

[28] HEYWOOD, J.G., PADULA, M.: On the existence of stedy flowsof viscous barotropic gas, In preparation.

[29] KAZHIKOV, A.: To a theory of boundary value problems for equations of one-dimensional non-stationary motion of viscous heat-conducting gases, *Boundary value problems for hydrodynamical equations*, **50** Inst. Hydr., Siberian Branch Akad. USSR, (1996) 327–362.

[30] KAWEON, J. R. & KELLOGG, R. B.: Compressible Navier–Stokes equations in a bounded domain with inflow boundary condition, *SIAM J. Math. Anal.*, **28** (1997), 94–108.

[31] KELLOGG, R. B.: Discontinuous solutions of the linearized steady-state, compressible, viscous Navier–Stokes equations, *SIAM J. Math. Anal.*, **19** (1988), 567–579.

[32] Kurtz, D. S., Wheeden R. L.: Results on weighted norm inequalities for multipliers, *Trans. Amer. Math. Soc.*, **255** (1979), 343–363.

[33] Ladyzhenskaja, O. L.: Investigation of the Navier–Stokes Equation for a Stationary Flow of an Incompressible Fluid, *Uspekhi Mat. Nauk.*, **14** (1959), 75–97.

[34] Ladyzhenskaja, O.L.: *The mathematical theory of viscous incompressible flows*, Gordon and Breach Sci. Publ. (1969).

[35] Ladyzhenskaja, O.L. & Solonnikov, A.V.: Determination of solutions of bounady value problems for steady–state Stokes and Navier–Stokes equations in domains having and unbounded integral, *Zap. Nauchn. Sem. Leningrad. Otdel. Mat. Inst. Steklov (LOMI)* **96** (1976), 81–116; english transl.: *J. Soviet Math.* **10** (1978), 257–286.

[36] Lax, P. D. & Phillips, R. S.: Symmetric positive linear differential equations, *Comm. Pure Appl. Math.*, **11** (1958), 333–418.

[37] Leray, J.: Etude de Diverses Équations Intégrales non Linéaires et de Quelques Problèmes que Pose l'Hydrodynamique, *J. Math. Pures Appl.*, **12** (1933), 1–82.

[38] Leray, J.: Sur le mouvement d'une liquide visqueux emplisant l'espace, *Acta Math.*, **63** (1934), 193–248.

[39] Lions, P. L.: Existence globale des solutions pour les equations de Navier–Stokes compressibles isentropiques, *C. R. Acad. Sci. Paris*, **316** (1993), 1335–1340.

[40] Lions, P. L.: Compacité des solutions pour les equations de Navier–Stokes compressibles isentropiques, *C. R. Acad. Sci. Paris*, **317** (1993), 115–120.

[41] Lions, P .L.: Limites inompressible et acoustiques pour des fluides visqueux, compressibles et isentropiques, *C. R. Acad. Sci. Paris*, **317** (1993), 1197–1202.

[42] Liu, B. & Kellogg, B.: Discontinuous solutions of the linearized steady-state, viscous, compressible flows, *J. Math. Anal. Appl.*, in press.

[43] Lovicar, V. & Straskraba, I.: Remark on cavitation solutions of stationary compressible Navier–Stokes equations in one dimension, *Czechoslovak Math. J.*, **41** (1991), 653–662.

[44] Matsumura, A.: Fundamental solution of the linearized system for the exterior stationary problem of compressible viscous flow, in *Pattern and*

Wawes. Qualitative Analysis of Nonlinear Differential Equations. NISHIDA, T., MISUDA, M, FUJII, H. eds., Studies in Mathematics and its Applications **18**, North Holland (1986), 481–505.

[45] MATSUMURA, A. & NISHIDA, T.: Exterior stationary problems for the equations of motion of compressible viscous and heat conductive fluids, *Proc. EQUADIFF* **89**. DAFERMOS, C., LADAS & PAPANICOLAU Eds, M. Dekker Inc. (1989), 473–479.

[46] MATSUMURA, A. & NISHIDA, T.: Exterior stationary problems for the equations of motion of compressible viscous and heat conductive fluids, manuscript (in Japanese) (1989).

[47] MATSUMURA, A. & PADULA, M.: Stability of the stationary solutions of compressible viscous fluids with large external potential forces, *Stab. Appl. Anal. Cont. Media*, **2** (1992), 183–202.

[48] MIRANDA, C.: *Istituzioni di Analisi Funzionale Lineare*, Unione Matematica Italiana, Oderisi Gubbio Editrice (1978)

[49] NAZAROV, S., NOVOTNY, A. & PILECKAS, K.: On steady compressible Navier–Stokes equations in plane domains with corners, *Math. Ann.*, in press.

[50] NAZAROV, S. & SPECOVIUS-NEUGEBAUER, M.: Approximation of exterior boundary value problems for the Stokes system, preprint (1997).

[51] NISHIDA, T.: Equations of fluid dynamics - Free surface problems, *Comm. Pure Appl. Math.*, **39** (1986), 221–238.

[52] NOVOTNY, A.: Steady flows of viscous compressible fluids. L^2-approach, *Proc. of EQUAM 92*, SALVI, R. & STRASKRABA, I. Eds. (1993).

[53] NOVOTNY, A.: About the steady transport equation. L^p-approach in domains with sufficiently smooth boundaries, *Comment. Math. Univ. Carolin.* (1996), in press.

[54] NOVOTNY, A.: Steady flows of viscous compressible fluids in exterior domains under small perturbations of great potential forces, *Math. Models Methods Appl. Sci.*, **3** (1993), 725–757.

[55] NOVOTNY, A.: Compactness of steady compressible isentropic Navier–Stokes equations via the decomposition method, *Preprint of the Univ. of Toulon* (1994).

[56] NOVOTNY, A.: Compactness of steady compressible isentropic Navier–Stokes equations via the decomposition method (the whole $\mathbb{R}^n$), *Preprint of the Univ. of Toulon* (1995).

[57] Novotny, A. & Padula, M.: Existence and uniqueness of stationary solutions for viscous compressible heat conductive fluid with large potential and small nonpotential external forces, *Siberian Math. J.*, **34** (1993), 120–146.

[58] Novotny, A. & Padula, M.: L^p-approach to steady flows of viscous compressible fluids in exterior domains, *Arch. Rational Mech. Anal.*, **126** (1994), 243–297.

[59] Novotny, A. & Padula, M.: Physically reasonable solutions to steady compressible Navier–Stokes equations in 3D-exterior domains ($\boldsymbol{v}_\infty = \mathbf{0}$), *J. Math. Kyoto Univ.*, **36** (1996), 389–422.

[60] Novotny, A. & Padula, M.: Physically reasonable solutions to steady compressible Navier–Stokes equations in 3D-exterior domains ($\boldsymbol{v}_\infty \neq \mathbf{0}$), *Math. Ann.*, **370** (1997), 470–521.

[61] Novotny, A. & Padula, M.: Note about decay of solutions of steady Navier–Stokes equations in 3-D exterior domains, *Differential Integral Equations* **8** (1995), 1833–1842.

[62] Novotny, A. & Penel, P.: An L^p-approach for steady flows of viscous compressible heat conductive gas I, II, *Math. Models Methods Appl. Sci.*, in press.

[63] Novotny, A., Padula, M. & Penel, P.: A remark on the well posedness of the problem of a steady flow of a viscous baarotropic gas in a pipe, *Comm. Partial Differential Equations*, **21** (1996), 23–34.

[64] Novotny, A. & Pileckas K.: On steady compressible Navier–Stokes equations in plane domains with corners, to appear.

[65] Oleinik, O. A.: Linear equations of second order with non negative characteristics form, *Amer. Math. Soc. Transl.*, **65** (1967), 167–199.

[66] Oleinik, O. A. & Radkevic, E. V.: Second order equations with non negative characteristic form, *Amer. Math. Soc. and Plenum Press.*

[67] Padula, M.: Existence and continuous dependence for solutions to the equations of a one-dimensional model in gas-dynamics, *Meccanica*, **17** (1981), 128–135.

[68] Padula, M.: On the uniqueness of viscous compressible steady flows, *Trends in Appl. of Pure Math. to Mech.*, vol. IV (Bratislava, 1981), Pitman (1983), 186–196.

[69] PADULA, M.: An existence theorem for steady state Navier–Stokes equations, *Proc. Symposium "Wavcs and Stability in Contiuum Media"*, ANILE, A. M., MOTTA, S. & PLUCHINO, S. Eds. Catania (1982), 276–278.

[70] PADULA, M.: Existence and uniqueness for viscous steady motions, *Proc. Sem. Fis. e Mat. "Dinamica dei fluidi e gas ionizzati"*, Trieste (1982), 237–260.

[71] PADULA, M.: Uniqueness theorems for steady compressible heat-conducting fluids: bounded domains, *Atti Acc. Naz. Lincei Rend. Cl. Sci. Fis. Mat. Natur.*, **74** (1983), 380–387.

[72] PADULA, M.: Uniqueness theorems for steady compressible heat-conducting fluids: exterior domains, *Atti Acc. Naz. Lincei Rend. Cl. Sci. Fis. Mat. Natur.*, **75** (1983), 56–60.

[73] PADULA, M.: Existence and uniqueness for viscous steady compressible motions, *Arch. Rational Mech. Anal.*, **77** (1987), 89–102.

[74] PADULA, M.: Stability properties of heat-conducting compressible regular flows, *J. Math. Kyoto Univ.*, **3** (1992), 1

[75] PADULA, M.: A representation formula for steady solutions of a compressible fluid moving at low speed, *Transp. Th. Stat. Phys.*, **21** (1992), 593–613.

[76] PADULA, M.: On the exterior steady problem for the equations of a viscous isothermal gas, *Comment. Math. Univ. Carolin.*, **34** (1993), 275–293.

[77] PADULA, M.: Mathematical properties of motions of viscous compressible fluids, *Progress in theoretical and computational fluid mechanics*, GALDI, G. P., MALEK, J. & NECAS, J. Eds. Pittman Reas. Notes in Math. Series **308** (1993), 128–173.

[78] PADULA, M. & PILECKAS, K.: On the existence and asymptotical behaviour of a steady flow of a viscous barotropic gas in a pipe, *Ann. Mat. Pura Appl.*, **172** (1996), 1–28.

[79] PADULA, M., PASSERINI, A. & PATRIA, C.: An existence theorem of steady solutions for the Poisson–Stokes equations in a pipe, In prepaation.

[80] PILECKAS, K. & ZAJACKOWSKI, W. M.: On the free boundary problem for stationary compressible Navier–Stokes equations, *Comm. Math. Phys.*, **129** (1990), 169–204.

[81] POISSON, S. D.: Mèmoire sur les équations gènêrales de l'équilibre et du mouvement des corps solides élastiques et des fluides, *J. Ecole Polytechnique*, **13** (1831), 1–174.

[82] SECCHI, P.: On a stationary problem for compressible Navier–Stokes equations, *Preprint Univ. Trento*, **351** (1991).

[83] SECCHI, P.: A symmetric positive system with non uniformly characteristic boundary, *Preprint Univ. Brescia* (1995).

[84] SERRIN, J.: Mathematical principles of classical fluid mechanics, in *Handbuch der Physik* (ed. C. TRUESDELL) VIII/1, 125–263.

[85] SERRIN, J.: The initial value problem for Navier–Stokes equations, *Nonlinear problems*, Langer, 67–98.

[86] SERRIN, J.: On the uniqueness of compressible fluid motions, *Arch. Rational Mech. Anal.*, **3** (1959), 271–288.

[87] SIMADER, C.: The weak Dirichlet and Neumann problem for the Laplacian in L^q for bounded and exterior domains. Applications, *Nonlinear Analysis, Function Spaces and Applications*, Teubner Texte Math. **4** (1990), 180–223.

[88] SOLONNIKOV, V. A.: On the solvability of boundary and initial-boundary value problems for the Navier–Stokes system in domains with noncompact boundaries, *Pacific J. Math.*, **93** (1981), 443–458.

[89] SOLONNIKOV, V. A.: Stokes and Navier–Stokes equations in domains with non-compact boundaries, *Collége de France Seminar*, Vol.IV, Pitman Research Notes in Math., **84** (1983), 240–349.

[90] SOLONNIKOV, V. A. & PILECKAS, K.: On certain spaces of solenoidal vectors and on the solvability of a boundary-value problem for the system of Navier–Stokes equations in domains with noncompact boundaries, *Zap. Nauchn. Sem. Leningrad. Otdel. Mat. Inst. Steklov (LOMI)*, **73** (1977), 136-1-51; English Transl.: *J. Soviet Math.*, **34** (1986), 2101–2111.

[91] SOLONNIKOV, V. A. & TANI, A.: Free boundary value problem for a viscous compressible flow with a surface tensionn, *Constantin Caratheodory: an international tribute, vol. I, II*, World Sci. (1991) 1270–1303.

[92] STEIN, E. M.: Note on Singular Integrals, *Proc. Amer. Math. Soc.* **8**, 1957, 250-254.

[93] STEIN, E. M. & WEISS, G.: Functional Integrals on n-dimensional Euclidean Space, *J. Math. Mech.*, **7** (1958), 503–514.

[94] STOKES, G. G.: On the theories of the internal friction of fluids in motion, *Trans. Cambridge Phil. Soc.* **8** (1845), 287–319

[95] STRASKRABA, I.: Asymptotic development of vacuums 1-dimensional Navier-Stokes equations of compressible flows, *Nonlinear–World*, **3** (1996), 519–535.

[96] TANI, A.: On the free boundary value problem for a viscous compressible flow, *J. Math. Kyoto Univ.*, **21** (1981), 839–859.

[97] TRUESDELL, C.: The mechanical foundations of elasticity and fluid dynamics, *J. Rational Mech. Anal.* **1** (1956), 125–200.

[98] TRUESDELL, C. & NOLL, W.: The non linear field theories of mechanics, in *Handbuch der Physik* (ed. C. TRUESDELL) III/3 (1957).

[99] VALLI, A.: Periodic and stationary solutions to compressible Navier–Stokes equations via a stability method, *Ann. Scuola Norm. Sup. Pisa*, **4** (1983), 607–647.

[100] VALLI, A.: On the existence of stationary solutions to compressible Navier–Stokes equations, *Ann. Inst. H. Poincaré*, **4** (1987), 99–113.

[101] WEINBERGER, H. F. : Variational properties of steady fall in Stokes flow, *J. Fluid Mech.*, **52** (1972), 321–344.

[102] ZEMANSKI, M. W.: *Heat and thermodynamics*, McGraw-Hill Book C. (1968).

On the magnetohydrodynamic stability

Salvatore Rionero

Contents

1. Introduction

The aim of this paper is to give an account of the stability questions concerning some fundamental magnetohydrodynamic motions. The paper consists of three Sections. The first one consists of two Subsections. First of all we introduce the M.H.D equations in the general case in which Hall and ion-slip currents are taken into account (Subsect. 2.1). In the second Subsection we study the stability of a basic steady motion, in the L^2-norm, and assume that the basic magnetic field is conservative. We show that

i) the Hall current does not give any contribution to the equation governing the norm of the perturbations

ii) the ion-slip current may only dissipate the energy of the perturbations and therefore may only have a stabilizing effect,

iii) the magnetic field may only stabilize the rest state.

Section 3 consists of four Subsections. In Subsection 3.1 we consider the Couette-Poiseuille flow $\mathcal{M}$ arising in a horizontal layer in the presence of Hall and ion-slip currents. The basic magnetic field of $\mathcal{M}$ is not conservative. Our aim is to show that even in this case, the ion-slip current has a strong stabilizing effect, at least with respect to laminar perturbations. Precisely after some preliminaries to stability of $\mathcal{M}$ (Subsect. 3.2), we determine the general condition ensuring the L^2−stability of $\mathcal{M}$ (Subsect. 3.3). Successively (Subsect. 3.4) we show that the embedding magnetic field has a strong stabilizing effect with respect to laminar perturbations. Section 4 is constituted by five Subsections. In Subsection 4.1 we introduce the classical Bénard problem (onset of natural convection), while in Subsection 4.2 we recall the magnetic Bénard problem (MBP) and the strong stabilizing effect of the magnetic field obtained in the linear stability via the normal modes analysis. Further we recall the stability results obtained in the nonlinear stability, via the direct method, when "generalized energies" are chosen as Liapunov functions.In Subsection 4.3 we reconsider the MBP, introduce two natural fields and determine their evolution equations. Successively (Subsection 4.4) we introduce, through these fields, a Liapunov function for the linear stability problem of the MBP. Finally in the last section we consider the variational problem arising in the linked variational problem and indicate how solving this problem one can obtain the same results of linear stability obtained via the normal modes analysis.

2. Equations of anisotropic MHD and some general properties

2.1 - Equations of anisotropic MHD.

The equations of anisotropic MHD are obtained by coupling the Navier-Stokes equations to the Maxwell's equations. Neglecting the displacement currents, assuming that a conservative force F (typically the gravity force) is acting on the fluid and taking into account the Lorentz force, in the Boussinesq approximation and for $(\boldsymbol{x}, t) \in \Omega \times \mathbb{R}^+$ it follows that

$$
\begin{cases}
\nabla \times \boldsymbol{H} = \boldsymbol{J}, \qquad \nabla \times \boldsymbol{E} = -\mu_e \boldsymbol{H}_t, \\
\boldsymbol{v}_t + \boldsymbol{v} \cdot \nabla \boldsymbol{v} = -\dfrac{1}{\rho}\nabla(p - \rho U) + \nu \Delta \boldsymbol{v} + \dfrac{\mu_e}{\rho} \boldsymbol{J} \times \boldsymbol{H} + \\
\qquad\qquad\qquad\qquad + [1 - \alpha(T - T_0)]\boldsymbol{g}, \\
\nabla \cdot \boldsymbol{v} = 0, \qquad \nabla \cdot \boldsymbol{H} = 0 \\
T_t + \boldsymbol{v} \cdot \nabla \boldsymbol{v} = k \Delta T,
\end{cases} \tag{2.1}
$$

where

Ω	=	region filled by the fluid,	$\boldsymbol{g}$	=	vertical gravity field,
$\boldsymbol{v}$	=	velocity field,	ρ	=	mass density,
$\boldsymbol{E}$	=	electric field,	μ_e	=	magnetic permeability,
p	=	pressure field,	ν	=	kinematic viscosity,
U	=	gravity potential,	$\boldsymbol{J}$	=	current density vector,
T	=	temperature field,	k	=	thermal conductivity,
T_0	=	reference temperature,	α	=	coefficient of thermal expansion.

When the fluid is an isotropic conductor of electricity, the classical constitutive equation for $\boldsymbol{J}$ is

$$\boldsymbol{J} = \sigma_e(\boldsymbol{E} + \mu_e \boldsymbol{v} \times \boldsymbol{H}), \tag{2.2}$$

where σ_e is the scalar electrical conductivity. Equation (2.2) is a particular case of the general constitutive equation [1,2]

$$\boldsymbol{J} = \boldsymbol{S} \cdot (\boldsymbol{E} + \mu_e \boldsymbol{v} \times \boldsymbol{H}), \tag{2.3}$$

where $\boldsymbol{S}$ is a double tensor denoting the anisotropic electrical conductivity. There are several cases of real physical interest in which the anisotropy cannot be neglected. This happens, for instance, for a weakly ionized gas in a strong magnetic field (when the mass fraction of the neutral particles is close to the unity and the product $\omega_c\tau$ of the cyclotronic frequency ω_c of the charged particles multiplied by the mean collision time τ is far greater than unity). In these cases equation (1.2) can be written [1,2]

$$(2.4)\quad \boldsymbol{J} + \mu_e\sigma_e\beta_H \boldsymbol{J}\times\boldsymbol{H} + \sigma_e\mu_e\beta_I \boldsymbol{H}\times(\boldsymbol{J}\times\boldsymbol{H}) = \sigma_e(\boldsymbol{E} + \mu_3 \boldsymbol{v}\times\boldsymbol{H} + \frac{\nabla p_e}{e n_e})$$

where

$$\begin{aligned} e &= \text{electron charge},\\ n_e &= \text{electrons number density},\\ p_e &= \text{electronic pressure},\\ \beta_H &= \text{Hall coefficient},\\ \beta_I &= \text{ion-slip coefficient.} \end{aligned}$$

From equations (2.1) and (2.4) it turns out the following well known mathematical model:

$$(2.5)\quad \begin{cases} \boldsymbol{v}_t + \boldsymbol{v}\cdot\nabla\boldsymbol{v} = -\nabla p^* + \nu\Delta\boldsymbol{v} + \dfrac{\mu_e}{\rho}\nabla\times\boldsymbol{H}\times\boldsymbol{H} + [1-\alpha(T-T_0)]\boldsymbol{g} \\ \boldsymbol{H}_t = \nabla\times(\boldsymbol{v}\times\boldsymbol{H}) + \eta_e\Delta\boldsymbol{H} + \beta_H\nabla\times(\boldsymbol{H}\times\nabla\times\boldsymbol{H}) + \\ \qquad + \beta_I\nabla\times[\boldsymbol{H}\times(\boldsymbol{H}\times\nabla\times\boldsymbol{H})], \\ \nabla\cdot\boldsymbol{v} = 0, \\ \nabla\cdot\boldsymbol{H} = 0 \\ T_t + \boldsymbol{v}\cdot\nabla\boldsymbol{v} = k\Delta T, \end{cases}$$

where $p^* = \dfrac{p-\rho U}{p}$ and $\eta_e = \dfrac{1}{\mu_e\sigma_e}$ is the magnetic resistivity.

To equations (2.5) initial and (suitable) boundary conditions must be appended. We consider $\partial\Omega$ rigid and electrically non conducting. Then for $(\boldsymbol{x},t)\in\partial\Omega\times\mathbb{R}^+$ it follows that

$$(2.6)\quad \begin{cases} \boldsymbol{v}(\boldsymbol{x},t) = \boldsymbol{v}_{\partial\Omega}(\boldsymbol{x},t) \\ \boldsymbol{H}_\tau(\boldsymbol{x},t) = \boldsymbol{H}_{\partial\Omega}(\boldsymbol{x},t) \\ T(\boldsymbol{x},t) = T_{\partial\Omega}(\boldsymbol{x},t), \end{cases}$$

where $\boldsymbol{H}_\tau$ is the tangential magnetic field and $\boldsymbol{v}_{\partial\Omega}$ and $\boldsymbol{H}_{\partial\Omega}$ are assigned vectors denoting respectively the velocity of $\partial\Omega$ and the tangential external magnetic field. $T_{\partial\Omega}(\boldsymbol{x},t)$ denotes an assigned temperature on $\partial\Omega$.

Remark 2.1 - The solvability of the problem (2.5)-(2.6), in suitable Sobolev and Holder's spaces, has been recently established [3,4]. In the sequel, however, we consider sufficiently smooth solutions.

2.2 - Equation governing the L^2-norm of perturbations to a basic flow.

We assume here $\beta_I = 0$ and $\partial\Omega$ rigid nonconducting and non-ferromagnetic. Therefore $\boldsymbol{H}$ can be considered continuous across $\partial\Omega$ and $(1.6)_2$ becomes

$$\boldsymbol{H}(\boldsymbol{x},t) = \boldsymbol{H}_{\partial\Omega}(\boldsymbol{x},t), \qquad (\boldsymbol{x},t) \in \partial\Omega \times \mathbb{R}^+ \tag{2.7}$$

where $\boldsymbol{H}_{\partial\Omega}$ now denotes the whole of external magnetic field.

Denoting by $(\boldsymbol{v},\boldsymbol{H},T,p)$, $(\boldsymbol{v}' = \boldsymbol{v}+\boldsymbol{u}, \boldsymbol{H}' = \boldsymbol{H}+\boldsymbol{h}, T' = T+\theta, p' = p+p^*)$, two solutions, from (2.5) it turns out that [5]

$$\begin{cases} \boldsymbol{u}_t = -\boldsymbol{u}\cdot\nabla\boldsymbol{v} - \boldsymbol{v}'\cdot\nabla\boldsymbol{u} + \dfrac{\mu}{\rho}(\boldsymbol{h}\cdot\nabla\boldsymbol{H} + \boldsymbol{H}'\cdot\nabla\boldsymbol{H}') + \\ \qquad\qquad + \nu\Delta\boldsymbol{u} - \alpha\theta\boldsymbol{g} - \nabla\Phi, \\ \dfrac{\partial\boldsymbol{h}}{\partial t} = \boldsymbol{h}\cdot\nabla\boldsymbol{v} + \boldsymbol{H}'\cdot\nabla\boldsymbol{u} - \boldsymbol{u}\cdot\nabla\boldsymbol{H} - \boldsymbol{v}'\cdot\nabla\boldsymbol{h} + \eta\Delta\boldsymbol{h} + \beta_H\boldsymbol{f}, \\ \theta_t = -\boldsymbol{v}'\cdot\nabla\theta - \boldsymbol{u}\cdot\nabla T + k\Delta\theta, \\ \nabla\cdot\boldsymbol{u} = \nabla\cdot\boldsymbol{h} = 0, \\ \Phi = \dfrac{1}{\rho}[p^* + \dfrac{1}{2}\mu(h^2 + 2\boldsymbol{H}\cdot\boldsymbol{h})], \\ \boldsymbol{f} = \nabla\times[\boldsymbol{H}\times(\nabla\times\boldsymbol{h}) + \boldsymbol{h}\times(\nabla\times\boldsymbol{H}')], \end{cases} \tag{2.8}$$

Now — denoting by $\boldsymbol{A}$, $\boldsymbol{B}$, $\boldsymbol{C}$ three vectorial fields — it follows that

$$\nabla\times(\boldsymbol{A}\times\boldsymbol{B}) = (\nabla\cdot\boldsymbol{B})\boldsymbol{A} - (\nabla\cdot\boldsymbol{A})\boldsymbol{B} + \boldsymbol{B} + \boldsymbol{B}\cdot\nabla\boldsymbol{A} - \boldsymbol{A}\cdot\nabla\boldsymbol{B} \tag{2.9}$$

$$\boldsymbol{C}\cdot\nabla\boldsymbol{A}\cdot\boldsymbol{B} = \nabla\cdot[(\boldsymbol{A}\cdot\boldsymbol{B})\boldsymbol{C}] - (\boldsymbol{A}\cdot\boldsymbol{B})\nabla\cdot\boldsymbol{C} - \boldsymbol{C}\cdot\nabla\boldsymbol{B}\cdot\boldsymbol{A}, \tag{2.10}$$

$$C \cdot \nabla A \cdot B = B \cdot \nabla A \cdot C + (\nabla \times A) \times C - B, \tag{2.11}$$

and therefore according to [5] it turns out that

$$\begin{cases} u_t \cdot \Delta u = 2\nabla \cdot (u \cdot d) - 2d : d, \\ h \cdot \Delta h = \nabla \cdot [h \times (\nabla \times h)] - (\nabla \times h)^2, \\ u \cdot \nabla h \cdot u = \dfrac{1}{2}\nabla \cdot (h^2 u), \\ u \cdot \nabla u \cdot u = \dfrac{1}{2}\nabla \cdot (u^2 u), \\ H' \cdot \nabla u \cdot h + H' \cdot \nabla h \cdot u = \nabla \cdot [(u \cdot h)H'], \\ h \cdot \nabla H \cdot u - u \cdot \nabla H \cdot h = (\nabla \times H) \times h \cdot u, \\ \theta\Delta\theta = \dfrac{1}{2}\nabla \cdot \nabla\theta^2 - (\nabla\theta)^2, \\ (\nabla \times h) \cdot \nabla H \cdot h - H \cdot \nabla[\nabla \times h] \cdot h = \\ \qquad = \nabla \cdot [(H \cdot h)\nabla \times h - (h \cdot \nabla \times h)H], \\ (\nabla \times H') \cdot \nabla h \cdot h - h \cdot \nabla(\nabla \times H') \cdot h = -h \cdot \nabla(\nabla \times H)h + \\ \qquad + \nabla \cdot \left[\dfrac{1}{2}h^2 \nabla \times H + h^2 \nabla \times h - (h - \nabla \times h)h\right], \end{cases} \tag{2.12}$$

where d is the symmetric part of ∇u.

On setting

$$\begin{cases} e = \dfrac{1}{2}(\rho u^2 + \mu h^2), \\ q = \dfrac{1}{2}\rho\theta^2, \end{cases} \tag{2.13}$$

it turns out that

$$\begin{aligned} e_t + v \cdot \nabla e = & -\rho(u \cdot \nabla v \cdot u + \alpha\theta u \cdot g + 2\nu d : d) + \nabla \cdot Y + \\ & + \mu[h \cdot \nabla\tilde{v} \cdot h + (\nabla \times H) \times h \cdot u - \eta(\nabla \times h)^2, \end{aligned} \tag{2.14}$$

$$q_t + v \cdot \nabla q = -\rho\theta u \cdot \nabla T - k\rho(\nabla\theta)^2 + \nabla \cdot Z \tag{2.15}$$

where

$$\begin{cases} Y = 2\nu u \cdot d + \eta h \times (\nabla \times h) - \dfrac{1}{2}(\mu h^2 + \rho u^2)u + \\ \qquad + \mu(u \cdot h)H' - \rho\Phi u + Y_1, \\ Y_1 = \mu\beta_H[(h^2 + H \cdot h)\nabla \times h + \dfrac{1}{2}h^2(\nabla \times H) - (h \cdot \nabla \times h)H'], \\ Z = \dfrac{1}{2}\rho(\nabla\theta^2 - \theta^2 u), \end{cases} \tag{2.16}$$

$$\tilde{v} = \boldsymbol{v} - \beta_H \nabla \times \boldsymbol{H}. \tag{2.17}$$

From (2.13)-(2.16) and the boundary conditions

$$\boldsymbol{u} = \boldsymbol{h} = \boldsymbol{0}, \qquad \theta = 0 \quad \text{on } \partial\Omega \tag{2.18}$$

it follows that

$$\begin{aligned}\frac{\mathrm{d}}{\mathrm{d}t}\|e\|^2 = &-\rho \int_\Omega [\boldsymbol{u}\cdot\boldsymbol{D}\cdot\boldsymbol{u} + \alpha\theta\boldsymbol{u}\cdot\boldsymbol{g} + \nu(\nabla\boldsymbol{u})^2]\,\mathrm{d}\Omega + \\ &+\mu\int_\Omega [\boldsymbol{h}\cdot\tilde{\boldsymbol{D}}\cdot\boldsymbol{h} + (\nabla\times\boldsymbol{H})\times\boldsymbol{h}\cdot\boldsymbol{u} - \eta(\nabla\boldsymbol{h})^2]\,\mathrm{d}\Omega,\end{aligned} \tag{2.19}$$

$$\frac{\mathrm{d}}{\mathrm{d}t}\|q\|^2 = -\rho\int_\Omega \theta\boldsymbol{u}\cdot\nabla T + k(\nabla\theta)^2]\,\mathrm{d}\Omega \tag{2.20}$$

where $\|\cdot\|$ denotes the L^2−norm and $\boldsymbol{D}$ and $\tilde{\boldsymbol{D}}$ are the symmetric parts of $\nabla\boldsymbol{v}$ and $\nabla\tilde{\boldsymbol{v}}$ respectively.

On adding (2.19) to (2.20), the equation governing the L^2−norm of the perturbation easily follows.

Remark 2.2 - We notice that

$$\nabla\times\boldsymbol{H} \equiv 0 \Rightarrow \tilde{\boldsymbol{v}} \equiv \boldsymbol{v} \tag{2.21}$$

therefore when the basic magnetic field is conservative, *the Hall current does not give any contribution to the L^2−norm of the perturbations.*

Remark 2.3 - When the basic motion is the rest state and the basic magnetic field is conservative, *i.e.*

$$\nabla\times\boldsymbol{H} \equiv \boldsymbol{v} \equiv 0 \tag{2.22}$$

$$\begin{aligned}\frac{\mathrm{d}}{\mathrm{d}t}[\|e\|^2 + \|q\|^2] = &-\rho\int_\Omega \theta\boldsymbol{u}\cdot(\alpha\boldsymbol{g} + \nabla T)\,\mathrm{d}\Omega + \\ &-\int_\Omega [\rho\nu(\nabla\boldsymbol{u})^2 + \mu\eta(\nabla\boldsymbol{h})^2 + \rho\boldsymbol{k}(\nabla\theta)^2]\,\mathrm{d}\Omega\end{aligned} \tag{2.23}$$

and therefore, in the L^2-norm, *the magnetic field cannot destabilize the rest state.*

Remark 2.4 - Even when $\beta_I \neq 0$, Remark 2.3 continues to hold [6]. In fact in this case one has to add the quantity $\beta_I f^*$ to the right hand side of $(2.8)_2$ where

$$f^* = \nabla \times [\boldsymbol{h} \times (\boldsymbol{H} \times \nabla \times \boldsymbol{H}) + \boldsymbol{H}' \times (\boldsymbol{H} \times \nabla \times \boldsymbol{h} + \boldsymbol{h} \times \nabla \times \boldsymbol{H}')], \tag{2.24}$$

which implies that to the r.h.s. of (1.19) one has to add the quantity

$$\beta_I \int_\Omega \{\nabla\times\boldsymbol{h}\cdot[\boldsymbol{h}\times(\boldsymbol{H}\times\nabla\boldsymbol{H})+\boldsymbol{H}'\times(\boldsymbol{h}\times\nabla\times\boldsymbol{H}')]\}\, d\Omega - \beta_I \|\boldsymbol{H}'\times\nabla\times\boldsymbol{h}\|^2 \tag{2.25}$$

Therefore when $\nabla \times \boldsymbol{H} \equiv 0$, *the ion-slip current cannot destabilize the motion.*

3. Stability of Couette-Poiseuille flows in the anisotropic MHD

3.1 - Couette-Poiseuille flows in an horizontal layer embedded in a coplanar magnetic field.

When the motion is isothermal and occurs in a layer Ω bounded by two rigid electrically non-conducting planes Σ_i (i=1,2), the lower Σ_1 being in rest and Σ_2 translating with the constant velocity $V\boldsymbol{e}_1$ ($V =$ const.> 0), the boundary conditions are

$$\begin{cases} \boldsymbol{v}(\boldsymbol{x},t) = 0 & \boldsymbol{x} \in \Sigma_1, \\ \boldsymbol{v}(\boldsymbol{x},t) = V\boldsymbol{e}_1 & \boldsymbol{x} \in \Sigma_2, \end{cases} \tag{3.1}$$

$$\begin{cases} \boldsymbol{H}_\tau = \boldsymbol{H}_{\Sigma_1} & \boldsymbol{x} \in \Sigma_1, \\ \boldsymbol{H}_\tau = \boldsymbol{H}_{\Sigma_2} & \boldsymbol{x} \in \Sigma_2, \end{cases} \tag{3.2}$$

where $\boldsymbol{H}_{\Sigma_i}$ $(i = 1, 2)$ denotes the tangential external magnetic field.

Denoting by H_i $(i = 1, 2)$ two constants, let us consider [1]

$$\begin{cases} \boldsymbol{H}_{\Sigma_1} = H_1\boldsymbol{e}_1 & \text{on } \Sigma_1, \\ \boldsymbol{H}_{\Sigma_2} = H_2\boldsymbol{e}_1 & \text{on } \Sigma_2, \end{cases} \tag{3.3}$$

[1] This happens, for instance, when Ω is embedded in a coplanar magnetic field.

We introduce a cartesian coordinate system $0xyz = (0, \boldsymbol{i}, \boldsymbol{j}, \boldsymbol{k})$ with the z-axis pointing vertically upwards and we assume that the fluid is confined between the planes $z = -d$ and $z = d > 0$. Then, in the set of the onedimensional laminar flows of the type

$$\text{(3.4)} \qquad \begin{cases} \boldsymbol{v} = v(z)\boldsymbol{e}_1, \\ \boldsymbol{H} = H(z)\boldsymbol{e}_1, \end{cases}$$

the boundary conditions (3.1)-(3.2) become

$$\text{(3.5)} \qquad v(-d) = 0, \qquad v(d) = V$$

$$\text{(3.6)} \qquad H(-d) = H_1, \qquad H(d) = H_2$$

From equations (2.5) it turns out that the flows (3.4) have to satisfy the system

$$\text{(3.7)} \qquad \begin{cases} \dfrac{\partial}{\partial x}(p^* + \dfrac{\mu_e}{2\rho}H^2) = -k, \\ \nu \dfrac{\mathrm{d}^2 v}{\mathrm{d}z^2} = -k, \\ \eta_e \dfrac{\mathrm{d}^2 H}{\mathrm{d}z^2} + \beta_I \dfrac{\mathrm{d}}{\mathrm{d}z}\left(H^2 \dfrac{\mathrm{d}H}{\mathrm{d}z}\right) = 0, \end{cases}$$

where $-k$ is a constant denoting the total pressure gradient.

In view of (3.7) then it follows that

$$\text{(3.8)} \qquad \begin{cases} p^* + \dfrac{\mu_e}{2\rho}H^2 = -kx + p_1^*, \\ v = \dfrac{V}{2d}(z + d) - \dfrac{k}{2\nu}(z^2 - d^2), \\ \beta_I H^3 + 3\eta_e H + c_1 z + c_2 = 0, \end{cases}$$

p_1^* and c_i $(i = 1, 2)$ being constants. Since the discriminant is always positive, exists one and only one real solution of $(2.8)_3$. Therefore, on taking into account conditions (2.7), it is easily seen [7] that the following Couette-Poiseuille flow $\mathcal{M}$ is allowed

$$(3.9) \qquad \begin{cases} v = \dfrac{V}{2d}(z+d) - \dfrac{k}{2\nu}(z^2 - d^2), \\ H = \sqrt[3]{f + \sqrt{f^2+\alpha}} + \sqrt[3]{f - \sqrt{f^2+\alpha}}, \\ p^* + \dfrac{\mu_e}{2\rho} H^2 = -kx + p_1^*, \end{cases}$$

where

$$(3.10) \qquad \begin{cases} f = -\dfrac{c_1 z + c_2}{2\beta_I}, \qquad \alpha = \left(\dfrac{\eta_e}{\beta_I}\right)^3, \\ c_1 = \dfrac{1}{2d}\left[\beta_I(H_1^3 - H_2^3) + 3\eta_e(H_1 - H_2)\right], \\ c_2 = -\dfrac{1}{2}\left[\beta_I(H_1^3 + H_2^3) + 3\eta_e(H_1 + H_2)\right], \end{cases}$$

3.2 - Preliminaries to stability of $\mathcal{M}$.

The stability of MHD Couette-Poiseuille flow has been studied in [8,9]. But the stability conditions obtained there appear not easy and very restrictive, even in the case of laminar perturbations. For these reasons one can fear for an instabilizing "focusing effect". This problem has been studied recently in [7] and has been shown that

i) *does not exist an instabilizing effect of the laminar perturbations,*
ii) *the embedding magnetic field has a strong stabilizing effect.*

Here and in Subsections 2.3, 2.4 we reconsider the question according to the guide-line of [7]. Let us denote by $(\boldsymbol{u}, \boldsymbol{h})$ a perturbation to the basic motion $\mathcal{M}$. Further, let $\mathcal{S}$ be the set (assumed not empty) of the smooth perturbations $(\boldsymbol{u}, \boldsymbol{h})$ such that

$$(3.11) \qquad \begin{cases} \boldsymbol{u} = u_1(z,t)\boldsymbol{e}_1 + u_2(z,t)\boldsymbol{e}_2, \\ \boldsymbol{h} = h_1(z,t)\boldsymbol{e}_1 + h_2(z,t)\boldsymbol{e}_2, \end{cases}$$

It is easily seen [8,9] that the following dimensionless equations and boundary conditions holds [1]

$$(3.12)\quad \begin{cases} \boldsymbol{u}_t = \sigma\Delta\boldsymbol{u} - \nabla\Phi \qquad (z,t)\in[-1,1]\times\mathbb{R}_+, \\ \dfrac{\partial h_1}{\partial t} = \dfrac{\partial^2 h_1}{\partial z^2} + \dfrac{1}{3}R\left[\left(3H^2h_1 + 3Hh_1^2 + h_1^3\right)_z + 3\left(H+h_1\right)h_2\dfrac{\partial h_2}{\partial z}\right]_z, \\ \dfrac{\partial h_2}{\partial t} = \dfrac{\partial^2 h_2}{\partial z^2} + \dfrac{1}{3}R\left[\dfrac{3}{2}h_2\dfrac{\partial}{\partial z}(H+h_1)^2 + \dfrac{\partial h_2^3}{\partial z}\right]_z, \end{cases}$$

$$(3.13)\qquad u_i(+1,t) = h_i(+1,t) = 0 \qquad t\in\mathbb{R}_+, \quad i=1,2$$

where $\sigma = \nu/\eta_e$, $R = (\beta_I\tilde{H}^2)/\eta_e$. We notice that $(2.12)_1$ implies $\|\boldsymbol{u}\|^2 \leq \|\boldsymbol{u}_0\|^2\exp(-\gamma\sigma t)$, $\gamma>0$ being the constant appearing in the onedimensional Poincaré inequality.

3.3 - Nonlinear stability of $\mathcal{M}$ with respect to the perturbations belonging to $\mathcal{S}$.

In view of (3.11)-(3.13), it follows that

$$\begin{aligned} \frac{1}{2}\frac{\mathrm{d}}{\mathrm{d}t}\|\boldsymbol{h}\|^2 = & -\left\|\frac{\partial\boldsymbol{h}}{\partial z}\right\|^2 - R\left[\left\|H\frac{\partial h_1}{\partial z}\right\|^2 + \left\|\boldsymbol{h}\cdot\frac{\partial\boldsymbol{h}}{\partial z}\right\|^2\right] + \\ & - R\int_{-1}^{1} H\left[\frac{\mathrm{d}H}{\mathrm{d}z}(h_1\frac{\partial h_1}{\partial z} + \boldsymbol{h}\cdot\frac{\partial\boldsymbol{h}}{\partial z}) + 2\frac{\partial h_1}{\partial z}(\boldsymbol{h}\cdot\frac{\partial\boldsymbol{h}}{\partial z})\right]\mathrm{d}z + \\ & - R\int_{-1}^{1} H\frac{dH}{dz}h_1(\boldsymbol{h}\cdot\frac{\partial\boldsymbol{h}}{\partial z})\mathrm{d}z \end{aligned}$$

and hence

$$(3.14)\quad \begin{aligned} \frac{1}{2}\frac{\mathrm{d}}{\mathrm{d}t}\|\boldsymbol{h}\|^2 = & -\left[\left\|\frac{\partial\boldsymbol{h}}{\partial z}\right\|^2 + R\left\|H\frac{\partial h_1}{\partial z} + \boldsymbol{h}\cdot\frac{\partial\boldsymbol{h}}{\partial z}\right\|^2\right] + \\ & - R\int_{-1}^{1}\left[\frac{\mathrm{d}H}{\mathrm{d}z}h_1(H\frac{\partial h_1}{\partial z} + \boldsymbol{h}\cdot\frac{\partial\boldsymbol{h}}{\partial z}) + H\frac{\mathrm{d}H}{\mathrm{d}z}\boldsymbol{h}\cdot\frac{\partial\boldsymbol{h}}{\partial z}\right]\mathrm{d}z. \end{aligned}$$

---

[1] We have set

$$z' = \frac{z}{d}, \quad \boldsymbol{u}' = \frac{1}{V}\boldsymbol{u}, \quad \boldsymbol{h}' = \frac{1}{\tilde{H}}\boldsymbol{h}, \quad t' = \frac{\eta_e}{d^2}t$$

where $\tilde{H}$ is a reference magnetic field. Further, for the sake of simplicity, in the equations (3.12)-(3.13) primes have been removed.

But (3.13) implies

$$\int_{-1}^{1} H\frac{\mathrm{d}H}{\mathrm{d}z}\boldsymbol{h}\cdot\frac{\partial \boldsymbol{h}}{\partial z}\mathrm{d}z = -\frac{1}{4}\int_{-1}^{1}\frac{\mathrm{d}^2H^2}{\mathrm{d}z^2}h^2\,\mathrm{d}z,$$

hence on adding and subtracting $\frac{1}{4}\left\|\frac{\mathrm{d}H}{\mathrm{d}z}h_1\right\|^2$, from (3.14) it turns out that

$$\frac{1}{2}\frac{\mathrm{d}}{\mathrm{d}t}\|\boldsymbol{h}\|^2 = -\left[\left\|\frac{\partial \boldsymbol{h}}{\partial z}\right\|^2 + R\left\|\boldsymbol{H}\frac{\partial h_1}{\partial z} + \boldsymbol{h}\cdot\frac{\partial \boldsymbol{h}}{\partial z} + \frac{1}{2}\frac{\mathrm{d}H}{\mathrm{d}z}h_1\right\|^2\right] + \tag{3.15}$$
$$+\frac{R}{4}\left[\left\|\frac{\mathrm{d}H}{\mathrm{d}z}h_1\right\|^2 + \int_{-1}^{1}\frac{\mathrm{d}^2H^2}{\mathrm{d}z^2}h^2\,\mathrm{d}z\right].$$

On removing the primes, the dimensionless form of the equation $(3.8)_3$ can be written

$$RH^3 + 3H + \gamma_1 z + \gamma_2 = 0 \tag{3.16}$$

where

$$\begin{cases} \gamma_1 = \dfrac{c_1 d}{\eta_e \tilde{H}} = +\dfrac{1}{2}\left[R(H_1^3 - H_2^3) + 3(H_1 - H_2)\right], \\ \gamma_2 = \dfrac{c_2}{\eta_e \tilde{H}} = -\dfrac{1}{2}\left[R(H_1^3 + H_2^3) + 3(H_1 + H_2)\right]. \end{cases} \tag{3.17}$$

Since

$$\begin{cases} \dfrac{\mathrm{d}H}{\mathrm{d}z} = -\dfrac{\gamma_1}{3(1+RH^2)}, \\ \dfrac{\mathrm{d}^2H}{\mathrm{d}z^2} = -\dfrac{2RH}{1+RH^2}\left(\dfrac{\mathrm{d}H}{\mathrm{d}z}\right)^2, \\ \dfrac{\mathrm{d}^2H^2}{\mathrm{d}z^2} = 2\left[\left(\dfrac{\mathrm{d}H}{\mathrm{d}z}\right)^2 + HH"\right] = 2\left(\dfrac{\mathrm{d}H}{\mathrm{d}z}\right)^2\left(1 - \dfrac{2RH^2}{1+RH^2}\right), \end{cases} \tag{3.18}$$

from (3.15) it follows that

$$\frac{1}{2}\frac{\mathrm{d}}{\mathrm{d}t}\|\boldsymbol{h}\|^2 = (R\mathcal{F} - 1)D_1 - D_2 \tag{3.19}$$

where

$$(3.20)\qquad \begin{cases} \mathcal{F} = \dfrac{I}{D_1}, \\[2ex] I = \dfrac{1}{4}\displaystyle\int_{-1}^{1}\left(\frac{\mathrm{d}H}{\mathrm{d}z}\right)^2(3h_1^2+2h_2^2)\mathrm{d}z - \frac{R}{4}\left\|\frac{\dfrac{\mathrm{d}H^2}{\mathrm{d}z}\boldsymbol{h}}{\sqrt{1+RH^2}}\right\|^2, \\[2ex] D_1 = \left\|\dfrac{\partial \boldsymbol{h}}{\partial z}\right\|^2, \qquad D_2 = R\left\|H\dfrac{\partial h_1}{\partial z} + \boldsymbol{h}\cdot\dfrac{\partial \boldsymbol{h}}{\partial z} + \dfrac{1}{2}\dfrac{\mathrm{d}H}{\mathrm{d}z}h_1\right\|^2. \end{cases}$$

Now we define R_E by

$$(3.21)\qquad \frac{1}{R_E} = \max_{I}\mathcal{F}$$

where

$$(3.22)\qquad I = \{\boldsymbol{h} \in C^2(-1,1) : \boldsymbol{h} = 0 \text{ when } x = \pm 1\},$$

therefore it turns out that

$$\frac{1}{2}\frac{\mathrm{d}}{\mathrm{d}t}\|\boldsymbol{h}\|^2 \le \left(\frac{R}{R_E} - 1\right)D_1 - D_2$$

and hence, by the Poincarè inequality, it follows that

$$R < R_E \quad \Rightarrow \quad \|\boldsymbol{h}\| \to 0 \quad \text{exponentially}$$

i.e.

$$(3.23)\qquad R < R_E$$

guarantees the nonlinear asymptotic exponential stability in the L^2 – norm.

3.4 - Stabilizing effect of the embedding magnetic field.

Owing to the high nonlinearity of the basic motion $\mathcal{M}$, the Euler-Lagrange equations of the variational problem (3.21) appear not easy. Nevertheless it is possible to determine some stability conditions which appear large and much less restrictive and involved than the conditions obtained in [8,9]

i) *Nonlinear stability in the case $H_1 = H_2$.*

Because of $(3.17)_1$-$(3.18)_1$, $H_1 = H_2 \Rightarrow \left\{\gamma_1 = 0, \frac{\mathrm{d}H}{\mathrm{d}z} = 0, \forall z \in [-1,1]\right\}$. Hence (3.14) implies

$$\|\boldsymbol{h}\|^2 \leq \|h(0)\|^2 e^{-2\pi^2 t} \tag{3.24}$$

ii) *Nonlinear stability for big R in the case $H_i \neq 0$ $(i = 1,2)$ and stabilizing effect of the embedding magnetic field.*

From (3.15) and (3.20) it follows that

$$\begin{aligned}\frac{1}{2}\frac{\mathrm{d}}{\mathrm{d}t}\|\boldsymbol{h}\|^2 \leq \int_{-1}^{1}\left[\frac{R}{4}\left(\frac{\mathrm{d}H}{\mathrm{d}z}\right)^2(3 - 4RH^2)1 + RH^2) - \pi^2\right] h^2\,\mathrm{d}z + \\ - R\left\|H\frac{\partial h_1}{\partial z} + \boldsymbol{h}\cdot\frac{\partial \boldsymbol{h}}{\partial z} + \frac{1}{2}\frac{\mathrm{d}H}{\mathrm{d}z}h_1\right\|^2.\end{aligned} \tag{3.25}$$

Therefore the condition

$$R > \frac{3}{H^2}, \qquad \forall z \in [-1,1] \tag{3.26}$$

guarantees the stability of $\mathcal{M}$ according to the exponential decay (3.24). We remark that, according to $(2.18)_1$, H is a monotone function of z. Therefore on defining

$$H_0 = \min(|H_1|, |H_2|), \tag{3.27}$$

when $H_0 \neq 0$ the condition (3.26) becomes

$$R > \frac{3}{H_0^2} \tag{3.28}$$

and shows *the stabilizing effect of the embedding magnetic field.*

iii) *Complementary conditions of nonlinear stability.*

From (3.25) it follows that the stability of $\mathcal{M}$ is guaranteed by

$$R\left(\frac{\mathrm{d}H}{\mathrm{d}z}\right)^2(3-\frac{4RH^2}{1+RH^2})\leq 4\pi^2,\qquad \forall z\in[-1,1] \tag{3.29}$$

and hence by

$$3R\left(\frac{\mathrm{d}H}{\mathrm{d}z}\right)^2\leq 4\pi^2+R^2(H\frac{\mathrm{d}H}{\mathrm{d}z})^2+4\pi^2RH^2,\qquad \forall z\in[-1,1] \tag{3.30}$$

From (3.18) it follows that

$$\left(\frac{\mathrm{d}H}{\mathrm{d}z}\right)^2=\frac{\gamma_1^2}{9(1+RH^2)^2} \tag{3.31}$$

Therefore (3.29) is satisfied when

$$R(3-RH_0^2)\leq\frac{36\pi^2}{\gamma_1^2}(1+RH_0^2) \tag{3.32}$$

and hence when

$$\gamma_1^2R<12\pi^2(1+RH_0^2) \tag{3.33}$$

On choosing suitably $\boldsymbol{e}_1$, we can assume $H_1>H_2$ and hence

$$\begin{cases} a=H_1^3-H_2^3>0,\\ b=H_1-H_2>0,\\ \gamma_1=\dfrac{1}{2}(aR+3b)>0, \end{cases} \tag{3.34}$$

Therefore (3.33) is satisfied when

$$R(aR+3b)^2\leq 48\pi^2 \tag{3.35}$$

Since the left hand side of (3.35) increases from 0 to ∞ when R runs from 0 to ∞, the following stability condition follows

$$(3.36)\qquad \begin{cases} R \le \overline{R}, \\ \sqrt{\overline{R}} \cdot (a\overline{R} + 3b) = 4\sqrt{3}\pi, \end{cases}$$

where[1]

$$(3.37)\qquad \overline{R}^{\frac{1}{2}} = \sqrt[3]{\frac{2\sqrt{3}\pi}{a} + \sqrt{\frac{12\pi^2}{a^2} + \left(\frac{b}{a}\right)^3}} - \sqrt[3]{\frac{2\sqrt{3}\pi}{a} - \sqrt{\frac{12\pi^2}{a^2} + \left(\frac{b}{a}\right)^3}}$$

Since (3.33) is also satisfied when

$$(3.38)\qquad \gamma_1^2 \le 12\pi^2 H_0^2$$

the stability condition

$$(3.39)\qquad R < \frac{4\sqrt{3}\pi H_0 - 3(H_1 - H_2)}{H_1^3 - H_2^3}$$

immediately follows.

On passing now to (3.30), we notice that it is satisfied when

$$(3.40)\qquad R^2 \left(H\frac{\mathrm{d}H}{\mathrm{d}z}\right)^2 - 3R\left(\frac{\mathrm{d}H}{\mathrm{d}z}\right)^2 + 4\pi^2 > 0, \qquad \forall R$$

and hence when

$$(3.41)\qquad 9\left(\frac{\mathrm{d}H}{\mathrm{d}z}\right)^2 - 16\pi^2 H^2 < 0$$

Therefore the stability condition

$$(3.42)\qquad |H_1| \exp\left[-\frac{4\pi(z+1)}{3}\right] \le |H| \le |H_1| \exp\left[\frac{4\pi(z+1)}{3}\right],$$

$\forall z \in [-1, 1]$ easily follows.

---

[1] Let us notice that, because of (3.34) the discriminant of (3.36) is positive.

iv) *A condition ensuring the nonlinear stability* $\forall R > 0$.

On coupling (3.28) to (3.39) [or to (3.36)], it is not hard to obtain conditions ensuring the nonlinear stability of $\mathcal{M}$, $\forall R > 0$. For instance, let be $H_1 > H_2 > 0$. On choosing suitably $\tilde{H}$, we may assume $H_0 = H_2 = 1$. Hence it follows that

$$\frac{4\sqrt{3}\pi H_0 - 3(H_1 - H_2)}{H_1^3 - H_2^3} = 4\sqrt{3}\pi H_0 H_1^3 - H_2^3 - \frac{3}{H_1^2 + H_1 H_2 + H_2^2} \geq \frac{4\sqrt{3}\pi}{H_1^3 - 1} - 1$$

Therefore

$$\frac{4\sqrt{3}\pi}{H_1^3 - 1} - 1 \geq 3$$

and hence

$$1 \leq H_1^3 < 1 + \sqrt{3}\pi$$

ensures the nonlinear stability of $\mathcal{M}$, $\forall R > 0$.

4. The onset of natural convection: Bénard problem

4.1 - Introduction.

Because of its relevance in many geophisical and industrial applications, the onset of convection has attracted - in the past as nowdays - the attention of many reserchers. According to [10] the essential feature of the phenomenon is as follows. Let S be a horizontal layer of fluid in the rest state and heated from below in such a way that an adverse temperature gradient β is maintained in S. Because of thermal expansions, the fluid at the bottom expands as it becomes hotter. When β reaches a critical value β_c, the buoyancy overcomes gravity, the fluid rises and a pattern of cellular motion may be seen. This is the onset of natural convection. The phenomenon - although recognized earlier by Rumford (1797) and Tomson (1882) - is called Bénard convection because of his experiments (1900) on this phenomenon. Of course, at the onset of convection the rest state loses stability.

Concerning the critical value β_c of β, we point out that it is not the exact parameter for determining the onset of convection. In fact, the onset of convection depends also on the layer depth d, and the correct non-dimensional parameter for describing this *threshold phenomenon* is the Rayleigh number[1]

$$R^2 = \frac{g\alpha\beta d^4}{k\nu}.$$

Rayleigh showed that the onset of convection happens when R^2 surpasses a certain critical value. We refer to [11] for the study of stability of the rest state by means of the method of linear stability via the normal modes analysis. The critical value R^2_L obtained there are contained in Table I.

TABLE I - *Critical value R^2_L of the Rayleigh number R^2 obtained by the normal modes analysis of linear stability*

R^2_L	**Nature of bounding surfaces**
657.511	Both free
1707.762	Both rigid
1100.65	One free and one rigid

For the nonlinear energy stability we refer to [12] and recall the result, first established by D.D. Joseph in 1965 , of the coincidence of the critical Rayleigh number R^2_L of linear stability and the critical Rayleigh number R^2_E of non-linear stability in the L^2-norm.

4.2 - Magnetic Bénard problem.

When the fluid is electrically conducting and embedded in a vertical magnetic field, in the isotropic M.H.D context the linear stability (normal modes analysis) predicts stabilizing effects of the magnetic field. The critical value of R^2 are contained in Table II.

[1] We notice that in Section 4, R^2 has a meaning completely different of the which one of Section 3

TABLE II - *Linear critical Rayleigh numbers R_L^2 obtained by the normal modes method of linear stability when: both bounding surfaces are free, the fluid is embedded in a vertical magnetic field and instability sets in as stationary convection; $Q=$ Chandrasekhar number measuring the vertical magnetic field of the rest state (Subsect. 4.3).*

Q^2	R_L^2
0	657.11
5	796.573
50	1762.04
500	8578.88
5000	63135.9

Remark 4.1 - It is to underline that the result of the linear stability, obtained by the normal modes analysis, are in agreement with the experimental ones [11].

Passing to the nonlinear energy stability theory in order to obtain the afore said effect Rionero [13] by using as Liapunov functional the standard energy (L^2-norm) of the perturbations obtained the non-destabilizing effect of the magnetic field. Successively a lot of efforts have been made in order to obtain the stabilizing effect of the magnetic field and the coincidence between the critical Rayleigh numbers of the L.S. and of N.L.E.S. In [14] the stabilizing effect of the magnetic field has been obtained, but the result given there fall short of those of L.S. In [17] the coincidence between the linear and nonlinear critical Rayleigh numbers has been obtained in the case $\{P_m < P_r,\ Q^2 \leq 105.18,\ R^2 \leq 2741.3\}$ where P_m and P_r are the magnetic and the usual Prandt numbers respectively.

The non-linear afore said results have been obtained by introducing the so called generalized energies i.e. Liapunov functionals V generalizing, in many aspects, the L^2-norm of the perturbations. Essentially a generalized energy V differs from the standard one because dipends on the spatial derivatives of the perturbations and is composed by two parts

$$V = V_0 + V_1$$

having different goals

i) V_0 *is a Liapunov functional of the linear problem and furnishes the critical Rayleigh number* R_E^2 *of L.S.(linear stability)*

ii) V_1 *dominates the nonlinear terms and governs the restrictions on the initial data under which* $R^2 < R_E^2$ *assures N.L.S.(nonlinear stability)*

Remark 4.2 - When the operator governing the linear problem is symmetric or symmetrizzable in a (suitable) functional space, then (in this space) one has $R_L^2 = R_E^2$ [10,19].

Remark 4.3 - The operator governing the linear problem of the M.B.P. is not symmetric in the L^2-norm [19].

4.3 - Two "natural" balances equations.

The introduction of a new balance equation in the study of the Bénard problem has been generated by D.D.Joseph [12]. This introduction opened a new way for obtaining results of nonlinear stability close to which ones of linear stability [14-18]. In particular in [20] (see also [10],[21]) by introducing a "natural" field - i.e. a field which appears in the equations governing the problem - it has been possible to obtain the coincidence between the critical values of R^2 of linear and nonlinear stability in the case of the rotating Bénard problem, when P_r =1. Recently by introducing two natural balances generating a system of two diffusion equation of the Dufour-Soret type, it has been reached the afore said coincidence in the

i) rotating Bénard problem for any P_r [22]

ii) Bénard problem for a mixture [23,24]

iii) magnetic Bénard problem in the free-free boundary conditions [25,26].

Our aim in this Part is to give an account of the problem iii), limiting ourselves in considering only the choice of V_0 in connexion with the L.S. via the Liapunov direct method. In other words, we give an account of the choice of the Liapunov functional V_0 for the linear stability which enables to reach the same critical value of R^2 obtained via the normal modes analysis.

We denote by $m_0 = (\tilde{\boldsymbol{v}} = 0,\ \tilde{\boldsymbol{H}} = H\boldsymbol{k}, \tilde{T} = -\beta z + \tilde{T}_0, \tilde{p})$ the rest state. The non-dimensional equations for a perturbation $(\boldsymbol{u}, \boldsymbol{h}, \theta, p_1)$ to m_0 are

$$(4.1)\qquad \begin{cases} \boldsymbol{u}_t + \boldsymbol{u}\cdot\nabla\boldsymbol{u} - P_m\boldsymbol{h}\cdot\nabla\boldsymbol{h} = -\nabla p_1 + R\theta\boldsymbol{k} + \Delta\boldsymbol{u} + Qh_z, \\ P_m(\boldsymbol{h}_t + \boldsymbol{u}\cdot\nabla\boldsymbol{h} - \boldsymbol{h}\cdot\nabla\boldsymbol{u}) = Q\boldsymbol{u}_z + \Delta\boldsymbol{h}, \\ P_r(\boldsymbol{\theta}_t + \boldsymbol{u}\cdot\nabla\theta) = Rw + \Delta\theta, \\ \nabla\cdot\boldsymbol{u} = \nabla\cdot\boldsymbol{h} = 0, \end{cases}$$

in the space-time cylinder $\mathbb{R}^2 \times (0,1) \times (0,\infty)$ and where

$$\begin{aligned} \boldsymbol{u} = (u, v, w) =&\ \text{perturbation in the velocity field,} \\ \boldsymbol{h} = (h_1, h_2, h) =&\ \text{perturbation in the magnetic field,} \\ \theta =&\ \text{perturbation in the temperature field,} \\ p_1 =&\ \text{perturbation in the pressure field (incorporating} \\ &\ \text{the magnetic pressure),} \\ P_r = \frac{\nu}{k} =&\ \text{Prandtl number,} \\ P_m = \frac{\nu}{\eta} =&\ \text{Prandtl magnetic field,} \\ Q^2 = \frac{\mu H d^2}{4\pi\rho\nu\eta} =&\ \text{Chandrasekhar number.} \end{aligned}$$

With the system (4.1) we adopt the typical boundary conditions of stress-free and not ferromagnetic boundary

$$(4.2)\qquad \begin{cases} u_z = v_z = w = \theta = h_1 = h_2 = h_z = 0, \\ w_{zz} = \Delta h_z = 0, \end{cases} \qquad \text{on } z = 0, 1.$$

We assume that the perturbations fields are periodic function of x and y of periods $\frac{2\pi}{a_1}, \frac{2\pi}{a_2}$ $(a_1 > 0,\ a_2 > 0)$ and denote by Ω the perodicity cell

$$\Omega = \left[0, \frac{2\pi}{a_1}\right] \times \left[0, \frac{2\pi}{a_2}\right] \times [0, 1]$$

We also require the "average conditions"

$$\int_\Omega u\,\mathrm{d}\Omega = \int_\Omega v\,\mathrm{d}\Omega = \int_\Omega h\,\mathrm{d}\Omega = 0. \tag{4.3}$$

We introduce the new fields

$$\begin{cases} \Psi = R\theta \boldsymbol{k} + Q\boldsymbol{h}_z, \\ \chi_1 = R\theta \boldsymbol{k} + p\delta Q\boldsymbol{h}_z, \end{cases} \tag{4.4}$$

where

$$p = \frac{P_m}{P_r}, \qquad \delta \in \mathbb{R}$$

We notice that $\boldsymbol{\Psi}$ is a "natural" field because appears in the equation $(4.1)_1$. In order to ensures a one-to-one correspondence between $(\boldsymbol{\Psi}, \chi_1)$ and $(\theta, \boldsymbol{h}_z)$ we request

$$p\delta \neq 1 \tag{4.5}$$

and then it follows that

$$R\theta\boldsymbol{k} = \frac{p\delta\boldsymbol{\Psi} - \chi_1}{p\delta - 1}, \qquad Q\boldsymbol{h_z} = \frac{\chi_1 - \boldsymbol{\Psi}}{p\delta - 1}. \tag{4.6}$$

The evolution equations of $\boldsymbol{\Psi}$ and χ_1 are found to be

$$\begin{cases} P_m\boldsymbol{\Psi}_t + P_m[R\boldsymbol{u}\cdot\nabla\theta\boldsymbol{k} + Q(\boldsymbol{u}\cdot\nabla\boldsymbol{h})_z - Q(\boldsymbol{h}\cdot\nabla\boldsymbol{u})_z] = \\ \qquad = pR^w\boldsymbol{k} + pR\Delta\theta\boldsymbol{k} + Q^2\boldsymbol{u}_{zz} + Q\Delta\boldsymbol{h}_z, \\ P_r\chi_{1t} + P_r[R\boldsymbol{u}\cdot\nabla\theta\boldsymbol{k} + p\delta Q(\boldsymbol{u}\cdot\nabla\boldsymbol{k})_z - p\delta Q(\boldsymbol{h}\cdot\nabla\boldsymbol{u})_z] = \\ \qquad = R^2w\boldsymbol{k} + R\Delta\theta\boldsymbol{k} + \delta Q^2\boldsymbol{u}_{zz} + \delta Q\Delta\boldsymbol{h}_z. \end{cases} \tag{4.7}$$

Linearizing (4.1) and (4.7) it follows that

$$\begin{cases} \boldsymbol{u}_t = -\nabla p_1 + \Delta\boldsymbol{u} + \boldsymbol{\Psi}, \\ \nabla\cdot\boldsymbol{u} = \nabla\cdot\boldsymbol{h} = 0, \\ P_m\boldsymbol{\Psi}_t = pR^2w\boldsymbol{k} + Q^2\boldsymbol{u}_{zz} + \dfrac{p^2\delta - 1}{p\delta - 1}\Delta\boldsymbol{\Psi} + \dfrac{1-\delta}{p\delta - 1}\Delta\chi_1, \\ P_r\chi_{1t} = R^2w\boldsymbol{k} + \delta Q^2\boldsymbol{u}_{zz}\dfrac{\delta(p-1)}{p\delta - 1}\Delta\boldsymbol{\Psi} + \dfrac{\delta - 1}{p\delta - 1}\Delta\chi_1. \end{cases} \tag{4.8}$$

Applying the operator $\nabla\times\nabla\times$ to $(4.8)_1, (4.8)_3$ and $(4.8)_4$ and on setting

$$\begin{cases} \Phi = -\boldsymbol{k}\cdot\nabla\times\nabla\times\boldsymbol{\Psi} = R\Delta_1\theta + Q\Delta h_z, \\ \chi = -\boldsymbol{k}\cdot\nabla\times\nabla\times\boldsymbol{\chi}_1 = R\Delta_1\theta + p\delta Q\Delta h_z, \end{cases} \tag{4.9}$$

$$\xi = \boldsymbol{k}\cdot\nabla\times\boldsymbol{u}, \qquad \Delta_1 = \frac{\partial}{\partial x^2} + \frac{\partial}{\partial y^2}, \qquad \xi^{(m)} = \boldsymbol{k}\cdot\nabla\times\boldsymbol{h} \tag{4.10}$$

it turns out that

$$\begin{cases} \Delta w_t = \phi + \Delta\Delta w, \\ P_m\Phi_t = pR^2\Delta_1 w + Q^2\Delta w_{zz} + \dfrac{p^2\delta - 1}{p\delta - 1}\Delta\Phi + \dfrac{1-p}{p\delta - 1}\Delta\chi, \\ P_r\chi_t = R^2\Delta_1 w + \delta Q^2\Delta w_{zz} + \dfrac{\delta(p-1)}{p\delta - 1}\Delta\Phi + \dfrac{\delta - 1}{p\delta - 1}\Delta\chi, \end{cases} \tag{4.11}$$

$$\begin{cases} \xi_t = \Delta\xi + Q\xi_z^{(m)}, \\ P_m\xi_t^{(m)} = Q\xi_z + \Delta\xi^{(m)}. \end{cases} \tag{4.12}$$

We notice that (4.12) immediately implies

$$\frac{\mathrm{d}}{\mathrm{d}t}\left[\frac{1}{2}\|\xi\|^2 + \frac{P_m}{2}\|\xi^{(m)}\|^2\right] = -\|\nabla\xi\|^2 - \|\nabla\xi^{(m)}\|^2 \tag{4.13}$$

and therefore $\|\xi\|$ and $\|\xi^{(m)}\|$ decrease and run exponentially to zero as $t\to\infty$.

4.4 - Linear stability via the Liapunov direct method.

We choice as Liapunov function for the linear stability the following one

$$V_0 = \frac{1}{2}[\lambda\|\Delta w\|^2 + P_m\|\Phi\|^2 + \mu P_r\|\chi\|^2]. \tag{4.14}$$

Because $\chi = \Phi = 0$ on $z = 0, 1$, along the solutions of (4.11) it follows that

$$\frac{\mathrm{d}V_0}{\mathrm{d}t} = I_0 - D_0, \tag{4.15}$$

where

$$(4.16)\qquad \begin{cases} I_0 = \lambda(\Phi, \Delta w) + \mu R^2(\Delta_1 w, \boldsymbol{\chi}) + \mu\delta Q^2(\Delta w_{zz}, \boldsymbol{\chi}) + \\ \qquad + pR^2(\Delta_1 w, \Phi) + Q^2(\Delta w_{zz}, \Phi), \\ D_0 = \lambda\|\nabla\Delta w\|^2 + \mu\dfrac{\delta - 1}{p\delta - 1}\|\nabla\boldsymbol{\chi}\|^2 \dfrac{p^2\delta - 1}{p\delta - 1}\|\nabla\Phi\|^2 + \\ + \dfrac{(p-1)(\mu\delta - 1)}{p\delta - 1}(\nabla\Phi, \nabla\boldsymbol{\chi}), \end{cases}$$

$$(4.17)\qquad (f, g) = \int_\Omega f g \, \mathrm{d}\Omega,$$

λ and μ being suitable positive parameters to be chosen later.

Remark 4.4 - On requiring

$$(4.18)\qquad \frac{p^2\delta - 1}{p\delta - 1} > 0, \quad \mu\frac{\delta - 1}{p\delta - 1} > 0, \quad (p-1)^2(\mu\delta - 1)^2 < 4\mu(\delta - 1)(p^2\delta - 1),$$

D_0 becomes positive definite.

Remark 4.5 - We assume $p < 1$ and choice $\delta < 1$. Then $p < 1$ implies that Hopf bifurcations cannot occur [11], while $\delta < 1$ implies $p\delta < 1$ and therefore $(4.18)_1 - (4.18)_2$ are verified.

On setting

$$(4.19)\qquad m = \max_{\mathcal{H}} \frac{I_0}{D_0}$$

$\mathcal{H}$ = space of admissible functions = $\{\boldsymbol{u}, \Psi, \Phi$, regular periodic fields, verifying (3.2)-(3.3); $0 < D_0 < \infty\}$, (14) gives

$$(4.20)\qquad \frac{\mathrm{d}V_0}{\mathrm{d}t} \leq (1 - m)D_0.$$

Assuming (4.18) it follows that exists a positive real number α_1 such that

$$(4.21)\qquad \begin{cases} \alpha_1(\|\nabla\Phi\|^2 + \|\nabla\boldsymbol{\chi}\|^2) \leq \mu\dfrac{\delta - 1}{p\delta - 1}\|\nabla\boldsymbol{\chi}\|^2 + \dfrac{p^2\delta - 1}{p\delta - 1}\|\nabla\Phi\|^2 + \\ \qquad + \dfrac{(p-1)(\mu\delta - 1)}{p\delta - 1}(\nabla\Phi, \nabla\boldsymbol{\chi}), \\ \alpha_1 = \dfrac{4\mu(\delta - 1)(p^2\delta - 1) - (p-1)^2(\mu\delta - 1)^2}{4(p\delta - 1)[p^2\delta - 1 + \mu(\delta - 1)]} > 0. \end{cases}$$

Therefore $\{m<1$, (4.20)-(4.21) and $(3.15)_2\}$ imply

$$\dot{V}_0 \le (m-1)[\alpha_1\|\nabla\Phi\|^2 + \alpha_1\|\nabla\boldsymbol{\chi}\|^2 + \lambda\|\nabla u\|^2]. \tag{4.22}$$

By using the

i) Poincare' inequality

$$\pi^2 \int_\Omega f^2\, d\Omega \le \int_\Omega |\nabla f|^2\, d\Omega \tag{4.23}$$

when $f=0$ on $z=0,1$,

ii) Wirtinger inequality

$$\pi_0^2 \int_\Omega f^2\, d\Omega \le \int_\Omega |\nabla f|^2\, d\Omega \tag{4.24}$$

with $\pi_0^2 = \min(\pi^2, a_1^2, a_2^2)$ when

$$\int_\Omega f\, d\Omega = 0, \qquad f_z = 0 \qquad \text{on } z=0,1 \tag{4.25}$$

it turns out that

$$\dot{V}_0 \le 2\pi_0^2\gamma_1(m-1)V_0 \tag{4.26}$$

where

$$\gamma_1 = \min\left(\frac{\alpha_1}{P_m}, \frac{\alpha_1}{\mu P_r}, 1\right). \tag{4.27}$$

Integrating (4.26), we obtain

$$m<1 \qquad \to \qquad V_0 \le V_0(0)\exp\{-2\pi_0^2\gamma_1(1-m)t\} \tag{4.28}$$

4.5 - Variational problem of linear stability via the Liapunov direct method and coincidence of the critical parameters.

The Euler-Lagrange equations associated to (4.18) are found to be

$$
\text{(4.29)} \quad \begin{cases}
\lambda\Delta\Phi + pR^2\Delta_1\Phi + Q^2\Delta\Phi_{zz} + \mu R^2\Delta_1\chi + \\
\qquad + \mu\delta Q^2\Delta\chi_{zz} + 2m\lambda\Delta\Delta\Delta w = 0, \\
\lambda\Delta w + pR^2\Delta_1 w + Q^2\Delta w_{zz} + 2m\dfrac{p^2\delta - 1}{p\delta - 1}\Delta\Phi + \\
\qquad + m\dfrac{(p-1)(\mu\delta - 1)}{p\delta - 1}\Delta\chi = 0, \\
\mu R^2\Delta_1 w + \mu\delta Q^2\Delta w_{zz} + 2m\mu\dfrac{\delta - 1}{p\delta - 1}\Delta\chi + \\
\qquad + m\dfrac{(p-1)(\mu\delta - 1)}{p\delta - 1}\Delta\Phi = 0.
\end{cases}
$$

In order to have non vanishing "plan form" solutions, it has to be

$$B_1 m^2 = A_1,$$

where $(n = 1, 2, \ldots)$

$$
\text{(4.30)} \quad \begin{cases}
A_1 = \dfrac{p^2\delta - 1}{p\delta - 1}\mu^2[\delta Q^2 n^2\pi^2(n^2\pi^2 + a^2) - R^2a^2]^2 + \\
\quad + \mu\dfrac{\delta - 1}{p\delta - 1}[-\lambda(n^2\pi^2 + a^2) - pR^2a^2 + n^2\pi^2Q^2(n^2\pi^2 + a^2)]^2 + \\
\quad - \mu\dfrac{(p-1)(\mu\delta - 1)}{p\delta - 1}[\delta Q^2 n^2\pi^2(n^2\pi^2 + a^2) - R^2a^2] \times \\
\quad \times [-\lambda(n^2\pi^2 + a^2) - pR^2a^2 + n^2\pi^2Q^2(n^2\pi^2 + a^2)], \\
B_1 = \lambda(n^2\pi^2 + a^2)^4\left[4\mu\dfrac{(p^2\delta - 1)(\delta - 1)}{(p\delta - 1)^2} - \dfrac{(p-1)^2(\mu\delta - 1)^2}{(p\delta - 1)^2}\right].
\end{cases}
$$

It is found that (cfr. [24])

i) m^2 is maximum when n=1

ii) exists a positive μ such that $(4.18)_3$ holds

iii) R^2 has to verify

$$\frac{1}{a^2}[Q^2\pi^2(\pi^2 + a^2)] < R^2 < \frac{(\pi^2 + a^2)}{a^2}[(\pi^2 + a^2)^2 Q^2\pi^2].$$

From iii) it turns out that the critical value $\tilde{R}_L^2$ of linear stability linked to the Liapunov function (4.14) is

$$\tilde{R}_L^2 = \frac{(\pi^2 + a^2)}{a^2}[(\pi^2 + a^2)^2 + Q^2\pi^2].$$

But it is well known that (cfr. [11], pp. 170-171) the critical value R_L^2 of linear stability obtained by the normal modes analysis is

$$R_L^2(a^2) = \frac{(\pi^2 + a^2)}{a^2}[(\pi^2 + a^2)^2 + Q^2\pi^2],$$

i.e.

$$\tilde{R}_L^2 = R_L^2.$$

Acknowledgments. M.U.R.S.T. (40 % and 60 % contracts) and the G.N.F.M. of the Italian C.N.R. are acknowledged.

References.

[1] PAI, S. I.: *Modern Fluidmechanics*, Van Nostrand (1981)

[2] SUTTON, G., SHERMANN, A.: *Engineering Magnetohydrodynamic*, Mc Graw-Hill (1965)

[3] MULONE, G., SOLONNIKOV, V. A.: On an initial boundary-value problem for equations of magnetohydrodynamics with Hall and ion-slip effect, *Zap. Nauchn. Sem. S. Peterburg. Otdel. Mat. Inst. Steklov. (POMI)*, **221** (1995), 167–184.

[4] MULONE, G., SOLONNIKOV, V. A.: On the solvability of some initial boundary value problems of magnetofluidmechanics with Hall and ion-slip effects, *Atti Accad. Naz. Lincei Rend. Cl. Sci. Fis. Mat. Natur.*, **6** (1995), 117–132.

[5] RIONERO, R.: Sulla stabilitá magnetofuidodinamica non lineare asintotica in media in presenza di effetto di Hall, *Ricerche Mat.*, **20** (1971), 285–296.

[6] MAIELLARO, M.: On the nonlinear stability of the anisitropic MHD Couette-Poiseuille flows, to appear on the *Proceedings of the IX Int. Conf. on Waves and Stability* (Incowascom 97, Bari-Capitolo di Monopoli, 6-11 October 1997).

[7] MAIELLARO, M., RIONERO, S.: On the stability of Couette-Poiseuille flows in the anisotropic MHD via the Liapunov direct method, *Rend. Accad. Sci. Fis. Mat. Napoli*, **62** (1995), 315–332.

[8] DE MITRI, M., MAIELLARO, M.: Couette-Poiseuille flows and their stability in anisotropic M.H.D., *Meccanica*, **19** (1984), 269–274.

[9] DE MITRI, M., MAIELLARO, M.: A note on nonlinear stability of the Poiseuille flows in anisotropic M.H.D., *Meccanica*, **22** (1987), 35–37.

[10] FLAVIN, J. N.,RIONERO, S.: *Qualitative estimates for partial differential equations. An introduction*, CRC Press, (1995).

[11] CHANDRASEKHAR, S.: *Hydrodynamic and hydromagnetic stability*, Oxford Univ. Press (1961).

[12] JOSEPH, D. D.: *Stability of Fluid Motions*, vol. I, II, Springer Tracts Nat. Philos. , **27**, **28**, (1976)

[13] RIONERO, S.: Sulla stabilità magnetoidrodinamica in media con vari tipi di condizioni al contorno, *Ricerche Mat.*, **17** (1968), 64–78.

[14] GALDI,G. P.: Nonlinear stability of the magnetic Bénard problem via a generalized energy method, *Arch. Rational Mech. Anal.*, **87** (1985), 167–186.

[15] GALDI, G. P., STRAUGHAN, B.: Exchange of stabilities, symmetry and nonlinear stability, *Arch. Rational Mech. Anal.*, **89** (1985), 211–228.

[16] GALDI, G. P., STRAUGHAN, B.: A nonlinear analysis of the stabilizing effect of rotation in Bénard problem, *Proc. Roy. Soc. London Ser. A*, **402** (1985), 257–283.

[17] MULONE, G., RIONERO, S.: A nonlinear stability analysis of the magnetic Bénard problem through the Lyapunov direct method, *Arch. Rational Mech. Anal.* **103** (1988), 347–368.

[18] GALDI, G. P., PADULA, R.: A new approach to energy theory in the stability of fluid motion, *Arch. Rational Mech. Anal.*, **110** (1990), 187–286.

[19] GALDI, G. P., RIONERO, S.: *Weighted Energy Methods in Fluid Dynamics and Elasticity*, Lecture Notes in Math., **1134**, Springer-Verlag, (1985).

[20] MULONE, G., RIONERO, S.: On the stability of the rotating Bénard problem, *İstanbul Tek. Üniv. Bül.*, **47** (1994), 181–202.

[21] MULONE, G., RIONERO, S.: Some recent results on the onset of convection, *Proceedings of the VIII Int. Conf. on Waves and Stability in Continuous Media* (Palermo 9-14 October 1995), Suppl. *Rend. Circ. Mat. Palermo*, **45** (1996) Part I, 465–476.

[22] MULONE, G., RIONERO, S.: The rotating Bénard problem: some stability results for any Prandtl and Taylor numbers, *Contin. Mech. Thermodyn.* (in press).

[23] MULONE, G.: On the non linear stability of the Bénard problem for a mixture: conditional and unconditional stability. to appear on the *Proceedings of IX Int. Conf. Waves and Stability in Continuous Media*, Bari-Capitolo di Monopoli 6-11 October 1997.

[24] MULONE, G., RIONERO, S.: On the nonlinear stability of the Bènard problem for a mixture: conditional and unconditional stability, (to appear).

[25] RIONERO, S.: On the influence of the magnetic field in the MHD stability, To appear on the *Proceedings of IX Int. Conf. Waves and Stability in Continuous Media*, Bari-Capitolo di Monopoli, 6-11 October 1997.

[26] MULONE, G., RIONERO, S.: Necessary and sufficient conditions for the nonlinear stability in the magnetic Bénard problem, to appear.

The Series *Quaderni di Matematica* is planned as a sequence of thematic volumes, each presenting one or more papers that deal with relevant problems in the same branch of mathematical research. The collected papers in each issue, further than new and meaningful results in their field, should also offer an uptodated picture of at least the recent researches about the problems they treat, together — if possible — with a quick look to their origin and relevance. Accordingly, will be published in the volumes of the Series only those papers whose Authors will have been explicitly invited by an Editor appointed by the Editorial Board, composed of the professors of the Department of Mathematics of the Second University of Naples.

Quaderni di Matematica publishes, as a rule, two volumes per year. The price of each volume is L. 60.000 in Italy and L. 80.000 abroad. Subscription requests and orders should be sent to

Aracne Editrice
via Raffaele Garofalo, 133
00173 Roma (Italy)
Telefax +39 (0)6 726722. 22–33
www.aracne.org

Any correspondence about exchange with other publications or any other matter should be sent to

Giulio Starita
Segretario di *Quaderni di Matematica*
Dipartimento di Matematica
Piazza Duomo, 81100 Caserta (Italy)
Tel. +39 (0)823 352618, Fax +39 (0)823 352724
e-mail: quaderni@unina.it

Finito di stampare nel mese di febbraio 1998
da "Industria Grafica Romana"